Research to Build and Present Knowledge: Chapters 3, 9, 10, 11, 13

7. Conduct short as well as more sustained research projects based on focused questions, demonstrating understanding of the subject under investigation.

8. Gather relevant information from multiple print and digital sources, assess the credibility and accuracy of each source, and integrate the information while avoiding plagiarism.

9. Draw evidence from literary or informational texts to support analysis, reflection, and research.

Range of Writing: Chapter 11

10. Write routinely over extended time frames (time for research, reflection, and revision) and shorter time frames (a single sitting or a day or two) for a range of tasks, purposes, and audiences.

Comprehension and Collaboration: Chapters 3, 4, 7, 8, 9, 12

1. Prepare for and participate effectively in a range of conversations and collaborations with diverse partners, building on others' ideas and expressing their own clearly and persuasively.

2. Integrate and evaluate information presented in diverse media and formats, including visually, quantitatively, and orally.

3. Evaluate a speaker's point of view, reasoning, and use of evidence and rhetoric.

Presentation of Knowledge and Ideas: Chapters 3, 4, 6, 8, 10, 12

4. Present information, findings, and supporting evidence such that listeners can follow the line of reasoning and the organization, development, and style are appropriate to task, purpose, and audience.

5. Make strategic use of digital media and visual displays of data to express information and enhance understanding of presentations.

6. Adapt speech to a variety of contexts and communicative tasks, demonstrating command of formal English when indicated or appropriate.

Conventions of Standard English: Chapter 4

1. Demonstrate command of the conventions of standard English grammar and usage when writing or speaking.

2. Demonstrate command of the conventions of standard English capitalization, punctuation, and spelling when writing.

Knowledge of Language: Chapters 4, 8

3. Apply knowledge of language to understand how language functions in different contexts, to make effective choices for meaning or style, and to comprehend more fully when reading or listening.

Vocabulary Acquisition and Use: Chapters 4, 8

4. Determine or clarify the meaning of unknown and multiple-meaning words and phrases by using context clues, analyzing meaningful word parts, and consulting general and specialized reference materials, as appropriate.

5. Demonstrate understanding of word relationships and nuances in word meanings.

6. Acquire and use accurately a range of general academic and domain-specific words and phrases sufficient for reading, writing, speaking, and listening at the college and career readiness level; demonstrate independence in gathering vocabulary knowledge when encountering an unknown term important to comprehension or expression.

Dear Readers,

When we set out to revise *Reading and Learning to Read*, our goal was to update this tenth edition with the latest thinking in the field of literacy while adhering to our core beliefs about literacy and learning. We hope you conclude that we have done that. Below we share with you some of the critical issues that have driven us to craft this new edition. These new issues are not in any particular order of importance. We invite you to think about them as you expand your knowledge and expertise regarding your current pre-clinical, clinical, and professional teaching experiences.

In this edition of *Reading and Learning to Read*, we address legislative influences throughout the text such as the Common Core State Standards (CCSS) initiative and the Response to Intervention (RTI) model. We recognize the importance of educating teachers with a core knowledge base that includes a focus on contemporary issues that influence national and statewide literacy decisions. Additionally, we aligned each chapter with the International Literacy Association Standards for Literacy Professionals 2017 to provide a connection between text content and literacy standards. In addition to inviting you, the reader, to think about contemporary topics regarding literacy, we provide you with practical strategies for assessing and engaging all students in the process of learning to read.

We continue to integrate classroom management in this new edition because we believe that teachers need to think about the many ways that they can organize language arts instruction as they learn to teach children how to read and write. There is no one best way to organize literacy instruction. As you will learn in our text, instruction depends on multiple factors: students' instructional needs, interests, background knowledge, linguistic proficiency, and so much more.

We have featured technology application and highlight transliteracies. *Transliteracy* is the understanding of traditional literacy components alongside the nuances that living in a touchscreen world brings. Throughout the text, we suggest classroom strategies that will broaden your understanding of transliteracies and the new skills we need to address as teachers of reading.

A new feature, Instructional Decision Making, encourages readers to review assessment data related to the chapter content and to make instructional decisions based on the assessment data presented. Encouraging the reader to engage in reflective decision-making is important to us. Reflection is also encouraged in another feature, Check Your Understanding. This feature encourages the reader to reflect upon the text content throughout each chapter in order to further develop understanding of reading and learning to read.

Finally, we again feature Viewpoint boxes in many of the chapters. We asked colleagues to share their stories and experiences on particular features of reading instruction in order to provide you with authentic anecdotes and classroom-tested strategies from real educators.

There is so much more included in this redesign that we hope you will take time to explore it and find new features for yourself. We are excited about this new edition and hope it serves you well in your quest to make a difference in the ways in which you teach children to read!

Our best,
Linda C. Burkey
Lisa A. Lenhart
Christine A. McKeon

Reading and Learning to Read

Tenth Edition

Jo Anne L. Vacca
Kent State University

Richard T. Vacca
Kent State University

Mary K. Gove
Cleveland State University

Linda C. Burkey
University of Mount Union

Lisa A. Lenhart
The University of Akron

Christine A. McKeon
Walsh University

 **Pearson**

330 Hudson Street, NY, NY 10013

Vice President and Editor in Chief: *Kevin M. Davis*
Portfolio Manager: *Drew Bennett*
Content Producer: *Miryam Chandler*
Development Editor: *Bryce Bell*
Portfolio Management Assistant: *Maria Feliberty*
Executive Product Marketing Manager:
  Christopher Barry
Executive Field Marketing Manager: *Krista Clark*

**Editorial Production and Composition
  Service:** *iEnergizer Aptara®, Ltd.*
Procurement Specialist: *Deidra Smith*
Cover Designer: *Cenveo, Carie Keller*
Cover Art: *James McKeon*
Media Producer: *Allison Longley*
Full-Service Project Manager: *iEnergizer Aptara®, Ltd.*
Text Font: *Palatino LT Pro, 9.5/13*

Additional text credits:
Links to www.readwritethink.org are provided courtesy of the International Literacy Association.
p. 10: CCSS Mission Statement © Copyright 2010. National Governors Association Center for Best Practices and Council of Chif State School Officers. All rights reserved.

Cataloging-in-Publication Data is available on file at the Library of Congress.

ISBN 10: 0-13-489464-2
ISBN 13: 978-0-13-489464-5

13 2022

About the Authors

Richard and Jo Anne Vacca are professors emeriti in the School of Teaching, Leadership, and Curriculum Studies in the College and Graduate School of Education, Health, and Human Services at Kent State University. They met as undergraduate English majors at SUNY–Albany and have been partners ever since. Jo Anne taught middle school language arts in New York and Illinois and received her doctorate from Boston University. Rich taught high school English and earned his doctorate at Syracuse University. He is a past president of the International Literacy Association.

The Vaccas have a daughter, Courtney; son-in-law, Gary; and grandsons, Simon, Max, and Joe. They volunteer, golf, and walk their toy poodles, Tiger Lily, Gigi, and Joely, in Vero Beach, Florida.

Mary Gove is an associate professor at Cleveland State University in the graduate literacy education program and served as a co-author on the early editions of *Reading and Learning to Read*. Her research interests include action research and how teachers' beliefs about teaching and learning influence classroom practice and teacher efficacy. Dr. Gove has also presented papers at various conferences and seminars worldwide. A recent area of focus for Dr. Gove has been ecological critical literacy (ECL), an approach to enhance how we read and critically think about published and broadcasted information about the present environmental depletion of natural resources.

Linda Burkey is a professor of education at the University of Mount Union in Alliance, Ohio. She is also the current appointee of the endowed Lester D. Crow Professorship in Education. Dr. Burkey teaches courses in the areas of reading methods, reading assessment, and special education. Prior to receiving her Ph.D. from Kent State University, Dr. Burkey taught special and elementary education. Her areas of interest in research include reading assessment and adolescent literacy. Dr. Burkey enjoys traveling and spending time with her family. She is a proud grandmother of Maura, Aubrey, and Ryan.

Lisa Lenhart is a professor of literacy in the College of Education at The University of Akron. She works with doctoral students and is the director of the Center for Literacy. As a former elementary school teacher and Title I reading teacher, Dr. Lenhart focuses her scholarship on early literacy development and has co-written several books, including *Oral Language and Early Literacy in Preschool* and *Early Literacy Materials Selector (ELMS): A Tool for Review of Early Literacy Program Materials*. Dr. Lenhart received her Ph.D. from Kent State University. In her free time, Dr. Lenhart enjoys hiking and reading. She is the mother of young adult daughters, Hannah and Emma.

Christine McKeon is a professor of early and middle childhood reading education at Walsh University in North Canton, Ohio. She holds a Ph.D. from Kent State University, where she studied under the mentorship of Drs. Rich and Jo Anne Vacca. Chris is a former second-grade teacher and Title I reading teacher, as well as high school reading teacher. She is a former co-editor of the *Ohio Reading Teacher*, an ILA-affiliated professional journal. She has also authored and co-authored numerous professional literacy articles and chapters in contemporary professional publications. Dr. McKeon's current interests focus on technology and new literacies. She is especially grateful to her son, Jimmy, for designing the cover for the tenth edition of *Reading and Learning to Read*!

May all who read this book embrace literacy as challenging, invigorating, necessary, and captivating. May you inspire children and young adolescents to read well, critically, and thoughtfully in the ever challenging ways that the twenty-first century expects readers to learn and learners to read.

Thank you to all who have supported our writing about reading and learning to read, especially:

Jo Anne and Rich Vacca
Bob, John, Ally, Maura, Aubrey, and Ryan Burkey
Hannah, and Emma Lenhart
Jimmy McKeon

Brief Contents

Contents

4 Foundations of Language and Literacy   76

5 Assessing Reading Performance   112

6 Word Identification   150

11 Reading–Writing Connections 311

12 Bringing Children and Text Together 342

13 Instructional Materials 369

Features

Student Voices

Preface

Evidence-based reading research, the essential components of reading instruction, and data-driven decision making—these concepts represent the direction in which literacy professionals currently focus attention. Fortunately, *Reading and Learning to Read* has always included philosophies, teaching strategies, and assessment practices that reflect the beliefs that underscore these concepts.

In the tenth edition of *Reading and Learning to Read*, there is a focus on the Common Core State Standards (CCSS) initiative. The CCSS are integrated throughout the text, and each chapter features the English language arts (ELA) standards respectively as they relate to the chapter content.

We continue to recognize legislative influences, standards for reading professionals, and research-based practices, as well as update the reader with new strategies that reflect alternative reading methodologies that we consider to be best practices. An additional feature, Instructional Decision Making, encourages the readers to review assessment data, interpret the data, and make instructional decisions. We updated Student Voices on reading and learning to read also support these practices. In addition, this edition reflects our dedication to struggling learners. We include features that demonstrate understanding and utilization of Response to Intervention (RTI). Also, we highlight the essential components of effective literacy instruction (phonemic awareness, phonics, fluency, vocabulary, and comprehension) and demonstrate how each component can be taught within meaningful contexts. In addition, we highlight elements of managing and organizing effective language arts classrooms.

The tenth edition continues to feature technology applications as they relate to literacy instruction, and also highlights transliteracies. The concept of transliteracies goes beyond linear print to include knowledge of fluid print such as hypertext, graphic design, visual literacy, music, and film interpretation. We recognize that transliteracies are transforming the way children comprehend and express their understanding of the world.

Finally, throughout each chapter a new feature, Check Your Understanding, was included to help support the reader's understanding and development as a literacy professional. The reader is asked a series of questions to encourage the reader to reflect upon the text and make connections. Feedback is provided to help the teacher understand the essential concepts being developed.

Core Beliefs at the Center of This Text

This tenth edition of *Reading and Learning to Read* is based on research, legislation, and current thinking about how children become literate. We continue to use our core beliefs about literacy learning to frame important questions related to the teaching of reading. In addition, we craft our beliefs to reflect topics that address current educationally related literacy issues relevant to the twenty-first century. We believe the following:

- Children use language to seek and construct meaning from what they experience, hear, view, and read.
- Reading, writing, speaking, listening, and viewing are interrelated and mutually supportive as children learn to become literate.
- Learning to read involves learning how to decode words quickly and accurately with comprehension as the main goal of word recognition instruction.

- Children learn to read as they read to learn. They need to view reading as enjoyable, a process of communication, a process of gathering knowledge, a venue for expressing opinions, and so much more.

- Children need to be exposed to a broad spectrum of reading materials and text, including fiction, nonfiction, informational, electronic, and texts that reflect new literacies (art, music, dance, graphics, comics, etc.) in a well-managed and organized literate classroom.

- Children develop skills and strategies through explicit instruction in purposeful, meaningful ways.

- Assessment techniques and processes need to mirror the authentic ways children demonstrate their continually developing literacy, and assessments should inform instruction.

- Children benefit from classroom communities in which materials, curricula, instruction, practice, and assessment recognize diversity.

- Teachers, parents, and administrators should work together as they make decisions based on how children learn and how they can best be taught.

New to This Edition

The tenth edition of *Reading and Learning to Read* continues to emphasize a comprehensive approach to teaching reading and writing. In maintaining this standard of excellence, this edition includes a number of additions and updates that reflect the changes in the field of literacy:

- **First Time as REVEL** This tenth edition is offered in a new immersive online format called REVEL that's been designed to accommodate twenty-first-century learning on laptops, tablets, and smartphones. REVEL offers a variety of interactive experiences:

  - **Learning Outcomes** The REVEL format guides the chapter structure. Specifically, we list learning outcomes at the beginning of each chapter, organize the chapter's content into sections addressing each learning outcome, and include self-assessments for each section.

  - **Classroom Videos** Important concepts in each chapter are illustrated in videos, showing you how teachers apply them in authentic classroom settings.

  - **Check Your Understanding** Self-assessments, appearing at the end of each major section of each chapter, help the reader reflect upon the chapter content. These multiple-choice self-assessments help verify comprehension and identify gaps in learning. Feedback is provided to further build understanding of the essential concepts being developed.

- The **Common Core State Standards (CCSS) for the English Language Arts** are aligned and integrated into each chapter to assist teachers with instructional and assessment decisions in order to help all children succeed.

- Chapter content is aligned with the **International Literacy Association Standards** for Literacy Professionals 2017.

- A new feature, **Instructional Decision Making**, encourages the reader to review and analyze data related to content in order to make data-based instructional decisions.

- The concept of transliteracy (contributed by Jeremy Brueck) is explored in the general text and in the **Transliteracies features**, which offer classroom strategies that go beyond linear print to include knowledge of fluid print such as hypertext, graphic design, visual literacy, music, and film interpretation. We recognize that transliteracies are transforming the way children comprehend and express their understanding of the world.

- Chapters 4 and 5 from the previous edition have been combined for a more comprehensive focus on young children and literacy development.

In addition to these global changes, discussions have been enhanced and new topics have been introduced within each chapter to reflect the latest trends and research in literacy education.

Additional Features of the Tenth Edition

With superior coverage of standards and an emphasis on comprehensive reading instruction, *Reading and Learning to Read*, Tenth Edition, remains an active learning tool that encourages future teachers to teach reading in ways that are both meaningful and reflective. Notable features of *Reading and Learning to Read* include the following:

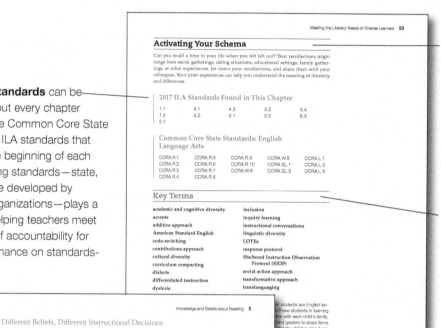

A Focus on Standards can be found throughout every chapter starting with the Common Core State Standards and ILA standards that are listed at the beginning of each chapter. Meeting standards—state, local, and those developed by professional organizations—plays a major role in helping teachers meet the challenge of accountability for student performance on standards-based tests.

Activating Your Schema at the beginning of each chapter acts as an advance organizer for critical thinking and reflective reading, providing schema-related questions that encourage readers to think about their own experiences in terms of their futures as reading and writing teachers.

Key Terms are linked to the glossary so that when students click on a key term, they will be taken to the definition for that term.

Student Voices boxes in every chapter provide students' perspectives as developing readers and writers and give insight into the ways in which their teachers make a difference in that development.

Research-Based Practices
boxes throughout the text
highlight relevant research that is
supported by theoretically sound
rationales or evidence-based
research. These boxes provide
general suggestions, strategies,
and approaches that are
supported by theory or scientific
research for reading instruction.

Viewpoint boxes introduce
the reader to the research and
opinions of respected teacher-
educators, researchers, and
authors about particular facets
of reading instruction.

Step-by-Step Lesson boxes
offer teacher-directed lessons
that can be imported directly
into the classroom as specific
lessons or as a series of lessons.

---

60 Chapter 3

BOX 3.3 | RESEARCH-BASED PRACTICES

Response Protocol in Mrs. Montler's Classroom

Mrs. Montler teaches third grade in a rural school district in Pennsylvania. She has 18 students in her class; three of her students are Hispanic. Carla, Marco, and Juanita have very limited conversational skills, so each day Mrs. Montler works with the students in a small group for 15 minutes in order to personalize conversation with them using response protocol. Here is how she uses research-based practices as she develops her lesson:

1. Mrs. Montler selects a focus theme that centers on communicating about an everyday topic in which the students have some background knowledge; for example, foods, hobbies, interests, or family.
2. Next, Mrs. Montler selects a picture or pictures that focus on the topic. For example, if the topic is foods, she might have pictures that represent ethnic and American foods.
3. Next, beginning with the pictures, she points to and models vocabulary associated with the pictures.
4. Next, Mrs. Montler models and prompts the students to discuss their associations with the pictures in a conversational dialogue.
5. She concludes the conversation by modeling a synthesis of the conversation with student participation.

Let's look at a lesson in which Mrs. Montler uses response protocol strategies (which are conversation elaboration strategies) with Carlos, Marco, and Juanita.

Mrs. Montler: Good morning, Carlos. Good morning, Marco. Good morning, Juanita.

Carlos, Marco, Juanita (in unison): Good morning.

Mrs. Montler: Today we have more pictures to talk about. These are pictures of things you might like to do. (Mrs. Montler points to the pictures.)

Mrs. Montler: This is a bus. This is a ball. This is a book.

Mrs. Montler: (She points to each picture.) What is this? What is this? What is this?

Carlos: Bike.

Mrs. Montler: Yes, this is a bike. What is this, Carlos?

Carlos: Bike.

Mrs. Montler: Yes, that's right, Carlos. This is a bike. What is this, Carlos?

Carlos: This is a bike.

Mrs. Montler: Yes, Carlos. This is a bike!

Mrs. Montler: Marco, what is this? (She points to the picture of the bike.)

Marco: A bike.

Mrs. Montler: Yes, Marco, this is a bike. What is this?

Marco: This is a bike.

Mrs. Montler: Yes, Marco, this is a bike!

Mrs. Montler: (Pointing to a ball) Juanita, this is a ball. What is this, Juanita?

Juanita: This is a ball.

Mrs. Montler: Yes, good job, Juanita, this is a ball! What is this? (Mrs. Montler points to the picture.)

Juanita: This is a ball!

Mrs. Montler: Yes, Juanita! This is a bike! I can ride my bike! (Mrs. Montler dramatizes riding a bike with actions.) Juanita, can you ride a bike?

Juanita: Yes.

Mrs. Montler: Yes, you can ride a bike! Can you ride a bike?

Juanita: Yes, I can ride a bike!

Mrs. Montler: Marco, can you ride a bike?

Marco: Yes, I can ride a bike.

Mrs. Montler continues the conversation by helping the children elaborate on what they can do with a bike, a ball, and a book. She uses prompts such as, "Can you tell me more? What else?" She also responds positively with comments such as, "Good job! That's right!"

CONTENT AREA PRACTICES It is well documented that ELLs take longer to learn academic language than social communication (Cummins, 2011)—approximately 5 to 7 years for children between the ages of 8 and 11 (Hadaway & Young, 2006). On the other hand, it is critical that ELLs learn to navigate in a world in which all people need to be able to critically think about complex content. In order to scaffold content learning, teachers need to explicitly teach the various formats associated with content text, such as *main headings, subheadings, italics, index, glossary, tables,* and *figures,* to name a few. Pacheco and Miller (2015) elaborate on how newspapers written in multiple languages can help young children realize text features such as *titles, authors,* and *captions.* In addition, strategies that include promoting LOTEs (languages other than English) in content area classrooms, such as taking notes and summarizing content in the first and second languages, can foster academic learning (Daniel & Pacheco, 2013).

Common Core Standard
CCRA.R.5

Meeting the Literacy Needs of Diverse Learners **63**

We believe that teachers need to go beyond limiting literacy lessons to celebrations or thematic units. Teachers of the twenty-first century need to provide students with authentic literacy and learning experiences that will supply them with the crosscultural knowledge and skills they will need as future adults in a nation that has become increasingly diverse. In Box 3.4, Patricia Schmidt shares the evolution of her beliefs about teaching diverse learners.

BOX 3.4 | VIEWPOINT

Patricia Ruggiano Schmidt
Teaching Diverse Learners

Patricia Ruggiano Schmidt is professor emerita of literacy at Le Moyne College in Syracuse, New York. She works with urban schools preparing teachers with the ABCs of cultural understanding and communication. From 2010 to 2013, she acted as principal and development director for Cathedral Academy at Pompeii, a preK through sixth grade urban school where 20 percent of the children are from Hispanic and African American backgrounds, and 80 percent of the children are from refugee and immigrant families who originated in Africa, Asia, and the Middle East.

As a reading teacher for 18 years in a suburban middle school in upstate New York, grades 5–8, I worked with students who had been diagnosed with difficulties in reading, writing, listening, and speaking. Each year I was also assigned the one or two new students from places such as Taiwan, Russia, Israel, Detroit, or Appalachia. Similar to other European American teachers in this suburban setting, I believed in the assimilationist perspective. I thought that students from ethnic or cultural minority backgrounds needed to fit into the mainstream to be successful academically

Diversity in our nation's schools is inevitable due to shifting world populations. Also, because the global economy affects all of us, our children will probably work in places very different from their home communities. Consequently, our present and future teachers must be prepared to work effectively with linguistic, cultural, and academic diversity. Since most teachers will have grown up in middle class European American suburbia and have had few opportunities to develop relationships with different groups, they may unconsciously rely on media stereotypes. Differences in the classroom may be viewed as problematic rather than opportunities for children to explore physical, linguistic, cultural, and academic differences and learn to appreciate individual talents and multiple perspectives. Therefore, the classroom as social context can begin to prepare children for an appreciation of differences that gives them social and economic advantages. But how do we do this?

A major means is through effective connections between home and school. Families who are actively involved in the classroom and school community feel comfortable and needed. They ... reach out to families who are culturally ... from the school and to families who ... because of their own emotional and ... who realize that families are the chil... value the family's knowledge and ... al. Therefore, I think that a teacher's ... connect with families and communi... groups of people will lead to closing

... to the relevance of materials and ... rs. When children see people like ... resources they are using and can ... own life experiences, they tend to ... rawing on home and community lit... es as well as children and young adult ... groups can be the means for con... r meaningful literacy development ... the European American culture are ... out diversity through literature and ... died in their classrooms.

---

158 Chapter 6

BOX 6.4 | STEP-BY-STEP LESSON

Synthetic Phonics Lesson

1. Teach a set of letter names; for example, *t, a, c.*
2. Teach the corresponding sounds for each letter.
3. Review and practice the sounds for each letter. For example, *t* makes the sound at the beginning of *table, tent, top; a* makes the sound at the beginning of *apple, action, after; c* makes the sound at the beginning of *cake, cup, cow.* Pictures and letter cards can be used to develop games.
4. Drill and practice until the students can rapidly elicit the sound associated with each letter.

5. Next, model how the individual sounds can be blended to make a word; in this example, the sounds of *c, a, t* make the word *cat.*
6. Continue with other letters, sounds, and blending activities.
7. Be sure to keep track of the letter sounds you have taught and review with blending activities.

There are similarities between analytic and synthetic phonics. Both approaches discuss isolated letter–sound relationships, break words apart, and put them back together again.

Teachers who engage children in the analysis of words must be well versed and knowledgeable in content and language of phonics. In Figure 6.2, we highlight the basic terminology associated with the content of phonics instruction. In Figure 6.3, we share word patterns that represent reasonably consistent vowel and consonant sounds depending on the locations of the letters.

SYLLABLES A *syllable* is a vowel or a cluster of letters containing a vowel and pronounced as a unit. Phonograms, for example, are syllables. The composition of the syllable signals the most probable vowel sound. Examine the following word patterns in Figure 6.3.

These patterns underlie the formation of syllables. The number of syllables in a word is equal to the number of vowel sounds. For example, the word *disagreement* has four vowel sounds and thus four syllables. The word *hat* has one vowel sound and thus one syllable.

There are three primary syllabication patterns that signal how to break down a word into syllabic units. Examine the patterns in Figure 6.4.

Although there is no one particular phonics sequence or program that is better than another (Cunningham, 2005), Bear, Helman, Templeton, Invernizzi, and Johnston (2007) suggest that early English learners begin with initial and final consonant sounds and short and long vowels by picture sorting, followed by blends, word families, and digraphs. In addition, they recommend:

- Talking with students as they perform activities such as drawing, painting, and playing with blocks
- Reading to students and talking about words and pictures
- Reading with students chorally, and using repeated readings and dictation activities

Helman's (2004) research on the English and Spanish sound systems reveals that the following consonants and vowels are shared between the two:

b, d, f, g, k, l, m, n, p, s, t, w, y

long *a, e, i, o, u* and short *o*

She also notes that Spanish does *not* include the following /s/ blends or clusters:

st, sp, sk, sc, sm, sl, sn, sw, scr, spl, spr, str, squ

2017 ILA Standard
2.2

Transliteracy boxes focus on how teachers can use technology to enhance literacy instruction. Readers will learn about using podcasts, wikis, and other software tools and programs that can make teaching and learning literacy skills motivating and engaging.

RTI for Struggling Readers sections at the end of each chapter highlight the influence of response to intervention on national and statewide literacy decisions, while reflecting current realities and concerns in today's schools.

Chapter-ending sections such as the **Summary** help students review, formulate, and extend their thinking about the concepts discussed in each chapter. In particular, the projects in **Teacher Action Research** challenge the reader to think critically about the information covered.

---

96 Chapter 4

BOX 4.6 | TRANSLITERACY

Jeremy Brueck

Creating a Simple E-Book with Young Children

Today's children are able to use new technologies with amazing ease. As a result, these tools are quickly becoming the medium through which students are learning and interacting. E-books, books in electronic format, are becoming popular in classrooms. They can be downloaded to a computer, a laptop, a handheld device, a smartphone, or any other reading tool and read on the screen. E-books can have page numbers, a table of contents, pictures, and graphics just like a traditional book. However, e-books have features traditional books do not. E-books allow students to connect with stories in ways never possible before; they can show links for easy access to more information, are searchable, and are interactive with audio, video, and animations, which can enhance the message the author is trying to convey. Fortunately for schools, many free e-books are available today. Teachers can log on to public library websites or other online sources to access e-books.

Personalized e-books are a lot of fun, too. However, the thought of creating an e-book can be intimidating, yet there are many online resources available to help you get started. Here is a basic overview on how to make your own e-book:

Step One: Planning and Preparation

1. To get started, think of the subject matter for your e-book. Select a simple plot by thinking about something that happens as a series, such as brushing your teeth or tying your shoe. For example, I made an e-book with my son, Aiden, about the home my dad lived in since Aiden was curious about where his grandpa lived. This helped him to see that Grandpa's house may look different, but it has all of the same things in it that ours does.

2. Next, create a simple storyboard on a piece of paper, or download and print a storyboard template from the Internet. Try to stick to six to eight pages for your first book. Remember to include a cover page! Here is a look at the start of my storyboard for Grandpa's house.

3. Once the storyboard is finished, you will need to search online for and install some essential story-creating applications on your tablet or computer. There are many apps to create stories and crop photos available online at no cost.

Step Two: Creating Media

Once your storyboard is complete and you have the apps downloaded, take a picture for each block on your storyboard and save it to your tablet camera. You could also use video.

Step Three: Assemble E-Book

No matter what app you've selected, you're now ready to use the media you've created to build your e-book. During this build, try to incorporate some of the tools that the e-book app provides in addition to your media. For example, you might have a child record the audio. Other apps allow you to insert text boxes and video. Explore the potential of the app as you build your e-book!

Step Four: Publication

Finally, take a moment to publish your e-book. Again, depending

---

Meeting the Literacy Needs of Diverse Learners 73

program "scripted"? If so, why was it selected? Was the population of our school and the expertise that would be needed to carry out the program considered? If so, how? Are there any political or business ties to the program that would benefit a constituency?

- What support systems does our school have in place to guide me in helping struggling students? Are there reading specialists to support classroom teachers? If so, *how* do they support teachers? If I am a first-grade teacher, where do I receive support for the students I perceive to be struggling readers? If I am a science teacher, what do I do with students who cannot read my textbook?

In essence, it is critical that teachers at all grade levels involve themselves in serious conversations about how to address students who are academically and cognitively challenged and the programs and strategies that are or might be implemented in classrooms. The questions listed can serve as a starting point for discussions by preservice teachers, continuing education and graduate-level students, and teachers in professional development programs.

| 2017 ILA Standard
| 6.3

Check Your Understanding 3.3: Gauge your understanding of the skills and concepts in this section.

RTI for Struggling Readers

Culturally and Linguistically Struggling Students and *Response to Intervention*

Historically, students from diverse cultures and languages who immigrated to the United States tended to be placed in programs that assumed they were or would be struggling learners. One of the underlying purposes of RTI is to avoid this labeling phenomenon. In an attempt to place culturally and linguistically diverse students within the framework of RTI, Klinger and Edwards (2006) suggest a four-tiered RTI model that addresses this concern. Here, we capture the gist of the model.

- *Tier 1*—Teachers need to be informed about culturally responsive teaching. This means teachers need to be aware of the linguistic similarities and differences of the languages their students speak as compared to the English language. They also need to be cognizant of cultural differences that may influence learning.
- *Tier 2*—For linguistically and culturally diverse students who do not respond to classroom initiatives that capture the purposes of Tier 1, classroom teachers need to evaluate why Tier 1 is not making an impact on student learning. What are the assessments used to evaluate culturally and linguistically diverse students? Are teachers uninformed about strategies that assist culturally and linguistically diverse students? Additional questions include the following: Are the teachers in Tier 1 expert teachers of reading for all students? Do they have the support of teachers who speak the native language(s) of the student(s)? In addition, Tier 2 ought to include more intensive instruction for culturally and linguistically diverse students from teams of teachers who participate in helping to plan, guide, and deliver instruction in the classroom to [meet] the "diverse" students' needs.

Summary

- We examined three dimensions of fluency: accurate word decoding, automaticity, and prosody. We looked at the close relationship fluency has with comprehension, serving as a bridge between word recognition and comprehension.
- Fluency can be taught through effective instruction, but should never be just for the sake of reading quickly. The goal of fluency instruction is always to preserve mental energy so that comprehension can take place. We shared strategies for groups of students,

pairs, and individuals, as well as ways to involve parents and older students.

- Assessing the components of fluency assists teachers in choosing appropriate text for various instructional purposes and provides information about areas in need of further instruction to assure accuracy.
- Silent reading, when managed appropriately, allows students time to practice reading. Research shows time spent reading increases reading achievement.

Teacher Action Research

1. Create a diagram that depicts the three dimensions of fluency and how they all work together and support comprehension. Be ready to share your diagram electronically with your peers.
2. Paired repeated readings have many benefits, and you'll want to use them often in your classroom. Create a guide to be used in your classroom to remind students of the steps in paired reading. It could take the form of a chart, a bookmark, or other form that is easily accessible to students.

3. Try out one of the assessment strategies you read about in this chapter on a young reader. What patterns of behavior do you notice? What strategies to develop fluency will you use based on what you learned from the assessment?
4. Based on what you learned about the benefits of independent reading time, write an email to your curriculum director, explaining why there should be time set aside for silent reading in the classroom. Be sure to use research to support your request.

Through the Lens of the Common Core

Students need word identification strategies such as phonics, structural analysis, and the use of context to figure out unknown words. But they also need fluency—the ability to read accurately and well in order to make meaning—so they can move on and maintain comprehension. Fluency is specifically included in the CCSS under Reading Foundational Skills. In this chapter we addressed why fluency matters and how the classroom teacher can

develop both oral and silent reading fluency by working with students on rate, accuracy, and automaticity. Knowing how to develop these three dimensions of fluency will allow teachers to scaffold students as they aim to read with sufficient accuracy to support comprehension, read grade-level text with purpose and understanding, and read with accuracy, appropriate rate, and expression—all of which are CCSS grade-level goals.

211

Support Materials for Instructors

The following resources are available for instructors to download on **www. pearsonhighered.com/educators**. Instructors enter the author or title of this book, select this particular edition of the book, and then click on the "Resources" tab to log in and download textbook supplements.

Instructor's Resource Manual and Test Bank (**0134448014**)

The Instructor's Resource Manual and Test Bank includes key topics for a robust variety of questions, activities, and critical-thinking reflective questions on topics such as the role of new technologies in the classroom, working with diverse learners, teaching middle school students, and teaching struggling readers. The test bank offers a large assortment of questions. Some items (lower-level questions) simply ask students to identify or explain concepts and principles they have learned. But many others (higher-level questions) ask students to apply those same concepts and principles to specific classroom situations—that is, to actual student behaviors and teaching strategies.

PowerPoint Slides (**0134519671**)

The PowerPoint slides include key concept summarizations to enhance learning. They are designed to help students understand, organize, and remember core concepts, skills, and strategies.

TestGen (**0134447743**)

TestGen is a powerful test generator available exclusively from Pearson Education publishers. You install TestGen on your personal computer (Windows or Macintosh) and create your own tests for classroom testing and for other specialized delivery options, such as over a local area network or on the web. A test bank, which is also called a Test Item File (TIF), typically contains a large set of test items, organized by chapter and ready for your use in creating a test, based on the associated textbook material. Assessments—including equations, graphs, and scientific notation—may be created for both print or testing online.

The tests can be downloaded in the following formats:

TestGen Test Bank file—PC

TestGen Test Bank file—MAC

Test Bank for Blackboard Learning System (application/zip)

Test Bank for Blackboard CE/Vista (application/zip)

Canvas Test Bank (application/zip)

Desire2Learn Test Bank (application/zip)

Moodle Test Bank (application/zip)

Sakai Test Bank (application/zip)

Acknowledgments

Foremost, we thank Jo Anne and Richard Vacca for the opportunity to co-author *Reading and Learning to Read*. This tenth edition is a tribute to their faith in us to carry on with their mission of intelligent, professional, and research-based practices regarding reading and learning to read.

This edition has evolved not only from the new information in the field of literacy, but also from the thoughtful response of our reviewers. We thank Mary Abouzeid, University of Virginia; Catherine N. Davison, Endicott College/American International College; Susan Massey, St. Thomas University; Merideth H. Van Namen, Delta State University; and Ken Winograd, Oregon State University. Throughout the revision process, each of us returned to their comments and feedback to focus our writing.

We also thank the teachers and colleagues who contributed to this tenth edition: Jeremy Brueck of the University of Akron for your expertise on transliteracy; Peggy Zufall from Alliance City Schools; Laura Schmidt of Plain Local Schools; Peter Schneller and Mandy Capel from the University of Mount Union; and Abby I. Montler, second grade teacher at Norwood Fontbonne Academy in Philadelphia, PA.

In addition, we thank all of the professionals at Pearson who guided us through the process of writing this tenth edition of *Reading and Learning to Read*. Genuine thanks to Editor Drew Bennett, Developmental Editor Bryce Bell, Content Producer Miryam Chandler, Executive Field Marketing Manager Krista Clark, and Procurement Specialist Deidra Smith. Thank you for all of your support.

And, of course, we would like to thank our families and friends for their loving support as we researched, crafted, and developed contemporary changes to this tenth edition. Their patience with us has indeed made the process a collaborative affair. A special thank-you to Jimmy McKeon for his creative cover design. You captured the essence of reading with the tree emerging from worldwide knowledge, which is the nature of reading and learning to read.

Finally again, we want to thank Jo Anne and Rich Vacca for the opportunity to continue the professional challenge of crafting this new edition of *Reading and Learning to Read*. Their initial invitation to write has motivated us to continue to develop literacy collaboratives, research-based inquiry, and a friendship that is priceless. Thank you, Jo Anne and Rich!

L. C. B.

L. A. L.

C. A. M.

Chapter 1
Knowledge and Beliefs about Reading

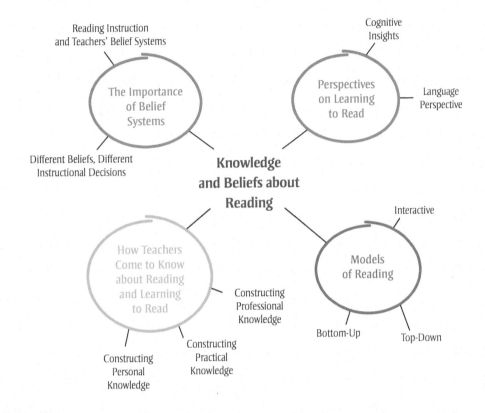

⌄ Learning Outcomes

In This Chapter, You Will Discover How to:

- ▪ Analyze how beliefs about literacy learning influence instructional decisions and practices.

- ▪ Explain how teachers use and construct personal, practical, and professional knowledge about literacy learning.

- ▪ Define language, social, and psychological perspectives on reading and explain how they inform knowledge and beliefs about literacy learning.

- ▪ Compare theoretical models of the reading process that describe what humans do when they engage in reading.

Activating Your Schema

Think about a teacher who had a positive influence on your reading development. What instructional reading strategies and materials did he or she use? Think about a teacher who did not have a positive impact on your reading development. What instructional strategies and materials did he or she use?

Think about your reading experiences outside the classroom. Focus on your home, family, and social experiences. How did these experiences influence your development as a reader?

2017 ILA Standards Found in This Chapter

1.1	2.1	4.2	5.2	6.2
1.2	3.2	4.3	5.3	6.3
1.3	4.1	5.1	6.1	6.4

Key Terms

alphabetic principle	literacy event
autobiographical narrative	metacognition
belief system	orthographic knowledge
best practice	professional knowledge
bottom-up model	psycholinguistics
constructivism	schemata
decoding	semantic cues
explicit	sociolinguistics
graphophonemic cues	syntactic cues
implicit	top-down model
interactive model	transliteracy
literacy coach	

During the beginning of each school year, Mrs. Zufall has the challenge of trying to encourage the children in her first-grade class to believe that they are readers and writers. Depending on the children's experiences and their developmental levels, some believe it easier than others. Some students like Maura read and write with ease, while Destanie finds that reading and writing are difficult tasks. Because of these differences, it is critical for Mrs. Zufall to create an environment that encourages all children to develop their confidence as beginning readers and writers.

Providing a literate environment where the children feel comfortable to read and write helps them to develop as readers and writers. Having multiple books in the classroom, using various writing materials, and providing uninterrupted time all help to develop a community of readers and writers. A writing activity that Mrs. Zufall likes to encourage regularly is letter writing. This activity encourages the children to freewrite and practice their writing skills.

One day after lunch, Destanie asks Mrs. Zufall, "Can I write a letter to you? I like to write letters." Mrs. Zufall tells Destanie that it is a good idea.

Maura overhears Destanie and requests permission to write a letter to her mom. "Certainly," Mrs. Zufall responds and then asks the other children whether they want to write letters, too.

The class responds with a resounding, "Yes, can we?" Mrs. Zufall decides to delay the spelling lesson until later in the day because there is an excitement for letter writing. She tells the students to think about how to write a letter, the other letters they have written, and to whom they would like to write. The first graders excitedly write their special letters.

The letters have a great deal to say about "literacy in the making." As innocent as it may seem on the surface, this activity reveals much about the children's literacy development. Just ask yourself, for example, "Do Maura, Destanie, and the others know what writing and reading are for? Do they get their message across effectively? Do they have a sense of being a reader?" And as language users, "Are Maura, Destanie, and the others empowered? Are they willing to take risks?" The answers to questions such as these are as revealing about Mrs. Zufall's first graders' literacy development as the grammatical and spelling errors they made.

Although Maura and Destanie misspelled words, their written approximations of *when, work,* and *favorite* are phonetically regular and close to the conventional spellings of the words. Though Maura neglected to use proper punctuation at the end of one sentence, Mrs. Zufall attributes the omission to fast writing rather than a lack of understanding the use of punctuation. Developmentally, Maura and Destanie write the way they talk. In time, they'll understand why it is important to use proper spelling and be grammatically appropriate.

After Mrs. Zufall collects all of the letters, she reads to the class *The Jolly Postman* by Janet and Allan Ahlberg. She builds anticipation for the story by inviting the students to think about the letters they have written and received. This book helps to demonstrate to the children that there are various kinds of letters and different purposes. Mrs. Zufall reinforces that letter writing is purposeful and conveys meaning.

Throughout the year, Mrs. Zufall's literacy program has centered on the development of confident and competent readers and writers. She continues to encourage her students to read and write and connect learning with literature. She wants her students to be motivated, thoughtful, and skillful as they engage in literacy learning. Although the school year is rapidly coming to a close, Mrs. Zufall thinks about the children's first few days in her class. She recalls students who hardly spoke and wrote a word. Yet today, they have blossomed into confident and competent readers and writers. Her decision to continue and extend the communication reflects not only what she knows about reading and learning to read but also what she believes about teaching, learning, and the process of becoming literate.

How teachers come to know and develop beliefs about reading and learning to read is the subject of this chapter. Examine the chapter overview. It depicts the connections between several key concepts related to the role of teacher knowledge and beliefs in reading instruction. A **belief system** represents a teacher's informed philosophy of reading and learning to read. What teachers believe about reading and learning to read is closely related to what they know about literacy learning and the teaching of literacy. As you study this chapter, pay close attention to how teachers come to know about literacy learning through (1) personal experiences—past and present—as readers and writers, (2) practical experiences and knowledge of their craft as they work with and learn from students, and (3) professional study that allows them to develop and extend their knowledge base about teaching and learning literacy.

2017 ILA Standard

1.1

Also in this chapter, we emphasize how different perspectives related to reading and learning inform teachers' knowledge and beliefs about literacy learning.

Language, social, and psychological perspectives are not mutually exclusive domains of knowledge. Often, effective literacy practice, sometimes referred to as **best practice**, requires teachers to use multiple perspectives as they plan and enact literacy instruction in their diverse, multidimensional classrooms. The final section of this chapter describes various theoretical models of the reading process. Understanding reading and learning to read within the context of theoretical models will enable you to connect knowledge and beliefs about reading to issues and approaches related to instructional practice.

The Importance of Belief Systems

■ **Analyze how beliefs about literacy learning influence instructional decisions and practices.**

Knowledge and beliefs about reading and learning to read are wedded in ways that influence almost every aspect of a teacher's instructional decisions and practices. To illustrate, consider what Mrs. Zufall does to help her students develop into confident readers and writers. Creating a literate environment where children feel comfortable to read and write and making connections with literature are essential. In addition, sharing the book with the class results in a "commercial" for another book, Janet and Allan Ahlberg's *The Jolly Christmas Postman*, which is part of the classroom library collection. Sharing literature encourages the children to read and write, which are integral parts of the literacy curriculum in this first-grade classroom.

All of the reading and writing activities that evolved from the unanticipated events of the morning provided children with a demonstration of the *intertextuality* of stories. Stories are products of the imagination, but the problems and themes they portray reflect the human experience. *Intertextuality* is a word used by literary theorists to describe the connections that exist within and between texts. Think about the personal connections made by Maura, Destanie, and their classmates. The children in Mrs. Zufall's class are exploring what it means to be *meaning seekers* and *meaning makers*. Their use of texts to construct meaning is the nexus by which they link the stories and explore a theme that will recur throughout their lives. They are developing a critical literary stance.

2017 ILA Standards

1.1, 1.2, 1.3

The work of teachers sometimes takes unexpected twists and turns—"teachable moments," if you will—that usually beget reasons for reading and writing. Yet taking advantage of a teachable moment, as Mrs. Zufall did, requires a philosophy of reading and learning to read. Some educators call a teacher's philosophical stance a *worldview*; others call it a *belief system*. For one reason or another, some teachers would probably have reacted differently to the children's letters. Perhaps another teacher would have praised Maura and Destanie for their efforts in writing the letters but, rather than extend the **literacy event**, would have concentrated on the misspellings or punctuation error. Another teacher might have been too busy or preoccupied with other matters to respond to Destanie's request in a manner that connects literacy learning to life in the classroom. Other teachers might simply have been oblivious to the teachable moment because they did not understand or appreciate the literacy event that occurred. Our point, therefore, is that a teacher's knowledge and beliefs about the nature and purposes of reading and the ways in which it should be taught contribute significantly to whatever decisions a teacher makes in a given situation.

Different Beliefs, Different Instructional Decisions

Just about every teacher we've ever talked to agrees on the main goal of reading instruction: to teach children to become independent readers and learners. Differences among teachers, however, often reflect varying beliefs and instructional perspectives on how to help children achieve independence. Because they view the reading process through different belief systems, teachers have different instructional concerns and emphases. The decisions they make will also vary based on research and societal influences.

2017 ILA Standards

1.1, 4.1, 4.2

In addition, effective reading teachers use their knowledge and beliefs about reading to adapt instruction to individual differences among children in their classrooms. The students they work with may have different academic, language, cultural, or physical needs. Student diversity in today's classrooms is greater now than at any time in this century. There are an increasing number of students whose first language is not English and whose culture does not reflect the beliefs, values, and standards of the mainstream culture in U.S. society. Moreover, inclusive classrooms, where students with "special needs" are included in regular classrooms, make it necessary that teachers become knowledgeable about the nature and purposes of reading acquisition.

No two teachers, even if they work with students at the same grade level and in classrooms next door to each other, teach reading in exactly the same way. Even though they may share the same instructional goals and adhere to literacy guidelines established within the school district or state department of education standards, teachers often make decisions and engage in practices based on what they know and believe to be worthwhile. In Box 1.1, Meghan, a high school student, reflects upon her experiences of learning to read. She recounts both positive and negative reading experiences, suggests characteristics of an effective reading teacher, and describes her beliefs on why teachers teach differently.

DIFFERING INSTRUCTIONAL DECISIONS Observe how Arch and Latisha, two first-grade teachers, introduce beginners to reading and learning to read. Arch invites his first graders to explore and experience the uses of oral and written language in a

---

BOX 1.1 | STUDENT VOICES

Meghan considers herself a good student and especially likes math. Overall she enjoys school, but she believes "It would be better if classes weren't so boring." As a high school student, Meghan has had many reading experiences and can identify characteristics that reading teachers exhibit that make them effective. Meghan believes "good teachers":

- Are caring and helpful
- Know what they are talking about
- Are professional
- Teach rather than assign
- Provide a variety of interactive, instructional activities
- Explain things well

- Provide a decent collection of interesting books in the classroom
- Know their students

She further explains that she has had "good" and "poor" reading teachers. Meghan believes that teachers teach differently because "Everyone has different personalities, backgrounds, cultural familiarity, college experiences, and everyday living occurrences."

Meghan's experiences and insights reflect how teachers exhibit different beliefs that influence instructional decisions. Students are affected by teachers' instructional styles in positive and negative ways. Consequently, it is important for teachers to be aware of their beliefs and understand how their instructional decisions affect students.

variety of instructional situations. He chooses all kinds of authentic and functional reading material—"anything that's real and important to the kids"—for reading and learning to read: signs, box tops, labels, poems, nursery rhymes, children's books, interactive stories, and computer games. His students also create their own texts, and these become the basis for reading. They write in journals about what they read, make books from original stories that they share with one another, and dictate stories that Arch captures on chart paper. In addition, Arch uses "big books" and storybooks to build concepts and skills related to reading. Often he begins a big-book lesson by reading the story aloud and discussing it with the class. Over the course of several days, he rereads the story in unison with the children once, twice, or even more times and then invites individual students to read parts of the story on their own.

2017 ILA Standard

2.1

Arch pays some attention to letter–sound relationships in the context of the writing and reading activities that children engage in. He encourages students to invent spellings during journal writing and other writing activities by helping them "spell the words the way they sound." In doing so, he responds individually to children's invented spellings. For words that he thinks a child should know how to spell correctly, he provides explicit intervention. For others, he accepts the child's invention if it approximates the conventional spelling. In addition, during big-book readings, Arch will periodically stop to point out and discuss initial letters and sounds, letter combinations, or endings. When students read aloud, Arch places little importance on word-perfect reading. He says, "I tell my kids not to let one or two words prevent them from reading; they might be able to understand what the story is about and to enjoy it without identifying all of the words."

Latisha also teaches reading to 6-year-olds. But her approach is different from Arch's. She believes quite strongly that beginning readers must start with letter–sound correspondences, translating print into speech. Other than occasional "experience charts" in the first weeks of the school year, Latisha doesn't attempt to introduce writing until most of her children make the monumental "click" between the black squiggly marks on a page (print) and the sounds they represent (speech).

Of the "click," Latisha says, "You can't miss it." When she sees children making the connection between print and speech, Latisha begins to aim for mastery.

The study of words in Latisha's class centers around story selections from the basal reading program that her school adopted several years ago. The basal program provides Latisha with "great literature, big books, everything that you need to teach reading." When she began teaching 15 years ago, Latisha taught letter–sound relationships by relying heavily on workbooks and worksheets from the basal program. Her students spent a lot of time on isolated drill and rote memorization of phonics rules. "I didn't know better then. Using workbook exercises was accepted practice by the teachers in my building, and I thought I was doing the right thing."

Today, however, Latisha bases much of what she does on research related to how children learn words. Each day she blocks out 15 to 20 minutes for word study. She still teaches letter–sound relationships in a direct and systematic manner but relies more on *explicit* instruction—that is, Latisha makes it a practice to *model* skills and strategies that children need to decipher unknown words, *explain* why it is important for students to learn the skill or strategy under study, and *guide* students in their acquisition of the skill or strategy. She makes sure, for example, at the beginning of the school year that her students have rudimentary skills related to hearing sounds in words, recognizing letters and sounds, and blending sounds into words. Latisha uses story selections from the basal reading anthology and big books to identify words for study and to provide practice and application in the use of the skill or strategy. Rather than dispense worksheets that require students to circle letters or draw lines to pictures, Latisha says, "I do a lot more teaching about phonics skills and strategies so that it makes sense to students as they learn to decode words."

The perspectives from which Latisha and Arch teach reading reflect different beliefs about learning to read that result in different instructional emphases and practices. Arch uses authentic, real-world literature such as children's books and functional materials such as signs and box tops. Latisha relies on materials from a basal reading program that includes literature anthologies and a wide range of ancillary materials. Latisha begins instruction with an emphasis on phonics skills and strategies. Arch begins with immersion in reading and writing. Comprehension is as important to Latisha as it is to Arch, but the two differ in belief. Latisha's understanding of reading suggests that when children decode words accurately and quickly, they are in a better position to comprehend what they read than children who are not accurate and automatic decoders. Arch's view is that children who engage in authentic literacy experiences will search for meaning in everything they read and write.

Reading Instruction and Teachers' Belief Systems

Latisha's style of teaching reading reflects beliefs that employ a systematic instructional approach. A systematic instructional approach includes direct teaching and a logical instructional sequence. This structure includes ample opportunities to practice specific skills and move along a defined trajectory related to the sequencing of skills. Arch's methods are the product of a belief system that reflects a broader constructivist view. This model is focused on the needs of the individual child. In this perspective, the role of the teacher is a facilitator who helps the child negotiate text by addressing the most immediate instructional needs. The progression of instruction or sequencing of skills is often centered on the student's individual progress. Language skills are practiced through application or embedded skills instruction.

In examining these two approaches to reading, it is clear that the implementation of reading instruction can be viewed from multiple perspectives. This ambiguity is further complicated as we look at the current movement at the national level that emphasizes teaching methods and curriculum standards, and demands that educators be accountable for result.

NATIONAL INITIATIVES   In April 1997, the National Institute of Child Health and Human Development (NICHD), in consultation with the secretary of education, was charged to convene a National Reading Panel (NRP) that would assess the status of research-based knowledge, including the effectiveness of various approaches to teaching children to read. The panel was asked to provide a summary of findings that included the application of this work to classroom-based instruction. The NRP built on the previous work of the National Research Council (NRC) published in *Preventing Reading Difficulties in Young Children* (Snow, Burns, & Griffin, 1998). In April 2000, the panel released its findings and made recommendations about teaching methods that are scientifically proven to increase student learning and achievement. The reauthorization of the **Elementary and Secondary Education Act (ESEA)** in 2001 includes the scientifically based reading instruction recommendations for preschool and primary grades.

Scientifically based reading research, as defined in the federal legislation, is the body of scientific evidence about reading methodologies drawn from experimental and quasi-experimental work. These studies include rigorous data analysis and measurements that provide valid data across observers and evaluators. The research must be accepted by a peer-reviewed journal or be approved by an independent panel of experts.

With the reauthorization of ESEA in 2001, the federal government set forward initiatives in an attempt to ensure that no child is left behind. **No Child Left Behind (NCLB)** requires districts to assess all subjects to determine the success of all students. This legislation challenges educators to use evidence-based research as a guide in the development of high-quality reading programs for students in preschool and the primary grades. Programs such as Reading First and Early Reading First clearly define the parameters and expected outcomes for educators and charge teachers to examine their teaching practices, tools, and materials. Reading First was established to improve K–3 reading achievement with the focus on explicitly teaching phonemic awareness, phonics, oral reading fluency, vocabulary, and comprehension. Early Reading First focuses on literacy development of preschoolers while also utilizing scientifically based reading research teaching approaches. These programs challenge reading teachers to rethink what it means to "teach and learn." The ESEA was reauthorized in 2015, with the objective of continuing No Child Left Behind's initiatives but reducing the role of the federal government and providing states, teachers, and parents with more decision-making responsibilities. It also had a focus on ensuring all students the opportunity to learn in spite of possibly disadvantaged backgrounds.

Continuing dialogue related to these current trends has resulted in recommendations from high-level organizations. The International Literacy Association (ILA), formerly known as the International Reading Association, released an Advocacy Position statement (2015) in support of the reauthorization of ESEA (2015). It focuses on quality education for all students no matter their backgrounds, dedicating funding for comprehensive literacy programs and professional development, and reducing reliance on standardized assessments. Previously, in the ESEA of 2001, the ILA raised questions about the notion of scientific research and calls for a broader perspective. This point of view stresses that "no single study ever establishes a program or practice as effective; moreover, it is the convergence of evidence from a variety of study designs that is ultimately scientifically convincing" (International Reading Association, 2002b, p. 1). The ILA supports evidence-based reading instruction as the way to enhance literacy development.

In light of the various positions on reading research, teachers need to be aware of programs and practices based on multiple types of research studies with a broad scope of topics reviewed. Research provides the reading professional with a foundation for effective reading instruction. It should broaden reading professionals' beliefs, not narrow them. There are more and more external mandates and legislative decisions regarding reading. A few legislative influences on literacy include **IDEIA** and the **LEARN Act**. These are briefly described in Figure 1.1.

2017 ILA Standard

6.4

The Common Core State Standard (CCSS) initiative set out to develop high-quality education standards in order to ensure that all students are college and career ready. With the focus on the CCSS established by National Governors Association and the Council of Chief State School Officers (2010), state-led curricular expectations were developed for content areas. The CCSS are rigorous, research-based

Figure 1.1 Legislative Influences on Literacy

The Individuals with Disabilities Education Improvement Act (IDEIA) — The 2004 reauthorization of IDEA (1997) established federal rules for special education. The reauthorization focused on more effective instruction for struggling students. Response to Intervention (RTI) was derived to provide intensive support and intervention.

Literacy Education for All, Results for the Nation Act (LEARN) — A proposed bill that would strengthen the literacy skills of all students from birth to grade 12. LEARN would support literacy programs for enhancing reading and writing skills at the local and state levels.

standards in reading, writing, listening, speaking, and mathematics. The Common Core State Standards for English Language Arts (CCSS-ELA) have created significant changes in literacy practices. Grade-specific standards require students to read more challenging texts—both narrative and informational—in order to help them reach more advanced literacy achievement levels (International Reading Association, 2012). CCSS-ELA standards include knowledge and skills in the domains of reading, writing, listening, speaking, and language, as well as the integration of the language arts across content subject areas in order to develop college- and career-readiness skills and strategies.

TEACHER PREPARATION   Students need to be prepared for college and career with a different set of skills than in the past. Developing higher-order thinking skills that require students to think critically is the focus of the standards. In order for students to develop these skills, teaching needs to be more personalized, relevant, applicable, and collaborative. Teachers are more empowered to utilize a variety of pedagogical strategies, digital tools, and resources to meet individual students' needs. Teachers are working more collaboratively with students to include them in the learning process. Additionally, data are utilized to set standard-based learning goals as well as instructional and assessment procedures.

Balancing literature and informational texts, building knowledge in content areas, using complex texts, relying upon evidence in text, developing academic vocabulary, fostering complex thinking skills, and relying upon a technological emphasis all have changed the literacy landscape. Teachers need to make decisions to develop reading, writing, listening, and speaking skills while they also cover the nonnegotiables in the area of teaching reading.

With today's views of reading content and reading instruction, teachers now more than ever need to make informed decisions based on their beliefs of reading and learning to read. Richard Vacca (see Box 1.2) emphasizes that teachers must make decisions for instructional approaches and strategies as well as materials. Teachers—not programs or mandates—produce effective reading instruction and achievement. It is ultimately the teacher who is responsible for providing successful reading experiences.

2017 ILA Standard

6.4

TRANSLITERACY   The teacher is responsible for providing reading experiences in a transliterate environment. Although difficult to define due to various interpretations of what constitutes **transliteracy** skills in the context of changing textual media, an understanding that best represents the viewpoint of this text is that of Brueck (2015), who suggests that being transliterate is the ability to read, write, and interact across a range of platforms, tools and media. It is becoming an essential disposition in modern society. With an increasingly wide range of communication platforms and tools

BOX 1.2 | VIEWPOINT

Richard T. Vacca

The Common Core State Standards: A Hot Button Issue Gets Hotter

Richard T. Vacca is past president of the International Reading Association, a member of the Reading Hall of Fame, and the author of many books and articles on reading instruction.

Teaching children to read has always been a challenge, even for the most skilled and experienced classroom teachers. After all, reading is a covert and complex human process that takes place in the head and heart of the reader. Who really knows what happens within a child (or adult) who picks up a book or goes online to engage in the very human activity that we call *reading*? The best that teachers can do is to involve learners in reading and learning to read through the use of instructional practices and strategies based on the best evidence from research and inquiry.

A standards-based curriculum is an important dynamic in the reading and learning to read journey that all students travel from the first day that they step into a kindergarten classroom. Why a standards-based curriculum? Standards define what students should learn and how they should learn it at designated grade levels. Since the mid-1990s, state-based standards have provided a road map to what students *should know* and *be able to do* at each grade level, not only for English language arts, but for other content areas as well. The underlying rationale for a standards-based curriculum is that high learning expectations—clearly stated and specific in nature—will lead to noticeable increases in student achievement. With high learning expectations comes an accountability system based on "high-stakes" testing to determine how well students meet the standards formulated in each content area. Most states tie high-stakes assessment to the threat of grade-level retention for students who perform below predetermined levels of proficiency in critical areas such as reading. Unfortunately, in some classrooms a proficient level of performance on high-stakes assessment becomes "the be-all and end-all" of classroom instruction.

The United States, unlike most countries, does not have a set of national education standards. Individual states have sole responsibility for determining what teachers should teach and students should learn. However, in 2010 the National Governors Association and the Council of Chief State School Officers released the Common Core State Standards (CCSS) for literacy and mathematics. According to the CCSS Mission Statement (2010):

> The Common Core State Standards provide a consistent, clear understanding of what students are expected to learn, so teachers and parents know what they need to do to help them. The standards are designed to be robust and relevant to the real world, reflecting the knowledge that our young people need for success in college and careers. With American students fully prepared for the future, our communities will be best positioned to compete successfully in the global economy. (p.11)

Frequently referred to as "the Common Core," CCSS originally was adopted by 46 states and the District of Columbia at the time that I first wrote this viewpoint for the previous edition. Fast forward 3 years since then, and we find ourselves in greater controversy over Common Core than ever before. Four states have since dropped out of participation of Common Core in favor of individual state standards. The Internet is ablaze with pro and con perspectives on the value of the closest thing we have to national standards in mathematics and English language arts. What was a hot-button issue has become even hotter!

The Common Core is the closest the United States has come as a country to adopting a national curriculum. From a teaching perspective, one of the real benefits of having states use the same core standards is the strong possibility for broad-based sharing of what works in the classroom and what doesn't. Because the Common Core does not come with rigid guidelines concerning implementation, it provides local school flexibility to decide how to best implement the standards at various grade levels. And therein lies the challenge—and the hope that the Common Core will make a real difference in the literacy learning of children and adolescents in today's schools.

From the very onset of schooling, the Common Core recognizes that learning to read and reading to learn are two sides of the same "literacy coin." From kindergarten onward, there is greater emphasis than ever before on the use of informational texts in the classroom. Gone forever is that false dichotomy that has plagued literacy instruction for years: *In grades K–3, children learn to read, and in grades 4 and beyond, they read to learn.* The real potential of the Common Core is that it positions students to become more active in their use of literacy skills: to better understand what they are reading about, writing about, talking about in classroom discussion, or viewing on a computer screen or video monitor.

Weaving literacy into the fabric of content area learning—for beginners as well as those who are developing in their abilities—is one of the looming challenges that will be faced by all teachers. Reading, writing, talking, and viewing are tools that students use to learn. Who is in a better, more strategic position to show students how to learn with all kinds of texts at a particular grade level than the teacher who guides *what* students are expected to learn and *how* they are to learn it? Are the CCSS the panacea for solving all of the literacy problems that teachers, parents, administrators, policy makers, and politicians have been praying for? Hardly! Yet the Common Core gives schools an opportunity to make decisions about the types of texts that will be used for literacy learning as well as instructional approaches and strategies at different grade levels. As I write this revised viewpoint, many school districts are engaged in ongoing professional development efforts, working diligently to improve the implementation of core standards.

The road map provided by the Common Core never guaranteed a smooth journey to reading and learning to read for all students. From the get-go, I predicted that there would be bumps in the road, detours, and digressions in the implementation of CCSS. Let's face it. There will always be critics and controversies. Such is the nature of the politics of most educational issues in the United States. Yet from my perspective, the journey is worth taking.

available to anyone, what it means to be a "literate" person is rapidly evolving. By examining the many dispositions our students need to possess, it becomes evident that a focused preK–12 transliteracy initiative can help provide a foundation for creating a new type of student learning experience that leverages the affordances of contemporary technology to create a new vision for literacy learning with technology. Being able to use, locate, and evaluate information from a web page; participate in an online discussion; listen to a podcast; and develop a video production are a few examples of new information and communication technologies that require students to be critical, active readers. Readers need a wide range of reading abilities in the twenty-first-century classroom (Tate, 2011). They rely on their foundational literacies to develop the skills and strategies needed to be critical readers (Coiro, Knobel, Lankshear, & Leu, 2008). Transliteracy provides opportunities for developing literacy skills and encourages students to work together.

The integration of technologically based reading and writing instruction is an important component in today's classrooms. The extent of developing transliteracy skills in the classroom is dependent on teachers' belief systems and relies on their professional expertise and their evaluation of current technology to successfully integrate technology in their classrooms. Teachers need to think about how they will develop foundational and critical literacy skills so their students can successfully read print and nonprint materials. Jeremy Brueck provides further insights on transliteracy and reading instruction in Box 1.3.

 In this video (https://www.youtube.com/watch?v=BpQrfPQA1Ao), Jeremy Brueck discusses how teachers can develop transliteracy skills. What methods are used to support the development of transliteracy skills?

2017 ILA Standards

5.2, 5.3

MULTIPLE APPROACHES TO READING INSTRUCTION   Why isn't there more consensus on how to teach children to read? Although it is perfectly natural to want to know the "right way" to do something, a comprehensive reading program—using several methods instead of just one approach—gives teachers the freedom to use their own professional expertise and judgment. The danger of buying into the "right way" to teach reading is that teachers can become dependent on others telling them how to help students develop as readers. If teachers are to be empowered as professionals, they must apply their knowledge and beliefs about reading and learning to read in deciding what practices are best for their students in order to help them be college and career ready.

In the pressured world of teaching, it is sometimes easy to lose sight of what we know and believe about children, reading, and how children learn to read. The common thread that runs through the literacy practices of Mrs. Zufall, Arch, Latisha, and countless other reading professionals is that they view reading and learning to read through belief systems that define and shape their roles as classroom teachers. Through what set of beliefs do you view reading and learning to read? How do you believe reading and writing should be taught in an effective literacy program? Throughout your teaching career, from the time you begin studying to become a teacher and all the while you practice your craft, you will be continually developing answers to these questions as you build and refine your knowledge and beliefs about what counts as literacy learning in your classroom.

Are some belief systems better than others? The answer to the question lies not with the authors of this or any comprehensive text on reading telling you the "right way" to think about teaching and learning to read but in the process of coming to know about literacy learning. The more you know about what readers and writers do

BOX 1.3 | TRANSLITERACY

Jeremy Brueck

Toward a Transliterate Future

Dr. Jeremy Brueck, visiting assistant professor at the University of Akron's LeBron James Family Foundation College of Education, shares his perspectives on the concept of transliteracy in schools.

What does *transliteracy* mean?

Originating within the past 10 years, *transliteracy* is a term used by educators to describe literacy as more than a function of foundational skills, such as reading and writing, but also including the ability to communicate across traditional and emerging platforms.

> *From early signing and orality through handwriting, print, TV and film to networked digital media, the concept of transliteracy calls for a change of perspective away from the battles over print versus digital, and a move instead towards a unifying ecology not just of media, but of all literacies relevant to reading, writing, interaction and culture, both past and present.* (Thomas, S. et al., 2007)

Simply put, transliteracy is the understanding of traditional literacy components alongside the nuances that living in a touch-screen world brings. Transliteracy puts aside the differences between traditional and emerging literacies to focus on the interconnected path of all literacies and the role they play in the development of a literate member of society. Students need to become fluent not only in their reading and writing practice, but also in the digital skills that are put to regular use in the world around them.

Reading and writing are at the core of transliteracy, as we interact with both traditional and digital print in our daily lives. Whether we are flipping through the pages of a favorite paperback or checking the weather on a smartphone, foundational reading skills (letter knowledge, sounds, and word reading) and meaning-based skills (comprehension, conceptual knowledge, and vocabulary) play an integral role. However, new skills, such as recognizing icons, setting up preferences, mastering multitap and swipe gestures, play a pivotal role becoming a transliterate individual.

With an increasingly wide range of communication platforms and tools available to anyone, what it means to be a literate person is rapidly evolving. In the past, educators have used terms like *digital literacy*, *media literacy*, and *new literacies* to describe these concepts. Whatever the term, we know that emerging technologies is a large component of the skills and dispositions we need to build in transliterate students.

What do students of all ages need to know about transliteracy and learning?

Literacy in a digital age is no longer a linear process; in fact, it is a hyperlinked experience in which we locate information, read, process, find links to other relevant information, and move on. Literacy in a digital age is much more than interacting with traditional print materials. In addition to books, newspapers, and magazines, we now interact with digital text, blogs, websites, video, and audio content.

With a diverse and increasingly online set of learning resources available to them, students no longer need to memorize and recall basic factual information. Searching, locating, and validating information is an increasingly important skill set for students to develop. Gone are the days of a single set of encyclopedias for classroom research, as students today are more inclined to search for a YouTube video or Wikipedia entry to find the information they need. Free, open, and easily accessible online resources present an incredible opportunity not only to answer questions and solve problems, but also for students to show what they know in new and creative ways with a global audience.

What do today's teachers need to know about transliteracy?

The students coming to classrooms are not the same learners they once were. Student literacy experiences are much different than those felt by today's teachers. Growing up in a digital age, with instant access to information and the sum of human knowledge at their fingertips, provides a whole new realm of literacy experiences for students. Educators should emphasize a seamlessly integrated approach to technology. Technology should not drive the curriculum nor determine content; rather, technology should be integrated at every available opportunity to take advantage of the expanded depth and breadth of student learning.

Teachers must look beyond literacy to the development of transliterate practices in their classrooms and in their daily lives to ensure they develop a thorough understanding of the skills and dispositions a transliterate individual possesses. Teachers can model these skills through the creation of new learning spaces that support and embrace information flow and communication beyond the walls of the classroom. Teachers must empower students to lead their own learning by shifting their pedagogical approaches and practices, taking risks, and learning alongside their students.

Educators who seek to bring transliteracy into their classrooms can begin by considering how to effectively merge content, pedagogy, and technology into their professional practice. The Technological Pedagogical Content Knowledge (TPACK) framework (Mishra & Koehler, 2006) is one resource that can assist teachers in understanding the dynamic relationship between content, pedagogy, and technology in the classroom. The TPACK framework requires teachers to develop understanding of the dynamic, transactional relationship between all three components. In this regard, TPACK "is an emergent form of knowledge" that teachers must develop beyond content, technology, and pedagogy alone (Mishra & Koehler, 2006, p. 1028).

and the roles that reading and writing play in the lives of children, the more empowered you are to respond to a question of such personal and professional importance.

Belief systems related to literacy learning are not a collection of naive assumptions and presuppositions but rather a set of beliefs that are grounded in research and current thinking about reading and writing. As suggested in the International Literacy Association's *Standards for Literacy Professionals* (ILA, 2017), beliefs are built on an organized and specific set of knowledge, skills, and dispositions that are needed to influence students' reading achievement. We as authors have core beliefs that underlie the writing of this text. Suffice it to say that we believe some aspects of reading and learning to read have changed considerably since we entered the teaching field, primarily because the *knowledge base* has changed. Nevertheless, there are some beliefs about children, teachers, teaching and learning, and how children learn to read and use reading to learn that have remained constant since we entered the teaching profession. If we were to characterize our worldview of reading and learning to read today, we would affirm that our beliefs are rooted in an *interactive* view of the reading process and a comprehensive view of reading instruction—concepts that will be developed in this chapter and throughout the text.

Check Your Understanding 1.1: Gauge your understanding of the skills and concepts in this section.

How Teachers Come to Know About Reading and Learning to Read

■ **Explain how teachers use and construct personal, practical, and professional knowledge about literacy learning.**

Teachers come to know in different ways. For example, in a lifetime of interaction with the world around us, we acquire knowledge about reading and learning to read by *building it from the inside* as we interact with people, processes, ideas, and things. Jean Piaget's theory of **constructivism** provides a compelling explanatory framework for understanding the acquisition of knowledge. Piaget, one of the preeminent child psychologists of the twentieth century, theorized that children do not internalize knowledge directly from the outside but construct it from inside their heads, in interaction with the environment. When constructivist thinking is applied to the acquisition of knowledge about teaching and learning, it holds that teachers engage in a process of seeking and making meaning from personal, practical, and professional experiences.

Constructing Personal Knowledge

Personal knowledge of reading and learning to read grows out of a teacher's history as a reader and a writer. Consider, for example, the influences in your life that have shaped the literate person you are. From birth, you have interacted with *people* (parents, teachers, siblings, friends, and significant others) and *things* (all kinds of literacy artifacts and texts, including books, signs, letters, labels, pencil and paper, word processors, e-mails, and the Internet) to construct knowledge about the *processes* of reading and writing. By engaging in reading and writing, you come to know in a very personal way what readers and writers do and the contributions that reading and writing make to a life. You belong to what Frank Smith (1988) calls the "literacy club" by virtue of the fact that you read and write.

The development of an **autobiographical narrative** is a powerful tool that helps you link your personal history as a reader to instructional beliefs and practices. Not all teachers like to read, even though they know how. Some may read well and be well

Figure 1.2 Developing a Reading Autobiographical Narrative

Reflect on how you learned to read, the reading habits you have formed, home and school influences on your reading development, and the kinds of reading you do. Prepare an autobiographical sketch that captures these personal memories. How did you learn to read? What home reading experiences do you recall? What kinds of instructional activities and practices were you involved in as an elementary school student? Which ones do you recall fondly? Which, if any, do you recall with regret? In retrospect, what belief systems and views of reading and learning to read did your elementary school teachers seem to hold? Were you effectively taught how to handle the variety of reading tasks you face in the real world?

read. But others may have struggled as readers and bear the emotional scars to prove it. How do these realities affect what teachers do in classroom situations?

An autobiographical narrative helps you inquire into the past in order to better understand what you do in the present and what you would like to do in future classroom situations. Teachers who engage in narrative inquiry explore mental pictures of memories, incidents, or situations in their lives. The inquiry allows teachers to reflect, make connections, and understand why some decisions are made.

To develop a reading autobiography, consider the questions in Figure 1.2. You may wish to share your narratives with others. What beliefs, values, and attitudes are an integral part of your stories? How do your personal histories of reading and learning to read influence where you are in your thinking about reading and where you would like to be?

2017 ILA Standard

6.3

Constructing Practical Knowledge

Teachers also construct practical knowledge, which is closely related to personal knowledge in that it grows out of experience both in and out of the classroom. The more you work with and observe students in literacy situations in classroom and community contexts and reflect on their behavior *and* your own, the more you develop theories about what is the best practice for the readers and writers with whom you work. Practical knowledge is characterized by the beliefs, values, and attitudes that you construct about readers and writers, texts, reading and writing processes, learning to read and write, and the role of the teacher in the development of children's literate behavior.

In teacher education programs, field experiences and student teaching are vehicles for acquiring practical knowledge. In addition, interactions with and observations of practicing teachers influence the way you might think about reading and learning to read in classroom situations. At times, preservice teachers may find incongruities between what is taught in education courses and what they observe in the field. These incongruities create conceptual conflict. This conflict is healthy because it helps reflective students of literacy think more deeply about their own understandings, beliefs, and practices.

The construction of practical knowledge extends beyond classroom situations and includes interactions within the cultural context of school and community. For example, a teacher's beliefs about reading and learning to read may be affected by the beliefs of colleagues and administrators, school board policies, curriculum guidelines, the publishing and testing industry, public opinion, and standards for teaching reading.

Constructing Professional Knowledge and Expertise

As an integral part of their professional development, teachers interact with the world of ideas. Professional education organizations, such as the ILA, refer to what teachers ought to know and be able to do in order to teach reading well as *standards* or the *knowledge base*.

Professional knowledge is knowledge acquired from an ongoing study of the practice of teaching. What teacher education programs do best is help preservice and inservice teachers build a knowledge base that is grounded in current theory, research, and practice. Throughout their professional development, the books and journals teachers read, the courses and workshops they take, and the conferences they attend contribute to the vision they have of reading and learning to read.

2017 ILA Standards

1.1, 6.1

The instructional differences among teachers reflect the knowledge they put to use in classroom situations. While few would argue that nothing is as practical as a good theory, we embrace the notion that there's nothing as theoretical as a good practice. Teachers construct theories of reading and learning to read based on their ways of knowing, which influence the way they teach, including the ways they plan, use, and select texts; interact with learners; and assess literate activity. In turn, the decisions teachers make about instruction influence students' reading performance and their perceptions of and attitudes toward reading, as illustrated in Figure 1.3.

Coming to know what readers do is no easy matter. Part of the challenge that teachers encounter comes from the complex, elusive nature of the reading process. Who can ever really know a process that takes place in the mind? The best we can do is investigate reading and learning to read by inquiring into literacy teaching and learning. The inquiry process can be made easier with assistance from a **literacy coach**. Using their expertise in reading and learning to read, literacy coaches provide professional development opportunities and resources. Literacy coaches help develop expertise in the classroom.

The role of the literacy coach varies. As reported in the **International Literacy Association's 2017 Standards for Literacy Professionals**, the primary role of the reading coach is to support teacher learning. Coaches provide a variety of activities while in a nonevaluative role, including developing curriculum with colleagues, making professional development presentations to teachers, modeling lessons, providing resources, and visiting classrooms to provide feedback.

2017 ILA Standards

6.2, 6.3

The responsibility of the literacy coach also varies across ages. According to Puig and Froelich (2007), the elementary coach's role focuses on promoting a more comprehensive literacy program, whereas in middle and high schools, literacy coaches support the teachers using reading and writing to develop content area knowledge. No matter how reading is taught, constructing professional knowledge is essential.

Figure 1.3 Relationships Between Teacher Knowledge, Decisions, and Actions and Students' Literacy Activity and Attitudes Toward Reading and Writing

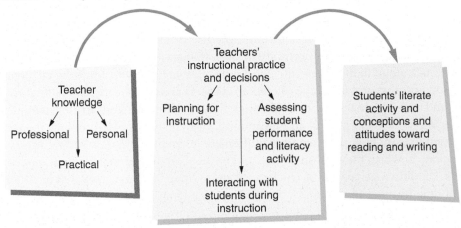

Personal, practical, and professional experiences are the stepping-stones to knowing about reading and learning to read.

A reading professional, whether novice or veteran, continually needs to study the knowledge base from *multidisciplinary* perspectives. Because reading and learning to read are complex processes, no one field of study provides all the answers. Understanding reading from multiple perspectives allows teachers to affirm, change, or let go of what they believe and value in light of new knowledge and research. Multidisciplinary perspectives on reading and learning to read enrich and broaden the knowledge base so that teachers are in the very best position to use their professional expertise and judgment to make instructional decisions.

Check Your Understanding 1.2: Gauge your understanding of the skills and concepts in this section.

Perspectives on Learning to Read

■ **Define language, social, and psychological perspectives on reading and explain how they inform knowledge and beliefs about literacy learning.**

A single discipline cannot provide a teacher with the insights and understandings needed to guide and support literacy learning in the modern world. The fields of education, linguistics, cognitive psychology, technology, sociology, and anthropology, to name a few, contribute in important ways to knowledge and beliefs about reading and learning to read. From a *cognitive* perspective, for example, an elementary teacher needs to understand, among other things, how children learn words in an alphabetic system of writing such as English; from a *language* perspective, how children's knowledge of written language emerges and develops naturally in early childhood to form the basis for literacy learning; and from a *sociocultural* perspective, how children's home language and community values influence language use and literacy learning.

Research on reading in the past three decades has centered primarily on the roles of cognition and language in reading acquisition. Cognitive studies have provided insights into how people comprehend and learn as they process written symbols. Cognitive scientists and researchers are interested in how reading works inside people's minds—how readers learn to *decode* words accurately and automatically in an alphabetic writing system, how readers use prior knowledge (*schemata*) to understand what they are reading, and how readers use and develop *strategies* to *regulate* and *monitor* comprehension as they learn from written language.

2017 ILA Standard

1.1

Language and literacy learning are inseparable. Learning to read needs to be understood in terms of learning to use written language effectively. One of the most important ways people learn is through the use of language—spoken, written, or signed. Children need the opportunity to share literacy experiences. Encouraging children to talk aloud in deliberate and substantive interactions with adults helps them to develop effective oral language (Biemiller, 2006). Shared book experiences, oral reading, and role playing are a few activities that connect oral and written language. Engaging students in playful and meaningful print activities also provides them the occasion to learn how print works. Children are inherently social, so setting up social situations in which they can share oral and written language enhances their language skills. If children perceive little use for oral and written language, they will have a difficult time learning to read and write. However, if language is meaningful, the social and cultural situations in which it is used allow children to discern what reading and writing are all about.

Cognitive Insights into Reading and Learning to Read

A university colleague of ours, a cognitive psychologist by training, says he's been researching and studying the reading process for more than two decades because he's interested in "how the mind works." How the mind works is another way of saying that he's interested in understanding *cognitive* and *metacognitive processes* involved in reading. His inquiries into the reading process embrace a psychological perspective. One of the important contributions from cognitive psychology focuses on beginning readers' discovery of the **alphabetic principle** in languages such as English. Learning to read English involves learning how an alphabetic writing system works.

2017 ILA Standards

1.1, 1.3

THE ALPHABETIC PRINCIPLE AND LEARNING TO READ   The alphabetic principle suggests that there is a correspondence between letters (*graphemes*), which are the basic units of writing, and sounds (*phonemes*). Tunmer and Nicholson (2011) report that in order for children to connect graphemes and phonemes, adult interaction to facilitate development is required. The teacher has an active role in this process. Therefore, a teacher needs to understand how beginning readers come to master the alphabetic system and use their knowledge of English writing to identify words.

However, before you consider how beginners learn to identify words accurately and quickly, participate in the two demonstrations that follow. These demonstrations make clear what *skilled* readers know about the alphabetic system and how they use their knowledge for accurate and automatic word identification.

Suppose the following lines were flashed on a screen in half-second intervals, and you were asked to write down what you could remember after each line was flashed.

Line 1   ─O─ □ ⊗ ⌐ ⊔ ╪ ⌐┘ ⊔

Line 2   Xmrbacdy

Line 3   Boragle

Line 4   Institution

Line 5   flour wiggle come stove investigate girl door yell

Line 6   the beautiful girl ran down the steep hill

What can we learn from this demonstration? Human beings can make about four fixations per second with their eyes (Smith, 1985). When looking at the flashed items, skilled readers use about 50 milliseconds of visual intake and then use 200 milliseconds to process the intake. During the intake, they can probably attend to only about five to seven items—the range of items most human beings can hold in short-term memory. When looking at each of the six lines for a half second, the limitations of short-term memory (being able to recall five to seven items) operate. What changes line by line is the nature of the items. Skilled readers are able to recognize some of the items quickly and accurately because they are able to perceive them as letter patterns or units of written language. These patterns are recognized by skilled readers as familiar *spelling patterns* or *sight words*.

In line 1, skilled college-level readers are unable to group the "squiggles" into meaningful patterns. The reason is simple: They have no prior knowledge of the squiggles, which have not been learned as an *orthography*. Skilled readers have internalized the shapes of alphabetic letters, their names, and the sounds they symbolize. But they aren't the least bit familiar with the shapes of these individual squiggles or whether they function as written symbols that represent sounds.

In line 2, the black squiggly marks are recognized as individual letters in English writing. However, within the time constraint of a half-second interval, college readers cannot group all of the letters into meaningful letter patterns. As a result, they have difficulty holding all the letters in short-term memory.

In lines 3, 4, and 5, skilled readers can group the letters into familiar spelling patterns. *Boragle* and *institution* are easily recalled by most college students when flashed on a screen. Even though *boragle* is a nonsense word, the letter patterns are consistent and predictable. *Institution* is recalled as a known sight word.

Most college students cannot in a half second recall all of the words in line 5 because these words cannot be strung together into a meaningful utterance. However, the students stand a greater chance of recalling line 6 precisely because the string of words makes a meaningful sentence that they are able to decode, based on their immediate sight recognition of known words.

Identifying Letter Patterns   Now read these two lists, both containing nonwords:

List 1	List 2
Scrass	tblc
Sook	gfpv
Tolly	oeaiu
amittature	rtbm
lanfication	Gdhtaiueo

Which list is easier to read? Use what you learned from the first demonstration to respond to the question.

List 1, of course, is fairly easy for skilled readers to read, but list 2 is nearly impossible. The reason, as you might have surmised, involves your skill at identifying letter patterns. "English is an alphabetic system that consists of mapping between graphemes and phonemes within words" (Ehri, 2011, p. 232). Skilled readers can connect written English letter patterns to sounds. They know that *scr* is likely to occur in English writing but that *tblc* is not likely to occur. When skilled readers encounter multisyllabic words (or even nonwords that contain common orthographic patterns), they depend on their ability to group these patterns into syllables. This is done by using their knowledge of likely and unlikely letter sequences. We know that the letters *lan* would go together to pronounce "lan," and that *fi, ca,* and *tion* should be treated as clusters of letters that we chunk together or treat as a group. Cognitive studies show that skillful readers chunk words into syllables automatically, *in the course of perceiving letters.* Skilled readers are able to do this because of their knowledge of likely spelling patterns, or **orthographic knowledge**. This knowledge is so thoroughly learned that skilled readers devote less attention to encoding and put less energy into identifying words (Templeton, 2011).

Use of Spaces   From an instructional perspective, then, it is important to know how to help beginning readers develop into skilled readers who can identify words quickly and accurately as they read. When young children begin reading, their eyes encounter three units of written language: letters, words, and sentences. The visual display of words on the page makes the learning of words easier. This can be determined in the following:

Readingandwritingarecomplexprocessesthatrequireexplicitinstruction.

Because of the use of spaces—a print convention that evolved with Gutenberg's invention of the printing press in the fifteenth century—the visual display of written language creates a system of distinct, perceptual units called *words.* According to Ehri (1995), during the course of learning to read, the eyes come to favor written words over letters and sentences: "The advantage of words over sentences is that words can be assimilated in one glance. The advantage of words over letters is that written words correspond more reliably to spoken words than letters correspond to sounds" (p. 171). Because words are the primary units of written language, helping beginners develop word-reading skill is one of the important instructional responsibilities of teachers in learning to read. Other print conventions—directionality, upper- and lowercase usage, and punctuation—all need to be considered and will affect students' ability to form words and read accurately and fluently. Although beginners have developed some knowledge of written language prior to first grade, explicit instruction becomes essential as children progress through various phases of word-reading development and develop strategies to read words quickly and accurately.

How children think and reason with print is an important concern in this text. A cognitive view of reading suggests that the reader's ability to construct meaning is at the core of the process. The constructive processes characteristic of reading comprehension have been of intense interest to cognitive psychologists and reading researchers for more than a decade. In particular, they have studied the role that schemata play in comprehending texts.

2017 ILA Standard

1.1

SCHEMA THEORY AND READING COMPREHENSION   **Schemata** reflect the prior knowledge, experiences, conceptual understandings, attitudes, values, skills, and procedures a reader brings to a reading situation. Students use what they know already to give meaning to new events and experiences. Cognitive psychologists use the singular term *schema* to describe how humans organize and construct meaning in their heads. Schemata have been called "the building blocks of cognition" (Rumelhart, 1982) and "a cognitive map to the world" (Neisser, 1976) because they represent elaborate networks of concepts, skills, and procedures that we use to make sense of new stimuli, events, and situations. Rueda (2011) emphasizes that "Automatic processing of schemas requires minimal working memory resources and allows problem solving to proceed with minimal effort" (p. 93). Therefore, meaning making while reading becomes more efficient.

In order to help understand schema, for example, do you possess the schemata needed to interpret the following passage?

> When evidence of the failure is first observed, stop the subject immediately before more damage is done. Continue to observe the subject in more detail to determine the exact location and nature of the failure. In most cases the failure will be readily apparent, but for an inexperienced observer care must be taken to ensure the proper location is selected since the observer will most likely have only one opportunity to correct the failure.

Upon first reading the passage, it may seem difficult to understand unless you were able to activate an appropriate schema. How many of you recognized that the passage had to do with getting a flat tire? Once a schema for getting a flat tire is activated, the words and phrases in the passage take on new meaning. Now try rereading the passage. Upon rereading, you will probably react by saying, "Aha! Now that I know the passage is about getting a flat tire, it makes sense!" Ambiguous words such as *subject, opportunity,* and *failure* are now interpreted within the framework of what you know about having a flat tire. The more you know about flat tires, the more comprehensible the passage becomes. When readers activate appropriate schemata, *expectations* are raised for the meaning of the text. Your expectations for the passage help you anticipate meaning and relate information from the passage to things you already know.

The more we hear, see, read, or experience new information, the more we refine and expand existing schemata within our language system.

Schemata, as you can see, influence reading comprehension and learning. For comprehension to happen, readers must activate or build a schema that fits with information from a text. When a good fit occurs, a schema functions in at least three ways to facilitate comprehension. First, the schema provides a framework that allows readers to *organize* text information efficiently and effectively. The ability to integrate and organize new information into old facilitates retention. Second, the schema allows readers to *make inferences* about what happens or is likely to happen in a text. Inferences, for example, help children predict upcoming information or fill in gaps in the material. And third, the schema helps readers *elaborate* on the material. Elaboration is a powerful aspect of reasoning with print. When children elaborate on what they have read, they engage in cognitive activity that involves speculation, judgment, and evaluation.

METACOGNITION AND LEARNING **Metacognition**, defined generally by Ann Brown (1985), refers to knowledge about and regulation of some form of cognitive activity. In the case of reading, metacognition refers to (1) *self-knowledge*—the knowledge students have about themselves as readers and learners; (2) *task knowledge*—the knowledge of reading tasks and the strategies that are appropriate given a task at hand; and (3) *self-monitoring*—the ability of students to monitor reading by keeping track of how well they are comprehending.

Consider the following scenario, one that is quite common when working with struggling readers: When reading orally, a student comes to a word in the text that he doesn't recognize. Stymied, he looks to the teacher for help. The teacher has at least four options to consider in deciding how to respond to the reader: (1) Tell him the word, (2) ask him to "sound it out," (3) ask him to take an "educated guess," or (4) tell him to say "blank" and keep on reading.

What would you do? A rationale, based on what you know and believe about teaching reading, can be developed for each of the options or, for that matter, a combination. For example, "First, I'd ask him to sound out the word, and if that didn't work, I'd tell him the word." Or, "First, I'd ask him to take a good guess based on what word might make sense, and if that didn't work, I'd ask him to say 'blank' and keep on reading."

Options 2 through 4 represent strategies to solve a particular problem that occurs during reading—identifying an unfamiliar word. Sounding out an unfamiliar word is one strategy frequently taught to beginners. When using a sounding-out strategy, a reader essentially tries to associate sounds with letters or letter combinations. An emphasis on sounding out in and of itself is a limited strategy because it doesn't teach or make children aware of the importance of monitoring what is read for comprehension. A teacher builds a child's metacognition when sounding out is taught in conjunction with making sense. For example, a teacher follows up a suggestion to sound out an unfamiliar word by asking, "Does the word make sense? Does what you read sound like language?"

Option 3, taking an educated guess, asks the reader to identify a word that makes sense in the context of the sentence in which the word is located or the text itself. The **implicit** message to the reader is that reading is supposed to make sense. If a child provides a word other than the unfamiliar word but preserves the meaning of the text, the teacher would be instructionally and theoretically consistent by praising the child and encouraging him to continue reading.

The fourth option, say "blank" and keep on reading, is also a metacognitive strategy for word identification because it shows the reader that reading is not as much a word-perfect process as it is a meaning-making process. No one word should stop a reader cold. If the reader is monitoring the text for meaning, he may be able to return to the word and identify it or decide that the word wasn't that important to begin with.

The teacher can make the implicit messages about reading strategies **explicit**. Throughout this text, we will use terms associated with explicit instruction: *modeling,* *demonstrating, explaining, rationale-building, thinking aloud,* and *reflecting.* From an instructional point of view, these terms reflect practices that allow teachers to help students develop *metacognitive awareness* and *strategic knowledge.* For example, Arch, the first-grade teacher discussed earlier in this chapter, chooses to engage the reader—after she has taken a good guess at the unfamiliar word and completes reading—in a brief discussion of the importance of identifying words that "make sense" and "sound like language" in the context of what's being read. Such metacognitive discussions have the potential to build self-knowledge and task knowledge and also to strengthen the reader's self-monitoring abilities.

Self-Knowledge   Do children know what reading is for? Do they know what the reader's role is? Do they know their options? Are they aware of their strengths as readers and learners? Do they recognize that some texts are harder than others and that all texts should not be read alike? Questions such as these reflect the self-knowledge component of metacognition. When readers are aware of *self* in relation to *texts* and *tasks,* they are in a better position to use reading strategies effectively (Armbruster, Echols, & Brown, 1982).

Task Knowledge   Experienced readers are strategic readers. They use their task knowledge to meet the demands inherent in difficult texts. For example, they know how to analyze a reading task, reflect on what they know or don't know about the text to be read, establish purposes and plans for reading, and evaluate their progress in light of purposes for reading. Experienced readers are often aware of whether they have understood what they have read. And if they haven't, they know what to do when comprehension fails.

Self-Monitoring   Reading becomes second nature to most of us as we develop experience with and maturity in the process. Experienced readers operate on "automatic pilot" as they read, until they run into a problem that disrupts the flow. For example, read the following passage:

> The boys' arrows were nearly gone, so they sat down on the grass and stopped hunting. Over at the edge of the woods they saw Henry making a bow to a little girl who was coming down the road. She had tears in her dress and also tears in her eyes. She gave Henry a note, which he brought over to the group of young hunters. Read to the boys it caused great excitement. After a minute but rapid examination of their weapons, they ran down the valley. Does were standing at the edge of the lake, making an excellent target. (author unknown)

Now reflect on the experience. At what points during reading did a "built-in sensor" in your head begin to signal to you that something was wrong? At what point in the passage did you become aware that some of the words you were misreading were homonyms and that you were choosing the inappropriate pronunciations of one or more of the homonyms? What did you do to rectify your misreadings? Why do you suppose the "sensor" signaled disruptions in your reading?

As experienced readers, we expect reading to make sense. And as we interact with a text, the metacognitive "sensor" in each of us monitors whether what we're reading is making sense.

What reader hasn't chosen an inappropriate pronunciation, come across a concept too difficult to grasp, or become lost in an author's line of reasoning? What experienced reader hasn't sensed that a text is too difficult to understand the first time around? The difference, of course, between the experienced and inexperienced reader is that the former knows when something's wrong and often employs correction strategies to get back on track. The strategic reader also has the confidence and belief that he or she can succeed in understanding what is read, leading to more motivation and engagement in the reading process (Vacca, 2006). This is what monitoring comprehension is all about.

Metacognitive ability is related to both age and reading experience (Stewart & Tei, 1983). Older students are more strategic in their reading than younger students, and good readers demonstrate more ability to use metacognition to deal with problems that arise during reading than readers with limited proficiency. Nevertheless, the instructional implications of metacognition are evident throughout this text. Becoming literate is a process of becoming aware not only of oneself as a reader but also of strategies that help solve problems that arise before, during, and after reading. A classroom environment that nurtures metacognitive functioning is crucial to children's literacy development.

Reading from a Language Perspective

Cognition and language are crucial components of human development. Although the acquisition of language is a complex process, many children understand and use all of the basic language patterns by the time they are 6 years old. A child's apparent facility with language is best understood by recognizing the active relationship between cognition and language.

Jean Piaget (1973) spent most of his life observing children and their interactions with their environment. His theory of cognitive development helps explain that language acquisition is influenced by more general cognitive attainments. As children explore their environment, they interpret and give meaning to the events they experience. The child's need to interact with immediate surroundings and to manipulate objects is critical to language development. From a Piagetian view, language reflects thought and does not necessarily shape it.

2017 ILA Standards

1.1, 1.3

Lev Vygotsky (1962, 1978), the acclaimed Russian psychologist, also viewed children as active participants in their own learning. However, at some point in their early development, children begin to acquire language competence; as they do so, language stimulates cognitive development. Gradually, Vygotsky believed, they begin to regulate their own problem-solving activities through the mediation of egocentric speech. In other words, children carry on external dialogues with themselves. Eventually external dialogue gives way to inner speech.

According to both Piaget and Vygotsky, children must be actively involved in order to grow and learn. Merely reacting to the environment isn't enough. An important milestone in a child's development, for example, is the ability to analyze means–ends relationships. When this occurs, children begin to acquire the ability to use language to achieve goals.

The linguistic sophistication of young children cannot be underestimated or taken for granted. Yet the outdated notion that children develop speech by imitation still persists among people who have little appreciation or knowledge of oral language development. The key to learning oral language lies in the opportunities children have to explore and experiment with language toward purposeful ends. As infants grow into toddlers, they learn to use language as an instrument for their intentions: "I want" becomes a favorite phrase. No wonder M. A. K. Halliday (1975) described learning oral language as a "saga in learning to mean."

When teachers embrace reading as a language process, they not only understand the importance of learning oral language but also are acutely aware that written language develops in humans along parallel lines. Children learn to use written language in much the same manner that they learn to use oral language—naturally and purposefully. As Goodman (1986) put it, "Why do people create and learn written language? They need it! How do they learn it? The same way they learn oral language, by using it in authentic literary events that meet their needs" (p. 24).

2017 ILA Standards

1.1, 1.3

Ultimately, there's only one way to become proficient as a writer and reader, and that's by writing and reading. When opportunities abound for children to engage in real literacy events (writing and reading), they grow as users of written language.

When language is splintered into its parts and the parts are isolated from one another for instructional purposes, learning to read becomes more difficult than it needs to be. The whole language concept, originated by Kenneth and Yetta Goodman (1986), reflects the way some teachers think about language and literacy. They plan teaching activities that support students in their use of all aspects of language in learning to read. Keeping language "whole" drives home the point that splintering written language into bits and pieces, to be taught and learned separately from one another, makes learning to read harder, not easier. Support for more holistic teaching comes from two areas of language inquiry: **psycholinguistics** and **sociolinguistics**.

PSYCHOLINGUISTICS AND READING   A psycholinguistic view of reading combines a psychological understanding of the reading process with an understanding of how language works. Psycholinguistic inquiries into the reading process suggest that readers act on and interact with written language in an effort to make sense of a text. Reading is not a passive activity; it is an active thinking process that takes place "behind the eyes." Nor is reading an exact process. All readers make mistakes— "miscues" as Kenneth Goodman (1973) calls them. Why? Miscues are bound to occur because readers are continually *anticipating* meaning and *sampling* a text for information cues based on their expectations. In fact, readers search for and coordinate *information cues* from three distinct systems in written language: the **graphophonemic**, the **syntactic**, and the **semantic**.

2017 ILA Standards

1.1, 1.2, 1.3

Graphophonemic System   This system relies upon the print itself in order to provide readers with a major source of information: The graphic symbols or marks on the page represent speech sounds. The more experience readers have with written language, the more they learn about regular and irregular letter–sound relationships. Experienced readers acquire enough knowledge of sounds associated with letter symbols that they do not have to use all the available graphic information in a word in order to decode or recognize it.

Syntactic System   This system depends on readers' possessing knowledge about how language works. *Syntactic information* is provided by the grammatical relationships within sentence patterns. In other words, readers use their knowledge of the meaningful arrangement of words in sentences to construct meaning from text material.

The order of words provides important information cues during reading. For example, although children may be able to read the words "ran race the quickly children the," they would make little sense out of what they read. The meaning is not clear until the words are arranged like so: "The children quickly ran the race." In addition, readers use syntactic information to anticipate a word or phrase that "must come next" in a sentence because of its grammatical relationship to other words in the sentence. For example, most children reading the sentence "I saw a red ___." would probably fill in the blank with a noun because they intuitively know how language works.

Semantic System   This system of language stores the schemata that readers bring to a text in terms of background knowledge, experiences, conceptual understandings, attitudes, beliefs, and values.

▶ In this video (https://www.youtube.com/watch?v=CckjFEDluLg), you will learn how the brain identifies words during the act of creating meaning with print or reading utilizing the three language cueing systems. Which system or combination of systems best reflects your teaching beliefs?

SOCIOLINGUISTICS AND READING   In the child's first several years, skill in spoken language develops naturally and easily. Children discover what language does for them. They learn that language is a tool they can use and understand in interactions with others in their environment. They also learn that language is intentional; it has many purposes. Among the most obvious is communication. The more children use language to communicate, the more they learn the many special functions it serves.

2017 ILA Standards

1.1, 1.2, 1.3

Halliday (1975) viewed language as a reflection of what makes us uniquely human. His monumental work explored how language functions in our day-to-day interactions and serves the personal, social, and academic facets of our lives. Language plays a central role in learning. Use and context of oral and written language influence literacy development. Some uses include communicating, information seeking, self-expression, enjoyment, and perpetuating information. These functions of language are context dependent. How one uses language in school, home, community, and informal environments influences the meaningfulness of oral and written language.

Because reading is uniquely human, learning to read requires sharing, interaction, and collaboration. Parent–child, teacher–student, and student–student relations and participation patterns are essential in learning to read. To what extent do children entering school have experience operating and communicating in a group as large as that found in the typical classroom? Children must learn the ropes. In many cases, kindergarten may be the first place where children must follow and respect the rules that govern how to operate and cooperate in groups. Not only must they know how and when to work independently and how and when to share and participate, but they must also learn the rules that govern communicative behavior. This is essential for students of all ages.

Communicative competence, as defined by Hymes (1974), develops differently in different children because they have not all had the same set of experiences or opportunities to engage in communication in the home or in the community. Some preschoolers have acquired more competence than others as to when and when not to speak and as to what to talk about, with whom, where, and in what manner. The sociolinguistic demands on a 5- or 6-year-old are staggering. As students age, more communicative competence develops. However, although middle school students have increased communication competence, motivation to participate in the social context of the classroom may be lacking. Opportunities for middle grade students to be involved in independent thought and language are closely linked to students' motivation for and engagement in reading and writing activities (Many, Ariail, & Fox, 2011). Therefore, literacy instruction needs to be focused on students' motivation, interests, and developmental needs.

Because a large part of learning to read will depend on the social and cultural context of the classroom, opportunities must abound for discussions and conversations between teacher and student and among students. Within this context, students must demonstrate (1) an eagerness to be independent; (2) an unquenchable zest to explore the new and unknown; (3) the courage to take risks, try things out, and experience success as well as some defeat; (4) the enjoyment of being with others and learning from them; and (5) a willingness to view themselves as readers.

2017 ILA Standard

5.1

Check Your Understanding 1.3: Gauge your understanding of the skills and concepts in this section.

Models of Reading

■ **Compare theoretical models of the reading process that describe what humans do when they engage in reading.**

Models of the reading process often depict the act of reading as a communication event between a sender (the writer) and a receiver of information (the reader). Generally speaking, language information flows from the writer to the reader in the sense that the writer has a message to send and transmits it through print to the reader, who then must interpret its meaning. Reading models have been developed to describe the way readers use language information to construct meaning from print. *How* a reader translates print to meaning is the key issue in the building of models of the reading process. This issue has led to the development of three classes of models: *bottom-up, top-down,* and *interactive.*

2017 ILA Standard

1.1

Bottom-up models of reading assume that the process of translating print to meaning begins with the print. The process is initiated by **decoding** graphic symbols into sounds. The reader first identifies features of letters; links these features together to recognize letters; combines letters to recognize spelling patterns; links spelling patterns to recognize words; and then proceeds to sentence-, paragraph-, and text-level processing.

Top-down models of reading assume that the process of translating print to meaning begins with the reader's prior knowledge. The process is initiated by making predictions or "educated guesses" about the meaning of some unit of print. Readers decode graphic symbols into sounds to "check out" hypotheses about meaning.

Interactive models of reading assume that the process of translating print to meaning involves making use of both prior knowledge and print. The process is initiated by making predictions about meaning and/or decoding graphic symbols. The reader formulates hypotheses based on the interaction of information from semantic, syntactic, and graphophonemic sources of information.

The terms *bottom-up, top-down,* and *interactive* are used extensively in the fields of communication and information processing. When these terms are used to describe reading, they also explain how language systems operate in reading.

Models of reading attempt to describe how readers use semantic, syntactic, and graphophonemic information in translating print to meaning. It is precisely in these descriptions that bottom-up, top-down, and interactive models of reading differ. Figures 1.4 and 1.5 show the flow of information in each reading model. Note that these illustrations are general depictions of information processing during reading

Figure 1.4 Bottom-Up and Top-Down Models

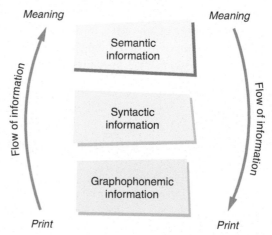

BOTTOM-UP PROCESSING:
The act of reading is triggered by graphophonemic information such as letters, syllables, and words in order to construct meaning from print.

TOP-DOWN PROCESSING:
The act of reading is triggered by the reader's prior knowledge and experience in order to construct meaning.

Figure 1.5 Information Processing in Interactive Models of Reading

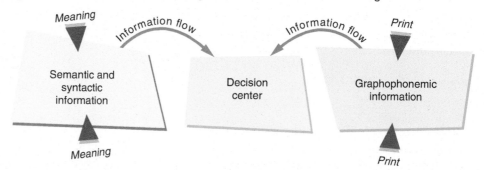

INTERACTIVE PROCESSING: The act of reading is triggered by the reader's prior knowledge and experience as well as graphophonemic information in order to construct meaning.

and do not refer specifically to models such as those in Singer and Ruddell's *Theoretical Models and Processes of Reading* (1985).

Bottom-Up Models

As illustrated in Figure 1.4, the process of deriving meaning from print in bottom-up models is triggered by graphic information embedded in print. This is why bottom-up models are described as being "data-driven." Data in this case are the letters and words on the page. A prototype model for bottom-up processing was constructed by Gough (1985), who attempted to show what happens in "one second of reading." In Gough's model, reading involves a series of steps that occur within milliseconds in the mind of the reader. The reader takes one "linguistic step" after another, beginning with the recognition of key features in letters and continuing letter by letter, word by word, and sentence by sentence until reaching the top—the meaning of the text being read. The reading model by Samuels (1994) is also essentially bottom-up. However, the Samuels model incorporates the idea of *automaticity*. The concept of automaticity suggests that humans can attend to only one thing at a time, but may be able to process many things at once as long as no more than one requires attention. Automaticity is similar to putting an airplane on automatic pilot and freeing the pilot to direct his or her attention to other things.

In reading, *decoding* and *comprehending* vie for the reader's attention. Readers must learn to process graphophonemic information so rapidly that they are free to direct attention to comprehending the text material for meaning. Readers need accurate, automatic word recognition. Promoting the development of automaticity is foundational for the proficient reader (Ehri, 2005).

The young reader is similar to the novice automobile driver. When learning to drive a car, the beginner finds the mechanics of operating the automobile so demanding that he or she must focus exclusively on driving. However, with practice, the skilled driver pays little conscious attention to the mechanics of driving and is able to converse with a passenger or listen to the radio. Likewise, the beginning reader must practice decoding print to speech so rapidly that decoding becomes automatic. As beginners become more fluent in decoding, they can devote their attention to comprehending the writer's message.

Top-Down Models

Top-down models emphasize that information processing during reading is triggered by the reader's prior knowledge and experience in relation to the writer's message. Obviously, there are no pure top-down models because readers must begin by focusing on print. As opposed to being data-driven, top-down models are said to be conceptually driven. That is to say, ideas or concepts in the mind of a reader trigger information processing during reading. As Frank Smith (1985) put it, "The more you already know, the less you need to find out" (p. 15). In other words, the more readers know in advance about the topic to be read, the less they need to use graphic information on the page.

To get a better idea of how reading is conceptually driven, read the following story:

Flan and Glock

Flan was a flim.

Glock was a plopper.

It was unusual for a flim and a plopper to be crods, but

Flan and Glock were crods. They medged together.

Flan was keaded to moak at a mox. Glock wanted to kead

there too. But the lear said he could not kead there.

Glock anged that the lear said he could not kead there

because he was a plopper.

Although you've never heard of Flan and Glock and don't know what a flim or a plopper is, it is not difficult to interpret from this short story that Glock was discriminated against. How did you figure this out? Your knowledge of capitalization may have led you to hypothesize that Flan and Glock are proper names. Knowledge of grammar, whether intuitive or overt, undoubtedly helped you realize that *flim, plopper, crods,* and *mox* are nouns and that *medged* and *keaded* are verbs. Finally, your knowledge of the world led you to predict that since the lear said, "Glock could not kead there because he was a plopper," Glock is probably a victim of discrimination.

Note that these interpretations of the story are "educated guesses." However, both prior knowledge and graphophonemic information were required to make these guesses. From our perspective, reading is rarely totally top-down or bottom-up. A third class of models helps explain the interactive nature of the reading process.

Interactive Models

Readers use neither prior knowledge nor graphophonemic information exclusively. Interactive models, as illustrated in Figure 1.5, suggest that the process of reading is initiated by formulating hypotheses about meaning *and* by decoding letters and words. According to Kamil and Pearson (1979), readers assume either an active or a passive role, depending on the strength of their hypotheses about the meaning of the reading material. If readers bring a great deal of knowledge to the material, chances are that their hypotheses will be strong and they will process the material actively, making minimal use of graphophonemic information. Passive reading, by contrast, often results when readers have little experience with or knowledge of the topic to be read. They rely much more on the print itself for information cues.

Effective readers know how to interact with print in an effort to understand a writer's message. Effective readers adapt to the material based on their purposes for reading. Purpose dictates the strategies that readers use to translate print to meaning. Two of the most appropriate questions that readers can ask about a selection are "What do I need to know?" and "How well do I already know it?" These two questions help readers establish purposes for reading and formulate hypotheses during reading. The questions also help readers decide how to *coordinate* prior knowledge and graphophonemic information.

Note that the models of reading just described don't take into consideration the social nature of reading and learning to read. In this sense, they're incomplete. However, models are useful in some respects: They help you reflect on your beliefs, assumptions, and practices related to reading instruction.

Check Your Understanding 1.4: Gauge your understanding of the skills and concepts in this section.

RTI for Struggling Readers

Understanding *Response to Intervention*

Response to Intervention (RTI), derived from the Individuals with Disabilities Education Improvement Act (IDEIA) of 2004, is a systematic approach to identification and instruction of struggling readers. With RTI, the identification process for learning disabilities shifts from a focus on the discrepancy between achievement and intellectual ability to the emphasis of early support and intervention. School districts have the option to use alternative approaches that employ research-based classroom interventions. If needed, more intensive small group and even individualized instruction are implemented prior to evaluation and identification of a learning disability. The focus of this process is on providing interventions and assessments to develop reading and writing skills and strategies for all students.

Although there are several available RTI models, a three-tiered approach strategy for intervention is used in many school districts. The process within each tier is dependent on each school and its administrative decisions.

- *Tier 1*—All students are provided research-based instruction differentiated to meet each student's needs. In Tier 1, intervention is considered preventive and proactive.
- *Tier 2*—More intensive work is provided to learners who have not been successful in traditional classroom learning situations. Therefore, more focused small group interventions are implemented with frequent monitoring to measure progress. Regular classroom teachers receive support from special educators and literacy coaches.

- *Tier 3*—Learners receive intensive, individualized intervention targeting specific deficits and problem areas. Regular classroom teachers are responsible for the intervention and assessment processes; special educators and literacy specialists provide support.

2017 ILA Standards

2.1, 3.2, 4.1, 4.2, 4.3, 6.2

This multitiered process involves a collaborative process in which all stakeholders—parents, teachers, literacy specialists, special education teachers, and students—work together to meet the literacy needs of struggling learners.

What About . . .

Standards, Assessment, and Knowledge and Beliefs about Reading?

Teachers should understand the theoretical and evidence-based foundations of the reading and writing processes. In addition, they need to make the connection between theory and instructional practices. Teachers who relate major theories and research to support their beliefs are able to utilize the components of reading and writing and literacy development to create an effective learning environment.

Knowledge and beliefs about the teaching of reading and writing have changed over time, especially with the ever-changing legislative influences and curricular demands. The pendulum of thought about what, how, and whom to teach moves continuously. It is therefore critical for literacy professionals to reevaluate their beliefs about the instruction of reading and writing on an ongoing basis. Teachers need to rely on multiple sources of information and other professionals to help guide instructional planning that improves reading and writing achievement of all students.

Summary: Knowledge and Beliefs about Reading

- Belief systems bring into focus what teachers know, believe, and value—not only about their roles as classroom teachers of reading but also about reading, readers, curriculum standards, instruction, and new literacies.
- Teachers develop belief systems about reading and learning to read through personal, practical, and professional study and experience.
- Because we believe that all teachers are theorists in that they have reasons for their instructional decisions, we examined the reading process from language, social, and psychological perspectives.
- Reading models have been developed to describe the way readers use language information to construct meaning from text. This has led to teaching models of the reading process.

Teacher Action Research

Teachers who engage in reflection and inquiry find themselves asking questions and observing closely what goes on in their classrooms. Action research is a way for teachers who want to reflect and inquire to better understand within the context of their own teaching more about themselves as teachers and their students as learners. Several ideas for action research are presented. Some are intended to be done in the field; others are for the classroom.

1. Observe a teacher in an elementary school. Record what you see and hear during reading instruction time. Based on the interactions recorded between

teacher and students, what did you learn about the teacher's knowledge and beliefs about literacy?

2. Using the idea of the reading autobiography, prepare an autobiographical narrative following the directions in Figure 1.2. Share your autobiographical sketch with other members of the class or with colleagues in your school, or with a family member or roommate. What differences in reading development and attitude are evident? What similarities exist?

3. Suppose you are going to be a guest speaker to a group of preservice teachers. The topic is "Theoretical Influences on Reading Instruction." You have time for a 15-minute presentation. What would you say? Why?

4. Develop your philosophy for the teaching of reading. Include the model of reading you closely align with. Discuss.

Through the Lens of the Common Core

The Common Core State Standards for English Language Arts (CCSS-ELA) provide schools a recommended curriculum in order to develop literacy skills. Richard Vacca (see Box 1.2) pointed out that the standards give "schools an opportunity to make decisions about the types of texts that will be used for literacy learning as well as instructional approaches and strategies at different grade levels." Many decisions will need to be made by the teachers to navigate the "road map" provided by the CCSS. Teachers will need to reflect and articulate their belief system in order to develop the high learning expectations of the standards.

Chapter 2

Approaches to Reading Instruction

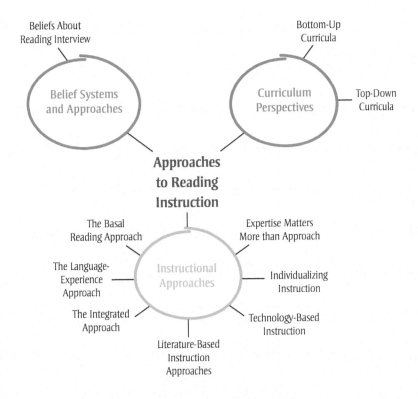

Learning Outcomes

In This Chapter, You Will Discover How to

- Recognize the relationship between belief systems and approaches to instruction.

- Identify curriculum perspectives of reading.

- Distinguish between instructional approaches in the teaching of reading.

Activating Your Schema

Reflect on something you've learned to do lately, outside of school. Were you successful at it, or did you fail? If you were successful, what was in place that helped you to succeed or absent that caused you to fail? Was there one single approach that helped you have success, or was it a variety of approaches that led to your accomplishment? This chapter is about the different approaches teachers take when it comes to teaching reading, writing, and spelling. Probably just like you, most teachers use a variety of approaches when it comes to teaching in order to meet the individual needs of their students.

2017 ILA Standards Found in This Chapter

1.1	2.1	4.3	5.4
1.2	2.2	5.2	6.1
1.3	2.3	5.3	6.2

Common Core State Standards: English Language Arts

CCSS.R.10

Key Terms

basal reading approach	language-experience approach (LEA)
comprehensive approach	leveled books
explicit strategy instruction	literature-based instruction
guided reading	technology-based instruction
instructional scaffolding	units of language
integrated approach	whole language

Premala attended classes to become a teacher after having raised three children. She had a strong sense of what children need in order to be able to read after spending thousands of hours on bedtime stories, homework assignments, and PTA involvement; and her teacher education program was aligned with her beliefs about teaching children to read.

Premala's first job was teaching second grade at a school with a literacy coach who was a strong proponent of guided reading practice using only authentic literacy. The population in the school was diverse, but the school had an English language learner (ELL) specialist who would support the children in-class. Premala thrived in this environment and had an 80-minute-a-day literacy block. She taught a reading-and-writing workshop alternate days, and then integrated word study in minilessons 2 days per week. Each day, students read or wrote independently for approximately 40 minutes. During that time, Premala conferenced with students and held guided reading groups, which were sometimes based on reading level and other times based on skill need, such as word study groups. She used journals to record students' knowledge concerning word patterns. After independent work time, students presented book talks or reviewed the day's minilesson. At the end of each class, Premala read aloud, selecting novels or short stories that would stretch the students' ability to infer meaning and apply reading strategies. This was her favorite time of day.

Now, due to relocation across several states, Premala teaches at a school where about 70 percent of the children come from minority backgrounds, and 20 percent of those are ELLs. The methods for teaching children to read come from a very different philosophy. The principal believes an "effective school must maintain high expectations for student achievement, an orderly climate, and a rigorous program in phonics instruction." She indicates that it is okay to try out new teaching strategies, "as long as you are teaching the skills the children need and use the state-approved core reading program." How well children score on state assessments is one of the main indicators of a teacher's success in the school.

Premala feels the pressure of having to teach skills in isolation with a newly adopted core reading program, which promises to "transform literacy instruction for twenty-first-century classrooms." The program features instruction based on 4-week units, with assessments after every two units. It has differentiated small books at four levels, decodable readers, practice response journals for strategy and phonics work, and another for skill practice. In addition, there is a "take home companion workbook" to foster home–school connections.

This approach, she admits, is "not what I believe in," but she feels obligated to "follow the lead of all of the other teachers." She is especially concerned about her ELL students being taught in this manner. "I know that if I start with the children's native language and build on it, I'll help them expand their English vocabulary. I can't do that with a skills workbook."

Prior to the opening of school, Premala spent weeks planning what she was going to do. One of her first tasks was to fix up the room so that it would be a vibrant, fun place to learn. The reading corner has a rainforest theme to start the year, with a large green canopy over it and vines hanging down. There is an area rug, bins of leveled books, and an assortment of pillows. The writer's nook has a round table and a laptop, and is filled with all kinds of supplies to stimulate writing. She remembers being excited about getting the children in the writer's nook and publishing on the Internet.

The reality of teaching reading skills in isolation is omnipresent, despite Premala's attempts to provide meaningful experiences for her second graders. After every two units, she is required to assess mastery of the skills, and she must also use a test preparation booklet to prepare them for the state achievement tests. Learning the online component of the new core reading program on top of the decodable readers, practice response journals, and phonics and skills workbooks has been a steep learning curve.

In practice, Premala teaches the skills using the workbooks and decodable text in the morning, and then she does individual conferencing on independent reading whenever she can find the time. Needless to say, Premala goes home each day exhausted and frustrated. She complains to her family she spends more time assessing children than she spends on instruction, and the instruction she does do "is not authentic." The reading corner and writer's nook are underused, and she hasn't even had time to think about the notion of creating a class blog. "At least," Premala says, "I still read to the class every day. I know this is important for building vocabulary for all of the children, especially the English language learners."

Although she tries to combine skills teaching with more top-down activities, Premala's instruction is out of balance. Her philosophical stance is in direct conflict with the principal's beliefs about learning to read. The pressure to conform to the principal's expectations for skills instruction and required assessments forces Premala to put her knowledge and beliefs about learning to read on hold. Although she attempts to mesh literature and language-rich activities and new ways to use technology with skills instruction, it simply doesn't work for her because she is caught between contrasting instructional methodologies. Her efforts simply create a disjointed hodgepodge of instructional activity.

Belief Systems and Approaches to Literacy Instruction

■ **Recognize the relationship between belief systems and approaches to instruction.**

In the search to build a comprehensive literacy program, it is critical for teachers to be aware of the needs of students, because there is no single approach to reading instruction that can successfully teach all children to read. Teachers must have a strong knowledge of multiple methods for teaching reading coupled with an understanding of how students learn so they can design and deliver instruction matched to the needs of the students within the class.

2017 ILA Standards

1.1, 2.1, 2.2, 6.2

Literacy programs require an informed philosophical stance. A teacher's philosophical stance, or belief system, is crucial to achieving balance in the teaching of reading because instruction involves the kinds of decisions that teachers make based on how children learn to read and how they can best be taught. Perhaps the Common Core State Standards (CCSS) can be seen as an opportunity for teachers to think about beliefs surrounding reading and learning to read. The CCSS tell us *what* students need to be able to do, but not *how* to do it. As teachers, you will need to have the knowledge and skills to decide how to best meet the needs of each student.

Teachers' beliefs and understandings of teaching and learning play an important role in their classroom practices. As Harste and Burke (1977) hypothesized, teachers make decisions about classroom instruction in light of beliefs they hold about teaching and learning. Teachers' beliefs influence their goals, procedures, materials, and approaches to instruction. Similarly, Richards and Rodgers (2001) affirmed that teachers possess assumptions about language and language learning, and that these provide the basis for a particular approach to language instruction. One way to examine your beliefs about reading and learning to read is to connect them to theoretical models of the reading process. Does your philosophical stance reflect a bottom-up view of reading? Top-down? Interactive? Throughout this text, we contend that teachers who use a more integrative, balanced, or **comprehensive approach** to teaching reading will meet the needs of their students when their instructional decisions and practices reflect the interactive nature of the reading process. Integrative models underscore the important contributions that both the reader *and* the text make in the reading process.

One important way to define who we are as teachers of reading is by talking about *what* we do and *why* we do it, or by observing one another in a teaching situation and asking *why* we did what we did. Another way is through self-examination and reflection. The tool that follows will help you examine your beliefs about reading in relation to instructional practices.

In Box 2.1, we hear from Kate, a first grader, and her perceptions about teaching someone to read.

Beliefs About Reading

Beliefs about how students learn to read in all likelihood lie on a continuum between concepts that reflect bottom-up, top-down, and interactive models of reading.

By participating in the Beliefs About Reading Interview (Gove, 1983) in Box 2.2, you will get a *general indication* of where your beliefs about learning to read lie on the continuum illustrated in Figure 2.1.

Belief Systems Your responses to the Beliefs about Reading Interview will often mirror **units of language** emphasized for instructional purposes. For example, the smallest units of written language are letters; the largest unit is the text selection itself. In Figure 2.2, concentric boxes help illustrate units of written language. The largest

BOX 2.1 | STUDENT VOICES

Kate, who learned to read before kindergarten, is now in the first grade and loves to read. When asked how she would teach someone else to read, she said, "I would read a bunch of books to them. And then I would help them sound out the words."

Kate's comments reveal that she believes in using several different approaches to teaching reading. In it, we see she believes children need a teacher's assistance and phonics instruction to learn to read. She's also a proponent of immersing them in reading "a bunch of books." Most teachers are similar to Kate, in that they believe that it takes a more than just one approach for good instruction to take place.

BOX 2.2 | VIEWPOINT

What Do You Believe About Reading and Learning to Read?

Use this opportunity to express your views and beliefs about reading.

If you are a preservice teacher studying reading for the first time, you may find it difficult to answer some of the questions. However, we encourage you to respond to all of the questions based on any sources of knowledge and beliefs you currently hold about the reading process and how it should be taught. Knowledge sources may include your own school experiences, observations in the field, experiences as a reader, and previous study. Toward the end of the semester, you may wish to respond to the interview questions again. This will provide a good measure of the growth you have made in thinking about reading and learning to read. Study the directions and respond to the questions in the Beliefs About Reading Interview.

Use Appendix A to analyze and interpret your beliefs about reading and learning to read. Appendix A will provide you with a general framework for determining whether you view reading and learning to read from a bottom-up, top-down, or interactive perspective.

Beliefs About Reading Interview

Directions: Respond to each question, thinking in terms of your own classroom—either the one in which you plan to teach or the one in which you now teach. As you respond to each question, explain what you (would) do and why you (would) do it.

1. Which goals for reading instruction do you feel most confident about making progress in during the school year?
2. Suppose that a student is reading orally in your class and makes a reading error. What is the first thing you do? Why?
3. Another student in your class is reading orally and doesn't know a word. What are you going to do? Why?
4. You have read about and probably tried out different kinds of strategies and activities for teaching students to read. Which ones do you feel will be the most important in your classroom? Why?
5. What kinds of activities do you feel your students should be involved in for the majority of their reading instructional time? Why?
6. Here are the typical steps in a directed reading activity as suggested in many commercial program manuals: (1) introduction of vocabulary, (2) motivation or setting purposes, (3) reading, (4) questions and discussion after silent reading, and (5) skills practice for reinforcement. Rank these steps in order from most important to least important (not necessarily in the order you will follow them).
7. Is it important to introduce new vocabulary words before students read a selection? Why or why not?
8. Suppose your students will be tested to give you information to help you decide how to instruct them in reading. What would this diagnostic test include, and what kind of information would you hope it gives you about your students?
9. During silent reading, what do you hope your students will do when they come to an unknown word?
10. Look at the oral reading mistakes that are underlined below on these transcripts of three readers. Which of the three readers would you judge as the best or most effective reader?

Passage: The product did not sell well because it was <u>ineffective</u>. People did not want machines that were <u>ineffective</u>.

Reader A: The product did not sell well because it was <u>defective</u>. People did not want machines that were <u>defective</u>.

Reader B: The product did not sell well because it was -<u>in</u>, <u>inner</u>. People did not want machines that were <u>inner</u>.

Reader C: The product did not sell well because it was -<u>in</u>, <u>inner</u>. People did not want machines that were <u>ineff</u>.

box represents the text as a whole. It may be a story, a poem, or an article on the Civil War. This unit of language is made up of *paragraphs,* which are made up of *sentences,* which are made up of *words,* which are made up of *letters.*

Teachers who possess a bottom-up belief system believe that students must decode letters and words before they are able to construct meaning from sentences, paragraphs,

Figure 2.1 Beliefs about Reading Visualized as a Continuum

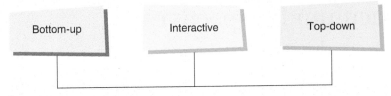

Figure 2.2 Units of Written Language

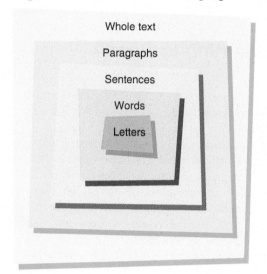

and larger text selections. Consequently, they view reading acquisition as mastering and integrating a series of word identification skills. Letter–sound relationships and word identification are emphasized instructionally. Because recognizing each word is believed to be an essential prerequisite to being able to comprehend the passage, accuracy in recognizing words is seen as important. If you hold a bottom-up set of beliefs, you may consider the practice of correcting oral reading errors as important in helping children learn to read. Or you may believe that helping students read a passage over and over is an important instructional activity because they develop accurate word recognition. Teachers who hold bottom-up belief systems often emphasize the teaching of skills in a sequential and systematic manner.

Teachers who have a top-down belief system consider reading for meaning an essential component of all reading instructional situations. They feel that the majority of reading or language arts instructional time should involve students in meaningful activities in which they read, write, speak, and listen. These teachers may also emphasize the importance of students choosing their own reading material and enjoying the material they read. Sentences, paragraphs, and text selections are the units of language emphasized instructionally. Because recognizing each word is not considered an essential prerequisite to comprehending the passage, word errors during oral reading may not be corrected. Instead, the teacher may advocate noninterference during oral reading or encourage a student to use the context or meaning of the passage to identify unrecognized words.

Teachers who hold an interactive view of reading and learning to read fall between bottom-up and top-down belief systems on the beliefs continuum. Such teachers recognize that a reader processes both letter–sound cues and meaning cues during reading. Reading as a meaning-making activity is utmost in their thoughts about reading and learning to read, but they also believe that readers must be able to identify words quickly and accurately if they are going to make sense of what they read. They know that phonics is one part of reading. Moreover, teachers with interactive belief systems integrate reading, writing, speaking, and listening activities; in the process of doing so, they *scaffold* children's literacy experiences. Scaffolding, as you will learn in more detail later in the chapter, suggests that teachers provide instructional support and guidance in the development of skills and strategies. Because they recognize the importance of teaching skills and strategies, interactive teachers blend *explicit* instruction with children's immersion in various reading and writing activities. Teachers who possess interactive belief systems are likely to achieve an equilibrium in the teaching of reading because they strike a balance between children's immersion in reading and writing experiences and their development as skillful and strategic readers and writers.

2017 ILA Standards

2.1, 2.2, 2.3

Table 2.1 summarizes the beliefs defining bottom-up, top-down, and interactive belief systems.

Check Your Understanding 2.1: Gauge your understanding of the skills and concepts in this section.

Curriculum Perspectives

■ Identify curriculum perspectives of reading.

The term *curriculum* has various shades of meaning in education. The word as it is defined from its early Latin origins means literally "to run a course." In its broadest

Table 2.1 Defining Bottom-Up, Top-Down, and Interactive Beliefs About Reading

	Bottom-Up Beliefs About Reading	Top-Down Beliefs About Reading	Interactive Beliefs About Reading
Relationship of Word Recognition to Comprehension	Believe students must recognize each word in a selection to be able to comprehend the selection.	Believe students can comprehend a selection even when they are not able to identify each word.	Believe students can comprehend by identifying words quickly and accurately.
Use of Information Cues	Believe students should use word and letter–sound cues exclusively to identify unrecognized words.	Believe students should use meaning and grammatical cues in addition to letter–sound cues to identify unrecognized words.	Believe students process letter–sound and meaning cues simultaneously to identify unrecognized words.
View of Reading	Believe reading requires mastering and integrating a series of word identification skills.	Believe students learn to read through meaningful and authentic activities in which they read, write, speak, and listen.	Believe students learn to read by developing skills and strategies in meaningful contexts.
Units of Language Emphasized Instructionally	Emphasize letters, letter–sound relationships, and words.	Emphasize sentences, paragraphs, and text selections.	Emphasize letters, letter–sound relationships, words, sentences, paragraphs, and text selections.
Where Importance Is Placed Instructionally	View accuracy in identifying words as important.	View reading for meaning as important.	View accurate word identification as contributing to meaningful reading.
Assessment	Think students need to be assessed on discrete skills.	Think students need to be assessed on the kind of knowledge constructed through reading.	Think students need to be assessed on the basis of their performance in meaningful contexts. Assessment informs instruction.

Complete the drag-and-drop activity to test your understanding of the material.

sense, a curriculum may refer to all courses offered at a school—a set of courses and their content. In the United States, the CCSS, which have been adopted by all but a couple of states, call for the new standards to be taught within the context of a content-rich curriculum. However, the CCSS do not stipulate what content students need to learn. Responsibility for developing a curriculum falls to schools, districts, and states. In many states, model curricula have been developed that are aligned with the new standards to ensure that the academic content and skills specified for each grade level are taught to students. Curriculum maps provide not only curricular and instructional guidance but also instructional strategies and resources.

A more dynamic conception of curriculum, however, is that it reflects what teachers and students *do* as they engage in classroom activity. If curriculum represents what teachers and students actually do in the classroom, a teacher's beliefs about literacy learning invariably contribute to curriculum decisions. These decisions involve, among other things, (1) the instructional objectives or target the teacher emphasizes for the classroom literacy program; (2) the materials the teacher selects and uses for instruction; (3) the learning environment the teacher perceives as most conducive to children's development as readers and writers; (4) the practices, approaches, and instructional strategies the teacher uses to teach reading and writing; and (5) the kinds of assessment the teacher perceives are best to evaluate literacy learning.

Curriculum-related questions every teacher has struggled with (or is struggling with) concern the teaching of literacy skills and strategies: What should children know and be able to do as readers and writers? Which skills and strategies are important? How do I teach skills and strategies? Answers to these questions will differ, depending on the curriculum perspective underlying the literacy program. Two curriculum perspectives—bottom-up and top-down—each supported by differing assumptions and principles about learning to read and write, have resulted in dramatically different objectives, materials, practices, and decisions related to literacy instruction.

Bottom-Up Curricula

The term *bottom-up curricula* refers to a reading model that assumes the process of translating print to meaning begins with children learning the parts of language (letters) to understanding whole text (meaning). Teachers who adhere to a bottom-up belief begin instruction by introducing letter names and letter sounds, advance to pronouncing whole words, then show students how to connect word meanings to comprehend texts.

READERS AND TEXTBOOKS   Teachers haven't always had a say in how to teach reading and writing. *The New England Primer*, the first textbook reader ever printed in America, was used to teach reading and Bible lessons in our schools until the twentieth century. In fact, many of the Founders and their children learned to read from it. Published for American colonists in the late 1600s, the *Primer* followed a strong bottom-up model of instruction. The alphabet was taught first; then vowels, consonants, double letters, italics, capitals, syllables, and so on were presented for instruction, in that order. Words were not introduced systematically in basal readers until the mid-1800s. Colonial children might meet anywhere from 20 to 100 new words on one page!

By the mid-1800s, the word method, silent reading, and reading to get information from content were introduced in these textbooks also known as basals. Basal readers are textbooks designed to teach reading in an organized, sequential way. The classics, fairy tales, and literature by U.S. authors became the first supplementary reading materials. Colored pictures, subjects appealing to children's interests, and the teacher's manual had all been introduced by the 1920s. It was then that a work pad was used for seatwork and skills practice in grades 1 through 3.

Publishing companies began to expand and add new components or features to their basal reading programs around 1925. Materials designed to teach reading readiness skills were added to the basal program to introduce beginning readers to the series and build a beginning reading vocabulary (i.e., words recognized on sight). Inside illustrations and outside covers also became increasingly colorful. Word lists became the standard for choosing readers' vocabulary.

Instruction in basal reading programs depended in part on a strict adherence to the scope and sequence of reading skills. Teacher's editions were coordinated with children's books, and diagnostic and achievement tests were developed. Basal reading programs had become more sophisticated and, to many teachers, unwieldy.

Until the 1960s, books in reading series were arranged according to grade placement. Grades evolved into levels, which went anywhere from 15 to 20 levels. By the 1970s, teachers and curriculum committees in general sought clarification about levels in relation to grades. As a result, publishers used the term *level* and cross-referenced this with its traditional grade equivalent.

The reading series used in schools in the twenty-first century are a far cry, in both appearance and substance, from the first readers. Nevertheless, current reading books retain some of the features that were once innovative. The new basal reading series have grown noticeably in size and price. Though not prescribing the bottom-up teaching approach that was used in the 1600s, today's teacher's manual presents a dilemma that is at the same time intriguing, interesting, and a bit daunting: It often purports to include *everything* that any teacher will ever need to teach reading.

Top-Down Curricula

The top-down model of teaching reading is in direct opposition to the bottom-up model. Although classroom descriptions of top-down practices vary from teacher to teacher, some basic principles guide every teacher's actions. For example, top-down teachers believe that language serves personal, social, and academic purposes in children's lives. Language therefore cannot be severed from a child's quest to make sense; language and meaning making are intertwined. In addition, top-down teachers recognize that oral and written language are parallel; one is not secondary to the other. Language, whether oral or written, involves a complex system of symbols, rules, and constructs that govern the content and form of language in the context of its use. For the top-down teacher, this means keeping language "whole" and not breaking it into bits and pieces or isolating the subsystems of language for instructional emphasis.

Respect for the child as a learner is paramount to a successful classroom environment. Top-down teachers believe that children are natural learners who learn how to read and write best under natural conditions. Because learning to read and write involves trial and error, top-down teachers hold firm to their convictions that children must learn to take risks in classroom contexts.

Classrooms are "communities" in a top-down curriculum. Teacher and students come together as a community of learners to engage in reading, writing, and other collaborative acts of meaning making. Language learners help one another. They talk to each other about what they are writing and what they are reading. They engage in partnerships around projects and thematic studies. They share their understandings of how to solve problems encountered while reading and writing.

Whole language, the belief system that seriously challenged the bottom-up perspective in the late twentieth century, was a progressive, child-centered movement that took root in the 1960s with the whole word approach and blossomed in the 1980s. One major rationale for the whole word approach was irregularities in the pronunciation of common words such as *shoe*, which violates the pattern *toe, doe, foe*. Since the correspondence isn't always reliable, the argument was that the focus should always be on the whole word. A whole language curriculum reflects the belief that students learn to read through meaningful experiences. These experiences include students' reading, writing, speaking, and listening about things important to them. Whole language is considered a solid top-down philosophy.

Many teachers today continue to maintain a whole language perspective and believe in weaving authentic texts for children to read, discuss, listen to, or write about into their teaching. They stress comprehension, use of quality literature, and the integration of reading and writing in authentic ways. One of the main goals of a whole language curriculum is to support children in the skillful use of language. They develop skills and strategies, but they do so in the context of meaningful learning. Some children will experience periods of accelerated learning followed by plateaus in their development. Some may need more time than others to "roam in the known" before they make noticeable progress in their use of language. It is only while students are using language that teachers can observe the student's control of the subsystems, and plan appropriate strategies to assist them with their needs. A whole language approach to teaching reading is based on a constructivist learning theory. Opponents of whole language cite the lack of structure traditionally supplied in basal programs through scope and sequence charts, sequenced lessons and activities, and leveled text.

Regardless of where you stand on these issues—top-down or bottom-up—one thing is clear: Literacy experts continue to discuss, debate, and ask questions about reading and writing well into the twenty-first century. **LinguaLinks** (http://www.sil.org) is designed to support work in the field of language and defines many of the terms used throughout this chapter, such as *top-down, bottom-up, interactive,* and *basal approach.* The site provides background information such as major proponents as well as examples to help facilitate understanding of concepts.

CLASSROOM CONDITIONS FOR LEARNING Brian Cambourne (1988) proposed that children acquire early competence with oral and written language most easily when certain conditions are present in their environments. He discovered certain conditions must be in place for oral language acquisition to take place. Take a minute and think about something you do well. How do you know you do it well? How did you learn to do it well? You might have learned because someone showed you how to do it (demonstration). Maybe you were encouraged as you tried it (response), or perhaps you learned by trial and error (approximations). The same things happen in the classroom. These conditions, since further described by Cambourne (2001) and others, hold true to a top-down philosophy. We contend that when these conditions are operating at an optimal level, learning is powerful and durable. So what does this look like in the classroom? Table 2.2 highlights these universal conditions and suggests applications.

Over the years, Cambourne (2016) found that teachers apply the conditions that then create cultures of learning that support deep engagement with literacy learning. He identified six "expectation messages" continually repeated and reinforced in the dialogue of teachers who support their students to become effective users of literacy. These teachers tell their students:

- Becoming an effective reader, writer, speller, and talker is worthwhile, and will greatly enhance the quality of your life.
- All members of the learning community are capable of becoming effective readers, writers, and spellers.
- The best way to become an effective user of literacy is to share and discuss the processes and understandings you are developing with other members of the learning community.

Table 2.2 Conditions for Learning

Immersion	Students need to be surrounded by high-quality literature and many different kinds of text (e.g., charts, labels, magazines) and be read to every day.
Engagement	Students must be active participants in their learning, which needs to be relevant. Help them become active learners who see themselves as potential readers and writers. Set up an environment where they can experiment with language and literacy. Provide paper, pencils, crayons, markers, books, and other literacy materials.
Expectation	Set realistic expectations for language and literacy development. Become familiar with the developmental stages of literacy, and support students in appropriate tasks. Expect that they will become accomplished readers and writers in their own time.
Responsibility	Students should take an active role in their own learning through choices. Establish an environment to promote problem solving and decision making. Provide easy access to books and literacy materials on low shelves and in baskets, and show them how to take care of them.
Response	Listen to students, and then give constructive feedback. Welcome their comments and questions and extend their use of oral language.
Approximation	With trial comes error. Allow students to make mistakes when learning to read and write. Guide them gently into accuracy and soon they will begin to self-correct.
Use/Employment	Create a climate for functional and meaningful uses of oral and written language. Give students time to use their strengths and abilities in meaningful ways, including engaging in a lot of conversations.
Demonstration	Teachers need to model reading and reading processes for students and demonstrate the role that literacy plays in their lives. Let them see you writing notes, letters, stories, recipes, and lists. Make sure they notice you reading to yourself, for pleasure, for information, for directions, and for other purposes. Show them how to hold a book, turn the pages, and read aloud.

Complete the drag-and-drop activity to test your understanding of the material.

- It is safe to take risks and try things out in this setting.
- Everyone is responsible for his or her own learning.

Cambourne (2016) states that the expectations can inform teaching practice and be adapted to any kind of teaching or learning setting.

2017 ILA Standards

1.1, 1.2, 1.3, 2.1, 2.2, 2.3, 5.4

Check Your Understanding 2.2: Gauge your understanding of the skills and concepts in this section.

Instructional Approaches

■ **Distinguish between instructional approaches in the teaching of reading.**

Approaches to reading represent general instructional plans for achieving goals and objectives in a literacy curriculum. Instructional approaches respond to curriculum-related questions concerning content, methods, and materials in the teaching of reading. When striving for a comprehensive program, teachers are likely to draw on their knowledge of different approaches in order to make decisions about instruction. Often, however, these decisions are consistent with teachers' beliefs about reading.

This section of the chapter examines the major approaches of teaching reading and writing, which fall into two basic categories. First, the top-down or meaning-based approach assumes that if children engage in meaningful reading and writing activities with the support of teachers and peers, they will become literate. Terms such as *emergent literacy, whole language, literature-based approach*, and *language experience approach* are related to this perspective.

Second, a bottom-up or skills-based approach to reading is one where the emphasis of instruction is on skills such as phonics, alphabet recognition, fluency, and spelling—all of which help students write and decode texts. In a skills-based view, the assumption is that once students are taught to recognize words, they will in turn comprehend the texts they read. The goal of both approaches is the same: fluent reading with good comprehension that supports the reader to effectively understand the author's message. The many instructional approaches are depicted in Figure 2.3. However, no single program addresses the needs of all learners. Students need teachers who know how to teach and have multiple ways of addressing individual needs.

Figure 2.3 The Many Instructional Approaches Teachers Draw From

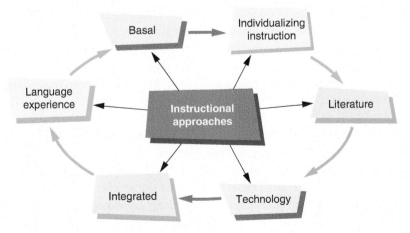

The Basal Reading Approach

A **basal reading approach** is an all-inclusive set of commercially produced materials for providing classroom reading instruction. Basal readers are used widely across the United States and are typically organized to illustrate and develop specific skills that are presented systematically in sequential order and taught continuously throughout all grades. The teacher's editions are also highly organized and contain suggestions for prereading and postreading activities and assessments, as well as scripted questions to ask students at specific points in a story. Traditionally, basal readers came with one set of books for students, but now typically include leveled books categorized into stages of difficulty for teachers to match text to ability.

Today's commercial programs contain more informational text than ever before and encompass a wide variety of genres. They include whole-group interactive lessons and small-group differentiated lessons and feature leveled texts, formative assessments, practice books, and online components such as interactive support for struggling readers, virtual field trips, games to practice vocabulary and comprehension, and digital copies of all materials. The traditional scope and sequence charts of skills and strategies to be taught at various levels are still included.

Depending on your beliefs, basal instruction could be considered a bottom-up approach, presenting skills to be taught in a sequence, or an interactive program, featuring unedited children's literature selections, authentic informational text, strategy instruction, and writing opportunities.

The Language-Experience Approach

Teachers often use the **language-experience approach (LEA)** in combination with other approaches to reading; it is especially prevalent in preK and kindergarten classrooms.

2017 ILA Standards

1.3, 4.3, 5.1

LEA is often associated with *story dictation,* recording the language of students on chart paper and using what they say as the basis for reading instruction. There is more to LEA, however, than just recording the ideas of students after they have taken a trip to the zoo or watched a baby chick hatch. LEA includes planned and continuous activities such as individual- and group-dictated stories, the building of word banks of known words, creative writing activities, oral reading of prose and poetry by teacher and students, directed reading–thinking lessons, the investigation of interests using multiple materials, and keeping records of student progress. It is most frequently used as a supplement to other programs and is especially useful with students who are in the beginning stages of learning to read.

LEA has been used in early childhood, elementary, middle, and secondary classrooms because it can provide opportunities for meaningful text for students from diverse backgrounds. The main feature of a language-experience approach is that it embraces the natural language of children and uses their background experiences as the basis for learning to read. This makes it a useful approach for meeting the needs of ELLs. Landis, Umolu, and Mancha (2010) used LEA with Nigerian secondary students who lacked appropriate texts for reading, and the effects were positive. The authors found LEA to be very effective in building their students' vocabulary, developing their reading comprehension, and studying spelling and phonics patterns with material that was both interesting and relevant. LEA is also widely used by teachers who work with students with hearing impairments. Students draw or take a pictures of an experience, and then the teacher translates the students' expressions in sign language into written English. The teacher regularly signs each sentence back to the student to make sure it is correct. Then the teacher makes additional small copies of the text for everyone to share with friends and families and to read again and again during the year. Schleper (2002) describes a middle school classroom where students made bread during a unit on Native Americans. The students researched how to make the bread and then dictated the directions in American Sign Language to the teacher, who documented the information on chart paper and then used it to do an extended vocabulary lesson.

Technology is playing a prominent role in facilitating and transforming LEA into the digital-language-experience approach, or Digital-LEA, and was first documented by Labbo and her colleagues (Labbo, Eakle, & Montero, 2002; Labbo, Love, & Ryan, 2007). Teachers are creatively using apps that allow for easy LEA content creation, which updates and brings more power to this classic approach. Students are able to use software that combines drawings, photos, voice, and text to create stories that can be used for LEA lessons. Glenn and Modla (2010) documented the successful use of Digital-LEA with emergent learners. They found that not only did it provide another opportunity for young students to explore their language and learn new skills in an exciting and engaging way, but LEA, coupled with digital storytelling techniques, can provide preservice teachers the opportunity to learn and adapt the time-honored approach of LEA with more technologically advanced applications.

Whether digital or in print, LEA is a compelling approach to teaching reading and writing. It helps students make sense of language as they communicate experiences that are highly personal and motivating.

> ▶ LEA is more than just dictating stories. In this **video** (www.youtube.com/watch? v=kz1bBZoWMQI), notice what this special education teacher does before the students dictate their personal stories. How did the teacher incorporate technology into LEA?

Literature-Based Instruction Approaches

The implementation of the CCSS has brought a renewed focus on using high-quality literature as a powerful teaching tool. A clear emphasis on the role literature should play is included in the standards document in the Appendix, which provides text examples of the level of complexity and quality required of all students in a given grade band. **Literature-based instruction** approaches accommodate individual student differences in reading abilities and at the same time focus on meaning, interest, and enjoyment. In literature-based instruction, teachers encourage their students to select their own trade books (another name for popular books) for independent reading. Many teachers are taking a cue from the standards and blending fiction and informational reading as they phase in the Common Core. In schools nationwide, teachers are finding ways to include historical documents, speeches, essays, and other nonfiction into the curriculum. The rationale is that an important part of classroom life should be *reading*: reading literature and other texts that make children wonder, weep, laugh, contemplate, and gasp.

2017 ILA Standard

5.2

Self-selection of literature for independent reading is integral in a literature-based program. It personalizes reading and is a good way to motivate and engage students. Teachers often hold conferences with individual students about what they are reading and ask questions that encourage students to think about the text. They may ask students to make predictions, discuss a difficulty they had while reading, or share an interesting fact they read in a piece of nonfiction text. The goal of conferencing is always to help students become strategic, thoughtful readers in order for deep comprehension to take place.

Some teachers depend widely on literature for **guided reading**, a widespread approach to teaching reading that uses **leveled books**. A leveled book collection is a large set of books organized by level of difficulty from the easy books that an emergent reader might begin with to the longer, complex books that an advanced reader will select. In some schools, the collection is housed in a central book room where teachers can make careful text selections. There are multiple copies of many books in the book-room. There might be 10 levels for grades K–1 and three or four levels for each later grade. Teachers provide support for small, flexible groups of readers based on ongoing teacher assessment and observation of students' needs using leveled books.

Common Core State Standard

CCSS.R.10

Pieces of literature are also used as springboards for writing in a literature-based approach. Children can write different endings for stories or incidents in their own lives that reflect conflicts similar to ones they have read about. Students also look at story structures and devise stories using the same kinds of structures. Further, the con-flicts between characters in literature can be used to help students gain insights into their own life situations.

> In this series of **videos** (https://www.youtube.com/watch?v=vXvefHR9qWl), watch how this fifth grade teacher uses guided reading in her classroom. What are the procedures she must put into place for all of her students in order to effectively hold guided reading groups?

Other forms of organization are also used. For example, a group of students might read and respond to the same piece of literature. Or students read different books with similar themes and then share and compare insights gained. Reading instruction deliv-ered in this way emanates from assumptions about the reading process that are inter-active and top-down. Literature-based approaches depend on teachers who know children's literature and classroom organization.

Technology-Based Instruction

Technology-based instruction can make a dramatic difference in students' literacy learning. Digital networked learning has changed the way we locate, communicate, and disseminate information; how we approach reading and writing; and how we think about people becoming literate. Students are as likely to swipe, tap, or scroll as they are to turn a page in a book.

Online opportunities abound that are easily integrated into the classroom and can greatly enhance student learning. Students can videoconference with authors or students from different parts of the world, or create video clips, iMovies, class blogs, e-books, and online collaboration documents. They might take pictures of what they are learning and upload them to the class account, often using a smartphone. Web-based applications allow students to access and retrieve information immediately, construct their own texts, and interact with others, using laptops, tablets, and mobile devices. With the proliferation of tools, the number of games, apps, and software available to help students learn to read and increase their literacy skills is growing fast. And as technology continues to evolve, those tools are becoming more interac-tive, animated, and sophisticated. Some of the major trends in digital reading media include e-books with games and multimedia, digital storybooks, software and apps that automatically scaffold instruction to meet students' ability levels, story creation software that uses voice recordings to allow students to create and tell their own stories in digital formats, and tools to engage parents and their child in reading-related experiences.

Technology is also infiltrating the classroom through the traditional basal reading program. Most programs have digital packages that feature student e-books that allow students to respond to questions, record verbal responses, highlight text, or take notes online. Some have videos embedded that introduce a topic, pique student interest, and create a framework for thinking about the text they will be reading. Student dashboards give learners access to a wealth of resources, such as interactive digital lessons or up-to-date informational articles related to unit topics. Teacher dashboards deliver performance data and analysis without interrupting instruction to administer an assessment. Programs included are able to predict year-end performance and provide teachers with a data-driven action plan to help differentiate instruction and step-by-step lessons on specific skills each student needs.

When teachers are meeting with small groups of students regarding specific skills or strategies, they might use class tablets and mobile devices that allow students to read to themselves, read to someone else, listen to fluent reading, compose writing, or practice word work. There is virtually an app for any classroom task. In Transliteracy Box 2.3, Jeremy Brueck shares some examples of technology-based instruction.

TECHNOLOGY-BASED INSTRUCTIONAL CONSIDERATIONS   As information and communication technology become more accessible to teachers and students, technology's impact on classroom organization and instructional practices increases. Teaching and learning are being defined by the technologies within the classroom environment. Technology increases the availability of reading materials, changes the

BOX 2.3 | TRANSLITERACY

Jeremy Brueck
Hyperlinked Writing

The author Donald J. Sobol first published his adventures of boy super sleuth "Encyclopedia" Brown in 1963. All 29 books in this popular series presented the reader with a set of short mysteries, each including factual disparities somewhere within. Young readers were encouraged to read the text closely to try to identify the "slip-up" that breaks the case and then turn to the "Answers" section in the back of the book to verify their finding.

An important part of writing in digital spaces is the use of "hyperlinks." In their most basic form, a "link," or hyperlink, is word, phrase, or image on a web page that instructs a computer to move to another relevant web page. Much like Sobol's "Answers" section linked readers to the facts that solved each case, hyperlinked writing provides links that are pertinent to a piece of writing on the web and help to strengthen the writing by providing direct access back to source documents and related materials for the writer's audience.

Increasingly important to digital texts, understanding hyperlinked writing is a valuable transliteracy skill to develop in students, beginning even in the preschool years. While they may not be familiar with the terminology associated with hyperlinks, young children almost innately understand the point-and-click

component of navigating hyperlinked content; therefore, teaching young children the vocabulary associated with hyperlinked writing is crucial. Parents and teachers can model this vocabulary as children are actively engaged with digital content by responding with phrases like, "Look what happened when you clicked the link! You opened a new page," or "If you want to move one, click on the link on the bottom of the screen." Infusing vocabulary with associated play activities is a great way to provide early exposure to the principles of hyperlinked writing.

In the primary grades, students can begin to use blogs to draft, edit, and publish writing responses that include hyperlinks. Teachers will need to begin by modeling for students the discrete skills of hyperlinking. For example, a teacher might begin by composing the phrase, "Brown bear, brown bear, what do you see?" As part of the predictable response, "I see a ___ looking at me," the teacher demonstrates how to insert a link to a picture of the animal included in the response. After repeated modeling, the teacher can then integrate student-created (and hyperlinked) responses into writing center activities. As an additional support, teachers can create step-by-step guides for the hyperlinking process that include screenshots for students to reference.

way in which reading takes place, provides individual learning opportunities, and encourages students to use good judgment in locating and using information.

Although the integration of technology for teaching and learning is increasing, its uses and benefits depend on how much teachers value technology and their comfort level with it. A teacher's belief system will guide the integration of technology into teaching and learning practices. It is important that support and resources be provided for teachers as technology continues to change. This support includes staff development to help ensure that teachers are prepared to integrate information and communication technologies into the curriculum. Teachers need to know how to organize instruction in order to take advantage of technological benefits.

2017 ILA Standards

2.2, 5.2, 5.3

Instructional Decision Making 2.1: Apply your understanding of the concepts in this section.

Individualizing Instruction

The term *individualizing,* more so than *individualized,* connotes the process of providing differentiated instruction to students. It reflects the accumulation of previous knowledge and direct experiences in reading classrooms over the years. Many teachers of reading subscribe to this process, which originated as the individualized instruction approach. Its relevance today is due in part to the inclusion movement, which worked to meet the needs of and adapt the curriculum for students with special needs. A significant part of selecting appropriate instructional approaches is understanding the learning profile of an individual. This is especially true for students with learning disabilities. **Learning Disabilities Association of America** (http://ldaamerica.org) has information on various approaches to teaching reading and considerations for classroom teachers. Often misunderstood, the term *individualized instruction* means different things to different people. To some, it means programmed, prescriptive instruction; to others, it means flexible grouping for instruction.

Individualized instruction evolved out of a 150-year-old U.S. goal of providing free schooling for everyone. Its biggest impetus came with the development of reading tests in the early part of the twentieth century. It spawned many experiments in education, such as ability grouping, flexible promotions, and differentiated assignments. Many of the plans followed the ideas outlined in the Dalton and the Winnetka plans, which allowed children to work in reading and content areas at their own pace (Smith, 1965).

Gradually, individualized instruction went beyond children's learning rates and reading achievement. The child's interest in reading, attitude toward reading, and personal self-esteem and satisfaction in reading expanded the goal of instruction (Smith, 1965). Terms associated with individualization ranged from *individual progression* in the 1920s to *individualized instruction* in reading to *self-selection* in reading to *personalized reading.* Today, we might add *objective-based* and *prescriptive learning.* An interesting irony is that procedures used in the original individualized classrooms did not vary widely.

Two variations of the original individualized approach to instruction are often found in today's classrooms: (1) Individualized procedures are one part of the total program (e.g., one day a week), or (2) parts of individualized reading are integrated into another reading approach (e.g., self-selection during free reading). Individualization can refer to instruction that is appropriate for the student regardless of whether it occurs in a one-to-one, small group, or whole class setting. Individualization is a process of personalizing teaching to provide instruction that recognizes and responds to the unique learning needs of each child. Although individualized instruction as an approach or a program for reading instruction is not as widespread as others, its influence on reading teachers has been pervasive because assessment of the individual reader's strengths and weaknesses is at the very core of effective reading instruction. This tenet cuts across the delivery of reading instruction, regardless of classroom organization pattern.

The Integrated Approach

In the 1960s, the federal government founded the United States Cooperative Research Program in First-Grade Reading Instruction (Bond & Dykstra, 1967, 1997), a large government-funded study commonly referred to as the "First-Grade Studies." These studies were launched nationally in an effort to identify the best approaches to the teaching of reading. These instructional approaches included phonics, linguistic readers, basal programs, initial teaching alphabet, literature-based reading, language experience, and various grouping schemes and combinations of instruction. The First-Grade Studies found that *no instructional approach was superior to the others* for students at either high or low levels of readiness. Richard Allington, at the 2013 Conference of the International Reading Association, stated, "every study since the First-Grade Studies says the same thing: good teaching matters. It is not the material. It is expert teaching"(Allington, 2013b). The First-Grade Studies, more than anything else, underscored the importance of the "teacher variable" in children's reading achievement. Combinations of approaches were recommended, using the best features of all approaches.

An **integrated approach** to instruction suggests that the best way to teach is to use the best features of all of the approaches. For example, it embraces the concept of language experience throughout the grades by immersing students in reading, writing, talking, listening, and viewing activities and can cut across subject matter areas. From the individualized approach, there may be the emphasis on student self-selection of reading materials. From the basal approach, there may be the inclusion of some organization built into the teaching of skills and strategies. Integrated teaching brings together different pieces of approaches to best meet student needs. Teachers who use an integrated approach determine *what* to teach using the CCSS and then, considering all of their options, decide *how* to teach it. They use their professional knowledge and judgment to determine the instructional needs of their students and then adapt programs to meet those needs. An integrated approach combines the best features of all the other approaches.

Expertise Matters More than Approach

Teachers who know the art and science of teaching reading are able to provide skillful, effective reading instruction and can help students who need it overcome obstacles that keep them from becoming readers. In Box 2.4, Mary-Rollins describes how she uses a variety of approaches in her classroom.

2017 ILA Standards

1.1, 1.2, 1.3, 2.1, 2.2, 2.3, 6.1

Most reading problems can be prevented by teachers who are able to provide effective instruction. We know from years of research how to teach children to read. A series of studies have confirmed what was probably obvious from the beginning: Good teachers matter much more than particular curriculum materials, pedagogical approaches, or reading programs (Allington, 2013a; Pressley, Allington, Wharton-McDonald, Block, & Morrow, 2001; Sanders, 1998; Taylor, Pearson, Clark, & Walpole, 2000). There are no programs or materials that will teach every child to read; only expert teachers can do that. Consider the following:

- Effective teachers provide **explicit strategy instruction**, directly teaching students what they need to know and providing opportunities for practice until the student applies the skill independently. They model and demonstrate useful strategies

BOX 2.4 | VIEWPOINT

Mary-Rollins Dunagan Lothridge
My Approach to Teaching Reading

Mary-Rollins Dunagan Lothridge is a third-grade teacher at the Centennial Arts Academy (Gainesville City Schools) in Gainesville, Georgia.

I have almost 15 years' experience in K–3 classrooms and have learned how to use a variety of approaches to teach reading. I teach two reading blocks daily, each for 60 minutes with 16 students in each class. While my preference is to have a 90-minute block, my school tried something different this year by pulling our gifted and ELL students for reading and math. This leaves a smaller group for homeroom teachers to instruct during the block but also limits the time to an hour due to manpower.

I begin each class with a minilesson on either word study using the week's spelling words or the introduction of a new comprehension skill. This minilesson can vary but usually includes me modeling the activity on the interactive whiteboard followed by a 10-minute independent or partnered activity. Whatever the skill (cause and effect, comparing two passages from the same author, main idea, elements of genre, etc.), it is reinforced at my literacy centers and in small-group guided reading throughout the week. This is also a good time to use formative assessments and pull students for quick progress monitoring for Response to Intervention, or RTI.

After the whole group minilesson and exercise, I pull two 20-minute guided reading groups. These groups are homogeneously formed by guided reading level, and depending on the group's needs, we work on fluency, comprehension, or both, using various genres throughout the year. I also use short texts designed to be read quickly and meaningfully for students who are struggling with reading fluency. We also use this group time to practice test-taking skills and reflective writing, but my ultimate goal in these groups is to give my third graders the opportunity to read on a level they are successful at. This helps build confidence and fluency, and with our discussions and writings supports comprehension. Because I strive to choose texts that are connected to our work in science, social studies, and character education, these texts are often ones that spark interest with my students, which I strongly believe is key to comprehension and learning the joy of reading.

Each 8 to 9 weeks, I assess students on their reading level to determine progress and regrouping needs. I also use miniassessments as formative assessments for the skills specifically taught from the Common Core Curriculum, and we give a unit assessment each 8 to 9 weeks, as well. Because third grade is the first year for the Georgia state assessments and students must pass the reading portion for promotion, we spend more time on assessment preparation and assessments than I would like to, but my system does a good job at keeping these windows to a minimum.

When students are not in small group with me, they are at a center (one per day) that supports our standards. For example, some might be at a computer station for online practice using a commercial program or doing research; others might be at the listening center using a book and CD, or an app on a tablet. They might be buddy reading with a partner, journal writing, or doing word work (this center varies week to week). I also believe that students need to learn the skill of working independently at the level at which they are capable, and this is their opportunity to do that. I try to keep the centers consistent in order to cut down on reading group disruptions due to students asking questions, and to create a structured environment that supports their independence.

That being said, my class is designed for changes regarding the progress of my students. Groups and activities change periodically to support this progress and the needs of my students.

In reflection, my viewpoint on reading and reading development in elementary aged children is that exposure to appropriately leveled text is key. As a mother of a kindergartner who, like many early readers, finds books to be intimidating, I realize this more than ever. As a reading teacher, it is my charge to expose my students to different types of texts in order to build interest, and at a level that is attainable for the student to help build confidence and momentum.

that good readers employ. These exemplary teachers routinely offer direct, explicit demonstrations of the cognitive strategies used by good readers when they read. In other words, they model the thinking in which skilled readers engage. Thus, these teachers take on the responsibility of crafting explicit demonstrations of skill and strategy use.

- Effective teachers realize one size does not fit all and adapt instruction based on assessment results. Teachers differentiate instruction by continually assessing students' individual progress to help them identify strengths and needs, then plan instruction for small groups of students to target those needs. These teachers offer strategy lessons to the whole class, to targeted small groups, and to individual students in side-by-side instruction. Effective teachers monitor progress regularly, reteach as needed, adapt instruction for students who struggle (and for high-achieving students as well), and use **instructional scaffolding** to support development. They teach specific skills and strategies students need to learn based on both formal and informal assessment data. They know a variety of ways to teach reading, when to use each method, and how to combine the methods into an instructional program.

- Effective teachers provide students with opportunities to apply skills and strategies in reading and writing using meaningful text. Extensive reading is critical to the development of reading proficiency, and practice provides the opportunity for students to combine the skills and strategies teachers work to develop. Children should be reading two-thirds of the time set aside for reading. Only one-third of the reading time should be spent with teacher talk.

- Effective teachers know a critical part of reading instruction is explicitly teaching students how to use efficient reading strategies. Students need a multitude of tools or strategies to sound words out, look for parts of a word they know, and then know how to use context to check and see whether it makes sense. Students must also be encouraged to identify strategies they know and use these strategies independently toward becoming a skillful reader. Students must know how to problem solve and how to get past strategy roadblocks when reading on their own in order to grow as a reader during independent reading time.

- Effective teachers recognize students need large quantities of reading experiences with an assortment of texts and genres, which they can read with accuracy, fluency, and comprehension in order to become independent, competent readers. They provide large amounts of text at the appropriate instructional levels, which are not too easy or too hard.

As you consider the instructional approaches presented in this chapter, keep in mind the usefulness of a certain instructional practice may depend on the skill level of each student. Strategies that help one student may be ineffective when applied to another with different skills. We need schools where every teacher understands reading and writing development and has the support necessary to become a reading expert who can design and deliver instruction matched to the individual needs of each student within the class. **ReadWriteThink** (http://www.readwritethink.org) is a partnership between the International Literacy Association (ILA), the National Council of Teachers of English (NCTE), and the Verizon Thinkfinity Foundation that works to provide educators access to high-quality practices and resources in reading and language arts instruction.

Check Your Understanding 2.3: Gauge your understanding of the skills and concepts in this section.

RTI for Struggling Readers

Differentiating Instruction as *Response to Intervention*

For RTI implementation to work well, it is critical that all students receive high-quality, differentiated instruction, but there is no single approach to instruction that can address the broad and varied goals and needs of all students, especially those from different cultural and linguistic backgrounds. There is no silver bullet—the problems of struggling readers are not solved by simply adopting a particular instructional approach or program. What teachers emphasize from various programs and approaches and how they deliver instruction matters a great deal. Knowledgeable teachers who provide quality classroom reading instruction can make a big difference for all readers, especially those who struggle. Knowing how to use different approaches and strategies in a comprehensive program that meets individual student needs is the hallmark of an effective teacher.

Watch this **video** (www.youtube.com/watch?v=a2-DXXoenAg), and notice how the staff uses data to inform their RTI processes. Based on this data, teachers differentiate lessons to support the needs of struggling readers. What approaches from this chapter do you recognize in the classrooms featured on the video? Do you notice a bottom-up, top-down, or more interactive approach to teaching readers?

What About . . .

Standards, Assessment, and Approaches to Reading Instruction?

For years, there has been controversy regarding the best way to teach children how to read. In this chapter, we highlighted the major approaches of teaching reading and concluded there is no one best way to teach all children. The CCSS determine what skills and concepts students are expected to learn in each grade. They do not tell teachers *how* to teach; they simply specify the skills that should be taught. For example, the CCSS do not dictate which books should be taught in fourth-grade English/language arts, but they do say that each fourth grader should learn how to describe in depth a character, setting, or event in a story or drama, drawing on specific details in the text. The best understanding of what works in the classroom comes from the teachers who are in them. That's why these standards will establish what students need to learn, but they will not dictate how teachers should teach. Schools and teachers will decide the best instructional approach to help students meet the standards.

Summary

- Teachers should determine their philosophical stance or beliefs about reading because beliefs impact classroom instruction. Awareness of belief systems helps achieve balance in the teaching of reading because instruction requires teachers to make decisions based on how children learn and how they can best be taught.
- The bottom-up and top-down curriculum perspectives were explored because they reflect what teachers and students do as they engage in learning. Teachers' beliefs about literacy invariably contribute to

curriculum decisions such as instructional objectives, materials selected, the learning environment, instructional approaches and practices, and the kinds of assessments used to evaluate learning.
- Approaches to reading instruction represent the general plans for achieving goals in the classroom. Six broad instructional approaches to teaching reading were presented in this chapter. Teachers draw from these various approaches to achieve a comprehensive program that meets the needs of all students.

Teacher Action Research

1. After completing the Beliefs About Reading Interview (Box 2.2), reflect on your beliefs, and then create a simple graphic that summarizes your beliefs about teaching reading. Your graphic might include multiple images. Share your graphic with a partner, and explain the images.
2. Study Table 2.2, Cambourne's Conditions for Learning. How can families and teachers use Cambourne's

eight conditions of literacy development to help children develop language and literacy in pleasurable and meaningful ways? For example, the condition of *expectation* could be met by expecting every student will become an accomplished reader and writing in their own time. This would include knowledge of the developmental stages of literacy and setting realistic expectations.

3. Watch this video (www.youtube.com/watch?v= d6DvFPc9FM8) to hear a second-grade teacher talk about using a basal reader in her classroom. As you watch, take notes on the routines that are included in the program. Also, what materials do you observe that accompany the basal approach to reading?

Through the Lens of the Common Core

In this chapter, we remind teachers that the CCSS tell *what* teachers must teach, but *how* they go about incorporating the standards is still their decision. A variety of instructional approaches need to be used by knowledgeable teachers to ensure that all children reach the goal of college and career readiness. The CCSS require equal outcomes for all students, but they do not require equal contributions. Teachers need to vary the amounts and types of instruction provided to students to ensure success.

Chapter 3
Meeting the Literacy Needs of Diverse Learners

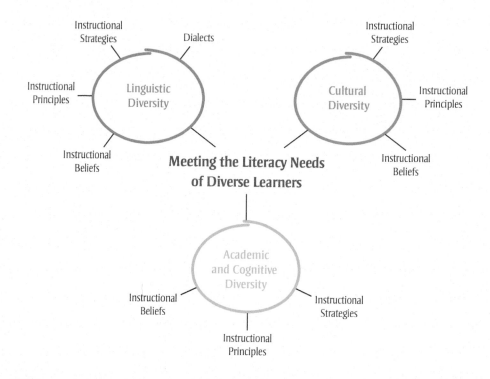

Instructional Strategies — Dialects — Instructional Principles — **Linguistic Diversity** — Instructional Beliefs

Instructional Strategies — Instructional Principles — **Cultural Diversity** — Instructional Beliefs

Meeting the Literacy Needs of Diverse Learners

Instructional Beliefs — **Academic and Cognitive Diversity** — Instructional Strategies — Instructional Principles

Learning Outcomes

In This Chapter, You Will Discover How to

■ Identify instructional beliefs, principles, and strategies for teaching students with linguistic diversity, including an appreciation for students who speak in different dialects.

■ Identify and appreciate the nature of cultural diversity, including core principles and instructional strategies for teaching students from diverse cultures.

■ Recognize that students have diverse academic needs and that teachers need to be aware of instructional principles and strategies that address cognitive differences.

Activating Your Schema

Can you recall a time in your life when you felt left out? Your recollections might range from social gatherings, dating situations, educational settings, family gatherings, or other experiences. Jot down your recollections, and share them with your colleagues. Your prior experiences can help you understand the meaning of diversity and differences.

2017 ILA Standards Found in This Chapter

1.1	4.1	4.3	5.2	5.4
1.2	4.2	5.1	5.3	6.3
2.1				

Common Core State Standards: English Language Arts

CCRA.R.1	CCRA.R.5	CCRA.R.9	CCRA.W.8	CCRA.L.1
CCRA.R.2	CCRA.R.6	CCRA.R.10	CCRA.SL.1	CCRA.L.3
CCRA.R.3	CCRA.R.7	CCRA.W.6	CCRA.SL.5	CCRA.L.5
CCRA.R.4	CCRA.R.8			

Key Terms

academic and cognitive diversity

accents

additive approach

American Standard English

code-switching

contributions approach

cultural diversity

curriculum compacting

dialects

differentiated instruction

dyslexia

inclusion

inquiry learning

instructional conversations

linguistic diversity

LOTEs

response protocol

Sheltered Instruction Observation Protocol (SIOP)

social action approach

transformative approach

translanguaging

Nikki teaches second grade at an urban school, and several of her students are English language learners (ELLs). She realizes that not only must she engage these students in learning English, but she must also build and maintain respectful relationships with each child's family. As part of her routine, Nikki provides time each day for several second graders to share items from home for a "show and tell" activity. The class sits in a circle, and the children take turns talking about the articles. The classmates are invited to ask questions. In order to encourage her ELL students to use this as a time to share their cultural backgrounds and traditions, Nikki meets with the parents at the outset of the school year to explain the activity and to encourage the ELLs to share cultural artifacts such as clothing, games, pictures, and food.

Maria, one second grader, is from Mexico, and she shared with pride a Spanish costume that was worn by her grandmother during a festival. As she pointed to the parts of the costume, she taught her classmates the Spanish words for skirt, blouse, and sleeve. Nikki took the opportunity to share other visuals of Spanish clothing through pictures she found on the web.

Since cultural background and self-concept influence student learning, teachers need to be aware of each child's cultural identity and background. It is necessary to build a learning community where all students' experiences are valid regardless of the differences. Providing ELLs with a safe, friendly, caring learning environment where diversity is celebrated enables them to become confident learners.

This vignette illustrates how one teacher strives to meet the diverse needs of her students in a caring, knowledgeable, and professional way. Multiple factors contribute to the diverse nature of today's classrooms and the challenges that teachers face in the twenty-first century. Generally, these factors fall into three categories:

1. *Linguistic diversity.* The language in which the student feels most comfortable communicating is not the language of instruction in the school.
2. *Cultural diversity.* The student's home, family, socioeconomic group, or culture differs from the predominant (often middle-class) culture of the school
3. *Cognitive and academic diversity.* The child learns at a pace or in a style different from that expected at the school.

These factors influence how, when, and under what circumstances students will best learn to read and write.

2017 ILA Standards

4.1, 4.3

In addition to linguistic, cultural, and cognitive or academic diversity, socioeconomic diversity compounds the complex nature of today's classrooms. Although school success or failure is not exclusively determined by economic factors such as poverty, students who come from family contexts in which they do not have easy access to books may be at risk for reading failure (McCabe & Tamis-LeMonda, 2013). In addition, limited access to meaningful print in schools may also contribute to low reading achievement for students with linguistic, cultural, or cognitive differences (Lazar, 2004). Students whose family contexts include a cycle of low literacy miss early literacy experiences such as shared reading. The more knowledge about literacy that students gain *before* entering school, the more likely they will experience success.

The instructional decisions teachers must make in teaching students to learn to read and write are multifaceted. Further complicating the choices teachers must make in the classroom is the complex nature of diversity. There is no one African American experience, just as there is no one Hispanic American experience or European American experience. Moreover, no two students who are identified with learning disabilities are alike. Students come from different socioeconomic backgrounds, geographic locations, levels of parental education, and cultural backgrounds, and have varying levels of language skills. All of these factors influence student success or lack of success in learning to read. Next, we discuss instructional beliefs associated with linguistic, cultural, and academic diversity. We also suggest teaching principles and strategies for teachers as they address the diverse needs of their students.

Linguistic Diversity in Literacy Classrooms

■ **Identify instructional beliefs, principles, and strategies for teaching students with linguistic diversity, including an appreciation for students who speak in different dialects.**

The demography of the United States has changed dramatically over the decades, and the **linguistic diversity** of our nation has a tremendous impact on our schools.

According to the U.S. Census Bureau (2015), at least 350 languages are spoken in homes nationwide, with large metropolitan areas ranging from nearly 200 languages recognized in the New York City area to at least 185 in Los Angeles, 153 in Chicago, and 146 in Philadelphia. According to the U.S. Census Bureau (2012), the Hispanic and Asian populations are expected to double by 2060. In addition, regional variations in language usage, commonly known as dialects, pose another challenge for literacy and language arts teachers. What are the beliefs regarding teaching students who speak linguistically diverse languages and dialects? What instructional principles and strategies work for these students?

Instructional Beliefs About Linguistic Diversity

Although the United States has a long history of non-English-speaking immigrant students attending public school, **American Standard English** has been the traditionally acceptable language of instruction in schools because it is viewed as a critical tool for success in the United States. Additionally, the Common Core State Standards for English language arts (2010) specify the importance of students' knowing the conventions of Standard English as indicated in the College and Career Readiness Anchor Standards for Language. Furthermore, in addition to learning a second language, ELLs need to learn complex content with academic texts (Hakuta, Santos, & Fang, 2013), as well as critical literacy skills (Leu, 2012). They need to be able to synthesize, infer, analyze, criticize, and compare and contrast complex text.

2017 ILA Standard

4.1

Common Core Standards

CCRA.R.1, CCRA.R.2, CCRA.R.3, CCRA.R.7, CCRA.R.8, CCRA.R.9, CCRA.R.10, CCRA.L.1, CCRAL.3, CCRAL.5

How do teachers address the needs of ELLs in the twenty-first century? Next, we address multiple instructional principles that teachers need to consider as they support learners from diverse language backgrounds.

Instructional Principles for Students Speaking Diverse Languages and Dialects

Language is largely cultural in nature, and when students maintain a strong identification with their culture and native language, they are more likely to succeed academically and they have more positive self-concepts about their ability to learn (Cummins, 2011; G. E. Garcia, 2000; Hadaway & Young, 2006; Reyes, 2012). In fact, the International Reading Association (2001) recommends that reading instruction be conducted in a student's native language. Moreover, Bauer (2009) and McCabe and Tamis-LeMonda (2013) contend that students benefit from opportunities to connect what they know about literacy in their primary language to their new language. Hence, a contemporary concept for educators to consider is **translanguaging** (Garcia, 2009), a view of English language learning that is characterized by speakers moving from one language (for example, English) to other languages when they communicate. This phenomenon, also referred to as **LOTEs** (languages other than English), is based on the belief that language is not something that a child simply "has," but rather reflects ways to communicate based on one's purpose, audience, and social context. When teachers allow students to integrate their heritage language into social as well as instructional conversations in the classroom, translanguaging can not only provide a safe environment for ELL students, but it can also foster academic achievement (Daniel & Pacheco, 2015).

2017 ILA Standards

4.1, 4.3

Although the ideal development of second-language literacy would have each native speaker receiving instructional support in the home language while learning to master English, the reality is often quite different. However, teachers should strive to provide an environment in which both languages are used in multiple and meaningful contexts (McCabe & Tamis-LeMonda, 2013). In addition, the principles that guide language and literacy learning in a first language should guide literacy learning in a second language.

The following second-language acquisition principles for classroom practice relate to alphabetic languages (e.g., Spanish and German) as well as nonalphabetic languages (e.g., Chinese and Japanese):

- The social context for learning a second language must be a setting in which students feel accepted and comfortable.

- Students in small groups and pairs should have natural opportunities for meaning-making and authentic communication.

- Students need time to listen and process without the pressure of oral and written production. They are often rehearsing and creating systems while silent.

In addition, teachers need to understand that English language learners often face unique challenges such as limited background knowledge and vocabulary constraints, and they are often unfamiliar with the text structures found in academic content books (Mora, 2006). On the other hand, motivation can play a key factor in ELLs learning to read and speak English (Protacio, 2012). See Box 3.1 to read how one ELL student views learning English.

BOX 3.1 | STUDENT VOICES

José is a typical ELL third grader who performs very well in school. He was interviewed by his ELL teacher, Miss Sue. José did not speak English when he first entered school in 2013. He arrived from Peru with his close-knit family—his parents and two older siblings. His parents do not speak English, but they expect their children to participate and work hard in school.

José attends an ELL class 12 periods per week for instruction in English. He attends all other classes with his homeroom. In the ELL class, José is given support in science, social studies, and math when necessary. He is an outgoing, pleasant, conscientious student who has a good sense of humor. He said that he enjoyed going on a tour of the facility when he first arrived, which helped him learn basic vocabulary associated with the school.

During his interview, José shared his perceptions about learning to speak English. He remembered the beginning of the school year when he thought to himself, "What is she saying? I don't understand." He only knew several English words and felt sad because he couldn't understand what was being said. At first José was reluctant to speak English because he was afraid to make mistakes. Newcomers often go through a silent period when entering school as non-English speakers. At this point,

after 6 months in the United States, José feels much more confident speaking English and has become very sociable. He has become so comfortable that he became a "buddy" to assist a new student from Turkey.

When asked what the teacher has done to help him develop oral language in the ELL class, José shared many insightful comments that are synthesized here:

- Provide a safe environment whenever he is in the ELL classroom.

- Build vocabulary using flash cards and a picture dictionary.

- Provide the opportunity to socialize with peers and practice speaking English in the ELL class during informal, structured play time.

- Demonstrate that the ELL teachers are caring and helpful.

- Offer support and "wait time," which allows students time to respond.

José recommended that teachers not be hesitant to teach more difficult vocabulary. Most important, José said that his ELL teacher loves him. He ended the interview with a hug.

2017 ILA Standard

2.1

The Common Core State Standards (CCSS) (National Governors Association Center for Best Practices, Council of Chief State School Officers, 2010) present a challenge for teachers of ELLs, especially when it comes to reading complex text (Fillmore & Fillmore, n.d.). Literacy, language, and content experts, however, recognize the importance of developing sound principles for assisting ELLs as they strive to meet the standards (Hakuta, Santos, & Fang, 2013; Protacio, 2012). Next, we address instructional strategies that support learners from diverse language backgrounds.

Instructional Strategies for Students Speaking Diverse Languages

Learning a second language should not mean losing a first language. Teachers can support the first language of ELLs in the following ways:

- Include environmental print from the child's first language in the classroom. Label objects in the first language and in English so that everyone is learning a second language.
- Make sure that the classroom and school libraries have books in languages other than English as well as books written in English representing the cultures of the children.
- Encourage children to bring in and share artifacts, music, dance, and food from their cultures, and encourage their parents to participate in selecting the artifacts (Protacio & Edwards, 2015).
- Help children publish and share their writing in their first language.
- Enlist the help of bilingual aides—other students, parents, teacher aides, or community volunteers.
- Use commercial or student-produced videos and computer software to support language learning and improve self-esteem.
- Help ELLs find support on the Internet. There are chat rooms, available 24 hours a day, in which students can meet others speaking their first language. They can engage in peer discussions as well as share ideas about learning English.
- Connect with the families. Welcome them into the classroom to observe and to share their language and culture. Even though their English may be limited, they often enjoy teaching the numbers, days of the week, greetings, and other common expressions.

Watch this **video** (https://www.youtube.com/watch?v=jnR5FDL0NCs&list=PLoU659 hwTdDYnuHRcZgFPjMaoAS8b09J1&index=3) to learn how one school engages the children in English language learning.

SHELTERED ENGLISH ADAPTATIONS   There are techniques that teachers can use in *sheltered English settings*, those in which the teacher is not proficient in the student's language and the student is not proficient in the teacher's language. Nonverbal communication is maximized. The following adaptations are recommended:

- Give students time to express what they know by drawing pictures, pointing, or manipulating objects.
- Demonstrate concepts with body actions. Make use of all the senses, including sounds and smells.

- Give students more wait time. They may need more processing time to answer questions or discuss topics.
- Keep language simple; rephrase information using body actions and objects.
- Adapt materials by adding pictures, diagrams, charts, and graphic organizers.

2017 ILA Standards

5.1, 5.2

A widely recognized model for sheltered English is the **Sheltered Instruction Observation Protocol (SIOP)**, designed to provide teachers with an effective framework for instruction for ELLs (Echevarria, Vogt, & Short, 2012). The protocol is organized around three major categories: teacher preparation, teacher instruction, and assessment. Preparation includes being sure the objectives are clear and meaningful. Instruction includes considering students' background knowledge, using appropriate language during your instruction, giving students many opportunities to use the strategies you are teaching, providing students with a variety of ways to interact with the concepts you are teaching, and ensuring that students are engaged. Assessment focuses on review of concepts taught with regular feedback to your students.

In this **video** (https://www.youtube.com/watch?v=IVGbz4EqyGs), you will see the SIOP model in action with English language learners. Think about how the categories in the SIOP model support ELLs' language acquisition and development.

INSTRUCTIONAL CONVERSATIONS   Instructional conversations are another effective way to engage students in diverse language classrooms. During **instructional conversations**, teachers facilitate students' prior knowledge and experience about a topic, build on the students' backgrounds, engage in extensive discussion, and guide understanding. Teachers also scaffold learning rather than expect correct yes or no answers. For example, by allowing students to respond to more divergent, high-order, and affective questions, teachers provide students with opportunities to express reactions to content on a personal level; this is a critical component of the CCSS. By minimizing teacher talk, teachers can encourage students to role-play, carry out small activity-oriented tasks, or use dramatic presentations to express understanding. See Box 3.2 on how Miss Yin uses instructional conversations with her ELL second graders as she works with them on a classroom job for the week.

Common Core Standard

CCRA.SL.1

RESPONSE PROTOCOL   Teachers often try to engage English language learners in talking by asking questions; sometimes the students' responses are one word, simple phrases, or simply body-language reactions such as nodding the head. In order to encourage productive talk in the classroom that fosters ELLs' social as well as academic language development, Mohr and Mohr (2007) suggest how teachers can elaborate on student language using **response protocol**. The design provides a framework for teachers to elaborate on ELLs' responses. For example, if the teacher points to an object and asks the student, "What is this?" and the student replies with a one-word answer, the teacher would expound on the response. The teacher might say, "Yes, this is a(an) _____," encouraging the student to repeat the expanded response. If the teacher asks a student to describe an object or activity, the teacher would use prompts such as "Can you tell me more?" In Box 3.3, the teacher, Mrs. Montler, engages three of her ELL students, Carla, Marco,

BOX 3.2 | STEP-BY-STEP LESSON

Instructional Conversations in Miss Yin's Classroom

Each week, Miss Yin assigns classroom jobs for her second-grade students, who work in pairs to complete the daily tasks. She uses instructional conversations with her ELL students to foster language learning in a meaningful context. In particular, she "walks and talks" the students through the task as it is completed; on the final day of the week, they illustrate and share their pictures about the task. Below is Miss Yin's step-by-step process and an example of the daily task of taking care of the plants in her classroom.

Day 1

Introduce the task, and "walk and talk" the students through the steps.

"Your job this week is to water the plants. Here are the plants. There are four plants."

Prompts: What are these? (Plants) Yes, these are plants.
How many plants are there? (Four) Yes, there are four plants.

"Your job is to water the plants."

Prompts: What is your job? (Water) Yes, you will water the plants.

"Here is the watering can. Here is the sink. We turn on the water. We fill the watering can with water."

Prompts: What is this? (Can) Yes, this is the watering can. What is this? (Sink) Yes, this is the sink.

"Let's turn on the water. Let's fill the watering can with water." (Demonstrate)

"We are watering the plants."

Prompts: What are we doing? (Watering) Yes, we are watering the plants.
How many plants are there? (Four) Yes, we are watering four plants.
The conversation may continue with additional prompts.

Day 2

Repeat the conversation in a similar manner.

Day 3

Repeat the conversation with fewer prompts, encouraging the students to "walk and talk" through the steps of the task.

Day 4

Repeat the conversation with fewer prompts.

Day 5

Repeat the conversation with prompts only as needed. Have the students illustrate the task. Next, the students talk about the task by referring to their pictures. The pictures are kept in notebooks for the students. Picture "walk and talks" are reviewed periodically for practice. The notebooks can be sent home for additional practice.

---

and Juanita, in a conversation in which she prompts the students and encourages them to elaborate on their communications.

2017 ILA Standard

5.1

WORDLESS BOOKS   Wordless picture books can serve as an effective way to foster meaning-making and reading comprehension with emergent readers (Lysaker & Hopper, 2015), and they can also be used to foster language development for ELLs. Using the pictures can nurture vocabulary development as the students learn to use dialogue about what they see in the illustrations. For example, "I see a house. What do you see?" or "This person looks happy. How does this person look?" In addition to learning vocabulary through the pictures, ELLs can talk about the actions occurring on each page and eventually be encouraged to tell the story based on the pictures. Wordless picture books can also be used with older children who are developing their English skills; in fact, pictures of any sort work with ELLs: newspaper photos, pictures from nonfiction books, cartoons, photographs from home, magazines, and posters. Resources for pictures are limitless and can serve as effective visual ways to engage ELLs in learning English, as well as encourage them to share vocabulary and experiences based on their individual backgrounds.

BOX 3.3 | RESEARCH-BASED PRACTICES

Response Protocol in Mrs. Montler's Classroom

Mrs. Montler teaches third grade in a rural school district in Pennsylvania. She has 18 students in her class; three of her students are Hispanic. Carla, Marco, and Juanita have very limited conversational skills, so each day Mrs. Montler works with the students in a small group for 15 minutes in order to personalize conversation with them using response protocol. Here is how she uses research-based practices as she develops her lesson:

1. Mrs. Montler selects a focus theme that centers on communicating about an everyday topic in which the students have some background knowledge; for example, foods, hobbies, interests, or family.
2. Next, Mrs. Montler selects a picture or pictures that focus on the topic. For example, if the topic is foods, she might have pictures that represent ethnic and American foods.
3. Next, beginning with the pictures, she points to and models vocabulary associated with the pictures.
4. Next, Mrs. Montler models and prompts the students to discuss their associations with the pictures in a conversational dialogue.
5. She concludes the conversation by modeling a synthesis of the conversation with student participation.

Let's look at a lesson in which Mrs. Montler uses response protocol strategies (which are conversation elaboration strategies) with Carlos, Marco, and Juanita.

Mrs. Montler: Good morning, Carlos. Good morning, Marco. Good morning, Juanita.

Carlos, Marco, Juanita (in unison): Good morning.

Mrs. Montler: Today we have more pictures to talk about. These are pictures of things you might like to do. (Mrs. Montler points to the pictures.)

Mrs. Montler: This is a bike. This is a ball. This is a book.

Mrs. Montler: (She points to each picture.) What is this? What is this? What is this?

Carlos: Bike.

Mrs. Montler: Yes, this is a bike. What is this, Carlos?

Carlos: Bike.

Mrs. Montler: Yes, that's right, Carlos. This is a bike. What is this, Carlos?

Carlos: This is a bike.

Mrs. Montler: Yes, Carlos. This is a bike!

Mrs. Montler: Marco, what is this? (She points to the picture of the bike.)

Marco: A bike.

Mrs. Montler: Yes, Marco, this is a bike. What is this?

Marco: This is a bike.

Mrs. Montler: Yes, Marco, this is a bike!

Mrs. Montler: (Pointing to a ball) Juanita, this is a ball. What is this, Juanita?

Juanita: This is a ball.

Mrs. Montler: Yes, good job, Juanita, this is a ball! What is this? (Mrs. Montler points to the bike.)

Juanita: This is a bike!

Mrs. Montler: Yes, Juanita! This is a bike! I can ride my bike! (Mrs. Montler dramatizes riding a bike with actions.) Juanita, can you ride a bike?

Juanita: Yes.

Mrs. Montler: Yes, you can ride a bike! Can you ride a bike?

Juanita: Yes, I can ride a bike!

Mrs. Montler: Marco, can you ride a bike?

Marco: Yes, I can ride a bike.

Mrs. Montler continues the conversation by helping the children elaborate on what they can do with a bike, a ball, and a book. She uses prompts such as, "Can you tell me more? What else?" She also responds positively with comments such as, "Good job! That's right!"

CONTENT AREA PRACTICES It is well documented that ELLs take longer to learn academic language than social communication (Cummins, 2011)—approximately 5 to 7 years for children between the ages of 8 and 11 (Hadaway & Young, 2006). On the other hand, it is critical that ELLs learn to navigate in a world in which all people need to be able to critically think about complex content. In order to scaffold content learning, teachers need to explicitly teach the various formats associated with content text, such as *main headings, subheadings, italics, index, glossary, tables,* and *figures,* to name a few. Pacheco and Miller (2015) elaborate on how newspapers written in multiple languages can help young children realize text features such as *titles, authors,* and *captions.* In addition, strategies that include promoting LOTEs (languages other than English) in content area classrooms, such as taking notes and summarizing content in the first and second languages, can foster academic learning (Daniel & Pacheco, 2015).

Common Core Standard

CCRA.R.5

Finally, to help students learn English academic language that is required by the CCSS, systematic coordination among content area teachers and ELL teachers is vital (Hakuta, Santos, & Fang, 2013). Teachers need to share what they are teaching and how they are teaching it. In some ELL programs, students meet with the ELL teacher outside the classroom several days a week. In other programs, the ELL teacher co-teaches with content area teachers in the classroom. In any program, the ELL teacher needs to be actively involved in team planning sessions so that there is congruency in the program. In addition, teachers need to use concrete examples to help ELLs understand content concepts as they relate prior knowledge and experiences to those concepts.

Instructional Decision Making 3.1: Apply your understanding of the concepts in this section.

Dialects

Dialects are variations of the same language spoken by members of a specific area, region, or community. The differences are typically characterized by distinctive sounds, pronunciations of words, grammar usage, and vocabulary. Regional dialects primarily differ in the pronunciation of vowels, while social dialects are typically characterized by differences in consonant sounds (Gollnick & Chinn, 2013). Grammar usage is typified by variations in patterns of speech such as subject–verb agreement, past tense, negatives, and plurals (Wheeler & Swords, 2006). Vocabulary differences are characteristically informal, nonstandard uses of words that are, at times, coined "slang." Sometimes dialects are confused with accents. **Accents**, however, are simply linguistic variations in the pronunciations of sounds; the grammar remains standard.

Although there is no consensus as to how many dialects are actually spoken in the United States, we all speak a **dialect** of English, although it may be much easier for us to see our own speech as natural and the speech of everyone else as the dialect. These variations of language are culturally specific, governed by rules, learned in social settings, reflective of the linguistic norms of a region or community, and significant to cultural identity, self-worth, and pride. For a time, it was thought that beginning readers who spoke a variation of Standard English, the dialect found in textbooks, would read poorly because the language was different from their own. However, this idea is unfounded.

Society in general fails to recognize that speakers of other dialects are using their cultural norms for communicating. Negative attitudes regarding some dialectics include judgements of intelligence, competence, socioeconomic status, and morality, which can foster feelings of low self-esteem (Zuidema, 2005). Hence, while teaching the norms of Standard English, it is important for teachers to understand the manner in which students from diverse cultures use language at home and in social settings and to nurture respect for linguistic differences. Rather than characterizing Standard English as "good" and a dialect as "bad," teachers should promote the belief that all linguistic variations are equal in social settings, but that Standard English is used in other settings (Gollnick & Chinn, 2013). For example, one would speak to a judge in a courtroom differently than one would communicate with a friend on a baseball field.

CODE-SWITCHING   Teachers can nurture positive attitudes toward linguistic differences by providing insight into the functions of language in particular settings and with particular audiences. Rather than characterizing Standard English as "right" and correcting a dialect as "wrong," the students contrast how language is used in particular settings and situations, and for specific purposes. In essence, students are encouraged to see that formal language (Standard English) is appropriate in certain circumstances, whereas informal language is suitable in other settings. The process of moving from one variation of a language to another or between dialects and Standard English is called **code-switching** (Wheeler & Sword, 2006). When teachers have students translate from informal (dialectical) English to formal (Standard) English, they provide them with a powerful way to examine language uses by contrasting them depending on the situation. Teachers can provide scenarios where students are asked to write or speak in their dialect first, then rewrite or communicate a similar message in Standard English; they can role play situations in which they code-switch; they can develop charts that compare and contrast ways to express ideas (Crotteau, 2007; Wheeler & Sword, 2006).

DIALECTICAL MISCUES   When reading aloud, children often substitute one word for another. Such errors, or miscues, can help teachers understand how—and how successfully—a child is constructing meaning from a text. Language choices are not random; miscues help a teacher decide which cueing system a reader is using to comprehend the text. In oral reading, when a child substitutes words from his or her dialect for the word printed on the page (for example, reading *he don't* for *he doesn't*), the miscue probably shows that the reader is reading the text for meaning. Such a substitution would be impossible if the reader had not comprehended the text. We know that reading revolves around the experiences and language the reader brings to the text to make sense of it; hence, it is important to consider dialects when evaluating how children read.

Teachers need to draw on a children's background knowledge, gather culturally relevant materials, effectively monitor oral reading, use language experiences, and bring the study of different language patterns into the classroom. When these components are central to literacy instruction, all children have the opportunity to successfully develop their reading, writing, listening, and speaking skills.

Check Your Understanding 3.1: Gauge your understanding of the skills and concepts in this section.

Cultural Diversity in Literacy Classrooms

■ **Identify and appreciate the nature of cultural diversity, including core principles and instructional strategies for teaching students from diverse cultures.**

Culture refers to the traditions, customs, beliefs, language, dress, cuisine, music, and social habits of a group or society of people. **Cultural diversity** refers to the differences that groups of people have toward these dispositions. Cultures have different rules that are culturally defined and culturally specific, and teachers need to make decisions regarding how to include these diversities in the classroom. In literacy settings, cultural diversity is inextricably linked to language and linguistic diversity. Purpose, context, and background experiences all affect how we make sense of language and cultural differences.

Teachers need to be aware of instructional principles and strategies for addressing the literacy needs of students from diverse cultures. What are the contemporary beliefs about cultural diversity and engaging students in literacy learning? What pedagogical principles does research suggest, and which instructional strategies work for students from diverse cultures?

Instructional Beliefs About Cultural Diversity

The rapidly changing demographics of the United States and our heightened awareness of cultural diversity have influenced the way school programs attempt to transform the curriculum. Four approaches that characterize school programs are the **contributions approach**, the **additive approach**, the **transformative approach**, and the **social action approach** (Banks, 2014). The contributions approach focuses on holidays and festivities that are celebrated by a particular culture; the additive approach focuses on thematic units about different cultures that are integrated into the curriculum; the transformative approach is more social in that students read and discuss various cultural perspectives; the social action approach focuses on projects that are culturally driven.

2017 ILA Standards

1.1, 4.1, 4.2

We believe that teachers need to go beyond limiting literacy lessons to celebrations or thematic units. Teachers of the twenty-first century need to provide students with authentic literacy and learning experiences that will supply them with the cross-cultural knowledge and skills they will need as future adults in a nation that has become increasingly diverse. In Box 3.4, Patricia Schmidt shares the evolution of her beliefs about teaching diverse learners.

BOX 3.4 | VIEWPOINT

Patricia Ruggiano Schmidt
Teaching Diverse Learners

Patricia Ruggiano Schmidt is professor emerita of literacy at Le Moyne College in Syracuse, New York. She works with urban schools preparing teachers with the ABCs of cultural understanding and communication. From 2010 to 2013, she acted as principal and development director for Cathedral Academy at Pompeii, a preK through sixth grade urban school where 20 percent of the children are from European American and African American backgrounds, and 80 percent of the children are from refugee and immigrant families who originated in Africa, Asia, and the Middle East.

As a reading teacher for 18 years in a suburban middle school in upstate New York, grades 5–8, I worked with students who had been diagnosed with difficulties in reading, writing, listening, and speaking. Each year I was also assigned the one or two new students from places such as Taiwan, Russia, Israel, Detroit, or Appalachia. Similar to other European American teachers in this suburban setting, I believed in the assimilationist perspective. I thought that students from ethnic or cultural minority backgrounds needed to fit into the mainstream to be successful academically and socially. Therefore, my task was to help them learn Standard English as quickly as possible. Some students did. They also made friends, followed peer dress codes, and were involved in school activities. They began to look and act exactly like their classmates. However, other students who maintained their cultural identities took longer to speak and read Standard English. They were often isolated both in and out of the classroom. Their families noticed the difficulties and enlisted my assistance.

During the school year, home visits and conferences revealed unfamiliar languages and dialects and diverse cultural perspectives. I began to understand their struggles in making new community connections. I realized that our school was ignoring the rich resources that the new families offered. Reading and study led me to the realization that the additive perspective (Cummins, 1986), which encourages the inclusion of differing languages and cultures in the classroom, could be the approach to guide connections between home and school. Those connections could help the children maintain their own cultural identities as well as see the relevance of the school culture. In addition, students in the mainstream who are unfamiliar with diversity would be gaining from the different people and cultures. So what does this experience mean for our children and schools?

Diversity in our nation's schools is inevitable due to shifting world populations. Also, because the global economy affects all of us, our children will probably work in places very different from their home communities. Consequently, our present and future teachers must be prepared to work effectively with linguistic, cultural, and academic diversity. Since most teachers will have grown up in middle-class European American suburbia and have had few opportunities to develop relationships with different groups, they may unconsciously rely on media stereotypes. Differences in the classroom may be viewed as problematic rather than opportunities for children to explore physical, linguistic, cultural, and academic differences and learn to appreciate individual talents and multiple perspectives. Therefore, the classroom as social context can begin to prepare children for an appreciation of differences that gives them social and economic advantages. But how do we do this?

A major means is through effective connections between home and school. Families who are actively involved in the classroom and school community feel comfortable and needed. They see themselves as contributors to their children's education. The task for teachers then is to reach out to families who are culturally and linguistically different from the school and to families who fear and dislike the school because of their own emotional and academic failures. Teachers who realize that families are the children's first teachers and who value the family's knowledge and contributions to the child's literacy development soon begin to communicate in positive ways. Therefore, I think that a teacher's ability to communicate and connect with families and communities from underrepresented groups of people will lead to closing the academic gap.

Another key factor relates to the relevance of materials and activities for diverse learners. When children see people like themselves pictured in the resources they are using and can connect an activity with their own life experiences, they tend to stay focused on learning. Drawing on home and community literacy activities and materials as well as children and young adult literature related to diverse groups can be the means for connecting home and school for meaningful literacy development. Furthermore, children from the European American culture are enriched when they learn about diversity through literature and materials introduced and studied in their classrooms.

Instructional Principles for Students from Diverse Cultures

English language learners who are recent immigrants undergo an assortment of adjustments and reactions ranging from mixed emotions to excitement, fear, and conflict (Hadaway & Young, 2006). First, there are several background factors that teachers of ELLs should consider, including the country of origin, the extent of ties to the country of origin, the reasons for immigration, the amount and quality of schooling in the native language, and the length of residence in the United States. Next, teachers should focus on what the students can do.

Learning about the cultures of ELL students and developing communications with the families is critical. It is recommended that teachers read about the culture through books and the Internet, learn about the arts associated with the culture, hold discussions with other members of the culture to grasp information about perceptions and beliefs, get involved with community events that are held by immigrants, and perhaps even learn the language of the culture (Banks, 2014; Lynch, 2004; Teale, 2009).

Moreover, teachers of students from diverse cultures should plan a curriculum that supports the cultural diversity represented in their classrooms, use cooperative learning strategies that foster cross-cultural understanding, and establish collaborative relationships with the home. It is also important that teachers develop a network of support from state and regional organizations that provide a wide variety of instructional resources for teachers of diverse learners (Banks, 2014). Next, we share instructional strategies for culturally diverse students.

2017 ILA Standard
4.2

Instructional Strategies for Culturally Diverse Students

Teachers need to be cognizant of the cultural differences represented in their classrooms, respect the diverse cultures, and include them in the curriculum. When instruction is inclusive, students from diverse ethnic backgrounds feel valued and are more likely to succeed.

DETERMINING CULTURAL EXPECTATIONS An awareness of cultural educational expectations can help teachers engage students from diverse backgrounds. This is particularly important because when home expectations of students in school differ from teachers' expectations in the classroom, students experience conflicting messages. How can a teacher decide whether cultural misunderstandings are interfering with learning in the classroom? Three things to look for are lessons that continually go awry, an extended lack of student progress, or a lack of student involvement.

Lynch (2004) suggests that teachers consider "value sets" that are common across cultures as a way to think about cultural diversity. Figure 3.1 identifies categories of cultural beliefs and questions to consider when learning about new cultures.

BACKGROUND KNOWLEDGE AND MOTIVATION Connecting the known to the new has long been considered a way to motivate and focus students, as well as a means of evaluating the existence of background knowledge. When a teacher draws on a child's prior experiences and helps the child connect those experiences to new vocabulary, story concepts, and content, this provides a basis for making meaning. Because we use our prior knowledge of the world to help us construct the meaning of what we read, it is only sensible that students with different experiences will have different understandings and viewpoints. Our cultural schemata, or the beliefs we hold about how the world is organized, influence comprehension.

Figure 3.1 Categories of Cultural Considerations and Questions to Ask

Family	How is the family situated? Do elders live in the home? As a teacher, would you be welcomed into the home as a resource?
Traditions	What traditions and symbols characterize the culture? What holidays are celebrated? What religious beliefs are held? Are there any foods that are forbidden or celebrated? Is there a particular mode of dress that characterizes the culture? What characteristics of music and instrumentation represent the culture? Are there visual arts that are associated with the culture?
Children	What roles do children have in the family? Is independence encouraged? Are there specific expectations at home for the children?
Gender	Are roles in the family gender specific?
Beliefs About Schooling	What are the viewpoints regarding education? Is parental involvement encouraged? Can you expect the parents to participate in conferences? Will they feel free to ask you for help? Will they understand what homework is?
Language	Do the parents speak any English? What language is spoken at home? Can the parents read English? Can the parents read to their children? Can they read newsletters you might send home? Will they be able to read and sign permission forms?
Body Language	How is eye contact viewed? Is it okay to look directly at the person? How is play viewed? Are playground activities limited? How is touching viewed? For example, is it appropriate to shake hands?

Complete the drag-and-drop activity to test your understanding of the material.

Helping students *build* background knowledge before reading remains an important task for teachers in classrooms with culturally diverse students. Asian students will have varying experiences and languages depending on their home country, their social class, and the geographic region from which they come. Hispanics in the United States have vastly divergent backgrounds, ranging from Mexican American and Puerto Rican to Chilean and Peruvian.

Using illustrations, drawing pictures, and dramatizing can help build prior knowledge about unfamiliar concepts. Peer-led discussions in which students share firsthand experiences not familiar to immigrants can also foster background building. Developing compare–contrast charts and Venn diagrams that help students associate the known and unknown is another effective strategy.

USING CULTURALLY RESPONSIVE READ-ALOUDS   When teachers read culturally relevant literature aloud to linguistically diverse learners and converse with the students about the vocabulary and storyline, they provide the students with an authentic, meaningful way to engage them in learning. Culturally relevant literature reflects the background, experiences, interests, and values of the students; hence, teachers need to get to know their students, build relationships with them, and learn about their countries of origin. Giroir, Grimaldo, Vaughn, and Roberts (2015) provide guidelines for using read-alouds with ELLs that include chunking the text, selecting relevant vocabulary from the chunk, activating students' prior knowledge about the vocabulary, and teaching words within the context of the story. The story is read multiple times with vocabulary and comprehension discussion occurring before, during, and after each reading.

As teachers capture the interests and prior experiences of ELLs through literature that reflects their cultures, they create an environment in which the students can take ownership of their learning. When children see books and materials with characters that look and sound like themselves, their lives are validated.

CHOOSING QUALITY MULTICULTURAL LITERATURE   Teachers who use high-quality multicultural literature in the classroom help students recognize the unique contributions of each culture and the similarities of the human experience across cultures. At the same time, they help nonmainstream cultures appreciate and value their heritage and give all students the benefit of understanding ways of knowing about the world that are different from their own. Choosing quality multicultural literature, however, is complex. Although Appendix B of the CCSS (2010) provides a list of text exemplars for teachers, the resource falls short of including adequate examples of multicultural literature (Boyd, 2012/2013). How, then, do teachers find quality multicultural literature, and what criteria should they use to select the works?

One approach to locating exemplary and culturally appropriate fiction and nonfiction is to search for award-winning literature that recognizes different cultures. Examples include the Corretta Scott King Award sponsored by American Library Association, the Arab American Book Award sponsored by the Arab American National Museum, and the American Indian Youth Literature Award sponsored by American Indian Library Association (Boyd, Causey, & Galda, 2015), to name a few.

Asking several questions can also help teachers choose those books that will be most useful to the students in their classrooms (Louie, 2006; Yokota, 1993): Does the literature accurately reflect the culture? Can the students relate to the characters in authentic ways? Are authentic cultural values reflected? Choosing books that reflect the insider's perspective not only helps students from nonmainstream cultures read about and validate their own experiences, but it also helps children understand diverse experiences of groups other than their own.

FOSTERING ETHNIC, NATIONAL, AND GLOBAL IDENTIFICATION Teachers need to help all students develop ethnic, national, and global identification (Banks, 2014). For students from diverse cultures, ethnic identification means providing them with opportunities to develop positive self-images of themselves and their rich cultural heritage, as well as learn about American traditions. Protacio (2012) found that ELLs are motivated when they are provided with opportunities to read about American culture so that they have background knowledge to connect to their peers. Planning for home–school collaborations in which parents share customs, traditions, holidays, and special events is another important component of the multicultural classroom. Teachers can help students develop a sense of pride in family heritage by inviting family members as guest speakers, encouraging family demonstrations of traditional customs, and including activities that involve ethnic foods, clothing, and music.

Teachers also need to help students develop a sense of national identification (Banks, 2014). Schools should foster a commitment to democratic ideals such as equality, human dignity, freedom, and justice through activities in which the students, for example, become involved in community service projects. When teachers encourage students to read about local issues and problems and design service activities that address those issues, they are helping students develop a sense of civic responsibility.

Global identification is also important, and teachers need to help students develop a sense of world cooperation among nations. Banks (2014) suggests that students must first develop a sense of ethnic identification, followed by national identification. Only when students have developed these can they truly understand their role in the world community.

TECHNOLOGY-ENHANCED INSTRUCTION With increased attention to the multiple ways that technology changes as well as enhances literacy learning, using technologically mediated instruction with ELLs has drawn considerable attention. Cummins, Brown, and Sayers (2007) suggest that technological innovations can enhance "curiosity, imagination, and social commitment while also promoting academic achievement . . . foster[ing] identity development, and encourage[ing] critical awareness" (p. 114). Danzak (2011) describes how ELLs created technological representations of their immigration stories; Smythe and Neufeld (2010) share the value of student-generated podcasts as a way to foster a community of learners for ELLs; and Black (2009) emphasizes the importance of providing ELLs with online learning experiences.

2017 ILA Standard

5.2

Check Your Understanding 3.2: Gauge your understanding of the skills and concepts in this section.

Academic and Cognitive Diversity in Literacy Classrooms

- Recognize that students have diverse academic needs and that teachers need to be aware of instructional principles and strategies that address cognitive differences.

Reading is the key to academic as well as personal success for all students. In fact, research indicates that students who experience early reading difficulty will often maintain or increase below-level performance (Stanovich, 1986). The prestige and power associated with cultural and societal definitions of literacy add to the importance of helping students become literate. In the next section, we discuss how instructional beliefs about diverse academic abilities have evolved and what implications this has for assisting students who struggle with reading.

Instructional Beliefs About Academic and Cognitive Diversity

Beliefs about **academic and cognitive diversity** are often grounded in definitions, categories, and labels. For example, disabilities characterized as low-incidence include hearing and visual impairments, autism, and developmental delay, to name a few. On the other hand, high-incidence disabilities include significant learning difficulties more specifically related to language arts and mathematical skills (Friend & Bursuck, 2011). Beliefs about academic and cognitive diversity have resulted in legislation that provides guidelines for instructional policies.

Several significant pieces of federal legislation reflect beliefs about the instruction of students with disabilities. Public Law 94-142, the Education for All Handicapped Children Act, passed in 1975 and since amended, is based on several principles that remain in effect today. For example, evaluation procedures must not be discriminatory; all children are entitled to a free and appropriate education; and an individualized education program (IEP) must be designed for all children with disabilities.

Since 1975 the law has been restructured. The Individuals with Disabilities Education Act (IDEA) 2004 added, among others, the following stipulations: "special education teachers must be highly qualified" (Friend & Bursuck, 2011, p. 13), and the states must consider a child's response to scientifically based interventions or alternative research procedures for identifying students with specific learning disabilities. These criteria lay the groundwork for Response to Intervention (RTI).

In addition, many states have enacted laws regarding **dyslexia**. Descriptions, classifications, and characteristics of dyslexia have evolved over decades of research, and the intent of dyslexia laws vary from state to state. The International Dyslexia Association (IDA), an association with a long history of research on dyslexia, has adopted a definition that is recognized by the National Institute of Child and Human Development (NICHD); many states have adopted this definition as well. In essence, dyslexia is defined by IDA as a specific reading disability in which individuals have difficulty in processing the phonological components of language (International Dyslexia Association, 2002). Some state laws include early screening for dyslexics, intervention strategies, and teacher preparation requirements. Regardless of the laws enacted by individual states, dyslexia is a specific learning disability associated with differences in the ways people process language.

With respect to the academic and cognitive diversity among linguistically and culturally diverse students, issues of dialect among diverse languages and definitions of cultural diversity tend to complicate matters for teachers. Although diverse dialects are recognized as legitimate language systems, teachers struggle with issues regarding Standard English. A major concern among educators is that there is a disproportionate number of students of color and from various ethnic backgrounds in special education programs (Banks, 2014; Garcia, 2002; Heward, 2012).

Exceptional students by definition also include those identified as gifted or talented, although they are not included in the IDEA legislation. Giftedness is defined in a variety of ways. Gardner (1993; 2006) defines giftedness as abundant talent in any of seven intelligences. Just as the number of ethnic and minority students in special education programs is disproportionately high, ethnic and minority students are not adequately represented in gifted or talented programs. In the next section, we address major instructional principles regarding academic and cognitive diversity.

Instructional Principles for Academic and Cognitive Diversity

In the highly publicized National Reading Panel report *Teaching Children to Read* (National Institute of Child Health and Human Development, 2000), the essential components of an effective literacy program include instruction in phonemic awareness, phonics, vocabulary, comprehension, and fluency. Needless to say, we agree that these essentials are critical. In addition, we recognize other vital components that are important for all learners, including those with diverse literacy needs. Below we suggest guidelines that capture our beliefs about what literacy learning for all students should include. In essence, teachers should:

- Assess students regularly, and focus instruction on critical literacy strengths and weaknesses.
- Use authentic learning experiences, and provide students with multiple opportunities to make connections.
- Use students' interests as a focus of instruction to capture meaningful experiences with text.
- Provide students with positive feedback no matter how small their steps are toward progress.
- Engage parents in the learning process, and keep them informed of their students' growth.

2017 ILA Standard
5.4

INCLUSION Another principle of instruction for students with diverse academic and cognitive abilities is the concept of **inclusion**. In the past, students with special educational needs based on academic competence were mainstreamed into regular education classes in which they could possibly accomplish some tasks with little or no help from the teacher. In a sense, these students were considered "guests" in the classroom; their primary instruction took place outside the regular education program. The concept of inclusion, however, means that children with special needs are included in the regular classroom and receive assistance from the regular education teacher as well as the special education teacher. This allows the students to experience instruction that focuses on their strengths and to have more opportunities to set higher goals for themselves (Friend & Bursuck, 2011; Scala, 2001). Additionally, collaborations between special education and regular classroom teachers in inclusive settings provide them with opportunities to work as teams as they address appropriate accommodations and modifications for special education students. When this concept is embraced, the special education students in regular education settings have opportunities to learn from their peers and to develop friendships and social skills, and to accept challenges that they would not encounter in noninclusive settings. Additionally, their classmates learn about the nature of differences in the real world: how some people have differences in learning, while others have atypical social skills and different needs to be productive members of society.

For students from diverse linguistic and cultural backgrounds who experience difficulties with reading, the same principle of inclusion applies. Teachers need to understand that students from diverse backgrounds will vary in their competency levels, their background knowledge, and their linguistic abilities. Cultural and linguistic diversity should not be used as a benchmark for determining difficulty in learning to read or for placing students in special education programs (Banks, 2001; Diaz, 2001). In fact, the CCSS (National Governors Association Center for Best Practices, Council of Chief State School Officers, 2010) specify that all students be able to read, interpret, analyze, infer, and assess complex text.

Common Core Standards

CCRA.R.1, CCRA.R.2, CCRA.R.3, CCRA.R.4, CCRA.R.5, CCRA.R.6, CCRA.R.7, CCRA.R.8, CCRA.R.9, CCRA.R.10

CURRICULUM COMPACTING   What about gifted students? They, too, constitute a diverse group of learners. Providing students who are academically advanced with instruction that challenges their capabilities is sometimes neglected in schools due to funding issues and seemingly more concerted efforts to focus on students who are struggling. Many gifted students, however, have mastered the content and skills that are taught at grade level and are at risk for being bored or disengaged in classroom work. In order to provide instruction for gifted students with more challenging in-depth content, one principle of instruction is **curriculum compacting**, in which the curriculum is compressed (Renzulli & Smith, 1979). Typically teachers first examine the curriculum and identify content, objectives, and outcomes. Next, students who are identified as gifted are assessed on their knowledge and skills based on the teacher's objectives for the lesson, the theme, or the unit. Subsequently, when a student indicates sufficient mastery of the content, the teacher and student collaborate on ways to enrich student knowledge by deciding on alternative accelerated avenues of learning. These might be project-oriented, research-based, or focused on the student's interests.

Teachers can also accommodate gifted students through an enriched curriculum with thoughtful and innovative methods that include technology applications. In addition, teachers can provide gifted students with internships and mentor programs outside the classroom.

DIFFERENTIATED INSTRUCTION   A presumption of **differentiated instruction** is that there are differences in what individuals know and how they learn. Differentiated instruction is based on assessing students' needs on a regular basis, implementing multiple approaches to learning, and blending whole class, small group, and individual instruction (Tomlinson, 2001). Teachers can differentiate based on students' modality preferences, levels of readiness for a topic, abilities, and interests. Rather than teaching to the whole class, teachers tailor lessons that include problem-solving, hands-on activities, and multiple ways that students can express what they discover. For example, students may communicate what they have learned through journal entries, artistic representations, oral reports, or dramatic renditions of new knowledge.

Instructional Strategies for Students with Diverse Academic and Cognitive Abilities

Instructional strategies that require students to be actively involved in constructing meaning, using all the cueing systems of written language, are especially important for struggling readers. Moreover, although gifted readers do not automatically learn without instruction, they learn quickly and need to be sufficiently challenged beyond reading instruction planned for average readers. With appropriate and innovative modifications, there are strategies that will benefit both readers who have difficulty, as well as gifted readers. Next we examine several approaches that address cognitive diversity.

MULTISENSORY PHONICS STRATEGIES   For students who struggle with the phonological components of reading, such as blending sounds and segmenting words into phonemes, engaging them in visual, auditory, kinesthetic, and tactile strategies is an effective way to teach phonemic awareness and phonics. There are many published programs, some of which are scripted, that feature multisensory strategies in which direct, explicit, and sequential phonics instruction is at the core.

Finger tapping is a kinesthetic strategy in which the students tap the sounds that are heard in words. For consonant-vowel-consonant words, such as *cat, sit,* and *bad,* the students use one hand and tap the index finger to the thumb as they say the first sound; next, they tap the middle finger to the thumb as they say the second sound; finally, they tap the ring finger to the thumb as they say the final sound. This strategy helps students learn how to segment phonemes.

Tracing is a tactile activity that can assist students as they learn to associate sounds with letters. Teachers can use a variety of textures to engage students in tracing letters as they learn to associate graphemes with sounds. Some examples of tangible resources are sandpaper squares, sand or salt trays, plastic screens, and puffy glue, to name a few.

Auditory activities incorporate rhyming games, poetry, and read-aloud books that play with language, such as *Mucky Ducky* (Brindley, 2003) and *Chicka Chicka Boom Boom* (Martin, 2009). Phonemic awareness tasks such as tapping and clapping to phonemes is another popular strategy.

Visual supports for learning include flash cards, word walls, labels of objects in the classroom, environmental print, and big books. Children can also use highlighters, markers, colored chalk, crayons, and paint to create letters as they learn to associate sounds with print.

Although these strategies can be useful for all students, teachers working with learners who have a specific disability, such as dyslexia, find that multisensory phonics instruction is effective for learners who struggle. We concur that phonics instruction should be taught in an orderly sequence and that multisensory strategies are indeed engaging; however, when teachers implement these activities, they should be sure the instruction occurs within a balanced literacy curriculum that also focuses on reading comprehension, vocabulary learning, and fluency.

TECHNOLOGY-BASED DIAGNOSTIC STRATEGIES   There is a wide array of computer-based reading programs in which students are assessed and, based on the results, targeted to work on instructional lessons based on their reported literacy needs. The diagnostic assessments are often subskills of reading proficiencies in the early grades, such as the ability to recognize consonant sounds, vowel sounds, digraphs, and blends, and the ability to use context clues. In addition to the technology-based lessons, teachers are often provided with appropriate strategies to include in small group and individual instruction. The resources are helpful for teachers of struggling readers, as well as for teachers who have advanced students.

One advantage of computer-based diagnostic testing and learning is that each student's progress can be individually monitored on a regular basis, and individual students' needs can be addressed systematically. However, teachers need to realize the relationship between social collaboration and individualized learning; therefore, opportunities for students to interact in small and large group settings is essential. Hence, we concur that technology-based diagnostic programs are indeed beneficial, but should not be the only avenue for teaching reading.

INQUIRY LEARNING **Inquiry learning**, a classroom approach for teaching math and science, can challenge gifted students in literacy learning, as well as those with special needs. Inquiry learning and teaching is based on the constructivist approach (Confrey, 1990; Fosnot, 1996; Piaget, 1970) and focuses on learning as a meaning-making process. Children experiment, solve problems, and discover how the world functions. They are encouraged to become active classroom participants as they connect with their own environment and the context at hand and formulate high-level questions. In Figure 3.2, we suggest prompts teachers can use to foster inquiry learning.

For academically and cognitively gifted students, inquiry learning can be enhanced immensely by using the Internet and computer software. As students brainstorm what they know and want to learn, they can explore virtual reality and informational web sites, communicate electronically with experts, and use sophisticated computer software that helps them express and demonstrate their curricular interests and goals (Heward, 2012).

2017 ILA Standard

5.3

TRANSLITERACIES **Transliteracies** refer to fluid representations of knowing beyond traditional linear text. Examples include visual representations, artistic interpretations (e.g., drama, painting, photography), auditory demonstrations, and multiple technological representations of text (Anstey & Bull, 2006; International Reading Association, 2000a; Karchmer-Klein & Shinas, 2012; Kist, 2010). Without a doubt, these

Figure 3.2 Prompts for Inquiry Learning

Initial Prompt	Follow-Up Prompts
What do you think?	What makes you think that? What else?
What have you heard about . . . ?	Do you believe what you heard? Why or why not? How can you find out more?
What do you wonder about . . . ?	What makes you wonder that? Why kinds of questions do you have about . . . ? Where can you find out more? Where else?
What do you think this means?	Why? How do you know? Are you sure? How can you find out more?
What would you like to discover about . . . ?	Why? What else would you like to discover? How can you find out what you want to know?
What is the problem?	How do you know? Are you sure? How do you solve the problem? How else?

Complete the drag-and-drop activity to test your understanding of the material.

transliteracies, as they are construed in the twenty-first century, open endless opportunities for students with diverse cognitive and academic abilities to express their understanding of concepts required by the CCSS. In Box 3.5, see how Jeremy Brubeck explores the possibilities that e-books hold for struggling readers.

There are countless instructional programs and strategies for struggling K through 12 readers, many of which claim to be evidence-based. Although scientifically based research is critical to informing teachers about what works, there are no specific prescriptions for specific problems. Moreover, there should *not* be such a list of programs and strategies that correlate with specific reading difficulties because the learning process is quite varied and unique for each individual. So what are classroom teachers to do? As a starting point, we suggest that teachers ask themselves the following questions:

- How will I identify my struggling readers? Will I request referrals from the previous year's teachers? Will I use standardized assessment scores? Will I assume that a student who was in an intervention program as "at risk" is still "at risk"? What will *that* really tell me about this student? Will the information I have be specific enough to work with the student on weaknesses? Or should I design a more informal assessment that captures my students' needs? If I am a Social Studies teacher, how will I determine those students who might struggle with my textbook?

- Has our school system "bought into" a particular intervention program? If so, who made the decision and on what was the decision based? Did the decision makers consider the price of the program as a key point? Was the decision to purchase the program based on reported scientifically based results? How informed were the decision makers about the nature of scientifically based programs? Is the

BOX 3.5

Leveraging E-books to Address Academic and Cognitive Diversity

Literacy is no longer confined to a standard print format. There is an increasing integration and adoption of digital texts and e-books in school libraries and classrooms across the United States. Compared to their print counterparts, e-books are portable, facilitating the easy transport of sizable libraries with little physical effort. The mobility of e-books allows them to be used in any place at any time via handheld or mobile devices.

E-books for young children are in some ways like storybooks we know and love. While features of e-books mirror those we see in traditional children's literature, e-books add new digital features. These digital additions to print are different in a manner that is profoundly changing the storybook as a piece of early literacy learning. As a result, e-books can be used to develop transliterate practices in the classroom that address academic and cognitive diversity in learners.

E-books offer an engaging medium for young struggling readers, ease of implementation for classroom teachers, and opportunities for individual practice for all students. Early studies suggest that multimedia features in e-books can improve inference skills in story reading and that game-like interactivity can stimulate story comprehension and word learning, especially when children's attention is guided to these purposes. E-books

have also been shown to motivate children to be active readers. When using e-books, children tend to more naturally investigate words, images, and interactives in the reading environment. It seems the e-book may invite play, and Gee (2003) indicates this is a powerful motivator for engaging with print.

Numerous theories of reading development recommend scaffolding as a foundational means to promote literacy development. In addition to features found in a print book, e-books provide scaffolding through narrations, animations, and interactive media, which support young children who are developing emergent literacy skills. Scaffolds in e-books include searching capacity, hyperlinks, audio and visual enhancements, and in some cases, hot-spot pop-up definitions for words. For users with learning difficulties or disabilities, e-books offer text-to-speech capabilities, print highlighting, and changes in font size, features that are not possible in print books. Early readers and students with learning disabilities can benefit from the use of e-books due to the ability to explore literature with digital scaffolding supports. The digital scaffolds found in e-books provide additional opportunities for independent practice and interactive exploration of a text, available even when an adult is not present to read with a child.

program "scripted"? If so, why was it selected? Was the population of our school and the expertise that would be needed to carry out the program considered? If so, how? Are there any political or business ties to the program that would benefit a constituency?

- What support systems does our school have in place to guide me in helping struggling students? Are there reading specialists to support classroom teachers? If so, *how* do they support teachers? If I am a first-grade teacher, where do I receive support for the students I perceive to be struggling readers? If I am a science teacher, what do I do with students who cannot read my textbook?

In essence, it is critical that teachers at all grade levels involve themselves in serious conversations about how to address students who are academically and cognitively challenged and the programs and strategies that are or might be implemented in classrooms. The questions listed can serve as a starting point for discussions by preservice teachers, continuing education and graduate-level students, and teachers in professional development programs.

2017 ILA Standard

6.3

Check Your Understanding 3.3: Gauge your understanding of the skills and concepts in this section.

RTI for Struggling Readers

Culturally and Linguistically Struggling Students and *Response to Intervention*

Historically, students from diverse cultures and languages who immigrated to the United States tended to be placed in programs that assumed they were or would be struggling learners. One of the underlying purposes of RTI is to avoid this labeling phenomenon. In an attempt to place culturally and linguistically diverse students within the framework of RTI, Klinger and Edwards (2006) suggest a four-tiered RTI model that addresses this concern. Here, we capture the gist of the model.

- *Tier 1*—Teachers need to be informed about culturally responsive teaching. This means teachers need to be aware of the linguistic similarities and differences of the languages their students speak as compared to the English language. They also need to be cognizant of cultural differences that may influence learning.

- *Tier 2*—For linguistically and culturally diverse students who do not respond to classroom initiatives that capture the purposes of Tier 1, classroom teachers need to evaluate why Tier 1 is not making an impact on student learning. What are the assessments used to evaluate culturally and linguistically diverse students? Are teachers uninformed about strategies that assist culturally and linguistically diverse students? Additional questions include the following: Are the teachers in Tier 1 expert teachers of reading for all students? Do they have the support of teachers who speak the native language(s) of the student(s)? In addition, Tier 2 ought to include more intensive instruction for culturally and linguistically diverse students from teams of teachers who participate in helping to plan, guide, and deliver instruction in the classroom that captures the nature of the "diverse" students' needs.

- *Tier 3*—If collaborative planning, instructional guidance from other team members, and professional development workshops don't seem to address the students' needs, Tier 3 might be appropriate. This could include a pull-out program that focuses on more intensive individual instruction.

- *Tier 4*—If Tier 3 does not result in effective growth, Tier 4 would focus on special education.

What About . . .

Standards, Assessment, and Diversity?

Standards-based education and high-stakes assessment are realities for all of today's students, including cognitively, linguistically, and culturally diverse learners. The CCSS (National Governors Association Center for Best Practices, Council of Chief State School Officers, 2010) place high expectations for all learners, and include incredible challenges for linguistically, culturally, and academically diverse students. This makes it critically important for teachers to be knowledgeable of appropriate assessments that inform instruction. Although assessments vary depending on state requirements, teachers need to consider multiple factors when administering assessments that may characterize students as having "disabilities." Teachers need to consider the home environment, the culture, and the social and educational literacy experiences of every student. The ultimate goals of assessments for ELLs and all students should be to help teachers determine what to teach and to provide ways to measure progress.

Summary

- Students from linguistically diverse backgrounds need to feel accepted and comfortable as they learn the new language. When teachers implement strategies such as sheltered English adaptations, instructional conversations, response protocol, and thematic teaching, they assist students in making the transition.

- Cultural diversity is closely related to linguistic diversity. Teachers need to become aware of the cultural differences students bring to the classroom, including beliefs about education and parenting. Fostering collaborative learning, implementing technology-enhanced instruction, and incorporating multicultural literature are several ways teachers can address cultural differences.

- Students with diverse cognitive and academic abilities need to be engaged in authentic learning experiences in which they view learning as meaningful and purposeful. Teachers should consider a range of principles that address cognitive diversity in their classrooms, such as inclusion, curriculum compacting, and differentiated instruction. Additionally, all teachers need to study, learn how to implement, and determine the effectiveness of strategies and programs that are intended to help struggling as well as gifted students. Some areas to consider are multisensory phonics programs, technology-based diagnostic programs, and inquiry approaches to learning.

Teacher Action Research

1. Observe a classroom in which ELLs are self-contained. Take field-based notes regarding how the teacher addresses linguistic diversity. Identify strategies that you observe, and share your observations with colleagues. Discuss the effectiveness of the strategies, and ask for input from others who have observed classrooms that include ELLs. Synthesize your discussion, and share your summary with your colleagues.

2. Select a diverse culture that may be predominant in your local community. Study significant characteristics of the culture, and compare and contrast them to your own.

3. Interview the curriculum directors in two school districts regarding the programs implemented to teach dyslexics. Compare and contrast your findings, and share with your colleagues.

Through the Lens of the Common Core

The CCSS raise the stakes for all learners; however, they pose significant challenges for students from diverse languages, cultures, and abilities. Teachers owe it to their students to foster instructional goals and practices that meet the standards while meeting their needs. Teachers need to embrace the belief that all children can learn and that all children can achieve at sophisticated levels of learning.

They need to provide instruction that focuses on analysis of complex text, problem solving, synthesis of information, and close reading. Instruction for diverse learners need not be watered down; teachers need to examine their beliefs about diversity and ensure that all children are provided with opportunities to develop the complex skills needed to achieve in the twenty-first century.

Chapter 4
Foundations of Language and Literacy

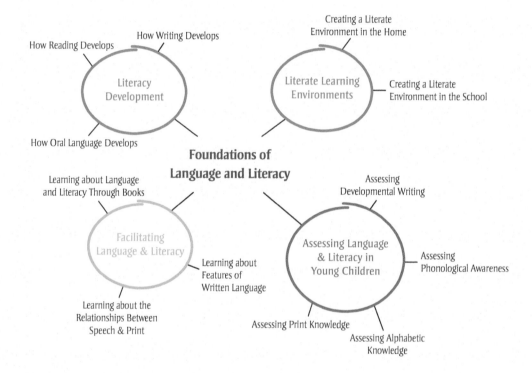

Foundations of Language and Literacy

Literacy Development
- How Reading Develops
- How Writing Develops
- How Oral Language Develops

Literate Learning Environments
- Creating a Literate Environment in the Home
- Creating a Literate Environment in the School

Facilitating Language & Literacy
- Learning about Language and Literacy Through Books
- Learning about Features of Written Language
- Learning about the Relationships Between Speech & Print

Assessing Language & Literacy in Young Children
- Assessing Developmental Writing
- Assessing Phonological Awareness
- Assessing Print Knowledge
- Assessing Alphabetic Knowledge

 Learning Outcomes

In This Chapter, You Will Discover How To

- Recognize literacy development.
- Identify core language and literacy skills.
- Create literate environments at home and school.
- Provide instruction for beginning readers and writers.
- Assess core language and literacy skills in beginning readers.

Activating Your Schema

How do you think children first learn to read and write? Why do you think that? Do you think adults, like teachers and parents, transmit knowledge about reading and writing, or do you think young children construct the knowledge on their own? Do you remember how you were taught to read and write? Think about these things as you read this chapter.

2017 ILA Standards Found in This Chapter

1.1	2.1	3.3	5.3
1.2	3.1	3.4	5.4
1.3	3.2	5.2	

Common Core State Standards: English Language Arts

CCRA.L.3	CCRA.L.6	CCRA.W.6	CCRA.SL.1
CCRA.L.5	CCRA.R.10	CCRA.W.9	

Key Terms

alphabet knowledge	oral language
big books	phonemic awareness
emergent literacy	phonemic segmentation
environmental print	phonological awareness
language-experience activities	print knowledge
linguistic awareness	scribbling
literacy play center	shared reading
literate environment	shared writing
observation	storybook experiences

When Aarav was just three, he looked at his aide's sweatshirt and said, "Hannah, what does e-a-s-t-e-r-n-u-n-i-v-e-r-s-i-t-y spell?" She told him it spelled "Eastern University" as she pointed to the letters, and explained it was the name of the university where she went to school. When he was four, he greeted her on Valentine's Day with a hug and a paper heart with the words, "Hannah, I love you. Aarav" printed very carefully in his best handwriting with the help of his mother. Since birth, Aarav has been read to by his parents, caregivers, and teachers, and he loves books. He has dozens of books in his bedroom, and his favorites are Cynthia Rylant's *Poppleton* (Rylant, 1997) and *Brown Bear, Brown Bear, What Do You See?* (Martin, 1992). When Aarav reads *Brown Bear* to Hannah, he likes to tell stories about each of the animals. For example, when he gets to the page with the white dog, he might say, "This white dog is in a cave. He's looking for his mom." Aarav has a long, rich history of experiences that have positioned him well for beginning reading and writing in a school setting. Fortunately, his preschool teacher, Ms. Blanchard, recognizes that her students come to school with varying degrees of literacy development, and she invites all of her students to be readers and writers. While reading the big book *Hattie and the Fox* (Fox, 1992), she encourages everyone to chime in with the repetitive text: "'Good grief!' said the goose. 'Well well!' said the pig. 'Who cares?' said the sheep. 'So what?' said the horse. 'What next?' said the cow." After one reading, she passed out paper to all and encouraged them to draw a picture of the story. She then walked around and prompted students to use language to talk about their drawings. A few, like Aarav, can write letters, letter-like forms, and some words, so Ms. Blanchard encouraged them to do so. But others were simply making marks on the page, so Ms. Blanchard asked for a description and then wrote it under the picture. Ms. Blanchard knows that when young children identify themselves as part of a community of readers and writers, and are accepted as such, they will build on the literacy knowledge they bring to school.

This chapter is about language and literacy. It is forged on the dynamic and powerful connections between children's oral language (speaking and listening) and written language (reading and writing) development. Oral language provides the base and foundation for literacy. Written language, on the other hand, builds on oral language. Printed symbols represent spoken words that in turn represent meaning. As you begin the chapter, keep in mind several main ideas about learning to read and write in early childhood. First, there is a continuum of children's development in early reading and writing. Young children develop as early readers and writers from birth as they progress from awareness and exploration in their early childhood years to independent and productive reading and writing by the end of the third grade. Second, early readers and writers develop core literacy skills as they participate in authentic and meaningful activities. And third, speaking, listening, viewing, writing, and reading are interrelated, mutually supportive activities. Language experiences provide the foundation for learning to read and write.

Research studies have demonstrated that learning achieved during the early years is likely to be sustained throughout the primary school years and is an important basis for successful early performance in school (Scarborough, 1998, 2001). *Developing Early Literacy: The Report of the National Early Literacy Panel*, published by the National Institute for Literacy (2008), confirmed that alphabet knowledge, phonological awareness, oral language, and writing/name writing demonstrated by four- and five-year-old children are the best predictors of later success in literacy achievement.

In this chapter, we start by explaining how literacy develops from birth, followed by a description of a print-rich home and school environment. The essential early literacy skills that prime young children for learning to read are described, followed by some instructional routines to support these foundational skills that lay the groundwork for later conventional reading. We conclude the chapter with informal assessments that can be used to monitor the progress of young children.

Literacy Development

■ **Recognize literacy development.**

The importance of the early years was underestimated for a very long time. However, we now know from a large body of research there is a link between successful achievement in early literacy and later school success (Strickland, 2013). **Emergent literacy**, a term used at the preK level, is a concept that supports learning to read as a result of a home environment where children begin learning about reading and writing from birth by observing and interacting with adults and other children as they use literacy in their everyday lives in meaningful ways. It assumes children are always becoming readers and writers and that they are born ready to learn about literacy and continue to grow in their understandings throughout life (Bennett-Armistead, Duke, & Moses, 2005). According to this social constructivist view, literacy acquisition has much in common with oral language development.

How Oral Language Develops

Speaking and listening in early childhood build the foundation for literacy development and future academic success (Roskos, Tabors, & Lenhart, 2009). Oral language development includes critical skills that allow children to communicate, to understand words and concepts they hear, to acquire new information, and to express their own ideas and thoughts. Babies listen to and become aware of sounds of spoken words by the people around them. In fact, language development begins before birth, and children exposed to more than one language in utero separate the two languages from each other and actively process both (Byers-Heinlein, Burns, & Werker, 2010). Very early on, babies begin to communicate their own needs through sounds and gestures. By about five months, they might even say "ma-ma" or "da-da." Around 11 months, they begin to use one word, such as "juice," to mean "I want juice" or "I see juice."

Toddlers use language to express themselves and to get information. They begin to talk in simple sentences, ask questions, and give opinions about what they do and do not like. A toddler might use two-word phrases such as "me juice" or "want more juice" to communicate the desire for juice. Parents accept these approximations with responses such as, "Yes. You want more juice. Daddy will be happy to give you more juice to drink."

Common Core State Standards

CCRA.L.5 CCRA.L.6

Preschoolers, then, build a large vocabulary from listening to language from the people around them and from exposure to books. Their sentences become longer and more complex, and they are able to talk about their experiences. Most preschoolers continue to learn more new words every day, and by the time they enter kindergarten, many have a vocabulary of 10,000 words or more. It is through these early experiences with different aspects of language and different activities that children develop rich oral language. Children with rich oral language experiences at home tend to become early readers (Dickenson & Tabors, 2001) and have high levels of reading achievement throughout the elementary grades (Wells, 1986).

Importantly, however, not all children go to school with the same number of words in their vocabulary. While children from different backgrounds typically develop language skills around the same age, the rate of vocabulary growth is strongly influenced by how much parents talk to their children. Language development, specifically the level of vocabulary development between birth and age three, significantly correlates with reading ability and school achievement in third grade. Equally important, children's outcomes are supported through the amount and types of language input that their environments provide (Hart & Risley, 1995). Hart and Risley's (1995) landmark study found that children from professional families talk to their children more, which means those children gain vocabulary at a quicker rate than their peers in working-class and welfare-recipient families. Children of professional families hear an average of 2,153 words per hour, while children in working-class families hear an average of 1,251 words per hour. Children of welfare-recipient families hear an average of 616 words per hour. This means that, in a year, children in professional families hear an average of 11 million words, children of working-class families hear an average of 6 million words, and children in welfare families hear an average of 3 million words. By age three, children of professional families know about 1,100 words, children of working-class families know about 750 words, and children of welfare-recipient families know just 500 words. The amount of talk that goes on moment-by-moment between young children and their parents and caregivers is critical to oral language development, which is the foundation for successful achievement in literacy and educational success. In Figure 4.1, we outline suggestions for promoting oral language development every day.

Figure 4.1 Promoting Oral Language Development Every Day

Parents and other caregivers should talk to their children throughout the day. Talk about what the child is doing and things of interest. Conversation should be frequent and meaningful.
- Use rich and abstract vocabulary.
- Ask questions that require children to use language to express themselves.
- Repeat, extend, and restate what the child says so the child can hear his or her own ideas.
- Give full attention and eye contact when listening and speaking.
- Provide explanations for why a child needs to do something.
- Read books and nursery rhymes aloud.

| Common Core State Standard
| CCRA.SL.1

How Reading Develops

Just as oral language is developmental, learning to read is also; all children do not begin to read at the same age. As explained in the last section, children may enter school at about the same chronological age, but their stages of reading development vary widely. As a result, teachers need to be cognizant of the developmental stages of learning to read so all students can be successful. Most children follow a similar pattern and sequence of reading behaviors as they learn how to read—from print awareness to pretend reading, identifying alphabet letters, and beginning reading. There are distinct stages of development across this continuum of learning to read, and specific reading behaviors can be identified at each of these stages. Researchers have used various labels and terms to identify the stages of reading development, but the literature indicates there are five stages to learning to read (Chall, 1983; Dorn & Soffos, 2001; Snow et al., 1998). Figure 4.2 illustrates the phases of children's development on the reading–writing continuum. As you study the figure, keep in mind that children will function at a variety of phases; grade levels are an approximation. These developmental stages give teachers an estimate, based on observations of reading behaviors and of each student's beginning instructional level.

PHASE 1: AWARENESS AND EXPLORATION The awareness and exploration phase begins at birth and progresses through a child's preschool years. Children explore their environment and build the foundations for learning to read and write. This marks the time when children become curious about print and print-related activities. For example, they enjoy listening to and talking about stories and understand that print carries a message. They demonstrate *logographic knowledge* by identifying labels, signs, cereal boxes, and other types of environmental print. Children see written language all around them—in books, supermarkets, department stores, and fast-food restaurants; on television, the computer, and signs; and in a variety of printed materials from video games to labels on household products. **Environmental print** is everywhere. Children may also see family and others using written language to read recipes, follow directions, do homework, solve problems, acquire information, or enjoy a story. The plethora of print that confronts young children on a daily basis plays a subtle but important role in their desire to understand written language and use it for personal and social means.

They also begin to *pretend-read* during their preschool years and engage in paper-and-pencil activities that include various forms of scribbling and written expression. Another literacy accomplishment in this phase occurs when young children begin to identify some letters and letter–sound relationships and write letters or approximations of letters to represent written language. In Box 4.1, Harper shows characteristics of phase 1 reading.

PHASE 2: EXPERIMENTAL READING AND WRITING Early awareness and exploration lead children to experiment with oral and written language. Children enter the experimental phase of the reading–writing continuum right around the

Figure 4.2 Phases of Children's Development in Early Reading and Writing

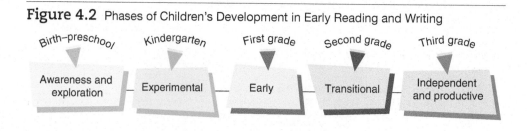

BOX 4.1 | STUDENT VOICES

Harper is three years old and has been read to since birth. Her parents interact with her all the time and call her amusing remarks "Harperisms." Recently, Harper was "reading" a book and said, "Mom, I love this book, but not this page, so I just skip it!" This "Harperism" demonstrates quite a bit about Harper's literacy development. First, she has books in her house that are accessible to her, and she views herself as a reader (and is accepted as one). She enjoys books and sees them as a worthwhile activity to occupy her time when her mom is doing something else. Further, she knows books carry meaning. In fact, when she doesn't like a certain page, she chooses to "skip it"—something she's undoubtedly seen her parents do.

time they enter kindergarten. This phase reflects their understanding of basic concepts of print, such as left-to-right, top-to-bottom orientation. Young children enjoy being read to and begin to engage in sustained reading and writing activities. They also continue to recognize letters and letter–sound relationships, become familiar with rhyming, and begin to write letters of the alphabet and high-frequency words.

PHASE 3: EARLY READING AND WRITING   The early phase of children's development usually occurs in first grade when instruction becomes more formal. Children begin to read simple stories and can write about topics about which they have much prior knowledge and strong feelings. They can read and retell familiar stories and begin to develop strategies for comprehension, such as predicting. They are beginning to develop accurate word identification skills through their increasing knowledge of letter–sound patterns. In addition, children's ability to read with fluency becomes more evident, as does their ability to recognize an increasing number of words on sight. Moreover, their writing shows awareness of punctuation and capitalization knowledge as they continue to engage in writing about topics that are personally meaningful to them.

PHASE 4: TRANSITIONAL READING AND WRITING   By second grade, students begin to make the transition from early reading and writing to more complex literacy tasks. They are reading with greater fluency and using cognitive and metacognitive strategies more efficiently when comprehending and composing. During the transitional phase, children demonstrate an ever-increasing facility with reading and writing in all facets of activity, including use of word identification strategies, sight-word recognition, reading fluency, sustained silent reading, conventional spelling, and proofreading what they have written.

PHASE 5: INDEPENDENT AND PRODUCTIVE READING AND WRITING   As children progress from the transitional phase, they engage in a lifelong process of becoming independent and productive readers and writers. The third grade marks the beginning of their journey into independent and productive learning as they use reading and writing in increasingly more sophisticated ways to suit a variety of purposes and audiences. From this point on in their development as readers and writers, children extend and refine their literacy skills and strategies.

The quality of interaction that the child has with family members—whether they are parents, grandparents, aunts, uncles, or siblings—figures heavily in reading development. Research has shown that when siblings engage in literacy together, both benefit from the interaction (Lenhart & Roskos, 2003; Murdoch, 2016). Often, however, assistance in learning to read is not consciously given. Instead, significant others, such as parents, read to children repeatedly (by reading certain stories again and again) and *answer questions that children ask about reading*. There is no better way to help the child make the connection that print is meaningful than to respond to the question, "What does this say?" as the child points to a printed page.

2017 ILA Standards

1.1, 1.2

How Writing Develops

Some young children are prolific with pencil and paper. Others are just as handy with crayon, marker, or paintbrush. Sometimes a convenient wall or refrigerator door substitutes nicely for paper. Still others take to the computer keyboard. The common denominator for "paper-and-pencil kids" is a strong desire and a need for self-expression and communication.

The noted Russian psychologist Lev Vygotsky (1962) suggests that an infant's gestures are the first visible signs of writing: "Gestures are writing in air, and written signs frequently are simply gestures that have been fixed." As infants learn about the power of signs and symbols, there is, in Vygotsky's words, "a fundamental assist to cognitive growth."

Young children learn writing through exploration. The key to early writing development is found not in a child's motor development or intelligence but in the *opportunities* the child has to explore print. According to Clay (1988), new discoveries about writing emerge at every encounter a child has with paper and pencil: Young children write "all over the paper in peculiar ways, turning letters around and upside down and letting the print drift over into drawing and coloring from time to time. We should be relaxed about this exploration of spaces and how print can be fitted into them" (p. 20). The importance of scaffolding and praising preschoolers' attempts at writing has been well recognized by researchers (Levin & Bus, 2003; Aram & Levin, 2004; Bindman et al., 2014). Writing attempts should be supported and applauded long before traditional writing begins. In a recent study, researchers (Bindman et al., 2014) found that caregivers who gave their children high levels of writing support had children with higher fine motor and decoding skills. Other researchers (Aram & Levin, 2004) found that children whose mothers assisted them with early writing skills (e.g., graphic formation of letters, explaining spelling fundamentals) and encouraged independent attempts at writing attained higher overall literacy rates in kindergarten and beyond.

Figure 4.3 Aiden's Scribbling

THE IMPORTANCE OF SCRIBBLING Scribbling is one of the primary forms of written expression for very young children. In many respects, scribbling is the source for writing and occurs from the moment a child grasps and manipulates a writing tool. Children take their scribbles seriously and learn to differentiate scribbling from writing as they develop (Schickedanz & Collins, 2013).

Early Scribbling Early or uncontrolled scribbling is characterized by children making random marks on paper. Evidence of early scribbling can be gathered for most youngsters before their first birthday. Very young children who scribble soon learn that whatever it is that is in their hands, it can make marks. Early scribbling is comparable to babbling in oral language development. Aiden, at a little over three years old, loves to scribble and likes to express what he's thinking as he writes. He told his dad that the scribble in Figure 4.3 is "people." He pointed to the two "heads" on the left hand side and said the long lines are the "bodies."

Because early scribbles are not usually representational (i.e., they do not convey meaning), parents and teachers should suppress the urge to ask a child, "What is this?" Instead, encourage a child to make markings on paper without pressure to finish a piece of work or tell what it's about, unless the child is eager to talk about it.

Controlled Scribbling   Movement away from early scrawls becomes evident in children's scribbles as they begin to make systematic, repeated marks such as circles, vertical lines, dots, and squares. Controlled scribbling occurs in children's written work between the ages of three and six. The marks are often characterized as *scribble writing* in the sense that the scribbles are linear in form and shape and bear a strong resemblance to the handwriting of the child's culture. Harste, Woodward, and Burke (1984) demonstrated this when they asked three four-year-olds from different countries to "write everything you can write." The children produced print that reflected their native languages—English, Arabic, and Hebrew. According to Harste and his collaborators, Dawn, the child from the United States, had controlled scribbles that looked undeniably like English. When Najeeba, from Saudi Arabia, finished her writing, it was distinctly Arabic looking. She said, "Here, but you can't read it because it is in Arabic." Najeeba went on to point out that in Arabic, one uses "a lot more dots" than in English. Dalia is an Israeli child whose whole writing bears the look of Hebrew. Kindergarten and first-grade children build on their knowledge of written language by participating in planned and spontaneous writing activity. In doing so, they acquire knowledge about reading *by* writing.

Scribble Drawing   Scribble writing stands in contrast to *scribble drawing*, which is more pictographic in expression. Before the age of four, most children don't know the difference between writing and drawing. But soon they show signs of understanding that these are two different ways to represent ideas. Drawing is important because it assists both writing development and eye–hand coordination. Children between the ages of four and six use drawings or pictographs as a form of written expression in their work. In fact, they recognize using a combination of drawing, dictating, and writing to compose or narrate a single event as appropriate for kindergarteners.

Often when a child draws a picture, it's open to interpretation—that is, until we have the child use words to tell us about the picture; then the picture takes on a much richer meaning. Take a look at Figure 4.4. At first glance, it doesn't have a lot of meaning, does it? We notice some dark circles on top and then a large circle in the middle with a line coming out of the right side of it, and then a longer, twisted drawing along the left side. However, after talking to the child, we learn the significance of the objects, "This is me playing in the home center. This is the table [in the center], the watercolors [along the top of the page], and this is the spoon [the twisted lines to the left of the drawing]."

Common Core State Standard

CCRA.W.4

When teachers and parents talk to children about their drawings, children have the occasion not only to express themselves but also to learn that the written word conveys meaning. Taking the time to talk with children about their pictures helps them consider the meanings they want to communicate. Schickedanz and Casbergue (2009) recommend avoiding extensive questions or discussions about a drawing. Instead, they advise simply repeating the child's first remarks about the picture, or perhaps commenting on a specific detail in the drawing is enough to invite the child to tell more. For example, in the case of the home center drawing, it might look like this:

> **Teacher:** Oh. So this is the table in the home center. I see the leg right here. And the spoon is used in the home center.
> **Child:** Yeah. I'm making dark chicken with the spoon.
> **Teacher:** Oh. Dark chicken is good. I like dark meat and white meat, too.
> **Child:** Yeah. My Daddy likes dark so I'm going to make that for him.

Figure 4.4 Work Plans

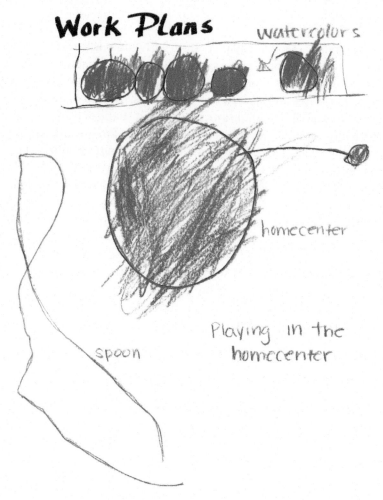

Providing the opportunity for the child to talk about the picture, expand on the experience, and convey meaning is just as important as writing the dictated words near the picture. Schickedanz and Casbergue (2009) remind us that graphic representations serve as placeholders until children's drawings and squiggles can stand on their own and convey meaning, which takes a long time. Until then, oral language allows children to tell us what they intend.

> ▶ In this **video** (https://www.youtube.com/watch?v=ILGVIHoZo-w), you will see how one kindergarten teacher encourages children to write about the pictures they have drawn. What is she doing to support young children's early attempts to communicate in writing?

When children start to figure out that writing and drawing are different, they begin to make great strides toward understanding the symbolic nature of writing. They start to understand that there are connections between letters and meaning and are soon on their way to making the transition from drawing writing to symbolic writing. They redefine what they think writing is and start to use letters and combinations of letters and letter-like forms to communicate ideas. Usually this begins with their name, a word that fascinates and intrigues them.

Name Scribbling   Name scribbling is an extension of scribble writing. Scribbles become representational to the child writer; the scribbles mean something. The first letters children are likely to know are from their name, and children probably become aware of both letters and words through engagement with their names.

When children differentiate between drawing and scribbling as a means of written expression, they begin to make great strides in their knowledge of print. Name scribbling underscores this differentiation and results in the formation of valuable concepts about written language—namely, that markings or symbols represent units of language such as letters and words, which in turn represent things and objects that can be communicated by messages. In this phase, there is no knowledge of the need to select and order letters to represent the order of sounds heard in spoken words. The intent is merely to make their writing look like words, and in fact they do believe they are words. They do not understand the alphabetic principle: Letters represent sounds. Yet it is very important for parents and teachers of young children to offer many opportunities for children to practice this. Drawing and writing tools should be available to children in various areas of a classroom and easily accessible in the home. Parent–child activities, such as the following, extend children's interest in and knowledge about written language by providing opportunities to observe, as well as participate in, meaningful, functional writing activities:

- Parents should encourage their children to help write the family shopping list.
- Parents and children may communicate with one another through written messages, such as writing notes. A bulletin board or a chalkboard provides a designated location for writing and receiving notes.
- Parents should create occasions to write, such as writing a grocery list or a letter to Santa. In the same vein, they should encourage children to correspond in writing or by e-mail with a responsive pen pal, perhaps a "best friend" or a relative living in another area who is about the same age. Writing invitations for a birthday party or a sleepover or writing the instructions to give to the person who will temporarily care for a pet provides a meaningful writing occasion.

2017 ILA Standard

1.3

While determining stages of oral language, reading, and writing development is helpful, individual differences in children's literacy development must be taken into account. Children are more diverse in their backgrounds, experiences, and abilities than ever before. Some kindergartners may have the skills characteristic of the typical three-year-old, while others might be functioning at the level of the typical seven-year-old. All young children, including dual language learners, need to have rich early language and literacy experiences from the very beginning of life. Important foundational literacy skills that serve as necessary precursors to conventional reading (Whitehurst & Lonigan, 1998) include oral language comprehension, vocabulary, phonological awareness, alphabet knowledge, developmental writing, and print knowledge. In this next section, we provide basic information about critical skills identified by research as those young children must have in order to become successful readers (Snow, Burns, & Griffin, 1998).

2017 ILA Standards

1.1, 1.2, 1.3

Common Core State Standards

CCRA.L.5, CCRA.L.6

Oral Language and Vocabulary

Oral language comprehension, the ability to listen and speak with understanding, is very important to later reading comprehension. This includes children's growing and diverse vocabulary of new and varied words. Oral language development is connected to children's cognition (thinking skills) in many important ways. As children's vocabularies increase, they demonstrate specific cognitive skills such as classification and categorization. Generally, children's receptive (listening) vocabulary—hearing and understanding the language or languages of an environment—is larger than their expressive (spoken) vocabulary, which involves making and using the sounds of a child's language or languages for communication. Children in poverty are at risk for having a smaller vocabulary of many fewer words than other children. A large vocabulary is important because it is the foundation for children learning to read and understanding what they read. When children lack exposure to rich language experiences, they quickly lose ground in the world of learning, and the word gap between them and their peers can widen substantially by age four (Hart & Risley, 1995). Vocabulary is important because it is a strong predictor of reading comprehension.

Phonological Awareness

To decode words a reader must know that each spoken word consists of a series of individual sounds. **Phonological awareness** involves hearing the sounds of language apart from its meaning, which is difficult for most children since they must be consciously aware of the structure of language, rather than simply using language to communicate. They need to learn how to listen with purpose for the number of words in sentences (I/ate/soup/for/lunch), the number of syllables in words (com-pu-ter), and the number of individual sounds in words (d/o/g). Phonological awareness is important because it is a strong predictor of future reading success and an essential skill for later phonics and spelling. Young children learn phonological awareness through interactions with such things as nursery rhymes, books with repetitive patterns, songs, and clapping syllables.

In this **video** (www.youtube.com/watch?v=ppB6g3_fteo), watch as this teacher works on phonological awareness with a group of five-year-old children. What strategies does the teacher use to support her young students' awareness of sounds?

Alphabet Knowledge

Decoding skill requires letter-name knowledge. **Alphabet knowledge** is the ability to name, write, and identify the sounds of the 26 letters of the alphabet. It supports children's understanding of letter–sound relationships and is the key to both reading and writing in English and many other languages. Letters are important building blocks of the English writing system and a predictor of success in beginning reading. Research suggests children don't learn the alphabet letter names in any particular order, although letters in their names are often the first identified. McGee and Richgels (2012) note that it takes many experiences with meaningful written language for children to learn letters of the alphabet.

Developmental Writing

Common Core State Standard

CCRA.W.6

From a very young age, children take an interest in writing and expressing themselves beginning with scribbling. With much experience and guidance, children gradually become more sophisticated in their invented spellings. Early writing supports later writing by developing children's understanding of the purposes and functions of written language and is one of the best predictors of children's later reading success (National Early Literacy Panel, 2008) because children develop understandings of both print (i.e., print concept and alphabet knowledge) and sound (i.e., phonological awareness) when they write.

Print Knowledge

Print knowledge is the ability to recognize print and understand that it works in specific ways and carries meaning and motivates the learn-to-read process. *Concepts about print* include the knowledge of such concepts as how to hold a book, turn a page, and read from left-to-right and top-to-bottom; or that the text, not the illustrations, carry the message. *Concepts about words* is the consciousness that words carry meaning, and stories and text are built from words. When a child has a concept of word, it means he understands that each word is separate, and that words have boundaries and are separated by a space within a sentence. Further, it is the ability to match spoken words to written words and later to determine that letters and words at the beginning of a sentence have a capital letter, and words at the end are followed by a punctuation mark. Knowledge of how print works is an indicator of literacy experience both at home and at school.

In the next section, we look at how literate environments, both at home and in the classroom, support young children in acquiring core knowledge and skills. It is here where routines and activities can engage children in language-rich activities that demonstrate how print and language work together.

Check Your Understanding 4.1: Gauge your understanding of the skills and concepts in this section.

Literate Learning Environments

■ **Identify core language and literacy skills.**

2017 ILA Standards

1.1, 5.1, 5.2, 5.3

From birth through preschool, young children begin to acquire basic understandings about reading and writing and their functions through experiences with print in the environment.

As you might surmise, a **literate environment** for young children is one that fosters interest in and curiosity about written language and supports children's efforts to become readers and writers. Early readers thrive in environments in which parents and other significant persons have a high regard for reading.

Within a literate environment, there is also a preoccupation with scribbling, drawing, and writing—so much so that Durkin (1966) characterized children who learn to read naturally as "paper-and-pencil kids." Early readers need to spend significant amounts of time expressing themselves through scribble writing, drawing, copying words, and inventing spellings for words. This means teachers, parents, and caregivers of young children need to intentionally create learning environments where core language and literacy skills can be explored. This happens only when thoughtful, purposeful planning takes place. In this section, we outline how to create rich environments both at home and in the early childhood classroom.

Creating Literate Learning Environments at Home

Studies of early readers indicate that learning to read is strongly associated with positive home environments (Pinto, Manuela, & Aguiar, 2013; Neuman & Roskos, 1993; Strickland & Morrow, 1990; Teale, 1978). There are large differences in how family environments support children's literacy development (Murdoch, 2016; Snow, Burns,

& Griffin, 1998). There are also significant differences among ethnic groups in how frequently families read to their children (Yarosz & Barnett, 2001).

Early readers have access to a variety of easy reading materials in the home, and they can also use the local library. Moreover, early readers are attracted to reading *anything* that interests them in their immediate everyday print environment, from labels on cans and cereal boxes, to TV listings, to recipes and bus schedules.

Although books, billboards, and package labels are all potential sources for reading in a young child's home environment, children must learn how print functions in their lives. In this respect, reading aloud to children is one of the most important contributing factors in the learning environment of early readers. Early readers' homes are frequently characterized by one or more parents and older siblings who read regularly.

As a result, children learn about reading by observing the significant people in their lives modeling reading behaviors naturally—for real purposes—in a variety of ways. As Vukelich and Christie (2009) note, children observe the literacy behaviors of significant others as they use literacy daily, such as creating grocery lists. They might see, for example, a parent reading a recipe while cooking or baking, a text from a friend, or the assembly instructions for a new bike. Some children will rivet their attention on the television screen as words flash before them during a commercial. Others quickly become aware that newspapers, the Internet, and magazines impart information about events occurring locally and in the world. Others realize that books may be read to learn and to entertain. Indeed, reading is part of their environment. Children need to become aware of the many purposes of reading and frequently become involved in different kinds of reading activity.

Parents are essential partners in their children's development of reading, writing, and talking skills. Years of research confirm children who read early have the following conditions in the home environment:

1. Parents provide access to a wide variety of print, such as books, magazines, and newspapers.
2. Parents demonstrate uses of written language for various purposes.
3. Parents are supportive of literacy efforts, assisting early attempts at literacy, and are willing to respond to questions about print.
4. Parents and siblings read to their child, which is positively related to outcomes such as language growth, early literacy, and later reading achievement.

Read about the impact a reading parent and literate environment had on Casey Taylor as a young child in Box 4.2.

Creating Literate Environments in the Classroom

A literacy learning environment in the classroom establishes ideal conditions for learning to read in much the same way that the home environment of the child establishes ideal conditions for learning to speak. In a classroom environment that promotes literacy development, children feel free to take risks because errors are expected and accepted. Risk taking is an important factor in literacy learning. Beginners should feel free to ask questions with the expectation that interested adults will listen and respond constructively. Effective teachers plan the environment so that children are engaged in interpreting and using print in meaningful ways.

DESIGN OF THE CLASSROOM ENVIRONMENT   High-quality classrooms are those in which literacy learning is grounded in all the ways that children learn and grow— physically, socially, emotionally, and cognitively. The environment in these classrooms is rich with print, representing language familiar to children and resulting from daily activities and thematic inquiry. The environment itself becomes a "teacher," providing opportunities for children to learn on their own and with peers. All areas of the room should serve as the learning environment, support children's learning, and allow children to learn from the environment itself.

BOX 4.2

The Power of a Literate Home Environment

Casey Taylor is studying to be an early childhood education teacher at the University of Akron in Ohio.

As a child, my earliest recollections of reading stem from memories of time spent alone with my mother. I was born with a heart condition that required me to undergo open-heart surgery at nine weeks old. As a result, I was in the hospital more often than not. My mother was always with me, and she loved to read to me. I found the sound of her voice soothing, and the stories she read were a welcome distraction from the physical discomfort I felt. When she read to me, I would close my eyes, become part of the story, and forget all about being in a hospital. My mother would read aloud using different voices and inflection for each character; she made reading look fun.

Due to my heart condition, I could not play the way other children could. It was important for my condition that I stay calm as often as possible, so as not to increase my heart rate. As a result, my physical activity was limited and I had to stay indoors for the better part of my childhood. When I was in the second grade, I came home from school one day to a surprise from my mother. She had converted the space underneath the staircase in our home into a special room for me. She called it "the book nook." The book nook was filled with comfortable pillows and shelves holding dozens of brand-new books. I spent countless hours in the book nook; I was always reading.

Throughout elementary school I would participate in school-sponsored summer reading programs. I won a prize for reading so many books during my third summer in the program. My teachers were very encouraging and supportive of my love for reading. They would allow me to go to the school library during recess and often engage in conversation with me about my favorite books. I was so proud of myself for being good at something that my heart condition could not take from me.

I lost my mother to brain cancer when I was 12 years old, and the memories I have of our times reading together are among the most important memories of my life thus far. She exposed me to reading at a time when she knew it was exactly what I needed. Since then I have saturated my life with an appreciation for books and learning through reading. I continue to read for pleasure. I have revisited many of the books I loved as a child, and each time I do I am whisked away, back to the second grade, back to my book nook, back to my mother's lap, back to a happiness I have not since known.

Watch this **video** (www.youtube.com/watch?v=Fm8PoT58Jk8) to tour a preschool classroom that is print rich. How has the teacher considered the needs of her students when planning the physical arrangement of the room, the instructional materials, the scheduling, and other factors that contribute to a literate learning environment?

Instead of decorating the room with commercially purchased materials as teachers have traditionally done, the environment should reflect print that supports the curriculum and promotes active engagement. There should be purposeful uses of print throughout the room so that children understand the uses and functions of print in their daily lives. For example, print should be put at eye level, the theme of the classroom should be evident, vocabulary should be reflected throughout, and overall the classroom should be intriguing and exciting. Doors and entryways are important learning spaces, too. Doors and entryways symbolize the threshold to learning and prepare children for what is going to happen in the room. In a way, they prime children for new adventures in learning. Christie and Burstein (2010) suggest the following areas for a supportive environment:

- *Book area.* A book area that is orderly and inviting with comfortable furniture for at least four children should be prominent in the classroom but away from the block and dramatic play areas. The books should range in difficulty, reflect the current classroom theme, and include both narrative and expository stories. Books should also be available in all centers such as dramatic play, science, block, and so on.

- *Listening area.* There should be a listening center where children can use headphones to listen to books on mobile devices. There are many free, downloadable e-books available for classroom use. This area, like the book area, should be comfortable and inviting.

Figure 4.5 Checklist for a Print-Rich Environment

Use a checklist similar to this one to assess the classroom print environment.
_____ Students have access to a variety of print materials around the room, such as books, menus, recipes, signs, and student work.
_____ Print is evident throughout the classroom.
_____ Print is clear, easy to read, and at children's eye level.
_____ Word walls with familiar words are displayed for children to copy or "read."
_____ Children's names are printed on their cubbies, desks, and other supplies.
_____ Children are encouraged to write their own names or letters from their names on a sign-in sheet and on paintings and drawings.
_____ Some print is written in languages other than English.
_____ Mailboxes exist for each child and family to encourage home–school communication and show children that print has meaning.

- *Computer area.* Software and online activities should be current and relevant. Children can use headphones to individually work at computers on meaningful activities that support language and literacy.

- *Writing area.* The writing area should be well stocked with a variety of paper and tools. Words—including the names of children—should be written on cards and available. The alphabet should be displayed at the children's eye level.

Opportunities for using the environment will emerge throughout the day as teachers plan for activities to make use of the print. In addition to planning for print, they also need to interact with children by responding to questions, extending their knowledge, modeling functions of print, and praising and encouraging attempts to read and write. See Figure 4.5 for a checklist for a print-rich environment.

LITERACY-RELATED PLAY CENTERS   Play is integral to exploration and instruction. In the section above, we told you about the essential skills for young children that can be taught via play: oral language comprehension, vocabulary, and writing. To accomplish this, a literate classroom environment is well-planned, but it is also playful. A play-centered environment allows young children in day care or early childhood classrooms to develop a "feel" for literacy as they experiment with written language. It is also a place where children's physical, social, emotional, and cognitive development can be pulled forward to higher levels of performance (Leong & Bodrova, 2012). For this reason, time for play should not be shortchanged.

Literacy play centers provide an environment where children may play with print on their own terms. Play provides a natural context for beginners to experiment with literacy and give children opportunities to observe one another using literacy for real reasons. Play centers are usually based around the classroom topic of study and change with each study. For example, a topic study on wheels may yield a play center that is a bike shop or an auto repair shop. If the topic study is food, the play center might be a Lebanese restaurant or a bakery. Each play center should contain both literacy materials and props to support the play. A bike shop might have an old bike in it and some tools so children can pretend to work on the bike. It could also have a cash register for paying, paper and pencils for writing orders and receipts, an appointment book, and various signs made by the children. Teachers can join the play in strategic ways to nudge children toward the literacy props. For example, the teacher who stops in the auto repair shop could ask the children for a receipt and to schedule her next oil change. These requests help children experiment with specific functions of writing and encourage them to use writing as part of their play. Box 4.3 has some examples of props found in play centers.

Teachers have a very important role in a play episode because without their support the play of many children will never reach its full potential. The main responsibility of the teacher is to facilitate literacy development by scaffolding play in the classroom (Leong & Bodrova, 2012), which involves appropriately intervening to create opportunities that expand language, promote social skills, and spark imagination

BOX 4.3

Examples of Props Found in Literacy Play Centers

Grocery Store

- Coupons
- Signs (open/closed, store name, sales, food, employee of the month, manager on duty, hours of operation)
- Notepads for shopping lists
- Brown paper bags with store name written by children
- Empty food boxes
- Grocery store ads
- Cash register and play money or debit cards

Flower Shop

- Flower delivery form
- Flowers and plants (real or play)

- Flower and seed catalogs
- Message cards
- Signs (open/closed, hours of operation, names of flowers, prices)
- Cash register and play money or debit cards
- Tissue paper to wrap flowers
- Ribbon or string
- Books about flowers
- Plastic vases
- Apron

during play. This may entail suggesting the need for making a list, recording an appointment, texting a friend, checking food labels, or reading a bedtime story. At times, teachers co-play and become directly involved in the play as a participant to model and extend language for the children, therefore supporting their literacy-related play. Other times the teacher may take on a more directive or leadership role and model specific behaviors of play such as introducing vocabulary or phrases into the play to be adapted by the children.

A home-centered, play-centered environment extends children's literacy learning in developmentally appropriate, creative ways. A language-centered environment provides language experiences that are crucial to a beginner's growth as a literacy learner. In Box 4.4, Yu-Ling Yeh writes about the efforts Head Start, America's largest preschool effort, is making to build rich language and literacy classroom environments.

Check Your Understanding 4.2: Gauge your understanding of the skills and concepts in this section.

BOX 4.4

Yu-Ling Yeh
Improving Literacy and Language for Young Children

Yu-Ling Yeh, an educational consultant in Akron, Ohio, provides some background on Head Start and Early Head Start.

Since Head Start's beginnings in 1965, many efforts have been made to improve the quality of teaching methods and the quality of language and literacy instruction for young children. In 2002, under the guidance of the No Child Left Behind Act and the Good Start, Grow Smart initiative, Project STEP (Strategic Summer Teacher Education Program) was launched with the goal of educating teachers about how best to promote children's emerging literacy, language, and cognitive development. In 2007, the Improving Head Start for School Readiness Act of 2007 was signed into law. In order to promote evidence-based practices for improving preschool

classroom teaching practices, Classroom Assessment Scoring System (CLASS) was selected to measure the quality of teacher–child interaction. CLASS has empowered the teaching staff to pay closer attention to the delivery of their instruction in the areas of the concept, language, and literacy development. In 2015, a comprehensive Early Learning Outcome Framework was rolled out to include children ages zero to five, instead of the previous focus on children three to five years old. The revised framework targets important domains that support our youngest children in preparing for school readiness and later success in life.

Facilitating Language and Literacy

■ **Create literate environments at home and school.**

Now we turn to some routines and practices that support these essential proficiencies, with books and other print materials at the core of instruction. We show you how teachers of young children support children's literacy and language learning through routines and activities that teach speech and print relationships, features of written language, and sounds and letters.

2017 ILA Standard

5.2

Common Core State Standards

CCRA.R.10, CCRA.W.9

Learning About Literacy Through Books

Books, in all of their various formats, are the heart of teaching young children about literacy. Teachers need to read often with children, read a variety of books, and reread favorites in order to maximize reading's impact on children's language and literacy development. There has been much documentation on reading aloud and how it helps children become familiar with language and literacy (Beck & McKeown, 2001; Cazden, 1983; Chomsky, 1972; Heisey & Kucan, 2010; Justice, Meier, & Walpole, 2005; Maloch & Beutel, 2010). In this section, we focus on five main categories of books: storybooks, nonfiction books, big books, e-books, and class-made books. In Box 4.5, we share tips for planning read-aloud experiences.

Storybooks

Reading aloud to children is powerful. Books unlock the mysteries of reading, rivet children's attention to print, and provide models of writing that build on and extend the young child's concepts of texts and how they work. Because books expose children to words beyond those they hear in their everyday lives, books both build vocabulary and

---

BOX 4.5 | RESEARCH-BASED PRACTICES

Planning for Read-Alouds

When planning to read aloud, be mindful of the following suggestions.

- Select high-interest books with rich language, well-developed plots and characters, and multiple layers of meaning.
- Select nonfiction books that extend vocabulary and have high-quality, realistic pictures.
- Preview the book before you read it. This will help you spot material you may want to shorten, take out completely, or expand on.
- Practice the book before reading aloud to children. Think about the story's structure (i.e., the setting, the sequence of events leading to plot conflict, and resolution), characters, descriptions, illustrations, themes, and the author's use of language if it's a piece of fiction. Consider how you will use your voice to convey meaning as you read.

- Consider features and structures you want to point out in the text, or what questions you want to ask.
- Determine whether there are any instructional goals you'd like to develop; then think about how you'd like to accomplish those goals.
- Decide on points in the story where you might pause to ask children to make predictions.
- Anticipate where you may need to build children's background knowledge so that they will understand concepts with which they may not be familiar.
- Include books that represent children's cultural heritage and provide opportunities to learn about similarities and differences among people.

allow children to experience people and places in situations they may never come across otherwise, building background knowledge. Repeated readings of books help children recognize words and connect speech to print. Read-alouds can support children's developing the ability to reason for themselves and with others if children are actively involved in discussions about the book being read. As children experience print through read-aloud events from adult models that use expression and show enjoyment of the text, they are motivated to interact within a social context to share information about books.

Immersing beginners in storybook reading experiences is an authentic way to accomplish a variety of instructional goals. For example, through reading aloud, modeling, and discussion, children learn that print has meaning, that print is read left to right, and that picture cues can help tell the story. They also learn that important skills such as prediction can be made around text and that one can use drawing and writing to respond to text. In classrooms where **storybook experiences** are an integral part of the school day, numerous literacy skills may be accomplished over time in combination or simultaneously. Hilden and Jones (2013) encourage the use of open-ended questions to scaffold comprehension and boost critical thinking skills. Storybooks can also be a way to spur writing in the classroom. Van Ness, Murnen, and Bertelsen (2013) suggest the use of storybooks to spark interest in personal journal writing in kindergarten.

There are many kindergarten and first-grade Common Core State Standards (CCSS) that can be learned through reading aloud. For example, read-alouds help young children become familiar with the direction of print; the sequence of letters; the role of the author and illustrator; and describing characters, settings, and major events (National Governors Association Center for Best Practices, Council of Chief State School Officers, 2010).

Nonfiction Books

Traditionally, the majority of early childhood teachers have used narrative text that tells a story during read-alouds or story time. However, the use of nonfiction with young children is getting more attention today than ever before. Children need to be exposed to fiction, but they also need to be exposed to nonfiction print, too. Think about what you've read over the past few days. How much of it was fiction, and how much of it was nonfiction, such as a recipe, newspaper article, text message, magazine article, or blog? Most of the reading that goes on outside school is nonfiction, so it only makes sense that children need to be exposed to nonfiction at an early age. And many children—particularly boys—enjoy reading informational books a great deal (Stead & Duke, 2005). Some adults think informational text is too difficult for young children. However, studies of young children's interactions with informational text demonstrate they are "capable of learning from, engaging in pretend reading with, and participating in sophisticated discussions about this type of text" (Yopp & Yopp, 2012, p. 481).

Are there other reasons to use nonfiction with young children? Research shows informational text contains more technical words than fiction, exposing children to a more diverse vocabulary (Price, Bradley, & Smith, 2012). Children can learn words such as *repel* or *attract* when reading a book about magnets. Nonfiction books help children acquire content knowledge they would not otherwise have access to (Schickedanz & Collins, 2013). For example, wasp nests are fascinating, and children might observe one from afar. But an informational book on wasps allows them to study a wasp up close and examine the papery, hexagonal cells of its nest. Other benefits of nonfiction include the expansion of background knowledge, high interest to children, connections to other content areas (such as science and social studies), and practice for the content area reading that is needed later in the intermediate grades (Duke & Bennett-Armistead, 2003). In addition to these benefits, reading quality informational books and other nonfiction texts provides a venue for children to think about the world around them, which encourages critical thinking.

The CCSS have placed a strong importance on nonfiction text, emphasizing engaging children with nonfiction texts equally with literary texts in grades K through 5. This means teachers of beginning readers need to adjust the read-aloud routines in the classroom to include informational texts and use them to teach CCSS skills such as using details in text to answer questions, locate key facts, and compare and contrast texts.

Common Core State Standard

CCRA.R.1

Big Books

Big books, big versions of children's books with large print and illustrations, are designed to further children's explorations with texts and to develop concepts related to print as well as strategies to construct meaning. The big book allows all children to see the text, enabling them to participate in the reading of the story.

Reading big books is one of the easiest and most effective ways to get beginners involved in the exploration of texts. The use of big books as an instructional resource began in the late 1960s in New Zealand, when teachers began to make their own big books from heavy brown butcher paper. Today's big books range in content from traditional tales, to books of poems, to nonfiction books in various content areas.

The predictability of the plot and language of narrative big books makes them easy to understand and remember. For example, after two or three readings, most children easily memorize Bill Martin Jr.'s *Brown Bear, Brown Bear, What Do You See?* and begin to chime in. Big books such as these, with their simple, repetitive refrains, colorful illustrations, and cumulative plot endings, allow children to make predictions and participate immediately in **shared reading** experiences.

In addition to the pleasure and enjoyment that children get when they participate in shared readings and rereadings of big books, big-book formats are versatile in helping to achieve all of the instructional goals for beginners. Nonfiction big books, now widely available, feature enlarged print and real-world photography for shared reading. The texts are written for whole class use with young children. Figure 4.6 suggests some of the activities that teachers and children engage in when they use big books.

E-Books

E-books, electronic or digital publications, are quickly finding their way into classrooms for authentic instructional purposes. E-books can be read online or downloaded onto personal devices or computers. Some e-books feature music, animation, hyperlinks to outside information, and word decoding. Others allow the reader to interact and explore by swiping or tapping the screen. Teachers and children are interacting with texts in whole new ways through e-books.

E-books are being used to support traditional print-based literacy programs in whole groups during shared reading time with touchscreen computers and independently by using tablets and handheld devices, which bring e-books into the palms of young children. Teachers can have children listen to stories, read along with text, look for familiar words or letters, and do virtually anything with an e-book that they can do with a traditional book. E-books are rapidly spreading into the early childhood world, inviting young children to interact with storybooks in new and different ways. Since e-books have audio features, highlighted words, and other assistive technology features, some teachers are finding them to be a good format for children with special needs, such as dyslexia.

2017 ILA Standard

5.3

Figure 4.6 Big Book Activities Before, During, and After Reading

What the Teacher Does	What the Child Does	Objective
Before Reading		
Stimulates discussion about relevant content and concepts in text.	Talks and listens to others talk about relevant content and concepts.	To focus listening and speaking on vocabulary and ideas about to be met in print. To activate background knowledge related to text.
Reads aloud title and author; uses words *title* and *author* and briefly explains what they mean.	Notes what the words on the book cover represent.	To build vocabulary and concepts: title, author, authorship.
Asks children what they think story might be about, based on title, cover. Thinks aloud about what she or he thinks this story might be about.	Uses clues from title and cover together with background knowledge to formulate predictions about the story. Or observes teacher model the above.	To use clues from text and background knowledge to make inferences and formulate predictions.
Shows pleasure and interest in anticipation of the reading.	Observes as teacher models personal interest and eagerness toward the reading.	To build positive attitudes toward books and reading.
During Reading (Teacher Reads Aloud)		
Gives lively reading. Displays interest and delight in language and story line.	Observes teacher evoke meaningful language from print.	To understand that print carries meaning.
Tracks print with hand or pointer.	Follows movement of hand or pointer.	To match speech to print. To learn directionality: left to right.
Thinks aloud about her or his understanding of certain aspects of the story (self-query, making predictions, drawing conclusions, etc.).	Observes as teacher monitors her or his own understandings.	To develop an understanding of the reading process as thinking with text.
Hesitates at predictable parts in the text. Allows children to fill in possible words or phrases.	Fills in likely words for a given slot.	To use semantic and syntactic clues to determine what makes sense.
At appropriate parts in a story, queries children about what might happen next.	Makes predictions about what might happen next in the story.	To use story line to predict possible events and outcomes.
After Reading		
Guides discussion about key ideas in the text. Helps children relate key concepts.	Participates in discussion of important ideas in the text.	To reflect on the reading: to apply and personalize key ideas in text.
Asks children to recall important or favorite parts. Finds corresponding part of the text (perhaps with help of children) and rereads.	Recalls and describes specific events and parts of text.	To use print to support and confirm discussion.
Guides group rereading of all or specific parts of text for errorless repetition and reinforcement.	Joins in the reading in parts he or she feels confident about.	To develop fluency and confidence through group reading.
Uses cloze activities (flaps to cover words) to involve children in meaningful (contextually plausible) offerings. Discusses response with children.	Fills in possible words for a given slot.	To use semantic and syntactic clues to determine which words fit in a slot and why.
After Reading, for Repeated Readings Only		
Focuses children's attention on distinctive features and patterns in the text: repeated words, repeated word beginnings (letters, consonant clusters), punctuation marks, etc. Uses letter names and correct terminology to discuss these features. Extends discussion to developmentally appropriate level.	Notes distinctive features and patterns pointed out by teacher and attempts to find others on her or his own.	To analyze a known text for distinctive features and patterns. To develop an understanding of the elements of decoding within a meaningful context.
Makes books and charts available for independent reading.	Selects books and charts for independent reading and reads them at own pace.	To increase confidence and understanding of the reading process by practicing it independently.

Source: Language, Literacy, and the Child, 1st ed., by L. Galda, B. Cullinan, and D. Strickland, pp. 102–103. Copyright © 1993 Wadsworth, a part of Cengage Learning, Inc. Reproduced by permission. www.cengage.com/permissions.

E-books are appealing to young children because they grab their attention. Music, narration, word highlights, and animation all enhance the visual and auditory experience, further heightening young children's attraction to the screen (Roskos, 2015). There are both pros and cons to e-books. On the positive side, children engage faster and stay engaged longer than with print books. Children—even those with lower attention spans—attend to text, storylines, and content longer when it's in digital form, and this increases their chances for learning (Roskos, Burstein, Shang, &

Gray, 2014). However, studies also show that e-books can be attention-splitters. The physical play of touching, swiping, poking, and tapping can overwhelm the child and diminish the opportunity for learning from e-books (Takacs, Swart, & Bus, 2015). Roskos (2015) suggests the following tips for using e-books effectively and purposefully with young children:

Preview

Carefully assess the literary and technical qualities of the e-book. Pay close attention to any reading aids available, as well as distractors that may detract from the storyline or content.

Explore

Introduce the book by reading the name of the title and author. Show children the special features on the menu or toolbar.

Listen or read

As you listen to or read the book, turn the pages, pausing to demonstrate how any digital features work to support the story.

Invite children to lead

Allow children to swipe to turn the pages or tap to hear sounds. Ask them to talk about the page on the screen, and encourage them to make connections between text and illustrations.

Have fun

Ask children to return to their favorite parts and try to read the text on their own. Adults can encourage children to book browse and reread familiar selections while also practicing their emerging literacy skills.

2017 ILA Standards

1.2, 2.1

Common Core State Standards

CCRA.SL.5, CCRA.W.6

Class-Made Books

Teacher, student, and class-made books can provide opportunities for meaningful text for students, especially those from diverse backgrounds. Teachers take dictation or record language of children on chart paper to create text. Some turn these dictations into classroom books, e-books, or big books. There is really no better way to help children understand what reading and writing is about than to show them how their language is transcribed into print.

This dictated, personal text provides many opportunities for explicit instruction in which teachers demonstrate early writing strategies. When children help with the writing, it is known as **shared writing**. Taberski (2010) says that through this activity, she and her students work out the conventions of print, spelling, and grammar. Following steps associated with the language-experience approach, the teacher becomes a scribe for a text dictated by the children and shares the pen with them, creating text together. The focus, first and foremost, is always on composing the text. The teacher, as well as the children who volunteer, will often read, then reread, the text for emphasis and make additions and changes to clarify meaning. Within this meaningful, collaborative context, opportunities abound to demonstrate early writing strategies such as word-by-word matching, left-to-right directionality, use of space to create boundaries between words, and other print conventions. As children gain experience with the conventions of print, the teacher uses shared writing activities to focus on spelling patterns and word analysis.

Language-experience activities in beginning reading instruction permit young children to share and discuss experiences; listen to and tell stories; dictate words, sentences, and stories; and write independently. The teacher can revolve language experiences around speaking, listening, visual expression, singing, movement, and rhythmic activities. There is no more appropriate way to help children understand what reading is all about than to show them how language is transcribed into print. A language-experience story is just what it implies—an account that is told aloud by a child and printed by another person. In the beginning of instruction, there are numerous ways to involve children in producing experience stories. For example, many of the suggestions for teaching about the uses of written language can serve to stimulate the child's dictation or, for that matter, a group-dictated story. Not only does an experience story vividly show the relationship between speech and print, but it also introduces children to the thrill of personal authorship. This can be especially true for children from diverse linguistic backgrounds because teachers who subscribe to the language-experience approach support children working with their *own* language.

Steps to Follow in Producing Language-Experience Stories

A child can dictate a complete story, or several children can collaborate on an account by contributing individual sentences. In either case, the first step is to provide a stimulus (e.g., a classroom guinea pig, a photo, concrete objects, an actual experience a child has had) that will lead to dictation. Whatever the stimulus, it should be unusual and interesting enough for children to want to talk about it and to remember it two or three days later when the dictation is reread.

Common Core State Standard

CCRA.W.4

HAVING STUDENTS DICTATE STORIES   As children dictate, it's important to keep their spoken language intact. Therefore, write down exactly what is said regardless of grammatical errors and incomplete sentences. By capturing language just as it is spoken, the teacher preserves its integrity and ensures the child's total familiarity with the print to be read.

Once the story is written down, the teacher should read it aloud several times, carefully but steadily moving left to right, top to bottom, and pointing to each word or line as it is read and then sweeping to the next line. After that, the account should be read in unison, with the teacher continuing to model left-to-right, top-to-bottom orientation to print.

The value of language experience lies in the physical ease by which text is produced *to achieve reading instructional goals.* When a child dictates, the physical burden of writing is removed. This often results in more of a child's ideas being put in print than would otherwise be possible in beginning situations. Through these language experiences, children increase phonological awareness, build oral language comprehension, and learn about print awareness. Producing student-written books is one way to support English language learners, since the natural language of the child is embraced. Books in a student's native language allow background experiences to be used as a basis for learning to read. Jeremy Brueck shares how he used his son's language to create a meaningful e-book in Box 4.6.

BOX 4.6 | TRANSLITERACY

Jeremy Brueck

Creating a Simple E-Book with Young Children

Today's children are able to use new technologies with amazing ease. As a result, these tools are quickly becoming the medium through which students are learning and interacting. E-books, books in electronic format, are becoming popular in classrooms. They can be downloaded to a computer, a laptop, a handheld device, a smartphone, or any other reading tool and read on the screen. E-books can have page numbers, a table of contents, pictures, and graphics just like a traditional book. However, e-books have features traditional books do not. E-books allow students to connect with stories in ways never possible before; they can show links for easy access to more information, are searchable, and are interactive with audio, video, and animations, which can enhance the message the author is trying to convey. Fortunately for schools, many free e-books are available today. Teachers can log on to public library websites or other online sources to access e-books.

Personalized e-books are a lot of fun, too. However, the thought of creating an e-book can be intimidating, yet there are many online resources available to help you get started. Here is a basic overview on how to make your own e-book:

Step One: Planning and Preparation

1. To get started, think of the subject matter for your e-book. Select a simple plot by thinking about something that happens as a series, such as brushing your teeth or tying your shoe. For example, I made an e-book with my son, Aiden, about the home my dad lived in since Aiden was curious about where his grandpa lived. This helped him to see that Grandpa's house may look different, but it has all of the same things in it that ours does.

2. Next, create a simple storyboard on a piece of paper, or download and print a storyboard template from the Internet. Try to stick to six to eight pages for your first book. Remember to include a cover page! Here is a look at the start of my storyboard for Grandpa's house.

3. Once the storyboard is finished, you will need to search online for and install some essential story-creating applications on your tablet or computer. There are many apps to create stories and crop photos available online at no cost.

Step Two: Creating Media

Once your storyboard is complete and you have the apps downloaded, take a picture for each block on your storyboard and save it to your tablet camera. You could also use video.

Step Three: Assemble E-Book

No matter what app you've selected, you're now ready to use the media you've created to build your e-book. During this build, try to incorporate some of the tools that the e-book app provides in addition to your media. For example, you might have a child record the audio. Other apps allow you to insert text boxes and video. Explore the potential of the app as you build your e-book!

Step Four: Publication

Finally, take a moment to publish your e-book. Again, depending on the app, there will be different options. Some export a file to a Dropbox account. Others allow you to e-mail a copy of the file or export directly to online bookstores. If possible, share a link to your e-book via Twitter.

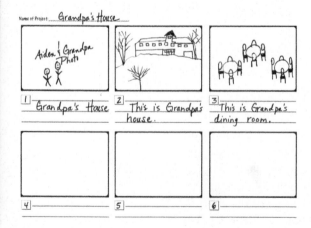

Jeremy Brueck

Learning About the Relationships Between Speech and Print

■ **Provide instruction for beginning readers and writers.**

Children must be able to figure out what spoken language and written language have in common. Without learning the relationship between speech and print, the beginner will never make sense of reading or achieve independence in it; children need to know what reading is for. Earlier we suggested that reading often to them, repeating favorite bedtime stories, and providing opportunities to draw, scribble, and interact with print in their immediate environment are some of the ways that children naturally learn to make sense out of reading and its uses. Nevertheless, many five-year-olds enter school with only vague notions of the purpose and nature of reading. They are not yet aware that what is said can be written, that written language is made up of words and sentences, or that reading involves directionality, attending to the spacing between words, punctuation cues, and other conventions of print. There are several ways of going about this important instructional task.

From the beginning of their school experience, children must learn that the value of reading or writing lies in its uses as a tool for communicating, understanding, and enjoying. The classroom should be filled with print to suit specific instructional goals. Print should be evident everywhere in the form of labels for classroom objects, simple messages, rules, directions, and locations where a specific activity takes place, such as a story-reading area or an art center. For example, the class can create a list of rules or directions to show how print can be used to regulate behavior. A joke-of-the-day can be posted to demonstrate how print can be used for entertainment. Classrooms should reflect a living example of written language put to purposeful ends. In Figure 4.7, we outline the uses of written language that should be evident in the environment and provide some examples of each.

Common Core State Standard

CCRA.L.3

Seizing the opportunity to help children recognize the value of reading and writing requires a certain amount of awareness and commitment from the teacher. Savvy teachers watch for opportunities for authentic reading and writing experiences and then take advantage of them.

Figure 4.7 Understanding the Uses of Written Language

Use of Written Language	Definition	Examples
Perpetuating Uses	Shows children how to bridge the gap between time and space through print.	Records and charts of daily activities such as weather charts, classroom helpers, or results from votes or polls conducted in the classroom.
Regulatory, Authoritative-Contractual Uses	Shows children how print can be used to control and direct behavior to establish rules and agreements.	List of classroom rules or directions for lining up for the bus. Contracts or agreements for classroom helper jobs.
Instrumental Uses	Shows children print can be used to express personal needs.	List of items to participate in an activity, such as a list on a chart of what is needed for phys ed class or a field trip.
Diversion Uses	Shows children the value of print as a tool for enjoyment or diversion.	Books with simple language patterns that introduce them to the rhythms of language. Tongue twisters, puns, jokes, and riddles.
Personal Uses	Shows children that written language can be used to express individuality, pride, and awareness of self.	Nametags for their desk or cubby that depicts things about them. An "All about Me" book with personal facts, drawings, or photos.

Learning About Features of Written Language

■ **Assess core language and literacy skills in beginning readers.**

Children's understanding of the relationship between speech and print is a vital first step in learning to read. They become aware of what reading is all about by recognizing the functionality of reading—that the purpose of reading, in its broadest sense, is to communicate ideas. A second step, or stage, is to become aware of the technical features of reading—of print knowledge, such as printed letters, words, sentences, syllables, sounds, punctuation marks, and so on. To understand the technical features of reading, children must develop **linguistic awareness**, the technical terms and labels needed to talk and think about reading.

Young children may not be aware that words are language units. Spoken language, after all, is a steady stream of sounds that flow one into the other. Words and other print conventions (e.g., punctuation marks) were created to better represent spoken language in print and thus facilitate the reading of written language. Have you ever heard a young child recite the alphabet, only to get to *l-m-n-o-p* and instead say, *elomenopee* as if it's a word, not individual letters? For the four-year-old, the six-word written message *Did you visit the fire station?* might sound like one big word—*Didjavisitthefirestation?* Even more difficult concepts for young children to learn are that spoken words are made up of smaller sounds (phonemes), that written words are made up of letters, and that in a written word, there is a close approximation between letters and sounds.

If children are to succeed in reading, they must acquire linguistic awareness and understand the language of reading instruction. They must learn the technical terms and labels that are needed to talk and think about reading and to carry out instructional tasks. What, for example, is the child's concept of "reading"? Of a "word"? Of a "sound"? Does the child confuse "writing" with "drawing" and "letter" with "number" when given a set of directions? Without an awareness of these terms, cognitive confusion in the classroom mounts quickly for the child. The teacher's job is to make explicit what each child knows implicitly about written language.

The technical features of written language are learned gradually by children and are best taught through real reading and reading-like activities and through discussions designed to build concepts and to untangle the confusion that children may have. Within the context of shared-book experiences, language-experience stories, and writing activities, children will develop linguistic sophistication with the technical features of print. These vehicles for instruction not only provide teachers with diagnostic information about children's print awareness but also form the basis for explicit instruction and discussion.

Learning About Letters and Sounds

Children must learn that a word can be separated into sounds and that the segmented or separated sounds can be represented by letters. Such learning involves the beginnings of *phonics*. The smallest sound unit that is identifiable in spoken language is known as a *phone*. Although phones describe all the possible separate speech sounds in language, they are not necessarily represented by the letters of the alphabet. *Phonemes* are the minimal sound units that can be represented in written language. The *alphabetic principle* suggests that letters in the alphabet map to phonemes. Hence the term *phonics* is used to refer to the child's identification of words by their sounds. This process involves the association of speech sounds with letters. In the beginning of reading instruction, key questions that need to be asked are "Is the child able to hear sounds in a word?" and "Is the child able to recognize letters as representing units of sound?"

Children can easily become confused when taught to identify sounds in words or correspond letters to sounds if they have not yet developed a concept of what a word is. Likewise, the level of abstraction in recognizing a word is too difficult for children if they have yet to make any global connection that speech is related to print. This doesn't mean that program goals for learning about letters and sounds are not worthwhile. However, learning letter–sound relationships must be put into perspective and taught to beginners in meaningful contexts and as the need or opportunity arises.

Recognizing Letters

Today's five-year-old undoubtedly brings more letter knowledge to beginning reading instruction than the five-year-old of a half-century ago. Educational television and the large number of computer games and apps for handheld devices are largely responsible for increasing children's letter awareness. However, even with all of the tools available today, some children still enter school with little knowledge or letters or their sounds. A good plan of instruction for teaching the alphabetic principle is to:

- Teach letter–sound relationships explicitly; don't assume that children will just pick it up.
- Provide opportunities for children to practice in meaningful written language contexts.
- Review previously taught relationships often and cumulatively.
- Plan opportunities daily to apply letter–sound relationships to the reading of phonetically spelled words that are familiar in meaning.

There are no set rules that govern how fast or how slow letter–sound relationships should be introduced. Each teacher must consider the group of students for whom the instruction is intended. Further, there is no agreed-upon order for introducing letter–sound relationships. However, most educators agree that those most commonly used should be introduced first so children can to begin reading as soon as possible, so it makes sense to start with high function letters such as *t, s, m, a, p, o*. With just these few letters, children can begin reading words like *sad, pat, top, dot, dad*, and numerous others. Consider the following instructional activities to help children learn letter recognition and discrimination:

- *Alphabet Books.* There are hundreds of alphabet books available today. Use them to have children find certain letters. Compare and contrast the illustrations of the letter in the different books. The children can illustrate their own rendition of the letter, and over time the class can develop its own alphabet book.
- *Environmental Print.* Have children search for the letter on labels of cans and other commercial products (e.g., Special K), and in magazines, newspapers, and other sources of print. Have them cut out the letters and make a letter collage by cutting out the letters they find and gluing them onto a big letter poster.
- *Magnetic Letters.* Use magnetic letters on cookie sheets to allow individual practice with letters. Have children sort letters from a pile and put them on their cookie sheet, or use them to spell simple words from known letters.
- *Use Children's Names.* Teach alphabet letter naming with children's names, since they are highly motivating. Write each child's name on a piece of heavy cardboard. Then write each letter of the child's name on a different clothespin. Have the child pin the clothespin with the corresponding letter in their name onto the cardboard above it, saying each letter as they attach it. Or give a child letter tiles that match the letters in their name and have them put them in order, saying each letter as they do.

Phonological Awareness

Earlier in this chapter we identified phonological awareness, or the ability to hear, recognize, and play with the sounds in language, as one of the essentials for later reading success. This is because children who have well-developed skills in phonological awareness, and more specifically **phonemic awareness**, have an easier time learning to read. A recent study (Cunningham & Carroll, 2015) evidenced a direct connection between phonological awareness and the ability to read accurately, and children with poor phonological awareness skills are at more danger of developing literacy deficits than children with poor language skills.

Phonological awareness is the recognition that sounds in English can be broken down into smaller and smaller parts: sentences, words, rimes, and syllables. Phonological awareness is auditory; students can do most phonological awareness activities with their eyes closed. Phonological awareness can be taught and is important for *all* students. Phonological awareness includes knowing that:

- Sentences can be segmented into words.
- Words can be segmented into syllables.
- Words can be segmented into their individual sounds.
- Words can begin or end with the same sounds.
- The individual sounds of words can be blended together.
- The individual sounds of words can be manipulated (added, deleted, or substituted).

Phonological awareness is a broad term that involves working with the sounds of language at the word, syllable, and phoneme levels; it is an umbrella term that includes rhyming, alliteration, sentence segmenting, syllable blending and segmenting, and phonemic awareness. These skills should be taught, so teachers should start with the larger units (rhymes) and move to smaller units of sounds like blends or individual sounds.

- Rhyming—Matching the ending sounds of words, called rimes, like *hat, cat, bat, rat.*
- Alliteration—Producing groups of words that begin with the same initial sound, like *two tall trees.*
- Sentence segmenting—Understanding sentences are composed of separate words.

The pig is fat.

1 2 3 4

- Syllable blending and segmenting—Blending syllables to make words and segmenting words into syllables help students distinguish distinct units of sounds: /mag/ /net/; /kick/ /ball/.
- Phonemic awareness—This is the most complex phonological skill. It is the ability to segment words into sounds, blend them back together, and manipulate the sounds to make new words:/c/ /a/ /t/; /sh/ /i/ /p/.

Figure 4.8 depicts the phonological awareness continuum.

Phonemic Awareness

Phonemic awareness is an advanced skill in phonological awareness and is the ability to hear and manipulate sounds in spoken words, the understanding that spoken

Figure 4.8 Phonological Awareness Continuum

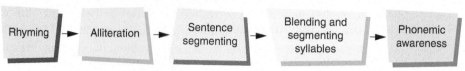

words consist of a sequence of speech sounds, and an awareness of individual sounds (phonemes). Beginning readers must become aware that a word is made up of a series of sounds. Phonemic awareness is important because it plays a causal role in learning to read, primes the reader for print, and helps make sense of phonics instruction. Young children are unaware that the spoken utterance *mat* is a word that is made up of a series of sounds, or phonemes, /m/, /a/, and /t/. The lack of phonemic awareness contributes to children's inability to identify unknown words. If beginners are to benefit from phonics instruction, they must first develop an ability to manipulate sounds in words. Research on early reading acquisition clearly demonstrates that phonemic awareness is a powerful predictor of young children's later reading development (Ehri et al., 2001; Juel, 1988; Schuele & Boudreau, 2008; Torgesen, Wagner, Rashotte, Herron, & Lindamood, 2010).

Why is phonemic awareness such an important ability in learning to read and spell? The orthographic system of the English language is based on the alphabetic principle, so children must have an understanding of how spoken language maps to written language. Phonemic awareness helps a child grasp this understanding. Without phonemic awareness, a child might be able to learn letter–sound relationships by rote but will not understand how to use and coordinate letter–sound knowledge to read or spell new words. As a result, phonemic awareness plays a critical role in the development of skills required in the manipulation of phonemes—namely, phonics and spelling skills.

Several kinds of tasks are involved in phonemic awareness. Children should be able to perform these tasks as a precursor to phonics and spelling instruction.

- *Phoneme isolation.* Children recognize individual sounds in a word. For example, the first sound in *dog* is /d/. This is a simple task of phonemic awareness.
- *Phoneme identity.* This is the recognition of the same sounds in different words, such as *six, sun,* and *sat.* The first sound, /s/, is the same.
- *Phoneme categorization.* This task requires children to recognize a word in a set that doesn't fit or has an odd sound. A teacher might ask, "What word doesn't sound like the others—*dot, big, doll?*"
- *Blending.* A more difficult task involving phonemic awareness requires children to blend a series of orally presented sounds to form a word; for example, given the separate sounds /k/, /a/, /t/, the child says *cat.*
- *Segmenting beginning and ending sounds in words.* Children who have developed the capacity to hear sounds in words are able to perform phonemic awareness tasks that require them to isolate and identify the sound at the beginning or end of a word. A teacher might ask, "What sound do you hear at the beginning of the word *pig?*" or "What sound do you hear at the end of the word *hit?*"
- *Segmenting separate sounds in a word.* This is the most difficult of the phonemic awareness tasks. Children who can segment separate sounds in a word are considered to be phonemically aware.
- *Phoneme deletion, addition, and substitution.* These phoneme manipulation tasks require children to take away or add something to make new words. For example, *stack* without the /s/ is *tack.* If you have *rain* and add a /t/ to it, you have *train.* These types of activities all require children to manipulate sounds in spoken words.

DEVELOPING PHONEMIC AWARENESS IN CHILDREN   Instruction has its greatest impact on phonemic awareness when teachers balance a high level of interaction with print and explicit instruction in various tasks related to manipulating sounds in words. Consider the following practices in the development of a child's phonemic awareness.

Play with Language Through Read-Alouds   Use read-aloud books, nursery rhymes, riddles, songs, and poems that play with language and manipulate sounds in natural and spontaneous ways. Choose language-rich literature such as nursery rhymes, songs, and stories that have playful speech sounds using rhyme, alliteration, assonance, and other forms of phoneme manipulation. In doing so, draw children's attention to the sounds of spoken language and examine language use.

Create Games and Activities to Reinforce and Extend Children's Awareness of Sounds in Words   As children develop a familiarity with the concept of rhyme, make or purchase games that use rhyming words. For example, make a bingo-style board on which children cover pictures that rhyme with those drawn from a bag or a box. Have children clap the number of syllables heard in a name or a word. Use tongue twisters to build awareness of the sounds in beginning letters. Have children say tongue twisters as quickly, and as slowly, as they can. Once children can recite tongue twisters from memory, write them on poster boards. Direct children's attention to the beginning sounds. Have children line up for lunchtime or recess by the beginning sound in their names. For example, say, "Anyone whose name begins with /b/, please line up."

Engage Children in Numerous Occasions to Write   Provide children with many opportunities to experiment with language through writing. Daily writing experiences may be beneficial for children who lack phonemic awareness. The more children write, the better they become at hearing sounds in words as they attempt to invent spelling. As they become more adept at segmenting sounds in words, encourage children to approximate spelling based on the way words sound. Teacher–child interactions should provide as much instructional support as the child needs to approximate the spelling of a word.

Teach Children to Segment Sounds in Words Through Explicit Instruction   Individual children who may be having trouble segmenting sounds in words may benefit most from explicit instruction. *Elkonin boxes,* often called *sound boxes,* are an outstanding **phonemic segmentation** strategy. Because they help fix phoneme–grapheme correspondences in children's minds, Elkonin boxes support children's spelling, reading, and writing development (Moats, 2006). The following procedures can be incorporated into individual or small group instruction once the children are identified as ready for training in phonemic segmentation. To benefit from such instruction, children must have developed strong concepts of print as "talk written down" as well as a concept of "word." Because the initial stages of training in segmenting a word into sounds is totally aural, children need not be aware of letters to profit from this type of instruction. Eventually, children learn to attach letters to sounds that are separated.

1. *Give the child a picture of a familiar object.* A rectangle is divided into squares according to the number of sounds in the name of the object. Remember that a square is required for every sound in a word, not necessarily every letter. For example, if the picture were of a boat, there would be three squares for three sounds:

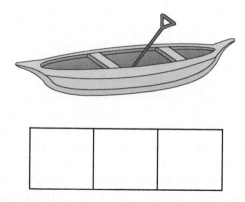

2. *Next, say the word slowly and deliberately, allowing the child to hear the sounds that can be naturally segmented.* It is easier to hear syllables than individual phonemes in a word.

3. *Now ask the child to repeat the word, modeling the way you have said it.*

4. *Continue to model.* As you segment the word into sounds, show the child how to place counters in each square according to the sounds heard sequentially in the word. For example, with the word *boat*, as the teacher articulates each sound, a counter is placed in a square:

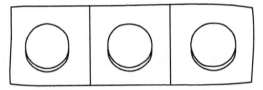

5. *Walk the child through the procedure by attempting it together several times.*

6. *Show another picture and then the word.* Ask the child to pronounce the word and separate the sounds by placing the counters in the squares. The teacher may have to continue modeling until the child catches on to the task.

7. *Phase out the picture stimulus and the use of counters and squares.* Eventually, the child is asked to analyze words aurally without teacher assistance.

In time, the teacher should combine phonemic segmentation with letter association. As the child pronounces a word, letters and letter patterns can be used instead of counters in the squares. The child can be asked, "What letters do you think go in each of the squares?" At first, the letters can be written in for the child. Clay (1985) suggests that the teacher accept any correct letter–sound relationship the child gives and write it in the correct position as the child watches. She also recommends that the teacher prompt the child with questions such as "What do you hear in the beginning?" "In the middle?" "At the end?" and "What else do you hear?"

Hearing sounds in words is no easy reading task for young children. As we suggested earlier, helping children sound out words may be premature if they are not yet phonemically aware. That is why it is important to assess children's ability to manipulate sounds in words.

> In this **video** (www.youtube.com/watch?v=dTf5gxF8-Sw), three activities for reinforcing phonemic segmentation are demonstrated. How does the teacher incorporate blending into each of these activities, and why is that important?

Check Your Understanding 4.3: Gauge your understanding of the skills and concepts in this section.

Assessing Language and Literacy in Young Children

2017 ILA Standards

3.1, 3.2, 3.3, 3.4

Effective teachers use multiple forms of assessment to find out what children know and can do. In fact, teachers can use **observation** to assess many of children's emerging literacy accomplishments. With young children, it is best to use ongoing informal assessments that monitor progress in the areas known to predict later reading success. For example, as you interact with children, observe children's print knowledge by noting if children are able to point to words as you read them, thereby demonstrating knowledge of directional patterns of print. Can they circle a word and letter in the book? In this section, we revisit the core skills children need and recommend assessments.

Assessing Print Knowledge

Marie Clay (1979) developed the *Concepts about Print Test* to assess children's print awareness, such as how print and books work. This assessment is individually administered to a child. To administer this widely used test, the teacher usually engages the child in a conversation and asks the child whether he or she will help in the reading of a story. The teacher then proceeds to assess the child's concepts of print as they read the book together. For example, the teacher might say, "I'm going to read a story to you. Can you show me the front of the book so that I can get started?" or, once the book is opened, "Where should I start reading?" The child's responses reveal the knowledge of print he or she possesses. Use Figure 4.9 as a guide for evaluating concepts about print. It lists the types of reading-related and linguistics concepts teachers should follow as they assess print concepts.

Assessing Alphabet Knowledge

Alphabet knowledge is important because it is a predictor of success in early reading. To assess alphabet knowledge, you need a set of lowercase letters and a set of uppercase letters as well as a checklist similar to the one in Figure 4.10.

Figure 4.9 Assessing Concepts of Print

Print Concept	Child's Task
Front of book	Identifies the front of the book
Difference between a picture and a page of print	Identifies a page of text (and not the picture on the opposite page) as the place to begin reading
Left-to-right directionality	Identifies the direction of reading as a left-to-right process
Return sweep	Identifies the return sweep as the appropriate reading behavior at the end of a line
Word pointing	Points out words as a teacher reads a line of print slowly
Beginning and end	Identifies the first and last parts of a story, page, line, or word
Bottom of a picture	Identifies the bottom of a picture that is inverted (upside down) on a page
Inverted page of print	Identifies the appropriate place to begin, left-to-right direction, and return sweep
Line order	Identifies line sequence as the correct answer when asked, "What's wrong with this?" (The teacher reads a printed sentence in which the line sequence is jumbled.) *Example:* and began to swim. I jumped into the water
Left page begins a text	Identifies the left page as place to begin reading when two pages of text are side by side
Word order	Identifies word order as the correct answer when asked, "What's wrong with this?" (The teacher reads a printed sentence in which the word order is distorted.) *Example:* I looked and looked I but could not find the cat.
Letter order	Identifies that the letters in simple words are not sequenced properly when the teacher reads, as if correct, a text in which the letters of the words are out of order. *Example:* The dgo chased teh cat thsi way and thta way. The cta ran pu a tree.

1. Ask the child to identify the uppercase letters one at a time: "What letter is this?"
2. Do the same procedure for the lowercase letters, one letter at a time.
3. Place an X next to the letters the child identifies correctly. You might use a dash if the child incorrectly identifies the letter.

For an assessment of letters and their associated sounds, use a chart such as the one in Figure 4.11 periodically to determine letter and sound knowledge.

Assessing Phonological Awareness and Phonemic Awareness

Children who have well-developed skills in phonological awareness—the ability to hear, recognize, and play with the sounds in our language—have an easier time learning to read. Remember, phonological awareness is an auditory skill; students can do most phonological awareness activities with their eyes closed. Phonological awareness includes knowing that:

- Sentences can be segmented into words.
- Words can be segmented into syllables.
- Words can be segmented into their individual sounds.
- Words can begin or end with the same sounds.
- The individual sounds of words can be blended together.
- The individual sounds of words can be manipulated (added, deleted, or substituted).

The assessment in Figure 4.12 is often used in kindergarten classrooms to assess students' knowledge of the individual components of phonological awareness.

Figure 4.10 Alphabet Knowledge Checklist

Child's Name _____ Date _____

X if Correct	– if Incorrect	Comments
A	a	
B	b	
C	c	
D	d	
E	e	
F	f	
G	g	
H	h	
I	i	
J	j	
K	k	
L	l	
M	m	
N	n	
O	o	
P	p	
Q	q	
R	r	
S	s	
T	t	
U	u	
V	v	
W	w	
X	x	
Y	y	
Z	z	

In this **video** (www.youtube.com/watch?v=5C4tFlmv04M), you will watch a teacher assess a kindergarten child on several early literacy competencies, such as alphabet knowledge, letter–sound knowledge, and phonological awareness, similar to the assessments introduced in this section. How do you suppose the teacher will use the results of the assessment to plan effective, individualized instruction?

Instructional Decision Making 4.1: Apply your understanding of the concepts in this section.

Figure 4.11 Letter and Letter-Sound Knowledge

Letter	Can the child *name* the letter?	Can the child *make the sound* of the letter?	Does the child know words that start with the sound the letter makes?	Can the child identify the letters in print?
B				
A				
S				

Figure 4.12 Assessment of Phonological Awareness

#1 Word Awareness

Example: Tell the student that he/she will repeat what you say. Say, "I like kittens." Student repeats. Now tell the student, "You are going to count the words in the sentence, like this, 'I like kittens.'" (Model using counters. Push one counter for each word.) "There are three words. Now you try it." Have student count words.

Sentence	Student Response	Points
See the big dog. (4)	Able to Repeat? Y N Able to Count? Y N	2 1 0
I saw a little girl/boy. (5)	Able to Repeat? Y N Able to Count? Y N	2 1 0
Look at the moon. (4)	Able to Repeat? Y N Able to Count? Y N	2 1 0
I like to eat pizza. (5)	Able to Repeat? Y N Able to Count? Y N	2 1 0
		Total ____/8

#2 Rhyming

Example: "Tell me a word that rhymes with pig" (nonsense words are okay). "Now tell me a word that rhymes with…"

Words	Student Response	Points
pat		1 0 NR
tug		1 0 NR
hen		1 0 NR
sit		1 0 NR
		Total ___/4

#3 Syllable Awareness

Say, "Listen for each syllable or word part you hear in the word *sunflower*. How many syllables or word parts did you hear?" Demonstrate with clapping or tapping if necessary. "Listen to each word, and tell me how many syllables or word parts you hear."

Words	Student Response	Points
calendar (2)		1 0 NR
boat (1)		1 0 NR
computer (3)		1 0 NR
caterpillar (4)		1 0 NR
hopping (2)		1 0 NR
		Total ___/5

#4 Blending (Phonemic Awareness)

Say, "I'm going to put the beginning, middle, and ending sounds together: d/o/g = dog. Now you try it."

Words	Student Response	Points
m/a/t		1 0 NR
c/a/n		1 0 NR
b/i/t		1 0 NR
c/u/p		1 0 NR
s/i/t		1 0 NR
		Total ___/5

#5 Isolate and Pronounce Initial, Medial Vowel, and Final Sounds (Phonemic Awareness)

Say, "I am going to say a word: cat. c/a/t. I hear /c/ in the beginning, /a/ in the middle, /t/ in the end. Now you try it. Make sure to say the sounds, not the letters, like I did: c/a/t." (Circle the sounds the student can isolate and pronounce. One point for each correct sound.)

Words	Student Response	Points
man	m / a / n	3 2 1 0 NR
pet	p / e / t	3 2 1 0 NR
top	t / o / p	3 2 1 0 NR
cup	c / u / p	3 2 1 0 NR
chum	ch/u/m	3 2 1 0 NR
sheep	sh/ee/p	3 2 1 0 NR
		Total ___/18

Figure 4.13 Spellings by Three Kindergartners

Word	Monica's Spelling	Tesscha's Spelling	James's Spelling
monster	monstr	mtr	aml
united	unintid	nnt	em3321
dressing	dresing	jrasm	8emaaps
bottom	bodm	bodm	19nhm
hiked	hikt	hot	sanh
human	humin	hmn	menena

Assessing Developmental Writing

One of the first indications that children can analyze speech sounds and use knowledge about letters is when they invent their own spellings during writing. Invented spellings are a sure sign that children are beginning to be conscious of sounds in words, an essential early literacy skill.

Figure 4.13 records invented spellings from several samples of writing from three kindergartners, Monica, Tesscha, and James. Their spellings reflect varying levels of sophistication in hearing sounds in words and in corresponding letters to those sounds.

Monica's developmental writing demonstrates the most phonemic awareness, and James the least. Remember, phonemic awareness refers to an insight about oral language and the ability to segment and manipulate the sounds of speech. A perusal of Monica's list of words indicates that she has learned to distinguish sounds in sequence and can correspond letters directly to the surface sounds that she hears. Tesscha has also developed an awareness of sounds and letters, though not to the same extent as Monica. James is the least ready of the three to benefit from letter–sound instruction. For James (and other children at a similar level of development), analyzing sounds in words and attaching letters to those sounds is beyond present conceptual reach. Making initial reading tasks too abstract or removed from what James already knows about print will not help him progress in reading.

Check Your Understanding 4.4: Gauge your understanding of the skills and concepts in this section.

RTI for Struggling Readers

Response to Intervention and Our Youngest Learners

In this chapter, we emphasized that authentic beginnings are important for emerging readers, and we highlighted the important role the family plays in the early literacy development of all children. Additionally, we recognized that children come to school with varying experiences with print and stories. Some children, for example, come from home environments in which English is not the primary language; some may come from homes in which interactions with print are not evident; and some may not come from environments in which they are exposed to the joys of reading. A variety of factors such as these can place children at high risk for struggling with reading because they do not bring a schema for literacy learning that recognizes reading as an emergent, developing process.

An RTI process provides extra help at increasing levels of intensity depending on how much progress students are making, and can be used at any level, including preschool and kindergarten. The report *Roadmap to Pre-K RTI: Applying Response to Intervention in Preschool Settings*, available from www.rtinetwork.org (http://www.rtinetwork.org), provides early childhood experts, policy makers, advocates, and others an explanation of how the essential components of RTI—universal screening and progress-monitoring with research-based, tiered interventions—can be applied in preschool settings. In the document, parents are encouraged to get involved early on, because they are essential to the success of their children. Further, parents know their child's strengths and needs within the wider context of home, neighborhood, and community—all important for planning and providing appropriate supports. We encourage educators to help parents understand and get involved in the RTI process within their setting.

What About . . .

Standards, Assessment, and Beginning Readers and Writers?

Teachers are constantly assessing to inform their instruction. Assessing informally is not only an effective way to monitor beginners' progress but also a worthwhile way to gather information for planning future instruction. Ongoing, informal assessments can help teachers understand student progress in relation to the CCSS. For example, when teachers use a poem on a chart for a reading aloud, they have the opportunity to observe children and evaluate them. They might notice whether a child is participating, or if the child is able to predict a rhyming word or show where a word begins and ends if called upon to do so. Assessments inform teachers' ongoing efforts to help students reach the new standards and keep them on track for college and career readiness. Teachers need to assess students in relation to their ability to meet the standards before they can plan effective instruction. Examples of assessments for beginning readers include teacher observations, checklists, writing samples, story dictation, and rubrics.

Rigorous common assessments have been designed to match the CCSS beginning in grade 3. However, to help teachers measure student knowledge in the lower grades, an array of assessment resources has been developed that is also aligned to the Common Core. Teachers, school districts, and states have all created various grade-appropriate checklists, classroom activities, and rubrics that reflect foundational aspects of the CCSS. The K through 2 formative assessment tools aim to help create a foundation for students and put them on the track to college and career readiness from the start.

Summary

- Children progress through phases in literacy development, so it is crucial for them to be exposed to appropriate literacy experiences in order to acquire knowledge about written and oral language long before they go to school. Literacy learning starts early and persists throughout life; oral language is the foundation for literacy development.

- Beginning readers benefit from literate environments both at home and at school. Exploration with print should be home-centered, play-centered, and language-centered. Reading to children, sharing books, and

- assisting with reading are among the activities that nurture the development of young readers and writers.

- Storybooks, nonfiction books, big books, e-books, and class-made books are among the various ways teachers use books in the classroom to provide instruction for beginning readers in authentic ways.

- Informal assessment tools are available to teachers to assist in gauging the literacy development of young children.

Teacher Action Research

Literacy is a developmental process that begins in infancy. Parents, caregivers, and teachers of young children all play a crucial role in their development by creating a literate environment, reading to them, answering questions, and modeling literate behaviors. Try some of the following action research ideas to learn more about supporting our youngest readers and writers for later success.

1. Collect some writing samples from children ages zero through six. Put them in order from less to more sophisticated using the developmental writing stages presented in this chapter. Write a short description of the sample, noting what you observe about each.

2. Visit a classroom, and notice the way the teacher uses print to help children understand how written language works. Is print evident everywhere in the classroom? Are labels, simple messages, rules, and directions present in the environment? If allowed, take digital photos of print in the room. Evaluate the purpose of print using the section of this chapter called Understanding the Uses of Written Language.

3. Using books is likely the best way to teach essential early literacy skills, but there are many resources such as songs and apps that enhance early literacy learning. Search the Internet and visit your local library to learn about books, songs, rhymes, apps, and other materials to teach literacy. Make an annotated bibliography of these materials.

4. Administer one of the assessments in this chapter on letter knowledge, concepts of print, or phonological awareness. Based on the analysis of the assessment, what do you determine are the strengths and needs of the student? What would be your next steps as a teacher?

Through the Lens of the Common Core

In this chapter, we demonstrated the many ways critical literacy skills for beginners could be nurtured using authentic text and experiences in the classroom. Children can learn how books work, concepts of print, phonemic awareness, alphabet knowledge, and many other concepts by the efforts of a knowledgeable teacher who makes reading and interacting with print part of the daily routine. Virtually any CCSS can be taught within a print-rich environment. Try it out! Choose a piece of informational text to share with beginning readers. Go to the **Common Core Standards**. Study the CCSS for kindergarteners or first graders. What associated standards could you teach using the piece of informational text you selected? How will you go about this? Plan a lesson incorporating some of the CCSS and, if possible, try it out with a young child.

Teachers of young children need to ask three questions that underlie instruction and assessment in an early literacy program: (1) What do children already know about print? (2) What reading behaviors and interests do children already exhibit? and (3) What do children need to learn? Once these questions are answered, teachers can plan literacy instruction for children that will meet their individual needs in a nurturing, print-rich environment in both large and small group settings. When effective teachers provide opportunities for children to engage in meaningful literacy activities through interaction with adults and peers, and some explicit instruction, children are well on their way to becoming conventional readers and writers.

Chapter 5
Assessing Reading Performance

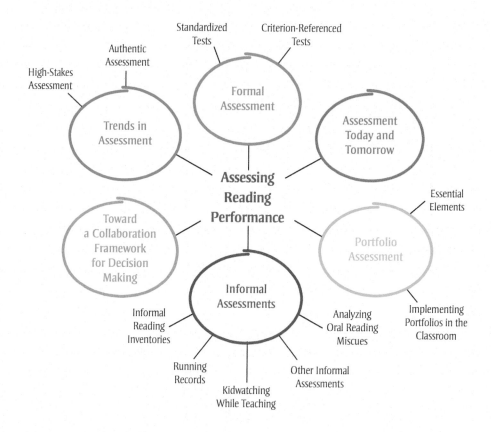

Learning Outcomes

In This Chapter, You Will Discover How to:

- Rationalize the importance of utilizing multiple assessment indicators.

- Compare the perspectives that support the use of high-stakes testing to the use of authentic assessments.

- Justify the purposes of utilizing formal testing for literacy assessment.

- Explain the commonalities between various informal assessments.

- Discuss the essential components of portfolio assessment as well as how to manage the portfolio process.

- Reflect upon how literacy assessment has changed over the years and will continue to do so.

Activating Your Schema

Do you consider yourself a good reader? How do you know? How did your teachers know whether you were or not? Think about the various ways your teachers assessed your reading skills in primary school. What about middle school? High school? Which ways positively affected you? Negatively?

Think about your experiences with standardized assessments. Have your thoughts changed over time? How will your experiences influence the assessment process you plan to implement in your classroom?

2017 ILA Standards Found in This Chapter

1.1	3.2	3.4	6.3
3.1	3.3	4.1	

Key Terms

anecdotal notes

authentic assessment

checklist

criterion-referenced tests

Developmental Reading Assessment (DRA)

diagnostic test

digital portfolio

Dynamic Indicators of Basic Early Literacy Skills (DIBELS)

formative assessment

high-stakes testing

informal assessment

informal reading inventory (IRI)

interviewing

kidwatching

miscue analysis

norms

portfolio

progress monitoring

reliability

retelling

running record

self-assessment

standardized reading test

survey test

validity

words correct per minute (WCPM)

It was springtime, and Ally Shultz smiled as she looked through a folder with assessment information on John, a "low" reader in her third-grade classroom. How her assessment of him had changed between early fall and now! She noted that on a *formal,* standardized reading test, given in October, John had scored in the 32nd percentile, which meant that he was below average in comparison to other third graders. Although she did not think this score was particularly useful to her in deciding how to work with John, Ms. Shultz knew that her principal examined these scores. She also noted that on a more *informal* assessment related to his attitude toward reading, John viewed himself positively. He also did well on a section from another informal reading assessment in which he picked questions from a list that he thought would help a person understand the important ideas about a selection. This reminded her of yesterday's social studies lesson on explorers. John and other students had raised some insightful questions as the class previewed the chapter, and created a list of questions that might be answered as they worked on the chapter.

At the start of the school year, Ms. Shultz had decided to work with John in a second-grade basal reader, along with four other students. Initially, her decision was based on a conversation with John's second-grade teacher and her review of the *skill mastery tests* administered as part of the basal reader program. One of these tests assessed students' ability to associate the hard and soft sounds of the letter *g*. John didn't reach mastery of this particular skill. In other words, he didn't score correctly on 80 percent of the items related to the skill objective; in fact, he answered only six out of ten items correctly. This puzzled Ms. Shultz, because just the day before, John had shared a part of a book he was reading about an animal sanctuary, which included seeing monkeys, *giraffes*, and *goats*. John didn't experience difficulty reading passages containing words with soft and hard *g* sounds. Later in October, she had a *miscue analysis* compiled from a *running record* of John's oral reading during small group instruction. She had noted no difficulties in his reading of either soft or hard sounds.

Ms. Shultz decided back then to capitalize on John's strength of raising questions about material read both in his reading group and in social studies and science units. She decided *not* to use additional instructional time working on the soft and hard sounds of *g*, even though he had not achieved mastery for this objective on the basal reader test. In fact, in November she thought that John was functioning well enough in the second-grade basal reader to reassign him to the third-grade reader. The bottom line is that Ms. Shultz considered information from informal and formal tests *and* her observations of John in actual reading situations. She then made decisions based on *multiple data sources.* Corroborating her instructional decisions was John's *portfolio* of work in progress: some stories and poems he was working on in response to their literature theme unit on tall tales and his personal reading list for sustained silent reading. By using examples of John's actual reading and actual writing, Ally Shultz had made an *authentic assessment* of John's *performance in literacy*—a reason to smile.

We know that good teachers have a comprehensive reading program that is guided by the assessment process. Through the use of formal and informal assessments, teachers learn about their students and the impact of the instructional program. Assessment, therefore, is an integral part of teaching and learning.

2017 ILA Standard

3.2

As depicted in the chapter overview, we support making instructional decisions using multiple ways to assess authentically the *processes* students are engaged in as they read and learn. Formative assessment *and* teaching allow teachers to gather information in order to make inferences about a student's reading ability and performance. Tests provide one perspective for becoming knowledgeable about a student's performance; actual teaching situations provide another perspective; and portfolios of student work provide still another.

Toward a Collaborative Framework for Decision Making

■ **Rationalize the importance of utilizing multiple assessment indicators.**

The process Ally Shultz used to develop an authentic assessment of John is another example of how teachers screen and filter information about students' performance through their concepts and beliefs about reading and learning to read. Ms. Shultz holds an interactive view of the reading process. She believes that reading acquisition involves coordinating and integrating many skills during actual reading situations. A child learns to read the way Ms. Shultz first learned to use a stick shift in a car with manual transmission. What she needed to learn was how to coordinate the use of the clutch pedal, gas pedal, brake, and stick in shifting from gear to gear. A beginner may practice pushing the clutch pedal in and out in an isolated drill, or simulate shifting from gear to gear. However, actually experiencing stick-shifting in traffic makes the difference in learning how to coordinate and integrate the skills.

And so it is with John in his learning to become a fluent reader. When contrasting his performance on the test with his performance in a real reading situation, Ms. Shultz chose to weigh the information from the teaching situation more heavily than the score on the test. Because her students keep portfolios of their work in reading and writing, they, too, understand their progress in literacy and are learning to evaluate their own strengths and weaknesses in various reading and writing tasks. Portfolios also helped Ms. Shultz plan the kinds of instruction that would move her students toward more mature reading and writing. The student portfolios, works in progress in literacy, are a record of the process of learning in reading and writing for each student. They contain valuable data about growth and progress in literacy performance, and, where weaknesses exist, they are useful in planning the instructional next step. Portfolios have become an important aspect of authentic assessment of literacy performance.

Assessment in reading involves understanding and appreciating *how* children interact with print in authentic reading situations and *why*. "To be authentic, the texts the students read need to relate to things that are interesting and real—that are meaningful for the student" (Farr & Tone, 1998, p. 19). Being authentic is important because data from the assessment process affect teaching and learning.

We advocate using *multiple indicators* of student performance for assessment. Based on the *Standards for the Assessment of Reading and Writing* (2010), multiple perspectives and sources of data are essential in the assessment process. Any single indicator—whether it involves commercially prepared or teacher-made tests or observation—provides a perspective, one means of attesting to the accuracy of the score or phenomenon under examination. Multiple indicators, however, build a *corroborative framework* that strengthens decision making. As teachers we must constantly make decisions. Multiple indicators of reading strengthen our decision making as information from one data source builds on or contrasts with information from other data sources. The result is a rich knowledge base for understanding how and why students perform in reading.

2017 ILA Standards

1.1, 3.1

Because reading takes place in the mind, the process is not directly observable and therefore not directly measurable. Yet one of the important functions of reading assessments, whether formal or informal, should be to help teachers understand a human process that is essentially hidden from direct examination. What are the latest trends and legislation that assist in or direct this assessment process? To what extent do standardized, criterion-referenced, informal, or teacher-made tests play a constructive role in the classroom?

How do teachers keep a running record of performance-based assessments in their classrooms? Finally, how can the process of portfolio assessment involve parents, teachers, students, and administrators in communication about the growth students are making in reading, writing, and language?

Check Your Understanding 5.1: Gauge your understanding of the skills and concepts in this section.

Trends in Assessment

■ **Compare the perspectives that support the use of high-stakes testing to the use of authentic assessments.**

Discontent among the public and within the field of education over the state of assessment has reached a fever pitch. Legislative decisions and funding opportunities impact assessment processes, as noted in Figure 5.1. Requirements for specific forms of assessment systems and accountability plans in order to assess literacy development are included. On the one hand, the public wants assurances that students will

Figure 5.1 Legislative Influences on Literacy Assessment

Every Student Succeeds Act (ESSA)—The 2015 reauthorization of the *Elementary and Secondary Education Act (ESEA)* required that states utilize state assessment systems and accountability plans in the areas of reading and mathematics in grades 3–8 and once in high school. It focused on the use of quality assessments for all students no matter their diverse background and reducing reliance on standardized assessments. The assessment data gathered must be broken into subgroups of students, such as English language learners (ELLs), students in special education, racial minorities, and those in poverty. States are responsible for holding schools and districts accountable.

The Individuals with Disabilities Education Improvement Act (IDEIA) of 2004—Response to intervention (RTI) was derived to provide intensive support and intervention. It requires the utilization of assessments to screen, diagnose, and monitor intervention of students' progress. Additionally, assessment results are used to plan and direct literacy instruction.

Literacy Education for All, Results for the Nation Act (LEARN)—This bill requires utilizing diagnostic, formative, and summative assessments to improve instruction and student learning at all age levels.

leave school well prepared to enter the workforce or embark on postsecondary education. On the other, educators are calling for better, more authentic assessment practices that reunite goals for learning with classroom instruction and assessment. These trends are nearly opposites. As Tierney (1998) explains it, there are two different orientations: one focuses on "something you *do to* students," and the other focuses on "something you *do with* them or help them *do for themselves*" (p. 378). Assessment, therefore, needs to provide information for public accountability as well as instructional decision making.

2017 ILA Standards

3.3, 3.4, 6.3

High-Stakes Testing

Today's standards-based education system relies on high-stakes testing. As a result of the *Every Student Succeeds Act* (2015), states are responsible for submitting accountability plans to the U.S. Education Department. These plans must address proficiency on tests, closing gaps in achievement, and other indicators such as graduation rates and English language proficiency. States require the administration of reading and mathematics standardized assessments and mandated reading tests that are considered high stakes. The premise of **high-stakes testing** is that consequences, whether good or bad, including promotion or retention decisions, are linked to test performance. Referred to as *proficiency tests* in the 1990s, high-stakes tests are known today as *achievement and graduation tests*. High-stakes testing is intended to provide the public with a guarantee that students can perform at a level necessary to function in society and in the workforce. Of course, there are no guarantees in life itself, let alone on any test, especially a test based on a one-time performance. High-stakes testing can provide information about program evaluation, but it cannot provide information to help with instructional decision making and learning opportunities for all students (Flippo, 2014).

2017 ILA Standards

3.3, 3.4, 6.3

Nevertheless, this trend is increasing. Johnston and Costello (2005) report that the "United States has currently reached the highest volume of testing and the highest stakes testing in its history" (p. 265). With this increase in standardized testing, Afflerbach (2004) expressed his concern with the use of high-stakes testing because of the lack of research linking the use of standardized assessments to increased reading achievement. The International Literacy Association (ILA) opposes high-stakes testing and high-stakes decisions based on single test scores. As emphasized in their position statement *Using High-Stakes Assessment for Grade Retention and Graduation Decisions (2014)*, high-stakes tests "do not provide a complete picture of students' literacy knowledge and accomplishments and should not be used to make decisions about students' grade retention or high school graduation" (ILA 2014, p. 5). Assessments should be relied on to improve instruction and benefit the students and not to punish schools or students.

Compounding this demand for more standardized testing is the problem that the tests themselves are not adequate, given what we now know about literacy. Children's abilities, prior educational experiences, interests, and knowledge influence how a child approaches reading and the reading task. Other learning dimensions include language diversity; family and cultural experiences; and motivation, aspirations, and goals (Flippo, 2014). Expecting all students at the same chronological age level to perform the same way and have the same skills is unrealistic. Students' performances vary considerably from task to task as well as student to student (Afflerbach, 2004). This inconsistency is especially true for English language learners.

Literacy assessment for English language learners is often seen as inequitable (Garcia & Beltran, 2003; Jimenez, 2004). Garcia and Beltran (2003) explain that the problem for ELLs with most standardized assessments is that the assessments compare the development of content for ELLs with the same standards as native English speakers. Standardized assessments also typically assess one's English ability rather than ability to utilize the various skills and strategies needed to create meaning. Therefore, the result is that ELLs score below grade level. A more appropriate means of assessment, such as the supplemental use of authentic assessments and adjusting assessments to the student's English proficiency, will provide a more complete perspective of an ELL's abilities. Utilizing multiple assessments to guide the instructional process is essential.

2017 ILA Standards

3.1, 4.1

What are some of the effects of this trend toward standard setting and high-stakes testing? Reliance on high-stakes assessment (in which students, teachers, and school districts are held accountable on the basis of their performance) eliminates the opportunity to track a student's progress in literacy as an individual. Instead, comparisons are made between groups of students, schools, and even school districts based on sets of state and national *standards* for performance in subject areas. In numerous states, newspapers publish "report cards" for school districts, and then rank them according to scores attained by their pupils on achievement tests, with special attention to the overall percentage passing. This in turn spawns the practice of "rewarding" districts that have higher rates of passing with awards and increased financial subsidies and "punishing" districts that have lower rates of passing with sanctions and decreased subsidies.

Another effect of this trend toward high-stakes testing is its impact on classroom life. Teachers are questioning their professional beliefs and abilities as well as instructional creativity when faced with the pressures of high-stakes testing (Bomer, 2005). The time spent preparing students to take these tests has actually replaced time that would normally be spent on teaching and learning activities. Likewise, the content of the curriculum itself is being examined for its "fit" with the content of the exams. School district personnel are at work trying to align the various subject matter curricula with the areas assessed by the standardized tests. Is this the best and most efficient way for teachers and administrators to spend their time and use their talent? And is this reallocation of classroom time in the best interests of students and their learning?

2017 ILA Standards

3.3, 3.4

> ▶ In this **video** (https://www.youtube.com/watch?v=_L-320WWIWg), Sydney Smoot, a nine-year-old fourth grader in Hernando County, Fla., delivered a speech about Florida's new standardized test, the Florida Standards Assessment. She says that a test does not measure her abilities and is stressful for no good reason. How do you think other students feel? What can teachers and administrators do?

Perhaps an even better question to consider is what kinds of assessment are most useful for providing students with the best possible instruction. If, for instance, high-stakes test scores were no longer an issue, what kinds of assessments would be effective and efficient? For countless teachers, the answers to this and similar questions are not found in their districts' report cards; they are unfolding as teachers become more involved in the assessment process.

Authentic Assessment

The second major trend in assessment is a movement in which teachers are exercising their empowerment as they recapture the vital role they know well—making and sharing decisions about instruction and assessment. What do we mean by *authentic*? Several criteria connote **authentic assessment**, as described by Farr and Tone (1998, pp. 18–19): Students are doing reading and writing tasks that look like real-life tasks, and students are primarily in control of the reading or writing tasks. These two criteria then lead to a third: Students develop ownership, engage thoughtfully, and learn to assess themselves. Classroom assessment of reading must be valid and reliable so the meaning constructed from the information gathered from the assessment process is fair, accurate, and useful (Afflerbach & Cho, 2011). This can be seen in the **Straight from the Classroom narrative** as well as the **Straight from the Classroom sample rubric to evaluate a narrative retelling** shared by Mrs. Capel, a former kindergarten teacher. She assesses in-depth knowledge of story **retelling**. As noted in the sample rubric, Mrs. Capel goes beyond assessing the simple sequence of the story to include understanding the story and characterization. With a clear rubric, students can utilize the assessment tool to assess themselves, which helps to make the assessment authentic.

Authentic assessment of literacy—determining exactly what students can and can't do in real-life reading and writing—is one of the major trends in assessment.

Annie Pickert Fuller/Pearson Education

Today's teachers want to know more about factors that contribute to their students' literacy achievement (products) and about how the students themselves think about their reading and writing (process). Some teachers strive for more authenticity in *performance-based assessment* by "requiring knowledge and problem-solving abilities" representative of real-world purposes (Leslie & Jett-Simpson, 1997, p. 4).

Teachers have many expectations for assessment. Information gathered should be useful in planning classroom instruction and guiding students to become reflective in order to help them assess their own strengths and weaknesses. Such assessment becomes **formative assessment** when the information gathered is used to adapt instruction to meet students' needs (Black, Harrison, Lee, Marshall, & Wiliam, 2004; Walker, 2008). Students demonstrate literacy growth by completing everyday tasks and activities. Participating in group projects and reader's theatre, taking teacher-made tests, and sharing reading and writing are all formative assessments (International Reading Association, 2013). Teachers use focused observations and anecdotal notes, as well as student work samples, to document student learning. Formative assessment involves noticing details of literate behavior, interpreting students' understanding and perspective, and knowing what the reader knows (Johnston & Costello, 2005). It is purposeful, collaborative, dynamic, and descriptive, and contributes to improvement in teaching and learning (McLaughlin & Overturf, 2013a, 2013b).

2017 ILA Standards

3.1, 3.2

Teachers need to be able to diagnose reading and writing problems and monitor the progress of each student, often referred to as **progress monitoring**. Progress monitoring is usually completed in a regular, preplanned schedule to evaluate rate of progress. This process helps to measure student performance, as well as improvement or responsiveness to instruction. It can help to document reading growth for the Response to Intervention (RTI) process, and it especially helps to identify the specific learning needs of all readers, including those who have difficulties with English learning.

> In this video (https://www.youtube.com/watch?v=zHFrvnHzzdU), you will learn what reading assessment should be like. Throughout the animated presentation you will learn do's and don'ts regarding effective reading assessment. What do's and don'ts have you seen? What additional do's and don'ts should be added to the lists?

Instructional Decision Making 5.1: Apply your understanding of the concepts in this section.

Authentic assessment also helps readers to think about their own learning and to use **self-assessment** strategies. "Student self-assessments are a process-driven evaluation system where students have the ability to use assessments to change their behaviors, set goals, and redirect their learning efforts" (Turner & Hoeltzel, 2011, p. 330). Chappuis (2005) believes students learn to answer such questions as "Where am I going?" "Where am I now?" and "How can I close the gap?" (pp. 40–42). These questions lay the foundation for students to identify their strengths and weaknesses and help provide a plan for intervention. Having students take an active role in the assessment process broadens the view of literacy development.

As teachers learn more about the developmental nature of reading and writing acquisition, they are likely to want more tools that authentically assess. They will seek ways to collect performance samples (both informally and formally produced), observation techniques, anecdotal records, checklists, interviews, conferences and conversations with students, writing folders, and portfolios. The use of technology can facilitate the assessment process. A middle school teacher who teaches Spanish has her students record messages on smartphones or iPads and send the recordings as a voice memos. She then goes to iTunes to listen to and assess the recordings. This saves her time in the classroom for instruction. She believes that it is really easy, that all students know how to do it, and that the files produced are small and easily saved.

2017 ILA Standard

3.1

Recording ELLs is especially important to help document language development and use. A variety of authentic assessments are easily integrated into the classroom. Although teachers will continue to be required to administer standardized tests and assign letter grades, they can confidently rely on their professional beliefs and abilities to meet their students' literacy needs.

Technology in Assessment

Assessment is multidimensional and multifaceted in order to assess the wide variety of literacy skills readers possess. As discussed earlier, high-stakes assessment is based on a static definition of literacy that does not include transliteracies. Assessment needs to be dynamic and formative to assess all skills and strategies that students utilize in order to construct meaning. Formative assessment needs to go beyond assessing individual work. It includes how students learn technology literacies and how they learn technology literacies from others, as well as how they communicate and collaborate with each other in order to construct meaning. Digital formative assessments can be used to gather this information. A few digital tools are shared by Jeremy Brueck in Box 5.1.

2017 ILA Standard

3.1

Check Your Understanding 5.2: Gauge your understanding of the skills and concepts in this section.

BOX 5.1

Digital Tools for Formative Assessment

Formative assessment is one of the most important strategies teachers use to check student understanding and plan future instruction. When used as checkpoints of understanding on a student's learning path, formative assessment shows where students need more help and allows teachers to effectively understand what students have and have not learned.

Most teachers are comfortable implementing formative assessment in their classrooms through the use of surveys, polls, asking questions, and writing assignments. However, with the growth of the web and explosion of mobile devices in schools, a new crop of digital formative assessment tools are available for teachers to add to their repertoire. Many of these tools are highly engaging for students, offering interactive content, game-like play, and real-time feedback for teachers. Using digital tools to frequently assess student mastery of standards also helps save time, since they provide teachers access to student responses without having to manually grade. Let's look at a few digital tools teachers can use for formative assessment:

Kahoot! (http://getkahoot.com) is a game-based formative tool built around social engagement. Teachers can build quizzes,

called *kahoots*, created from a series of multiple-choice questions that can include text and images. Kahoot! offers the choice of randomizing questions as students work individually or in teams to complete the quiz on a mobile device. It also allows teachers the option to have students move at their own pace or participate in a timed game.

Pear Deck (http://peardeck.com) is an interactive presentation system with an integrated response system. Teachers can create several slides of content, including embedded images and videos, and follow up with student response questions. Individual results are not made public to the students, but the responses can be downloaded in spreadsheet form for the teacher to review and use to inform future instruction.

Socrative (http://socrative.com) provides opportunities for teachers to create quizzes, tests, exit tickets, surveys, games, and other digital formative assessments. Question types include multiple choice, true/false, graded short answer, or open response. Students can use a mobile devices to respond and receive immediate feedback. Teachers are able to view results in real time and access student reports to help inform instruction after data have been collected.

Formal Assessment

■ **Justify the purposes of utilizing formal testing for literacy assessment.**

Pressures for accountability have led many school districts and states to use formal reading tests as a means of assessment. Formal tests may be norm-referenced or criterion-referenced. Many of the recent standardized tests give *both* norm-referenced and criterion-referenced results of students' performance. Norm-referenced test results, in particular, appear to meet stakeholders' needs for making comparisons.

Standardized Tests

Standardized reading tests are machine-scored instruments that sample reading performance during a single administration. Standardized test scores are useful in making comparisons among individuals or groups at the local, state, or national level. A *norm-referenced test* is constructed by administering it to large numbers of students in order to develop **norms**. It's inefficient and difficult, if not impossible, to test every student in an entire population. Norms therefore represent average scores of a sampling of students selected for testing according to factors such as age, sex, race, grade, or socioeconomic status. Once norm scores are established, they become the basis for comparing the performance of individuals or groups to the performance of those who were in the norming sample. These comparisons allow you to determine whether a child or group is making "normal" progress or performing in "normal" ways.

2017 ILA Standards

3.1, 3.2

Normal progress or performance, of course, depends on the *representativeness* of the norming sample. Therefore, the norms of a test should reflect the characteristics of the population. Moreover, it's important to make sure that the norming sample used in devising the tests resembles the group of students tested. Some norm-referenced tests provide separate norms for specific kinds of populations (e.g., urban students). The technical manual for the test should contain information about the norming process, including a description of the norming group.

In developing norm-referenced tests, the scores in the norming sample are distributed along a *normal, or bell-shaped, curve.* That is to say, scores cluster symmetrically about the *mean*, the average of all scores. In Figure 5.2, notice that the majority of the scores (about 68 percent) are concentrated within *one standard deviation* above or below the mean.

Figure 5.2 A Bell Curve

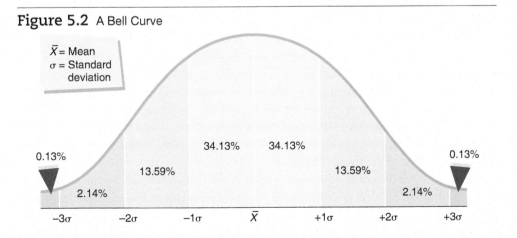

The standard deviation is an important measure because it represents the variability or dispersion of scores from the mean. The standard deviation, roughly speaking, can help you interpret a child's performance. You can judge how well a child performed on a test by examining a score in relation to the standard deviation. A score that falls more than one standard deviation below the mean on a reading test would probably be a cause for concern. Recognize, however, that standardized tests aren't error-free: There are measurement problems with any test. Some tests are better than others in helping teachers interpret performance. The more *reliable* and *valid* the reading test, the more likely it is to measure what it says it does.

Reliability refers to the stability of the test. Does the test measure ability consistently over time or consistently across equivalent forms? The reliability of a test is expressed as a correlation coefficient. Reliability coefficients can be found in examiner's manuals and are expressed in numerical form with a maximum possible value of +1.0. A reliability coefficient of +1.0 means that students' scores were ranked exactly the same on a test given on two different occasions or on two equivalent forms. If students were to take a test on Monday and then take an equivalent form of the same test on Thursday, their scores would be about the same on both tests, if the test were indeed reliable. A test consumer should examine reliability coefficients given in the examiner's manual. A reliability coefficient of +0.85 or better is considered good; a reliability coefficient below +0.70 suggests that the test lacks consistency.

A statistic tied to the idea of reliability is the *standard error of measurement*. The standard error of measurement represents the range within which a subject's *true score* will likely fall. A true score is the score a test taker would have obtained if the test were free of error. Suppose the standard error of measurement was 0.8 for a reading test. If a student achieved a score of 4.0 on the test, his or her true score would fall somewhere between 3.2 and 4.8. Rather than assume that a score received by a student is precisely accurate, the teacher should identify the standard error of measurement in the test manual and interpret each score as falling within a range.

Validity is probably the most important characteristic of a test. It refers to how well a test measures what it is designed to measure. A test developer will validate a test for general use along several fronts. First, the test should have *construct validity*. To establish construct validity, the test developer must show the relationship between a theoretical construct such as *reading* and the test that proposes to measure the construct. Second, the test should have *content validity*. Content validity reflects how well the test represents the domain or content area being examined. Are there sufficient test items? Are the test items appropriate? Third, the test should have *predictive validity*. In other words, it should accurately predict future performance. For test developers, predictive validity is most important in order to predict reading outcomes.

TYPES OF TEST SCORES To make interpretations properly, you need to be aware of differences in the types of scores reported on a test. The *raw*, or *obtained*, *score* reflects the total number of correct items on a test. Raw scores are converted to other kinds of scores so that comparisons among individuals or groups can be made. A raw score, for example, may be converted into a *grade-equivalency score*. This type of conversion provides information about reading performance as it relates to students at various grade levels. A grade-equivalency score of 4.6 is read as "fourth grade, sixth month in school." Therefore, a student whose raw score is transformed into a grade equivalency of 4.6 is supposedly performing at a level that is average for students who have completed six months of the fourth grade.

The idea behind a grade-equivalency score is not flawless. When a score is reported in terms of grade level, it is often prone to misinterpretation. For example, don't be swayed by the erroneous assumption that reading growth progresses throughout the school year at a constant rate—that growth in reading is constant from month to month. Based on what is known about human development generally and language growth specifically, such an assumption makes little sense when applied to a human process as complex as learning to read.

One of the most serious misinterpretations of a grade-equivalency score involves making placement decisions. Even though a child's performance on a test or subtest is reported as a grade level, this doesn't necessarily suggest placement in materials at that level. Suppose a student received a grade-equivalency score of 2.8 on a comprehension subtest. The score may represent information about the student's ability to comprehend, but it doesn't mean that the student should be placed at the second grade, eighth month of basal reading or library materials. First, the standard error of the test indicates that there is a range within which 2.8 falls. Second, the test's norms were in all likelihood not standardized against the content and level of difficulty of the basal reading curriculum in a particular school or library of books. In the early 1980s, the International Reading Association cautioned teachers on the misuse of grade equivalents and advocated the abandonment of grade-equivalent scores for reporting students' performance, and they continue today with these warnings. In place of grade-level scores, the use of *percentile scores* and *standard scores* such as *stanines* provides a more appropriate vehicle for reporting test performance.

Percentiles refer to scores in terms of the percentage of a group the student has scored above. If several second graders scored in the 68th percentile of a test, they scored as well as or better than 68 percent of the second graders in the norming population. Whereas grade-equivalency scores are normed by testing children at various grade levels, percentile norms are developed by examining performance only within a single grade level. Therefore, percentile scores provide information that helps teachers interpret relative performance within a grade level only. For this reason, percentiles are easily interpretable.

Stanine is one of several types of standard scores. A standard score is a raw score that has been converted to a common standard to permit comparison. Because standard scores have the same mean and standard deviation, they allow teachers to make direct comparisons of student performance across tests and subtests. Specifically, *stanine* refers to a *standard nine*-point scale. When stanines are used to report results, the distribution of scores on a test is divided into nine parts. Therefore, each stanine represents a single digit with a numerical value of 1 to 9. A stanine of 5 is the midpoint of the scale and represents average performance. Stanines 6, 7, 8, and 9 indicate increasingly better performance; stanines 4, 3, 2, and 1 represent decreasing performance.

TYPES OF TESTS Different norm-referenced tests have different purposes. Two broad types of tests are frequently used in schools. An assessment that is based on a **survey test** represents a measure of general performance only. It does not yield precise information about an individual's reading abilities. Survey tests are often used at the beginning of the school year as screening tests to identify children who may be having difficulties in broad areas of instruction. A survey test may be given to groups or individuals.

A standardized **diagnostic test**, by contrast, is a type of formal assessment intended to provide more detailed information about individual students' strengths and weaknesses. The results of a diagnostic test are often used to profile a student's strengths and weaknesses of reading performance. Some diagnostic tests are individual; others are designed for group administration.

2017 ILA Standard

3.1

Most diagnostic tests are founded on a bottom-up subskills view of reading. Therefore, diagnostic tests are characterized by a battery of subtests that uses large numbers of items to measure specific skills in areas such as phonics, structural analysis, word knowledge, and comprehension.

The concern today is with the type of information provided by the test: What is it for? How useful is it for instructional purposes? In what ways does it apply to culturally diverse populations? Until teachers can readily answer these questions to their own satisfaction, controversy will continue to surround the use of standardized achievement tests in U.S. education. The uses and misuses of standardized tests for reading, writing, and language assessment continue to spur debate.

USES OF STANDARDIZED TEST RESULTS   Critics of formal testing tend to argue against the uses to which the standardized test information is put. As noted earlier, scores from formal testing shouldn't be used as the *only* source of information considered in making instructional decisions. Other inappropriate uses of standardized test scores are in the evaluation of teachers and programs, and the distribution of resources.

2017 ILA Standards

3.2, 3.3, 3.4

Some critics call into question whether there is any worth at all to formal testing. For example, Afflerbach and Cho (2011) argued that it is important to assess reading skills and strategies. However, there is a missed opportunity to understand how students use and understand reading, motivation, goals, and affective development. Multiple-choice tests, the common format of standardized tests, inform teachers about learning constrained skills of reading but do not provide data regarding higher-order thinking skills (Afflerbach, Cho, Kim, & Clark, 2010). Therefore, important elements of reading are not being assessed.

Most test developers assert that their tests can provide accurate and reliable information about groups of 25 or more. From this perspective, scores can show public accountability by reporting schoolwide trends and differences among groups within a school. Standardized test results can also be used to get an idea of how students in a school compare to other students across the country or indicate whether a school as a whole is increasing or decreasing in general reading achievement. What large-scale single-test batteries cannot do, despite the claims of some test designers, is recommend appropriate instructional or curriculum objectives for schools, classrooms, or students.

In the meantime, state-by-state comparisons of student achievement in reading and other subject areas, using norm-referenced test scores, are widespread. The **National Assessment of Educational Progress (NAEP)** and the **National Center for Educational Statistics** periodically make available to the public data on large-scale reading and writing performance. On what is sometimes called the "nation's report card," NAEP compares several age groups over time and by geographic and other factors. It's important to keep in mind, however, that even though NAEP data make front-page news, it's not appropriate to report large-scale assessment results for individual pupils, classes, or schools. Reporting procedures that focus on ranking rather than performance can create adverse consequences for schools and students (International Reading Association and National Council of Teachers of English, 2010).

2017 ILA Standards

3.2, 3.3, 3.4

Criterion-referenced testing is another kind of testing conducted in schools, and the assumptions underlying it are different from those of norm-referenced testing. Rather than comparing a student's test performance to that of a norming sample, performance on a criterion-referenced test hinges on mastery of specific reading skills. Let's examine criterion-referenced assessment and how test information is used in classroom decision making.

Criterion-Referenced Tests

Criterion-referenced tests have been used in formal situations for district-wide purposes, in classroom situations, and more recently in statewide testing. The major premise behind criterion-referenced testing is that the mastery of reading skills should be assessed in relation to specific instructional objectives. Test performance is measured against a criterion, or acceptable score, for each of the objectives. Suppose, for example, that there are 10 test items for each skill objective. Eight to 10 correct items on the test would suggest a level of mastery as specified by the objective. A score of six or seven correct items would signal that additional practice and review of the skill under examination are needed. Fewer than six correct items could mean that a student is deficient in the skill and needs extensive reteaching to achieve mastery.

Performance on a criterion-referenced test, unlike a norm-referenced situation, is judged by what a student can or cannot do with regard to the skill objectives of the test. The test taker isn't compared to anyone else. The rationale for assessment, then, is that it will indicate strengths and weaknesses in specific skill areas. Whereas norm-referenced test scores are used to screen students and to make general grouping decisions, results from a criterion-referenced assessment are used to make instructional decisions about reading skills development. This same feature is viewed as a restriction by some teachers who want to plan individual instruction on variables other than test-identified weaknesses.

2017 ILA Standards

3.1, 3.2

Criterion-referenced tests often measure students' performance on a large number of objectives. Because the number of objectives tested is large, the number of items testing each objective may be as low as four or five. Such a practice leads to questions of how *reliable* the measurement of each skill can be with such a small number of items. It's possible that students who perform poorly on a criterion-referenced test won't perform poorly in another situation that assesses the same skill. For example, will a child who cannot count syllables in a word be unable to break down similar words into pronounceable parts when reading orally? Will a child who cannot answer inferential questions as directed on a test be unable to make inferences from a story in an oral retelling?

Test makers assume that mastery of specific skills leads to better reading ability. This is at best a tenuous assumption. A teacher must ask, "Do test items really measure what they are supposed to measure?"

What does mastery performance mean on a criterion-referenced test? For example, are comprehension skills ever mastered? Comprehension is an ongoing, developing process, as we have maintained throughout this text. To test for mastery of a comprehension skill would provide a teacher with misleading information at best.

Criterion-referenced tests are similar to standardized diagnostic tests in the sense that both attempt to identify strengths and weaknesses in specific skill areas. They share many of the shortcomings of norm-referenced testing and raise new objections among educators (Farr & Tone, 1998). The teacher must recognize that a criterion-referenced test provides only one perspective for understanding children's reading performance. Other indicators of reading should be weighed carefully when teachers plan instruction.

Check Your Understanding 5.3: Gauge your understanding of the skills and concepts in this section.

Informal Assessment

■ **Explain the commonalities between various informal assessments.**

Informal measures of reading such as *reading inventories, miscue analyses,* and *running records* yield useful information about student performance that can be used to inform and guide instruction. As the name implies, an **informal assessment** doesn't compare the performance of a tested group or individual to a normative population. Instead, informal assessments may be given throughout the school year to individuals or groups for specific instructional purposes.

2017 ILA Standards

3.1, 3.2

Informal reading assessments gauge performance in relation to the student's success on a particular reading task or a set of reading tasks. In this respect, they are similar to criterion-referenced measures. One of the best uses of informal assessments is to evaluate how students interact with print in oral and silent reading situations. We will explore how these measures can be used to inform decision making and strengthen inferences about students' reading behavior and performance.

Informal Reading Inventories

The **informal reading inventory (IRI)** is an individually administered reading test. It usually consists of a series of graded word lists, graded reading passages, and comprehension questions. The passages are used to assess how students interact with print orally and silently. According to the standards set for reading professionals by the International Reading Association (2010b), classroom teachers across all grade levels and special education teachers should have a basic understanding of multiple forms of assessment, including formal and informal reading inventories.

The information gathered from an IRI should allow teachers to pair students with appropriate instruction materials with some degree of confidence. Moreover, an analysis of oral reading miscues helps to determine the *cueing systems* that students tend to rely on when reading. In short, IRI information can lead to instructional planning that will increase students' effectiveness with print.

IRIs are commercially available, although teachers can easily construct one. Selections from a basal reading series may be used to make an IRI. When making and using an IRI, at least three steps are necessary:

1. Duplicate 100- to 200-word passages from basal stories. Select a passage for each grade level from the basal series, pre-primer through grade 8. Passages should be chosen from the middle of each basal textbook to ensure representativeness.

2. Develop at least five comprehension questions for each passage. Be certain that different types of questions are created for each graded passage. Avoid the following pitfalls:

   • Questions that can be answered without reading the passage (except for on-your-own questions)

   • Questions that require yes or no answers

   • Questions that are long and complicated

   • Questions that overload memory by requiring the reader to reconstruct lists (e.g., "Name four things that happened …")

3. Create an environment conducive to assessment. Explain to the student before testing why you are giving the assessment. In doing so, attempt to take the mystery out of what can be a worrisome situation for the student.

ADMINISTERING AN IRI   Commercially published IRIs have graded word lists that can be used for several purposes: (1) to help determine a starting point for reading the graded passages, (2) to get an indication of the student's sight-word proficiency (e.g., the ability to recognize words rapidly), (3) to get an indication of the student's knowledge of letter–sound relationships in order to attack unfamiliar words, and (4) to identify the student's word identification strategies.

When giving the IRI, the teacher may simply estimate placement in the graded passages instead of using word lists. Select a passage (narrative and/or expository) from the inventory that you believe the student can read easily and comprehend fully—for example, a passage two grade levels below the student's present grade. If the passage turns out to be more difficult than anticipated, ask the student to read another one at a lower level. However, if the student reads the passage without difficulty, progress to higher-grade-level passages until the reading task becomes too difficult.

Oral reading is usually followed by silent reading. In both oral and silent reading situations, the student responds to comprehension questions. However, an excellent variation is first to require students to retell everything they recall from the reading. Note the information given and then follow up with aided-recall questions such as the following:

What else can you tell me about _____ and _____?

What happened after _____ and _____?

Where did _____ and _____ take place?

How did _____ and _____ happen?

Why do you think _____ and _____ happened?

What do you think the author might have been trying to say in this story?

Do not hurry through a retelling. When asking a question to aid recall, give the student time to think and respond.

RECORDING ORAL READING ERRORS   During the oral reading of the passage, the teacher notes reading errors such as mispronunciations, omissions, and substitutions. As the student reads, the teacher also notes how fluent the reading is. Does the student read in a slow, halting, word-by-word fashion? Or does the student read rapidly and smoothly? Errors are recorded by marking deviations from the text on a copy of the passages read by the student. A *deviation* is any discrepancy between what the student says and the words on the page.

The following coding system can be used to mark oral reading errors:

1. *Omission.* An omission error occurs when the reader omits a unit of written language—that is, a word, several words, parts of words, or one or more sentences. Circle the omitted unit of language.

    Example   Erin was ⟨still⟩ at school. She never played ⟨after school.⟩

2. *Substitution.* A substitution error is noted when a real word (or words) is substituted for the word in the text. Draw a line through the text word, and write the substituted word above it.

    Example   The ~~lion~~ *monkey* looked lonely.

3. *Mispronunciation.* A mispronunciation miscue is one in which the word is pronounced incorrectly. Follow the same procedure as for a substitution error, writing the phonetic spelling above the word in the text.

    Example   Because he was a ~~frog~~ *frag*, we called him Hoppy.

4. *Insertion.* The insertion miscue results when a word (or words) is inserted in the passage. Use a caret (^) to show where the word was inserted, and write the word.

Example   Dan adjusted the ∧ knob on the DVD player.
                          turning

5. *Repetition.* In repetition, a word or phrase is repeated. Treat the repetition of more than one word as a single unit, counting it as one miscue. Underline the portion of text that is repeated.

Example   <u>This is a</u> tale about a man who is blind.

6. *Reversal.* The reversal error occurs when the order of a word (or words) in the text is transposed. Use a transposition symbol (a curved mark) over and under the letters or words transposed.

Examples   He went ⁀no his trip.

"See you later," ⁀said Sue.

7. *Pronunciation.* A word (or words) is pronounced for the reader. Place the letter *P* over the word pronounced.

Example   This was a startling development in his life.
                          𝒫

In addition to marking errors, you should also code the reader's attempts to correct any errors made during oral reading. Self-correction attempts result in repetitions, which may have one of three outcomes:

1. *Successful correction.* The reader successfully corrects the error. Corrected miscues are coded in the following manner:

Example   I did (not know <u>where</u>) I was going.
                  © 1. why   2. where

2. *Unsuccessful correction.* The reader attempts to correct an error but is unsuccessful. Unsuccessful correction attempts are coded in the following manner:

Example   He felt |compelled| to leave.
                  (UC) 1. complied   2. completed

3. *Abandoned correct form.* The student reads the text word (or words) correctly but then decides to abandon the correct form for a different response. Code this behavior in the following manner:

Example   Chris |wondered| if the tracks were made by a bear.
                  (AC) wandered

Familiarity with a coding system is important in marking oral errors. To ensure accurate coding, record the student's reading. You can then replay the student's reading to check whether all errors are recorded accurately. Moreover, audio recording will help in analyzing the student's responses to comprehension questions or a retelling of the material.

DETERMINING READING LEVELS   The following reading levels can be determined for individual students by administering an IRI.

- *Independent level:* The level at which the student reads fluently with excellent comprehension. The independent level has also been called the *recreational reading level* because not only will students be able to function on their own, but they also often have high interest in the material.

- *Instructional level:* The level at which the student can make progress in reading with instructional guidance. This level has been referred to as the *teaching level* because the material to be read must be challenging but not too difficult.

- *Frustration level:* The level at which the student is unable to pronounce many of the words or is unable to comprehend the material satisfactorily. This is the lowest level of reading at which the reader is able to understand. The material is too difficult to provide a basis for growth.
- *Listening capacity level:* The level at which the students can understand material that is read aloud. This level is also known as the *potential level* because if students were able to read fluently, they would not have a problem with comprehension.

The criteria used to determine reading levels have differed slightly among reading experts who have published IRIs. However, the most recommended over the years have been the Betts criteria, named for Emmett Betts (1946), the "father" of the IRI. Betts recommended that when students are reading instructional-level materials, the percentage of unknown words is estimated to be in the range of 1 to 5 percent.

In making decisions about a student's reading level, teachers should be cognizant of two powerful correlates that determine whether children will find material difficult. First, there is a strong relationship between a student's interest in a topic and reading comprehension. Second, a strong case has been built throughout this text for the relationship between background knowledge and reading comprehension. If students do poorly on a particular passage because they have limited knowledge or schemata for its content, it's easy to err by underestimating reading level.

2017 ILA Standard

3.2

The point to remember is that reading levels are not chiseled in stone. Levels do fluctuate from material to material depending on a child's schemata and interest in the passage content. The placement information that an IRI yields gives an approximate figure, an indication. Placement decisions should rest on corroborative judgment, with IRI results an important source of information but not the sole determinant.

Analyzing Oral Reading Miscues

Oral reading errors are also called miscues. The terms *error* and *miscue* essentially describe the same phenomenon—a deviation or difference between what a reader says and the word on the page. During the 1970s, the Goodmans and others popularized the term *miscue* to replace the term *error*. A miscue provides a piece of evidence in an elaborate puzzle; it helps reinforce a positive view of error in the reading process for teachers and students alike. Differences between what the reader says and what is printed on the page are not the result of random errors. Instead, these differences are "cued" by the thoughts and language of the reader, who is attempting to construct what the author is saying.

Miscues can be analyzed *quantitatively* or *qualitatively*. A quantitative analysis involves counting the number of errors; it pivots on a search for *deficits* in a student's ability to read accurately. A quantitative analysis is used, for example, to determine the reading levels previously discussed. In addition, a tallying of different types of errors has traditionally been a strategy for evaluating the strengths and weaknesses of a child's ability to analyze words. For example, does the reader consistently mispronounce the beginnings of words? An analysis based on this question helps pinpoint specific difficulties. Does the reader consistently have trouble with single consonants? Consonant clusters?

2017 ILA Standard

3.2

In a quantitative analysis, each miscue carries equal weight, regardless of the contribution it makes to a child's understanding of the material read. A qualitative miscue analysis, by contrast, offers a radically different perspective for exploring the strengths of students' reading skills. A qualitative miscue analysis is a tool for assessing what children do when they read. It is not based on deficits related to word identification but rather on the *differences* between the miscues and the words on the page. Therefore, some miscues are more significant than others.

A miscue is significant if it affects meaning—if it doesn't make sense within the context of the sentence or passage in which it occurs. Johns (1985, p. 17) explained that miscues are generally significant in the following instances:

- When the meaning of the sentence or passage is significantly changed or altered and the student does not correct the miscue
- When a nonword is used in place of the word in the passage
- When only a partial word is substituted for the word or phrase in the passage
- When a word is pronounced for the student

Miscues are generally *not* significant in these circumstances:

- When the meaning of the sentence or passage undergoes no change or only minimal change
- When they are self-corrected by the student
- When they are acceptable in the student's dialect (e.g., "goed" home for "went" home; "idear" for "idea")
- When they are later read correctly in the same passage

We agree with Johns that only significant miscues should be counted in determining reading levels according to the Betts criteria. He recommended subtracting the total of all dialect miscues, all corrected miscues, and all miscues that do not change meaning from the total number of recorded miscues.

Miscue analysis can be applied to graded passages from an IRI or to the oral reading of a single passage that presents the student with an extended and intensive reading experience. In the case of the latter, select a story or informational text that is at or just above the student's instructional level. The material must be challenging but not frustrating.

Through miscue analysis, teachers can determine the extent to which the reader uses and coordinates graphic–sound, syntactic, and semantic information from the text. To analyze miscues, you should ask at least four crucial questions:

1. *Is the meaning changed?* If it isn't, then it's *semantically acceptable* within the context of the sentence or passage. Here are some examples of semantically acceptable miscues:

   - I *want* to bring him ^back home.

   - Marcus went to the ~~store~~ shop.

   - His feet are firmly planted ~~on~~ to the ground.

   - ~~Mother~~ Mom works on Wall Street.

These are examples of semantically unacceptable miscues:

   - Jacob went to ~~camp~~ court for the first time.

   - The mountain ~~loomed~~ leaped in the foreground.

   - The summer had been a ~~dry~~ quiet one.

2. *Are the miscues nonwords or partial words?* If they are not, then they are not *syntactically acceptable* within the context of a sentence or passage. Miscues are syntactically acceptable if they sound like language and serve as the same parts of speech as the text words. The above examples of semantically acceptable miscues also happen to be syntactically acceptable. Here are two examples of syntactically unacceptable miscues.

- Estelle ~~reached~~ *carefully* for the book.

- I have ~~a~~ *to* good idea.

3. *Are the miscues similar to the text words in structure and sound?* Substitution and mispronunciation miscues should be analyzed to determine how similar they are in approximating the graphic and pronunciation features of the text words. High graphic–sound *similarity* results when two of the three parts (beginning, middle, and end) of a word are similar, as in this miscue:

- He was ~~getting~~ *going* old.

- Scooter ~~ran~~ *run* after the cat.

4. *Did the reader self-correct?* Self-corrections are revealing because they demonstrate that the reader is attending to meaning and is aware that the initial miscuing did not make sense.

A profile can be developed for each reader by using the summary sheet in Figure 5.3. Study the following passage, which has been coded, and then examine how each miscue was analyzed on the summary sheet.

Sheepdogs ~~work~~ *walk* hard on a farm. They must ~~learn~~ (C) *lean* to take the sheep from place to place. They *must* (C) *mostly these* see that the sheep do not run ~~away~~ (C) *always*. And they must see (that) the sheep do not get ~~lost or~~ *loose and* killed.

Sometimes (these) dogs are ~~trained~~ *trying* to do other ~~kinds~~ *kind* of farm work. They (earn) (UC) *learn* the right to be called good ~~helpers~~ *helps*, too.

Can you think of ~~one other~~ *another* kind of ~~work~~ *working* dog? He does not need a coat or strong legs like the sheepdog('s) *dog*. He does not ~~learn~~ *leave* to work ~~with~~ *and* a *sled* in the deep, cold snow. He ~~does not~~ *doesn't* learn to be a farm worker.

To determine the percentage of semantically acceptable miscues, count the number of yes responses in the column. Then count the number of miscues analyzed. (Do not tally successful self-corrections.) Divide the number of semantically acceptable miscues by the number of miscues analyzed and then multiply by 100.

To determine the percentage of syntactically acceptable miscues, proceed by counting the number of yes responses in the column. Divide that number by the number of miscues analyzed (less self-corrections) and then multiply by 100.

Figure 5.3 Qualitative Miscue Analysis Summary Sheet

Text	Miscue	Context — Semantically Acceptable	Syntactically Acceptable	Self-Corrections	Graphic–Sound Similarity — Beginning	Middle	Ending	Graphic–Sound Summary
work	walk	no	yes		✓		✓	high
learn	lean			yes				
must	mostly			yes				
the	these	yes	yes		✓	✓		high
away	always			yes				
that								
lost	loose	no	yes		✓			some
or	and	no	yes					none
these								
trained	trying	no	yes		✓			some
kinds	kind	yes	yes		✓	✓		high
earn	learn	no	yes	no		✓	✓	high
helpers	helps	yes	yes		✓	✓		high
one other	another	yes	yes			✓	✓	
work	working	yes	yes		✓	✓		high
dog's	dog	yes	yes		✓	✓		high
learn	leave			yes				
with	and	no	no					none
sled	sleep	no	yes		✓			some
does not	doesn't	yes	yes					

Percentage of semantically acceptable miscues	= 50 percent
Percentage of syntactically acceptable miscues	= 93 percent
Percentage of successful self-corrections	= 80 percent
Percentage of miscues with high graphic–sound similarity	= 50 percent
Percentage of miscues with some graphic–sound similarity	= 21 percent

To determine the percentage of successful self-corrections, tally the number of yes responses in the column and divide the number by the number of self-correction attempts and then multiply by 100.

To determine the percentage of high or some graphic–sound similarity, analyze mispronunciations and substitutions only. Divide the total of high-similarity words by the number of words analyzed and then multiply by 100. Follow the same procedure to determine whether some similarity exists between the miscues and text words.

A final piece of quantitative information to be tabulated is an estimate of the extent to which the reader reads for meaning. This is calculated by determining the number of miscues that were semantically acceptable or that made sense in the selection *and* the number of successful corrections. Divide this number by the total number of miscues. This percentage gives you an estimate of the extent to which the reader reads for meaning. When referring to Figure 5.4, this percentage also becomes a quick measure of the reader's effectiveness in using reading strategies.

2017 ILA Standard

3.2

Figure 5.4 The Effectiveness of Using Reading Strategies

Effectiveness of Using Reading Strategies	Miscues that Did Not Change the Meaning of the Passage and Miscues That Were Successfully Self-Corrected
Highly effective	60 to 100 percent
Moderately effective	40 to 79 percent
Somewhat effective	15 to 45 percent
Ineffective	No more than 14 percent

Inferences can be drawn about oral reading behavior once the miscues are charted and the information is summarized. Although the reader of the passage miscued frequently, his strengths are apparent: He reads for meaning. Half of the miscues were semantically acceptable. When attempting to self-correct, the reader was successful most of the time; when combined, over 60 percent of his miscues were semantically acceptable or were successfully self-corrected; most of his miscues sounded like language. Moreover, the great majority of his substitution and mispronunciation miscues reflected knowledge of graphic–sound relationships.

Miscue analysis is time-consuming. However, when you want to know more about a student's processing of print, miscue analysis is very useful. McKenna and Picard (2006/2007) believe that although miscue analysis is beneficial, it does not give a complete perspective of word identification skills and strategies. They believe that miscue analysis is best utilized for determining students' reading levels, for determining inadequate decoding, and for determining use of contextual clues. Other word identification skills and strategies such as analogies, sight recognition, and structural analysis should be assessed in different ways.

In order to understand English language learners' miscues, it is essential for teachers to recognize that their miscues in English generally do not reflect their native language. Rather the miscues are associated with the fact that ELLs have not mastered the English language (Weaver, 2002). Weaver continues to emphasize that these miscues typically demonstrate language growth. Therefore, there needs to be appropriate assessment and analysis of ELLs' reading.

Throughout this chapter, reliance on *multiple indicators* has been emphasized. This is especially important when determining a child's progress in becoming literate. Assessments need to show a student's growth rather than simply to compare a student to other students of similar age. In addition to the IRI, running records and kidwatching help teachers keep track of students' progress.

Running Records

Keeping track of students' growth in reading, their use of cueing systems of language—semantics, syntax, and graphophonemics—can help teachers understand the process that goes on in readers' minds. When readers try to construct meaning as they read aloud, teachers can begin to see the relationship between the miscues readers make and comprehension. This in turn influences the teacher's instructional decision-making process.

A **running record**, originally developed by Marie Clay (1985), is an assessment system for determining students' development of oral reading fluency and word identification skills and strategies. Running records are used by teachers to guide a student's approach to learning when needed at frequent intervals, but not daily (Clay, 2001). With running records, the teacher calculates the percentage of words the student reads correctly and then analyzes the miscues for instructional purposes. The various types of decisions Clay recommends are to (1) evaluate material difficulty, (2) group students, (3) monitor individual progress of students, and (4) observe the particular difficulties of struggling readers.

2017 ILA Standard

3.2

ADMINISTERING A RUNNING RECORD   A running record can be completed with only a blank sheet of paper, making it especially good for collecting data about a student's oral reading during regular classroom activities. When administering a running record, the following guidelines are recommended by Clay (2001):

1. Sit next to the student to view the student's text (it is preferable to use text materials that are part of the everyday program) and the reader's observable reading behaviors.
2. Record everything the student says and does on a blank sheet of paper (in place of a blank sheet of paper, you can use a duplicate copy of the pages the student will read).
3. Make a record of the student reading three book selections (a sample reading of 100 to 200 words from each text is recommended, as is choosing readings from one easy, one instructional, and one difficult text).
4. Mark a check for each word the student says correctly, matching the number of checks on a line of the paper with the number of words in a line of the text being read.
5. Record every error (substitution, insertion, omission, repetition, mispronunciation, and prompt) and self-correction. Deviations from print are marked in much the same way as in other miscue analysis procedures. The sample coded running record passages in Figure 5.5 display a coding system for marking oral reading errors and self-corrections.
6. Record all observable behaviors.

Figure 5.5 A Sample Coded Running Record

Teachers of beginning readers (who read aloud more often, read slowly, and read shorter, less complicated texts) often prefer the use of a running record because it does not require special preparation or disrupt the flow of the classroom lesson. As students read faster and read more complicated texts, however, running records become more difficult for the teacher to administer. Nevertheless, no matter what the level, running records can be a natural part of the classroom when teachers practice with the procedures in order to become comfortable with the process. Suggestions from other teachers and working with a literacy coach will assist the teacher in becoming proficient with running records.

ANALYZING RUNNING RECORDS   In order to determine appropriate material connections and instructional decisions from running records, Clay (1985) recommends that the teacher calculate the words read correctly, analyze the student's errors, and identify patterns of errors. Clay (2005) also recommends that the teacher give close attention to self-corrections. To determine the percentage of words read correctly, the total number of errors is divided by the total number of words in the selection. Then multiply this total by 100 in order to convert to a percentage. Finally, subtract the percentage from 100 to obtain the percentage correct. As shown in Figure 5.6, if the student reads 95 percent or more of the words correctly, the reading material is considered easy or at the student's independent reading level. If the reader reads 90 to 94 percent of the words correctly, the material is at his or her instructional level. Finally, the reading material is considered difficult or at the student's frustration level if less than 90 percent of the words are read correctly.

Running records provide insights into students' strengths and weaknesses by allowing teachers to analyze patterns of miscues. This information provides the teacher with an understanding of the cueing systems the reader relies on. Analyzing oral reading miscues and patterns helps teachers determine the extent to which the reader uses and coordinates graphophonemic, syntactic, and semantic information from the text. To assist in this analysis process, as suggested with informal reading inventories, it is important to ask the crucial questions recommended by Clay (2005): Did the meaning or the messages of the text influence the error? Did the structure (syntax) of the sentence influence the number of error responses? Did visual information from the print influence any part of the error—letter, cluster, or word? (p. 69). Clay also recommends that the teacher scan the response record to answer two additional questions: Did the child's oral language produce the error with little influence from the print? Was the child getting phonemic information from the printed letters? (p. 70). Asking these questions will help the teacher get a more holistic view of the reading process.

It is important for the teacher to consider the pattern of responses in order to analyze errors and self-corrections. Categorizing this information based on the cueing systems helps the teacher to identify a student's specific strengths and needs. Figure 5.7 is a sample running record sheet completed with a second grader reading a passage from *Days with Frog and Toad* by Arnold Lobel (1979). The teacher, Stacy Bricker, generated this summary sheet to help categorize and analyze the data. As shown in the summary sheet, Miss Bricker totaled the miscues for each line and then categorized the miscue as syntactic (S), semantic (M), or graphophonemic (G), and also determined the number of self-corrections. As shown in the analysis of the

---

Figure 5.6 Reading Levels Determined by Running Records

Reading Level	Percentage Correct
Independent	95 to 100 percent
Instructional	90 to 94 percent
Frustration	Below 90 percent

Figure 5.7 Sample Running Record Sheet

Student Name: _Tamiko_   **Age:** _8_

Grade: _2_   **Text:** _Days with Frog and Toad_

Teacher: _Miss Bricker_   **Date:** _November 10_

Level: Independent   (Instructional)   Frustration

Page		Total	S	M	G	SC
4	Today / Toad ☑ ☑	1			1	
	That / Drat ☑ ☑	1			1	
	☑ ☑ ☑ ☑					
	☑ ☑ ☑ ☑ ☑ ☑					
	☑ ☑ throw/through ☑ ☑	1			1	
	☑ ☑ ☑					
	☑ ☑ ☑ ☑ ☑					
	☑ ☑ ☑ (used picture clue)					
	☑ ☑ ☑					
5	☑ ☑ ☑ torn SC/tomorrow					1
	☑ ☑					
	☑ ☑ ☑ ☑ ☑					
6	☑ ☑ ☑ ☑					
	☑ ☑ ☑ (used intonation)					
	☑ ☑ ☑ coat/jacket	1		1		
	☑ standing/lying ☑ ☑ ☑	1	1			
	☑ ☑ ☑					
	☑ uncle/under ☑ ☑	1			1	
	☑ ☑ ☑					
	☑ ☑ ☑ ☑ plates/dishes	1		1		
	☑ ☑					

student sample (Figure 5.8), Tamiko's teacher determined that he had difficulty with identifying unknown words and with oral reading fluency. Miss Bricker also noted that Tamiko read with hesitation and did not rely on a specific word identification strategy when he came to an unknown word. Miss Bricker used this information in addition to other assessment indicators for instructional intervention and material placement. She decided to work with Tamiko on word identification skills such as context clues and decoding, and placed him with reading material at approximately the second-grade level.

Figure 5.8 Analysis of Sample Running Record Sheet

Analysis

Total number of words in passage: _87_

Total number of miscues in passage: _7_

Accuracy rate: _92 percent_ *(instructional level)*

Number of syntactic miscues: _1_

Examples: standing / lying

Miscue fits grammatically in the sentence.

Number of semantic miscues: _2_

Examples: coat / jacket   plates / dishes

Miscue fits the meaning in the passage.

Number of graphophonemic miscues: _4_

Example: Today / Toad   That / Drat   throw / through   uncle / under

Attention to graphic cues.

Number of self-corrections: _1_

The student read the text with some hesitation and had some general overall understanding of the passage. When trying to pronounce unknown words, the student had limited word identification skills. Therefore, specific instructional activities to develop word identification skills and strategies (context clues, decoding skills) are needed.

2017 ILA Standard

3.2

The approximate reading level suggested by an informal reading inventory and running records, along with other information on how a reader uses the cueing systems of language to construct meaning, can help teachers understand a student's progress in becoming literate.

Kidwatching While Teaching

Observing how students interact with print during the instructional process is what "kidwatching" is all about. The term *kidwatching* was coined to dramatize the powerful role of observation in helping children grow and develop as language users. Yetta Goodman (1978) maintained that teachers screen their observations of children through their concepts and beliefs about reading and language learning.

In many classrooms, kidwatching is an ongoing, purposeful activity. Because language learning is complex, it's impossible to observe everything that happens in the classroom. It is especially difficult to document slow growth of young readers; also, assessment is complicated by the introduction of new kinds of learning or when complex activities are being learned (Clay, 2005). Systematic observation is a way to document the development progress of all readers. They need to be observed frequently and regularly. Nichols, Walker, and McIntyre (2009) recommend that "multiple observations are needed to establish reliability and to recognize patterns" (p. 258). The first essential step in observing students' reading and language use is therefore to decide what to look for in advance. Clearly, teachers need to watch for signs that signify growth in reading behavior. For example, probably the clearest indicator of word identification difficulties is failure to self-correct. Consequently, this is a behavior that the teacher as an expert process evaluator would take note of as students read orally.

2017 ILA Standard

3.1

Because it is unobtrusive and does not interfere with ongoing activities, kidwatching enables teachers to catch students in the act, so to speak, of literate behaviors. But knowing what it is that we see and what it means in terms of our students' progress takes practice and good judgment. To be an effective observer, the teacher must have an understanding of reading milestones and established standards. Understanding contextual influences, the development of reading process, and the expected year-end standards are key for kidwatching.

Watching students interacting with others, participating in small group and whole class instruction, and choosing books in formal and informal situations all provide the teacher with essential information. Reading behaviors, skills and strategies, motivation, and interests are exhibited while developing as a reader. While kidwatching, the teacher is able to answer: What do students know how to do well? What kind of patterns have evolved? What do they need to learn or to practice?

> In this **video** (https://www.youtube.com/watch?v=Vq9_HOv2W2g), you will see teachers assessing with the use of structured and controlled observation tasks such as running records. Reading and writing observation activities are demonstrated, and they include structured and informal techniques with the use of anecdotal notes. What observation techniques do you believe are appropriate for students in various grades? What is the best way to manage classroom observations?

ANECDOTAL NOTES Teachers write short **anecdotal notes** that capture the gist of an incident that reveals something the teacher considers significant to understanding a child's literacy learning. Anecdotal notes are intended to safeguard against the limitations of memory. Record observations in a journal, on charts, or on index cards. Sticky notes and other small pieces of paper that are easily carried about and transferred to a student's folder are perfect for writing on-the-spot anecdotal records. These jottings become "field notes" and will aid the teacher in classifying information, inferring behavior, and making predictions about individual students or instructional strategies and procedures.

It isn't necessary or even realistic to record anecdotal information every day for each student, especially in classes with 25 or 30 children. However, over a period of time, focused observations of individual children will accumulate into a revealing and informative record of literacy and language learning.

Charts are particularly useful for keeping anecdotal records. Charts can be devised to record observations in instructional situations that are ongoing, such as participation in reading and writing activities, small and large group discussions, book sharing, and silent and oral reading. For example, the chart in Figure 5.9 was developed to record observations of students' participation in journal-writing sessions.

In addition, charts can be used to record certain behaviors across instructional activities. A good strategy for developing a permanent record for each child in class is

Figure 5.9 Observational Chart for Journal Writing

Mrs. Carter

Grade: 2

Time Period: *March 27 – April 2*

Name:	Date:	Writing Strategies:	Date:	Writing Strategies:
George	3/27	Frequently asks for assistance with spelling.	4/2	Appears to be writing more independently but still worries about correct spelling of words.
Alejandro	3/27	Revising draft of April Fool's story; has lots of ideas.	3/29	Writes fluently; ready to publish.
La Shawna	3/28	Copied a recipe from a cookbook.	4/2	Wrote first original story; was very anxious to have story read; wanted to begin another story.
Maxine	3/29	Draws pictures to rehearse before writing; concentrates on handwriting and neatness.	4/1	Wrote a riddle; wants to share it with class.

to cut observations apart from the individual charts and then place each student's notes into a permanent growth record. With improved technology, some data management systems afford teachers the opportunity to use handheld computers to chart kidwatching as it occurs. The information documented can be used during conferences with students or with parents.

Some teachers find that writing anecdotal information can be unwieldy and time-consuming, especially if they are observing students over long stretches of time. An alternative to ongoing anecdotal notes is the use of checklists.

CHECKLISTS Using a **checklist** is somewhat different from natural, open-ended observation. A checklist consists of categories that have been presented for specific diagnostic purposes.

Checklists vary in scope and purpose; they can be relatively short and open-ended or longer and more detailed. To be useful, checklists should guide teachers to consider and notice what students can do in terms of their reading and writing strategies. The DR–TA checklist in Figure 5.10 can reveal how a group of students interacts with a text. Collaboratively designed checklists serve the added purpose of helping teachers develop and refine their beliefs about what constitutes important literacy performance.

When Mr. Niece began using an open-ended checklist designed to show evidence of creative thinking and leadership skills on the part of his fifth graders, he noticed an unanticipated benefit. "It was easy for me to overlook quiet students who were more peer-centered or who kept to themselves but out of trouble. But if I didn't have an annotation for a particular student for a few days, I had to stop and ask myself why. What did I need to do to make sure that all of my students were included in activities? I'm more aware of who I watch and why I watch them."

Figure 5.10 Directed Reading–Thinking Activity Checklist

Teacher: _Mr. Niece_   Grade: _5_

Time Period: _Fourth Period_   Group: _Niece's Nikes_

Reading Behavior During DR–TA	Student Name					
Reading Title of a Selection	Eduardo	Miguel	JoAnne	Sophia	Rich	Emma
1. Participates in predicting/is cooperative.	☑	☑	☐	☐	☑	☑
2. Makes some predictions with coaxing.	☑	☑	☐	☐	☐	☐
3. Initiates own predictions eagerly after prompting with title.	☑	☐	☐	☐	☐	☐
4. Low risk taking/reluctant.	☐	☑	☐	☑	☐	☐
5. Predictions are numerous.	☐	☐	☑	☐	☐	☐
After Reading Sections of a Selection						
1. Retelling is accurate.	☑	☐	☑	☐	☑	☐
2. Retelling is adequate.	☐	☑	☐	☐	☐	☑
3. Retelling is minimal.	☐	☐	☐	☑	☐	☐
4. Confirms or refutes past predictions.	☑	☐	☑	☐	☐	☑

INTERVIEWING Through **interviewing**, the teacher can discover what children are thinking and feeling. Periodic student interviews can lead to a better understanding of (1) reading interests and attitudes, (2) how students perceive their strengths and weaknesses, and (3) how they perceive processes related to language learning. Using a variety of questions related to the students' thoughts and experiences with reading and writing is important. A few sample questions include (1) Are you a good reader? How do you know? (2) Who is a good reader? Why do you consider him or her a good reader? and (3) If another classmate were having a difficult time with reading, what would you tell him or her in order to help? All questions can then be reworded to relate to writing in order to learn about the student's writing experiences. It is important to remember when asking students questions to allow them time to think through each question and permit the students to share true thoughts and feelings.

2017 ILA Standard

3.1

While interviewing, the teacher can learn about the whole child. This is especially important for middle school students. Teachers learn through interviews how motivation plays into the struggling reader's illiteracy. Nichols, Walker, and McIntyre (2009) warn that classifying a struggling reader as being illiterate may be overgeneralizing the student's ability. Rather, the student may have the skills but is not demonstrating his or her abilities by choice or due to lack of motivation.

Interviews provide a rich source of information. When coupled with observations made during teaching, interviews strengthen data from formal and informal tests of student performance. Moreover, interviews may reveal information that will not be provided by other means of assessment.

2017 ILA Standard

3.1

Other Informal Assessments

Other informal assessments to monitor oral reading development include words correct per minute (WCPM), Dynamic Indicators of Basic Early Literacy Skills (DIBELS), and Developmental Reading Assessment (DRA). **Words correct per minute (WCPM)** assessment involves children reading aloud for 1 minute from materials used in their reading lessons. As the student is reading the text, the teacher crosses out any word read incorrectly onto a copy of the text. To calculate the score, the teacher counts the number of correctly read words, records, and then graphs the score in order to track changes in rates and accuracy over time. Repeated samples of oral reading over time will help to document student growth. In addition to documenting progress in rate and accuracy, the teacher can also determine the appropriateness of the difficulty of a text.

Dynamic Indicators of Basic Early Literacy Skills (DIBELS) includes a series of oral reading skill assessments. Short measures are used to monitor early literacy skills and provide feedback to inform instruction. The various measures include (1) letter naming fluency recommended for kindergarten and beginning first grade, (2) initial sound fluency recommended for preschool through middle kindergarten, (3) phoneme segmentation fluency recommended for mid-kindergarten through first grade, (4) nonsense word fluency recommended for mid-kindergarten through first grade, and (5) oral reading fluency recommended for middle first grade through third grade. A few optional assessments that may be included in the DIBELS process are oral reading fluency retell and word use fluency.

When administering and utilizing the scores from DIBELS, teachers need to be cautious about what is being assessed. Although the subtests are called fluency measures when administered as directed, fluency is regarded as speed and accuracy. What teachers learn from the subtests is how fast children can name letters, identify sounds, read words, and read passages aloud (Allington, 2009). Goodman (2006) also warns that reading is not considered the ability to read words rapidly and accurately, and that comprehension is essential.

Developmental Reading Assessment (DRA) includes a series of leveled texts that assess fluency and comprehension (Beaver & Carter, 2005). Students read aloud while the teacher takes a running record of the reading. By **retelling** and answering various types of questions, oral comprehension levels are determined. This assessment helps to monitor progress because it is typically administered two to three times a year.

Garcia and Bauer (2009) report the difficulty of assessing ELLs when administrating any oral reading assessment or assessments in general. They emphasize that (1) ELLs demonstrate more comprehension of English reading when they are permitted to respond in their native language; (2) ELLs need more time to complete assessments; (3) ELLs have limited English vocabulary related to test instructions or test items; (4) ELLs have limited English vocabulary; (5) ELLs should be assessed on how they use language in real-life situations rather than taking a sample of skills related to oral language development; and (6) ELLs should be assessed on academic language that is needed for learning new concepts rather than social language. Therefore, the assessment process for all learners must be appropriate to the students themselves, as well as the literacy process.

Along with understanding of the unique needs of individual students, the teacher must address the use of accommodations in classroom assessment. Federal laws and mandates have identified appropriate assessment accommodations for those who qualify. They are varied and are determined by the student's needs and abilities. Such modifications include reading of the test instructions, use of dictionaries, and taking an extra time allotment, to name a few. Accommodations help to make the assessment process effective and fair.

No matter which informal assessment process is used, it is essential that the teacher utilize the information gathered. Keeping a record of the assessment data need not be an overwhelming task. A folder for each child or a notebook with a page for each child that contains a collection of information about his or her literacy learning helps teachers organize the information they collect for assessment. Assessment folders or notebooks could also contain information from informal reading tests, miscue analyses, and observational data. Because it is difficult to remember classroom events, we recommend writing down anecdotal records or using a checklist to record important incidents.

The assessment folder that teachers keep for their own use or to share with parents or students is one type of portfolio. As the interest in developing authentic assessment to match our understanding of the constructive nature of the reading process grows, portfolios have emerged as important avenues of assessment.

Check Your Understanding 5.4: Gauge your understanding of the skills and concepts in this section.

Portfolio Assessment

■ **Discuss the essential components of portfolio assessment as well as how to manage the portfolio process.**

Through the process of portfolio assessment, teachers seem to have discovered a way to connect instruction and assessment by involving students in reflecting on and making decisions about their work. **Portfolios** are collections that "document the literary development of a student" and include "evidence of student work in various stages" (Noden & Vacca, 1994, p. 292). It is an important summative tool that offers insights into the process of students' development (Afflerbach, 2007). Portfolios include literacy information from various contexts and sources and are organized in a variety of formats. Three-ring binders, file folders, and digital are a few of the organizational types. The evidence that goes into student portfolios is collaboratively chosen by teachers and students and is more likely to represent a process or activity rather than a product. Portfolios provide an opportunity to involve students in the assessment process because they can require students' input and encourage them to think about their own literacy growth (Turner & Hoeltzel, 2011).

2017 ILA Standards

3.1, 3.2

The items in a portfolio are selected with care. As teachers and students reflect on work samples, they choose those that show merit as examples of significant growth, effort, and achievement, especially those representing clear learning goals. Looking through portfolios, the teacher or parent sees a fairly complete picture of students as learners. Portfolios contain work samples that cross many curriculum areas and take many forms, from essays, letters, stories, poems, and anecdotal records to photographs, videos, recordings, and DVDs. Other technology-based language arts samples that reflect students' daily lives should also be included. Technology such as videotapes or digital audio or video on computers provides parents and teachers samples of the reading skills and strategies the reader relies on. It is best with technology and other portfolio content to include samples from different times of the academic year to document literacy growth over time.

Electronic portfolios, known as e-portfolios or digital portfolios, are also standard-driven assessments. **Digital portfolios** are multimedia collections of student work stored and reviewed in digital format (Niguidula, 2005; Waters, 2007). They may contain similar items found in a traditional portfolio but multimedia technologies are used to present the material (Jones & Shelton, 2011). Scanned worked samples, sample blogs, wikis, instant messages, e-mails, and the like all can be archived in a searchable digital portfolio (Coiro & Castek, 2011). Additionally, communication and collaboration skills can be documented, especially with collaborative projects, research, and presentations from different times throughout the school year, which also further document language arts development.

No matter what format is utilized, portfolios serve many purposes and vary accordingly, but their underlying value is a commitment to students' assessment of their own understanding and personal development. They are fair and objective and work especially well for culturally and linguistically diverse students, who may struggle with more traditional evaluation formats (Nichols et al., 2009). Above all, portfolio assessment is a powerful concept that helps teachers and students alike work toward developing standards, reflecting on growth, and taking responsibility for learning.

2017 ILA Standards
3.1, 4.1

Essential Elements of Portfolios

Although portfolios differ from each other as literacy profiles of individual learners in different classrooms, they are more authentic than traditional, formal assessment procedures. To varying degrees, they measure the process of the construction of meaning. What makes a portfolio authentic? Portfolio assessment doesn't mandate or prescribe that all portfolios contain the same elements; that would be contrary to the thoughtful collaboration that is central to this process and makes it so appealing. The following elements are associated with portfolios:

- Varied types of work, often completed over time
- Written and artistic responses to reading
- Writing in several genres
- Teacher-assigned and student-generated work
- An introduction, summary, or self-reflection by the student about the nature of the piece or what it demonstrates about his or her literacy
- Collaborative decision making between teacher and student on work assigned and chosen
- Work in progress, documenting changes and growth in literacy
- Best work, selected for showcasing based on input from teachers and peer conferencing during times set aside to discuss what students are doing and planning, writing and reading, and thinking
- Notes in a reading log or response journal
- List of books read, updated regularly
- Work demonstrating transliteracies
- Students' self-reflections

Portfolios in essence are multiple stories of what individuals can do, both within the language arts of reading, writing, listening, and speaking and across the curriculum. With the input from others, they document change and help communicate assessment information to parents, school officials, and the public. Ultimately, a portfolio "represents a creation of self ... its contents, like items in a scrapbook, are tangible pieces of the story. Everything is connected" (Kieffer & Morrison, 1994, p. 417).

Implementing Portfolios in the Classroom

Getting started in the implementation of the portfolio assessment process, whether in grade 1 or grade 7, calls for certain decisions and logical steps. Here are a few suggestions:

- Introduce the notion of portfolios, the concept itself, and the connection with instructional activities. Show some examples from other occupations and fields; show sample items that might be found in portfolios.
- Explain your model for assessment: What is the purpose of the portfolio? Is there more than one purpose? Why are we going to use them? Who are we going to show them to?

- Decide what types of items will be included and how they will be selected for inclusion. Who gets to choose? Approximately how large will the portfolio become, and what size will it be? What format will it take? Will different designs be permitted (or even encouraged)? What is the time frame—start date and end date?

- Consider in advance appropriate ways to communicate clear explanations of portfolios to your colleagues, your principal, your students' parents, and possibly others in your school district or community.

- Develop an array of possible contributions that are most appropriate for your class, the range of students, the language arts, or a reading or writing emphasis: writing samples, videos, conference notes, tests, quizzes, self-evaluations (see Figure 5.11), peer evaluations, daily work samples, personal progress sheets, writing conference logs (see Figure 5.12), semantic maps, inventories, journal entries, observation information, interviews, and so on.

When Julie Poyser, who has been relying upon portfolio assessment for many years, gets ready to implement the process with a new group of students in the fall, she discusses the management of portfolios with the students. She encourages the students to creatively think about how best to manage the artifacts. In the most recent years, Julie has used cereal boxes as containers for her portfolios in her classroom. They are motivational, and the students take ownership of their "box." (Follow the procedures she describes in the **Straight from the Classroom** narrative on how to develop cereal box portfolios.) Keep in mind that Julie made numerous adjustments over the years; she suggests talking to teachers who already do this and starting out slowly with one or two new ideas a semester.

As teachers take a more direct, hands-on approach to assessment, they should try to match their beliefs about literacy and instructional practice with the assessment tools they implement. Therefore, teachers who are intent on using portfolio assessment and want to increase the likelihood for success may find certain things particularly useful to do with their students. Be sure to offer guidance, set expectations, monitor portfolio content, conference with each student, and encourage regular self-evaluations in order to facilitate the assessment process. The bottom line is that when a student's work is judged by the standards of growth and positive change and when students play a role in the assessment of their own literacy processes and products, the teacher's role is apt to change. This role of facilitator is one of the many roles a teacher must take on in the assessment process.

Check Your Understanding 5.5: Gauge your understanding of the skills and concepts in this section.

Figure 5.11 Fifth-Grade Internet Inquiry Project: Criteria for Self-Evaluation

Name: _____

Directions: Evaluate your group's performance in each of the following categories. Be honest. Please also make comments about parts of this project you found successful and parts you found unsuccessful.

Content	Points Possible	Points Earned	Comments
Selection of topic	5		
Evidence of planning	10		
Bibliography of print resources (minimum of three per person)	15		
Critical evaluation of websites	10		
Websites (minimum of five): usefulness, appropriateness	20		
Website summaries	30		
Quality of writing	10		
Total	100		

Figure 5.12 Writing Conference Log

WRITING CONFERENCE LOG FOR: *Megan O.*

Date:	Title:	Focus of Conference:	Genre:
Jan. 15	*Plot Comparison for Story of Three Whales & Humphrey the Lost Whale*	*Compare/contrast*	fiction (nonfiction)

Progress observations:

Strengths
1) was able to correctly compare/contrast stories
2) able to complete the sentences

Spelling development: *Examples of spelling*
thay ✓
traped ⟩ *transitional*
banged
lived ⟩ *conventional*

Areas to work on
1) more details for the story endings

Developmental stage
* work on double consonants
* able to add "ed" endings

Date:	Title:	Focus of Conference:	Genre:
Jan. 20	*Double-Entry Journal for Whales Song*	*reflection/sharing ideas*	(fiction) nonfiction

Progress observations:

Strengths
1) Megan easily identified passages she liked!
2) She picked meaningful passages
* Do more double entries! Megan would benefit!!!

Spelling development: *Examples of spelling*
deskripting
used, good, words

Areas to work on
1) identifying more reasons for her choices, connecting to personal life (possibly)
2) risk-taking

Developmental stage
transitional
conventional

Date:	Title:	Focus of Conference:	Genre:
Jan. 28	*Whales*		fiction (nonfiction)

Progress observations:

Strengths
1) many details
2) topic sentence
3) lists mammal traits
4) good closing sentence

Spelling development: *Examples of spelling*
bowhead, whale
favit (favorite)
diffrnt (different)
boty (body)
tempcer (temperature)
mammel

Areas to work on
commas – for lists

Developmental stage
conventional

transitional

Assessment Today and Tomorrow

■ **Reflect upon how literacy assessment has changed over the years and will continue to do so.**

As we have discussed, the assessment of literacy is a complex process. "Not only is literacy complex and social but also the literate demands of the world keep changing with exponential acceleration" (Johnston & Costello, 2005, p. 257). State-mandated common core standards have federal, state, and local officials searching for ways to make assessment meaningful. Multistate consortiums like Smarter Balanced have developed a balanced assessment process to provide data to inform instruction as well as to provide accurate information for program and professional development. With the demands of accountability, Common Core State Standards, instructional decision making, and transliteracies, new recommendations and trends in assessment will come about. It is important to remember that the assessment process needs to be flexible. The use of multiple assessments can help provide a broader perspective of literacy development.

2017 ILA Standards

3.1, 3.2

Utilizing multiple assessments is especially important to Chris (see Box 5.2). As a high school senior, Chris reflects on the various assessment experiences he has had throughout his schooling. He points out that assessments have specific purposes and should be utilized at different stages of learning.

Recommended by the IRA Literacy Research Panel (2012), the assessment process will need to change in order to assess students engaged in complex reading tasks. The panel suggested that because of the limitations of assessments, teachers need to connect assessment and instruction. With this connection teachers can link the goals of reading and assessment so that the assessment process does not interfere with literacy development. Alignment of assessments with standards has influenced and continues to influence assessment utilization. When aligning the assessment, it is important that each assessment is linked to a specific objective or purpose. However, aligning assessments with state standards does not mean creating assessments that mimic the content and format of the annual test. An alignment that is too close gives the state tests more focus and narrows the curriculum (Herman & Baker, 2005). Rather, assessments that look at standards and test formats holistically measure student learning more accurately and provide the appropriate information needed for instructional decision making.

2017 ILA Standard

3.2

BOX 5.2 | STUDENT VOICES

Chris is a successful student and reader. He recognizes that his home experiences, accessibility to interesting books and magazines, and the encouragement of his mother have all contributed to his reading success.

When reflecting on his assessment experiences, Chris recalls that in his early years being assessed in reading mainly included reading aloud. Chris said, "Teachers would test me and the other classmates' knowledge of reading by having us read passages aloud to the class." He further explains that as he grew older, he started to take "more comprehensive tests on passages and other short stories." Finally during his high school years, the connection of reading and writing was emphasized. Chris points out that "reading skills are tested through papers and essays."

With regard to standardized assessments, Chris believes, "The purpose is to compare students in their state and other students around the nation." He continues, "Teachers use these

tests to discover weaknesses in students' abilities." Chris believes that this type of assessment "does not accurately tell about the abilities of everyone who takes these tests."

Chris recommends the use of multiple assessments by teachers so they can learn about their students' reading abilities. He cautions about the use of multiple-choice tests because it allows for guessing. He is also concerned about assessments that require students to "memorize dates, names, quotes, and other pieces of information in the books or stories." Chris believes knowing major details are important to evaluate comprehension skills; however, "minute details that are not mentioned more than a few times measure memorization skills more than how well a student can read."

Chris has had a variety of assessment experiences throughout his years in school. His insights provide teachers important information to reflect on as they develop an assessment process.

If literacy assessment is to guide reading and writing instruction, then the assessment utilized needs to reflect the process of literacy learning. Teachers must also be cognizant of societal demands and the requirements of accountability. Most important, assessment practices need to reflect the values and beliefs of the teachers as well as focus on the needs of the learners.

Check Your Understanding 5.6: Gauge your understanding of the skills and concepts in this section.

RTI for Struggling Readers

Assessment and *Response to Intervention*

A combination of informal assessments is regularly utilized for the Response to Intervention (RTI) initiative. As described previously, RTI is a systematic approach to provide intensive support and intervention for struggling readers. Differentiated and intensified language and literacy assessment and instruction are key to the RTI framework, especially for academically and linguistically diverse students. As recommended by the International Reading Association (2010a), RTI assessment guidelines include the following:

1. The assessment process is aligned with the multidimensional nature of literacy, language, and students.
2. Assessments and techniques reflect authentic language and literacy activities.
3. Appropriate assessments and techniques are aligned with purposes and language abilities.
4. Assessment is a layered approach to include screening, diagnosis, and ongoing progress monitoring.
5. Teachers and literacy specialists have a critical role in conducting assessments to plan instruction and monitor the students.
6. Assessments should be aligned with the *Standards for the Assessment of Reading and Writing* (2010b) developed by IRA and NCTE.

Literacy assessments are utilized to determine reading skills students need and to identify the skills that would be at risk. The assessment process also measures students' responses to intervention and monitors their progress. Finally, the assessment process involves utilizing results to plan instruction. Assessment is truly multifaceted.

2017 ILA Standards

3.1, 3.2, 4.1

What About . . .

Standards, Assessment, and Reading Performance?

Assessing students is a process of gathering and using multiple sources of relevant information for instructional purposes. Two major approaches to assessment prevail in education today: a formal, high-stakes one and an informal, authentic one. Pressure from federal and state policy makers and other constituencies has resulted in the adoption of curriculum standards specifying goals and objectives in subject areas and grade levels in most states. Hence student performance on state-mandated tests must be considered by teachers when making instructional decisions based on their students' content literacy skills, concepts, and performance.

An informal, authentic approach is often more practical in collecting and organizing the many kinds of information that can inform decisions, including students' prior knowledge and students' use of reading strategies and other communication strategies. Knowing the assessment type, purposes, and strengths and limitations all can help teachers make the appropriate decisions from assessment data to plan and evaluate instruction.

Summary

- Reading is a process that takes place inside the mind; it isn't directly observable or measurable through any one instrument or procedure. To make an authentic assessment of a human process that's essentially hidden from direct examination, teachers need to base decisions about instruction on multiple indicators of reading performance.

- Trends in reading assessment are almost at cross-purposes with one another. Very different perspectives are held by educators who support standard setting and high-stakes testing and those who promote authentic, performance-based assessment.

- The uses of formal types of assessment were considered for both norm-referenced and criterion-referenced tests. We examined how to interpret test scores and provided information about reliability and validity of standardized tests.

- We explored informal assessment, beginning with informal reading inventories. Observation and interview, informal reading inventories, miscue analysis, and running records also contribute to teachers' understanding of students' learning. They all are useful for matching students with appropriate materials and in determining how they interact with print in oral and silent reading situations.

- The utilization of portfolios is a way to document literacy development. Essential components of portfolio usage include teacher-assigned and self-selected work. Additionally, portfolio layout and purpose need to be determined for proper implementation in order to make it an assessment tool.

- Assessment is a complex process and is used for different purposes. Mandates at the federal and state levels influence assessment selection, especially when data from the assessments are utilized to determine achievement of standards.

Teacher Action Research

1. Look at whole class data from multiple sources that have been gathered relating to standards and literacy development. What patterns of student learning do you notice? What additional information do you need? Create instructional lessons based on the data. Be sure to defend the decisions you make.

2. At a parent–teacher conference, you were asked to explain the difference between high-stakes testing and authentic assessment. What would you say to the parents? Explain.

3. Create a visual of the differences and similarities between the purposes of formal and informal assessments.

4. Complete a miscue analysis with a primary or middle school student to find out more about the student's processing of print. Or ask a classmate to read a passage and purposely make miscues; record the reading. Then follow the procedures in this chapter for conducting miscue analysis to determine the percentage of semantically acceptable miscues, and so forth. Analyze to what extent the reader was able to use and coordinate graphophonemic, semantic, and syntactic information from the text.

5. Collaborating with a partner, develop a method of portfolio assessment that you believe would serve to show students' growth in literacy. What would be the essential elements of all of the portfolios? What elements would you leave open to student selection? Design a cover sheet to help organize and explain the portfolio's content. Determine the criteria for evaluating the content of the portfolio.

6. Interview an administrator from a local school district in order to discuss his or her beliefs about effective methods to assess and how assessment has changed. Then interview teachers on different grade levels, inquiring about their beliefs on how to assess literacy. Compare the recommendations and beliefs. Discuss why you believe each person interviewed responded the way he or she did.

Through the Lens of the Common Core

With the adoption of the Common Core State Standards (CCSS) at the state level, there is a push for a consortium of state educators to develop a common assessment system. Utilizing a common assessment system will encourage comparison across students, schools, and states, which takes away from the purpose of assessment and does not focus on teaching and learning.

Until the common assessment is determined, assessing the Common Core State Standards for English Language Arts (CCSS-ELA) varies among the states. Some states rely upon standardized assessments while others utilize authentic assessments.

What is important for this varied process is the utilization of the data received. Assessments are to provide teachers information about the students' learning. Utilizing multiple assessments is key due to the nature of the assessment process and the uniqueness of each child. Assessing the CCSS with multiple means helps to give schools the opportunity to make decisions about literacy learning as well as instructional approaches and strategies.

Chapter 6
Word Identification

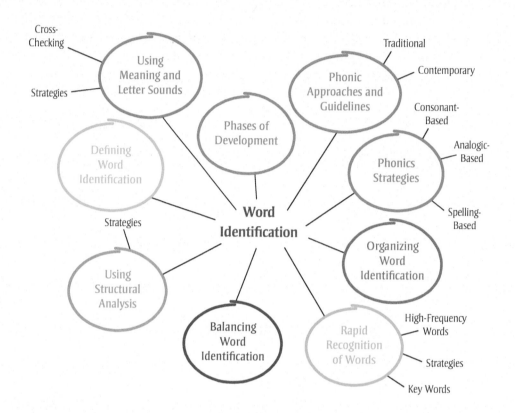

In This Chapter, You Will Discover How to

- Define word identification, and synthesize associated terminology.

- Characterize various phases of development in children's ability to identify words.

- Compare and contrast traditional and contemporary approaches and guidelines for teaching phonics.

- Explain strategies for teaching phonics, including consonant-based and analogic-based strategies.

- Describe strategies that combine using meaning and letter–sound information to identify words.

- Characterize strategies that use structural analysis to identify words.

- Identify strategies that teach rapid recognition of words.

- Organize word identification instruction according to identifiable principles.

- Balance word identification instruction through multiple approaches.

Activating Your Schema

Read each of these words: *the* and *frontimity*. Did you know the first word? Why? Could you pronounce the next word? If yes, how did you do it? What helped you to read that word? Now read the following sentence: *When the car sped down the four-lane frontimity the police officer pulled the driver over for speeding.* Even though you have never seen the word *frontimity*, what do you think it means in this sentence? Discuss with a partner how you identified each of the words to begin thinking about how we recognize words.

2017 ILA Standards Found in This Chapter

1.1	2.2
2.1	5.2

Common Core State Standards: English Language Arts

CCRA.R.4	CCRA.L.4	CCRA.L.5	CCRA.L.6

Key Terms

analogy-based phonics instruction	onset
analytic phonics	phonics
cloze procedure	phonograms
context clues	rime
cross-checking	self-monitoring
embedded phonics instruction	semantic gradients
high-frequency words	spelling-based strategies
incremental rehearsal	structural analysis
inflected endings	synthetic phonics
key words	word banks
morpheme	word ladders
multisensory activities	word walls

At age three, Jimmy, one of our children, commented while driving through the mountains of Pennsylvania on a trip to his grandparents' home, "So, where is the *pencil* in Pennsylvania?" Another time, when knocked over by a wave in the ocean (visiting his other grandparents on the East Coast), he stormed out of the water and exclaimed in childhood moodiness, "I don't like that *sexy* ocean!" Still another time, when Jimmy was running around in circles in the living room, his mother asked, "What are you doing, Jimmy?" "I'm catching pneumonia!" he earnestly replied. Hence, a young child's observations of oral language.

Jimmy also had a keen sense of the *visual* components of language. At age three, he was adept at completing a puzzle of the United States and could name each state while working with a plastic template. When walking him in a stroller through the mall one day, he seemed to be intrigued by the "map" of the mall and wanted to know "What is Utah doing in Sears?" The shape of Utah actually resembled the shape on the mall map of the Sears store. Interesting observation. Still another time, when visiting a restaurant in southern Ohio, a sign on the building captured Jimmy's interest as a three-year-old. Jimmy wanted to know what "OHIO" was doing in a sign that advertised "CHICKEN." (If you close the Cs of the word CHICKEN, they become Os—hence, OHIO). And when asked what he was doing with pencil and paper at the dining room table, he candidly replied, "I'm doing the taxes."

These are examples of one young child's observations of the world of language and print. Not all children at age three, however, are as observant of the purposes and components of literacy as Jimmy. Although children enter school with a broad range of literacy concepts, teachers need to have a wide repertoire of instructional strategies that teach children how to *read* print and *identify* words. Although teachers have different instructional approaches, they have the same instructional goal in mind: They want their students to achieve independence in word identification. *How* teachers invest their time in helping readers identify words is an important instructional question; although there are differences in practice, it is philosophical differences that seem to predominate (Stahl, 1992; Stahl, Duffy-Hester, & Stahl, 1998).

In this chapter, we suggest strategies that reflect two broad instructional goals of word identification instruction. The first is that children should learn how to identify unfamiliar words *rapidly* and *independently*. If children cannot quickly recognize new words on their own, reading soon becomes tedious, if not overwhelming. Misty, a first grader, put it this way: "I'm in big trouble if I miss words when I'm reading." Furthermore, if word identification takes up most of the reader's energy and attention, comprehension and enjoyment will suffer (Samuels, 1994).

A second goal of instruction is that readers should develop *multiple strategies* for word identification. Readers must have an adequate sight vocabulary and know how to use phonics, the structure of words, and context clues to help them identify words.

2017 ILA Standard

1.1

Defining Word Identification

■ **Define word identification, and synthesize associated terminology.**

Several terms have been associated with identifying words: *word attack, word analysis, word recognition,* and *decoding.* These terms are often used interchangeably. Figure 6.1 illustrates the relationship of these terms to word identification. *Word identification* means putting a name or label on words that are encountered in print. It is a comprehensive term that encompasses the use of multiple cues to identify unfamiliar words.

Word recognition suggests a process that involves *immediate identification.* Immediately recognized words are retrieved rapidly from *lexical memory.* Word recognition is sometimes referred to as *sight-word recognition* or *sight vocabulary.* These terms suggest a reader's ability to recognize words rapidly and automatically. In this chapter, we use *immediate word recognition* to describe rapid recognition. Keep in mind, however, that the process of immediate word recognition is far more complicated than merely recognizing words on flash cards. When a word is retrieved rapidly from memory, the process is often triggered by the application of letter–sound knowledge. Learning to read words rapidly involves making associations between particular spellings, pronunciations, and meanings by applying knowledge of letter–sound relationships (Ehri, 1995). Skilled readers use the strategy of immediate word recognition on 99 percent of the printed words they encounter.

Figure 6.1 Terms Related to Word Identification

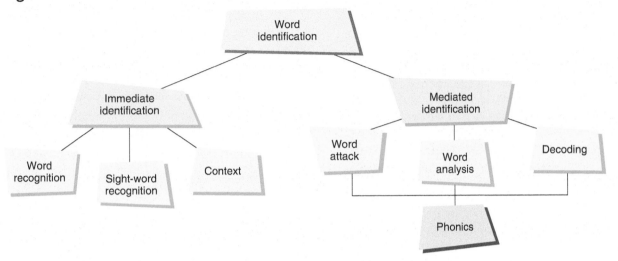

Word identification also includes strategies in which pictures and surrounding text assist the reader in recognizing words.

The terms *word attack, word analysis,* and *decoding* suggest the act of translating print into speech through analysis of letter–sound relationships. These terms have been used frequently with what is commonly referred to as *phonics.* **Phonics** provides readers with a tool to pronounce words by associating sounds (phonemes) with letters (graphemes). Phonics involves *mediated word identification* because readers must devote conscious attention to "unlocking" the alphabetic code.

Teachers are in the most strategic position to make decisions about the word identification strategies children actually use to read and write well. Effective teachers ask *when, how, how much,* and *under what circumstances* word identification strategies should be taught. Understanding the phases of development that children progress through in their ability to identify words is important knowledge that teachers can use to make decisions about instruction. See Box 6.1 to learn Tim Rasinski's viewpoint on word identification.

BOX 6.1 | VIEWPOINT

Timothy Rasinski

Word Identification Involves More than Teaching Phonics

Timothy Rasinski is a professor of literacy education at Kent State University.

I am glad that you have chosen to use the term *word identification* to identify the contents of this chapter. In recent years, the term *word identification* has been supplanted by *phonics* in many literacy-related educational circles. I prefer *word identification* as it is a broader term that refers to all the ways that a reader can *decode* words. Certainly phonics, using one's knowledge of the letters and letter combinations and the sounds they represent, is one way to unlock the pronunciation of a word. However, there are other strategies that readers use to decode words— the meaningful context that surrounds words, knowledge of meaningful prefixes and suffixes, and the reader's knowledge of English root words that are derived from other languages, par-

ticularly Latin and Greek. Word identification embraces all these strategies. Good readers have access to and use multiple decoding strategies, not simply phonics. Of course the ultimate goal of a good word identification program is for readers to maximize their sight vocabulary—words that have been memorized by sight and sound. I'd like to suggest that the goal of any word identification or phonics program is to get students to the point where they don't have to use phonics—identifying a word using phonics or other strategies uses cognitive energy that could be better used for comprehending the text. Very little cognitive energy is used when the words that a reader encounters are recognized by sight.

In my opinion, word identification needs to be taught daily, directly, and in engaging ways to students. A person cannot read if he or she is unable to decode the words in print. However, this does not mean that I endorse the use of a daily packet of worksheets that has been the traditional tool for teaching word identification. This approach, I believe, is not terribly effective—it sends the message to students that words and the study of words is a dry subject filled with learning activities that are boring.

I am a constructivist at heart, and I feel that students best learn words when they are guided by their teacher in learning how words work—how words are made and how the various elements of words represent sound and meaning. Pat Cunningham's instructional strategy *Making Words* and my variation called *Making and Writing Words* are particular favorite strategies of mine and the students I work with in our university reading clinic. **Word ladders** are another form of guided word construction that students love and through which students learn words. Here is a word ladder that is based on the title of this text (students respond with the word in parentheses):

Read   Change a letter in *Read* to make a word that means to "be in charge."

(Lead)   Change a letter in *Lead* to make a word that means "to rest against an object for support OR a person or animal with very little fat."

(Lean)   Add a letter to *Lean* to make a word that describes what happens when you read.

(Learn)!

I have found that word identification instruction seems to be most engaging, authentic, and effective when it feels like a game for students and teachers. Think of all the games that we play as adults that involve words in one form or another—Scrabble, Boggle, Scrabble Slam, crossword puzzles, Upwords, Wheel of Fortune, Buzz Word, Taboo, and so on. If adults love games that involve words, why wouldn't students? Indeed, that's what we have found. Making words, word ladders, word sorts, word bingo, developing word walls, and the like all have the feel of a game that makes the students want to engage in the study and play of words.

Word identification needs to be taught. However, when teachers are empowered to design their instruction and the word study curriculum in ways that are engaging and fun for their students, they will not only be developing good readers, they will also be developing *lexophiles*—people who love words.-

Keep in mind, however, that word identification is only one part of the total reading curriculum. In addition to word study, students need daily instruction in reading fluency, comprehension, study strategies, and so on. Effective reading instruction involves all aspects of the reading process.

2017 ILA Standard

2.2

Check Your Understanding 6.1: Gauge your understanding of the skills and concepts in this section.

Phases of Development in Children's Ability to Identify Words

■ **Characterize various phases of development in children's ability to identify words.**

It is through frequent experiences with books and print that children develop knowledge about reading and writing prior to school. They do so at different rates, in different ways, and in different settings. When young children engage in frequent book and print experiences, their development of word knowledge may emerge during the preschool years without much, if any, formal instruction. Yet the ability to read words cannot be left to chance. Teachers must build and expand on the word-reading knowledge that children bring to school. See Box 6.2 to read about one student's perceptions of learning to read English.

Children progress through various developmental phases of word identification while learning to read (Ehri, 1991, 1994). In the course of their development, they first learn to identify some words purely through *visual cues*, such as distinctive graphic features *in* or *around* the words. As children continue to grow as readers, they use their developing knowledge of letter–sound relationships to identify words. The development of word learning can be divided into four phases: the *prealphabetic,*

BOX 6.2 | STUDENT VOICES

Kathia is an 11-year-old Hispanic fourth grader from Honduras. She is an average fourth-grade student who has experienced academic challenges. Kathia has attended both public and private schools and is currently attending a parochial school. She was interviewed by Mr. Smith, who knows Kathia through a cooperative learning experience with preclinical teachers. According to Mr. Smith, Kathia has truly "opened up" during this school year and was enthusiastic to share her thoughts about learning.

When asked to share her experiences about learning to speak and read English, Kathia said, "I was never too good in school before. I stay after school to get tutored sometimes, but mostly I do a lot better in school now." She explained that when she first began school in America, she didn't understand anything, she didn't have any friends, and she thought that everyone made fun of her. When she switched schools (to the private one), Kathia became more confident because she had a friend she met at camp who was in the same class. Kathia explained that because she had a friend, "I knew I would do better in school. The teacher lets me ask Wuendy [another Hispanic student] something if I don't know, but mostly I know everything now."

When Mr. Smith asked Kathia about learning to read English, she shared that she likes to be part of the story. "I close my eyes and pretend to be one of the characters. I mostly like to be the best character because they get to do a lot of fun things. I like to act out the story, too, and maybe put on a play and we can pretend to be part of the story." Kathia continued, "When I grow up I want to be a teacher. I will let the students talk about the stories after we read them. That will help them remember the story." As far as trying to figure out new words, she shared that if she doesn't know something, she can read it again and that helps her figure it out.

Kathia gives us quite a powerful message in her interview! The focus of this chapter is word identification. This 11-year-old Hispanic child expresses the power of learning words through listening, speaking, and sharing her thoughts. What does this tell us as teachers of all students? Perhaps that we should listen, probe, and allow children to share their understanding of learning words through conversations with our students.

---

partial alphabetic, full alphabetic, and *consolidated alphabetic* phases (Gaskins, Ehri, Cress, O'Hara, & Donnelly, 1997).

The *prealphabetic phase,* which has also been called the *logographic* or *visual cue* phase, occurs before the development of alphabetic knowledge. Children are able to recognize some words at sight during this phase because of distinctive visual and contextual cues in or around the recognized words. The ability to read cereal box labels, restaurant logos, and other kinds of environmental print is one of the first literacy accomplishments of a preschool child. The octagonal shape of a stop sign, for example, may prompt preschoolers to shout "stop" as a parent slows down at the sign. In addition, young children learn to attend to visual cues in words. For example, a child might recognize the word *ball* because of the tall letters at the beginning and end of the word.

ba̲l̲l̲

Children progress to the *partial alphabetic phase* when they begin to develop some knowledge about letters and detect letter–sound relationships. For example, at four and a half years old, Simon reads his name by remembering that the letter *s* looks like a snake and makes a hissing /s/ sound; and the letter *i* sounds like its name. The partial alphabetic phase emerges during kindergarten and first grade for most children, when they acquire some knowledge of letters and sounds. They remember how to read specific words by detecting how a few letters correspond to sounds in the word's pronunciation. For example, a child might read the word *run* because he knows the sounds of *r* and *n*.

ru̲n̲

Early readers who function at the partial alphabetic phase are likely to misread some words sharing the same partial letter–sound cues—for example, misreading *kitchen* as *kitten.* This is especially the case when the word is read in isolation rather than in the context of a story.

The *full alphabetic phase* emerges in children's literacy development when readers identify words by matching all of the letters and sounds. They have developed enough knowledge about letter–sound relationships to unlock the pronunciations of unknown words. For example, a child would recognize all of the actual sounds in the word *cake*.

<u>cake</u>

Sounding out letters and blending them into words may be laborious and slow at the beginning of the full alphabetic phase, but as children become more accomplished at decoding unknown words, they progress to more rapid word analysis. Some children enter first grade with the capacity to analyze words fully. Others do not and will benefit from explicit, carefully planned lessons that help them make discoveries about letter–sound relationships in words (Gaskins et al., 1997).

As children become more skilled at identifying words, they enter the *consolidated alphabetic stage*. They rely less on individual letter–sound relationships. Instead, they use their knowledge of familiar and predictable letter patterns to speed up the process of reading words. They do so by developing the ability to analyze chunks of letters within words (Johnston, 1999; Moustafa & Maldonado-Colon, 1999). For example, when reading the word *ship*, the child sees the *sh* as a chunk and *ip* as a rime.

<u>sh</u> <u>ip</u>

The recognition of predictable letter patterns begins to emerge in the first grade as children engage in reading and begin to recognize many words with similar spelling patterns. Readers at the consolidated alphabetic phase would be able to segment the words into sound units known as **onsets** (the initial consonants and consonant patterns that come at the beginning of syllables) and **rimes** (the vowel and consonants that follow them at the end of syllables). The recognition of letter patterns in the consolidated alphabetic phase eventually allows children to analyze multisyllabic words rapidly.

Although teaching children whose primary language is not English to read is a complex issue, Bear, Helman, Templeton, Invernizzi, and Johnston (2007) synthesize research by providing general instructional principles for English language learners (ELLs). They suggest that word study should be explicit and systematic, yet should allow students to make connections to prior knowledge. In addition, instruction should include active engagement and focus on interaction with others. Lenters (2004/2005) recommends providing opportunities for children to demonstrate what they know in their first language and suggests that parents read to their children in first-language books.

Next, we discuss the teaching of phonics in more depth. As you read about phonics instruction, however, keep in mind that phonics is only one part of a comprehensive reading program.

Check Your Understanding 6.2: Gauge your understanding of the skills and concepts in this section.

Approaches and Guidelines for Teaching Phonics

■ **Compare and contrast traditional and contemporary approaches and guidelines for teaching phonics.**

Approaches to phonics instruction have been classified as traditional or contemporary (Stahl et al., 1998). As Stahl and colleagues put it, traditional approaches to phonics instruction "are approaches that were in vogue during the 1960s and 1970s but seem to be returning as teachers grapple with how to teach phonics" (p. 344). Contemporary approaches to phonics instruction, however, are approaches that emerged in the 1990s and continue to develop in the 2000s. Today, teachers who hold a comprehensive and contemporary literacy philosophy do not adhere to a single approach; they plan instruction using a variety of strategies and materials.

Traditional Approaches

Traditional phonics instruction includes the *analytic* and *synthetic* approaches to teaching word recognition. These approaches are favored by teachers who devote large chunks of time to *early, intensive,* and *systematic* instruction designed to help master the sounds of the letters. The instructional emphasis is often on the teaching of isolated letter–sound correspondences separate from meaningful activities. Implicit in this "phonics first" approach is a bottom-up belief that children must learn letter–sound correspondences *early* in their school experiences in order to build a foundation for reading meaningful texts.

Word identification needs to be taught in meaningful contexts in which students are engaged.

Annie Pickert Fuller/Pearson Education

Intensive and *systematic* are tandem concepts often mentioned in the same breath by proponents of traditional phonics approaches. The word *intensive* suggests a thorough and comprehensive treatment of letter–sound correspondences. *Systematic* implies that phonics instruction should be organized sequentially and in a logical order through structured lessons. Key findings from the National Reading Panel (2000) support early, intensive, systematic phonics instruction.

2017 ILA Standard

2.2

ANALYTIC PHONICS INSTRUCTION   **Analytic phonics** is characterized as "whole-to-part" instruction. The children learn a whole word first and then analyze the individual parts. See Box 6.3 for a step-by-step lesson on how to teach an analytic phonics lesson.

Analytic lessons typically rely heavily on the use of workbooks and practice exercises. A criticism of the analytic approach is that teachers invest too little time on the initial teaching of alphabetic relationships and students spend too much time on paper-and-pencil exercises. Oral instruction from the teacher simply serves as an introduction to worksheets rather than to help students clarify relationships and make discoveries (Durkin, 1988; Stahl et al., 1998). Teachers need to ensure that the students understand that reading needs to make sense in authentic contexts.

SYNTHETIC PHONICS INSTRUCTION   **Synthetic phonics** is teaching sounds in isolation, followed by blending the sounds to form words. See Box 6.4 for a step-by-step lesson that teaches synthetic phonics.

BOX 6.3 | STEP-BY-STEP LESSON

Analytic Phonics Lesson

1. Decide on a one-syllable word to teach as a whole word; for example, *cat*. Teach the word by associating it with a picture.
2. Once the student can read the word *cat* as a whole, decide on a phonetic element to teach; for example, the initial sound *c*.
3. Segment the *c*, and teach the initial sound alone as /k/. Have the child associate other words that begin with that sound; for example, *car, cake, cow*. If the child says *kite*, tell the child that the sound is the same, but another letter makes that same sound.
4. You do not need to elaborate here about the other letter.
5. When the child knows the sound of *c*, add the letter back to the *at*, for *cat*.
6. Decide on another phonetic sound to teach based on the word *cat*. For example, you could teach the initial sound of *t* as in *tap, table, tip*; or the initial sound of short *a* as in *apple, after, at*.
7. As you teach the sounds in isolation, be sure to review them regularly.

BOX 6.4 | STEP-BY-STEP LESSON

Synthetic Phonics Lesson

1. Teach a set of letter names; for example, *t, a, c.*
2. Teach the corresponding sounds for each letter.
3. Review and practice the sounds for each letter. For example, *t* makes the sound at the beginning of *table, tent, top*; *a* makes the sound at the beginning of *apple, action, after*; *c* makes the sound at the beginning of *cake, cup, cow.* Pictures and letter cards can be used to develop games.
4. Drill and practice until the students can rapidly elicit the sound associated with each letter.
5. Next, model how the individual sounds can be blended to make a word; in this example, the sounds of *c, a, t* make the word *cat.*
6. Continue with other letters, sounds, and blending activities.
7. Be sure to keep track of the letter sounds you have taught and review with blending activities.

There are similarities between analytic and synthetic phonics. Both approaches discuss isolated letter–sound relationships, break words apart, and put them back together again.

Teachers who engage children in the analysis of words must be well versed and knowledgeable in content and language of phonics. In Figure 6.2, we highlight the basic terminology associated with the content of phonics instruction. In Figure 6.3, we share word patterns that represent reasonably consistent vowel and consonant sounds depending on the locations of the letters.

SYLLABLES A *syllable* is a vowel or a cluster of letters containing a vowel and pronounced as a unit. Phonograms, for example, are syllables. The composition of the syllable signals the most probable vowel sound. Examine the following word patterns in Figure 6.3.

These patterns underlie the formation of syllables. The number of syllables in a word is equal to the number of vowel sounds. For example, the word *disagreement* has four vowel sounds and thus four syllables. The word *hat* has one vowel sound and thus one syllable.

There are three primary syllabication patterns that signal how to break down a word into syllabic units. Examine the patterns in Figure 6.4.

Although there is no one particular phonics sequence or program that is better than another (Cunningham, 2005), Bear, Helman, Templeton, Invernizzi, and Johnston (2007) suggest that early English learners begin with initial and final consonant sounds and short and long vowels by picture sorting, followed by blends, word families, and digraphs. In addition, they recommend:

- Talking with students as they perform activities such as drawing, painting, and playing with blocks
- Reading to students and talking about words and pictures
- Reading with students chorally, and using repeated readings and dictation activities

Helman's (2004) research on the English and Spanish sound systems reveals that the following consonants and vowels are shared between the two:

b, d, f, g, k, l, m, n, p, s, t, w, y

long *a, e, i, o, u* and short *o*

She also notes that Spanish does *not* include the following /s/ blends or clusters:

st, sp, sk, sc, sm, sl, sn, sw, scr, spl, spr, str, squ

2017 ILA Standard

2.2

Figure 6.2 A Primer on the Content and Language of Phonics

Consonants. *Consonants* are all the sounds represented by letters of the alphabet except *a, e, i, o, u.* Consonants conform fairly closely to *one-to-one correspondence*—for each letter there is one sound. This property of consonants makes them of great value to the reader when attempting to sound out an unknown word. There are some consonant anomalies:

The letter *y* is a consonant only at the beginning of a syllable, as in *yet.*
The letter *w* is sometimes a vowel, as in *flew.*
Sometimes consonants have no sound, as in *know.*
The letters *c* and *g* each have two sounds, called hard and soft sounds:

Hard *c: cat, coaster, catatonic* (*c* sounds like /k/)
Soft *c: city, receive, cite* (*c* sounds like /s/)
Hard *g: give, gallop, garbage* (*g* sounds like /g/)
Soft *g: giraffe, ginger, gym* (*g* sounds like /j/)

Consonant Blends. *Consonant blends* are two or three consonants grouped together, but each consonant retains its original sound. There are several major groups of blends:

l blends: *bl   cl   fl   gl   pl   sl*
r blends: *br   cr   dr   fr   gr   pr   tr*
s blends: *sc   sk   sm   sn   sp   st   sw*
three-letter blends: *scr   spr   str*

Consonant Digraphs. When two or more consonants are combined to produce a new sound, the letter cluster is called a *consonant digraph.* The most common consonant digraphs are these:

ch as in *chin*	*ph* as in *phone*
sh as in *shell*	*gh* as in *ghost*
th as in *think*	*nk* as in *tank*
wh as in *whistle*	*ng* as in *tang*

Vowels. *Vowels* are all the sounds represented by the letters *a, e, i, o, u.* The letter *y* serves as a vowel when it is not the initial sound of a word. Sometimes *w* functions as a vowel, usually when it follows another vowel. There is *rarely a one-to-one correspondence* between a letter representing a vowel and the sound of the vowel. Vowel sounds are influenced heavily by their location in a word and by the letters accompanying them. Several major types of vowel phonemes are worth knowing about.

A *long vowel* sound is a speech sound similar to the letter name of the vowel. A *macron* (-) is sometimes used to indicate that a vowel is long. *Short vowel* sounds are speech sounds also represented by vowel letters. Short sounds are denoted by a *breve* (˘). An example of the long and short sound of each vowel letter follows:

Short Vowel Sound	**Long Vowel Sound**
/ă/ as in *Pat*	/ā/ as in *lake*
/ĕ/ as in *bed*	/ē/ as in *be*
/ĭ/ as in *pit*	/ī/ as in *ice*
/ŏ/ as in *hot*	/ō/ as in *go*
/ŭ/ as in *hug*	/ū/ as in *use*

Often when a vowel letter initiates a word, the short sound will be used; for example, *at, effort, interest, optimist,* and *uncle.*

Vowel Digraphs. *Vowel digraphs* are two vowels that are adjacent to one another. The first vowel is usually long, and the second is silent. Vowel digraphs include *oa, ee, ea, ai,* and *ay,* as in *boat, beet, beat, bait,* and *bay.* There are notable exceptions: *oo* as in *look, ew* as in *flew, ea* as in *head.*

Vowel Diphthongs. *Vowel diphthongs* are sounds that consist of a blend of two separate vowel sounds. These are /oi/ as in *oil,* /oy/ as in *toy,* /au/ as in *taught,* /aw/ as in *saw,* /ou/ as in *out,* and /ow/ as in *how.* Generally, children do not need to be taught these formally.

Consonant-Influenced Vowels. The letter *a* has a special sound when followed by an *l,* as in *Albert* or *tallow. R*-controlled vowels occur when any vowel letter is followed by an *r: star, her, fir, for,* and *purr.*

Phonograms. *Phonograms* (also called *rimes*) are letter patterns that help form word families or rhyming words. Letter clusters such as *ad, at, ack, ag, an, ap, ash, ed, et, ess, en, ine,* and *ike* can be used to develop families of words; for example, the *ad* family: *bad, dad, sad, fad,* and so on. Phonograms may be one of the most useful letter patterns to teach because they encourage children to map speech sounds onto larger chunks of letters.

Contemporary Approaches

Contemporary approaches to phonics instruction do not emphasize an overreliance on worksheets, skill-and-drill activities, rules, or rote memorization. Instead, contemporary approaches are rooted in constructivist principles of learning and the fact that children can learn phonics through meaningful engagement with reading real texts. Compared to traditional approaches to phonics instruction during which phonics is

Figure 6.3 Word Patterns

Long vowels	CV	*be*
	CVe	*like*
		rote
	CVVC	*paid*
		boat
Short vowels	VC or CVC	*it*
		hot
R-controlled	Vr	*art*
	CVr	*car, her*
Digraph/diphthong variations	VV	*saw, book*
		boil, out

Figure 6.4 Syllabication Patterns

- *VCCV.* When there are two consonants between two vowels, the word is usually divided between the consonants: *hap-pen, mar-ket, es-cape.* However, we do not split consonant digraphs such as *sh* or *th* or *ng,* as in *sing-er, fa-ther.* There is a variation of this pattern—the VCC*le* pattern. A word with this pattern is still divided between the consonants: *sad-dle, bot-tle, rat-tle, pud-dle.*
- *VCV pattern 1.* When one consonant is between two vowels, the division is before the consonant: *re-view, o-pen, be-gin.* Again there is a slight variation with the VC*le* pattern, but still divide before the consonant: *peo-ple, ta-ble, cra-dle.*
- *VCV pattern 2.* If using VCV pattern 1 does not result in a familiar word, divide after the consonant, as in *sal-ad* or *pan-el.*

often treated as a separate "subject," contemporary approaches integrate the learning of sound–symbol relationships within the context of meaningful activities.

Next, we examine two approaches to teaching phonics from contemporary points of view. These perspectives are more holistic and reflect a "top-down" philosophy. By that, we mean they begin with the learner, what the learner knows, and what teachers need to teach based on that knowledge.

2017 ILA Standard

2.2

ANALOGY-BASED PHONICS INSTRUCTION In **analogy-based phonics instruction,** children are taught to recognize onsets and rimes as they learn to decode unfamiliar words. Underscoring analogic-based instruction is the notion that children learn to read words in context better than out of context and that "chunking words" by letter patterns is what good readers do (Cunningham, 2000; Goswami, 1986). Research suggests that we use letter patterns to read, rather than looking at individual letters and blending them (Cunningham, 2005, 2009; Treiman, 1985). Analogic phonics focuses on having children compare and contrast words that they already know in order to figure out unknown words (Gaskins et al., 1997).

Analogic phonics instruction is favored by teachers who believe that children need to actively engage in word study to make words, learn spelling patterns, and draw analogies between known and unknown word parts. See Box 6.5 for a step-by-step procedure on how to teach an analogic phonics lesson.

EMBEDDED PHONICS INSTRUCTION **Embedded phonics instruction** is often associated with holistic, meaning-centered teaching. In literature-based instruction, for example, students learn phonics skills in the context of stories that make sense. First, a story is read; next, word identification of letters, words, and phrases is studied within the context of text.

The National Reading Panel (2000) criticized the concept of embedded phonics, claiming that it is not systematic and intensive enough, and tends to be incidental. However, we believe that children need to be cognizant of what they are learning, and

BOX 6.5 | STEP-BY-STEP LESSON

Analogic-Based Phonics Lesson

1. Decide on the letter pattern(s) you are going to teach. For example, *-an* and *-at.*
2. Select literature that includes examples of the letter pattern. For example, *Angus the Cat* contains words with the letter patterns *-an* and *-at.*
3. Read the story aloud for enjoyment, and discuss the story line.
4. Introduce the letter patterns, and reread the story as children listen for words that contain those patterns.
5. Reread the story a third time. During this reading, pause as each word that contains the pattern is read and record the words on a chart or word wall.
6. Continue instruction by providing opportunities for the students to write the words, use them in sentences, complete cloze passages, and engage in sorting activities.
7. Provide other books that contain the letter patterns, and encourage the children to partner read, silent read, or read the books in small groups.

teaching must be multifaceted and meaning centered. Hence, we believe that teachers can teach phonics systematically through meaningful literature. Systematic phonics instruction means implementing a logical, sequential plan. When teachers determine the sequential order for phonics instruction, they will use (easy to more difficult) and the order of letters and sounds to be learned. It makes sense that using literature to introduce the phonics elements that are featured in the literature can be a natural, meaningful way to introduce the phonics elements. In fact, a simple Google search of books that teach a particular phonics sound provides teachers with multiple books for engaging students in meaningful connections through literature.

GUIDELINES FOR CONTEMPORARY PHONICS INSTRUCTION   Here are five guidelines for contemporary phonics instruction that work both in classrooms where the basal reader is the core text and in classrooms where reading instruction centers on literature-based programs.

1. Phonics instruction needs to build on a foundation of phonemic awareness and knowledge of the way language works. Young children differ in their phonemic awareness of sounds in spoken words.
2. Phonics instruction needs to be integrated into a total reading program. No more than 25 percent of the time, and possibly less, should be spent on phonics instruction and practice (Stahl, 1992).
3. Phonics instruction needs to focus on reading print rather than on learning rules. Skilled readers do not refer to phonics rules but see words in terms of patterns of letters. Adams (1990) points out that they recognize new words by comparing them to words and patterns they already know.
4. Phonics instruction needs to include the teaching of onsets and rimes (Morris, 2015; Treiman, 1985). An *onset,* or the part of a syllable before the vowel, is a consonant or consonant blend or digraph; a *rime* is the rest of the syllable. Consonant letter–sound associations are fairly consistent. In addition, **phonograms** or rimes have been found to be generalizable. One early study found that of the 286 phonograms that appear in primary-grade texts, 95 percent were pronounced the same in every word in which they were found (Durrell, 1963). According to Wylie and Durrell (1970), nearly 500 primary-grade words can be derived from only 37 consistent rimes. Fry (1998) provides a useful resource of the 38 most common phonograms for teachers.
5. Phonics instruction needs to include invented spellings. When children are encouraged to write and to use invented spellings, they use their knowledge of letter–sound relationships. Writing with invented spelling improves children's awareness of phonemes, an important precursor to learning to decode words.

Check Your Understanding 6.3: Gauge your understanding of the skills and concepts in this section.

Strategies for Teaching Phonics

■ **Explain strategies for teaching phonics, including consonant-based and analogic-based strategies.**

The preceding five guidelines are broad statements of principles by which teachers can become actively involved in the teaching of phonics based on contemporary approaches to instruction. These principles are grounded in research related to the phonics children use to identify words. Contemporary phonics approaches support children's ability to identify words through explicit strategy-based instruction and integrated learning during reading and writing activities.

2017 ILA Standard
2.2

Consonant-Based Strategies

Recognizing and naming letters is one of the important accomplishments of early readers because it sets the stage for beginners to become involved in more sophisticated manipulations of graphemes and phonemes. Consonant letters represent all of the individual phonemes associated with letters of the alphabet except for the vowels *a, e, i, o,* and *u.* Because consonants generally have one sound for each letter, they lend themselves well to instructional strategies that allow children to make discoveries about words. Once children have developed a good grasp of consonant letter–sound relationships, they can engage in activities that will help them recognize consonant digraphs and blends. Consider the following consonant-based phonics instructional strategies and activities.

MULTISENSORY ACTIVITIES   **Multisensory activities** are instructional strategies that involve the senses, namely the visual, auditory, kinesthetic, and tactile modalities. Children who struggle with reading, including dyslexics, benefit from instruction that taps all of the senses; students see, hear, move, and touch or write as they are learning. Although there are many commercial phonics programs that utilize multisensory activities, teachers can implement these techniques regardless of the reading curriculum.

The visual modality involves the sense of vision, including viewing images. Visual aids for learning phonics can include pictures, illustrations, photographs, cartoons, posters, and multimedia representations to name a few; the use of color can also be beneficial. For example, an illustration, a photograph, or an animated cartoon of a *cat* might represent the initial consonant sound *c.* Auditory activities can include singing, clapping, stomping, and tapping. For example, when children work with phonemes, they often clap to them as they decode words. Kinesthetic activities include physical actions as they are associated with letters and sounds, such as *pointing to letters* and moving markers in Elkonan boxes. Other instructional strategies include drama, floor games, and activities that include body movements such as finger-tapping to the phonemes heard in words. Tracing is a tactile activity in which teachers can use textures to help children associate graphemes with phonemes. Materials that are useful for tactile lessons include sand or salt trays, plastic screens or templates, sandpaper, colored chalk, glitter, and so forth. Teachers should not reserve multisensory activities for students who struggle. All learners can benefit from multimodal instruction.

> ▶ Watch this video (https://www.youtube.com/watch?v=uGr-N7A4ZQI) to learn how Dr. Susan Nolan clarifies kinesthetic and tactile multisensory learning. See what new information she shares about the concept of multisensory instruction.

Instructional Decision Making 6.1: Apply your understanding of the concepts in this section.

BOX 6.6 | STEP-BY-STEP LESSON

Consonant Substitution

The consonant substitution strategy actively involves students in learning words that rhyme or belong to the same word family. The basic steps for consonant substitution are as follows:

1. Select a word family for instructional emphasis; for example, *ack.*
2. Create a set of word cards that include the *ack* word family, such as *back, tack, sack, rack.* Underline the word family *ack,* or write it in a different color.
3. Ask students to identify the first word in the set; for example, *back.* If the students do not know the word, tell them. Then have them read the word after you. Place the word in a pocket chart so that it is visible to the students.
4. Display the next word, *tack.* Invite them to read the word, and if they don't know it, tell them. Place the word in the pocket chart next to the first word. Help students discover the similarities and differences between the first two words, and discuss how the pronunciation of each word changes when the consonant letter is substituted.
5. Repeat the activity with the remaining word cards, and provide assistance as needed as you engage in discussion.
6. As the students learn word families, develop a word wall for choral review and practice.
7. Help students develop silly sentences that focus on each word family. For example: The rack had a sack with a tack.
8. Continue the strategy with other high-frequency word families.

CONSONANT SUBSTITUTION As students develop consonant letter–sound knowledge, you can use numerous activities to assist them with learning to read words that rhyme or belong to the same *word family.* These activities involve consonant substitution. The step-by-step lesson featured in Box 6.6 outlines a basic procedure for consonant substitution.

FLIP BOOKS Another strategy is to create flip books (see Figure 6.5). Flip books are made from sentence strips, which are ideal for creating small booklets for word study. One large sentence strip is used for writing the rime (on the right side of the strip). Strips that are half the size of the larger one are cut for the onsets. Consonants, consonant blends, and consonant digraphs are written on these smaller cards and then stapled or attached with binding to the longer card. Students flip through the booklet, reading each word. *Man* is changed to *can* or *ran* with the flip of the page.

MAKING WORDS Flip books make students aware of their word-making capability when they substitute different consonants at the beginning of a rime. To engage children in the process of making words, consider these steps (Cunningham, 2005; 2009):

1. Decide on the rime that you wish students to practice, and develop a rime card for each of the students.

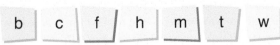

2. Develop a set of consonant letter cards for each student that can be used to make words with the rime that has been targeted for practice.

3. Direct students to use the letter cards to make the first word, *ball.*
4. Invite students to now change the word to make *call.*
5. Repeat the activity until all of the words have been made.

In addition to letter and rime cards, students could use letter tiles to make words. Decide on the rime you would like students to study. Select the letter tiles

Figure 6.5 Flip Books

Figure 6.6 Pocket Holders

for the rime and a number of consonants on additional tiles. Have the students construct the words on their desks or a carpet square. Also use slate squares or mini-chalkboards for consonant substitution. Students write the rime and then change the initial consonant to make words.

Other variations are possible: Use magnetic letters on a filing cabinet, cookie sheet, or chalkboard to make words. Fill a cookie sheet with sand or gelatin mix. Students write the words in the medium, changing only the beginning of the word. To erase the entire word, simply tap the sides of the tray lightly. This activity works well as a learning center. Remember to have a list of the rimes on hand for the children to refer to.

Finally, create pocket holders for cards. Large tag boards can be folded to hold letter cards in a bottom pocket. The sides can be folded in to create a trifold effect (see Figure 6.6). The teacher can call out a specific three-letter word to be formed. Students slip the letter cards into the appropriate pockets. When the words are formed, the teacher calls out, "Show me." Students turn their pocket folders around for the teacher to check. The following short-vowel rimes are ideal for this activity:

an   ap   ar   ab   ad   ag   am   at
ed   en   et
id   in   ig   im   ip   it
ob   od   op   og   ot   ow
ub   ug   um   un   ut

WORD LADDERS   This is a game in which students add, delete, or replace letters in words to create new words that are prompted by clues (Padak & Rasinski, 2009; Rasinski 2005a, 2005b). Students begin with one given word and are guided through the steps toward creating new words. The final word is typically related to the initial word. The game is a fun way to foster students' engagement with words. Below are two examples:

Initial word	sweater (take away two letters; this is a word that tells what you do if you are too hot)
	sweat (take away a letter; this is what you sit on)
	seat (change a letter; this is the sound a drum makes)
	beat (change a letter; this is something that floats in water)
	boat (change a letter; this is something you wear outside)
Final word	coat
Initial word	brain (change a letter; this is something you can ride)
	train (take away a letter; this happens when you see clouds)
	rain (take away two letters and add a letter; this is in a pen)
	ink (add two letters; this what you do with your brain)
Final word	Think

CUBE WORDS   Consonant substitution activities can also be developed using letter cubes (see Figure 6.7). Students roll the cubes, using four to six cubes, depending on their ability level. Words are formed with the letters that are rolled. Words are recorded on a sheet of paper that is divided into columns marked with the numbers one through five. Words with one letter are recorded in the first column, words with two letters in the second, and so on. Students can work independently or in pairs. Students who work in pairs may take turns rolling the cubes, forming the words, and writing the words in the appropriate columns. A sand clock or egg timer may be used. When time is up, students review the words and count up the total number of letters used as the score (Bear, Invernizzi, Templeton, & Johnston, 2008).

Once the children have a strong understanding of consonants, they are ready to begin work with consonant digraphs and blends. Many of the same activities done with consonants can be adapted for the digraphs and blends.

Analogic-Based Strategies

One of the ways that readers identify unknown words is to compare the patterns to known words. An analogic-based strategy is based on the premise that words with similar onset and rime patterns also have similar pronunciations. For example, if a reader knew the word *cat*, she would be able to separate it into the *c* onset and *at* rime. Furthermore, the reader would also identify other *c* words such as *cap*, *call*, and *cut*, as well as other *at* words such as *sat*, *hat*, and *rat*.

Justin, a first grader, was reading the following poem that the teacher and students constructed during an interactive writing lesson.

Figure 6.7 Letter Cubes

> In winter it's so nice,
> To slip and slide on the ice,
> Slip-sliding once,
> Slip-sliding twice,
> On ice that's white as rice.

His class had written the poem in their poetry notebooks and recited it each morning as a part of their morning poetry time. Justin was reading through his poems during quiet reading time and was slowly pointing to the words as he read. Each time he came to a word with the *ice* rime, he paused as if deep in thought. His teacher, who was close by, made these observations.

> Justin was experiencing an "aha" moment. He was piecing together what we had been talking about in class. He was making connections between the rhyming words and their letter patterns. It was almost as if I could see his mind separating the onsets and rimes and joining them back together. Justin would pause and say "n-ice," "r-ice," and "tw-ice." Later that day he came upon the word *mice* in a story he was reading. Immediately, he said, "Look, this is another *ice* word." He turned to the poem in his poetry notebook and carefully wrote the word *mice* at the bottom.

Each time that Justin pronounced the *ice* words, he left the rime intact. He automatically saw the letters *i-c-e* as a unit. He discovered that it was easier to pronounce the entire rime than to pronounce each sound separately. Because the pronunciations of rimes are consistent from word to word, it is wise to teach them in this way.

Rimes are so numerous that teachers will need to select the most frequent patterns their students will encounter. The following list of 38 phonograms, compiled by Fry (1998), provides teachers with a useful resource of high-frequency rimes:

ay ag ot ain op ow ob im
ill ack ing eed in ew ock uck
ip ank ap y an ore ake um
at ick unk out est ed ine
am ell ail ug ink ab ight

All syllables have a rime. Whereas single-syllable words have only one rime and one onset, multisyllable words have any number of onset and rime combinations. Some words, such as *at* and *it*, have only a rime. To determine the onsets and rimes

Figure 6.8 Examples of Onsets and Rimes in Single-Syllable and Multisyllable Words

Single-Syllable Words				
onset	+	rime	=	word
l	+	ive	=	live
d	+	ark	=	dark
		and	=	and

Multisyllable Words									
onset	+	rime	+	onset	+	rime	+	onset	+	rime	=	word
gr	+	and	+	f	+	a	+	th	+	er	=	grandfather
f	+	or			+	est					=	forest
g	+	ar	+	d	+	en					=	garden
b	+	e	+	y	+	ond					=	beyond
m	+	ead	+		+	ow					=	meadow

within a word, simply break the word apart into syllables. The number of syllables will be equal to the number of vowel sounds heard during the pronunciation of the word. For example, the word *finish* has one onset, *f*, and two rimes, *in* and *ish*. Examples of single and multisyllable words are shown in Figure 6.8.

POETRY Children's poetry is ideal for teaching onsets and rimes. Poems can be printed on large chart paper and posted in the classroom so that the rime patterns can be identified. When students have individual copies of the same poems, they can circle or highlight the letter patterns with colorful markers. Some favorite poets include Dorothy Aldis, Dorothy Wise Brown, Shel Silverstein, and Jack Prelutsky.

MAKING AND WRITING WORDS USING LETTER PATTERNS Rasinski and Padak (2001) recommend a strategy for older students in which the teacher selects a multisyllabic word that contains several onsets and rimes. Using a template with boxes that contain the onsets and rimes, the students are directed to write words using the patterns. For example, beginning with the word *habitat*, the following onsets would be recorded in boxes at the top of a form sheet: *h, b, t*; the following rimes would also be recorded: *ab, it, at*. Other onsets and rimes would be added, such as *r, s, m*, and *ake*. Using the preceding letter combinations, some words that can be made include *cab, tab, sat, bat, lei, bet*, and *lit*. This activity provides students with practice in using word patterns to decode longer words. See Figure 6.9 for an example of a template for this activity.

Figure 6.9 Using Onsets and Rimes to Make New Words

Key word: habitat	
ONSETS: h b t	RIMES: ab it at
New words:	
Tab	
Hit	
Hat	
Bat	
Bit	
NEW ONSETS: st sl fl	
New words:	
Stab	
Slab	
Flab	
Flat	
Slat	
Slit	
Slat	

2017 ILA Standard

2.2

Spelling-Based Strategies

Spelling-based strategies for word identification are designed to engage children in word study through the use of *word banks, word walls*, and *word sorting* strategies.

WORD BANKS Word banks are boxes or collections of word cards that individual students are studying. Word banks are a natural extension of the language-experience approach in which students learn to read words from dictated stories. Students make word cards from the words in their language-experience stories and study them. A quick way of helping students begin a word bank without using dictation is to have them read a selection that is fairly easy for them. The students underline words they cannot immediately recognize, words they cannot figure out, as well as words they consciously used context or mediated strategies to figure out. The students then write each of these words on cards. Words for word banks can also be gleaned from basal readers, trade books, signs, labels, and other print with which the children are involved. Words in the word banks can then be used in word sorting activities.

WORD WALLS   Another way to study words and word patterns is through **word walls**. A word wall may be started when students notice words that rhyme but are not spelled with the same letter patterns. For example, in Susan Valenti's second-grade classroom, the students participated in a shared-book experience as the teacher read Shel Silverstein's "Enter This Deserted House." In this poem, the poet rhymes the words *do, too, blue,* and *few* as he creates for readers young and old the eerie feeling of entering a deserted house.

As Susan read the poem, the students noticed that *do, too, blue,* and *few* all rhymed but were not spelled with the same letter pattern. So Susan and her class started a word wall for this sound. The word wall was constructed on a sheet of shelf paper hung on the wall. Students were asked to find words for each of the spellings of the sound /oo/. The following are some of the words they found:

do	*too*	*blue*	*few*
to	tool	clue	dew
	fool	Sue	

Intermediate and middle-level teachers often target homophones, compound words, or commonly misspelled words for students to reference. Words that are part of a theme or topic may also be emphasized for word study on a classroom word wall. A sixth-grade class studying the Civil War included words such as *slavery, Confederate, secede, union, soldier,* and *battlefield* on the word wall.

Word walls may be permanent or temporary. They may stay up for the entire school year or for only a particular unit of study. They can be written on sentence strips, word cards, poster board, or chart paper. Charts are ideal for classrooms with limited space. They may be displayed when needed and then stored away when not in use. The charts can be put back on display for review or comparisons with other word study charts.

Portable word walls can be made with file folders. Manila folders can be divided into categories according to alphabet, letter patterns, rimes, themes, and so on. Students can copy words onto the folder for personal reference at home or school. This technique may be especially helpful for intermediate grades in which students are in different classrooms each day. In addition, word walls can be individually created by ELLs as they develop their personal study of words.

WORD SORTING   Word sorting activities are another way to engage students in studying words. When sorting words, students look for similarities in words, including letter pattern similarities.

There are two kinds of word sorts: open and closed. In both, children are guided toward *discovering* similarities in words, rather than *being told* how they are alike.

For open word sorts, the following steps are suggested:

1. Each child in a small group has a word bank. Sorting activities can be done with children seated on the floor or at a table.
2. The children are asked to go through their word banks and group some words that go together in some way.
3. After grouping words, each child shows what words he or she has grouped. Then another student "reads his or her mind" by telling how the group of words is alike.
4. In open word sorts, there is no one correct answer. Students just have to be able to explain why they grouped words as they did. For example, Jill grouped *top, tickle,*

to, and *terrible* because they all begin with the letter *t*. John sorted *tomato, potato, tomorrow*, and *butterfly* because they all have three syllables. Sue sorted *mother, father, sister*, and *brother* because they are all family members. Helen classified *pretty, ugly, green*, and *fat* together because they all describe something. Notice that students can sort words by attributes concerning letter–sound relationships, the meanings of the words, or their functions in sentences.

In closed word sorts, the students try to group words according to a specific attribute the teacher has in mind. There is a correct way to sort the words in closed sorts. The students figure out what that correct way is.

The ability to generalize from the known to the unknown is a fundamental aspect of all word analysis. The closed word sort is an excellent way to get students to think about similarities among words. As students are learning the consonants and consonant blends, they can sort pictures of objects beginning with those phonics elements.

Students can also group words by letter patterns. The purpose of having students sort words by letter patterns is to encourage them to look for graphic similarities in words. Students can also be given word cards with letter patterns that are not similar, or a harder task is to have students sort word cards with letter patterns that are somewhat similar.

Common Core State Standards

CCRA.L.4, CCRA.L.5

Check Your Understanding 6.4: Gauge your understanding of the skills and concepts in this section.

Using Meaning and Letter–Sound Information to Identify Words

■ **Describe strategies that combine using meaning and letter–sound information to identify words.**

As children develop as readers, they learn to use with greater sophistication various kinds of *meaning and letter–sound information from the text itself*. When readers use information surrounding unknown words as an aid to word identification, they are using context or **context clues**. Although the issue of reliance on context for word identification has been the focus of debate among reading researchers, there is agreement that skilled readers understand that reading must make sense (Juel & Minden-Cupp, 2000; Snow, Burns, & Griffin, 1998). The Common Core State Standards (CCSS) specify that it is critical for students to use context for word identification in order to identify the meaning of text.

2017 ILA Standard

2.2

Common Core State Standard

CCRA.L.4

Strategies for Teaching Context

Readers use meaning clues to identify words they have heard but may not have experienced visually in print. When readers can combine meaning clues with phonic information, they have developed a powerful tool for word identification. The following activities help show readers how to use the *context* of a sentence or passage.

CLOZE PASSAGES   The **cloze procedure** is a strategy in which words or letters are omitted from the text and students are required to fill in the blanks using information from the passage. Cloze passages can be constructed from materials that are at first relatively easy to read. The material used can be stories, informational text, and poems from anthologies, language-experience stories, other student-written products, or subject matter texts. Gradually, the difficulty of the reading material can be increased. Although cloze-type materials are available commercially from publishing companies, teachers often produce the most effective cloze passages because they are in the best position to gear the material to the needs of their students.

Cloze activities can contain as few as one deletion in a sentence or up to 20 deletions in a passage. There are different deletion systems: selective word deletion, systematic word deletion, and partial word deletion. The kind of deletion system used determines what aspects of the passage students should focus on as they complete the cloze passages and discuss their responses.

Using *selective word deletion*, important nouns, verbs, adjectives, and adverbs can be left out. These words carry the meaning and context of what the author is saying. When selected nouns, verbs, adjectives, and adverbs are deleted, the focus is on using meaningful information from the passage to determine an appropriate response.

In *systematic word deletion*, every *n*th word in a passage is deleted—for example, every fifth, tenth, or twentieth word. When such a cloze deletion system is used as a teaching device, many function words will be deleted. Consider the following examples: "Bill went _____ the hill." Did Bill go up, down, or around the hill? The students must deduce appropriate words from the context of the rest of the passage.

In *partial word deletion*, every *n*th word or selected word is partially deleted. Three types of partial deletions can be used: (1) Initial consonants, initial consonant blends, digraphs, or initial vowels are given, and all other letters are deleted. (2) The letters mentioned in option 1 plus ending consonants or ending consonant digraphs are given, and all other letters are deleted. (3) Consonants are given, and vowels are deleted. Examples of partial deletions are:

1. The m____ was m_____ the lawn.
2. Would you like to w____k to the p_____k with me?
3. The b_y pet the d_g.

Cloze passages in which only the initial letters are given help children understand that initial letters serve to reduce the number of meaningful substitutions available.

CLOZE WITH CHOICES GIVEN   If students find it difficult to complete cloze activities, giving choices for the deleted words makes the task easier. This is called the maze procedure. Here are some different procedures to use in devising the choices for the cloze blanks.

1. The incorrect item, or *foil*, can be a different part of speech as well as different graphically.

   The doctor was _____ that the patient got better so quickly.

   MONKEY/AMAZED

2. The foil can be graphically similar to the correct item but a different part of speech.

   The doctor was _____ that the patient got better so quickly.

   AMAZON/AMAZED

3. The foil and the correct answer can be graphically similar and the same part of speech.

   The doctor was _____ that the patient got better so quickly.

   AMUSED/AMAZED

4. Three choices can also be given: the correct response, a word of the same part of speech that is graphically similar, and a word of a different part of speech that is graphically similar.

   The doctor was _____ that the patient got better so quickly.

   AMAZED/AMUSED/AMAZON

A discussion of these particular cloze examples would include a discussion of why a doctor would be more likely to be amazed than amused by a patient's progress in getting well. Students would also note that "The doctor was amazon that the patient got better so quickly" makes no sense.

GUESSING GAMES   Guessing games can be played to help students use visual and meaning clues to identify unknown words. Teachers can read riddles and have students guess solutions based on visual hints, such as beginning letters, as well as meaning hints. For example, a teacher might say, "I am thinking of a color word that begins with *r*. Apples are often this color." For older students, Hall (1995) devised a guessing game in which students work in teams to guess sentences of seven to fifteen words. A variation of the activity works like this:

1. The teacher selects sentences from stories or constructs sentences that have strong meaning clues (e.g., "This evening we played baseball, and our team lost").
2. One key word is selected from the sentence to provide a schema (e.g., *baseball*).
3. Blank lines that represent each word in the sentence are written on the board and numbered. The key word is written in the appropriate blank.

   _____ _____ _____ _____ baseball, _____ _____ _____ _____

      1   2   3   4   5   6   7   8   9

4. Two "free" cards are given to each of two or three teams that they can use to ask the teacher the beginning letters of two words during the game.
5. Members of each team discuss possible words, and when it is a team's turn, a spokesperson calls out a number and guesses a word. If the word is correct, the team scores two points (e.g., if the spokesperson said that number eight is *team*, two points would be scored). If the word is not correct, it is the next team's turn.
6. Teams may ask for a beginning letter of a word (e.g., What does number nine begin with? Answer is *l*). If the team guesses the correct word after the letter is given, one point is scored. Free cards may also be used to ask for the second letter of a word if the first letter is already given.
7. The game continues until the sentence has been correctly identified. Points are tallied for each team.

During this game, the teacher encourages students to use graphic as well as meaning clues to guess words. The purpose of the game is to foster an awareness of meaning clues that can be used to identify unknown words.

Common Core State Standards

CCRA.R.4, CCRA.L.4, CCRA.L.5, CCRA.L.6

SEMANTIC GRADIENTS AND CONTEXT CLUES   A **semantic gradient** is a collection of related words placed along a continuum (Blachowicz & Fisher, 2006; Greenwood & Flanigan, 2007). The words are not synonyms; rather they are terms that have a concept in common and are placed along a line that goes from one extreme to the other. A continuum that suggests words that might characterize an *idea, decision,* or *statement* could look something like this:

Profound	Weight	Deep	Heavy	Important	Basic	Trivial

→

Greenwood and Flanigan (2007) suggest two ways that teachers can have students work with semantic gradients so that they understand the concept: selection and generation. *Selection* involves providing a continuum with the extreme words given on opposite sides and the other words given in a box. The students complete the continuum by placing the boxed words in order from one extreme to the other. The box for the example above would look like this:

Heavy   Weighty

Basic   Deep

Important

Generation involves providing the same sort of initial continuum without the box of choices.

After the students understand the concept of semantic gradients, cloze sentences are introduced in which the students select words from continuums to fill in the blanks based on basic contexts; these are contexts in which several choices are possible. Richer contexts are sentences that provide specific clues as to which word or words make the most sense. Below are examples of cloze sentences using the words in the accompanying continuum with boxed choices already added to the band.

Hollered   Shouted   Yelled   Announced   Stated   Whispered   Murmured

$\longrightarrow$

- Matthew _____. (many appropriate choices)
- Matthew _____ that he would be home after three o'clock. (*announced* or *stated* are probably most appropriate)
- Matthew _____ his secret to Jim. (probably *whispered*)
- Matthew was reluctant to give his answer in class. He _____ something that couldn't be understood. (*murmured*)
- The room was noisy. When Matthew saw his friend across the room, he _____ to him. (*hollered, shouted,* or *yelled* could be appropriate)

As students select their answers, they should explain what context (or lack of context) helped them decide. Students can also develop their own gradients and accompanying sentences. This can be done in small groups or with partners. The purpose of this strategy is to make students aware of the subtle meanings that words have and how to use context to select an appropriate choice.

2017 ILA Standard

2.2

Cross-Checking and Self-Monitoring Strategies

Cross-checking and *self-monitoring* strategies help readers combine letter–sound and meaning information to make sense while reading. **Cross-checking** simply involves rereading a sentence or two to "cross-check"—confirm, modify, or reject—probable pronunciations of unknown words encountered during reading. If the sentence makes sense, the meaning confirms the reader's cross-checking; if the sentence doesn't make sense, the reader tries again.

The cross-checking strategy takes little preparation and is very effective for teaching word identification in meaningful contexts. For example, notice how cross-checking brings together students' knowledge of digraph sounds and the use of context clues for decoding words. On large chart paper, sentence strips, or the projector or whiteboard, write sentences similar to the ones given here. Cunningham (2009), a proponent of cross-checking, notes that children love to see their names used in the sentences, so make sure to include them.

- Roderiquez likes to eat <u>chocolate chip</u> cookies.
- Kate likes to have <u>wheat</u> bread for her sandwiches.
- Zachary likes to eat <u>sherbet</u> on a hot day.
- Tamika is good at <u>throwing</u> Frisbees.
- Miguel <u>cheers</u> for his team to win.

Cover the underlined word in each sentence with a sticky note or index card. Have the students read the sentence and predict what words would make sense in the blank spot. Reveal just the initial digraph, and have the children check their predictions, crossing out any that do not begin with the specific digraph. Record new words that make sense and begin with the digraph. Finally, uncover the word, and see whether any of the predictions match the original word.

Cross-checking, even at the earliest stages of development, is crucial in learning to read. When a teacher places a high premium on students' word-perfect oral reading performance, young developing readers are at risk of not developing strategies for **self-monitoring**. Such readers become dependent on the teacher or other able readers to help them when they encounter a hard word.

Another way to help children self-monitor is to discuss with them what to do when they come to unknown words. When children attempt to figure out unknown words in text, encourage them to use meaning and letter–sound information. Help children monitor their searches by using a chart similar to the one in Figure 6.10. Explain the procedures listed on the chart and let children practice using them.

Common Core State Standard

CCRA.L.4

Check Your Understanding 6.5: Gauge your understanding of the skills and concepts in this section.

Figure 6.10 Figuring Out an Unknown Word

What do you do when you come to a word you don't know?

1. Say "blank" and skip it.
2. Read at least to the end of the sentence.
3. Go back and look at the word and see if you can think of a word that makes sense and has these letters.

If you can't figure it out, don't let the word bug you. Maybe you can understand the selection without it.

Using Structural Analysis to Identify Words

■ **Characterize strategies that use structural analysis to identify words.**

Structural analysis involves identifying words through meaningful units such as prefixes, suffixes, and root words. The smallest meaningful unit of a word is a **morpheme**. In the word *unhappy*, there are two morphemes: *un*, which means "not," and *happy*, which means "joyful." The CCSS include the importance of being able to identify and understand word parts. Kieffer and Lesaux (2007) suggest four principles for teaching morphology. First, teach within the context of rich vocabulary instruction that includes multiple ways of knowing words. Second, have students select words they don't understand; study the words based on the meanings of prefixes, suffixes, and root words; make educated guesses about the meaning of the words; and check guesses about the meanings of words based on the contexts in which they are written. Third, explicitly teach common prefixes, suffixes, and root words. These can be displayed as wall charts or word walls. Fourth, for students who speak Spanish as their primary language, help them see the similarities between words in both languages.

2017 ILA Standard

2.2

Structural analysis also includes **inflected endings**, which are suffixes that change the tense or degree of a word but not its meaning. Examples of inflected endings are listed below:

ing as in *going*	*s* as in *books*
d as in *saved*	*es* as in *dresses*
ed as in *looked*	*ly* as in *slowly*
er as in *smaller*	*est* as in *tallest*

In addition, structural analysis includes compound words and contractions.

Strategies for Teaching Structural Analysis

When word identification strategies include teaching children how to identify prefixes, suffixes, root words, inflected endings, compound words, and contractions, children have a larger repertoire of methods to help them recognize unknown words. The following activities will help children use structural analysis.

WORD STUDY NOTEBOOK   Model for students how prefixes and suffixes can change the meanings of words and help determine the meanings of other words. For example, *bi* + *cycle* = a two-wheeler, and *tri* + *cycle* = a three-wheeler. As prefixes, suffixes, and root words are introduced, have students brainstorm other words that contain the same elements and add them to a word study notebook that has a section reserved for this type of word analysis. Following is a list of some of the more commonly used prefixes, suffixes, and root words and their meanings (Bromly, 2007; Savage, 2004).

Prefixes

re	again	*anti*	against
auto	self	*com*	together, with
un	not	*dis*	apart
ex	out	*pre*	before

Suffixes

ly	the quality of	*less*	without
ist	one who does	*ful*	full
ment	quality or act	*ship*	ability or skill
able	capable of	*er*	more

Roots

dict	say	*port*	carry
scrib	write	*cred*	believe
vid	see	*spect*	look
aud	hear	*rupt*	break

WALL CHART CAROUSEL   Tack four sheets of chart paper on each of four walls of the classroom. In the center of each sheet of paper, print a prefix large enough for everyone to see. Divide the class into small groups of four or five, provide each group with a marker, and allow one person per group to be the "recorder." Each group should stand by one of the prefix charts. At the signal "go," each group should record as many words as they can on the chart, making a web. Allow 1 minute. At the signal "stop," the students should rotate to the next chart, and when they hear "go" they should record additional words. Continue until each group has rotated to each chart. Discussion can take place regarding the meanings of the recorded words. For the prefix *un*, for example, the following words might be recorded: *unlike, unnecessary, unlock, uncover, undo, unhappy, unsaid, untrue*, and discussion would focus on the meaning *not* for each word. As a follow-up to the activity, a guessing game can be played with each chart. Using the above words, the teacher (or a student) might say, "I spy a word that means *sad*. What could it be?" or "I spy a word that means *not needed*. What could it be?"

COMPOUND WORD CUPS   Large Styrofoam coffee cups, when stacked in sets of two, are easy to twist when their lips fit together (Rasinski & Padak, 2001). On the lip of the inner cup, write with indelible marker the first half of a compound word. On the lip of the outer cup, write the second half of the word. For example, on the inner lip write *base*, and on the outer lip write *ball*. Other words on the same set of cups might include *bedroom, toothbrush, cupcake, doorbell, wallpaper*. A variety of activities can be played depending on how many cup sets are available. For example, if everyone in the class or group has a cup set, a variation of musical chairs can be played. Sitting in a circle, when music is played, each student passes his cup to the left. When the music stops, each person must form a compound word by twisting the cups and taking turns reading the words. In addition to playing the game, a word wall is a useful way for students to share compound words that they find in printed material during the school day.

CONTRACTION SEARCH   To foster quick identification of contractions and word pairs that can be transformed into contractions, distribute junk mail, old newspapers, or magazines and have the students highlight all of the contractions and word pairs that can become contractions that they find. Using a section of a word study notebook, students can keep track of the contractions by recording them in two columns: One column contains a list of contractions; the other consists of the word pairs.

Check Your Understanding 6.6: Gauge your understanding of the skills and concepts in this section.

Rapid Recognition of Words

■ **Identify strategies that teach rapid recognition of words.**

There is more to rapid word identification than flashing a sight-word card and requiring an instant response. Immediate identification of words is the result of *experience with* reading, seeing, discussing, using, and writing words.

Durkin (1980) suggested whole word methodology at the outset of reading instruction on the following grounds: Whole word learning allows children to sense "real reading" quickly. It can also be of greatest interest to most children, because they are apt to be familiar with the concept of a *word* rather than linguistic concepts associated with phonics, such as *letter* or *sound.*

In addition, Helman and Burns (2008) elaborate on the relationship between ELLs' acquisition of sight-word vocabulary and their proficiency in oral language production. They strongly recommend that teachers be aware of the oral language skills that ELLs have and tailor the teaching of reading, including sight-word vocabulary, based on those skills. Once teachers determine the oral proficiency of ELLs, Helman and Burns propose that the number of sight words that an ELL can learn, based on language proficiency, ranges from three new words for students who are just beginning to learn the language to five new words for students who are characterized as intermediate ELLs.

High-Frequency Words

High-frequency words are words that appear over and over in print. Numerous lists of high-frequency words have been compiled. E. W. Dolch (1948) developed and published a well-recognized list of 220 high-frequency words. The words are listed as pre-primer, primer, and first-, second-, and third-grade words. See Johns and Lenski (2010) for a revised Dolch list. Figure 6.11 contains another well-renowned list, Edward Fry's (1977) 300 "instant words." According to Fry (1980), the first 100 instant words on his list make up half of all written material, and the 300 words make up 65 percent of all written text.

High-frequency word lists contain a large number of words that are grammatically necessary—words such as articles, conjunctions, pronouns, verbs of being, and prepositions that bind together information-bearing words. These words are called *function words*; they do much to help a sentence function, but they do not get across the meaning of a passage by themselves. Nouns, action verbs, adjectives, and adverbs are *content words*; they supply the content or information of the topic.

Compare the following paragraphs to get a better idea of how these two types of words work together in running print.

Paragraph 1

Once upon a _____ there was a _____ _____ _____ _____. One _____ _____ _____ an _____ in the _____ _____ _____. "An _____ _____ has a _____ of _____. I'll _____ this _____ _____ me to his _____ of _____."

Paragraph 2

_____ _____ _____ time _____ _____ _____ mean man named Grumble. _____ day Grumble saw _____ elf _____ _____ woods. Grumble said, "_____ elf always _____ _____ pot _____ gold. _____ make _____ elf take _____ _____ _____ pot _____ gold."

Figure 6.11 The Instant Words

First Hundred			
Words 1–25	**Words 26–50**	**Words 51–75**	**Words 76–100**
the	or	will	number
of	one	up	no
and	had	other	way
a	by	about	could
to	word	out	people
in	but	many	my
is	not	then	than
you	what	them	first
that	all	these	water
it	were	so	been
he	we	some	call
was	when	her	who
for	your	would	oil
on	can	make	now
are	said	like	find
as	there	him	long
with	use	into	down
his	an	time	day
they	each	has	did
I	which	look	get
at	she	two	come
be	do	more	made
this	how	write	may
have	their	go	part
from	if	see	over

Common suffixes: *-s, -ing, -ed*

Second Hundred			
Words 101–125	**Words 126–150**	**Words 151–175**	**Words 176–200**
new	great	put	kind
sound	where	end	hand
take	help	does	picture
only	through	another	again
little	much	well	change
work	before	large	off
know	line	must	play
place	right	big	spell
year	too	even	air
live	mean	such	away
me	old	because	animal
back	any	turn	house
give	same	here	point
most	tell	why	page
very	boy	ask	letter
after	follow	went	mother
thing	came	men	answer
our	want	read	found
just	show	need	study

Figure 6.11 The Instant Words *(Continued)*

Second Hundred			
Words 101–125	**Words 126–150**	**Words 151–175**	**Words 176–200**
name	also	land	still
good	around	different	learn
sentence	form	home	should
man	three	us	America
think	small	move	world
say	set	try	high

Common suffixes: *-s, -ing, -ed, -er, -ly, -est*

Third Hundred			
Words 201–225	**Words 226–250**	**Words 251–275**	**Words 276–300**
every	left	until	idea
near	don't	children	enough
add	few	side	eat
food	while	feet	face
between	along	car	watch
own	might	mile	far
below	close	night	Indian
country	something	walk	real
plant	seem	white	almost
last	next	sea	let
school	hard	began	above
father	open	grow	girl
keep	example	took	sometimes
tree	begin	river	mountain
never	life	four	cut
start	always	carry	young
city	those	state	talk
earth	both	once	soon
eye	paper	book	list
light	together	hear	song
thought	got	stop	leave
head	group	without	family
under	often	second	body
story	run	late	music
saw	important	miss	Color

Common suffixes: *-s, -ing, -ed, -er, -ly, -est*

When reading paragraph 1, can you tell what the paragraph is about? All of the content or information-bearing words were taken out. When reading paragraph 2, at the very least you know that the story is about a mean man named Grumble and an elf. By studying paragraph 2, you might even have figured out that Grumble wanted to take the elf's pot of gold.

2017 ILA Standard

2.2

Teaching Function Words

Function words, high-frequency words, or sight words, such as *was, there, the, has,* and *of,* should be taught as whole words early in children's reading instruction. The rationale for teaching rapid recognition of these words is this: Beginning readers who can quickly and accurately identify high-frequency words will more readily read across *any line of print,* because these words make up 65 percent or more of *all* written material. Another reason children need to be taught high-frequency function words as sight words is that a large number of these words are not phonically regular. Words such as *the, one,* and *of* do not conform to predictable letter–sound associations.

> ▶ Watch this video (https://www.youtube.com/watch?v=PSSbhgpOYDY) to learn one approach for teaching sight words. After viewing the video, compare this strategy with other approaches that we discuss. What are your thoughts on these strategies? How would you implement them in a first-grade classroom?

Next, consider the following strategies for teaching high-frequency words.

INCREMENTAL REHEARSAL **Incremental rehearsal** is a drill ratio procedure that teaches children new words by interspersing them with known words. The most effective ratio is to teach one unknown word along with nine words that the student knows (Joseph, 2006; MacQuarrie, Tucker, Burns, & Hartman, 2002). The procedure works like this:

1. Using a list of words, let's say a section of the Fry list, assess the student's knowledge of the words by using flash cards.
2. Set aside nine known words, and add one unknown word.
3. Make a pile of the words with the unknown word first, followed by the other nine.
4. Show the student the unknown word, and you read it orally.
5. The student repeats the word after you.
6. Flash the next card (known word), and have the student read it aloud.
7. Have the student read the unknown word aloud again, followed by the first and second known words. Repeat the procedure with the unknown word, followed by the first, second, and third known words.
8. When the student knows the unknown word, add it to the pack of cards and remove the ninth known word.
9. Continue to introduce unknown words by repeating the process until 10 new words have been learned.

It is important that in addition to teaching new words using the procedure, the words are practiced in meaningful sentences.

LANGUAGE-EXPERIENCE STRATEGY After providing the students with an experience, the teacher has students dictate captions describing the activities that are written on chart paper. For example, following a nature walk, Jan, a first-grade teacher, had her students dictate what they saw.

> I *saw* an oak tree.

> I *saw* a squirrel.

> I *saw* some poison ivy.

The students can read the story in unison, or the teacher can provide individual copies of the captions. Students can highlight the word *saw* in this example, locate the word *saw* in books and poems, or write the word *saw* in personal dictionaries. Language-experience activities provide students with a meaningful context in which to learn high-frequency words.

WORD WALLS   After introducing sight words in meaningful contexts, teachers can display the words on a wall or chart paper so that the words can be viewed and practiced. As high-frequency words are added to the word wall, teachers can have the students chant the words in loud voices, soft voices, happy voices, and so on. The word wall also becomes an instant reference for high-frequency words when the children are writing. In addition, teachers can provide students with individual word walls of sight words that are kept in folders or word banks for easy reference.

ENVIRONMENTAL PRINT   As teachers introduce high-frequency words, children can locate the words in environmental print. Teachers can provide students with junk mail, magazines, newspapers, cereal boxes, and paper place mats, for example. The students can circle words they are learning or highlight the words with markers. When environmental print sources are laminated, they can be reused with washable markers and placed in a learning center. This activity provides students with practice reading the words in a meaningful context.

WORD GAMES   Children enjoy word games when they are learning word identification skills. Adaptations of games such as bingo, Go Fish, Concentration, and Memory can serve as motivating ways to help children practice sight-word recognition. Teachers can, for example, provide students with blank bingo grids on which the children write words from a word wall. As the teacher calls words, the students use markers to identify them.

LITERATURE AND POETRY   After introducing several sight words, teachers can provide children with a variety of books and poems. Students are encouraged to "spy" the sight words in the literature and read sentences and phrases in which the sight words are found. A word wall chart can be used to record the sentences and phrases the students "spy." Students can then highlight the words on the chart.

When teaching high-frequency words, it is important that teachers provide children with multiple opportunities to read the words in meaningful contexts. Children need to see that these words occur in print in a variety of settings.

Teaching Key Words

One of the quickest and most interesting ways to ease children into reading is through key word teaching. **Key words** are a fundamental aspect of language-experience instruction. Key words are charged with personal meaning and feeling, for they come out of the experience and background of the child. The concept of key words emerged from the work of Sylvia Ashton-Warner (1959, 1963, 1972). Key words become the core of what might be traditionally called *sight-word development*. The emphasis in learning words is to tie instruction to meaningful activity through *seeing, discussing, using, defining,* and *writing* words.

Ashton-Warner (1972) suggested that each child keep a file or word bank of special personal words drawn from both personal experiences and experiences with literature. The word cards could be used in the following way. The personal word cards of a group of children are jumbled together. The children sort out their own word cards and read them to each other before placing them back into their files. Cards that are not recognized are left out for further study. Thus the words kept by each child retain personal meaning and use.

2017 ILA Standard

2.1

GROUP ACTIVITIES WITH KEY WORDS   There are many useful strategies for key word instructional activities in small groups. Consider the following, all of which are excellent word-learning activities for ELLs.

- *Classifying words.* Select a topic according to a classification (e.g., desserts, television characters, funny words, places, scary words). All of the children who have a dessert word, for example, would stand in one area of the room. The teacher might want to label the area with a sheet of paper marked *dessert.* Children who have words of other classifications also stand in their designated areas.

- *Relating words.* If one child has the word *cake* and another the word *knife,* a child might relate the words by saying, "A knife can cut a cake." The teacher should try to get the children to relate words by asking questions such as "What can my word do to the cake?" "How can my word be used with the cake?" The teacher can continue this by asking the children, "Does someone else have a word that can be used with the word *cake?*"
- *Learning a partner's words.* Each child chooses a partner, and the partners teach each other their own words.
- *Coauthoring.* Two or more children get together and combine their words or ideas to make longer words or stories from their original words or ideas.
- *Acting out words.* If the key word is conducive to acting out, a child could dramatize the word for the other children to guess.

2017 ILA Standard

5.2

Check Your Understanding 6.7: Gauge your understanding of the skills and concepts in this section.

Organizing Word Identification Instruction

■ **Organize word identification instruction according to identifiable principles.**

There is no one best way to organize reading instruction, but teachers *do* need to be organized! As you probably realize, teaching children to read, identify, and recognize words is a complex task. The goal of teaching students how to *read* words is, of course, so that they will be able to focus on understanding what they are reading. So how can teachers organize word identification instruction? We believe that three principles will help teachers get started. In addition to each principle, we share scenarios that serve as examples of how the principles are implemented.

PRINCIPLE 1 *Remember that identifying words does not mean just "sounding them out."* Phonics is only one part of the word identification process. Other ways to identify words are by sight (instantly), using parts of words (structural analysis and onsets and rimes), and through context (identifying words through surrounding information, including sentences and other clues). Teaching children to read words is not an incremental process. In other words, teachers don't teach phonics first and then sight words. The process occurs simultaneously, and it should be meaningful to the children.

Common Core State Standard

CCRA.L.4

Scenario: Mrs. Simons is a first-grade teacher, and most of her students are just learning to read, although several can do so somewhat fluently. She initially organizes her word identification instruction by developing her students' sight vocabulary, as well as teaching letter–sound relationships (phonics). She begins with stories. Below is one of her strategies for teaching word identification:

5 minutes	Read a story using a big book so that all of the students can see the print.
2 minutes	After reading the story, talk about the sight words the students have already learned by pointing out the words in the story.
1 minute	Introduce a new "high-frequency" word to learn from the story.
2 minutes	Practice reading the word chorally from the big book in context. Add the new word to the word wall. Practice all sight words chorally from the word wall.
1 minute	Review a phonics element within the context of the story (e.g., the initial sound of the letter *b* in the word *bear*). Introduce another consonant sound.
1 minute	Play with other words that begin with the new sound.
2 minutes	Play with the story, and talk about other words that begin with the consonant sounds learned thus far.

PRINCIPLE 2 *Use assessment and kidwatching to guide grouping.* Grouping students for reading instruction is a common practice in many classrooms. This practice, however, is often misused when students are placed in what has been characterized as low, middle, and high groups. Often this labeling leads to low self-esteem issues for the "low" readers; teachers fail to acknowledge student growth and lockstep students into groups that are no longer appropriate; and often instruction is uninformed—teachers use programs with low-achieving students that are scripted—not a good thing. Assessment need not be formal. It can simply involve students reading short lists of words and evaluating the strategies students use to identify them. Do they know how to chunk words? Do they read high-frequency words accurately? See how Mr. Thomas uses kidwatching for word identification instruction to guide a group of students.

> *Scenario:* Mr. Thomas is a third-grade teacher. Most of his students can read on grade level, but there are several who struggle with identifying words. He noticed that these students tend to sound out most words that they don't know. Mr. Thomas realizes that these students do not understand that there are ways to "unlock" unknown words other than phonics. He organized a "group game" time for these students. During this time (15 minutes several times a week), Mr. Thomas scaffolds his students as he plays sight-word games and matching activities with them that teach prefixes and suffixes. He conducts minilessons before the games; his viewpoint is that teaching and playing word games *together* is what scaffolding is all about.

PRINCIPLE 3 *Teach and reinforce word identification in meaningful contexts.* It is critical that teachers use real-life examples as they instruct students in the multiple ways that words can be recognized. Students need to understand the importance of the word-learning strategies they are learning and how they connect to the world of reading. Drill work that is workbook based—and disconnected from what students know about, are interested in, and care about—doesn't make much sense. In essence, it is essential that teachers develop word identification lessons that reflect meaningful contexts, which help students capture why they are learning to read words. Below, see how Miss Emily develops her lesson for teaching the /at/ rime.

Informal assessment and kidwatching guide teachers toward effective small group word identification instruction.

Annie Pickert Fuller/Pearson Education

> *Scenario:* Miss Emily is a first-grade teacher who understands that one of her goals of teaching word identification is to provide her students with contexts that make sense to them. Her organization for teaching the /at/ rime is as follows:

1. Miss Emily reads *The Cat in the Hat* by Dr. Seuss. She engages the students by encouraging them to share their favorite parts and make connections to the story.
2. Miss Emily focuses on the title of the story as she introduces the /at/ rime. She explains that there are sounds and sound patterns that help you read words in stories.
3. The students make flip books that feature the /at/ rime, and they practice reading the books to each other. The /at/ rime is then added to her word wall.

Students need to be aware of what they are learning and why. Miss Emily does a good job of teaching in a meaningful way.

2017 ILA Standard

2.1

Check Your Understanding 6.8: Gauge your understanding of the skills and concepts in this section.

Balancing Word Identification Instruction

■ **Balance word identification instruction through multiple approaches.**

Learning to read cannot be limited to experiences with words alone. We believe that children need to have ample experiences with books, frequent encounters with oral and printed language, and early opportunities to write. Furthermore, teaching students word recognition strategies ought to relate to their developmental needs. There is no "one-size-fits-all" approach to teaching word identification. Some kindergartners come to school reading; some middle school students are not proficient readers. Teachers need to observe how their students approach words and text and make instructional decisions based on those observations. Observe how Mrs. Bourn, the literacy coach in Box 6.7, coaches first-grade teacher Chuck in developing his own teaching skills in order to make instruction for the children more effective.

BOX 6.7 | VIEWPOINT *THE LITERACY COACH*

Using Phonics Instruction Effectively

It is October, and Chuck, a newly hired first-grade teacher, is required to use a scripted phonics program. He is frustrated because many of the first graders are not engaged during the lessons. He asked Mrs. Bourn, the literacy coach, to observe a lesson and guide him toward motivating his students to enjoy learning to read.

During the 20-minute lesson, Mrs. Bourn observed Chuck read a script that focused on the /at/ rime. Although he read the script accurately, his voice was monotone and she noticed that Chuck did not seem particularly involved with the lesson. Mrs. Bourn also observed that although the majority of the children were initially on task as Chuck prompted them to recite words such as *bat, cat, rat*, and *fat*, midway through the lesson several of the students were yawning or had their heads on their desks.

After the lesson, the following conversation took place between Mrs. Bourn and Chuck:

Mrs. Bourn: Well, what did you think about the lesson, Chuck?

Chuck: Frankly, I don't like these scripts. The children don't seem to understand the purpose of reciting them, and they appear bored.

Mrs. Bourn: Okay. What could we do to help them understand the purpose of the lessons? How could we make the lessons more meaningful?

Chuck: I really don't know. We are required to read them 20 minutes a day but it seems like a waste of time since they don't "get it."

Mrs. Bourn: Well, let's talk about the purpose of this particular lesson. It was to teach the /at/ rime, correct?

Chuck: That's right.

Mrs. Bourn: But you don't think the students understood the idea?

Chuck: No, I don't think so. Maybe some of them did.

Mrs. Bourn: What do you think is the purpose of teaching rimes, Chuck, in this case the /at/ rime?

Chuck: So they can read words that have that rime.

Mrs. Bourn: Okay. Maybe we could locate or write some poetry that uses the rime. Or maybe we could find a Dr. Seuss book. The idea would be to engage the children in a fun read-aloud first, then point out words that use the /at/ rime and explain to the children that grown-ups use this rime to read poetry and books. Next, it might be a good idea to explain that we are going to practice reading /at/ words so they can read the poetry or book by themselves.

Following the scripted lesson, the children could practice reading copies of the poetry or selections from the book with a buddy. Do you think that would work?

Chuck: Sure sounds like it might. I'll give it a try. Thanks, Mrs. Bourn!

What is the teacher doing well? What evidence of this would we see? How might you guide the teacher to improve his skills?

BOX 6.8

Word Identification and E-books

In their most basic form, children's e-books are computer files that act much like a book. They have traditional conventions like a title, pages, and chapters. However, they also can contain illustrations and hotspots that provide a navigation mechanism for the reader. A deeper look at children's e-books reveals a more complex form, a type of software that includes animations, sounds, videos, and a read-aloud function.

Early studies suggest that multimedia features in e-books can improve inference skills in story reading and that game-like interactivity can stimulate story comprehension and word learning, especially when children's attention is guided to these purposes. E-books have also been shown to motivate children to be active readers. When using e-books, children tend to more naturally investigate words, images, and interactives in the reading environment. It seems the e-book may invite play, and this is a powerful motivator for engaging with print. These digital additions to print are different in a manner that is profoundly changing the digital storybook as a piece of early literacy learning.

As teachers begin to incorporate e-books into their early literacy instruction, it is critical they are aware of the multimedia functions available in these resources and leverage them to support student learning. It is becoming more common for e-book designers utilize multimedia to aid in word identification. For example, Figure 6.12 shows a screen where words are

Figure 6.12 Words Are "Discoverable" When Children Tap on Them.

"discoverable" when children tap on them. The tap produces a pop-up screen that introduces the word to the child through an audio pronunciation of the word accompanied by a dictionary definition.

Teachers who incorporate e-books into their classrooms should introduce this word identification feature and model its use for their students. Children have a tendency to reuse the same method repeatedly for initiating an action, so a minor investment in this instruction can benefit students in an ongoing fashion while helping to support word identification.

In addition, engaging children and young adolescents with software and applicable websites can enhance word identification and literacy skills. Many children and young adolescents are motivated by computer activities that are designed to teach reading skills

There are countless websites that reinforce word recognition skills. Teachers can download stories, interactive games in which students can engage in active learning, and word recognition resource materials for teachers including lessons, flash cards, and ideas for games. In Box 6.8, see what Jeremy Brueck has to say about word identification and e-books.

Check Your Understanding 6.9: Gauge your understanding of the skills and concepts in this section.

RTI for Struggling Readers

Word Learning and *Response to Intervention*

Because RTI practices involve evidence-based instruction by expert literacy teachers, in this section we share several tips about word instruction based on research conducted by Williams, Phillips-Birdsong, Hufnagel, Hungler, and Lundstrom (2009). These tips focus on small group instruction based on students' developmental writing abilities.

- It is suggested that teachers first assess students' word-learning abilities by conducting informal spelling inventories such as the Elementary Spelling Inventory (Bear et al., 2008), as well as examining the children's writing samples.
- After examining the results of the assessments, it is recommended that the students are grouped by developmental spelling levels.
- Teachers need to plan instruction so that children learn *about* words and how they work..They should use assessment results to develop explicit lessons that reflect developmental spelling levels.
- Interactive writing helps students practice what they know about words in an authentic setting. Teachers should model by writing the spelling patterns that the students are learning.
- Suggested teaching strategies include using rhyming words; saying words slowly; clapping, then writing the sounds heard in words; comparing new words to known words; and using word walls to reinforce working with words.

Finally, it is recommended that assessment occur regularly to document growth as well as struggles. Assessment and specific instructional lessons based on the assessment results are key components when thinking about RTI.

What About . . .

Standards, Assessment, and Word Identification?

In order to comprehend text, readers identify words rapidly, automatically, and accurately. The CCSS recognize that students learn to identify words by using a variety of strategies, including phonics, sight recognition, structural analysis, and context. In addition, according to the International Literacy Association's (ILA) *Standards for Reading Professionals* (2010b), reading teachers must be versed in a wide range of strategies for teaching word identification.

Teachers need to be cautious about assessing word identification skills in isolation. For example, students who can read sight-word flash cards with accuracy may not be able to identify the same words in the context of a story. Others may not be able to identify words in a list but readily understand those same words in the context of a meaningful story. Real reading takes place within meaningful contexts, and having students read lists of words may not be an accurate assessment of word identification skills.

Summary

- Initially, this chapter synthesized for teachers the concept of word identification, which is the ability to associate words or labels to print. In addition, related terms associated with the concept were discussed, including word attack and word recognition.

- Next, we looked at word identification abilities within the context of the developmental phases associated with children's ability to identify words: the prealphabetic, partial alphabetic, full alphabetic, and consolidated alphabetic phases.

- Additionally, this chapter outlined explicit guidelines and approaches for teaching phonics as a strategy for teaching word identification. These approaches include traditional strategies such as analytic and synthetic phonics instruction as well as contemporary approaches such as analogy-based and embedded phonics instruction.

- Consonant-based strategies for teaching phonics— such as multisensory activities, making words, flip books, and cube words—were explained with practical examples. In addition, analogy-based strategies that use word patterns and spelling-based strategies, such as word banks and word walls, were described. It is important that teachers understand that no one strategy is better than another.

- Word identification strategies also include teaching students how to use context clues. Guessing games, cloze procedures, and introducing the concept of semantic gradients are strategies that foster the use of context clues.

- Using structural analysis involves the ability to use affixes, inflected endings, compound words, and contractions to identify words. Strategies such as word study notebooks, wall chart carousels, compound word cups, and contraction searches assist students in using structural analysis as they examine print.

- It is critical that students develop the ability to read high-frequency words. These are words that bind sentences together, such as articles, conjunctions, prepositions, and verbs of being. A list of common high-frequency words is included in this chapter, as well as strategies such as word walls, the language-experience approach, word games, and using literature and poetry.

- Three principles for word identification were presented. These include understanding that phonics is only one way to recognize words, and should not be overemphasized at the expense of other strategies; being conscious of what strategies work for students and grouping children accordingly based on their strengths and weaknesses; and realizing that instruction on how to identify words needs to make sense to the students. Using meaningful contexts should be a priority.

- We emphasized that teachers need to balance word identification instruction with oral language experiences, writing, and exposure to quality literature. Teachers also need to be aware of the strengths and weaknesses that children bring to the classroom; not all students will respond to word identification instruction the same way.

Teacher Action Research

1. Analyze the word identification strand of a basal reading program. How is decoding or word identification defined? What are the major components of the strand?

2. Collect several samples of writing from a child in primary school. Analyze the writing to determine the child's letter–sound knowledge. Then interview the child's teacher to determine his or her perceptions of the child's strengths and gaps in reading and writing. Does your analysis match the teacher's perceptions? Why or why not?

3. Examine a literature-based anthology. How is phonics taught—for example, is phonics taught analytically or synthetically? Develop a synthesis of your findings.

4. Examine a literature-based anthology. What provisions are made to help children develop multiple strategies for identifying unknown words? How comprehensively is phonics taught and reinforced?

5. Examine a literature-based anthology. Develop a graphic organizer that captures multiple ways that students are taught how to use context clues to identify unknown words.

6. Examine a grade 3 through 6 literature-based anthology. Develop a template of 5 to 10 strategies that feature teaching structural analysis. Share the strategies that you found, and demonstrate one. Discuss the strategy with your colleagues, and share adaptations that might be used with younger children.

7. Select a piece of children's literature, and type 100 words from the selection. Using Fry's instant word list, highlight each word on the list that you locate in the piece of literature, and calculate the percentage of words that are high frequency. Repeat the same procedure using a college textbook. What did you find?

8. Interview a teacher in the primary grades, and inquire how he or she organizes word identification instruction. Does the teacher use a separate phonics program? The lessons found in a literature-based anthology? Share and compare with your colleagues.

9. Examine the language arts curriculum in your school district, and develop a resource for technology-based applications that are used for teaching word identification. Share with your colleagues.

Through the Lens of the Common Core

The main goal of reading is to understand the print. In order to understand print, however, the CCSS recognize the need to be able to interpret the multiple meanings of words and the relationships between words, and understand how words function in a variety of contexts. Although a primary goal of teaching children how to identify words is to read them quickly and automatically so that they can focus on comprehension, it is also critical that we teach children how to use parts of words (structural analysis) and context clues when they encounter unknown words. Hence, when teaching word identification skills, it is important to teach them in meaningful contexts. If there is no context, there is nothing to comprehend.

Chapter 7
Reading Fluency

 Learning Outcomes

In This Chapter, You Will Discover How to

- Define fluency, its dimensions, and the relationship of fluency to comprehension.

- Explain how to implement effective strategies for developing fluency.

- Articulate how to assess all aspects of oral reading fluency.

- Explain how to conduct a silent reading program that supports oral reading fluency.

Activating Your Schema

Do you remember when you were in school, and the teacher had other students take turns reading out loud? It might have been called *around the world, popcorn reading*, or *round-robin reading*. Or were you the person who had to read out loud and you struggled with most of the words in front of your peers? What was that experience like for you as a listener, or you as the struggling reader? Was it a positive experience? Were you able to comprehend the text? What was it about the reading that wasn't fluent? Learning how to read fluently is important, because fluent reading results in more time devoted to making sense and comprehending text.

2017 ILA Standards Found in This Chapter

1.1	2.2	3.1	3.4
1.3	2.3	3.2	5.1

Common Core State Standards: English Language Arts

CCRA.R.10   CCRA.SL.1.1

Key Terms

automated reading	oral recitation lesson (ORL)
automaticity	paired reading
choral reading	predictable text
cross-age reading	reader's theater
fluency	repeated readings
fluency development lesson (FDL)	support reading strategy

Carlito, a fourth grader, can read fluently in his native Spanish. Like many English language learners (ELLs) who live in homes where the family speaks only the native language, Carlito never hears or speaks English at home. However, he now lives in Kansas and is finding reading in English to be tricky. He is deceptively fast and accurate in his reading because he was a good reader in his primary language. His decoding skills are strong, but he demonstrates little understanding of the text. His teacher, Abe Williams, has tried reading the text to Carlito because that has been helpful for his native speakers, but it just doesn't seem to help with Carlito's comprehension. Abe is at a loss as to what to do to help Carlito, since in this case fluency is an inaccurate indicator of comprehension.

Abe's colleague connected him with an expert at an area university who specializes in teaching English to second language learners. She told him it is not unusual for an ELL to read a passage beautifully and then not be able to correctly answer more than a couple of comprehension questions. She explained that native speakers who struggle with decoding often comprehend text that is read to them better than text that they read themselves. That's because when someone else is doing the reading, they can focus on meaning without having to struggle to get the words off the page. However, she said that comprehension problems for ELLs are often associated with limited vocabulary and background knowledge. This means that listening to text read by someone else won't improve comprehension. She suggested Abe give Carlito a chance to practice reading out loud using independent level texts that he can practice again and again. She also suggested Carlito practice reading a passage with a certain emotion or to emphasize expression, intonation, and inflection based on punctuation to help with meaning. Finally, she explained that Abe needs to pre-teach key vocabulary and that he could have his student discuss the topic at home with his parents in his own language.

Abe is now sending topics of study home with Carlito and encouraging him to talk about them with his family. He is also using the read-aloud feature in the class's e-book collection so Carlito can practice reading along with the text. This is helping with his use of punctuation and phrasing, and over time seems to be helping with his comprehension.

In this chapter, we underscore the value of having readers develop fluency in oral and silent reading situations. We begin by defining reading fluency as *reading easily and well with a sense of confidence and knowledge of what to do when things go wrong.* By examining the concepts of immediate word identification and automaticity, we see that fluent reading is far more than reading words smoothly out loud; fluency is the core of comprehension. After considering how materials influence fluency development, we describe teaching strategies and routines to teach fluency, as well as ways to monitor and assess oral reading fluency. Included are descriptions of best practices that help orchestrate the teaching and training of fluency with the teaching of comprehension.

Common Core State Standard

CCRA.SL.1.1

Defining Oral Reading Fluency

■ **Define fluency, its dimensions, and the relationship of fluency to comprehension.**

The term *fluent* is often associated with doing something easily and well. When applied to reading, **fluency**, in everyday terms, means reading easily and well. However, fluency is not simply reading fast. In response to a decade of defining fluency based on reading rate and accuracy, Samuels (2012) states, "The essential characteristic of fluency is the ability to decode and comprehend at the same time. The less important characteristics are accuracy and speed." (p. 14). Rasinski (2015) writes, "Success in real world reading is not measured by how fast a person can orally read a short text. Rather, reading success is more likely to be an outcome of how well a person can engage in meaningful, close, silent readings of lengthy, complex, and challenging material for extended periods of time" (p.v).

Common Core State Standards

CCRA.R.10, CCRA.SL1.1

Rasinski (2004) explains that fluency has three dimensions.

1. The first dimension is *accuracy in word decoding*. Readers must be able to sound out words (using phonics and other word decoding strategies) in text with few errors.
2. The second dimension is *automatic processing*. This is when the reader uses as little mental effort as possible in the decoding of text, saving mental energy for comprehension.
3. The third dimension is *prosody* or *prosodic reading*. Prosody is a linguistic concept that refers to such features in oral language as *intonation, pitch, stress, pauses,* and the *duration* placed on specific syllables. These features signal some of the meaning conveyed in oral language.

2017 ILA Standard

1.1

Fluent readers first exhibit accurate reading, then reading with automaticity, and finally the use of prosody, which is likely the result of reading comprehension (Schwanenflugel, Hamilton, Kuhn, Wisenbaker, & Stahl, 2004).

Effective fluency instruction has three parts: instruction, practice, and assessment.

1. Fluency *instruction* should incorporate the teaching of basic skills such as phonemic awareness and phonics. It should also model what fluency looks and sounds like.

2. Fluency *practice* includes the use of decodable text and other independent-level texts to strengthen the sounds and spelling that are taught in the classroom. Strategies such as repeated readings, covered later in this chapter, should be utilized often. Instruction in fluent oral reading produces readers who move from word-by-word reading to more efficient phrase reading (Chomsky, 1976; Samuels, 1979). Fluency instruction has also resulted in improved reading achievement, assessed through measures of comprehension (Dowhower, 1987). Rasinski (2003) explains that because fluent readers do not have to spend time decoding words, they are able to spend time and energy on making sense of and comprehending a text.

3. The final component of fluency is *assessment*. Assessing fluency needs to include assessing all dimensions: accuracy, automaticity, and prosody. Without the focus of all three, readers will simply be word callers. Additionally, the role of assessment is not only to monitor students' progress but also to inform instruction.

Accuracy in Word Decoding

Students need to recognize or identify words rapidly. The general belief is that children can read a text successfully when they know at least 95 percent of the words. Accuracy refers to the ability to recognize or decode words correctly. To do this, students need an understanding of the alphabetic principle and the ability to blend sounds together. Knowledge of a large bank of high-frequency words is required for word-reading accuracy (Hudson, Lane, & Pullen, 2005). When a word is retrieved rapidly from long-term memory, the process is often triggered by well-developed schemata that the reader has developed for a word. In immediate word identification, semantic or physical features in a word (e.g., a single letter or a letter cluster) trigger quick retrieval of that word.

Immediate word identification is the strategy used by skilled readers on 99 percent of the printed words they meet. It is also the method used by children when they identify their first words. Often one of the first words children learn to identify in print is their name. Jessica, a four-year-old, can recognize her printed name but may not attend to each individual letter. She recognizes her name because some distinctive feature triggers rapid retrieval from long-term memory.

When words cannot be read accurately from memory as sight words, they must be analyzed. In order to do this, students need to have word identification strategies such as phonics, structural analysis, and the use of context to figure out unknown words in order to move on and maintain comprehension. Students who struggle, such as those with dyslexia, need some direct instruction and intervention on decoding. For dyslexics, the most common deficit among children who can't read is phoneme awareness: the ability to see letters and sound them out efficiently to form words (Wolf, 2007). These students need one-on-one tutoring to tackle their reading disability in order to read accurately.

How do skilled readers reach the point at which they read fluently and don't have to rely on word identification strategies? Researchers are finding that *repetition is extremely important in learning to recognize words.* The amount of repetition needed for beginning readers to be able to recognize words immediately has not been appreciated. Traditionally, repetition of reading texts has not been systematically included in reading instruction. Today, reading familiar text is considered a key component of a comprehensive literacy program.

Automatic Processing

Word recognition needs to be accurate and *automatic*. To explain the term **automaticity**, an analogy is often made to driving a car. Most of the time, a skilled driver will focus little attention or use little mental energy while driving. Skilled drivers frequently daydream or ponder happenings in their lives as they drive, yet they still manage to drive in the appropriate lane at an appropriate speed (most of the time!). They drive on automatic pilot. Nevertheless, when the need arises, a driver can swiftly focus attention on driving—for example, when a warning light goes on or when weather conditions suddenly change. In other words, most of us drive with automaticity, with little use of mental energy, but when necessary, we're able to refocus rapidly on what we're doing as drivers.

When readers are accurate but not automatic, they put considerable amounts of mental energy into identifying words as they read. When readers are both accurate and automatic, they recognize or identify words accurately, rapidly, easily, and with little mental energy. Like the skilled driver, the skilled reader can rapidly focus attention on a decoding problem but most of the time will put energy into comprehending the text. In general, fluent readers read at least 100 words per minute; however, reading quickly is not the same as reading fluently.

Fluency strategies are also one way of getting rid of the "uh-ohs" that are a part of learning any new skill. When taking tennis lessons, the beginner often makes mental comments such as "Uh-oh, I need to hit in the middle of my racket" or, "Oh, what a crummy backhand shot." Each hit is judged as either good or bad. Children are also prone to struggling with the "uh-ohs" when learning to read. This happens especially when they think about which words they can and cannot identify. Like the beginning tennis player, the beginning reader often gets anxious because the "uh-ohs" interfere with constructing meaning from the text. Developing automaticity is one way to give beginning readers a feel for reading without anxiety.

Prosody

Prosody has a close relationship with comprehension since it incorporates the characteristics of oral reading that allow it to sound expressive. Have you ever sat in a class or been to a presentation when the speaker used few prosodic cues while speaking? Sometimes it's difficult to focus on what the person is trying to say or what the person means. In the same way, reading with expression, or using prosodic features while reading orally, has the potential of conveying more meaning than reading without expression. In addition, prosodic cues convey moods and feelings. Children generally know instantly when a parent is irritated with them. A mother's tone of voice (intonation) is usually enough to signal, "Mom is mad."

In learning to understand oral language, children rely on prosodic features. Similar conditions appear to be necessary in learning to understand written language. Schreiber (1980) found that students learned how to put words together in meaningful phrases, despite the fact that a written text provides few phrasing cues and uses few graphic signals for prosodic features in print. In classrooms we often hear teachers tell students to "read with expression." This suggestion is a hint that the reader should rely on intuitive knowledge or prosodic features in oral language, not only to help convey meaning to others but also to help the reader's own understanding of what is being read.

 In this **video** (http://www.youtube.com/watch?v=KnuCq5KWOjo), the teacher uses several techniques for teaching prosody. What are some of the ways she does this?

Predictability of Reading Materials

For children to develop into confident, fluent readers, they need to read lots of texts that are easy for them. For first and second graders, **predictable text** can be read with ease. Predictable books have a context or setting that is familiar or predictable to most children. The pictures are supportive of the text; that is, there is a good match between the text and the illustrations. The language is natural, meaning that common language patterns are used. The story line is predictable. There is a repetitive pattern such as the mother rocking the child at night regardless of the trials during the day. There is also repetitive language in the refrains. Further contributing to the predictability of the book is the rhyme of language. There are several different kinds of predictable texts.

- *Chain or circular story.* Plot is interlinked so that the ending leads back to the beginning. Laura Numeroff's *If You Give a Mouse a Cookie* is a good example of a circular story.
- *Cumulative story.* Each time a new event occurs, all previous events in the story are repeated. The well-known tale of the Gingerbread Man is a good example of a story that is cumulative.
- *Pattern story.* Scenes are repeated throughout the story with some variation, as in the fairy tale *The Three Billy Goats Gruff.*
- *Question and answer.* The same or similar questions are repeated throughout the story. *Brown Bear, Brown Bear, What Do You See?* by Bill Martin is a good example of this type of text.
- *Repetition of phrase.* Word order in a phrase or sentence is repeated. Margaret Wise Brown's classic *Goodnight Moon* is an example.
- *Rhyme.* Rhyming words, refrains, or patterns are used throughout the story, such as *Is Your Mama a Llama?* by Deborah Guarino.
- *Songbooks.* Familiar songs have predictable elements, such as repetitive phrase. The classic song "Over in the Meadow" has many predictable elements.

Predictable texts are particularly helpful in developing fluency because children can rely on these characteristics of predictability. With predictable stories, less able readers can use intuitive knowledge of language and sense rather than rely on mediated techniques that draw on their mental energy. Using predictable texts, readers can develop fluency by reading them repeatedly with less and less assistance.

 Watch this **video** (www.youtube.com/watch?v=YMaiL1UtVl8) to listen to an expressive reading of the predictable, repetitive story *Chicken Little*. What does the narrator do that makes listening to the story so enjoyable? What portions of the story would the children chime in and read along with the narrator?

2017 ILA Standards

1.1, 1.3, 2.2, 2.3

Check Your Understanding 7.1: Gauge your understanding of the skills and concepts in this section.

Developing Oral Reading Fluency

■ **Explain how to implement effective strategies for developing fluency.**

Children learn to become fluent in environments that support oral reading as communication. Mindless classroom situations in which children take turns reading in round-robin fashion accomplish little that is constructive. In round-robin reading, the teacher

BOX 7.1 | STUDENT VOICES

Kara is a college junior enrolled in a teacher preparation program. In a recent class she was asked to reflect on her journey as a reader, and this is what she had to say:

> Reading was never one of my favorite things growing up. In fact, I would avoid it as much as possible. I struggled everyday with reading and writing. I could not read as well as the other students, and my spelling was horrible. I was always in the lower level reading groups all throughout elementary school, which made me feel even more insecure about my reading. I would do anything to get out of reading out loud in class. I remember when we would have to read out loud in class and we all had to go around the classroom and read a part of the book in round-robin or popcorn reading. I would

figure out which paragraph or page I had to read and then read that page over and over until it was my turn. I was so nervous about messing up and getting made fun of when I would do this that I did not pay attention to anyone else reading because I was concentrating on my section.

Kara experienced an outdated practice known as round-robin reading, in which the teacher calls on children to read unrehearsed text in front of the class. Teachers need to learn about and implement routines and strategies that foster fluency during oral reading, not simply word-perfect portrayals of text. The goal of fluency is always comprehension.

randomly calls on students to read a section of text "cold" in front of the class. When teachers utilize this traditional practice, students often do not view their role as that of tellers of a story or as communicators of information. Instead, since their role is to be word perfect, they focus on accuracy, not automaticity or comprehension. In Box 7.1, Kara tells us just how little is accomplished during round-robin reading.

We've asked our students what they recall from their school years about reading aloud in front of peers, and it always begins a rich conversation about this outdated practice. Andrew's poignant story in Box 7.2 is one of them. Although we are strong proponents of oral reading in classrooms, the emphasis during oral reading must be on communication and comprehension, not word-perfect renderings of a reading selection. We suggest that students, especially ELLs, have the opportunity to practice text silently before they read aloud.

BOX 7.2 | VIEWPOINT

Andrew Pinney
My Reading History

Andrew is a middle school Social Studies teacher who is passionate about using reading strategies in his content area teaching. When people ask him why he cares so much about teaching students to read texts, he tells them his story.

I remember the day and event that happened 30 years ago like it was yesterday. Part of this day feels 30 years ago, for I can't recall my teacher's name, but the pain I felt is still very palpable. I was in my second-grade class, and it was the first day we were put into reading groups. I sat there and waited, well aware of what it meant to be in the *yellow* group, as opposed to the "smart kids" in the *red* and *blue* groups. I remember waiting my turn and hoping for at least a shot in the *blue* or "average smart" *red* group. Then I heard her, "Andrew, go to the *yellow* group." I felt dumb. I was humiliated in front of all my classmates. Whether or not this was effective differentiated instruction or just plain de facto sorting, I can't say, although today I tend to think it was the latter. Little did I know at the time, this turned out to be a defining moment, not only in my reading history, but in my life—I let the event become a self-fulfilling prophecy. Since I was put in the "slow readers" group, I felt I was no good at reading. While some students may want to strive to improve from this point and use it

to motivate them, I chose the path of proving that the teachers were correct. I gave up.

From this point forward I hated to read, and there didn't seem to be any intervention at school or at home. The third- to the sixth-grade years seem to be a blur, except for incessant daydreaming. By the time of the sixth-grade class production of *Julius Caesar*, I was the only child in the class without a speaking part. This stung in a way that my teacher, or others for whom learning came easy, could probably never understand. But I still remember how it felt today.

I spent the next few middle school years being embarrassed daily by my mispronouncing easy words during "popcorn" or round-robin reading. By this time, I had had enough of trying, and I dealt with it by the only way acceptable to my peers: getting into trouble. From this point forward, it was going to be fun to get bad grades in school and be a smart aleck in class. Also in middle school, the real sorting of students began. I had the same teacher for seventh, eighth, tenth, and eleventh grades. She was given the kids who were unmotivated or lacking in "college potential"—in other words, kids like me. Maybe she was given us because no one else wanted us or because the administration figured the better teachers should teach the college-bound students—I don't know. But I do know that I spent four crucial years with a teacher who expected nothing from me, and I delivered exactly that. I can honestly say that outside round-robin reading in class, I read *nothing*. To compound this, I wrote one paper in those four years, and it was about the designated hitter in baseball, a two-page piece of trash with illustrations taking up most of the paper. I was exposed to no literature, other than the in-class reading that was never comprehended. My senior year I actually had a teacher who cared and expected me to learn something, but by this time I didn't see the point in it, so I slept in several days a week so I could miss her class. Needless to say, I did not attend college out of high school.

I finally did attend college after coming to the realization that I might want a future that did not consist of sanding boards on an assembly line. College was a struggle, and for four-plus years I taught myself how to read for comprehension, how to write, and how to study. It took most of my undergraduate years to learn to read with comprehension, not get distracted and daydream and then have to constantly reread the pages. I finally broke through at some point toward the end of my undergraduate studies. Now, 30 years after being put in the "slow reading"

group, I devour books one after another. My comprehension is to a point that I can read a book while watching a ball game on television yet still manage to comprehend the written words.

This self-fulfilling prophecy stripped me of the enjoyment of reading for 10 critical, developmental years of my life. It took six years of extreme difficulty to break the cycle of "slow reading" while also trying to earn a bachelor's degree so that I could become a teacher.

Today I have two young daughters of my own, and I read to them all the time. Before we read I ask them to guess what they think the story will be about, and throughout the story I often stop and have them retell me what we've read. I tell them to use the pictures and other clues in the story to help them make sense, and I tell them they should be forming pictures in their heads as they are reading.

As a teacher, I believe the experience has given me empathy for students who have the same kind of difficulties I had. I often share parts of my story with them so they know that I understand what it's like to struggle with reading. I tell them that if they find that they are daydreaming when they are reading, it doesn't mean they're dumb; it just means they have to learn how to think with text and comprehend it. I incorporate reading strategies in my teaching, and I *never* have kids read unfamiliar text out loud in front of others. I hope I can take my understanding of and compassion for these students and combine it with literacy practices that will change *their* reading history.

Rasinski (2010) suggests teachers develop oral reading proficiency by (1) modeling fluent, expressive reading so students can hear how it sounds; (2) providing scaffolding for students by using partners or whole group assisted reading; (3) practicing fluency using phrases since fluent readers read in phrases, not word-to-word; and (4) repeatedly practicing reading text to get better. Research shows what students learn from the repeated reading of one passage partially transfers to the new passage; and word recognition, accuracy, automaticity, comprehension, and attitude toward reading improve with repeated readings (Dowhower, 1994; Kuhn & Stahl, 2000; Rasinski, Reutzel, Chard, & Linan-Thompson, 2011).

Strategies for Groups of Students

To really improve fluency, students need explicit instruction focused on accuracy in word decoding, automatic reading, prosody, and how to self-monitor in order to improve their own fluency. Let's take a closer look at some classroom routines and strategies that can help foster fluency.

CHORAL READING   Telling students to read with expression is not enough for many developing readers. Rather, many children need to listen to mature readers read with expression and interpret and practice different ways of orally reading selections. **Choral reading** is an enjoyable way to engage children in listening and responding to the prosodic features in oral language in order to read with expression. In essence, through the use of choral reading techniques, students consider ways to get across the author's meaning using prosodic cues such as pitch, loudness, stress, and pauses. For ELLs, choral reading provides practice in a nonthreatening atmosphere, allowing them to build meaning from text and learn more about language.

Choral reading is reading aloud in unison with a whole class or group of students. After hearing the teacher read and discuss a selection, students reread the text together.

Choral reading helps build students' fluency (Dowhower, 1987; Hasbrouck, 2006; Schreiber, 1980), self-confidence, vocabulary knowledge, motivation, and enjoyment of literature. In addition, it provides a legitimate and fun way for children to practice reading a text that leads to a decreased number of oral reading miscues. Reading in unison can be difficult because the entire group speaks all the lines and responds to the prosodic cues simultaneously. Timing, parallel inflections, and consistent voice quality are of prime importance; otherwise, there is a singsong effect. This points to the need for the teacher to model how to read a selection with expression and to discuss how to use stress, pitch, intonation, and loudness when reading in unison.

In preparing for a choral reading of a text, the teacher models one way the selection can be read while the children listen. Then students identify how the teacher read the passage. Were parts read loudly or softly? What was the tempo? Did the teacher emphasize particular syllables? Was his or her voice pitched higher or lower in different parts of the passage? Students are then invited to try different ways of reading or interpreting a part, and they may want to respond to the mood or feeling that each interpretation imparts.

There are different ways to conduct choral reading. Once children are comfortable with the procedure, you might create variations, dividing the children into different groups to alternate reading. Sometimes you might have students read the refrain only. Other times you might encourage children to take turns reading lines or only read the parts that are dialogue.

ECHO READING   Echo reading is a method of modeling oral reading in which the teacher reads a line of a story and then the students echo by reading the same line back, imitating the teacher's intonation and phrasing. This strategy allows the teacher to provide learners with a great deal of support, or scaffolding, which is why we suggest you choose a text that is challenging for your students that will allow you to provide the most support.

To conduct echo reading, the teacher should select a text of approximately 200 words that is above the students' reading level. The teacher reads the first line of the text, accentuating appropriate phrasing, rate, and intonation. Next, the students read the same line from the text, modeling the teacher's example. The teacher and the students read the entire passage in echo fashion, increasing the amount of text when the students can imitate the model. Echo reading also works well with small groups and individuals.

FLUENCY-ORIENTED READING INSTRUCTION (FORI)   Fluency-Oriented Reading Instruction (FORI) (Stahl & Heubach, 2005) was developed for whole group instruction with a grade-level basal reader, although many teachers have used the strategy with grade-level trade books. FORI incorporates the research-based practices of repeated, assisted reading with independent silent reading within a three-part classroom program. The three components are a reading lesson that includes teacher-led, repeated oral reading and partner reading, a free-reading period at school, and home reading.

In FORI a basal reading selection is read to the students by the teacher and then followed by a brief discussion of the story to ensure that they understand what has been read. The teacher reviews key vocabulary from the story and has students participate in comprehension exercises built around the story. The students then take the story home to read to their parents or other listeners. For struggling readers, a single story may be sent home additional times. On the second day, the students reread the story with a partner. One partner reads a page as the other monitors the reading. Then the partners switch roles until the story is finished. Following partner reading, the teacher engages students in some extension activities and moves on to another story. On the third day, the students might chorally read the text and on the fourth day partner-read. The students also take the text home for additional reading practice, but if the students are already fluent with the selection, they are asked to read alternative material. The week ends with extension activities such as written responses to the week's selection or a second discussion of the text.

The purpose of the FORI is to build fluency and comprehension of grade-appropriate text through repeated reading, text-related discussion, and teacher support and guidance before and after reading. Additionally, FORI uses teacher read-aloud and repeated reading as a scaffold so students can access grade-level reading material that would normally be too difficult.

2017 ILA Standards

1.1, 1.3, 2.2, 2.3

READER'S THEATER Another way to involve children of all ages in orally reading literature to other children is through **reader's theater**. Reader's theater is the oral presentation of drama, prose, or poetry by two or more readers. Reader's theater differs from orally reading a selection in that several readers take the parts of the characters in the story or play. Instead of memorizing or improvising their parts, as in other types of theater productions, the players read them. Because the emphasis is on what the audience *hears* rather than sees, selection of the literature is very important. Reader's theater scripts generally contain a great deal of dialogue and are often adapted from literature. Researchers have found that the use of reader's theater promotes fluency and interest in reading (Griffith & Rasinski, 2004; Young & Rasinski, 2009). Because reader's theater has repeated readings of the text, students increase sight-word vocabulary and the ability to decode words quickly and accurately (Carrick, 2006, 2009). Also, repeated readings permit students to practice appropriate phrasing and punctuation, which helps them spend less time on decoding and more on comprehension (Pikulski & Chard, 2005). Although fluency instruction is most often emphasized in the early grades, middle and high school students also have much to gain from becoming more fluent readers. Older students can become more fluent readers through repeated reading practice, which is best accomplished through performance-based activities such as reader's theater. An example of a portion of a reader's theater script is illustrated in Figure 7.1. Be sure to include stories that reflect culturally and linguistically diverse characters.

During a reader's theater program, the members of the audience use their imagination to visualize what is going on, because movement and action are limited. Although there is no one correct arrangement of the cast in presenting reader's theater, an effective procedure is to have the student readers stand in a line facing away from the audience and then turn toward the audience when they read their part.

Reader's theater is not simply reading a selection of text over and over and then performing it for an audience. Effective teachers know that following several key features will yield much better results from this research-based instructional strategy. Notice in the following guidelines how parts are not assigned until the entire class has practiced the text:

1. Introduce the piece, and have the students read it through once (chorally) to become familiar with the words.
2. Direct students to look for places where they could add things like feeling, expression, pauses, and enunciation.
3. Ask students to model suggestions for the class for enhancing the text.
4. Practice the piece of text together, phrase by phrase.
5. Read the entire piece as a class using the suggested expression.
6. Stop the process when necessary to reteach, model, or discuss fluency issues.
7. Assign reader's theater parts to students.

Figure 7.1 Excerpt from Reader's Theater Script: *The Three Billy Goats Gruff*

Cast:
1. Little Billy Goat Gruff
2. Middle Billy Goat Gruff
3. Big Billy Goat Gruff
4. Narrator
5. Angry Troll
6. Bridge

Vocabulary:	gruffly, meadow, troll, bridge, hillside, wicked, underneath
Narrator:	This is the story of the three Billy Goats Gruff. One day, a little Billy goat, known as Little Billy Goat Gruff, saw a beautiful meadow on a hillside across a bridge. The meadow looked so green, and it had peach trees. He wanted to go over. All of the grass on his side of the bridge was gone, and he was very, very hungry.
Little BGG:	Oh. That looks so good! I am going to cross that bridge and go to the meadow and eat that green grass so I can grow big like my brothers.
Narrator:	So Little Billy Goat Gruff started to walk across the bridge.
Bridge:	*Trip trap, trip trap, trip trap.*
Narrator:	Just as Little Billy Goat Gruff got halfway across the bridge, a wicked old troll popped up from underneath!
Troll:	(*Gruffly*) Who is walking on my bridge?!
Little BGG:	It is me, Little Billy Goat Gruff.
Troll:	This is MY bridge. You can't cross it! I am going to eat you for lunch!
Little BGG:	I just want to cross the bridge and eat some grass in the meadow. Please don't eat me. I'm just a little Billy goat. Wait until my brother comes along. He is MUCH bigger than me.
Troll:	Well … okay. Go ahead and cross the bridge. I will wait and eat your brother.
Little BGG:	Thank you very much, Troll!
Narrator:	And he crossed over the bridge into the meadow.
Bridge:	*Trip trap, trip trap, trip trap.*
Narrator:	Just then a second Billy goat, Middle Billy Goat Gruff, started to walk over the bridge.
Troll:	(*Gruffly*) Who is walking on my bridge?!

8. Practice individual reader's theater parts.
9. Perform reader's theater.
10. Ask students to self-assess: "What did you do this time that was better?"
11. Confirm their comments, offering suggestions.

After students have presented several reader's theaters using teacher-made or commercially prepared scripts, students can write their own scripts, either adapting literature, poetry, plays, song lyrics, or speeches they enjoy or using stories they have written. Here's how to guide students to develop their own scripts: Once children have read a story, they transform it into a script through social negotiation. The writing of a story into a script requires much rereading as well as knowledge and interpretation of the text. Once the script is written, the children formulate, practice, and refine their interpretations. Finally, the reader's theater is presented to an audience.

Reader's theater motivates children to read the same material repeatedly to increase fluency. Many children will rehearse a part enthusiastically to present it to an audience.

 Watch this **video** (www.youtube.com/watch?v=4g_KqjZQ43Q) to watch children from Taiwan perform a reader's theater. Do you think they had to read the text repeatedly in order to perform?

FLUENCY IDOL Building on best practices in fluency instruction, Fluency Idol (Calo, Woolard-Ferguson, & Koitz, 2013) was created as a way to encourage repeated readings, practice at home, supportive feedback, and performance. To use this strategy, the teacher selects a poem at each child's independent reading level and has the students practice the poems in pairs and at home with family throughout the week. Teachers select several students to Fluency Idol and record the performance so fluency can be assessed later. The class completes a secret ballot, voting on the student who made the reading most enjoyable by using the components of fluency to make listening gratifying and easy to understand.

Strategies for Pairs and Individual Students

When you need to work more intensely with a student, perhaps in Response to Intervention (RTI) work, you will need to know about strategies that are designed specifically for this type of instruction. Following are some strategies that model fluent reading and encourage repeated readings while incorporating other important aspects of reading at the same time.

REPEATED READINGS **Repeated readings** increase reading fluency. Rasinski (2015b) blogs that it is regular practice, where a student reads a text several times until he or she achieves a certain level of automaticity that improves speed and comprehension. Repeated readings involve simply having a child read a short passage from a text more than once with differing amounts of support. Reading poetry is a natural way to develop fluency. Children of all ages enjoy and respond to the rhythm of poetry, and it can be incorporated easily into the classroom routine. In order to read or share a poem for the class, students need to practice the poems using repeated reading, thus developing reading fluency. However, Shanahan (2016) cautions that since the point of fluency instruction is to help students read all kinds of text fluently, teachers should typically use prose texts the majority of the time. Repeated readings have been beneficial for many students and ELLs with learning disabilities (Rubin, 2016).

In Box 7.3, Jeremy Brueck describes how digital audio recording can improve reading fluency.

Samuels (1979) proposes the method of repeated readings as a strategy to develop fluent oral reading. Here are several steps Samuels suggests when using repeated readings:

1. Students choose short selections (50 to 200 words) from stories that are difficult enough that students are not able to read them fluently.
2. Students read the passage several times silently until they are able to read it fluently.
3. The teacher can involve students in a discussion of how athletes develop athletic skills by spending considerable time practicing basic movements until they develop speed and smoothness. Repeated reading uses the same type of practice.
4. Samuels suggests that students record their first oral rendition of the passage as well as their oral rendition after practice so that they can hear the difference in fluency.
5. Students continue practicing until they can read the passage with accuracy and fluency.

Studies on repeated readings fall into two categories: *assisted* repeated readings, in which students read along with a live or taped model of the passage, and *unassisted* repeated readings, in which the child engages in independent practice (Dowhower, 1989). In both assisted and unassisted repeated readings, students reread a meaningful passage until oral production is accurate and smooth and resembles spoken language. Both assisted and unassisted readings can be used to develop reading fluency, beginning initially with assisted reading.

BOX 7.3 | TRANSLITERACY

Digital Audio Recording to Improve Reading Fluency

Fluent readers develop over time with plenty of practice. Many students (and parents) mistakenly equate fluent reading with fast reading. Teachers must work to help students and parents understand that reading quickly with little expression or in a monotone voice is not fluent reading (CCSS.ELA-LITERACY.RF.1.4.B). One way transliteracy skills can assist in this process is through the use of digital audio recording. Many digital audio recording tools exist that teachers can use to help students develop into more fluent readers.

Chirbit (http://www.chirbit.com/) is a social audio sharing tool that can be used for recording, hosting, and streaming audio. It is available as a free web-based application and a free mobile app available for both Android and iOS devices, although audio files are limited to five minutes in length. Chirbit allows audio recordings to be shared on numerous social platforms and includes an option to get a QR code for each file. Other digital audio recording options include **Soundcloud** (https://soundcloud.com/) and **AudioBoom** (https://audioboom.com/).

To get started in your classroom, determine what device students can access and use to record themselves. Will they be recording at a desktop computer? A laptop? A tablet device? Once you've made this determination, you can decide which digital audio recording tool to use. The tools listed above offer one-button recording options, which make them easy for students of all ages to use, although teacher modeling of the recording process for students is critical.

Next, ask students to pick a familiar book that they feel they can read fluently, and have them read it aloud once before recording. After their practice read, students can launch Chirbit on the computer or mobile device. When they are ready to begin, they use the one-button recording feature to get started. Ask them to start each recording by reading the title, author, and illustrator of the book. If desired, students can use the one-button feature to pause the recording when they need to turn the page. After they have finished, teachers can assist students with publishing their digital audio recording, making sure to use the title of the book and the student's first name when naming the file. Each digital audio recording completed in this fashion will be uploaded to your class Chirbit page, where you can access them at a later time.

Finally, use the QR code option to share the recording with others. Email QR codes to parents so they can listen to their child's oral reading and track fluency development at home. QR codes could also be added to your classroom website for others to access. You might even try printing QR codes on self-adhesive labels, affixing them to your classroom books, and encouraging students to scan the QR codes during your classroom literacy block so that they can follow along in the book as they listen!

When teachers talk about the repeated-reading strategy, they frequently wonder whether students find repeated readings of the same story boring. To the contrary, teachers who have used repeated readings find that young children actually delight in reading favorite stories over and over, especially when they know the repetitive parts and can chime in and feel like a reader. Children plead to have their favorite bedtime story read again and again. In the same vein, they get very involved in practicing a story with the goal of reading it accurately and fluently and are eager to share their story with parents and classmates.

PAIRED REPEATED READINGS In paired repeated readings, students select their own passage from the material with which they are currently working. The passage should be about 50 words in length. Students, grouped in pairs, should each select different passages, which makes listening more interesting and discourages direct comparison of reading proficiency. The material should be predictable and of a level at which mastery is possible.

When working together, the students read their own passage silently and then decide who will be the first reader. The first reader then reads his or her passage out loud to a partner three different times. Readers may ask their partner for help with a word. After each oral reading, the reader evaluates his or her reading. A self-evaluation sheet might ask the reader, "How well did you read today?" Responses to be checked might range from fantastic, to good, to fair, to not so good. The partner listens and tells the reader how much improvement was made after each rendition of the reading, such as whether the reader knew more words and read with more expression during the final reading.

THE FLUENCY DEVELOPMENT LESSON   The **fluency development lesson (FDL)** was devised for primary teachers to help students increase reading fluency (Rasinski, Padak, Linek, & Sturtevant, 1994). The FDL takes about 10 to 15 minutes to complete. Each child has a copy of the passage of 50 to 150 words. The steps in the fluency development lesson are as follows:

1. Read the text expressively to the class while students follow along silently with their own copies. This step can be repeated several times.
2. Discuss the content of the text with attention to developing comprehension and vocabulary as well as the expression the teacher used while reading to the class.
3. Together, read the text chorally several times. For variety, the students could read in groups of two or more or echo read.
4. Have the class practice reading the text in pairs. Each student takes a turn reading the text to a partner multiple times. The partner follows along with the text, provides help when needed, and gives constructive feedback.
5. Have a brief word study activity with words chosen from the passage. Match the words to those on the world wall, for example.
6. Have volunteers perform the text as individuals, pairs, or groups of four. Arrangements can be made for students to read to the principal, the secretary, the custodian, or other teachers and classes. Students should also read the text to their parents. In this way, students are given much praise for their efforts.

Evanchan (2015) used FDL routinely in her second-grade classroom and found it resulted in an increase in comprehension. Read how she implemented it in Box 7.4.

BOX 7.4 | VIEWPOINT

Gail Evanchan, PhD
Fluency Instruction in the Classroom
Gail Evanchan is a teacher in Summit County, Ohio.

My interest in fluency began my first year of teaching, when I had to complete report cards for the first time. Imagine seeing the word *fluency* and having no idea about how to teach or assess it! I had a slight idea of what the word meant, but looked it up in the dictionary because I was too embarrassed to ask a colleague. The teacher manual I had was of no help; fluency was rarely mentioned, if at all. Well, as that first year teacher, I did assign a fluency grade by listening to my students read and judging them as objectively as I could. However, I felt a real sense of guilt knowing that if I did not teach or assess fluency, how could I, in good conscience, assign a grade?

My observations of students through the years led me to the realization that fluency is very important. Students who read poorly were the same students who spent much time decoding, which made their comprehension break down. These observations and my ignorance on the subject of fluency led to my research on oral reading fluency and its relation to comprehension. Many opportunities and approaches for good fluency instruction in the classroom exist. I found the Fluency Development Lesson (FDL) (Rasinski, Padak, Linek, & Sturtevant, 1994) to be very effective for me. It takes about 15 minutes to administer, and I learned it was best to do it first thing in the morning. FDL can be done using any passage, but poetry is a good

choice of text because it has rich and playful language and encourages children to want to have fun reading (Faver, 2009). I tried to correlate poems with curricular themes or seasonal activities; they can also align with the Common Core State Standards (CCSS). This is how FDL looked in my classroom over the course of a week:

Day 1: Introduce the poem to the class. Discuss the content, the meaning, and the poet's purpose and style. Read the poem as the students follow along with their own copies. Identify rhyming words, onomatopoeias, or alliteration. Students can also discuss the quality of your reading.

Day 2: Read the poem chorally a few times. While students read aloud, listen to and analyze their reading. Then lead a discussion on what a fluent reader looks and sounds like or the characteristics of a fluent reader.

Day 3: Repeat readings of the text with some variation, such as having boys read a stanza and then the girls, or students taking turns reading a line. You might discuss words from the poem that may cause difficulties, sort words phonetically, or add words of interest to a word bank.

Day 4: Students are each given a copy of the poem to add to their poetry notebook. They listen as you read the poem again, and then partners practice reading the poem to one another. Individuals, pairs, and groups volunteer to perform the poem for the class. Students take the poem home and read it to a "lucky listener," and write a response to the poem on the back, which adds a writing component to the FDL with a focus on comprehension.

Day 5: Collect the "lucky listener" homework and respond to it. A volunteer performs the poem and is recorded while reading. As a class, discuss the quality of the reading, and

have the reader self-evaluate his or her reading after listening to the recorded reading.

I found FDL to be very successful, and students made great progress in their reading fluency. In addition, the students seemed to enjoy and look forward to the lessons. As students became successful at reading FDL texts, my hope was that they transferred that success to other, unfamiliar texts.

2017 ILA Standards

1.1, 1.3, 2.2, 2.3

PEER TUTORING   Another way to organize fluency practice is to use a **paired reading** strategy with peer tutoring. This is a particularly useful strategy in second and third grades, where differences between the most fluent and the least fluent readers become evident.

Topping (1989) noted that the collaborative work of children in pairs has enormous potential, but teachers must be able to organize and monitor this activity carefully. He advocated structured pair work between children of differing ability in which a more able child (tutor) helps a less able child (tutee) in a cooperative learning environment.

Teachers often recognize the value of extra reading practice in a paired reading situation for less able children but sometimes express concern about the worth of the activity for more able students. Research reviews on the effectiveness of peer tutoring with paired reading have shown that the more able reader accelerates in reading skill at least as much as the less able reader (Fuchs, Fuchs, & Burish, 2000; Sharpley & Sharpley, 1981).

To maximize growth in fluent reading, teachers need to pair students carefully. One way to do this is to match the most able tutor with the most able tutee. This procedure seems to aid in matching students with an appropriate *relative competence* to each other, which maximizes the success of using this technique.

Here's a general plan for paired reading with peer tutoring: The tutee chooses a book that has been read to the children or used in direct instruction. The book needs to be within the tutor's readability level (i.e., 95 to 98 percent accuracy level). The tutor and the tutee discuss the book initially and throughout the reading. They read together aloud at the tutee's pace. If the tutee happens to make a word error, the tutor says the word correctly. The pair continues reading together. When the tutee wants to read alone, he or she signals nonverbally—for instance, with a tap on the knee. The tutor praises the tutee for signaling, then is silent and the tutee reads alone. The tutor resumes reading when requested by the tutee. If the tutee makes an error or does not respond in 5 seconds, they use the correction procedure just described, and then the pair continues to read together. At the conclusion, the pair discusses the story based on questions developed by the tutor before the session.

This procedure allows tutees to be supported through the text with higher readability levels than they would attain by themselves. The text level also ensures stimulation and participation for the tutor, who promotes discussion and questioning on the content of the text.

AUTOMATED READING   Another practice that supports children as they increase oral reading fluency is **automated reading**, or listening while reading a text. An automated reading program employs simultaneous listening and reading (SLR), a procedure suggested by Carol Chomsky (1976). In the SLR procedure, a child reads along with a recording of the story. To use the SLR, students listen individually to recorded stories, simultaneously reading along with the written text. They read and listen repeatedly to the same story until they can read the story fluently. Students need to choose a book that is too hard to read right away but not out of range entirely. When students feel ready to read the text fluently, they read it to the teacher. The teacher can listen or take a running record or other informal assessment. Students are encouraged to evaluate themselves on how fluently they read the selection they have prepared.

When students are able to read the story fluently, they need to be given opportunities to read the story to their parents, the principal, or fellow students. Students using this strategy could not present the story without having a book to follow, so they have not really memorized the book. However, a combination of memorization and reading enables students to experience successful, effective, fluent reading. These techniques are effective with students of all ages, including those in middle school. To provide further fluency practice, the SLR strategy can be used with computer software, e-books, or other online resources. Some "talking books" read the text to the child, allowing the child to slow down and speed up the reading speed, to click on text to have it reread, to click on a word to be given help, and to click on an illustration to learn additional information or activate animation.

The use of voice recording devices and automated reading has great promise for independent practice for ELLs. Koskinen and his colleagues (1999) found that most ELL students reported that they practiced almost daily reading with the books and recordings, and that the least proficient ELL readers were most likely to use the recorded materials to practice and improve their reading at home.

THE ORAL RECITATION LESSON   The **oral recitation lesson (ORL)** provides a useful structure for working on fluency in daily reading instruction (Hoffman, 1985). ORL has two components: direct instruction and student practice. The first component, direct instruction, incorporates comprehension, practice, and then performance. The second phase, indirect instruction, involves practicing until mastery is achieved. Here are the steps for ORL:

1. The teacher models fluency by reading a story to the class.
2. Next, the teacher leads a discussion of the story, and asks students to summarize what happened. (As a variation, the children can predict what will happen as the story unfolds. Hoffman emphasizes that predictable stories should be used in the ORL.)
3. The class discusses what expressive oral reading is like—that it is smooth, not exceedingly slow, and demonstrates an awareness of what punctuation marks signal.
4. Students read in chorus and individually, beginning with small text segments and gradually increasing the length of the segment.
5. The teacher chooses individual students to select and orally read a portion of the text for their classmates. Other class members provide positive feedback to students on the aspects of expressive oral reading discussed.

Students should continue to practice oral reading of the same text to achieve reading fluency. Hoffman suggests that second graders should reach the goal of reading 75 words a minute with 98 percent accuracy with expression before moving to another story. This component takes from 10 to 15 minutes, with students doing soft or whisper reading. The teacher checks on individual mastery and maintains records of students' performance on individual stories.

Boxes 7.5 and 7.6 highlight two more strategies to use with pairs and small groups: **support reading strategy** and **cross-age reading**. Both of these strategies emphasize specific aspects of fluency training and integrate the teaching of fluency with other important aspects of reading, such as comprehension and word recognition. Box 7.6 explains how fluency instruction differs for ELLs.

BOX 7.5 | RESEARCH-BASED PRACTICES

The Support Reading Strategy

The support reading strategy was designed to integrate several aspects of fluency growth into traditional basal instruction over a 3-day period.

The first day, the teacher reads a story to a small group of children in a fluent, expressive voice. Throughout the reading, the teacher stops and asks the children to clarify what is happening in the story and then to predict what will happen next. The teacher and children echo read the story, with the students reading their own books. The teacher monitors each child's reading and provides assistance where needed.

The next day, the teacher pairs the readers, and the pairs reread the story; each reader reads alternating pages. Each pair is then assigned a short segment from the story to practice reading orally with fluency.

The third day, while the class is working individually or in small groups on writing or other tasks, individual children read the story to the teacher. The teacher monitors the reading by taking a running record, a procedure for monitoring word recognition strategies.

BOX 7.6 | STEP-BY-STEP LESSON

Cross-Age Reading

Cross-age reading provides middle school readers with a lesson cycle that includes modeling by the teacher, discussing the text, and allowing for opportunities to practice fluency. It also provides a legitimate reason for practicing for an oral reading performance. It provides middle school students with purposeful activities to develop reading fluency, and provides younger students with valuable literary experiences.

1. The teacher helps the older student select an appropriate book.
2. The older student practices the text with repeated readings. He or she might even be paired with a peer in order to receive constructive feedback about his or her fluency.
3. The teacher works with the older student about how he or she will present the book. For example, how to determine

stopping points in the story, or what questions he or she might ask the student.

4. After a great deal of practice, the older student meets the younger student and reads the book to him or her.
5. After reading, both students can share about the experience. The older student can write a reflection on the encounter, specifically on the quality of the reading interactions. The reflective nature of these reflections can also help students develop strategies to improve for next time. Cross-age reading can involve having the middle school children write stories for the younger children to read and then to write stories with the younger children. Other programs have both the older and younger students read the stories to their parents or some other adult.

Involving Parents

The subject of reading is often perceived by parents as too complicated for them to teach their children. However, the success of a literary program, to a certain extent, depends on the literacy environment at home and involving parents as an essential part of literacy instruction (Morrow, Kuhn, & Schwanenflugel, 2007). In fact, when Don Holdaway (1979) conceived the shared book experience used in the majority of primary classrooms today, he was trying to mimic the authentic oral reading experiences of parents and children when children were read to at home.

Many teachers develop home reading programs that motivate parents to read to their children on a regular basis. Some hold evening workshops where they model simple strategies such as echo reading, choral reading, and repeated readings and then engage parents in discussions on the significance of the methods (Morrow et al., 2007; Rasinski & Fredericks, 1991). Others simply send home leveled classroom books and expect parents to read to or with their child daily. Although family involvement events vary from classroom to classroom, the following guidelines should be present for a successful program (Morrow et al., 2007).

- Use proven and effective strategies to maximize the effectiveness of the time parents have to work with children.
- Make the activities easy to understand and initiate for quick results.
- Provide a forum such as a workshop for parents to report on what they are noticing.
- Use content that is nonthreatening and fun.
- Encourage parents to use expression while reading so that the text comes alive and children hear fluent reading.
- Provide materials. Some parents don't have reading materials available—don't let this cause your plan to be unsuccessful.

2017 ILA Standard

5.1

WHAT PARENTS CAN DO TO HELP AT HOME   Children become fluent readers through lots of practice; they need a lot of opportunities to read and be read to at home. Following are some practical suggestions for parents to follow to encourage fluency at home.

- *Read more.* Research tells us that the best way to become a better reader is to spend more time reading. Anything parents do to encourage their children to spend more time with print will help make them better readers.
- *Read aloud.* Express the importance of parents reading aloud to children of all ages. Suggest they read aloud while their child watches the page. Encourage them to use free, online e-books while the child follows along.
- *Reread familiar texts.* Children love to read old favorites. While it may not be interesting to parents, rereading favorite books helps children become fluent and therefore should be done frequently.
- *Echo read.* Echo reading is a rereading strategy designed to help students develop expressive, fluent reading. The teacher or parent reads a short segment of text (sentence or phrase), and the student echoes back the same sentence or phrase while following along in the text.
- *Use predictable books.* To build fluency, parents should read books with children that have predictable, rhythmic patterns so the child can "hear" the sound of fluent reading as he or she reads the book aloud.

BOX 7.7 | VIEWPOINT

Fluency and English Language Learners

Fluency instruction can be helpful for ELLs because the strategies that enhance fluency also contribute to oral language development in English. While all students are taking part in fluency activities such as choral reading, echo reading, and assisted reading, the ELL student is gaining valuable skills in the areas of print concepts, vocabulary, and listening comprehension—all important concepts for learning to read English. Taking part in fluency instruction immerses the ELL in rich language settings.

However, caution must be taken when assessing the fluency of ELLs. What might look like nonfluency with a native English-speaking student may not be with an ELL. For example, it is easy to mistake language differences for weaknesses in reading knowledge so dialect should be ignored. And because some ELLs are good readers in their native language, they may have strong decoding skills and be accurate in word knowledge in English yet demonstrate little understanding of text. It is not unusual for an ELL to read a passage beautifully and then not be able to answer comprehension questions. For this reason decodable text that makes no sense isn't the best text for students.

For all students, but especially ELLs, fluency instruction must be carefully balanced. Give ELLs extra time to preview or rehearse a passage before reading aloud. Ask comprehension questions after each fluency reading, spend extra time on vocabulary of passages to make sure the students understand word meanings, and allow them to ask questions about what they are reading.

To improve their English, have them read text that is at an independent reading level so they can practice it repeatedly. Make sure they use prosody, stressing expression, intonation, and articulation.

2017 ILA Standards

3.1, 3.2, 3.3, 3.4

 In this **video** (www.youtube.com/watch?v=ek-UXokHiJQ), you will observe a student participating in an oral reading fluency assessment. What are the advantages and disadvantages of this type of fluency assessment? What other methods can be used to assess students' reading fluency?

Check Your Understanding 7.2: Gauge your understanding of the skills and concepts in this section.

Assessing Oral Reading Fluency

■ **Articulate how to assess all aspects of oral reading fluency.**

Reading rate, or the number of words read per minute, has become the standard measure of reading fluency. This is likely because studies have shown high correlations between rate and reading. This research has grown into a definition of fluency as reading fast, and as a result, fluency instruction has become a quest for speed (Rasinski, 2012b). It is important to remember that fluency is not just about reading fast. Fluency is about decoding words and comprehending at the same time (Samuels, 2012). Simply recognizing words quickly is not fluency. All aspects of fluency—accuracy, automaticity, and prosody—need to be assessed since readers need all of these skills to be considered fluent. However, most tools available to assess fluency rely heavily on assessment of accuracy and rate but not prosody, even though all components of fluency should be measured (Dowhower, 1991; Fuchs, Fuchs, Hosp, & Jenkins, 2001; Hudson, Pullen, Lane, & Torgeson, 2010; Kuhn, Schwanenflugel, & Meisinger, 2010). Researchers are currently developing comprehensive measures of reading fluency that include prosody as well as accuracy and rate (Benjamin et al., 2013). In Box 7.8, Gail Evanchan shares how she assessed all areas of fluency in her classroom.

In this **video** (www.youtube.com/watch?v=4n_MfxQzfhs), watch a teacher administer the 3-minute reading assessment. What do you notice she tells the student prior to reading?

Accuracy and Automaticity

Rasinksi (2015b) blogs that word recognition automaticity, as measured by reading speed, is critical for reading success. However, it should be taught through authentic and meaningful reading experiences, not through reading experiences that aim to increase reading speed. He writes, "I know of no compelling research that has shown that instruction to improve reading speed actually leads to profound and lasting improvement in reading comprehension or overall reading proficiency" (Rasinski, 2015).

With the above caution in mind, the easiest way to assess fluency is to take timed samples of students' reading and compare their performance with published oral reading fluency norms or standards. The number of correct words per minute assesses both accuracy (the number of words the reader is able to identify) and automaticity, also known as *reading rate*. Rasinski's (2003) 1-minute reading sample is an easy assessment to administer, and the number of words read correctly in a minute is considered to be one of the best indicators of reading rate. To obtain a words-correct-per-minute

BOX 7.8 | VIEWPOINT

Gail Evanchan, PhD
Assessing Oral Reading Fluency

Oral reading fluency instruction must include all elements of oral reading fluency, and assessing oral reading fluency needs to also include all components of fluency. When looking at the effect reading fluency has on comprehension of texts, Rasinski and Padak's (2005) *3-Minute Reading Assessments, Word Recognition, Fluency & Comprehension* is one option for teachers. The purpose of the assessments is to measure the fluency and comprehension development of students in grades 1 through 4. This teacher-friendly assessment helps teachers to determine whether fluency instruction has resulted in adequate student progress and how well each student is able to read grade-level texts. The assessment can be done at regular intervals three or four times during the school year. It takes less than 5 minutes to administer, and it gives teachers information on accuracy of decoding skills, reading rate, expression, and comprehension. If fluency is defined to include accuracy, rate, prosody, and comprehension, then an assessment of fluency should incorporate all of these; this assessment does that.

The directions for the assessment are easy to follow. The student is given a copy of the passage that corresponds with the grade level and time of year. The teacher will tell the student that at end of the reading, the student will tell the teacher what she or he remembers about the passage. The student reads for 60 seconds. The teacher keeps a copy of the passage in front of her or him and marks any uncorrected errors. The teacher marks the place the student reached after 60 seconds, and then reads the text aloud as the student follows along silently. If the student reads the text with few errors, they can finish the passage silently on their own. At the end of the reading, the teacher takes the passage away and asks the student to do a retelling. The assessment is finished and ready to be scored.

Scoring guides are provided for each area in the assessment. There is a procedure for figuring out word recognition accuracy, a chart for measuring a fluency reading rate, and a scale for determining fluency through expression. In addition, a rubric is available for determining comprehension.

(WCPM) score, students are assessed individually as they read aloud for 1 minute from an *unpracticed, unfamiliar, grade-level* passage of text.

To calculate the WCPM score, subtract the total number of errors from the total number of words read in 1 minute. An error includes any word that is omitted, mispronounced, or substituted for another word. It's best to take several samples and average the score on different passages to account for any text-based differences. If standardized passages are used (text that has been carefully controlled for difficulty), a score from a single passage may be sufficient.

To determine whether the student's score is on target, compare the WCPM score to an oral reading fluency norms chart to determine whether your student is reading above, below, or on grade level. The Hasbrouck-Tindal Oral Reading chart in Figure 7.2 is one example of a norm chart. It shows the oral reading fluency rates of students in grades 1 through 8, and can serve as an indicator of reading proficiency (Hasbrouck, 2016).

Technology available today is making an impact on how teachers across the country assess fluency. Instead of assessing fluency with a timer and paper and pencil and then entering the data manually, teachers are using handheld devices to administer assessments. With this technology, data are immediately entered and teachers are able to view the results at once in several formats (including charts and graphs) on their handheld computers and then sync them to their desktop computers. Teachers we have talked with report that once they learn how to use these new devices, they enjoy the efficiency that handhelds bring to the process. They value the ease of administration and all-inclusiveness of the tool, as well as the accuracy it provides since they don't have to worry about managing a timer while marking responses. They also value the easy-to-read graphics and display of data that are immediately entered into a central system.

Prosody

When students' speed and accuracy are at appropriate levels, reading with proper phrasing, expression, and intonation should be the next goal. As we mentioned earlier, this allows for better comprehension of text, which is always the goal of reading.

Figure 7.2 Oral Reading Fluency Norms Chart

Grade	Percentile	Fall WCPM*	Winter WCPM*	Spring WCPM*	Avg. Weekly Improvement**
1	90	—	81	111	1.9
	75	—	47	82	2.2
	50	—	**23**	**53**	**1.9**
	25	—	12	28	1.0
	10	—	6	15	0.6
2	90	106	125	142	1.1
	75	79	100	117	1.2
	50	**51**	**72**	**89**	**1.2**
	25	25	42	61	1.1
	10	11	18	31	0.6
3	90	128	146	162	1.1
	75	99	120	137	1.2
	50	**71**	**92**	**107**	**1.1**
	25	44	62	78	1.1
	10	21	36	48	0.8
4	90	145	166	180	1.1
	75	119	139	152	1.0
	50	**94**	**112**	**123**	**0.9**
	25	68	87	98	0.9
	10	45	61	72	0.8
5	90	166	182	194	0.9
	75	139	156	168	0.9
	50	**110**	**127**	**139**	**0.9**
	25	85	99	109	0.8
	10	61	74	83	0.7
6	90	177	195	204	0.8
	75	153	167	177	0.8
	50	**127**	**140**	**150**	**0.7**
	25	98	111	122	0.8
	10	68	82	93	0.8
7	90	180	192	202	0.7
	75	156	165	177	0.7
	50	**128**	**136**	**150**	**0.7**
	25	102	109	123	0.7
	10	79	88	98	0.6
8	90	185	199	199	0.4
	75	161	173	177	0.5
	50	**133**	**146**	**151**	**0.6**
	25	106	115	124	0.6
	10	77	84	97	0.6

*WCPM = Words correct per minute

**Average weekly improvement* is the average words per week growth you can expect from a student. It was calculated by dividing the difference between the fall and spring scores by 32, the typical number of weeks between the fall and spring assessments. For grade 1, since there is no fall assessment, the average weekly improvement was calculated by dividing the difference between the winter and spring scores by 16, the typical number of weeks between the winter and spring assessments.

Source: Hasbrouck-Tindal Table of Oral Reading Fluency Norms, retrieved from www.readnaturally.com/howto/orftable.htm. Based on "Oral Reading Fluency Norms: A Valuable Assessment Tool for Reading Teachers," by J. Hasbrouck and G. A. Tindal, 2006, *The Reading Teacher, 59*(7), pp. 636–644. Reprinted by permission of Jan Hasbrouck.

Measuring prosody is not always an easy task because measurements of smoothness, phrasing, pace, and expression are subjective and therefore variable. One way to measure the quality of a student's prosody is to use the National Assessment of Educational Progress (NAEP) Oral Reading Fluency Scale (Daane, Campbell, Grigg, Goodman, & Oranje, 2005). This four-level scale focuses on the level of skill a student demonstrates in phrasing and expression while reading aloud and is shown in Figure 7.3. After listening to an individual student read aloud, the teacher rates the student's reading according to the level that best describes the overall performance. While the scale is a helpful tool, it is the anecdotal notes the teacher makes as the student is reading that will give the fullest picture of the student's reading ability. These

Figure 7.3 National Assessment of Educational Progress Fluency Scale

Fluent	Level 4	Reads primarily in larger, meaningful phrase groups. Although some regressions, repetitions, and deviations from text may be present, these do not appear to detract from the overall structure of the story. Preservation of the author's syntax is consistent. Some or most of the story is read with expressive interpretation.
Fluent	Level 3	Reads primarily in three- or four-word phrase groups. Some small groupings may be present. However, the majority of phrasing seems appropriate and preserves the syntax of the author. Little or no expressive interpretation is present.
Non-Fluent	Level 2	Reads primarily in two-word phrases with some three- or four-word groupings. Some word-by-word reading may be present. Word groupings may seem awkward and unrelated to larger context of sentence or passage.
Non-Fluent	Level 1	Reads primarily word-by-word. Occasional two-word or three-word phrases may occur but these are infrequent and/or they do not preserve meaningful syntax.

Source: Fourth-Grade Students Reading Aloud: NAEP 2002 Special Study of Oral Reading, by M. C. Daane, J. R. Campbell, W. S. Grigg, M. J. Goodman, and A. Oranje, NCES 2006-469, U.S. Department of Education, Institute of Education Sciences, National Center for Education Statistics (Washington, DC: Government Printing Office, 2005).

notes assist teachers in documenting the growth of students as well as identifying specific needs to target. Practice instructional decision making related to fluency using a teacher's anecdotal notes and these scales.

Instructional Decision Making 7.1: Apply your understanding of the concepts in this section.

2017 ILA Standard

1.1

Check Your Understanding 7.3: Gauge your understanding of the skills and concepts in this section.

Silent Reading Fluency

■ **Explain how to conduct a silent reading program that supports oral reading fluency.**

Research confirms that independent reading for pleasure enhances comprehension (e.g., Cox & Guthrie, 2001), language (e.g., Krashen, 2004), vocabulary development (e.g., Angelos & McGriff, 2002), general knowledge (e.g., Cunningham & Stanovich, 1998), and compassion for others (e.g., McGinley et al., 1997), as well as their self-confidence as readers, motivation to read throughout their lives, and positive attitudes toward reading (e.g., Allington & McGillFranzen, 2003; Eurydice Network, 2011). This also applies to ELLs, regardless if they read in English or their native language. There can be little doubt that demands for efficient silent reading have increased as the amount of information available via the Internet and social media increases. Most of the reading that adults, adolescents, and even middle- and upper elementary-grade students do is silent reading. Silent reading fluency matters, and is a complementary form of reading that reflect students' developmental growth as readers. In this section we discuss the role silent reading has on fluency and provide guidelines for successful implementation in the classroom.

Developing Silent Reading Fluency

Fluent readers are seasoned readers, just as some individuals are considered to be seasoned runners. A seasoned runner has knowledge of what it is like to run for long periods of time, and a seasoned reader knows how to read for long periods of time and stay focused on the text. Although seasoned runners have developed patterns of running, they choose when, where, and how far to run. Readers do the same thing; they choose what they are going to read, for what purpose, and how long they need to read to suit those purposes. Runners have gained much knowledge about themselves, how to assess how they feel so they do not run too far, and what they can do to protect themselves from a running injury. Self-knowledge contributes to self-confidence as a runner. They know the task of running and about themselves as runners, and how to monitor themselves during running. Readers know that on some days and with some reading materials, they probably won't be able to concentrate as well as on other days with other materials. Like runners, they know about the task of reading, about themselves as readers, and how to self-monitor their reading. Fluent readers perceive themselves as able readers. They engage in the task with confidence.

An independent, **silent reading** program is important to the development of fluency. Fluent readers grow by leaps and bounds from silent reading experiences, because the more children read the more proficient they become. Also, when students are motivated to engage in silent reading for intrinsic reasons such as pleasure, interest, or challenge (as opposed to extrinsic reasons such as grades or competition), their reading comprehension increases (Guthrie, Hoa, Wigfield, Tonks, & Perencevich, 2006).

However, silent reading should have some structure to it because, as Stahl (2004) argues, all practice is not equally effective. Sanden (2014) suggests a period of time set aside daily for students' non-monitored reading of self-selected books with 15 minutes of independent reading in challenging texts at the upper limits of the reader's lexile range (https://lexile.com) followed by 5 minutes of teacher-led sharing of personal reading by students either with the whole class or in small groups or pairs.

Reutzel, Jones, Fawson, and Smith (2008) suggest scaffolding silent reading (SSR). They point out four areas of concern educators have about SSR: student self-selection, student engagement and time on task, student accountability, and interactions around text.

1. *Student self-selection.* Traditionally, students have had free choice when selecting reading materials for SSR. But research shows struggling readers often select books they cannot read (Donovan, Smolkin, & Lomax, 2000; Kelley & Clausen-Grace, 2006). Teachers who have classroom libraries with books of various levels and a wide variety of genres can help students choose books that will keep them motivated and engaged during silent reading.

2. *Student engagement and time on task.* Hunt (1970, 1971b) warns that there are all sorts of disruptive behaviors that can take place during SSR. For example, he mentions the *gossips* (students who talk instead of read), the *wanderers* (those who spend most for their time searching for something to read), and the *squirrels* (those who are so busy collecting books they have little time to read). Teachers need to establish firm guidelines for silent reading time so reading practice takes place.

3. *Student accountability.* Students must be accountable for reading practice during SSR time. This might mean they are expected to keep and turn in reading logs or journal entries. Some teachers start SSR time with a "status of the class" and have students quickly tell them what they are reading, what page they are on, and the like. Others spend SSR time circulating around the class and checking in with each student. During SSR teachers can quietly discuss a book with students. We have seen teachers quietly circulate the room, lean in, and very quietly check in with students about the book they are reading. Regardless of the technique, students will get more engaged reading practice if accountability is in place.

4. *Interactions around text.* Reutzel, Jones, and Newman (2010) report "the effectiveness of reading practice is increased when interactions around text are a consistent, integral part of SSR" (p. 134). These can be teacher-to-student interactions or peer-to-peer. In one class we witnessed "Sell a Book," where students, after finishing a good book, would tell others about it. They might tell why they liked it, what genre it was, and then read a small excerpt. Classmates could ask questions about the book and then decide whether it was something they might like to read in the future.

One further note about silent reading. Many teachers engage in silent reading with the students to serve as a model. However, research shows that teacher reading does not increase student engagement (Widdowson, Dixon, & Moore, 1996; Newman, 2007). Instead, teachers should use SSR time for conferencing, assessment, and instruction. Garan and DeVoogd (2008) found an increased effectiveness of SSR by including reading conferences and minilessons during this time.

Check Your Understanding 7.4: Gauge your understanding of the skills and concepts in this section.

RTI for Struggling Readers

Fluency and *Response to Intervention*

In this chapter, we stressed that reading fluency is important because improving reading fluency is necessary to improve reading comprehension. In addition, fluent readers are more likely to choose to read. Also worth noting is an extensive amount of research showing that a student's scores on reading fluency assessments help to predict that student's likelihood of success on other meaningful measures of reading, such as reading comprehension.

Studies show that progress monitoring in reading (oral reading fluency or word identification fluency in grades 1 and 2) increases teachers' awareness of students' current levels of reading proficiency and has a positive effect on the instructional decisions teachers make. Collecting and using progress monitoring data is a component of Tier 2 instruction.

In an RTI system, fluency is monitored frequently to provide information about students' learning rates and levels of achievement. These data are then used when determining which students need closer monitoring or intervention. For example, benchmark testing (usually done three times per school year) helps to identify students within Tier 1 who may be struggling and need Tier 2 intervention. Progress monitoring is then used to assess the effectiveness of the Tier 2 intervention that was put in place to help the students reach the benchmark.

What About . . .

Standards, Assessment, and Reading Fluency?

Fluency is specifically addressed in the CCSS under Foundational Skills and requires students to "read grade-level prose and poetry orally with accuracy, appropriate rate, and expression" (2010, p. 17). The expectation is that students should be well on their way to decoding automatically and reading with fluency by the time they finish second grade. Although progress in fluency should continue through third grade and beyond with increasingly more complex text, the first three years of instruction (K through 2) are the most critical for preventing students from falling behind and preventing reading failure. However, the reality is there is just one teacher in every classroom and children come to school with a myriad of issues related to reading.

The NAEP special study on fluency (Daane et al., 2005) shows that only 10 percent of fourth graders could read with phrasing that was in line with the author's syntax and had some expressiveness. Forty percent of fourth graders were unable to read with minimal fluency—clearly a concern because of fluency's connection to comprehension. We know the best way to increase fluency is for students to practice and have good fluency instruction. Adams (2013) argues no matter how hard classroom teachers try, they cannot give each student the individual, guided oral reading support he or she needs. She suggests if we want to meet the goals of CCSS, we must increase productivity, and the best way to do that is to develop speech recognition–based reading software for schools. She notes voice recognition technology exists and is used commonly in many areas except in education where it is needed most. Technology can be used to listen to students read and make records of their progress, helping teachers assess needs.

Without fluency, reading takes up too much mental energy. The use of technology in fluency would allow more individual instruction to take place for more students.

Summary

- We examined three dimensions of fluency: accurate word decoding, automaticity, and prosody. We looked at the close relationship fluency has with comprehension, serving as a bridge between word recognition and comprehension.
- Fluency can be taught through effective instruction, but should never be taught just for the sake of reading quickly. The goal of fluency instruction is always to preserve mental energy so that comprehension can take place. We shared strategies for groups of students, pairs, and individuals, as well as ways to involve parents and older students.
- Assessing the components of fluency assists teachers in choosing appropriate text for various instructional purposes and provides information about areas in need of further instruction to assure accuracy.
- Silent reading, when managed appropriately, allows students time to practice reading. Research shows time spent reading increases reading achievement.

Teacher Action Research

1. Create a diagram that depicts the three dimensions of fluency and how they all work together and support comprehension. Be ready to share your diagram electronically with your peers.
2. Paired repeated readings have many benefits, and you'll want to use them often in your classroom. Create a guide to be used in your classroom to remind students of the steps in paired reading. It could take the form of a chart, a bookmark, or other form that is easily accessible to students.
3. Try out one of the assessment strategies you read about in this chapter on a young reader. What patterns of behavior do you notice? What strategies to develop fluency will you use based on what you learned from the assessment?
4. Based on what you learned about the benefits of independent reading time, write an email to your curriculum director, explaining why there should be time set aside for silent reading in the classroom. Be sure to use research to support your request.

Through the Lens of the Common Core

Students need word identification strategies such as phonics, structural analysis, and the use of context to figure out unknown words. But they also need fluency—the ability to read accurately and well in order to make meaning—so they can move on and maintain comprehension. Fluency is specifically included in the CCSS under Reading Foundational Skills. In this chapter we addressed why fluency matters and how the classroom teacher can develop both oral and silent reading fluency by working with students on rate, accuracy, and automaticity. Knowing how to develop these three dimensions of fluency will allow teachers to scaffold students as they aim to read with sufficient accuracy to support comprehension, read grade-level text with purpose and understanding, and read with accuracy, appropriate rate, and expression—all of which are CCSS grade-level goals.

Chapter 8
Vocabulary Knowledge and Concept Development

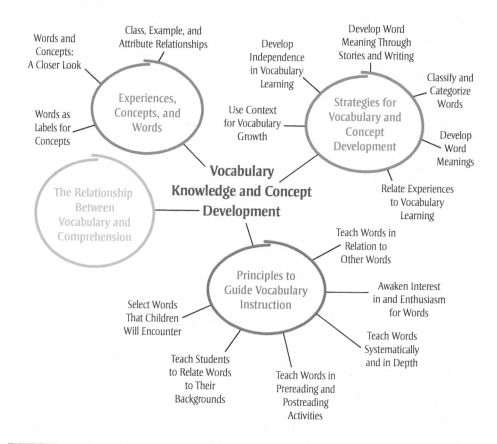

Learning Outcomes

In This Chapter, You Will Discover How to

■ Draw appropriate conclusions about the connection between vocabulary knowledge and comprehension.

■ Analyze the relationship among students' experiences, concepts, and words.

■ Explain and implement the principles that guide the teaching of vocabulary in elementary classrooms.

■ Give examples of instructional strategies for teaching vocabulary using a variety of activities promoting concept development.

Activating Your Schema

Think about when you were in the primary grades and middle school. When you came across a word while reading that you did not know the meaning of, what did you do then? What do you do now as an independent reader?

Think about the instructional strategies, activities, and materials utilized by your teachers in the past. What helped you to learn new vocabulary words? What did not help you to learn new words?

2017 ILA Standards Found in This Chapter

1.1	2.2	2.4	5.3
2.1	2.3	5.1	6.1

Common Core State Standards: English Language Arts

CCRA.R.4	CCRA.L.3	CCRA.SL.1	CCRA.L.4
CCRA.SL.2	CCRA.L.5	CCRA.SL.6	CCRA.L.6

Key Terms

analogy	prereading activities
antonyms	self-selection strategy
aptitude hypothesis	semantic mapping
categorization	subordinate
class relationships	superordinate
concept	synonyms
concept circles	think sheet
contextual search	vocabulary
definitional knowledge	vocabulary-building skills
instrumental hypothesis	word knowledge rating
knowledge hypothesis	word part connections
multiple-meaning words	words
paired-word sentence generation	word sorts
predictogram	

Maria, like so many children at the age of four, is curious about language and undaunted by the use (and misuse) of words. In her zest to learn, Maria plays with language, often experimenting and using words spontaneously to express herself or to describe new experiences and understandings. As her language expands, so does Maria's world. Ever since developing the concept of *word,* she does not hesitate to ask, "What's that word mean?" when she hears an unfamiliar word used in conversation or in media. No one in her family blinked when Maria asked, "What is a distracter?"

Maria and her family were visiting a friend's family on the Fourth of July to enjoy an afternoon of food and an evening of fireworks. During a conversation between Maria's mother and Terry, a family friend, Maria overheard Terry using the word *distracter.* Terry was explaining that it was difficult to get anything done at work because of all the distractions, and continued to explain that when she goes home there are many distractions and distracters. She talked about the difficulty of completing work around the house because of the many day-to-day distractions and referred to her two children as "distracters." Terry did not make reference to her children as "distracters" in a mean way—rather as a matter of fact.

Common Core State Standards

CCRA.SL.1, CCRA.SL.6

Later that afternoon, Maria's mother was sitting in a lounge chair in the backyard enjoying the picnic. Maria jumped up on her mother's lap and asked, "What is a distracter?" Her mother asked why she wanted to know, and Maria said that Terry called her children "distracters." Maria's mother proceeded to explain that a distracter is someone who takes someone else away from something that they were doing. Maria, satisfied with the explanation, jumped off her mother's lap and went to play with the other children. Later that evening after the fireworks, Maria's mother was gathering up their things to get ready to go home. Her mother went to Maria, who was busily playing with sparklers, and said that she needed to get ready to go home because it was late. Without hesitation Maria turned to her mother and said, "Mom, you are a distracter," and went back to playing with the sparklers.

It's like day and night, the difference between classrooms where children like Maria are allowed to experiment and play with words and classrooms in which the learning of words is focused on lists. Teachers in the former take advantage of children's natural spontaneity and creativity, knowing that part of the joy of teaching is the unpredictability of what children will say or do. These teachers create classroom environments in which opportunities to experiment with words abound. Every time a student makes a decision as to which word is best in a piece of writing, vocabulary learning takes place. Mark Twain said that the difference between the right word and the almost-right word is the difference between lightning and the lightning bug. Children experiment with words whenever they hear unfamiliar words read aloud in literature or whenever they encounter new words while reading. They develop an ear for language and an eye for the images created by language.

Nevertheless, teachers face real problems in developing vocabulary knowledge and concepts in their classrooms every day. As "children's vocabulary grows, their ability to comprehend what they read grows as well" (Rupley, Logan, & Nichols, 1999, p. 336). Beck, McKeown, and Kucan (2008) emphasize that vocabulary development is a predictor of both reading performance and school achievement. Children are likely to have trouble understanding what they read if they are not readily familiar with most words they meet in print. Shanahan, Fisher, and Frey (2012) reported that, "If you ask students what makes reading hard, they blame the words" (p. 59). A foundation in oral language and concept development is essential (Blachowicz & Fisher, 2010).

Too often we assume that children will develop an understanding of words from such staple activities as discussing, defining, and writing the words in sentences. We do little else instructionally. Yet students must not only be able to define words but also experience unfamiliar words in frequent, meaningful, and varied contexts. They need to know the word in order to use it appropriately in print as well as in oral language. Therefore, a major premise of this chapter is that *definitional knowledge* is necessary, but students must also develop *contextual* and *conceptual knowledge* of words to comprehend fully what they read.

Defining and using words in sentences are insufficient to ensure vocabulary learning. Teaching vocabulary through the memorization of short definitions and sentences suggests a "reductionist perspective," which contradicts the understanding of the reading process (Nagy & Scott, 2004, p. 574). Students need to be involved in *constructing* meaning rather than memorizing definitions. According to Nagy and Scott (2004), a reader who knows a word can recognize it, understand it, and use that understanding in combination with other types of knowledge to construct meaning from text. The more that students, including those from diverse backgrounds, encounter vocabulary in as many language contexts as possible, the more they will come to know and use words.

Have you ever heard a student who encounters a difficult word say with confidence, "I know what that word means!"? We share a concern that there are not enough children developing the I-know-that-word attitude. This chapter will emphasize ways to increase children's sensitivity to new words and their enjoyment in word learning. What instructional opportunities can be provided to influence the depth and breadth of children's vocabulary knowledge? What are the instructional implications of vocabulary for reading comprehension? How do students develop the interest and motivation to *want* to learn new words? How can students grow in independence in vocabulary learning? To answer these questions, we must first recognize that vocabulary development is not accidental. It must be orchestrated carefully not only during reading time but also throughout the entire day.

The Relationship Between Vocabulary and Comprehension

■ **Draw appropriate conclusions about the connection between vocabulary knowledge and comprehension.**

The relationship between knowledge of word meanings and comprehension has been well documented by researchers and acknowledged by children. Many students admit that sometimes they don't understand what they're reading because "the words are too hard." The seminal work of F. B. Davis (1944) and that of other early researchers such as Thurstone (1946) and Spearitt (1972) have identified vocabulary knowledge as an important factor in reading comprehension. This relationship continues to be documented (Blachowicz & Fisher, 2010; Graves, 2006).

2017 ILA Standard

1.1

Common Core State Standards

CCRA.R.4, CCRA.L.6

In this **video** (www.youtube.com/watch?v=BjE3XjBZsdl), a panel of experts discuss the importance of teaching vocabulary to students to strengthen comprehension skills. Instructional strategies emphasized include student engagement and connecting to literature. Relating to the sensory level, such as creating mental representations, is discussed for struggling and students with disabilities. What other activities can you think of to connect vocabulary and comprehension for all readers?

Various explanations are used to account for the strong relationship between vocabulary and comprehension. Anderson and Freebody (1981) proposed three hypotheses: the **aptitude hypothesis**, the **knowledge hypothesis**, and the **instrumental hypothesis**.

All three hypotheses have merit in explaining the relationship between word knowledge and comprehension. The implications of the aptitude and knowledge hypotheses signal the importance of reading aloud to children and immersing them in written language. Wide reading experiences develop a facility with written language. Further, the instrumental hypothesis is important to us as teachers: If word meanings are taught well enough, students will find reading material easier to comprehend. Unfortunately, some vocabulary instruction has provided contradictory evidence on this effect.

Many widely used methods generally fail to increase comprehension. Why might this be the case? One explanation may involve the very nature of practices associated with vocabulary instruction. This instruction usually involves some combination of looking up definitions, writing them down or memorizing them, and inferring the meaning of a new word from the context. These activities do not create enough *in-depth* knowledge to increase comprehension of difficult concepts. However, comprehension is facilitated when vocabulary is taught *in depth* before reading begins (Blachowicz & Fisher, 2010; Graves, 2006; McKeown & Beck, 2004). Multiple exposures to a word, deep processing, and the development of definitional and contextual knowledge are essential to enhance reading comprehension (Beck et al., 2008).

We've noticed that many teachers spend instructional time introducing vocabulary words *before* students read but do not spend much time on vocabulary *after* students have read. For example, few teachers encourage children to use significant vocabulary words *after* reading texts in activities such as retelling and written, oral, artistic, and dramatic responses to what has been read. Providing young students as well as middle school students opportunities to develop vocabulary throughout the reading process is essential.

Teaching vocabulary is not a simple process of teaching words but rather a systematic process that is multifaceted and influenced by various factors. Blachowicz and Fisher (2010) believe that teaching vocabulary involves "teaching particular words to particular students for a particular purpose" (p. 517). Therefore, teachers need to understand vocabulary acquisition, students' vocabulary needs and abilities, and how to facilitate vocabulary learning for each student.

2017 ILA Standards

1.1, 2.3, 5.1

In order to produce the desired rates of learning vocabulary for struggling readers and English language learners (ELLs), vocabulary development must go beyond simple instruction and natural vocabulary acquisition. Students who need the most help are those whose home experiences have not given them support in vocabulary learning (Blachowicz & Fisher, 2010; Nagy & Scott, 2004). They are at a disadvantage in increasing their vocabulary if they are unable to use context to access word meanings and to do the amount of contextual reading required to develop their vocabulary.

Pearson, Hiebert, and Kamil (2007) stress the importance of connecting vocabulary instruction and assessment. When assessing vocabulary it is important to assess the in-depth knowledge of vocabulary. Therefore, assessments need to be authentic and performance-based, and occur in multiple contexts. For assessment and vocabulary instruction for ELLs, authentic reading materials that connect to real-life experiences in various contexts and are adjusted to the appropriate level of English proficiency are essential.

Words need to be taught directly and well enough to enhance comprehension. Students must have quick access to word meanings when they are reading, which can be achieved through a variety of strategies that make use of students' definitional, contextual, and conceptual knowledge of words.

Before examining instructional strategies, the relationships of students' experiences, concepts, and words need to be explored. What are concepts? What does it mean to know words?

Check Your Understanding 8.1: Gauge your understanding of the skills and concepts in this section.

Experiences, Concepts, and Words

■ **Analyze the relationship among students' experiences, concepts, and words.**

One way to define vocabulary is to suggest that it represents the breadth and depth of all the words we know—the words we use, recognize, and respond to in meaningful acts of communication. *Breadth* involves the size and scope of our vocabulary; *depth* concerns the level of understanding we have of words. **Vocabulary** is the panoply of words we use, recognize, and respond to in meaningful acts of communication. It is the understanding of concepts based on experiences.

2017 ILA Standard

2.1

Vocabulary has usually been classified as having four components: *listening, speaking, reading,* and *writing.* These components are often said to develop in breadth and depth in the sequence listed. Children ages five and six, for example, come to school already able to recognize and respond to thousands of spoken words. Children's first vocabulary, without much question, is listening vocabulary. However, as a child progresses through the school years, he or she eventually learns to identify and use as many written as spoken words. By adulthood, a person's reading vocabulary often outmatches any of the other vocabulary components.

An additional influence of vocabulary development includes students' exposure to transliteracies. The Internet and other technology have changed the access to print to include digital, multimodal, and interactive text. Because students need to be able to read critically and write functionally in various media, vocabulary development, regardless of the medium, is essential. A classroom that utilizes technology features daily work in multiple forms of representation.

Because of the developmental nature of vocabulary, it is more or less assumed that listening and speaking vocabularies are learned in the home, whereas reading, writing, and transliteracy vocabularies fall within the domain of school. Although this assumption may generally hold, it creates an unnecessary dichotomy between inside and outside school influences. It is much safer to assume that both home and school are profoundly influential in the development of all components of vocabulary.

2017 ILA Standard

5.3

Common Core State Standard

CCRA.SL.2

Words as Labels for Concepts

Although **words** are labels for concepts, a single **concept** represents much more than the meaning of a single word. It might take thousands of words to explain a concept. However, answers to the question "What does it mean to know a word?" depend on how well we understand the relationships among words, concepts, and experiences. Understanding these relationships provides a sound rationale for teaching vocabulary within the larger framework of concept development.

Concepts are learned through our acting on and interaction with the environment. Edgar Dale (1965) reminded us how children learn concepts best: through direct, purposeful experiences. Dale's Cone of Experience in Figure 8.1 depicts the levels of abstraction from the most concrete, nonverbal experiences beginning at the base of the cone to the most abstract and removed experiences at the tip of the cone—verbal symbols. For a child who has never ridden on a roller coaster, the most intense and meaningful learning would occur during a trip to an amusement park! The relationship of experiences to concepts and words sets the stage for an important principle of vocabulary instruction: To learn new or unfamiliar words, it is necessary to have experiences from which concepts can be derived.

2017 ILA Standards

1.1, 2.1, 2.2

Figure 8.1 Dale's Cone of Experience

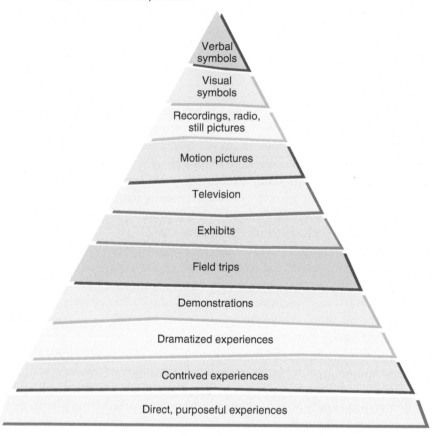

Words and Concepts: A Closer Look

One way of thinking about a concept is that it is a mental image of something. By *something*, we mean anything that can be grouped together by common features or similar criteria—objects, symbols, ideas, processes, or events. In this respect, concepts are similar to schemata.

Common Core State Standard

CCRA.L.5

Concepts are synonymous with the formation of categories. Categories are essential for concept development (Neuman, Neuman, & Dwyer, 2011; Neuman & Wright, 2013). We would be overwhelmed by the complexity of our environment if we were to respond to each object or event that we encountered as unique, so we invent categories (or form concepts) to reduce the complexity of our environment and the necessity for constant learning. Every canine need not have a different name to be known as a dog. Although dogs vary greatly, the common characteristics they share cause them to be referred to by the same general term. Thus, to facilitate communication, we invent words to name concepts.

Scan a page from any dictionary, and you will discover that most words are the names of concepts. The only place these words stand alone is on a dictionary page. In your mind, concepts are organized into a network of complex relationships. Suppose you were to fix your eyes on the word *baboon* as you scanned the entries in the dictionary. What picture comes to mind? Your image of *baboon* probably differs from that of another person. Your background knowledge of

Using pictures helps students understand concepts.

Annie Pickert Fuller/Pearson Education

baboon, or the larger class to which it belongs known as *primates,* will very likely be different from someone else's. So will your experiences with and interests in baboons, especially if you are fond of frequenting the zoo or reading books about primate behavior. The point is that we organize background knowledge and experiences into conceptual hierarchies according to class, example, and attribute relations. Let's take a closer look at these relationships.

Class, Example, and Attribute Relationships

We stated that the concept *baboon* is part of a more inclusive class called *primates,* which in turn is a member of a larger class known as *mammals,* which in turn is a member of an even larger class of animals known as *vertebrates.* These *class relationships* are depicted in Figure 8.2.

Class relationships in any conceptual network are organized in a hierarchy according to the **superordinate** and **subordinate** nature of the concepts. For example, in Figure 8.3, the superordinate concept is *animals.* There are two classes of animals, known as *vertebrates* and *invertebrates,* which are in a subordinate position in the hierarchy. However, *vertebrates* is superordinate in relation to *amphibians, mammals, birds,* and *fish,* which, of course, are types or subclasses of vertebrates. To complete the hierarchy, the concept *primates* is subordinate to *mammals* but superordinate to *baboons.*

Common Core State Standard

CCRA.L.5

By now you have probably recognized that for every concept, there are examples of that concept. In other words, an *example* is a member of any concept under consideration. A *nonexample* is any instance that is not a member of the concept under consideration. Class example relationships are reciprocal. *Vertebrates* and *invertebrates* are examples of *animals. Mammals, birds, fish,* and *amphibians* are examples of *vertebrates.* A *primate* is an example of a *mammal,* and so on.

To extend this discussion, suppose we were to make *primates* our target concept. In addition to baboons, what are other examples of primates? No doubt *apes, monkeys,* and *humans* come quickly to mind. These examples can be shown in relation to each other.

Figure 8.2 Example of a Concept Hierarchy

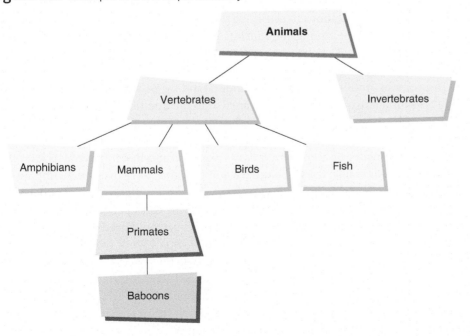

Figure 8.3 Class Example Relationships for the Target Concept "Primates"

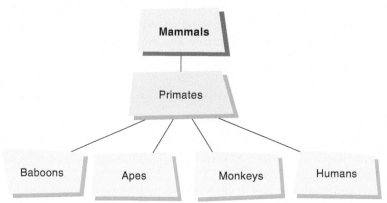

Note that the examples of primates given in Figure 8.3 are not exhaustive of all possible primates we could have listed. Nevertheless, we might ask, "What do baboons, apes, monkeys, and humans have in common?" Answers to this question would force us to focus on relevant *attributes,* the traits, features, properties, or characteristics that are common to every example of a particular concept. In other words, the relevant attributes of primates refer to the characteristics that determine whether baboons, apes, monkeys, and humans belong to the particular class of mammals called *primates.*

All primates, from baboons to human beings, have certain physical and social characteristics, but not every primate shares each of these features. Nearly every example of a primate can grasp objects with its hands or feet. Vision is a primate's most important sense. Most species of primates live in groups, but some live alone. A social group is often considerable in size and highly organized. Primates have the capacity to communicate with one another by means of signals based on scent, touch, vision, and sound. And, of course, primate infants depend to a large extent on their mothers.

This discussion began when we asked you to form a mental image of *baboon.* The clarity with which you were able to picture a baboon in your mind depended, as you may have surmised, on how familiar you were with the characteristics of primates in general and baboons specifically. Baboons, apes, monkeys, and humans share common characteristics, but they also differ.

In what ways are baboons similar to other primates? How are baboons different? These are important questions in clarifying your concept of *baboon* and sorting out the relationships that exist among the various examples. Concept learning involves a search for attributes that can be used to distinguish examples from one another and to differentiate examples from nonexamples.

To promote students' conceptual understanding of key vocabulary, Simpson (1987) calls for an instructionally useful answer to the question "What does it mean to know a word?" Suppose that a concept to be developed in a third-grade Social Studies unit was *wigwam.* Students would need to be able to generate the information that wigwam was a shelter or home for Native Americans and that it was not as sturdy as a house. They could relate the wigwam to a tent they may have used on a camping trip or a Scout outing, while noting that wigwams were made of lightweight wooden poles covered by layers of bark or reed mats. But suppose the concept in a science unit was a more abstract one, such as *energy.* In this case, students would need to be able to generate the information that they needed energy to play and work but that they did not need much energy to sleep or to watch television. As the concept *energy* was explored further, students would realize that our bodies need food to produce energy, just as cars and airplanes need fuel to keep running. Students could even come up with the notion that nuclear reactors split atoms to produce electrical energy, which lights their houses and runs their television sets and video games.

Students' reading development is enhanced when words are taught in meaningful semantic clusters (Roskos & Neuman, 2014). Through such understandings, children gain depth in their word learning. Next, before we examine teaching strategies, let's look at some guidelines for establishing vocabulary programs throughout the primary and middle grades.

Check Your Understanding 8.2: Gauge your understanding of the skills and concepts in this section.

Principles to Guide Vocabulary Instruction

■ **Explain and implement the principles that guide the teaching of vocabulary in elementary classrooms.**

In this section, we consider six principles to guide the teaching of vocabulary in elementary classrooms. They evolve from common sense, authoritative opinion, and research to theory on the relationship between vocabulary knowledge and reading comprehension.

2017 ILA Standards

1.1, 2.1, 5.1

Principle 1: Select Words That Children Will Encounter While Reading Text and Content Material

Readers can tolerate not knowing some words while reading; they can still comprehend the text selection. So vocabulary instruction that introduces a smattering of new words prior to a reading selection will boost comprehension. However, when vocabulary learning is centered on acquiring a large percentage of words appearing in actual selections that will be read in class, comprehension is likely to be enhanced significantly (Blachowicz & Fisher, 2010; McKeown & Beck, 2004). Which words are the best choices for vocabulary instruction? Which aren't?

Words shouldn't be chosen for instructional emphasis just because they are big or obscure. Teaching archaic or difficult words just because they are unusual is not a legitimate reason for instruction. A reader learns to use monitoring strategies to overcome such obstacles. Nor should difficult words be chosen in expository and narrative texts if they do not relate to the central meaning of the passage or important concepts in it. Choose words that students will read most often and that are useful to them (Blachowicz & Fisher, 2010; McKeown & Beck, 2004). Vocabulary words representing formal English are also important to develop for all learners. Maps or organizers of the reading material can be used to help identify the words for study. This is true for literature as well as for content area vocabulary instruction. For example, for the book *The Paperbag Princess* by Robert N. Munsch (1980), one teacher chose the vocabulary from a map she constructed (see Figure 8.4).

Common Core State Standards

CCRA.R.4, CCRA.L.6

Consider the following additional ways to choose words for instructional emphasis.

KEY WORDS   Key words come directly from basal, literature, Internet, or content text selections. These words convey major ideas and concepts related to the passage content and are essential for understanding to take place. Key words need to be taught, *and taught well*, because they present definite obstacles to comprehension that cannot be overlooked by the reader.

Figure 8.4 Map for *The Paperbag Princess*

Characters:

1. *Elizabeth: a princess with expensive clothes*
2. *Ronald: a prince*
3. *dragon: dragon smashed castle, burned Elizabeth's clothes, and carried off Ronald*

Problem:

Elizabeth wanted Ronald back.

Resolution:

Elizabeth outwitted dragon by telling him he was the "fiercest" dragon and got Ronald back. Ronald told her to "come back when dressed like a real princess." Elizabeth told Ronald he looked like a prince but he was a bum.

Big Ideas:

*Sometimes using your brains wins out over physical strength.

*At times what you do is more important than what you wear.

2017 ILA Standard

2.1

USEFUL WORDS   Useful words are relevant. Children encounter useful words repeatedly in a variety of contexts. In some cases, a child may be familiar with useful words, having learned them in earlier stories or units or in previous years. However, it cannot be assumed that these words are old friends; they may be mere acquaintances.

INTERESTING WORDS   Interesting words tickle the imagination and create enthusiasm, excitement, and interest in the study of words. Words that have unique origins, tell intriguing stories, or have intense personal meaning for students make good candidates for instruction. Children can get hooked on words through the study of interesting words.

VOCABULARY-BUILDING WORDS   Classroom instruction should include words that lend themselves readily to vocabulary-building skills. **Vocabulary-building skills** allow children to seek clues to word meanings on their own. Words should be selected for instruction that will show students how to inquire into the meaning of unknown words—through structural analysis (i.e., drawing attention to word parts) or context analysis (Vacca & Vacca, 2011).

Choosing the appropriate words for all learners is important. Fisher, Blachowicz, and Watts-Taffe (2011) explain the need to teach explicitly content-specific vocabulary (key words) and general academic vocabulary (useful words). Although content-specific or key words are typically taught more often, developing general academic or useful words is just as essential, especially for ELLs.

2017 ILA Standard

2.3

Principle 2: Teach Words in Relation to Other Words

Vocabulary words are often crucially tied to basic concepts. Children, as we contended earlier, develop definitional knowledge when they are able to relate new words to known words. When words are taught in relation to other words, students are actively drawn into the learning process. They must use background knowledge and experiences to detect similarities and differences. When words are taught within the context of concept development, children develop a greater sensitivity to shades of meaning in communication. Rather than learning words randomly, students, especially linguistically and culturally diverse students, should deal with words that are related semantically and belong to categories.

Common Core State Standard

CCRA.L.5

Henry (1974) outlined four basic cognitive operations associated with learning concepts and words. The first involves the act of *joining*, or "bringing together." Comparing, classifying, and generalizing are possible through the act of joining. Asking children to explain how words are related or having them sort through word cards to put words into groups involves the act of joining.

The act of *excluding* is another conceptual operation worth considering when teaching words in relation to other words. Children must discriminate, negate, or reject items because they do not belong in a conceptual category. When a child must decide which word does not belong in a set of words, the process involves exclusion. In this case, the child would search through his or her background knowledge to distinguish examples from nonexamples or relevant attributes from irrelevant attributes. So when a child is asked to decide which word does not belong in the list *flower, music, perfume, skunk,* on what set of criteria is a decision made? One immediate response may have been that music doesn't belong since it has little to do with the concept of smell.

A third conceptual activity or operation involves the act of *selecting*. Students learn to make choices and to explain why they made their choices based on what they have experienced, know, or understand. Synonyms, antonyms, and multiple-meaning words lend themselves well to the act of selecting. For example, select the *best* word from the choices given in the following sentence:

Tyrone's quiet behavior was mistaken for _____.

SHYNESS/MODESTY/TERROR

Any of the choices might be acceptable. Yet the value of the activity is in providing a rationale for your choice by judging the worth of several potentially correct answers.

A fourth aspect of thinking conceptually involves the act of *implying*. Is a child able to make decisions based on if–then, cause-and-effect relationships among concepts and words? Dupuis and Snyder (1983) contend that the most common form of vocabulary exercise using implication is the analogy. They believe that the act of completing an analogy is such a complex activity that it actually requires the use of joining, excluding, and selecting processes.

Principle 3: Teach Students to Relate Words to Their Background Knowledge

Judith Thelen (1986) likened children's schemata of differing subjects to having file folders inside the brain. Let's suppose a math text reads, "A negative number is on the left of a number line." If Joe has a well-developed file folder for some schema for *number line*, this explanation of a negative number will be useful to Joe. But suppose Shantell has heard of *number line* but has an underdeveloped file folder for the concept. In that case, the sentence defining negative numbers will have little meaning for Shantell.

Pearson (1984) admonished educators by saying that we have asked the wrong question in teaching vocabulary. Instead of asking, "How can I get this word into the students' heads?" we should be asking, "What is it that students already know about that they can use as an anchor point, as a way of accessing this new concept?" If we ask the latter question, we will always be directing our vocabulary instructions to the file folder issue—where does this word fit? Following Pearson's line of thinking, Joe and

Shantell's teacher could help each of them think, "How can I use what I know about a number line to learn what a negative number is?" In Shantell's case, the teacher needs to show her a number line and have her work with it to develop her notions of the concept. Blachowicz and Fisher (2010) recommend that when learning new words students use what they know to make initial predictions about the meaning of the word and then refine the meaning. Teaching students to relate words to their background knowledge is important for all students, especially for ELLs.

Common Core State Standards

CCRA.L3, CCRA.L.6

Principle 4: Teach Words in Prereading Activities to Activate Knowledge and Use Them in Postreading Discussion, Response, and Retelling

Through **prereading activities**, vocabulary words can be focused on *before* students read to help activate background knowledge in activities involving predicting. For example, Ms. Vizquel, a second-grade teacher, used vocabulary words she had chosen from *The Paperbag Princess* in a technique called Connect Two (Blachowicz, 1986). Her students predicted ways in which the terms would be connected in the story (see Figure 8.5). Then since the words she chose reflected the story line, her students used them quite naturally when responding *after* reading. Here is a retelling given by Omar, a second grader:

Common Core State Standards

CCRA.L.3, CCRA.L.6

Elizabeth was a princess who wore *expensive* clothes and was going to marry a prince named Ronald. A dragon *smashed* her castle and took Ronald. Elizabeth told the dragon, "Aren't you the *fiercest* dragon in the world?" and "Can't you burn up 10 forests?" and stuff like that. The dragon did this stuff and got so tired he went to sleep so Elizabeth got Ronald. Then Ronald told her, "Come back when you look like a real princess." Elizabeth told him he looked like a prince but he was a *bum*.

Figure 8.5 Example of the Connect Two Strategy for *The Paperbag Princess*

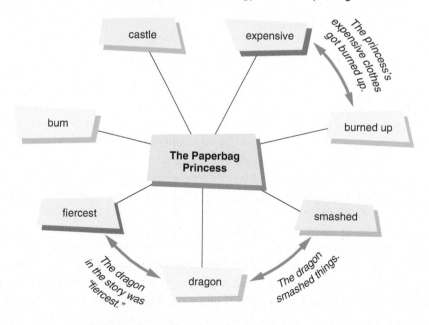

In this way, Omar was able to integrate the words *expensive, smash, fiercest,* and *bum* as he retold the story. He related vocabulary to text.

Prereading and postreading vocabulary activities that connect vocabulary words to content are more desirable than isolated vocabulary exercises, especially for ELLs. Freeman and Freeman (2003) emphasize that ELLs have more difficulty applying knowledge that they've gained through isolated drill. Therefore, they suggest that teachers rely more on reading-related vocabulary activities to help the ELLs make connections to text. According to Goldenberg (2011), "For English speakers and English Language Learners alike, word learning is enhanced when the words are taught explicitly, embedded in meaningful contexts, and students are provided with ample opportunities for their repetition and use" (p. 696). Acquiring and using vocabulary in a variety of activities before, during, and after reading, including conversation, help children develop language, vocabulary, and comprehension skills.

2017 ILA Standard

2.3

Common Core State Standard

CCRA.SL.1

Principle 5: Teach Words Systematically and in Depth

As discussed earlier in the chapter, vocabulary knowledge is applied knowledge. Knowing and teaching a word in depth means going beyond having students parrot back a definition. It means more than having students do something with a definition such as finding an antonym, fitting the word into a sentence blank, or classifying the word with other words. All these are excellent activities and do need to be a part of a systematic vocabulary program. However, researchers are finding that for students to process vocabulary *in depth,* they must *generate a novel product using the term:* They could restate the definition in their own words, compare the definition to their own experiences with the concept, or make up a sentence that clearly demonstrates the word's meaning. These novel products can be written. But, in fact, class discussion leads students to process words deeply by drawing connections between new and known information (Stahl, 1986).

According to Neuman and Roskos (2012), teachers need to provide opportunities for students to be involved in more intentional instruction in oral language development. Initiating conversations, asking open-ended questions, and providing substantive feedback promote student responses and develop expressive vocabulary. Students should have the opportunity to use vocabulary in everyday communication. "Talking with children purposefully integrating new words in daily conversations can help build children's vocabulary" (Wasik & Iannone-Campbell, 2012/2013, p. 321).

2017 ILA Standards

1.1, 2.1, 2.2, 2.4

Common Core State Standards

CCRA.L.6, CCRA.SL.2

By teaching systematically, we mean following a vocabulary program that includes 10 to 12 conceptually related words that are taught and reinforced over an extended period of time. Networks of meanings of these words, as well as links to students' experiences, are established. Students are engaged in words by hearing them, saying them, manipulating them, and playing with them (Blachowicz & Fisher, 2010). For

ELLs, a systematic vocabulary program by Hickman, Pollard-Durodola, and Vaughn (2004) features engagement through daily read-aloud sessions. This five-day program encourages the ELLs to preview the story and vocabulary, participate in guided discussions, reread passages, and extend their vocabulary knowledge.

> In this **video** (www.youtube.com/watch?v=-NMzKYWRBJg), you will see April Kelley introducing the word "violent" using various steps to teach vocabulary. She is utilizing active participation strategies. What specific strategies is Kelley using? What vocabulary instruction techniques do you believe are appropriate for students in various grades?

Principle 6: Awaken Interest in and Enthusiasm for Words

Too often in elementary classrooms, vocabulary learning is one of the dullest activities of the school day. Children tend to associate vocabulary instruction with dictionary drills: looking up words, writing out definitions, and putting words in sentences. Though these activities have some merit, they quickly become routine. Students need to know *why, when,* and *how* to use dictionaries. Dictionary usage is discussed later in the chapter.

Promoting students' interest and engagement helps to develop rich vocabularies, especially for less advantaged students (Graves, 2006). Nothing can replace the excitement about words that a good teacher can generate. The teacher's attitude toward vocabulary instruction can be contagious. What you do to illustrate the power of words is vital in improving children's vocabulary. Ask yourself whether you get excited by learning new words. Share words of interest to you with your students, and tell stories about the origin and derivation of words.

Help students play with words, as Cindy's third-grade teacher did. In one activity, her teacher, through discussion and demonstration, developed for the children the concept of facial expression, or "mugging." With a digital camera, she took "mug shots" of her students, downloaded them, and placed them prominently on the bulletin board. The children learned to "mug" for the camera by acting out "mug" words (e.g., happy mugs, sad mugs, angry mugs). The very last mug the children learned was the smug smile of satisfaction, or the "smug mug." Cindy's teacher explained that when a child knew something that no other person knew or took great pride in an accomplishment, he or she was to flash the "smug mug."

When students see that learning words can be fun, they become interested and curious about them. This results in the desire to learn more. Playing with words by utilizing various forms of media is important. Besides being motivational to students, playing with words helps students develop an understanding of how words work (Blachowicz & Fisher, 2010). Incorporating pictures, charts, audiotapes, videotapes, songs, and video clips allows students to learn vocabulary words in more than one format. These forms of media help to build connections between words and the students' experiences. Jeremy Brueck explains how to use word clouds to facilitate that connection in Box 8.1.

2017 ILA Standard

5.3

Common Core State Standard

CCRA.SL.2

Check Your Understanding 8.3: Gauge your understanding of the skills and concepts in this section.

BOX 8.1 | TRANSLITERACY

Using Word Clouds to Enhance Vocabulary Development

To develop a comprehensive vocabulary, students must build connections between words and cultivate sophisticated schemas of meaning. Teachers can use graphic organizers as a tool to help students visualize the interconnection between words to support this process. In the transliterate classroom, one way students can create powerful graphic organizers to support vocabulary growth is through the use of word clouds.

A word cloud is a compilation of words associated with a distinct idea that has been appropriated from a narrative or informational text on the topic. The words in the cloud often vary in print size and color. The more frequently a word is found in the text, the larger it appears in the cloud. A quick look at the cloud can help students preview a text passage, introduce key terms, and strengthen vocabulary.

Teachers and students can create word clouds using a number of free websites, most of which work in a similar manner.

Word Clouds, from ABCYa! (http://www.abcya.com), is a great place to get started with early elementary students. Begin by finding a passage of grade-level appropriate text online that you plan on having students read. Students can then type or paste the text into the word box, press the create button, and view the word cloud. After generating the word cloud, students can change the color, layout, and font of the words through an easy-to-use interface. ABCYa! word clouds can be saved or printed for later reference.

When teachers model the creation of word clouds using ABCYa! or a similar web application, they are not only offering opportunities to strengthen vocabulary, but also exposing students to critical transliteracy skills such as highlighting, copying, pasting, and "what you see is what you get" (WYSIWYG) editing. Teachers should be teaching the vocabulary associated with these technological tasks alongside academic vocabulary contained in the text.

Best Practice: Strategies for Vocabulary and Concept Development

■ **Give examples of instructional strategies for teaching vocabulary using a variety of activities promoting concept development.**

Vocabulary instruction should not be neglected in primary and middle school classrooms. Teachers in most grades worry that they "don't have the time to spend on vocabulary instruction." Direct vocabulary instruction need not take more than 20 minutes a day. Moreover, opportunities for incidental instruction and reinforcement arise in content area instruction throughout the school day. Isabella, a second-grade student, recognizes the need for various opportunities for vocabulary development during reading and content area instruction (see Box 8.2).

Best practice in vocabulary instruction begins with the teacher's commitment to teach words well. Start slowly and gradually build an instructional program over the

BOX 8.2 | STUDENT VOICES

Isabella is a confident young reader who enjoys school, especially second grade. She is aware of the need to develop vocabulary or, in Isabella's terms, "new words." Isabella believes that "it is hard to read a book if I do not know the words."

Learning new words for Isabella needs to be varied to include an assortment of activities. Isabella says, "I like to do lots of stuff." She explains that she likes her weekly list of words and definitions because "it helps me learn the words." However, learning new vocabulary words from a word list is not the only way Isabella learns. She notes that for reading, social studies, and science, she likes to learn new words by

- Playing hangman
- Playing SPARKLE (a spelling game)

- Playing word ball
- Drawing a picture
- Using the SmartBoard
- Using maps and pictures

As a developing reader Isabella demonstrates her metacognitive awareness of how she learns vocabulary. She is aware of instructional strategies that help her learn. Including direct instruction along with opportunities to "play" with new words is necessary. In reading and content area instruction, teachers need to include a variety of instructional strategies to meet the students' needs.

year. We have already recommended that words be selected for emphasis that come from the actual materials students read during the year—basal and literature selections as well as content area text selections. For best practice, the program should evolve from the instructional implications of the knowledge, instrumental, and aptitude hypotheses discussed earlier.

2017 ILA Standard

6.1

Relating Experiences to Vocabulary Learning

Dale's Cone of Experience (see Figure 8.1) is a good place to begin when planning and selecting vocabulary strategies that are experience based. The more direct, firsthand experiences students have, the better.

2017 ILA Standard

2.2

But different levels of vicarious experience can also establish bases for vocabulary learning. Vicarious experiences, though secondhand, are valuable in their own right. Dale's Cone of Experience indicates possibilities for planning experiences that are vicarious: demonstrations, simulations, dramatization, visual and audio media, reading to children, keeping vocabulary logs and reading on one's own.

The use of technology also provides opportunities for the students to see, hear, and use words. These experiences provide for in-depth vocabulary development. Through the use of various vocabulary development software (drill and practice, tutorial, and learning games), iPad applications, Internet sites, virtual field trips, and talking books, students learn to use words, understand concepts, and appreciate how words are related to the content being studied. Ebner and Ehri (2013) researched the benefits of vocabulary development through Internet usage. They concluded that the Internet provides students access to "multisensory and varied experiences with words" (p. 480). Reading online, seeing words in different contexts, and website resources are a few Internet activities to develop vocabulary skills. Teachers are encouraged to rely upon the various forms of technology as valuable instructional tools for vocabulary development.

2017 ILA Standards

2.2, 5.3

Common Core State Standard

CCRA.SL.2

Next we will consider how wide reading is useful for growth in vocabulary learning and how to help students use context to extend this growth.

Using Context for Vocabulary Growth

Teachers and experts know that in addition to defining new terms, students need some examples of the concept; that is, students need to hear the new words used in different contexts. Hearing a dictionary definition is not enough to learn a new word.

Defining a word and using the word in a sentence or a context is a common and useful practice. In studying sound, a third-grade class learned that the definition of *vibrate* was "to move rapidly back and forth." They also discussed different contexts for *vibrate*—how a violin string vibrates and how blowing into a bottle or a flute makes the air vibrate. Even though we know that using context while reading is an important avenue for vocabulary growth, we agree with Nagy (1988) that when teaching *new* meanings, context alone is not effective. We know that the context provided in most texts tells us something about the word's meaning, but seldom does any single context give complete information (Deighton, 1970; Shatz & Baldwin, 1986). Nevertheless, we suggest that *the instructional goal should be to teach students to use context to gain information about the meanings of new terms.* For example, Judy led a group of first graders in reading a book about the Skylab. First, when she asked the children what they thought a Skylab was, Jan said, "A lab in the sky, of course." Judy wrote this on the board. As Jan and the first graders read the book together, they made a list of what a Skylab is:

It is a space station.

A rocket takes a Skylab into space.

A Skylab goes around the earth.

Astronauts stay on a Skylab.

A Skylab has big solar collectors. Solar collectors change sunlight into electricity.

2017 ILA Standards

2.1, 2.2

Common Core State Standard

CCRA.L.3

Helping students learn to use context to gain information about words new to them is particularly important for struggling readers of any age. In addition, young students as well as middle school students need to know that they must accept partial word knowledge, some degree of uncertainty, and occasionally misleading contexts as they meet new words in their independent reading (Beck, McKeown, & McCaslin, 1983).

Instructional Decision Making 8.1: Apply your understanding of the concepts in this section.

We will examine ways to help children grow in independence by using different contexts to extend their vocabulary knowledge, but first we look at more direct instructional strategies to develop word meanings.

Developing Word Meanings

Definitional knowledge, or the ability to relate new words to known words, can be built through synonyms, antonyms, and multiple-meaning words.

Synonyms are words that are similar in meaning to other words. **Antonyms** are words that are opposite in meaning to other words. Synonyms and antonyms are useful ways of having children define and understand word meanings. Antonyms in particular can demonstrate whether children really comprehend the meanings of new words. Moreover, words that have multiple meanings tend to confuse students, especially when they are reading and encounter the uncommon meaning of a word used in a passage.

Common Core State Standard

CCRA.L.5

SYNONYMS Synonym instruction has value when a child has knowledge of a concept but is unfamiliar with its label—the new word to be learned. In such cases, the focus of instruction is to help the student associate new words with more familiar ones. This particular strategy is a good example of the cognitive principle of bridging the gap between the new and the known.

2017 ILA Standards

2.1, 2.2

For example, a fifth-grade teacher provided a synonym match for words that students were studying in a unit on ecology. Here are several of the matching items:

Column A: New Words	Column B: Words That You Already Know
Cultivate	Change
Erode	Surroundings
Environment	wearing away
Modify	Work

The students were directed to match the words from column B with the words from column A. A discussion followed, with students giving reasons for their matchups. The discussion led to further clarification of each new term and the realization, as one child put it, that "some words just look hard but really aren't."

In another synonym-related activity, students were given overworked or unimaginative words in sentences or paragraphs, and asked to supply alternative words that would make each sentence or the paragraph more descriptive and interesting. Words such as *nice, great,* and *neat* are good candidates for this type of activity.

Our trip to the zoo was *neat*. The entire family had a *swell* time. Dad thought that seeing the monkeys on Monkey Island was *fun*. So did I. But Mom said, "The monkeys were okay, but I liked the reptiles even more." The snakes were *terrific*. We all had a *great* time at the zoo.

This activity, and adaptations of it, can be used as a springboard for students to analyze a piece of their own writing, looking for overworked words and substituting more interesting and precise words.

Many word processing programs have a built-in thesaurus. Children can be shown how to use the thesaurus to help find "just the right word" for what they want to say. Teachers can also use the thesaurus to develop exercises in which students must decide which synonyms would fit best in specific contexts, such as the following:

Which synonym would you most likely find in a funeral announcement or an obituary?

Dead   Departed   Extinct

Exercises such as this one are a part of vocabulary instruction that promotes deep and fluent word knowledge.

ANTONYMS In addition to matching activities (in which students associate the target words with words that are opposite in meaning) and selecting activities (in which students select the best choice for an antonym from several listed), consider strategies that challenge students to work with antonyms in various print contexts.

For example, ask children to change the meanings of advertisements: "Change the ad! *Don't* sell the merchandise!" Children can ruin a good advertisement by changing the underlined words to words that mean the opposite. The following are examples of the antonym advertisement activity:

Today through Tuesday!

Save now on this <u>top-quality</u> bedding.

The <u>bigger</u> the size, the <u>more</u> you save.

<u>GREAT</u> truckload sale!

Just take your purchase to the checkout, and the cashiers will <u>deduct</u> 30 percent from the ticketed price.

Similar activities can be developed for a target word in a sentence or several new vocabulary words in a paragraph. You may devise an activity in which children work with sentence pairs. In the first sentence, the target word is underlined. In the second sentence, a child must fill in the blank space with an antonym for the target word.

1. The ship sank to the <u>bottom</u> of the ocean. The climbers reached the _____ of the mountain.
2. The <u>joyful</u> family reunion never had a dull moment. The funeral was the most _____ occasion I had ever experienced.

Sentence pairs will generate variations of antonyms. Therefore, children should be asked to defend their choices. In the first pair of sentences, *top, peak,* and *highest point* are acceptable antonyms for *bottom. Sad, solemn,* and *depressing* are all possible antonyms for *joyful.*

WORDS WITH MULTIPLE MEANINGS   **Multiple-meaning words** give students opportunities to see how words operate in context.

- The *hall* was so long that it seemed endless.
- The concert took place in a large *hall.*
- The Football *Hall* of Fame is located in Canton, Ohio.

Common Core State Standard

CCRA.L.4

In content area textbooks, students frequently run across common words that have different meanings (e.g., *mean, table, force, bank, spring*). These can lead to confusion and miscomprehension. A strategy for dealing with multiple-meaning words involves prediction and verification (Vacca & Vacca, 2011):

1. Select multiple-meaning words from a text assignment. List them on the board.
2. Have students predict the meanings of these words and write them on a sheet of paper next to each term.
3. Assign the reading selection, noting the numbers of the pages where students can find each word in the text reading.
4. Ask students to verify their original predicted meanings. If they wish to change any of their predictions, they can revise the meanings based on how each word was used in the selection.

Classifying and Categorizing Words

When children manipulate words in relation to other words, they are engaging in critical thinking. Vocabulary strategies and activities should give students the experience of *thinking about, thinking through,* and *thinking with* vocabulary. Working with relationships among words provides this opportunity.

2017 ILA Standards

2.1, 2.2

Through the aid of **categorization** and classification strategies, students recognize that they can group words that label ideas, events, or objects. Such strategies involve the processes of joining, excluding, selecting, and implying. Students will learn to study words critically and form generalizations about the shared or common features of concepts. Word sorts, categorization, semantic mapping, analogies, paired-word sentence generation, and collaborative learning exercises are all activities that help students, including those from diverse backgrounds, conceptualize as well as learn and reinforce word meanings.

Common Core State Standard

CCRA.L.5

WORD SORTS The process of sorting words is integrally involved in concept formation. A **word sort** is a simple yet valuable activity to initiate. Individually or in small groups, children sort through vocabulary terms that are written on cards or listed on an exercise sheet. The object of word sorting is to group words into different categories by looking for shared features among their meanings. The strategies can be used effectively at any grade level.

There are two types of word sorts: the *open sort* and the *closed sort*. In the *closed sort,* students know in advance what the main categories are. In other words, they must select and classify words according to the features they have in common with a category. The closed sort reinforces and extends the ability to classify words. The *open sort* stimulates inductive thinking. No category or grouping is known in advance of sorting, and students must search for meanings and discover relationships among words.

Fifth-grade students participating in a unit on the newspaper discovered the many functions of a newspaper: to inform and interpret, influence, serve, and entertain. A closed sort task that children participated in involved the completion of the following worksheet in small groups:

Directions: In your groups, place the topics below under the proper headings. You may use a topic more than once. Base your decisions on class discussions and what is found in today's newspaper.

the largest picture on page A-1	the Market at a Glance column (business)
Weather Watch	the Transitions column (sports)
News Watch	the Bridge column
the first full-page ad	the classified index
the first Focal Point story	display advertising
legal notices	death notices
the first letter to the editor	the headline on page A-1
Dear Abby	the crossword puzzle
the astrology column	

Informs or Interprets	Influences	Serves	Entertains

Ms. Prince modified word sorts when she introduced a science unit on fish. She had her third graders work in groups to brainstorm and list everything they could think of relating to the word *fish*. Their list included:

good to eat	fun to catch	slippery
pretty	water	bugs
fins	tail	shiny

While the students were still in groups, she then asked them to come up with one or more categories or groups that two of the words could go into. The students came up with the following categories:

- Fins and tail are *parts of a fish's body.*
- Pretty, slippery, and shiny describe *how fish look.*
- Good to eat and fun to catch tell about *things people like to do with fish.*

After the children had read the chapter on fish, Ms. Prince asked them to find words from the chapter that could go in the category or group that describes parts of a fish's body. The students very quickly added *scales* and *gills* to this category. In this way, Ms. Prince involved students in an open sort before reading and a closed sort (using a category identified by the children) after reading the text.

An excellent use of open sorting is to coordinate it with word banks. Word banks, closely associated with the language-experience approach, are collections of cards bearing words that a student does not recognize immediately.

CATEGORIZATION   Vocabulary activities involving categorization help students form relationships among words in much the same manner as open and closed sorts. The difference, however, lies in the amount of assistance a child is given. For example, a teacher may give students two to six words per grouping and ask them to do something with the sets of words. Different formats may be used to "do something" with the word sets. Consider giving the children sets of words and asking them to circle the word in each set that includes the meaning of the others. This exercise requires them to perceive common attributes or examples in relation to a more inclusive concept and to distinguish superordinate from subordinate terms. Children are involved in the cognitive process of joining.

Common Core State Standard

CCRA.L.5

Directions: Circle the word in each group that includes the meaning of the others in the group.

Generals	Ocean	Spicy
Troops	Lake	Sour
Armies	Water	Taste
Warriors	Bay	Salty

Directions: Cross out the word in each group that doesn't belong.

Meat	Earth	Judgment
Butter	Ground	Treasure
Oatmeal	Stable	Cash
Fish oil	Soil	Price

Other categorization exercises may direct students to cross out the word that does not belong in each set. This format forces students to manipulate words that convey the meanings of common items. In these activities, children learn to exclude words that are not conceptually related to other words.

The younger the children are, the more manipulative and directed the categorization activity might be. Word cards may be used instead of worksheets. Working with sets of cards, a teacher may place one set at a time on a worktable and call on a child to remove the card that doesn't belong. The other children around the table must then attempt to explain the child's choice. Manipulative activities that require cutting, pasting, or drawing also work well.

CONCEPT CIRCLES   A versatile activity appropriate for students at a wide range of grade levels, **concept circles** provide still another format and opportunity to study words critically and to relate words conceptually to one another. A concept circle simply involves putting words or phrases in the sections of a circle and then directing students to describe or name the concept relationship among the sections. In the example in Figure 8.6, Diane Burke asked her seventh graders, after they had read about climate, to determine the main idea of the concept circle.

Alternatively, you might invite students to shade in the section of a concept circle containing a word or phrase that *does not relate* to the other words or phrases in the

Figure 8.6 Example of a Concept Circle

What is the main idea of this concept circle?

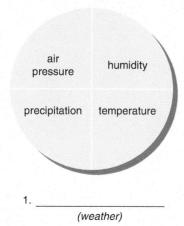

1. _____
(weather)

Figure 8.7 Variation on the Concept Circle

Directions:
Shade in the section that does not relate to the other sections. What is the concept?

1. _____
(economic rehabilitation)

circle's sections and then identify the concept they have in common. See Figure 8.7 for an example of a concept circle that Debbie Schmidt's eighth graders were asked to do in groups of three during their history lesson on Roosevelt's New Deal.

Other modifications include leaving one or more sections of the circle empty, inviting students to fill in the empty sections with a word or two relating in some way to the terms in the other sections. Students must then justify their choices by identifying the larger concept depicted by the circle.

Although these activities are similar to categorization exercises, students may respond more positively to the visual aspect of the sections in a circle than to category sorting because the circles seem less like tests.

SEMANTIC MAPPING Semantic mapping, or webbing, is a strategy that shows readers and writers how to organize important information. Semantic mapping can also revolve around vocabulary learning by providing a visual display of how words are related to other words. Earlier in this chapter, semantic mapping was used to make distinctions among class, example, and attribute relations. Similarly, students can use semantic mapping to cluster words belonging to categories and to distinguish relationships.

The first step in the semantic mapping of vocabulary is for the teacher to select a word central to a story or from any other source of classroom interest or activity and then write this word on the board. From this point, the procedures can vary, depending on the objective of the lesson. For example, the teacher can ask the students to think of as many words as they can that are in some way related to the word and jot them down. As students share the words they have written with the class, the words are grouped into categories on the board around the central concept. The students can suggest names for the categories and discuss the category labels, relating their experiences to the words on the board.

Common Core State Standard

CCRA.L.5

Semantic maps can be elaborately developed or kept relatively simple, depending on the sophistication of the class and grade level. In Figure 8.8, a group of beginning readers developed a concept of the five senses through a mapping strategy.

The teacher began the map by writing the target concept, *five senses,* in the middle of the board. She then presented the class with a familiar situation: "How often have you known that your sister was making a snack even before you got to the kitchen to see or taste it?" The children responded by saying they could smell food cooking or hear a sibling preparing the snack. The teacher praised the student responses and continued, "You were using your senses of smell and sound to know that a snack was being fixed." She then wrote *smell* and *sound* on the board and connected the words to the central concept.

The children's attention was then directed to the bulletin board display of five children, each employing one of the senses. Through a series of questions, the class gradually developed the remainder of the semantic map. For example, when the concept of smell was being developed, the teacher noted, "We call a smell 'scent,'" and connected *scents* to *smell* on the map. She then asked, "How do you think flowers smell?" "What words can you tell me to determine different types of smells?" As the students volunteered words, the teacher placed them on the map. When the teacher asked, "When you think of sound, what's the first thing that comes to your mind?" the children quickly said, "Noises." The teacher connected *noises* to *sound.* Further discussion focused on types of noises, both pleasant and unpleasant.

Figure 8.8 A Semantic Map of the Five Senses

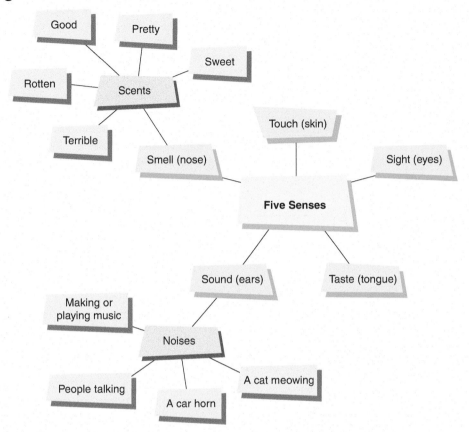

ANALOGIES An **analogy** is a comparison of two similar relationships. On one side of the analogy, the words are related in some way; on the other side, the words are related in the same way. Analogies probably should be taught to students beginning in the intermediate grades. If they are not familiar with the format of an analogy, they may have trouble reading it successfully. Therefore, give several short demonstrations in which you model the process involved in completing an analogy. The step-by-step lesson in Box 8.3 provides an outline for using analogies. In Figure 8.9, we illustrate some of the types of word relationships from which many analogies can be developed.

2017 ILA Standard

2.2

Common Core State Standard

CCRA.L.5

BOX 8.3 | STEP-BY-STEP LESSON

Teaching Analogies

Ignoffo (1980) explained the value of analogies this way: "Analogies are practical because they carry an implied context with them. To work the analogy, the learner is forced to attempt various … procedures that involve articulation, problem solving, and thinking" (p. 520). Consider the following steps when teaching vocabulary using analogies.

1. Begin by asking students to explain the relationship that exists between two words. For example, write on the board a simple class example relationship:

    apple   fruit

2. Ask students, "What is the relationship between the two words?" Explanations may vary greatly, but arrive at the notion that an apple is a type of fruit.

3. Explain that an analogy is a comparison of two similar sets of relationships. Write on the board:

   <u>Apple</u> is to <u>fruit</u> as <u>carrot</u> is to _____.

4. Suggest to students, "If an apple is a type of fruit, then a carrot must be a type of _____." Discuss the children's predictions, and provide additional examples.

5. Note that an analogy has its own symbols:

   apple:fruit::carrot: _____

6. Point out that the symbol : means *is to* and :: means *as*. Walk students through an oral reading of several analogies, saying, "An analogy reads like this." (The class reads the analogy in unison following the teacher's lead.)

7. Provide simple analogies at first, and gradually increase the complexity of the relationships.

8. Develop analogies from vocabulary used in stories, content area texts, or topics of interest in the classroom.

In order to assist ELLs or struggling readers with analogies, students can be given two or three words to choose from to complete the analogy. Then follow up by asking the students to explain why the word was chosen. Teachers can also encourage the use of a thesaurus to help determine the correct word.

Figure 8.9 Using Word Relationships to Form Analogies

Directions: Study each type of relationship, and for each example given, complete the analogy. Then compare your responses with a classmate or colleague.

1. **Purpose relationship**
   Teeth:chew::pen: _____
   Chair:sit::knife: _____

2. **Part-to-whole relationship**
   Antler:deer::tusk: _____
   Cat:feline::dog: _____

3. **Synonym relationship**
   Small:tiny::create: _____
   Copy:imitate::large: _____

4. **Antonym relationship**
   Black:white::day: _____
   High:low::morning: _____

5. **Place relationship**
   Book:bookcase::car: _____
   Flowers:vase::clothes: _____

6. **Attribute relationship**
   Rare:whale::common: _____
   Detective:clue::scientist: _____

7. **Cause-and-effect relationship**
   Furnace:heat::freezer: _____
   Seed:tree::egg: _____

In this **video** (https://www.youtube.com/watch?v=bbXR43hMSV8), you will learn what analogies are and about a few types of analogy relationships. How do you plan on teaching analogies? What type of analogy relationships should be taught?

PAIRED-WORD SENTENCE GENERATION Students often need many exposures to new and conceptually difficult words in order to begin using these words in their speaking and writing vocabularies (Duin & Graves, 1987). After students have classified and categorized words through word sorts or other strategies, **paired-word sentence generation** can spur them into using these words in their speaking and writing.

Common Core State Standards

CCRA.R.4, CCRA.L.5

Simpson (1987) described paired-word sentence generation as a task that could be used to *test* students' understanding of difficult concepts. We have taken her notion of paired-word sentence generation and developed it into a teaching strategy. In using this strategy, the teacher gives students two related words. The goal of the strategy is to generate *one* sentence that correctly demonstrates an understanding of the words *and* their relationship to each other. However, several steps in the process help elementary students reach this goal. We will describe these steps by illustrating how Mr. Fratello used the strategy with his fifth-grade class as they worked with the concepts *reptile* and *cold-blooded*. First, Mr. Fratello had each student write sentences with the terms *reptile* and *cold-blooded* in them. The class came up with sentences such as these:

- Reptiles are cold-blooded.
- Snakes, lizards, and turtles are reptiles.
- *Cold-blooded* means that when the air is warm, their bodies are warm, and when the air is cold, their bodies are cold.

Mr. Fratello then led the class in a sentence-combining activity to write a sentence that would give the reader information about what *reptiles* are and what *cold-blooded* means, as well as how the two concepts are related to each other. The class came up with sentences such as these:

- Reptiles, like snakes, lizards, and turtles, are cold-blooded because they are cold when the air is cold and warm when the air is warm.
- Snakes, lizards, and turtles are reptiles that are cold-blooded, which means they are warm when the air is warm and cold when the air is cold.

Mr. Fratello asked his fifth graders to generate paired-word sentences throughout the school year. They first worked as a whole class and later worked in groups of four made up of both high and low achievers. Finally, they worked alone, devising their own sentences.

In addition to being considered a classifying and categorizing strategy, as described in the previous illustration, paired-word sentence generation is also considered an instructional strategy for developing word meanings through stories and writing.

Developing Word Meanings Through Stories and Writing

Vocabulary functions differently in literature and in content material. First of all, when reading literature, knowing the meaning of a *new* word may not be necessary for understanding the gist of the story. In contrast, content area vocabulary often represents major concepts that are essential for comprehension and learning. For example, students who cannot give a definition of *stamen* after reading about the parts of a flower have not grasped important content. But they can understand a story about a band even if they glean from context only that a *tambourine* is a musical instrument but don't know what exactly it is like. Second, vocabulary in literature often involves simply learning a new label for a concept already possessed, such as learning that *desolate* means "very sad." In content areas, often the purpose of the text is to teach the concepts, as in the example of the second-grade science material labeling the parts of the flower, whereas this is not generally true in stories. Finally, in content texts, vocabulary terms often have a high degree of semantic relatedness—as the terms *nectar, pollen, anther, stamen, stigma,* and *style* do. With the increase of usage of informational text as a result of the Common Core State Standards (CCSS), students may encounter much more semantic relatedness. This is less likely to be true of vocabulary terms selected from literature (Armbruster & Nagy, 1992).

2017 ILA Standards

2.1, 2.2, 5.1

Common Core State Standards

CCRA.L.3, CCRA.L.5

Yet, as mapping the story *The Paperbag Princess* illustrates, story grammar can be used to develop word meanings. The following two strategies, semantic analysis to writing and predictogram, draw on insights from story grammar.

SEMANTIC ANALYSIS TO WRITING Because authors develop a theme through a series of related incidents, Beyersdorfer and Schauer (1989) reasoned that stories provide a situational context that could be used for rich development of word meanings. When using this strategy, the teacher narrows the selection of words to those semantically related to the theme. Students then develop definitions based on personal schemata for the theme.

In using *semantic analysis to writing:*

1. The teacher identifies the theme and composes a question involving critical thinking related to the theme.
2. The teacher selects words used by the author or consults a thesaurus to find about five words, both synonyms and antonyms, relating to the theme. (Words that are too closely synonymous are discarded.)
3. The teacher constructs a **think sheet** (see Figure 8.10) for discussion purposes as well as for writing.

Mr. Bradford, a sixth-grade teacher who was piloting a literature-based reading program, decided to involve his students in semantic analysis to writing with the thought-provoking book *A Wrinkle in Time* by Madeleine L'Engle. In this story, Meg Murry, along with her precocious brother, Charles Wallace, and their friend Calvin O'Keefe, hopes to rescue her father from a mysterious fate. The children travel through time to the planet Camazotz with the assistance of Mrs. Whatsit, Mrs. Who, and Mrs. Which. There they confront IT, the planet's intimidating force for conformity. Meg and friends find her father, but Charles Wallace gets swallowed up in IT. Meg's father cannot rescue Charles Wallace because he has been away from him so long that the familial ties are too weak: Meg has to go back to IT and rescue Charles Wallace.

Although many themes can be derived from this book, Mr. Bradford chose to use *self-reliance* in semantic analysis to writing because Meg, the main character, changed in terms of self-reliance through the many incidents in the book. Mr. Bradford found that the dictionary definition of *self-reliance* was "sure of oneself and one's ability; needing, wishing for, and getting no help from others."

Mr. Bradford then devised the questions "Was Meg in *A Wrinkle in Time* self-reliant?" "If so, how?" "What did she do that showed self-reliance?" "If not, what did she do that was not self-reliant?"

To make the think sheet, Mr. Bradford used a thesaurus and chose the following words and phrases:

- self-confidence
- certainty

Figure 8.10 Think Sheet for Extended Definition of Self-Reliance

Questions You Will Respond to in an Essay:

Was Meg in *A Wrinkle in Time* self-reliant? If so, how? What did she do that showed self-reliance? If not, what did she do that was not self-reliant? Further, did she change during the story?

What is self-reliance? _____

_____

Directions:

1. As a class, we will define the terms. Write down definitions as we do this.

2. To this list add two words (numbers 6 and 7) suggested during brainstorming. Consult your dictionary and record a definition.

3. Decide which of the seven words contribute an essential characteristic to your definition of *self-reliance.*

4. Find evidence from the story that proves that Meg did or did not demonstrate the characteristics. Give the page number and a phrase description of the event.

5. Using the order of importance, rank the essential characteristics.

6. Write an essay. Define *self-reliance* and support the definition with evidence from *A Wrinkle in Time.*

Term—Definition	Essential—Yes/No	Illustration—Story, Page Number
1. Self-confidence		
2. Certainty		
3. Trust in oneself		
4. Independence		
5. Conviction		
6. *Courage*		
7. *Determination*		

- trust in oneself
- independence
- conviction

Because he knew that the book would prove quite difficult for some of the readers in the class, Mr. Bradford read the book orally to the class over a two-week period. He knew that some of these same readers would write interesting essays on self-reliance. Each day as he read the chapters, students wrote in a response journal, and the class had lively discussions comparing their responses.

Students were now prepared for Mr. Bradford to involve them in the semantic analysis to writing strategy. As a result of class brainstorming and discussion, the terms *courage* and *determination* were added to the think sheet. Small group work then began in earnest to find incidents that showed that Meg was or was not self-reliant.

Next the class had an animated debate about whether Meg was or was not self-reliant, citing evidence for both positions. Many felt that Meg was not self-reliant and supported this with the incident when Meg finds her father and becomes disillusioned when her father is not able to get her brother, Charles Wallace, away from IT. Students who felt Meg became self-reliant cited the fact that Meg finally mustered the courage to attempt to save Charles Wallace from IT. Thus two different initial statements and story frames were formulated to help students begin writing their first drafts, after they had worked in pairs to rank the importance of their supporting evidence.

I think Meg in *A Wrinkle in Time* _____
self-reliant. I think this because _____. Further, _____.
In addition, _____
_____
In conclusion, _____
_____

Mr. Bradford took home many stimulating essays to read after his students had eagerly read them to each other. Many students later chose their self-reliant essay from all those accumulated in their writing folder to revise and edit.

PREDICTOGRAM   Story elements—including the setting, the incidents in the plot, characterization, the character's problem or goal, how the problem or goal is resolved, and the theme or larger issue to which the problem or goal relates—can be used to develop students' meaning vocabulary with the **predictogram** strategy.

Common Core State Standard

CCRA.R.4

In planning for a predictogram, teachers choose words from a story that they feel will be challenging to the students. The words and their meanings are discussed in class, and students relate their personal associations with the words. Finally, students work in groups to predict how they think the author might use each term in the story. Would the author use it to tell about the setting? The characters? The problem or goal or trouble the characters have? Would the author use the word to tell about how the problem or trouble was solved? Students then read to discover how the author did use the terms.

Mrs. Nowak, a fourth-grade teacher in the same school as Mr. Bradford, was also beginning to use a literature-based program with the basal reading program she had used for five years. She was planning for a group of students to read *Crow Boy* by Taro Yashima. The words she thought would be challenging included *forlorn, interesting, trudging, admired, announced, imagine, graduation, attendance, charcoal,* and *rejected.* To get students thinking about the problems in the story, she asked them to freewrite about their thoughts on the idea that "sometimes kids tease a classmate who is shy or different." The students shared their freewrites. Then Mrs. Nowak told them what was happening at the beginning of the story. She led them in a discussion concerning how the meanings of the terms related to personal experiences and predicting which of the words the author would use for each story element.

Figure 8.11 shows how the group completed the predictogram for *Crow Boy.* The students then read the story, looking to see how the author actually used the challenging vocabulary terms. Next we suggest ways to help children gain control over their own vocabulary learning.

Developing Independence in Vocabulary Learning

There is no question that wide reading and thus learning the meaning of words from context is an important way for people to extend their vocabularies. "Anyone interested in increasing students' vocabularies should see that they read as much and as widely as possible" (Graves & Watts-Taffe, 2002, p. 143). Fielding, Wilson, and Anderson (1986) found that the amount of free reading was the best predictor of vocabulary growth between grades 2 and 5. Nagy (1988) theorized that after third grade, for children who do read a reasonable amount, reading may be the single largest source of vocabulary growth.

In order to continue to develop student independence, teachers should next teach dictionary usage and the strategies of self-selection and word knowledge rating. The

Figure 8.11 Predictogram for *Crow Boy* by Taro Yashima

Directions: Discuss with members of your group how you think Taro Yashima would use the vocabulary words below. Would he use them to describe the characters? Or the problem or goal of the character? Or the solution to the problem? Place each word in the appropriate square. Be prepared to tell why you think so.

Vocabulary words:

forlorn	imagine
interesting	graduation
trudging	attendance
admired	charcoal
announced	rejected

Setting where the story took place	*charcoal* *interesting*
Characters the people in the story	*forlorn* *imagine* *trudging*
Problem or goal main character	*rejected*
Solution to problem or attainment *of goal*	*graduation* *attendance* *announced* *admired*

dictionary is an important tool for independent readers. Using a dictionary to effectively obtain information is a complex task and requires teaching students proper usage. Self-selection and word knowledge rating are two strategies that aid students in monitoring their own growth in vocabulary knowledge as they use context in reading and listening. The *self-selection* strategy helps students of all ages and abilities become sensitized to the many words they read and hear in school and at home that they can add to their meaning vocabulary. *Word knowledge rating* helps children develop an awareness of the extent to which they know the words they come across as they read and interact with others.

2017 ILA Standards

2.1, 2.2, 5.1

Common Core State Standards

CCRA.L.4, CCRA.L.6

DICTIONARY USAGE Interpreting definitions of words from a dictionary involves more than just choosing a synonym or the first definition from the word entry. It requires connecting word usage with context. Nagy and Scott (2004) believe that a real weakness of dictionary usage and definitions is that the definition may not provide needed information related to context. Many times children are looking up words in isolation from a list and do not look at the context and may choose a definition that may or may not relate to text. The use of the dictionary should not be a primary activity to develop vocabulary; rather, it should be used as a reference tool to verify the meanings of words to ensure that the meanings are syntactically and semantically suitable. Whether the student is using a text, smartphone, or iPad, teachers need to look at dictionary usage and the role it plays in their classrooms. A few Internet sites that provide dictionary-related activities and helpful resources include **Word Central** and **Oxford English Dictionary**.

A few activities that utilize the dictionary as a verification tool are contextual search and word part connections. With a **contextual search**, the teacher assigns a few words to each student. Each student is responsible for reading each word in three different contexts. It is recommended that the text in which the word was originally located is used as well as using the Internet. The student records the contextual usage from all three examples. The student predicts the meaning of the word from the information gathered and verifies the predictions with the dictionary. The definition is then shared with the class, and the student explains why he or she came up with the definition that was decided on. Breaking up a word into word parts in **word part connections** is another dictionary-related activity. Students are encouraged to analyze the unknown word and identify various word parts. Based on word parts such as root, prefix, or suffix, the student is to deduce the meaning of the word. The dictionary is used to verify the meaning of the word or word part. The vocabulary word is then read in context to ensure that the meaning is correct. If not, the dictionary may be used again to help the student determine the correct meaning of the word. The student should be prepared to explain the reasoning behind his or her definition. With contextual search and word part connections, using the dictionary to verify word meaning is key. Other instructional vocabulary activities discussed in the chapter when paired with the dictionary can be used to enhance word meaning.

2017 ILA Standards

2.1, 2.2

In order to make effective use of the dictionary, teachers should consider the management of the classroom. Students should have easy access to various types of dictionaries (picture, writing, spelling, thesaurus, etc.), as well as a variety of levels. Because of their varied reading and writing abilities, students should have options to choose from to fit their abilities and needs. Read **Straight from the Classroom** to see how a second-grade teacher encourages her students to develop their own vocabulary logs to help them with the development of word meanings.

SELF-SELECTION STRATEGY Words for the **self-selection strategy** can be drawn from basal readers, literature, content area instruction, or incidental learning experiences. As the name implies, children select the words to be studied. In describing how to use this strategy, Haggard (1986) explained that the first step is to ask students to bring to class one word they believe the class should learn; the teacher also chooses a word. These words are then written on the board, and students give the definitions they gleaned from the context in which they found the word. Class members add any information they can to each definition. The students and teacher consult pertinent references such as dictionaries (texts and CD-ROMs), glossaries, thesauri, dictionary Internet sites, and textbooks to add to definitions that are incomplete or unclear.

At this point, students can explain why they think a word is important to learn. Through this discussion, students narrow the list, agreeing to exclude terms that many already know or are not useful enough. The agreed-on terms and their definitions are recorded in vocabulary journals that are kept throughout the year. Students may also enter into their own vocabulary journal personal words that they chose but that were not chosen by the group. The class list of words is then used in activities such as word sorts, analogies, synonym matching, or any of the other activities that have been described. The class-selected words also become part of end-of-unit tests. By using this strategy, students become aware of many striking words that they see and hear in their daily lives.

WORD KNOWLEDGE RATING **Word knowledge rating** is a way to get children to analyze how well they know vocabulary words. Words chosen by the teacher or by the students in the self-selection strategy are written on a worksheet or on the board. We suggest students rate words using Dale's (1965) continuum to explain the degrees of word cognition.

- I've never seen the word.
- I've heard of it, but I don't know what it means.
- I recognize it in context. It has something to do with _____.
- I know the word in one or several of its meanings.

After students have rated themselves on their knowledge of the words, the teacher should lead them in a discussion using questions such as "Which are the hardest words?" "Which do you think most of us don't know?" "Which are the easiest?" "Which do you think most of us know?" (Blachowicz, 1986). The exchange could also involve consideration of the question "Which terms are synonyms for concepts we already know, and which are somewhat or totally new concepts to us?"

Through such discussions, students will begin to make judgments concerning the depth of their knowledge of vocabulary terms they have encountered, as well as the amount of effort needed to add the terms to their meaning vocabulary.

Check Your Understanding 8.4: Gauge your understanding of the skills and concepts in this section.

RTI for Struggling Readers

Vocabulary Development and *Response to Intervention*

Children learn many new words each year. Extensive reading and writing opportunities contribute to vocabulary expansion. Children learn most of their vocabulary from multiple interactions with the new words. As discussed earlier in the chapter, kindling an interest and enthusiasm for words is essential. "Playing" with words not only develops vocabularies but also improves reading development, especially for struggling learners.

To narrow the gap in vocabulary development between struggling and more able readers, teachers should consider including opportunities for students to play word games. Teacher-made games or adaptations of commercial games are easily incorporated into the classroom because of the students' familiarity with games. The following are a few games with or without adaptations that can develop word knowledge:

- Candy Land
- Boggle Junior and Boggle Master
- Memory/Concentration
- Taboo
- Jeopardy
- Pictionary Junior
- Outburst Junior
- Scattergories Junior
- Go to the Head of the Class

Teaching vocabulary words with games should not be "played" in isolation. Games should be connected to learning objectives and adapted to include the words being learned or reinforced. In order for vocabulary development to truly occur, the focus needs to be on word knowledge rather than word pronunciation. For Tier 1 and Tier 2 accommodations, direct instruction in whole class and small group intervention helps to scaffold student learning by modeling and providing opportunities for the students to "play" with words. The use of these as well as other vocabulary games encourages children to be active learners.

2017 ILA Standards

2.1, 2.2, 2.3, 5.1

What About . . .

Standards, Assessment, and Vocabulary Development?

The development of vocabulary knowledge and concepts is essential for students to comprehend and critically think about texts across the curriculum. It is also an essential component of the CCSS. Although most state and national content standards in the various academic disciplines do not explicitly state a standard for vocabulary learning, it is more broadly implied in content standards that relate to comprehension, interpretation, inquiry, and critical thinking. Some state achievement assessments may not have direct measures of word meaning related to specific disciplines, but they generally do have reading and language arts assessments.

Informal, authentic assessments are an important aspect of literacy instruction. Blachowicz and Fisher (1996), for example, recommend knowledge rating as a self-assessment/instructional strategy before students read a chapter or book in order to help students develop an awareness of the extent to which they know the words they come across when they read. Thinking about their own vocabulary knowledge and the content of the text helps students connect and comprehend text. The steps in knowledge rating include the following:

1. Develop a knowledge rating sheet to survey students' prior knowledge of vocabulary they will encounter in the text assignment.
2. Invite students to evaluate their level of understanding of key words on the knowledge rating sheet.
3. Engage in follow-up discussion, asking the class to consider questions such as "Which are the hardest words?" "Which do you think most of the class doesn't know?" "Which words do most of us know?" Encourage the students to share what they know about the words and to make predictions about their meanings.
4. Use the self-assessment to establish purposes for reading. Ask, "What do you think this book is going to be about?"
5. As the students read the text and refer to the words on the knowledge rating sheet as they are used in text. Have the students compare their initial word meaning predictions with what they are learning as they read.

Summary

- Vocabulary instruction is one facet of reading instruction about which there is minimal controversy. Educators agree that it is possible to extend students' knowledge of word meanings, and it is important to do so because of the relationship between this knowledge and reading comprehension.

- This chapter explored that relationship between students' experiences, concepts, and words. By utilizing instructional strategies such as word sorts, concept circles, and semantic mapping, the students gain depth in their word learning and conceptual understanding.

- Six principles for establishing vocabulary programs throughout the elementary grades were presented. The focus was on selecting words, teaching words, and teaching students strategies to learn words.

- For best practice, numerous strategies for vocabulary and concept development that capitalize on students' natural spontaneity, using direct instruction and small grouping as well as reinforcement activities, were suggested. These strategies can be adapted for teaching vocabulary through basal readers, literature, media, or content area texts.

Teacher Action Research

1. Observe various vocabulary lessons being taught in different classes. Listen for the connection to comprehension development. What types of connections are being made? Are they explicitly or implicitly expressed? Are the students making the connections? Discuss your experiences.

2. Talk with students from various grade levels. Ask them, "What is a word?" "What does it mean to know a word?" and "How is vocabulary in reading, writing, listening, and speaking similar and different?" Compare and contrast responses over grade levels.

3. Gather various lists of vocabulary words used in lessons over a two-week period of time. Analyze the words used. Discuss the principles utilized to guide vocabulary instruction. Which principles were relied upon the most? The least?

4. Choose any grade level, and plan a vocabulary lesson. Teach it to a small group of your classmates or children. The lesson should emphasize one of the following strategies discussed in the chapter: (a) relating experiences to vocabulary learning; (b) developing word meanings using synonyms, antonyms, or multiple-meaning words; and (c) classifying and categorizing words. In what ways did the strategy selected work well with the students?

Through the Lens of the Common Core

Vocabulary is an important element in the Common Core State Standards for the English Language Arts (2010b). Throughout this chapter various teaching strategies were suggested in order to facilitate vocabulary development. Teaching students to interpret and analyze word choice while reading various texts and to use vocabulary in various speaking and listening situations are critical components of the core standards. Instructional strategies for developing word meanings, word relationships, and acquiring and using various words for reading, writing, listening, and speaking were discussed in order to help teachers develop vocabulary knowledge and comprehension.

Chapter 9
Comprehending Narrative Text

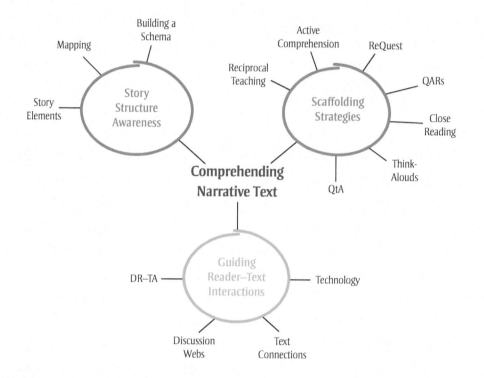

<img> Learning Outcomes

In This Chapter, You Will Discover How to

- Explain the importance of teaching story structure and story elements for comprehension.

- Scaffold comprehension strategies.

- Guide readers' interactions with text.

Activating Your Schema

Do you like to read stories? If so, what genre do you prefer? Romance? Science fiction? Mysteries? If you like to read stories, jot down the genres you prefer. If you don't like to read stories, jot down your thoughts about your dislike for this type of reading. What would you prefer to read if given a choice? Share your thoughts with your class-mates and begin a discussion about reading habits and preferences.

Now, if someone told you to read a story and analyze it, how would you feel about that assignment? If a teacher told you to express your personal feelings about a story, how would you feel? Jot down your thoughts, and share with your classmates. In this chapter you will be explore a variety of ways that teachers connect children with reading and the skills teachers need to help children comprehend what they read.

2017 ILA Standards Found in This Chapter

1.1	2.3	4.2
2.2	3.2	5.3

Common Core State Standards: English Language Arts

CCRA.R.1	CCRA.R.10	CCRA.R.5	CCRA.R.3	CCRA.R.9
CCRA.R.4	CCRA.SL.1	CCRA.R.8	CCRA.R.6	CCRA.W.8
CCRA.R.7	CCRA.R.2	CCRA.W.6		

Key Terms

active comprehension

annotating text

circular story maps

close reading

directed reading–thinking activity (DR–TA)

discussion webs

evaluative (or critical reading) questions

inferential questions

literal questions

narrative text

question–answer relationships (QARs)

questioning the author (QtA)

reciprocal teaching

ReQuest

scaffolded instruction

story frames

story grammar

story map

story schema

text connections

think-alouds

Third grader Anna ran into her classroom one Monday morning and said, "Mrs. Matthew, I just read the best book ever this weekend! It was about a princess who married a frog, and this is what happened! The frog turned into a real live man at the end! Can I share my book during sharing time? It's the best book I ever read!"

Mrs. Matthew assured Anna that she could indeed tell about her story during book-sharing that day. She smiled to herself; Anna was indeed becoming an avid reader.

When a child, such as Anna, is engaged with a story and wants to share with classmates, teachers cannot help but smile. After all, a love of reading is an intrinsic goal that language arts teachers hope to instill in their students. In order to reach this goal, teachers need to engage students in lessons that help them think as they read; reading a story can only become an enjoyable activity when the story is understood.

Exemplary teachers engage children in explicit strategy instruction through the use of well-planned lessons or *minilessons*. Minilessons allow teachers to take the mystery out of comprehension and learning by sharing insights and knowledge students might otherwise never encounter. Explicit strategy lessons create a framework that provides the instructional support students need to become aware of, use, and develop control over comprehension skills and strategies. Striking a balance between strategy instruction and readers' actual interactions with texts is the key to comprehension development.

Strategy lessons, practice with texts, and fostering students' interactions with texts is, however, only a minimal framework for teaching students to comprehend what they are reading. The Common Core State Standards (2010a) explicitly state that students need to read a wide variety of fictional and informational text in depth. In addition to being able to read for literal information, they need to be able to infer, analyze, problem solve, synthesize, summarize, criticize, evaluate, and create new ideas based on what they read. In essence, reading comprehension is much more than just answering the question, "Did I get it?" It involves deep thinking and being able to make decisions and turn new information into knowledge (Harvey & Goudvis, 2013; McLaughlin, 2012).

Common Core State Standards

CCRA.R.1, CCRA.R.2, CCRA.R.3, CCRA.R.4, CCRA.R.5, CCRA.R.6, CCRA.R.7, CCRA.R.8, CCRA.R.9, CCRA.R.10

Think about reading comprehension as a dialogue between the author of the text and the reader. Authors use written language to communicate their ideas or tell a good story to someone else—an audience of readers. Readers use *cognitive* and *metacognitive strategies* to engage their minds in the dialogue so that they can understand, respond to, question, and challenge the author's ideas. Students are in a strategic position to comprehend whenever they use their prior knowledge to construct meaning. Prior knowledge is the sum total of the student's world. It represents the experiences, conceptual understandings, attitudes, values, skills, and strategies that students put into play to comprehend what they are reading. Given the multicultural nature of today's school population, it is particularly important that teachers honor the diverse backgrounds from which their students come as they help them construct meaning from the texts they are reading. Today's teachers are challenged with the task of helping students from a wide variety of ethnic backgrounds and cultures identify with literature that reflects those backgrounds.

2017 ILA Standard

4.2

It is important that teachers take time for prereading activities that help build English language learners' (ELLs) background knowledge prior to reading and that teachers teach vocabulary that is critical to understanding concepts that are new to ELLs. In addition, teachers need to realize that ELLs may understand more than what they are able to verbalize about what they are reading (Manyak & Bauer, 2008).

Developing Readers' Awareness of Story Structure

■ **Explain the importance of teaching story structure and story elements for comprehension.**

Literature that tells a story is considered **narrative text** and is characterized as fiction. Essentially, the story line or text is not true. There are many genres of narrative text: mysteries, fantasies, fairy tales, science fiction, myths, and folk tales. Some narrative text can be a mixture of fiction and fact, hence the genre of historical fiction.

When teachers read stories aloud to children, they help them internalize the sense of a story. Stories typically have a setting or settings (where the story takes place). They include characters (people or animals or fantasy creations) that are central to carrying on the development of the story. Stories also include a plot (typically a problem, difficulty, or puzzle that needs to be solved). Finally, stories usually involve a solution to the problem, sometimes referred to as the point of view. Stories are central to children's reading comprehension development, and children's knowledge of stories begins to develop at an early age when they are engaged in read-alouds. When children hear stories, they develop a sense of **story schema**; they begin to understand that stories have beginnings and endings, problems and solutions.

Early instruction in reading comprehension typically includes dialogue about **story grammar**, which helps specify the basic parts of a story and how they tie together to form a well-constructed piece of literature. What do most well-developed stories have in common? Although individual story grammars may differ somewhat, most people would agree that a story's structure centers on *setting* and *plot*.

2017 ILA Standards

1.1, 5.3

Elements in a Story

The setting of a story introduces the main character (sometimes called the *protagonist*) and situates the characters in a time and place. The plot of a story is made up of one or more *episodes*. A simple story has a single episode. More complex stories may have two or several episodes, as well as different settings. Each episode is made up of a chain of events. Although the labeling of these events differs from story to story, the following elements are generally included:

- *A beginning or initiating event*—either an idea or an action that sets further events into motion
- *Internal response (followed by a goal or problem)*—the character's inner reaction to the initiating event, in which the character sets a goal or attempts to solve a problem
- *Attempts*—the character's efforts to achieve the goal or alleviate the problem; several attempts may be evident in an episode
- *One or more outcomes*—the success or failure of the character's attempts
- *Resolution*—the long-range consequence that evolves from the character's success or failure to achieve the goal or resolve the problem
- *A reaction*—an idea, emotion, or further event that expresses a character's feelings about success or failure in reaching a goal or resolving a problem or that relates the events in the story to some broader set of concerns

The events in the story form a causal chain. Each event leads to the next one as the main character moves toward reaching a goal or resolving a problem.

Mapping a Story for Instructional Purposes

An analysis of a story's organizational elements strengthens instructional decisions. A **story map** is a way of identifying major structural elements, both explicit and implicit, underlying a story to be taught in class. A chart such as the one in Figure 9.1 helps you map the relationships that exist among the major events in a story. Once these relationships are established, they form the basis for developing a line of questions that will help students grasp the story parts under discussion.

The following generic questions are easily applied to many stories.

Setting
Where did the story take place? When did the story take place? Who is the main character? What is _____ like? What is _____'s problem? What did _____ need? Why is _____ in trouble?

Internal Response and Goal/Problem
What does _____ decide to do? What does _____ need to do?

Figure 9.1 Mapping Story Structure

Chain of Events	
Time and place:	Character(s):

Chain of Events	
The beginning event that initiates the action	
Internal response and goal/problem	
Attempt(s) and outcome(s)	
Resolution	
Reaction	

Attempts and Outcomes

What did _____ do about _____? What happened to _____? What will _____ do now? How did it turn out?

Resolution

How did _____ solve the problem? How did _____ achieve the goal? What would you do to solve _____'s problem?

Reaction

How did _____ feel about the problem? Why did _____ do _____? How did _____ feel at the end?

When students have responded to questions related to the story line, engage them in discussion centered on other important aspects of the story, such as its theme, character development, and the reader's personal response to the story.

Theme

What is the moral of the story? What did you learn from the story? What is the major point of the story? What does this story say about _____? Why do you think the author wanted to write this story?

Characters

Why do you think _____ did that? What do you like about _____? Dislike? Does _____ remind you of anyone else you know?

Personal Response
Is there anything you would have changed in the story? How did the story make you feel? Happy? Sad? Angry? Bewildered? Was there anything about the story that didn't make sense?

For ELLs, Fitzgerald and Graves (2004) recommend a visual aid that resembles a "yellow brick road" to foster understanding the sequence of a story map. The activity resembles a game board in which each "brick" is numbered and corresponds to questions that identify the sequential organization of the story. It is suggested that ELLs can work in pairs to write answers to the questions and share in small groups.

Not only is story mapping useful for planning questions, but it also provides you with information about "break points" during reading. A break point occurs whenever students are asked to stop an in-class reading to discuss story content. When and where to stop reading is one of the most important decisions you can make when guiding reading.

Building a Schema for Stories

You can put story structure to good use in the classroom when students have access to reading materials that are written around recognizable story structures.

The following activities and suggestions will help students build a sense of story and reinforce their awareness of story structure.

READ, TELL, AND PERFORM STORIES IN CLASS   One strategy for building experience with stories or extending students' knowledge of how stories are put together is to have them read, tell, and perform stories in class on a regular basis. These types of experiences with stories are as paramount in the middle grades as they are in the beginning grades. For beginning ELLs, drama can help with understanding new ideas as they watch students enact story parts (Fitzgerald & Graves, 2004). In addition, tableau and pantomime are activities in which students can create scenes from stories as an expression of comprehension (Cornett, 2006).

SHOW RELATIONSHIPS BETWEEN STORY PARTS   Flowcharts reflect best practices for mapping relationships that exist between events in the story. Flowcharts give children a visual image of how stories are organized. Give students copies of a diagram without the story information. As information is discussed relating to the story parts depicted on the flowchart, students can write what is being said on their own copies.

Common Core State Standard

CCRA.R.3

Flowcharting can take many different forms, including the one illustrated in Figure 9.2. Study the generic flowchart and how a second-grade teacher adapted that format to develop a story map based on students' suggestions during discussion.

The value of flowcharting lies in the discussions that take place before, during, and after the activity. Discussions should revolve around the relationships of one event to another. The goal behind a discussion is to make students consciously aware that events in a story form a causal chain. With much teacher-led discussion, modeling, and guided practice, many students beginning in the second or third grade will grasp how to map story parts and make flowcharts on their own. Once this is the case, have students share their products with one another. Rather than emphasize accuracy during sharing sessions, ask for reasons and rationales. Encourage speculation and risk taking. Also, allow students the opportunity to revise or alter their individual efforts based on the discussion.

REINFORCE STORY KNOWLEDGE THROUGH INSTRUCTIONAL ACTIVITIES
Children's understanding of story structure can be extended through varied instructional tasks. Two examples include **story frames** and **circular story maps**.

Figure 9.2 Generic Flowchart for Mapping a Story and a Classroom Example of the Format

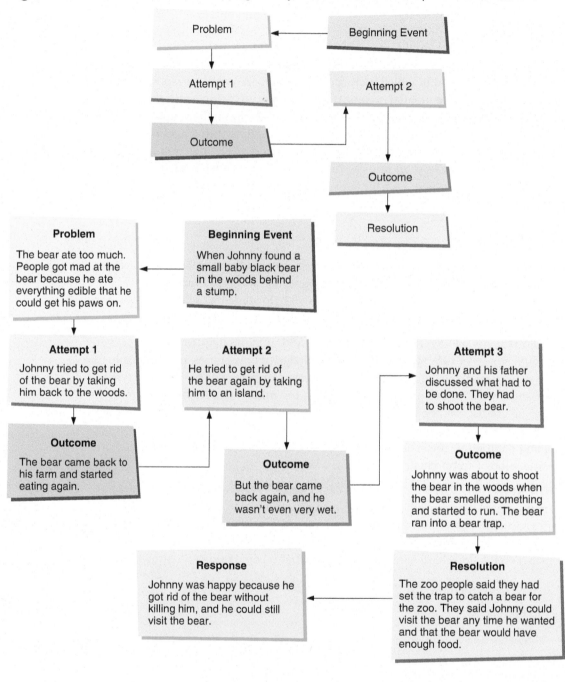

Story Frames Story frames present a way of heightening an awareness of stories. Fowler (1982) showed that story frames may be particularly appropriate in the primary grades or in situations in which students are at risk in their development as readers. A story frame provides the student with a skeletal paragraph: a sequence of spaces tied together with transition words and connectors that signal a line of thought. Fowler identified five story frames, each with a different emphasis: *plot summary, setting, character analysis, character comparison,* and the story's *problem.*

In Figure 9.3, examine how two third graders completed a frame for the story "Owl at Home." The frame centers on the story's problem. The children bring differing abilities to the task, yet both capture the central focus of the story. As students become familiar with using story frames, you may want to involve them simply in writing summary paragraphs that focus on different elements of the story.

Figure 9.3 Comparison of Story Frames for "Owl at Home"

Tanner's Frame

In this story the problem starts when *Owl thought the moon was following him home.*

After that, *He started walking and he said that the moon was still following him.*

Next, *He was almost home and he still thougt the moon was still following him.*

Then, *he went inside his house and he got his pJ's on.*

The problem is finally solved when *Owl looks out the window and says night to the moon and went to bed.* The story ends *with owl sleeping.*

Renee's Frame

In this story the problem starts when *everything was dark.*

After that, *a tip of the moon appeared over the seashore.*

Next, *Owl watched the moon go higher, higher.*

Then, *They became good friends.*

The problem is finally solved when *Owl went to bed*

The story ends *good*

Circular Story Map   A circular story map uses pictures to depict the sequence of events leading to the problem in the story. This strategy is useful for students whose strengths include visual representation. Using Latino literature, Smolen and Ortiz-Castro (2000) describe how individual figure drawings that represent the major story events can be glued in a circle on poster board to represent the story sequence. Refer to Figure 9.4 for an example of a circular story map based on the picture book *The Always Prayer Shawl* (Oberman, 1994). In this story, a young Jewish boy in Czarist Russia, Adam, moves to the United States during the revolution. Before Adam embarks on his journey, Adam's grandfather gives him a shawl that becomes part of a powerful family tradition passed from generation to generation.

Check Your Understanding 9.1: Gauge your understanding of the skills and concepts in this section.

Figure 9.4 A Circular Story Map Based on the Picture Book *The Always Prayer Shawl* (Oberman, 1994)

Illustrations by Matthew McKeon.

Scaffolding the Development and Teaching of Reading Comprehension Strategies

■ **Scaffold comprehension strategies.**

In order to develop students' comprehension abilities, teachers need to consider multiple levels of reading instruction, including decoding skills, vocabulary development, and context clues, as well as more specific comprehension strategy instruction based on what we know skilled readers do when they read (McLaughlin, 2012; Pressley, 2000). Good readers use an array of strategies in order to comprehend. They make connections as they read; they visualize, infer, and synthesize information; and they ask questions as they read. Teachers need to explicitly teach and demonstrate these strategies so that students know how to construct meaning before, during, and after reading.

2017 ILA Standard

2.2

When teachers explicitly teach strategies with the purpose of eventually fostering independent use of those strategies, teachers are scaffolding instruction. With respect to teaching comprehension, **scaffolded instruction** means that teachers model strategies step-by-step and explicitly demonstrate the processes of thinking before, during, and after one reads. Next, teachers provide the students with guided practice in the strategies, followed by independent practice and application. Strategies, however, should not be taught in isolation; students need to know how to use strategies in a variety of settings and for a variety of purposes. The Common Core State Standards (CCSS) challenge teachers to model strategies so that they will be able to read a myriad of multiple complex texts critically and reflectively (Hollenbeck & Saternus, 2013).

Common Core State Standard

CCRA.R.10

Brown (2008) characterizes the concept of scaffolded teaching as transactional strategies instruction (TSI), a framework for teaching reading comprehension that teachers can use in flexible ways. TSI includes four dimensions: the use of strategies, the gradual release of responsibility, collaborative learning, and interpretive discussion. In Figure 9.5, you will see examples of how teachers implement each dimension.

2017 ILA Standard

2.2

Active Comprehension and Asking Questions

A common comprehension strategy is to have children answer questions about what is read. Traditionally such questions have been organized into three categories:

1. Students answer **literal questions** by using information explicitly stated in the text.
2. Students answer **inferential questions** by using their background knowledge along with information from the text.
3. Students answer **evaluative (or critical reading) questions** by making judgments about what they read.

Figure 9.6 provides examples of each type of question.

When children are engaged in a process of generating questions and making connections throughout reading, they are involved in **active comprehension**. Athans and Devine (2008) recommend using fiction to teach question asking. They suggest that mysteries, science fiction, books with action, and historical fiction work well. See Figure 9.7 for guidelines for teaching questioning. A first-grade teacher, for example, might focus attention on a picture or an illustration from a book. Instead of asking, "What is the picture about?" the teacher poses a question that elicits questions in response: "What would you like to know about the picture?" or "What does this

---

Figure 9.5 Dimensions of Transactional Strategies Instruction

Strategy Instruction Dimension

- Teachers are knowledgeable of research-based strategies and how to teach them.
- Teachers explain why using strategies is important.
- Teachers share how they use strategies when they read.

Gradual Release Dimension

- Teachers model the strategies and explain how they help improve understanding of text.
- Teachers demonstrate how to select strategies to use when reading.
- Teachers cue students in their use of strategies and guide them toward independent practice.

Collaboration Dimension

- Teachers and students work together.
- Teachers encourage students to verify how strategies helped them understand.
- Teachers are flexible and base lessons on students' needs.

Interpretive Discussion Dimension

- Teachers encourage dialogues in which the students respect each other's viewpoints.
- Teachers encourage discussion among students and do not focus on one "correct" answer.
- Teachers encourage students to share what they are thinking and feeling as they use strategies.

Figure 9.6 Types of Questions

A woman walked into a university cafeteria. She was wearing high heels and a navy blue suit, and she was carrying a briefcase. The woman was also wearing a gold band on the fourth finger of her left hand. The woman placed her briefcase on a table and went to the counter to order a cheeseburger, French fries, and a milkshake. When the woman returned to the table, she opened her briefcase and took out a stack of papers and a red pen. There was also a picture drawn in crayon inside the briefcase.

- *Literal questions:* What was the woman wearing? Where was the woman?
- *Inferential questions:* What was the woman going to do with the papers and red pen? What was the woman's occupation?
- *Evaluative questions:* Was the woman eating a healthy meal? If the woman was going to grade papers, should she be using a red pen?

Figure 9.7 Guidelines for Teaching Questioning

The following guidelines will help teachers foster successful questioning by students:

- Help students focus on questions that are relevant to the text being read.
- Show students how to develop questions that make use of information stated earlier in the text.
- Model your curiosity as you read. Encourage students to verbalize their curiosity with phrases such as "I wonder," "What if," and "I'm not sure about . . ."
- Encourage questions that prompt additional questions.

picture remind you of?" In return, students might generate questions that focus on the details, main idea, or inferences from the illustration.

In this **video** (www.youtube.com/watch?v=psakxRT9hdA&list=PL5178787DB725559D), you will see how a teacher is conducting a lesson with young children on questioning as they read a story. How is she effectively engaging the children?

Generating Questions Not only do questions stimulate interest and arouse curiosity, but they also draw students into the story. In the process, students' reading comprehension will be more goal-directed. That is, they will read to satisfy purposes that *they*, not the teacher, have established. When selecting literature for active comprehension, it is important that teachers select stories that foster questions and understandings that reflect the diverse nature of their classrooms. In classrooms of mixed ethnic backgrounds, for example, teachers need to provide students with opportunities to respond to literature that reflects their culture. In addition, encouraging students to ask questions to clarify meaning is important. See how 11-year-old Jessie, a Hispanic student, views questioning in Box 9.1.

There are a variety of ways to encourage students to ask questions. Teachers, however, should be clear on the purpose of generating questions, as well as foster higher-order questioning (Peterson & Taylor, 2012). In the past, teachers typically asked questions after the text was read; this often led struggling readers to feel that the purpose of reading was to answer questions that would be posed by the teacher. Teachers tended to view this as an assessment process. Did the students understand the text or not? Modeling question asking *while reading* and encouraging students to ask *their own questions* fosters ownership in the reading process. The step-by-step lesson in Box 9.2 fosters a smooth transition from teacher-led questions to student-generated questions.

Highlighting sections of copied text, recording questions on sticky notes, developing question maps, and coding questions are several additional strategies that can be effectively used with all students. Harvey and Goudvis (2013) suggest that students can code their questions in the following manner:

BOX 9.1 | STUDENT VOICES

Jessie is an 11-year-old Hispanic fourth grader who experiences academic challenges.

When asked about reading comprehension, Jessie said, "My teacher tells me what I am supposed to know and lets us take it home to read." She also shared that she sometimes makes note cards to study vocabulary and definitions. Jessie was unsure about what strategies she uses to comprehend what she is reading, but she was very clear that she can ask her friend Wuendy, another Honduran student, for help when she doesn't know something. "Mostly Wuendy can help me because she is really smart." When probed further, Jessie shared, "I used to be afraid to ask questions because at my public school I was the only Hispanic in the classroom. But now I can ask. I get better grades now, and I'm not afraid to ask. Nobody really laughs at me anymore. I can speak the language a lot better now. Sometimes I ask someone sitting by me, and the teacher doesn't get mad if I do." Jessie shared that she thinks teachers should allow students to talk about stories after they read them: "I like to talk about the story. My teacher likes us to ask questions as we read, too. I like to do that."

This fourth grader clearly sends us a message about the social nature of learning. Jessie likes to talk, and she is comfortable asking questions. It appears that she is confident in her ability to speak English because she is allowed to converse and inquire about concepts that are unclear to her. The classroom environment for all students ought to foster using language in purposeful ways, and Jessie, as an ELL, confirms how this is important to her when it comes to comprehension and learning.

BOX 9.2 | STEP-BY-STEP LESSON

Teaching Question Generation

1. Discuss the importance of asking questions as you direct students' comprehension of text. Explain that asking questions helps readers "dig deeper" as they figure out what the author is saying.
2. Using a read-aloud, model the types of questions that can be asked about central story content, including the setting, main characters, problem or goal, and obstacles encountered while attempting to resolve the problem or achieve the goal. Include high-order prompts such as "Why?" and "Why not?"
3. As you work through the story, ask questions that require questions in response (e.g., "What would you like to know about the setting of the story?" "What else?" "What would you like to know about the main character?" "Why would you like to know that?" "What would you like to know about what happened next?"). Record questions on chart paper, and discuss the types of information that can be learned by asking questions. Spend several class periods guiding question generation in this manner.
4. Divide the class into small groups of four to six children. Have one student read a text selection aloud and one student play the role of the teacher by eliciting questions from the other members. Have another student record the questions. Circulate around the room to facilitate the process. Spend several class periods in small group question generation. Allow time toward the end of each class period for debriefing with students (e.g., "How did the questioning go?" "Were there any problems?" "Why does question asking make a story easier to read?"). Allow time for each group to share several questions.
5. Have students work in pairs, asking each other questions and recording the questions as they read.
6. Have students work on their own to generate questions. Students can use sticky notes to record their questions. Discuss the questions they raise as a whole group.

ELLs who speak the same language can initially work in their native language together while they master the strategy.

A	means that the question is answered in the text
BK	means it is answered from background knowledge
I	means it is inferred
D	refers to questions that can be answered by further discussion
RS	requires further research for an answer
Huh? or C	signals confusion

For example, while independently reading *The Best Christmas Pageant Ever,* a fourth grader in Ms. Mayer's class might have placed a sticky note labeled "Huh?" next to the word *toolbox* if it was not clear what a *toolbox* was. Another student might have placed a "D" next to the text that states, "The Herdmans were absolutely the worst kids in the history of the world," in hopes of generating a discussion about behaviors that characterize people as "bad." As Harvey and Goudvis suggest, helping students ask questions as they read is an important skill that enhances reading comprehension.

A technological way to encourage questions is through e-mail. In one study, McKeon (1999) found that 9- and 10-year-olds could effectively use e-mail to ask questions about stories they were reading with preservice teacher partners. The fourth graders were partners with education students for a 14-week semester, and they e-mailed weekly. After getting to know each other socially, the dialogue turned to electronic conversations about a book that the teacher had selected based on a social studies theme. Initially, the preservice teachers asked the students questions about the literature; eventually, the fourth graders were encouraged to ask questions of their own. The lowest level readers in this study did in fact ask the most questions.

Regardless of the approach used to develop students' ability to ask questions as they read, it is important that teachers model questions of their own. This is a crucial instructional component of enhancing the active comprehension of all readers. In addition, it is critical that teachers of ELLs select literature that is culturally relevant to the students. If learning to comprehend stories is to occur through the social interaction that asking questions demands, teachers need to be cognizant of the background knowledge of culturally diverse students. Drucker (2003) makes a case in point regarding this issue. If the students are reading a story about a birthday party, for example, can we assume that children from other cultures have the same schema for what a birthday party is? Hence, teachers of ELLs need to carefully select literature in which the students will have adequate prior knowledge that enables them to ask questions as they read. Next, we address additional strategies that involve students thinking and questioning as they read.

Reciprocal Questioning (ReQuest)

Reciprocal questioning, also known as **ReQuest**, is another strategy that encourages students to ask their own questions about the material being read (Manzo, 1969; Vacca & Vacca, 2011). Although ReQuest was originally designed for one-on-one instruction, it is easily adapted for small group work. Here's how it works.

- The teacher selects a story for the group to read and divides the literature into logical stopping points.
- The group, including the teacher, reads the first section silently with the intent of asking a question or questions after reading.
- The teacher models questions, and small group discussion takes place.
- The next section is read silently followed by another question or questions by the teacher and small group discussion.
- After the next section is read, the children begin asking their questions, followed by group talk.
- The procedure continues with the teacher and students taking turns asking questions.

Initially questions will tend to be literal. It is important for teachers to model higher-level questions such as *why, why not, how come, how do you know, what do you think?* After practice and guidance with the teacher, the children work in small groups as they craft their questions.

See how one group of children implements ReQuest in Box 9.3.

Whenever students are asked to generate questions, some will not know how to do so. Others will ask only literal questions because they don't know how to ask questions that will stimulate inferential or evaluative levels of thinking. One way to deal

BOX 9.3 | STEP-BY-STEP LESSON

Implementing Reciprocal Questioning (ReQuest)

This group of third graders has just read the beginning of the fairy tale *Cinderella*. See how they question each other.

Maria: What do you think about the setting?

Jon: I think the people are poor.

Maria: What about the setting?

Jon: Cinderella has a hole in her dress. She is poor.

Jack: I think the people are rich.

Maria: What about the setting? What tells you they are rich?

Jack: There is a big clock and lots of fancy furniture. Jon, why do you think they are poor?

Jon: Because Cinderella's clothes are all ripped.

Maria: But Jack said there is fancy furniture. How could they be poor?

Jon: Maybe Cinderella is just poor.

Maria: But what about the setting? Where does the story take place?

Jon: In a rich house because there is fancy furniture.

Jack: I think so, too. But I think Cinderella's clothes are torn because she is poor and she is working in a rich house.

Maria: How do you think Cinderella feels?

Jon: I think she is sad.

Maria: Why do you think she is sad?

Jon: Because she is crying quietly to herself.

Jack: I think she is sad, too. The mean sisters yelled at her.

Maria: How do you feel when someone yells at you?

Jon: It makes me mad.

Jack: Once my mom yelled at me because she thought I ate the last cookie and my brother did it. It made me sad that she thought I did it. But I wasn't really mad.

Be sure to include literature for which ELLs have prior knowledge.

---

with these situations is to provide a model that students will learn from. Prompts can be displayed in the classroom to assist students. Over time you will notice the difference in students' ability to pose higher-level questions.

Question–Answer Relationships (QARs)

When asking questions, special attention should be given to the most likely source of information the reader needs to answer the question. Certain questions can be thought of as *textually explicit,* or literal, because they promote recall or recognition of *information actually stated in the text.* Other questions are *textually implicit,* or inferential, because they provoke thinking. Readers must search for text relationships and think about the information presented. If students are to integrate ideas within a text, textually implicit questions are likely to be the most useful. Finally, some questions place the reader's knowledge of the world at the center of the questioning activity. Such questions are *schema based.* Because students' schemata will vary depending on the nature of their diverse backgrounds, teachers must be knowledgeable about the students' various cultures. And because students must rely on their own resources as well as the text to solve problems, discover new insights, or evaluate the significance of what was read, teachers should include reading material that reflects the students' backgrounds.

Question–answer relationships (QARs), as proposed by Raphael (1986), help learners know what information sources are available for seeking answers to different types of text questions. Through this strategy, readers become more sensitive to the different mental operations and text demands required by different questions. As a result, teachers and students become cognizant of the three-way relationships that exist among the question, the text to which it refers, and the background knowledge and information at the reader's disposal. QARs enhance children's ability to answer comprehension questions by teaching them how to find information they need to answer questions. Explicit instruction will make students sensitive to two information sources where answers can be found. The CCSS make it explicitly clear that these skills are critical for effective reading.

Common Core State Standard

CCRA.R.1

The first information source is the *text*. Some answers to questions can be found *right there* in the text. Other answers found in the text, however, demand a *think-and-search* strategy in which students *search* the text for information and *think* about the relationships that exist among the bits of information found. For example, if the question about a house is "What color is the house?" and the text reads, "The old house was white," the answer to the question is *right there* because it is directly stated. On the other hand, if the question about the house is "What characteristics of the house indicate that it is haunted?" the answer would involve *thinking and searching* for clues that the author gives about the house being haunted. Such clues might include "the house is spooky," "the residents claimed to feel the presence of ghosts," or "weird sounds could be heard at midnight."

The second information source is the *reader*. Some questions signal to the reader "I am on my own." Other questions may signal "It's up to the author and me." In either case, the text may help, but answers must come from inside the reader's mind. A question such as "How would you feel about being in a haunted house?" might elicit the response, "I would be scared. I was in a spooky house on Halloween once and it was creepy." This answer would be "on my own" because it reflects personal prior knowledge. The use of Right There, Think and Search, Author and You, and On My Own are mnemonics to help readers recognize question–answer relationships. A chart such as the one in Figure 9.8 can be used to make readers aware of QARs.

The research-based practices featured in Box 9.4 will assist students in their understanding and use of QARs.

See an example of a short narrative text selection with QARs in Figure 9.9.

Questioning the Author (QtA)

Questioning the author (QtA) is another instructional strategy that models for students the importance of asking questions while reading. Beck, McKeown, Hamilton, and Kucan (1997) devised the QtA strategy to demonstrate the kinds of questions students need to ask in order to think more deeply and construct meaning about segments of text as they read. The strategy is based on the notion that successful readers act on the author's message. If what they are reading doesn't make sense to them, successful readers raise questions about what the author says and means. QtA shows students how to read text closely as if the author were there to be challenged and questioned. A key feature of the CCSS is to ensure that students are able to analyze what the author is saying and critically evaluate the author's claims.

QtA places value on the quality and depth of students' responses to the author's intent. It is important that students keep their minds active while reading as they engage in a dialogue with an author. A successful reader monitors whether the author is making sense by asking questions such as "What is the author trying to say here?" "What does the author mean?" "So what? What is the significance of the author's message?" "Does this make sense with what the author told us before?" "Does the author explain this clearly?" These questions, according to Beck et al. (1997), are posed by the teacher to help students "take on" the author and understand that text material needs to be challenged. Through QtA, students learn that authors are fallible

Effective teachers help students make connections and question the author to clarify misunderstandings.

Annie Pickert Fuller/Pearson Education

Figure 9.8 Introducing Question–Answer Relationships

Think and Search

The answer is in the text, but the words used in the question and those used for the answer are not in the same sentence. You need to think about different parts of the text and how ideas can be put together before you can answer the question.

Right There

The answer is in the text. The words used in the question and the words used for the answer can usually be found in the same sentence.

or

In My Head

Author and You

The answer is not in the text. You need to think about what you know, what the author says, and how they fit together.

On My Own

The text got you thinking, but the answer is inside your head. The author can't help you much. So think about the question, and use what you know already to answer it.

BOX 9.4 | RESEARCH-BASED PRACTICES

Steps in the Development of Students' Understanding of QARs

The QAR instructional strategy enhances students' ability to answer comprehension questions. Raphael (1982, 1986) recommends the following steps for developing students' understanding of QARs:

Day 1

- Introduce the concept of QARs by showing students a chart containing a description of the basic question–answer relationships: Right There, Think and Search, Author and

You, On My Own. The chart should be positioned in a prominent place in the classroom so that students may refer to it whenever the need arises.

- Begin QAR instruction by assigning students three short passages (no more than two to five sentences in length). Follow each reading with one question from each of the QAR categories on the chart.

- Then discuss the differences between a Right There question and answer, a Think and Search question and answer, an Author and You question and answer, and an On My Own question and answer. Explanations should be clear and complete.

- Reinforce the discussion by assigning several more short passages and asking a question for each. Students will soon begin to catch on to the differences among the QAR categories.

Day 2

- Continue practicing with short passages, using one question for each QAR category per passage. First, give students a passage to read with questions *and* answers *and* identified QARs. Why do the questions and answers represent one QAR and not another?

- Second, give students a passage with questions and answers; this time they have to identify the QAR for each.

- Finally, give students passages, decide together which strategy to use, and have them write their responses.

Day 3

- Conduct a brief review. Then assign a longer passage (75 to 200 words) with up to five questions (at least one each from the QAR categories).

- Have students work in groups to decide the QAR category for each question and the answers for each.

- Next, assign a second passage, comparable in length, with five questions for students to work on individually.

Discuss responses either in small groups or with the whole class.

Day 4

- Apply the QAR strategy to actual reading situations. For each question asked, students decide on the appropriate QAR strategy and write out their answers. Here is an example:

What is Jack's problem?

_____ Right There
_____ Think and Search
_____ Author and You
_____ On My Own

Answer:

(Discussion follows.)

- Once students are sensitive to different information sources for different types of questions and know how to use these sources to respond to questions, variations can be made in the QAR strategy. For example, during a discussion, consider prefacing a question by saying, "This question is *right there* in the text" or "You'll have to *think and search* the text to answer" or "You're *on your own* with this one." Make sure that you pause several seconds or more for "think time."

Source: Based on "Teaching Question–Answer Relationships Revisited," by T. E. Raphael, 1986, *The Reading Teacher, 39,* pp. 516–522.

Figure 9.9 Short Narrative Text Selection with OARs

Anthony was very excited because his birthday was in just four days. He was going on another adventure with his grandparents, and they were going to collect rocks again. Anthony had quite a collection of rocks! He sure hoped the weather would be nice and warm and sunny. He already had his outfit picked out; he was going to wear a brand-new pair of blue jeans with a t-shirt that is special because his grandparents gave it to him last year at this time. Anthony figured he should bring a sweatshirt along in case the weather was cool. "Just in case!" he thought to himself. Anthony wondered and wondered what he should bring to gather the rocks this time!

Right There Questions

Why is Anthony excited? *[It says "right there" that his birthday is soon and he is going on an adventure with his grandparents.]*

What is Anthony going to do with his grandparents? *[It says "right there" that he is going to collect rocks with them.]*

Think and Search Question

How has Anthony prepared for this adventure? *[It says "here" that he has selected what to wear. It also says "here" what he will bring along in case the weather is cool. It says "here" he is wondering what he should bring to gather his rocks.]*

On My Own Questions

What do think is Anthony's hobby? *[Collecting rocks because when someone collects something it is often called a hobby.]*

How does Anthony feel about his grandparents? *[It seems like he loves them because he is excited to go on an adventure with them and appreciates that they are making his day special, and he is going to wear the t-shirt they gave him last year because it is meaningful to him. Usually when you feel that way about someone like your grandparents, you love them.]*

---

and may not always express ideas in the easiest way for readers to understand. QtA builds metacognitive knowledge by making students aware of an important principle related to reading comprehension: *Not comprehending what the author is trying to say is not always the fault of the reader.* As a result, students come to view their roles as readers as "grappling with text" as they seek to make sense of the author's intent.

Common Core State Standard

CCRA.R.8

Step by Step Lesson: Slide to hide and reveal the steps outlines the steps for planning QtA lessons for narrative or informational texts.

When using QtA to comprehend stories, pose *narrative queries.* Through the use of narrative queries, students become familiar with an author's writing style as they strive to understand character, plot, and underlying story meaning. The following queries help students think about story characters: "How do things look for this character now?" "Given what the author has already told us about this character, what do you think the author is up to?" Understanding the story plot can be accomplished with queries such as these: "How has the author let you know that something has changed?" "How has the author settled this for us?" The thoughtful use of queries is vital for classroom discussion. As students actively explore and clarify meaning, guide the discussion as you progress from one text segment to the next.

Close Reading

Close reading involves reading short selections of complex text multiple times and examining the text for evidence that answers text-specific questions. The concept is similar to the "Right There" and "Think and Search" approach implemented in QARs, as well the QtA strategy. A difference is that the same selection is read several times in order to locate, explain, identify, and be able to discuss and analyze the text in depth and support answers to questions with examples from the text. Hence, a purpose of close reading is to gain multiple levels of meaning for different purposes through analysis (Beers & Probst, 2013; Hinchman & Moore, 2013; Lapp, Moss, Johnson, & Grant, 2013).

A key focus of the CCSS is to foster **close reading** by developing a wide range of proficiencies including the ability to make logical inferences, to identify and summarize main ideas and details, to analyze text structure, and to interpret how words are used in texts; thus, an important purpose of close reading is teaching children how to read analytically.

Common Core Standards

CCRA.R.1, CCRA.R.2, CCRA.R.3, CCRA.R.4, CCRA.R.5, CCRA.R.6

Teachers can engage students in a variety of ways to document evidence as they read. **Annotating text** is a notetaking strategy in which students jot down thoughts within the actual text and margins that indicate the evidence that supports text-based questions. In addition, highlighters, colored pens, or pencils can be used to mark the selection. Some teachers have students use sticky-notes to make annotations; others use charts or notebooks. Using a "code" to mark information is also common. Question marks may indicate confusing sections; a W may indicate a word that is unclear; an exclamation point might indicate a surprising turn of events. Whatever strategy is used, in order to be effective, teachers need to model for students the process of annotating. See the step-by-step framework for getting started with close reading in Box 9.5.

Common Core Standard

CCRA.R.4

 In this **video** (www.youtube.com/watch?v=HDfv3B_JZQo), you will see a teacher conducting a close reading lesson. What characteristics of close reading do you observe?

BOX 9.5 | STEP-BY-STEP LESSON

Implementing Close Reading Instruction

No step-by-step lesson plan is "set in stone" for teachers as they assist students in the skills that capture close reading. However, the following guidelines support the purposes, and goals, of close reading instruction.

First, the teacher should select a short text or story that captures at least one or two of the CCSS that exemplify goals. The teacher needs to choose a selection that lends itself to reading the text for specific purposes. For example, one purpose might be to examine the author's choice of words to find evidence of a point of view. This step is critical. If teachers simply select a text or story at random, the goals of close reading will probably not be defined.

Second, the teacher should examine the text and develop focus questions to which the students can respond with evidence from the text based on the goals that were established in the first place. For example, what words or phrases give you a sense of the mood of the story?

Third, the teacher should establish ahead of time how the students will read the passage and document the evidence they find regarding the question. Will they annotate on a copy of the passage? Will they add thoughts in a notebook? Will they use sticky notes to document their evidence? For example, the students might highlight words that provide evidence of the mood.

Fourth, the teacher needs to decide how the evidence to questions will be shared. Will it be through small group discussion? Will it be through whole class participation? Will it be through one-on-one conferencing? For example, the students might work in small groups and develop a chart that captures words and phrases in the selection that indicate the mood of the story.

Fifth, the teacher needs to consider how learning will be documented. Will anecdotal records be used to informally report student progress? Will the teacher have a chart that records students' abilities to read closely based on specific criteria? Will the teacher videotape students' discussions and analyze their responses later? Will a predetermined rubric be used? Based on the example above, the teacher might simply observe the children in small groups and put a check mark next to students' names on a class list if they appear to grasp the initial goal of locating words that capture the mood of the story and take anecdotal notes on the students who seem to struggle.

Instructional Decision Making 9.1: Apply your understanding of the concepts in this section.

For decades, comprehension instruction has featured activating schema and encouraging children to share personal responses to literature as important components of engaging children in reading (Rosenblatt, 1978, 1982, 2004). Teachers activate schema, or prior knowledge, about a topic to help children relate to the story, and they are invited to share individual reactions to the story often based on those experiences. In close reading, however, activating prior knowledge is discouraged; the focus should be to gather information from the text itself, and personal responses are not considered important (Boyles, 2012, 2013; Dalton, 2013; Dobler, 2013; Serafini, 2013).

We believe that schema and personal responses to literature do have roles in teaching reading comprehension, depending on the nature and purpose of reading the story, as well as the instructional needs of the students doing the reading. The key word here is *purpose*. Activating schema should not simply be an activity that teachers "do" out of habit; the purpose should be related to the context of the reading selection. If, for example, the text is about an imaginary trip to the moon, discussing what students know about the moon and what they would expect to find would probably not be worthwhile. The purpose would be to read the story and *find out* what was discovered during the adventure. If, on the other hand, the theme of the story was about the *struggles* that a man experienced living in poverty in a slum in New York City, discussing what a "slum" is *might be* appropriate, depending on the characteristics of the class. Students living in a rural area surrounded by farms might have no idea what a slum is; hence the struggles of the man might not make any sense unless the concept was discussed first.

With respect to encouraging personal responses to literature, we agree that sometimes students get so engaged in sharing their own experiences that they do not rely on the text for explicit information. On the other hand, why would a teacher not allow children to share their individual responses to literature? After all, learning is social, and individual differences, experiences, and feelings are all part of the social realities of making sense of the world. Again, we believe that the key word is *purpose*. Certainly if the reason for reading a story or short text selection is to analyze what the author is saying, personal connections are less important. However, when the purpose of reading a story is to relate to the characters, the problem, or solution to the problem on an aesthetic level, the goal of reading the story changes. If students are always engaged in analyzing what the text "says," through closely reading a story over and over for evidence, it is very possible that students will become *disengaged* with reading (Snow, 2013). As such, we believe that teachers need to balance close reading with attention and opportunities for students to express their personal experiences, thoughts, and love of reading certain stories.

During reciprocal teaching, students assume the role of the teacher as they discuss the text.

Annie Pickert Fuller/Pearson Education

Reciprocal Teaching

Reciprocal teaching is an approach to scaffolding reading comprehension in which teachers introduce four strategies, model the strategies, and gradually encourage independent use of the strategies in small groups as students take on the role of the teacher (Palincsar & Brown, 1984; Rosenshine & Meister, 1994). The four strategies are (1) predicting what the text is about, (2) raising questions about the text, (3) summarizing the text, and (4) clarifying difficult vocabulary and concepts.

In reciprocal teaching, the teacher begins the lesson by modeling each of the four comprehension activities while leading a discussion of the text. During this phase of the lesson, the quality of the dialogue between teacher and students depends on how explicit the teacher is in demonstrating each of the comprehension activities.

After observing the teacher, students are invited to share or add to what the teacher has stated and then to teach the remaining sections of the text selection. For example, a student assumes the role of the teacher and proceeds to model one or more of the comprehension activities on the next segment of text. If the students run into trouble with any of the activities, the teacher reenters the lesson to provide support by adjusting the demands of the task. Gradually, the teacher withdraws support and the students continue teaching the lesson. In the step-by-step lesson featured in Box 9.6, we provide a framework for developing reciprocal teaching lessons.

2017 ILA Standard

2.2

Think-Alouds

A **think-aloud** is a strategy in which teachers and students share their thoughts, discuss what they wonder about and what confuses them, and make connections *as* they are reading. A prime opportunity to conduct think-alouds is when teachers read aloud to students (Santoro, Chard, Howard, & Baker, 2008; Scharlach, 2008). By modeling comprehension strategies that involve asking questions, making predictions, visualizing, making judgments, and sharing personal connections, teachers invite students to share their own thoughts. Hence, think-alouds during teacher read-alouds provide a window to view what is going on in the minds of the students as they read.

BOX 9.6 | STEP-BY-STEP LESSON

Framework for Developing Reciprocal Teaching Lessons

Explain to the students that they are going to learn four ways to be "the teacher." They are going to learn how to make predictions, how to ask questions, how to summarize, and how to talk about challenging words or parts of a story. Explain that these are four strategies what good readers think about when they read. Post a chart that is entitled "Ways to Think as I Read," and list the following words: *predict, ask questions, summarize,* and *talk about hard stuff.*

Next, explain that you are going to show the students the first step, how to make predictions, so they can practice being the teacher. After they learn the first step, you will teach them the other steps so they can practice each one.

Week One: Model How to Make Predictions

1. Select a picture book and do a picture walk, modeling how to make predictions using the illustrations.
2. Divide the students into small groups, and provide each group with a picture book; have each group practice making predictions using the illustrations. Allow each student a turn to be "the teacher."
3. Select a read-aloud, and model how to make predictions based on a portion of the text.

4. Using a class anthology or set of trade books, have the students follow along as you read aloud the beginning of a story. Model how to make predictions based on the text. Have the students work in their small groups as they continue to read the story and practice being "the teacher" by making predictions based on "stopping points" that you have selected.
5. Select another story, and have the students work with a partner to practice making predictions based on stopping points. You can have the students place sticky notes on the pages that indicate stopping points.
6. Provide ample time for the students to practice making predictions when they read independently. Teachers can conference with students during independent reading time about their predictions.

Continue the reciprocal teaching strategy by modeling how to ask questions, summarize, and clarify difficult words or concepts. Depending on the abilities of the students, some strategies may require more or less time. Regardless of the time it takes for the students to master each step, it is critical that they understand the purpose of each strategy and how to use it independently depending on the nature of the text. Be sure to include literature in which ELLs have sufficient schemata.

To conduct a think-aloud, the teacher should select a passage that elicits ambiguity, difficult vocabulary, or contradictions. As the teacher reads aloud, the students follow along silently and listen as the teacher describes what he or she is thinking. After modeling, the students are encouraged to describe their thoughts. Examine **Straight from the Classroom** to see how Beth uses a think-aloud to encourage visual imagery and discussion in a story. Students can also work with partners to share their thinking.

In summary, strategy instruction lets children in on the secrets of reading comprehension. What they discover through explicit instructional techniques like reciprocal teaching and QtA is that meaning doesn't lie hidden in text like buried treasure, waiting for readers to dig it out. On the contrary, readers must actively engage in reading to construct meaning. Reading comprehension is triggered by the knowledge that readers bring to print. Through explicit strategy instruction, teachers provide all students, including those from diverse backgrounds, with opportunities to make connections between what they are reading and their prior experiences. Culturally and linguistically diverse students especially benefit from instructional strategy demonstrations when they are modeled in small groups. In fact, the most effective programs for ELLs are those that include collaborative, interactive learning. In addition, middle school students who are exposed to increasingly difficult reading material need explicit strategy instruction in comprehension in all of their classes (Moore, Bean, Birdyshaw, & Rycik, 1999).

Check Your Understanding 9.2: Gauge your understanding of the skills and concepts in this section.

Guiding Interactions Between Reader and Text

■ **Guide readers' interactions with text.**

Literacy skills for the twenty-first century demand a myriad of critical thinking and problem-solving skills, including how to reason effectively, analyze, make judgments, evaluate evidence, interpret information, and draw conclusions, to name a few (Trilling & Fadel, 2009). In addition, the CCSS (2010a) require that students be able to read complex text on multiple levels (Lapp et al., 2013). Hence, elementary and middle school readers need to become deep thinkers who are aware of and skilled at interpreting dense text, as well as able to recognize when shifts in thinking occur during reading. The shifts may involve an author's transition to a new topic, changes in setting, twists in the plot, and so on. Or the author may put demands on the reader's ability to make inferences.

Common Core State Standard

CCRA.R.10

For whatever reason, many youngsters run into trouble while reading because they don't know *how* or *when* to adjust their thinking as a particular reading selection demands. Suppose you were teaching a class in which most of the students had appropriate background knowledge for the reading selection. Discussion before reading activates schemata, and students approach the selection with anticipation of what lies ahead in the material. But somewhere during reading, you sense that the readers are having trouble understanding the story. Some look confused as they read; a couple raise their hands to ask for clarification. Others just plow ahead; whether they are comprehending is anyone's guess.

Readers sometimes get lost in a jumble of details or bogged down in the conceptual complexity of the selection. The prereading activity initiated at the beginning of the lesson, though necessary, wasn't sufficient to maintain readers' interactions with the text. As a result, they're able to process only bits and pieces of information but fail to grasp the author's intent and message. How can you help? Or suppose you were teaching a class in which multiple cultures and languages were represented and the students had little background knowledge for the story. What would you do?

2017 ILA Standard

3.2

Assigning questions *after* reading may clarify some of the confusion but does little to show readers how to interact with the author's ideas *during* reading. This is why guiding reader–text interactions is an important part of comprehension instruction. In this section, we explain instructional strategies that teachers find useful for this purpose. It is important that teachers provide the purpose for learning each strategy and that students are given multiple opportunities to use the strategies with a variety of complex texts. Students need to understand that the strategies will help them think as they read (Brassell & Rasinski, 2008; Burkins & Croft, 2010; Fountas & Pinnell, 2012; Hollenbeck & Saternus, 2013).

2017 ILA Standard

2.2

Directed Reading–Thinking Activity

The **directed reading–thinking activity (DR–TA)** builds critical awareness of the reader's role and responsibility in interacting with the text. The DR–TA strategy involves readers in

Figure 9.10 Potential Stopping Points and Open-Ended Questions in a DR–TA

Title

What do you think this story is going to be about?

Why do you think so?

STOP

Setting, introduction of characters, and beginning event

What do you think is going to happen next?

Why do you think so?

STOP

Character's response and goal or problem

What do you think is going to happen next?

Why do you think so?

STOP

Attempts made to alleviate problem and achieve goal

What do you think is going to happen next?

Why do you think so?

STOP

Outcomes or attempts and resolution of problem

STOP

Character's reaction to events

the process of predicting, verifying, judging, and extending thinking about the text material.

Common Core State Standard

CCRA.R.1

To prepare a DR–TA for a story, analyze its structure first by mapping the important story parts; next, decide on logical stopping points within the story. In Figure 9.10, we indicate a general plan that may be adapted for specific stories.

Initial predictions are often off the mark. This is to be expected as students' predictions are fueled by background knowledge and experience. The DR–TA begins with very open-ended or divergent responses and moves toward more accurate predictions and text-based inferences as students acquire information from the reading. It is critical that teachers scaffold students' ability to read the text closely and justify predictions based on explicit and implicit information found in the text. See the step-by-step lesson featured in Box 9.7 for general procedures in using the DR–TA strategy.

Discussion Webs

Discussion webs require students to explore both sides of an issue during discussion before drawing conclusions (Alvermann, 1991). When classroom discussions occur, they can quickly become dominated by the teacher or a few vocal students. In an effort to move the discussion forward, the teacher may ask too many questions too quickly. Usually children are more reticent about participating or becoming involved when discussions are monopolized by teacher talk or the talk of one or two students. This can be particularly true for students from diverse linguistic and cultural backgrounds. Discussion webs help balance the conversation.

2017 ILA Standards

2.2, 2.3

The discussion web strategy uses a graphic aid to guide children's thinking about the ideas they want to contribute to the discussion. The graphic aid is illustrated in Figure 9.11. In the center of the web is a question. The question reflects more than one point of view. Students explore the pros and cons of the question in the No and Yes columns of the web—in pairs and then in groups of four. The main goal of the four-member group is to draw a conclusion based on the discussion of the web. Drawing conclusions and problem solving are critically important skills. A discussion web can visualize the process for the learner.

Common Core State Standard

CCRA.R.8

When students use discussion webs, there is usually a high degree of participation; they are eager to hear how other groups reach consensus and draw conclusions. In Gloria Rieckert's class, sixth graders use discussion webs to think about several dilemmas that Billy, the main character, faces in the book *Where the Red Fern Grows* by

BOX 9.7 | STEP-BY-STEP LESSON

Steps in the Directed Reading–Thinking Activity (DR–TA)

Two features that distinguish the DR–TA from some of the other instructional strategies for guiding reader–text interactions are (1) that the students read the same material at the same time and (2) that the teacher makes frequent use of three questions to prompt inquiry and discussion: "What do you think?" "Why do you think so?" and "Can you prove it?"

Steps in the DR–TA Plan

1. Choose an interesting narrative (informational text can also be used). If you choose a story, initiate the DR–TA by having students focus on the title and illustrations and ask them to predict what the selection will be about. Ask, "What do you think this story will be about?" "Why do you think so?"
2. Write students' predictions on chart paper or the marker-board so there is a visible record to which students can refer during discussion. Then invite students to read silently to a logical stopping point. Ask, "Now that you have had a chance to read the beginning of the story, what do you think it is about?" "Would anyone like to change predictions or make new ones?" Add and delete initial prediction on the chart. After students have made or refined predictions, ask, "How do you know? Read the lines that prove it." Redirect questions as needed.
3. When there are no more ideas, invite students to read the next text segment silently. Ask similar questions and other related ones. Add and delete responses to the chart.
4. Have students continue reading the text, stopping at logical points, and engaging in the same cycle of questions until the story is finished. Throughout the process, be sure to have students justify their predictions.

To assist ELLs in the strategy, the teacher can work with small groups of children. During the activity, the teacher should scaffold responses to the questions with prompts such as "Can you tell me more?" "What else?"

Figure 9.11 Discussion Web for *Where the Red Fern Grows*

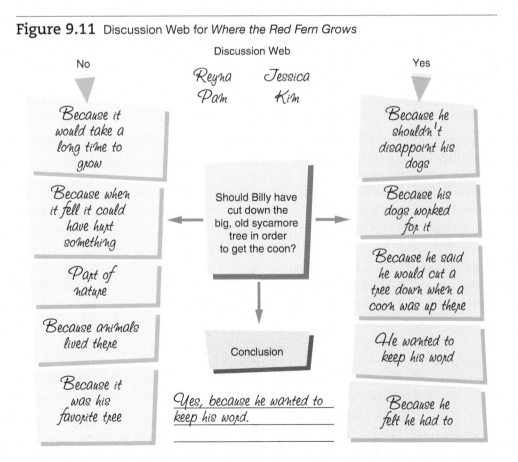

Figure 9.12 Dialogic Examples of Making Text Connections

Text-to-Self Connections Based on *Goldilocks and the Three Bears*
Teacher: Goldilocks reminds me of my sister. She has really long, blond hair.
Student: Goldilocks reminds me of my sister. She loves adventures.
Student: Goldilocks reminds me of me. I love to take hikes in the woods.

Text-to-Text Connections Based on *Cinderella*
Teacher: The part at the end reminds me of the book we read, *The Shoemaker and the Elves*, because that was about magical shoes, too, and both stories had happy endings!
Student: It reminds me of that nursery rhyme *The Old Woman in the Shoe.* That was about a shoe in a different way. That old woman had so many children. I don't know how she managed it!
Student: I don't have a connection about shoes, but I do remember a story that has magical stuff. It was *Peter Pan*, and Tinker Bell was magical to me. The fairy godmother in *Cinderella* was pretty magical, too.

Text-to-World Connections Based on *Little Red Riding Hood*
Teacher: This story makes me think about caring. My grandma needs help sometimes, and I have to take care of her. I think we need to take care of older people who need help.
Student: I think this reminds me of bad things that people do, like the wolf. He was mean.
Student: It makes me think about wood choppers. Are they real people? How do you learn to be a wood chopper? Where do they live? How much money do they make?

Wilson Rawls. The discussion web shown in Figure 9.12 asks the question, "Should Billy have cut down the big, old sycamore tree in order to get the coon?" Reyna, Pam, Jessica, and Kim reach a yes consensus on the question, but Reyna still has her doubts and Jessica clearly voices a dissenting view. Each member follows up the discussion by writing his or her response to the question.

Readers have an opportunity through discussion webs to view and refine their own interpretations of a text in light of the points of view shared by others. Students from diverse backgrounds benefit from multiple opportunities to express their points of view based on their cultural heritage (Spangenberg-Urbschat & Pritchard, 1994). They also benefit from instructional practices that include cooperative learning (Banks, 2014). Discussion webs afford students a collaborative way to enhance their comprehension by making connections to the story and listening to the connections made by other members of the group.

Text Connections

As you probably realize by now, a critical feature of teaching students to actively think while they read is to help them relate their prior knowledge to what they are reading. Teaching and encouraging students to relate what they are reading to their own experiences fosters comprehension as students relate what they are reading to themselves. An explicit way to teach children to do this is to model and provide opportunities for them to make **text connections.** Text connections can be thought of in three ways: text-to-self, text-to-text, and text-to-world (Harvey & Goudvis, 2007).

TEXT-TO-SELF   This is a text connection that asks the students to share what a piece of text reminds them of personally. For narrative text, this is typically related to the plot of the story, the actions of a character, the setting, the problem, or the solution. The possibilities are endless.

TEXT-TO-TEXT   This is a text connection that asks the students to recall *another text* that reminds them of the one they are reading. For example, a child reading *Goldilocks and the Three Bears* might make a connection that there are three characters in *The Story of the Three Little Pigs*, too. On more sophisticated levels students might recognize similar problems in stories, similar character traits, or similar settings. Again, the possibilities are endless.

TEXT-TO-WORLD   This type of connection is more inferential in nature because it asks the students to make connections beyond the story. What world issues does this story bring to mind? Does *Goldilocks and the Three Bears* bring up issues of theft? Does *The Story of the Three Little Pigs* bring up issues of starvation? The text-to-world connections should be reserved for older students who are capable of making higher-level inferences and connections. In Figure 9.12 you will find examples of text connections.

Technology and Twenty-First-Century Reading Comprehension Skills

New literacies, especially technological advances and access to the Internet, have significantly broadened contemporary viewpoints regarding reading comprehension (Coiro & Moore, 2012; Goldman, Braasch, Wiley, Graesser, & Brodowinska, 2012; Karchmer-Klein & Shinas, 2012; Leu et al., 2011). Below we highlight important differences that teachers need to consider when engaging students in online reading. Underlying these points are factors that will influence students' understanding of online text.

First, digital text is nonlinear. Whereas reading linear text (books, magazines, newspapers, etc.) essentially involves turning pages to make sense of what the author is presenting to the reader, online text is fluid and provides the reader with an infinite number of ways to navigate the story or information that include multiple resources and, hence, multiple skills. Although reading informational text such as the newspaper involves decision-making skills, such as "Where in the newspaper can I find the score of last night's baseball game?" searching for information on the web involves more complex decision-making abilities. The reader, for example, needs to decide which search engine to use, what key words to include in a search for information, and ultimately what results of the search to explore. Once an initial site for exploration is selected, a myriad of additional skills is needed: reading and clicking on menu items, selecting hyperlinks, browsing, close reading, clicking on video clips and images, to name a few.

These aptitudes also involve critically thinking about the credibility of multiple resources, how to evaluate information, how to synthesize findings, and what to do with the knowledge. These are significant skills that teachers need to address when engaging students with reading online. In addition, since the information on the web is endless, teachers need to prepare students in developing both specific and open-ended purposes for reading and how to organize new information with prior knowledge.

Common Core State Standards

CCRA.R.7, CCRA.R.8, CCRA.W.6, CCRA.W.8

Another essential set of skills necessary for successful online reading is the ability to communicate the information effectively, as well as to problem solve collaboratively (Leu et al., 2011). Online stories, for example, offer the reader (and teachers) myriad ways to respond and relate to text via the arts, videos, and creative renditions of the stories. Perhaps more importantly, students need essential skills that will help them to communicate and problem solve informational web-related information in a variety of formats such as blogs, wikis, and shared spaces. In essence, several of the critical goals for students of the twenty-first century, as indicated by the CCSS, are to be able to examine and evaluate new information, conduct research using multiple technological mediums, craft solutions to new problems, and communicate ideas effectively.

The enhancement of reading comprehension with the use of interactive CD-ROMs also demonstrates the complex implications that technology holds for teaching reading. For example, Pearman (2008) suggests that second graders who read with CD-ROMs significantly improve their retellings of what they read. Using interactive CD-ROMs can provide substantial benefits for struggling readers' comprehension, including work with vocabulary and word pronunciation, when highlighted words are clicked.

Common Core State Standards

CCRA.W.6, CCRA.W.8

BOX 9.8

Transliteracy and Comprehension

During the development of a literate society, literacy practices were very linear in nature. Consider a traditional piece of literature, like a book. It has a cover with the title and author. When we address these elements, we begin by decoding letters and words starting in the upper left and moving to the right across the first line to develop meaning and comprehend printed text. We then open the book, turn the page, and then again begin to read for meaning making, starting in the upper left, moving across to the right, and then down to the next line. This repetitive process reflects the literacy practices most of us have participated in since childhood.

Literacy in a digital age is much more than interacting with traditional print materials. In addition to the books, newspapers, and magazines we are all comfortable with, we now interact with digital text, e-books, blogs, websites, video, and audio. These additional components mean literacy in a digital age is not a linear process, but more of a hyperlinked experience where students need to locate information, read, process, find links to other relevant information, and move on. These transliteracy practices are beginning to merge traditional literacy components with the nuances of living in a touchscreen world. The understanding that information can be located, interpreted, and applied through a series of taps, touches, and swipes is indeed a new type of reading comprehension that educators must model and share with students of all ages.

At this time, we do not know a lot about the extent to which emerging digital materials, such as e-books, can support comprehension. In many cases, e-books possess digital features designed to provide evidence-based instruction. For example, an e-book or other online text that offers animations to support the text would be similar to an adult or teacher who offers explanations of what is happening within a story. Having students repeatedly use the Read-to-Me feature of an e-book would be akin to a teacher offering repeated reading of a text to support understanding of the plot. How effective these built-in digital scaffolds are in aiding student comprehension remains to be seen; however, one thing is certain. Teachers need to draw students' attention to digital features that can help support comprehension and to explicitly model how students can use them to bolster their learning.

2017 ILA Standard

5.3

In summary, as you begin to think about teaching reading comprehension strategies to your students, we suggest that you also consider the broader notion of reading comprehension that technology poses. As teachers of reading, we cannot ignore the implications for instruction that reading electronic text brings with it. See what Jeremy Brueck has to say about transliteracies and reading comprehension in Box 9.8.

Check Your Understanding 9.3: Gauge your understanding of the skills and concepts in this section.

RTI for Struggling Readers

Reading Comprehension and *Response to Intervention*

One of the purposes of RTI is to help create learning environments that support ELLs without assuming that they are or will be struggling readers. The CCSS (2010a) explicitly suggest that all learners, including ELLs, need to be prepared for college or careers. On the other hand, many classroom teachers are underprepared to teach ELLs. The complexity of these issues is rather massive.

2017 ILA Standard

4.1

Conversations are a natural way of communicating. We converse all the time about things that are second nature to us. Conversations are ways we use language to share thoughts and ideas, issues, and daily concerns. In essence, conversations are the way we communicate our social connections to everyday life. Beyond social and classroom conversations, however, ELLs need to learn how to respond to complex texts and how to problem solve, evaluate texts, and think as they read. We believe that enhanced conversations about complex text with ELLs can begin with questions that foster higher-level thinking skills. Instead of asking, for example, "What did the author or writer say?" teachers should focus on questions that go beyond literal information: "What do you think about this?" "What do you wonder about after reading this?" "Why do you wonder about that?" In addition, when students limit responses to several words, teachers need to include prompts such as "What else?" "Can you tell me more?"

Common Core State Standard

CCRA.SL.1

In essence, conversations and using higher-order questioning can help ELLs learn to understand what they are reading in a natural setting, which encourages them to use communication skills with which they feel comfortable (DaSilva Iddings, Risko, & Rampulla, 2009; Peterson & Taylor, 2012).

What About . . .

Standards, Assessment, and Reading Comprehension?

The CCSS (2010a) and other state standard documents—regardless of content domain or grade level—highlight the importance of comprehension, inquiry, and critical thinking. Critical thinking, interpretation, and analysis are highly valued in education in the United States. In the science standards developed by the National Science Teachers Association (NSTA), for example, science as inquiry is a critical dimension of what students should know and be able to do; the NSTA standards acknowledge that students at *every* grade level must have opportunities to engage in scientific inquiry and to think and act in ways that support inquiry. Similarly, the IRA and NCTE standards documents emphasize that students need to apply a wide variety of comprehension strategies that include (but are not limited to) interpreting, evaluating, and appreciating texts. Clearly, then, literacy standards nationally indicate that multiple levels of reading-comprehension instruction are critical at all levels of education.

What about assessing students and their abilities to reach these higher levels of comprehension? How can teachers ensure that students are learning to comprehend what they are reading beyond literal levels? How can teachers assess critical thinking skills in the classroom?

Throughout this chapter, we shared many instructional strategies for teaching students how to comprehend and think as they are reading. We suggest that teachers can use these strategies as authentic assessment practices that have the potential to provide them with real information about how their students comprehend what they are reading. For example, teachers can make anecdotal records as students "question the author" or engage in reciprocal teaching. Teachers can also evaluate students' abilities to think as they read by providing them with graphic organizers to complete while reading.

Keep in mind that, although national and state standardized tests tend to explicitly set minimum scores for specific grade levels, standardized assessments often do not tell teachers much about their students beyond overall achievement in comprehension. We believe that teacher observations regarding how students interact in meaningful ways with print can provide teachers with more specific information about how students comprehend and make sense of text.

Summary

- We explored how an awareness of story structure helps students comprehend narrative text. Strategies included teaching the elements of a story, mapping stories, and building a schema for stories.
- We discussed how to scaffold comprehension strategies through questioning strategies such as reciprocal questioning (ReQuest), question–answer relationships (QARs), questioning the author (QtA), close reading, reciprocal teaching, and think-alouds.

- We explored how to guide interactions between the reader and the text with strategies such as the directed reading–thinking activity (DR–TA), discussion webs, and text connections. We also discussed implications that technology holds for reading teaching reading comprehension.

Teacher Action Research

1. Choose a story from an anthology, and construct a story map using a chart similar to the one suggested in the chapter. Read the story to a group of children, and explain how a story map works; have them participate in completing the map as a group. Next have the group share in retelling the story based on the map. Share your observations with your colleagues.
2. Create and distribute a questionnaire to teachers in your school district regarding their understanding of *close reading*, **and if and how they implement the** **concept with their students. Analyze the results, and prepare your findings so that you can share them with your classmates.**
3. Select three picture books with a partner. Using sticky notes and the illustrations in the books, share your text-to-self connections with the first book, your text-to-text connections with the second book, and your text-to-world connections with the third book. Compare and contrast your connections with your partner.

Through the Lens of the Common Core

In this chapter we discussed the rigorous levels of reading comprehension that are addressed in the CCSS (2010a). We emphasized that in order for students to meet the standards, teachers need to focus on questioning skills that go beyond literal information. Students need to know how to infer, analyze, synthesize, problem solve, evaluate, criticize, compare, and contrast information. They need to know how to read closely, beyond the surface level of text, and they need to know how to generate new information based on what they read. In addition, students must be able to read complex text so that they will be college and career ready. These abilities will provide students with the skills they will need to meet the ever-changing literacy demands of the twenty-first century.

Chapter 10
Comprehending Informational Text

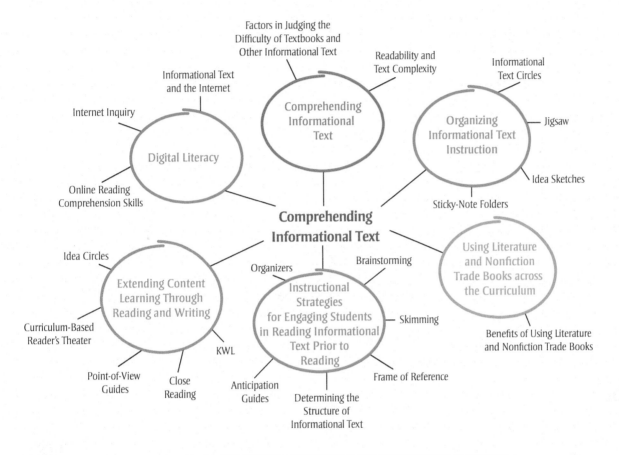

⌄ Learning Outcomes

In This Chapter, You Will Discover How to

■ Explain why content area textbooks and other sources of informational text are difficult for some students.

■ Demonstrate several ways to organize the reading of informational text.

■ Plan how to use literature and nonfiction trade books to enhance content area learning.

■ Model strategies that prepare students to read informational text.

■ Demonstrate informational text strategies that include reading and writing connections.

■ Understand and explain the importance and complexity that digital literacy holds for content area teachers.

Activating Your Schema

Think about the times when a teaches (elementary, high school, or college) gave you a reading assignment for a chapter or chapters in a textbook. How did you approach the assigned reading? Did you read it? Did you skim the chapter(s)? Did you hope that you would learn the textbook material from the teachers' class lectures? Did you high-light parts of the chapters? Did you take notes? Share your strategies for reading (or not reading) content area textbooks with a partner. What do you realize about content area reading as a result of the activity?

2017 ILA Standards Found in This Chapter

1.1	2.2	6.1
2.1	5.2	

Common Core State Standards: English Language Arts

CCRA.R.1	CCRA.R.4	CCRA.R.7	CCRA.R.9	CCRA.W.8
CCRA.R.2	CCRA.R.5	CCRA.R.8	CCRA.R.10	CCRA.SL.5

Key Terms

academic language	KWL
anticipation guide	literature across the curriculum
considerate text	mixed-text informational books
curriculum-based reader's theater	narrative informational texts
digital literacy	organizer
disciplinary literacy	point-of-view guide
expository informational books	readability
graphic organizer	signal words
idea circle	sticky-note folders
idea sketches	text complexity
informational text	text set
informational text circles	trade books
Internet inquiry	WebQuest
jigsaw strategy	

It is mid-October, and two eighth graders, Jimmy and Matt, are talking about science class as they walk home from school.

Jimmy: I sure don't like science class this year!

Matt: How come, man?

Jimmy: It's all about tests! Mr. Lee just keeps testing us on stuff I don't even know. He tells us to read the book but it's so boring. I just don't get it!

Matt: Wow! Maybe you could change teachers. I have Miss Smyth, and she's great. We haven't had one single test. We do hands-on science, and we work in small groups and talk about what we learned. Miss Smyth also gives us lots of choices about how we learn the stuff. We can read the chapter summaries, and we can look up information in the summaries on the Internet. Then we talk about it in class. It's cool!

Jimmy: Well, you're pretty lucky, Matt. I think it's too late to change teachers. I guess I'll have to just sweat it out.

Teaching children how to read words is one thing, but teaching children how to understand and learn from what they read is the primary goal of reading. Elementary teachers have a long history of viewing many of their responsibilities in reading instruction primarily in terms of skill and strategy development. Their actions are motivated by the question, "How can I help children become more skillful and strategic as readers?" Their main concern, then, was the *process*, or how to guide children's reading development. When children enter the middle school years, teachers are usually concerned with the content of subject matter and often spend little time on instructional strategies for helping young adolescents learn how to read the content. Note Jimmy's comments in the preceding scenario. However, it is critical that today's teachers focus on instruction in reading to learn from academic texts in K–12. Through expository texts, children gain an understanding of how the world works and how society functions; this is the key to success in school, in everyday life, and in the workplace (Common Core State Standards, 2010; Duke, 2004; Shanahan & Shanahan, 2014; Stratchan, 2015).

Teaching subject matter has historically been coined *content area reading* and has recently undergone discussion among professionals regarding the skills needed to teach the subject areas—hence the term **disciplinary literacy**. Disciplinary literacy fosters the notion that students need to be able to read math as mathematicians, history as historians, science as scientists, and so forth (Altieri, 2011; Buehl, 2011; Buehl & Moore, 2009; Moje, 2007, 2008; Shanahan & Shanahan, 2008; Vacca, Vacca, & Mraz, 2014). See Rich Vacca's viewpoint in Box 10.1. He places the discussion in a realistic context.

BOX 10.1 | VIEWPOINT

Richard T. Vacca
Content Determines Process

Richard T. Vacca is a professor emeritus in the School of Teaching, Learning, and Curriculum Studies in the College of Education, Health and Human Services at Kent State University.

Throughout the history of reading and learning to read, there has been a tendency for researchers, scholars, and practitioners to reinvent core concepts, strategies, and approaches to literacy instruction. Since the days of William S. Gray, one of the founding fathers of modern-day reading instruction, the concept of *reading in the content areas* (also known as *content area reading*) has been used to help learners better understand what they read across the curriculum. More than 90 years ago, Gray (1925) argued that each content area requires different sets of skills for effective reading and study of text material. These different skill sets are related to the learner's purpose for reading and the conceptual content of the text.

Researchers and scholars in the 1990s, however, reinvented the concept of content area reading to reflect the role that language plays in learning with print and digital texts. *Content literacy* became the "in" term to describe the ability of learners to use reading, writing, talking, listening, and viewing to learn subject matter in a given discipline (Vacca, Vacca, & Mraz, 2014). Content literacy is a broader, more inclusive concept than content area reading in that it entails the use of research-based skills and strategies designed to support reading, writing, thinking, and learning with all kinds of text.

In the first decade of the twenty-first century, *disciplinary literacy* is the new "in" term influencing the way researchers and educators are thinking about literacy and learning in content areas (Buehl & Moore, 2009; Lee, 2004; Moje, 2007, 2008; Shanahan & Shanahan, 2008). Proponents of disciplinary literacy argue that using literacy skills in a discipline is inextricably related to content knowledge and thinking. To become literate in a content area, students must learn to use the skills and strategies that an expert within a specific discipline uses to read, write, and think. Advocates of disciplinary literacy argue that teachers in specific content areas easily become frustrated by generic literacy practices often encountered in professional workshops and journal articles that may not be relevant to learning in their specific disciplines.

Learning to read and reading to learn go hand in hand. Students, beginning in the primary grades, must learn how to adapt reading skills and strategies to meet the peculiarities and conceptual demands of each discipline they study. My mentor and professional role model, Harold Herber, in 1970 wrote the first comprehensive textbook devoted solely to content area reading instruction: *Teaching Reading in Content Areas*. The underlying thesis in Herber's book is as powerful today as it was then: *Content determines process.* Disciplinary literacy, from my perspective, is a reinvention of the concept of content area reading, where content determines process in a given discipline. The underlying goal of a discipline-specific approach to literacy is to show students how to think and learn with text as they develop a deep understanding of concepts and ideas encountered. Each discipline poses its own challenges in terms of purposes for reading, vocabulary, concepts, texts, themes, and topics. How

students read, think, and learn with text more than likely varies from content area to content area.

Call it what you will: *disciplinary literacy, content area reading,* or *content literacy.* The conceptual demands and structure of a discipline-specific text determine how a reader will interact with that text, make sense of it, and learn from it. As Shakespeare reminds us in *Romeo and Juliet:* "What's in a name? That which we call a rose by any other name would smell as sweet."

Regardless of the terminology used, the Common Core State Standards (2010a) raise the literacy expectations for all students; they focus on high levels of thinking, reading, writing, speaking, listening, and viewing needed to prepare students for college and careers in the twenty-first century. Additionally, beginning in the early years, children are expected to read and interpret nonfiction; the Common Core State Standards (CCSS) explicitly state the skills students need to achieve in kindergarten through grade 5 for reading information. For grades 6 through 12, the CCSS (2010a) delineate more overtly the skills needed for reading history, social studies, science, and technical subjects. See how Abby Montler considers using informational text in her second grade classroom in Box 10.2.

BOX 10.2 | VIEWPOINT

Abby I. Montler
Using Informational Text in a Primary Classroom
Abby I. Montler teaches second grade at Norwood Fontbonne Academy in Philadelphia, PA

With an increased focus on integrating informational text into the classroom (Common Core State Standards, 2010a), as a second grade teacher, I have recently given more careful thought about this topic. These ponderings have led me to the conclusion that, not only do I love using informational text in the classroom, but I already do it more frequently than I realized. The standards specify that students should be able to read and comprehend nonfiction text on grade level independently and proficiently. I have found that the best way to teach toward this goal is to expose students to informational text in a variety of ways.

I start the year by filling students' book boxes with a variety of books on their independent reading levels. In these boxes, I include some high interest nonfiction books among other types of literature. Because these interests vary by student, I like to do a quick informal interview with each child at the beginning of the year. I find that a lot of students are interested in a particular type of animal, history topic, or sport. Each year, I am amazed by how the students often have a hard time returning their book boxes to the shelves because they want to explore them all the first day! I change the books frequently at the beginning of the year and then encourage the students to choose their own books based on their independent level. I usually find that my students choose an even mix of fiction and nonfiction based on this spark of interest at the beginning of the year.

One benefit to introducing nonfiction books at the students' independent levels is that it tends to make easier books

acceptable. I have had so many students complain about having to read "baby books," referring to fictional books on their level. However, due to the high interest level of informational books and the wide variety of levels, students do not see these texts as too juvenile.

In addition, with such a limited time to teach social studies and science, incorporating informational texts into language arts is necessary. Most comprehension strategies can easily be taught using informational texts; hence, this addresses many skills, as well as incorporates the content. I also like to expose my students to news articles for this reason. They are especially interested in articles that are relevant to them or those that can be controversial. For example, my students have loved reading about hover-board safety, school nutrition requirements, or technology innovations. These articles have spurred so many productive conversations about current events. Giving students these nuggets of information allows them to improve their conversational skills and, in turn, their overall confidence in knowing things that they may teach others about.

I have seen numerous positive outcomes by integrating informational text into my classroom. My students grow to love nonfiction, and they enjoy becoming authors of their own research pieces, often unprompted by me. They become familiar with the genre and become passionate about seeking their own answers. What a fantastic gift to give students: the tools and passion for becoming lifelong learners!

We next focus our attention on factors that make learning from textbooks and other sources of informational text challenging for many children. These include assumptions about vocabulary and prior knowledge, and the readability levels and complexity of informational texts.

2017 ILA Standard

1.1

Common Core State Standard

CCRA.R.10

What Is Informational Text, and What Makes It Challenging?

■ **Explain why content area textbooks and other sources of informational text are difficult for some students.**

Informational text is explanatory in nature and conveys factual information meant to increase an individual's knowledge of subject matter. There are a wide variety of genres that are considered informational text, including textbooks, technical texts such as "how to" books, manuals, newspaper and magazine articles, reports, summaries, and online resources, as well as books about science, history, social studies, and the arts.

Textbooks are a primary source of informational text in the classroom for most teachers; they rely heavily on an expository style of writing—description, classification, and explanation. However, by its very nature, a textbook is often dry and uninteresting to the novice reader. In fact, as young adolescents enter the middle school years, textbooks often become less and less appealing and more difficult for students. The curriculum, on the other hand, is often driven by textbook learning at the middle school level.

However, e-books and Internet resources are becoming commonplace for engaging students in learning subject matter. However, whether the venue is having the students grasp the content of a topic via a textbook or through online resources, the skills needed to read, understand, interpret, and use content area subject matter are challenging.

In addition, students from diverse ethnic, cultural, and linguistic backgrounds may find the complex content and new vocabulary in textbooks and online daunting. Teachers need to develop strategies for making subject area content manageable for these and actually all students; otherwise, students will get lost in a sea of meaningless text and quickly become frustrated.

The resurgence of children's nonfiction trade books in the twenty-first century underscores the importance of meaningful content and authentic texts in elementary and middle school classrooms. In addition to reading trade books in content area learning, children are learning to use electronic texts to read extensively and think critically about content. Reading and writing with computers allows children to access and retrieve information, construct their own texts, and interact with others. In fact, computer technologies have redefined our more traditional notions of literacy. Content area reading by means of the Internet, for example, has opened a plethora of opportunities for teachers to connect students to worldwide information about all subject areas.

Content learning also requires an understanding of **academic language**. Academic language refers to the words that are not typically used in everyday conversations, but rather vocabulary that relates to academic content. These are referred to as Tier 2 and

Figure 10.1 Common Academic Task Vocabulary

circle	summarize	predict
explain	infer	demonstrate
list	compare	identify
analyze	contrast	critique
prove	define	persuade

Tier 3 words. Tier 2 words are used across subject areas; words such as *alternate, represent, temporary,* and *frequent* are Tier 2 words. Tier 3 words are content specific (Beck, McKeown, & Kucan, 2002; Townsend & Kiernan, 2015). Content specific words are critical to understanding the new concepts being learned from informational text (Fisher & Frey, 2014; McKeown, Crosson, Artz, Sandora, & Beck, 2013). For example, words that students need to understand mathematics include *addition, subtraction, multiplication, theorem, cosine,* and *formula,* to name just a few. Social studies vocabulary would include terms such as *rural, urban, population, natural resources, citizen,* and *government.* Often the academic language is in italics or bold text. In addition, students are often asked to perform specific tasks when they are reading informational texts. Figure 10.1 lists common terms associated with frequent tasks students are required to complete in school.

Although e-texts and the Internet have become an integral part of teaching, content area textbooks are still a fundamental part of schooling. Yet elementary and middle school teachers often remark that children find textbooks and other sources of informational text difficult. When students have trouble reading texts, we are aware of the mismatch that can occur between the reading abilities students bring to text material and some of the difficulties of the text. This can be particularly true for English language learners (ELLs). In addition, many teachers find it difficult to use textbooks effectively (Vacca, Vacca, & Mraz, 2014). On the other hand, one might speculate that college textbooks will present students with even more complex reading skills. If one of the essential goals of the CCSS (2010a) is to prepare students for college reading, and students find middle school textbooks difficult, this presents quite a dilemma for all teachers. How are they to prepare students for college "reading" if the texts they read in middle school seem to be too difficult for them?

Some teachers are tempted to avoid difficult materials; however, once again, we know that the CCSS (2010a) stipulate that students need to be able to read complex text in order to prepare for college and careers and citizenship. This brings us to the issue of **text complexity**. What makes a text complex? This is a complex issue in and of itself. According to the CCSS, *text complexity* is a term that shares three elements:

1. One is a quantitative measure of the text's difficulty typically based on word and sentence length; this is commonly known as the readability level.
2. Another element is qualitative and focuses on the language and clarity of the text, as well as its structure.
3. The third element features the reader and his or her ability to complete the reading task (Fisher, Frey, & Lapp, 2012; Hiebert, 2013; National Governors Association Center for Best Practices, Council of Chief State School Officers, 2010a).

In addition to addressing the nature of what the CCSS deem "complex text," we also need to get answers to some very basic questions: How does a textbook or other informational text meet the goals of the curriculum? Is the conceptual difficulty of the text beyond students' grasp? Does the author have a clear sense of purpose as conveyed to this audience? How well are the ideas in the informational text organized? With answers to these and other questions, teachers of young as well as middle school students have some basis on which to make decisions about informational text–related instruction, allowing them to exercise their professional judgment.

2017 ILA Standard
2.1

Factors in Judging the Difficulty of Textbooks and Other Informational Text

As recognized by the CCSS (2010a), the difficulty of text material is the result of factors residing in both the reader and the text. Therefore, to judge well, you need to take into account several types of information when deciding what informational text to select.

- An initial source to consider is information about the publisher and author. Consider if the publisher or author provided descriptions of the design, format, and organizational structure of the text, along with grade-level readability designations.

- A second source is your knowledge of students in the class.

- A third source is your own sense of what makes the informational text useful for learning a particular subject.

Another important consideration is to define how the informational text will be used. Will it be used as the sole basis for information or as an extension of information? Will it be used in tandem with other informational books, other forms of children's literature, or online resources?

HOW DIFFICULT IS THE TEXT TO UNDERSTAND?   This question might be recast into a set of subsidiary questions: How likely are students to comprehend the text? How difficult are the concepts in the text? Has the author taken into consideration the prior knowledge that students bring to the text? The ability to understand the informational text, to a large extent, will be influenced by the match between what the reader already knows and the text itself. Background knowledge and logical organization of expository texts are crucial factors for comprehending new information. In addition, informational text poses difficult linguistic characteristics: The vocabulary is technical, abstract, dense, and authoritative in nature (Fang, 2008).

Teachers need to be aware that students from culturally, linguistically, and socially diverse backgrounds will bring a wide range of experiences to the classroom. These experiences will influence how students understand or fail to understand their textbooks and other informational text. Fitzgerald and Graves (2004) elaborate on factors associated with text difficulty for ELLs. They point out that while difficult vocabulary is relatively easy to identify, texts that contain "a lot of difficult words are likely to be harder for English-language learners" (p. 333). Although it is important that ELLs have access to text in which they will *learn* new words, when they are overloaded with new terminology, learning is impeded. Regarding vocabulary and informational texts, it is also important to realize that, although some ELLs have adequate conversational skills, their knowledge of academic English vocabulary is typically less developed. Read how one student views content area learning in Box 10.3.

In addition to vocabulary, it is important to consider the complexity of sentences as well as how the text sounds. Long and complex sentences can make reading difficult for all readers, including ELLs. On the other hand, short, choppy sentences can interfere with understanding. The length of a reading assignment is another factor to consider in terms of readability for ELLs, as well as how clearly examples are elaborated on, the coherence and unity of the text, and the structure and organization of the text (Fitzgerald & Graves, 2004).

2017 ILA Standard
2.2

HOW USABLE IS THE INFORMATIONAL TEXT?   To determine how usable an informational text is, you will need to consider its organizational features and its presentation

BOX 10.3 | STUDENT VOICES

Mia is a 10-year-old multiracial fourth grader who has documented attention deficit hyperactivity disorder (ADHD), but has consistently made satisfactory progress when compared with typically developing peers. She is a sensitive, imaginative child who prefers creative reading activities that allow her to express herself in artistic ways.

Mia characterizes herself as "not pro" at reading, but she thinks she is "pretty good." She said that she doesn't always know all the words, but she tries to sound them out. If she can't sound out words, Mia asks somebody (like her family, her friend, or her teacher). Mia shared that she *really* enjoys mysteries (fiction) and scary books, like *The Boxcar Children* and *Goosebumps*. She doesn't like to read at school because other kids often talk and she needs "peace and quiet" to read. Mia also shared that when she reads at school, she is allowed to move around the room and has the choice of sitting at her desk or on the floor, and she likes that.

When asked about subject area learning, Mia said that she does have to read textbooks for science and social studies, but that she would rather do projects like making/selling doughnuts for economics and dissecting flowers for science. She finds reading aloud during science and social studies class "annoying" because the teacher calls on her and she doesn't always know the words and she wants to figure them out first for herself. When she comes to difficult words in textbooks, Mia tries to sound them out using some of the rules she has learned, like "saying the word with the 'e' at the end and then without the 'e'—like *algae*." Mia also shared that when she tries to figure out an unknown word, she looks to see whether it is a compound word and then she counts the syllables (demonstrated by clapping). Her advice to content area teachers is that they have "little reading stations" to help students who have trouble reading the textbook.

Mia's interview reveals that her perception of content area reading focuses on her struggles with word identification. She shares that word pronunciation is challenging and that when her teachers have her read aloud in science and social studies, she is not confident; in fact, she finds that "annoying." Mia's message appears to be twofold: Reading content area vocabulary that she has never seen before is frustrating for her, and reading aloud in content area classes without having a chance to read the text silently is troublesome and makes her feel uncomfortable, to say the least. When content area teachers include textbook reading as part of their instruction, they need to understand that preteaching new subject area vocabulary is important.

of material. Remember that a variety of informational texts are available for teaching content reading. You may be using a textbook as the students' primary source of information; you may be using articles that support your content; you may be using documents that students need to analyze; you may be using online text. Your responses to the following questions will help you decide whether you are dealing with a **considerate text** or an *inconsiderate* one. Considerate text is distinguished by its user friendliness with respect to the organizational features and presentation of the material. For example, your responses may reveal the extent to which relationships among ideas in the text are clear and how well the logical organization between ideas and the use of *signal words* (connectives) make relationships explicit. To determine whether a text is *considerate* and *user-friendly*, ask yourself these questions:

- Does the table of contents or online menu clearly represent the organization of the content?
- Do the headings and subheadings appear helpful in assisting the students to think and learn about the content?
- Is there a glossary that will be useful in defining concepts? Does the online text highlight and define words?
- Do graphs, charts, illustrations, and electronic web links include useful information?
- Are there helpful study guides to assist students?

HOW INTERESTING IS THE INFORMATIONAL TEXT?   Informational text should appeal to students; the more relevant the text, the more interesting it will be. Illustrations and pictures should be appealing and informative and, depending on the nature of the content, convey up-to-date, culturally diverse images. Also consider the type sizes and fonts. Are they varied in a manner that helps the students understand the text? Does the boldface lettering of headings contrast with the lightface lettering of the ideas? Italics and numbering of words and phrases in lists are two other devices that can help make the printed page come alive for elementary as well as middle school students. In addition to the questions just raised, consider these as you analyze informational text for interest:

- Is the writing style of the text appealing to the students?
- Are the activities motivating? Will they make students want to pursue the topic further?
- Does the text clearly show how the knowledge being learned might be used by the learner in the future?
- Does the text provide positive and motivating models for both sexes as well as for all racial, ethnic, and socioeconomic groups?
- Does the text help students generate interest as they relate experiences and develop visual and sensory images?

Once you consider these multifaceted factors that may contribute to the difficulty of reading informational text, including textbooks, you are in a position to use professional judgment, but you should also be cognizant of and consider the approximate reading level on which the text is written.

Readability and Text Complexity

When teachers judge instructional content area materials and informational text, they frequently assess **readability**. Readability formulas can help *estimate* the difficulty of any text, but they are not intended to be precise indicators. Of the many readability formulas available, the most popular ones are relatively quick and easy to calculate on the computer. They typically involve a measure of sentence length and word length to ascertain a grade-level score for text materials. This score is meant to indicate the reading achievement level students would need to comprehend the material. Well-known readability formulas include the Fry Readability Graph (1968) and the Flesch-Kincaid (Flesch, 1948; Kincaid, Fishburne, Rogers, & Chissom, 1975); the Dale Chall (1948); and the Spache (1953). Teachers can easily access these formulas online with a Google search.

More recently, however, text complexity has been measured by Lexile scales that use word frequency and sentence length to determine the difficulty of a text or the level on which a child can read (MetaMetrics, 2000). Many book publishers now include Lexile levels in their descriptions of texts. Lexile scales provide a range of bands that designate grade levels, including easier text to more complex reading material according to reading levels. You do, however, need to be aware of limitations associated with using readability formulas and Lexiles.

Readability formulas and Lexile levels yield scores that are simply estimates, not absolute levels, of text difficulty. These estimates are often determined along a single dimension of an author's writing style: vocabulary difficulty and sentence complexity. They are measured by word and sentence length, or word frequency. These are variables most often used to predict the difficulty of a text. Nevertheless, they only *indirectly* assess vocabulary difficulty and sentence complexity. Are long words always harder to understand than short ones? Are long sentences necessarily more difficult than short ones?

Keep in mind that a readability formula or a Lexile level doesn't take into account the experience and knowledge that young, middle school, linguistically and culturally diverse, or struggling readers bring to content material. The reader's emotional, cognitive, and linguistic backgrounds are not included in readability estimates. Thus several factors that contribute to a reader's ability to comprehend text are not dealt with: purpose, interest, motivation, emotional state, environment, culture, and ability.

Other dimensions of text complexity involve the language and syntax of the text, as well as the tasks that readers need to understand, interpret, and ultimately use new content information. Hiebert (2013) offers a four-step model of how to assess texts and match them with readers. The model, Text Complexity Multi-Index (TCMI), includes benchmark texts that can be used as models for teachers as they explore what complex texts are and how to foster close reading of texts, as well as the multiple skills students will need to prepare for college and careers in the twenty-first century. You can access Hiebert's work and strategies for assessing text complexity, as well as an extraordinary array of resources, at **TextProject** (http://textproject.org).

Needless to say, there are myriad considerations that teachers need to think and learn about when addressing the CCSS (2010a) and the skills that we need to teach students in order for them to meet the literacy skills necessary to be productive citizens in the twenty-first century. One of the most important factors will be ongoing professional development. Teachers today will need to research, study, and explore the new literacy skills that will be essential tomorrow, next week, or a decade from now. Next, however, we suggest ways that teachers can organize content area reading instruction.

Check Your Understanding 10.1: Gauge your understanding of the skills and concepts in this section.

Organizing Informational Text Instruction

■ **Demonstrate several ways to organize the reading of informational text.**

Teachers across all curricular areas acknowledge that informational text presents multiple challenges, and yet it involves critical thinking skills that are essential for all students as we prepare them to be well equipped as adults when they leave school. How might teachers organize and develop constructive lessons that foster effective learning with textbooks and other informational text? Next, we explain strategies that address this issue.

Informational Text Circles

When teachers organize literature instruction, they sometimes use literature circles as an organizational way to foster engagement. Literature circles typically involve grouping students and having them assume roles as they read a story. In a group of five students, one student might, for example, assume the role of discussing vocabulary; another might summarize the story; another might illustrate main ideas. Other roles might include posing questions about a paragraph in the story or reading a quote to promote discussion. The roles are not set in stone. The primary point is to have each student focus on a particular purpose for reading the story or a selection of the story.

Literature circles can be effectively modified as a cooperative learning strategy in which informational text is shared in small groups; hence the name **informational text circles**. When given a section or sections of text to read in small groups, each student assumes a role or purpose for reading and is responsible for reporting to the rest of the group regarding that role after a prescribed amount of time. Altieri (2011), for example, suggests how a student can read science text and assume the role of a "visual expert" by examining the graphics or diagrams in a text, or a student can assume the role of a "mad scientist" by searching for related information via other resources. Wilfong (2009) suggests "textmaster" roles such as discussion director, summarizer, vocabulary enricher, and webmaster. The webmaster designs a graphic organizer that synthesizes the main points of the reading. It is important that teachers define the goals and model the purpose of each task to ensure that participation is effective and that the students are engaged in learning.

Following the reading, each student typically shares the information they have learned based on the assigned task. For example, a participant whose role was "vocabulary enricher" might share and discuss important academic language that was critical

Figure 10.2 Group Participation Rubric for Our Informational Text Circle

My Name:	Date:		Informational Circle Topic:	
	I really understood what the person shared.	I pretty much understood what the person shared.	I was a bit confused by what the person shared.	I really didn't get what the person shared.
Group Member "Summarizer"				
Group Member "Discussion Captain"				
Group Member "Word Explorer"				
Group Member "Question Crafter"				
My Role "Cartoon Creator"	My self-evaluation:			

Figure 10.3 Early Childhood Informational Text Circle Roles

Role	Task
Fact Finder	After reading, locate two important ideas you found. Explain why they are important.
Picture Talker	After reading, select two pictures and explain what the author is telling about them.
Questioner	After reading, prepare two questions for your classmates. Ask them where they found the answer.
Word Searcher	After reading, find two words that are important and explain what they mean.

to the reading. Group participation rubrics can be implemented to ensure that each member of the group contributes in a responsible manner. In Figure 10.2, we present an example of a group participation rubric that was cooperatively created by a fifth-grade class. See how one teacher characterizes the roles for an early childhood class in Figure 10.3. In Figure 10.4, one teacher explains more sophisticated roles that middle school students assume as they read an informational text selection.

You probably noticed that the roles for the students exemplified in Figure 10.4 are rather sophisticated. However, the example is meant to suggest that teachers need not follow a specific structure for engaging students in expository circles. Motivation, the purpose, and the nature of the students' ability should drive how you develop the roles.

Jigsaw

Jigsaw is another cooperative learning strategy in which students assume roles as they read and share their understanding of the content in small groups (Aronson, 1978). Much like informational text circles, the students are assigned a passage or section of text to read, but the organization is somewhat different. Each group consists of three to five students of mixed ability, and each student is given a copy of *the same* informational text or sections of a textbook to read. Copies of informational text are needed when textbooks are not the primary source of the content.

The students in the initial groups are characterized as "home groups." Although each *group* of students is reading the same informational text, the purpose for *individual* students in the home group is different. For example, if the topic under study is a particular country, let's say Italy, one student in each home group would have an informational topic about the culture of the country; another student in the group

Figure 10.4 Middle Childhood Informational Text Circle Roles

Role 1 Grabber	You will grab the main idea about what you learned, and toss the details to your classmates. You will share by drawing a circle with main idea in the center and adding information with lines that represent the details.

Role 2 Bulldog	You will challenge your classmates with at least two tough questions that you want to talk about. Your questions should focus on information in the text that your classmates should be able to provide evidence for. You should fill out your "Question Sheet" so that you are clear on what you want to ask and where *you* found the evidence. Jot down comments in the last column about your classmates' responses.		
	Question 1	My Evidence	How Did They Do?
	Question 2	My Evidence	How Did They Do?
Role 3 Sly Cat	You role is to select academic language (vocabulary) that is important to the reading. You will highlight at least two words after you read, and you will explain the importance of these words by sharing the definition or meaning. Your task is to have your classmates guess which academic word you are talking about. Write a comment about how you think your classmates did with your words. Did your clues for the words work?		
	Word 1	My Meaning of the Word	Did They Get It?
	Word 2	My Meaning of the Word	Did They Get It?
Role 4 Stumper	You will select three facts that you have read about, and you will develop true/false sentences about those facts. When you read the sentences, your classmates will have to guess if the facts are true or false and provide evidence in the text that supports their answers. Check the last box if your classmates got the answer correct.		
	Fact One	True or False Statement	Correct
	Fact Two	True or False Statement	Correct
	Fact Three	True or False Statement	Correct
Role 5 Wonder Master	As you read the text, your job is to think of questions that make you wonder about new information you would like to know. When you share your "wonders" with your classmates, you will ask them to think about what they wonder. What you all wonder about can be the focus of additional reading about this topic.		
	What I Wonder About:		
	What Do My Classmates Wonder About?		

might be reading about the climate; another about the geography; and still another student in the home group might be reading about exports and imports. While reading the selection, each home group member becomes the expert on the specific topic that was read.

Next, each expert in the home group joins with the other experts. In this scenario, each student who was the expert on culture would form a group; each expert who read about climate would gather together, and so on. The purpose of the expert groups is to share with each other and gather notes to insure they understood the topic content.

The next step is for each expert to reconvene with the home group to share and teach the other members about the topic. Each expert may also develop a graphic organizer or chart to synthesize the information. See Box 10.4 for a step-by-step jigsaw plan.

JIGSAW STRATEGY IN AN ELEMENTARY CLASSROOM

Watch this **video** (www.youtube.com/watch?v=mtm5_w6JthA) to learn how the jigsaw strategy works in an elementary classroom. What do you notice about how this teacher engages the students in the jigsaw strategy?

BOX 10.4 | STEP-BY-STEP LESSON

Jigsaw Plan

1. Select a topic in which the home group members will have assignments that are related. The tasks must be linked so that the jigsaw completes a total picture of the initial topic.

   For example, if the topic is lions, tasks might include reading to learn about the habitat, diet, physical features, and behaviors of lions.

2. Explain the technique, and assign each student to a home group that is heterogeneous; each person in the home group has a different task and will be the expert of the group for that task.

   For example, each home group will have one member who studies the lion's habitat, one member who finds out about the lion's diet, one member who studies the physical features of lions, and one member who learns about the behaviors of lions.

3. Provide each expert with appropriate resources to gather information.

   For example, the experts for learning about the lion's habitat might all be reading a section from a textbook; the experts for investigating the diet of lions might be reading an article from a children's magazine.

4. Prior to engaging the students in reading, you should guide them in constructive ways to locate and record information.

   For example, they might log the facts on sticky notes, index cards, notebooks, or graphic organizers, or they might annotate the text and highlight information.

5. Provide time for each home group to gather information. It is important that teachers give students ample time with management guidelines.

   For example, the teacher may allow 20 minutes to gather three significant facts. The time factor will depend on the nature of the task and the abilities of the students.

6. Next, reconfigure the students according to expert groups and have them compare and contrast what they learned about their area of investigation. Be sure to provide guidelines for sharing and for creating a final "product" that they will bring back to their home group.

   For example, all the students who read about the habitat of the lion would gather together and take turns contributing information. Each expert might complete a graphic organizer to share with the home group.

7. Next, have the students return to their home groups and peer teach to their classmates the information learned. Be sure to provide guidelines for peer teaching and remind students that they need to learn the content that is presented by each expert. This can occur in a variety of ways, and depending on time, this portion of the lesson might occur the next day.

   For example, during peer teaching, the home group members may complete a blank graphic organizer as the information is explained, or they may be required to write a summary.

8. Finally, be sure that you decide on how the students will be held accountable for the learning. This is critical because a final goal will motivate all of the students to attend to the process and actually learn from each other.

   For example, you might tell the students at the beginning of the activity that they will have a quiz on each topic, or they might be required to write a summary for each area of expertise. A final evaluative piece will help ensure that learning is taking place.

Idea Sketches

Idea sketches are graphic organizers that students complete in small groups as they read informational text. The purpose of the activity is for students to read a section of the text and focus on main ideas and supporting details, adding information to the organizers as they read. Here is how idea sketches work:

1. Introduce the overall topic under study, and activate the students' background knowledge through discussion. Point out the organization of the text by referring to main topics and subtopics.
2. Chunk the text by dividing it into manageable sections. Topic headings or subtopics work best for this.
3. Divide the class into small groups or pairs, and assign (or have students select) the chunk they will read.
4. Instruct the groups to place the topic of inquiry (topic or subtopic) in the center of a large poster board and circle it. This is the beginning of the "sketch." Model how

to construct a graphic organizer by sketching boxes, circles, triangles, diamonds, or other shapes to represent main ideas and details.

5. Each group reads its chunk of text either orally or silently, and together students sketch the information as they design a graphic organizer that represents the information read. At this time the teacher circulates among the groups to assist, guide, and clarify any misinformation.

6. Display the poster boards in chronological order according to the original text, and have the members of each group share what they learned. Add clarifying information as needed, and discuss the relationships among the poster board topics. Sticky notes for additional information or questions can be added to the boards.

Common Core State Standards

CCRA.R.1, CCRA.R.2, CCRA.R.4, CCRA.R.8, CCRA.R.9, CCRA.R.10

Sticky-Note Folders

Sticky-note folders is cooperative learning strategy that assists students in organizing and thinking about informational text by providing them with a way to manipulate and group concepts, and add additional information from other resources, such as online texts and trade books. Once the information is recorded, the students use the folders and sticky notes to interpret, analyze, evaluate, and organize the material. See the step-by-step lesson in Box 10.5 for a framework for sticky-note folders.

In order to document information, students can create logs on the front and back of the folders. Each side can be divided into three columns. The first column indicates a code that refers to the sticky note, A, B, C or 1, 2, 3. The middle column is used to cite the URL or trade book. The third column can be coded with a plus, minus, or question mark to indicate confirming, biased, or questionable information. A star can indicate essential main ideas.

BOX 10.5 | STEP-BY-STEP LESSON

Sticky-Note Folders

1. Explain to the students that they are going to work with a partner as they learn and record information about main ideas and details on sticky notes that they will place in folders. Tape a legal size folder on the wall, and use a simple example to demonstrate how this will be done.

    A simple example might be main ideas—kitchen and bedroom; write *kitchen* on a large sticky note in one color and place it at the top of the left side of the folder; write *bedroom* on another large sticky note in a different color and post it at the top of the right side of the folder. Brainstorm and record details for kitchen, such as sink, counter, refrigerator, and stove, on smaller sticky notes that are another color and post them under *kitchen*. Do the same for details about bedroom, such as bed, dresser, mirror, and lamp, in a different color.

2. Select two key related main concepts and important details to learn and think about based on your content area standards and the informational text you are having the students read.

3. Next, activate schema about the topics and guide students to formulate questions about related ideas and details. The purpose of this step is to assist students in thinking about prior knowledge regarding the content and to scaffold

questions that will lead to significant information about the concepts.

    During this step, record the information on chart paper. Divide the paper into four boxes. Title the top left box "What we think we know about . . . ." Title the top right box "Our questions about . . . ." Label the bottom boxes the same way with the second concept. For example, if the main idea is *oceans*, students might think there are five oceans but may wonder how big they are.

4. Partner the students, and provide each pair with a legal-size folder and sets of multicolored large and small sticky notes. The sticky notes will be used to record main ideas and details as they read the text and place them in the folders.

5. Assign the chapter or pages in the textbook or other informational text that include the main ideas and details; instruct the students to skim for information, record what they find on sticky notes, and place the sticky notes related to one concept on the left side of the folder and the second concept on the other side. During this step the students should document the page number(s) of the text where the information was located.

6. As the students work, scaffold by circulating among the students and assisting as needed.

7. Provide time for the students to share folders in groups of four to six. Encourage them to compare and contrast findings. During this step the students can add information on additional sticky notes and place them in the folders when they learn new information from other members of the groups.

8. During the next lessons, provide trade books and online resources about the same topics. As the students work to locate new information or content that confirms or questions what they have noted on the original sticky notes, provide additional colors so that they can add more information to the folder. The sticky notes can be color-coded. For example, yellow sticky notes might signify facts found online; green might signify examples from trade books; pink might signify additional information that needs to be located.

9. Once the students have recorded content information on the sticky notes, they can rearrange them in the folders according to a variety of categories, such as factual information, information that is not yet clear, contradictory information, or information that gives good examples. The new sticky notes should be coded in such a way that documents where the information came from. For example, each new sticky note can be labeled A, B, C, and so on and the resources can be listed on a separate sheet of paper.

This strategy can be conducted over several days or weeks. It will depend on the nature of the topics under study and the abilities of the students.

Manipulative activities can be created where students remove all of the sticky notes and trade folders with other groups. Each partnership discusses the information and re-creates new organization of the material.

2017 ILA Standard

2.2

Common Core State Standards

CCRA.R.1, CCRA.R.2, CCRA.R.3, CCRA.R.4, CCRA.R.5

In the next section we discuss how to use trade books to teach curriculum content. You will discover the benefits of using trade books, how to plan to use literature and informational texts in content area learning, as well as instructional strategies to implement in the classroom.

Check Your Understanding 10.2: Gauge your understanding of the skills and concepts in this section.

Using Literature and Nonfiction Trade Books across the Curriculum

■ **Plan how to use literature and nonfiction trade books to enhance content area learning.**

The use of children's literature and nonfiction **trade books** in elementary and middle school classrooms extends and enriches information provided in content area textbooks. Often textbooks cannot treat subject matter with the breadth and depth necessary to develop ideas and concepts fully. Literature and nonfiction trade books have the potential to capture children's imagination and interest in people, places, events, and ideas. And they also have the potential to develop in-depth understanding in ways that textbooks aren't equipped to do. The CCSS specifically place a strong emphasis on children's ability to read informational text. Neuman and Roskos (2012) point out that teachers need to use a variety of genres when considering informational texts; they recommend using **text sets** that include storybook formats. Text sets are groups of books that share related concepts in different formats.

Generally, there are three types of informational or nonfiction text types: narrative informational, expository informational, and mixed- or combined-text trade books (Chapman & Sopko, 2003; Kletzien & Dreher, 2004). In **narrative informational texts** the author typically tells a fictional story that conveys factual information. For example, in the book *Charlie Needs a Cloak* by Tomie dePaola, a make-believe shepherd goes through the steps of shearing a sheep and washing, carding, and spinning wool to make his cloak. This type of text often works well as a read-aloud and can be a motivating lead-in to a topic of study. **Expository informational books** do not contain stories; they contain information that typically follows specific text structures such as description, sequence, cause and effect, comparison and contrast, and problem solving. In addition, they often contain features such as a table of contents, a glossary, a list of illustrations, charts, and graphs. Whereas narrative informational texts are typically read from beginning to end, expository books do not have to be read in any particular order. **Mixed-text informational books**, sometimes referred to as *combined-text trade books*, narrate stories and include factual information in the surrounding text. For example, in *The Magic School Bus: Inside the Human Body* by Joanna Cole, the author takes the reader through an imaginary adventure through the human body; surrounding the story are true facts and illustrations about the body. With books of this type, it is important to help the students distinguish fact from fiction. A combination of texts is referred to as a text set.

For example, one book might be narrative in nature; another might relay the information in story format; another might primarily implement photographs to convey the information.

According to Moss (2002), informational book selections should be made on the basis of the "five A's": the *authority* of the *author*, the *appropriateness* of the book for the children in the classroom, the literary *artistry*, and the *appearance* of the book. Stephens (2008) provides a checklist for teachers that includes questions about the cover, illustrations, photographs, font size, and organizational features of the book. Others suggest strategies and activities that enhance the reading of informational texts and focus on specific skills such as organizing and analyzing information, summarizing, and visualizing, to name a few (Duke & Bennett-Almistead, 2003; Kletzien & Dreher, 2004; Moss & Loh, 2010; Olness, 2007). Nonetheless, having a wide array of literature and nonfiction trade books available for content area learning is necessary but not sufficient to ensure that children make appropriate use of trade books. Teachers must plan for their use by weaving trade books into meaningful and relevant instructional activities within the context of content area study.

Benefits of Using Literature and Nonfiction Trade Books

There are many benefits to using trade books and **literature across the curriculum**, either in tandem with textbooks or in units of study around a thematic unit. For one, trade books and other literature provide students with intense involvement in a subject; for another, they are powerful schema builders; third, they may be used to accommodate a wide range of student abilities and interests. With trade books, children may choose from a variety of topics for intensive study and inquiry. One benefit for the teacher, of course, is that literature may be used instructionally in a variety of ways. Picture books, for example, can provide elementary and middle school students with valuable background knowledge regarding diverse cultures. Hence picture books can provide students with a greater appreciation for the multicultural world in which we live.

2017 ILA Standard

2.2

Common Core State Standard

CCRA.R.9

INTENSE INVOLVEMENT A textbook compresses information. Intensive treatment gives way to extensive coverage. As a result, an elementary or middle school textbook is more likely to mention and summarize important ideas, events, and concepts than to develop them fully or richly. Brozo and Tomlinson (1986) underscored this point by illustrating the content treatment of Hitler, the Nazis, and the Jews in a fifth-grade social studies textbook.

> Hitler's followers were called Nazis. Hitler and the Nazis built up Germany's military power and started a campaign against the Jews who lived in that country. Hitler claimed that the Jews were to blame for Germany's problems. He took away their rights and property. Many Jews left Germany and came to live in the United States. The Nazis began to arrest Jews who stayed in Germany and put them in special camps. Then the Nazis started murdering them. Before Hitler's years in power came to an end, six million Jews lost their lives.

Combining trade books and informational texts provides students with intense involvement in a subject.

Annie Pickert Fuller/Pearson Education

A textbook, as you can surmise from this example, often condenses a subject to its barest essentials; the result often is a bland and watered-down treatment of the subjects. The paragraph on Hitler's treatment of the Jews is a vivid example of the "principle of minimum essentials" in textbook practice. The passage cited represents the entirety of this particular text's coverage of the Holocaust. Though it may be accurate, it takes one of the most tragic and horrifying events in world history and compresses it into a series of colorless and emotionless summarizing statements. On the other hand, trade books are an excellent vehicle for content study because they generate intense involvement in a subject (McTigue, Thornton, & Wiese, 2012). Here are some examples of children's books that capture the Holocaust in more intense ways:

- *Don't Forget* by Patricia Lakin (1994, Aladdin). As a young child prepares to bake a cake for her mother and collects the ingredients from various storekeepers, all of whom are Holocaust survivors, the child observes the numbers tattooed on their arms.
- *Let the Celebrations Begin* by Margaret Wild (1996, Orchard Books). This story captures how women made toys from scraps for child survivors after the war.
- *One Candle* by Eve Bunting (2002, HarperCollins). A grandma recalls her experience as a 12-year-old in a concentration camp.

A Google search of trade books for the content areas will provide teachers with a wealth of books for all grade levels and subject area topics.

SCHEMA BUILDING Intense involvement in a subject generates background knowledge and vicarious experience that make content area concepts easier to grasp and assimilate. As a result, one of the most compelling uses of trade books is as schemata builders for subjects under textbook study. Second-grade teacher Michelle Horsey not only uses informational texts to support her science and social studies curriculum, but she also integrates nonfiction trade books throughout the entire school to foster inquiry among her students (Maloch & Horsey, 2013). Her substantial library of informational texts provides the second graders with multiple resources for building schemata about subject matter.

The transition to informational text is smoother when students bring a frame of reference to textbook study. Reading literature strengthens the reading process because reading about a topic can dramatically improve comprehension of related readings on the same topic. The background knowledge acquired in the natural reading of trade books helps students comprehend related discourse.

ABILITIES AND INTERESTS When teachers use trade books in tandem with textbooks, there's something for everyone. A teacher can provide students with trade books on a variety of topics related to a subject under investigation. Books on related topics are written at various levels of difficulty. It is also clear that children of all ages find informational text motivating. Mohr (2003), for example, found that first graders had a strong preference for nonfiction trade books, and Coleman, Bradley, and Donovan (2012) found that second graders were motivated by visuals in informational texts.

VOCABULARY BUILDING   It is well recognized that students need multiple exposures to new vocabulary words in order to learn them. This is particularly true of learning new content vocabulary, which is often technical and difficult to pronounce. When teachers integrate trade books into their teaching of content, they provide students with opportunities to read new vocabulary in multiple contexts, and trade books often use synonyms for new words (Soalt, 2005).

Pollard-Durodola, Gonzalez, Simmons, Davis, Simmons, and Nava-Walichowski (2011/2012) describe how shared-book reading lessons can be used with preschoolers to foster content area vocabulary. Gregg and Sekeres (2006) suggest teaching new content vocabulary using realia—actual objects—and demonstrations. They recommend providing time for students to physically experience new ideas and concepts before introducing them to the new vocabulary in texts. Boyd and Ikpeze (2007) demonstrated how seventh-grade students wrote and performed skits that exhibited their understanding of new vocabulary. When students have opportunities to observe and experience new concepts in real life, they will be more motivated to read about them.

In essence, when fictional and nonfiction trade books are integrated into content area instruction, students have opportunities to become intensely involved with the subject matter, build their background knowledge by using meaningful text, tap their interests and abilities, and learn new and often difficult vocabulary. In the research-based practices featured in Box 10.6, you will find guidelines for selecting literature to augment content area instruction. Lesson development suggestions are featured in Figure 10.5.

Box 10.6 provides guidelines for selecting children's literature to enhance content area reading instruction.

Check Your Understanding 10.3: Gauge your understanding of the skills and concepts in this section.

BOX 10.6 | RESEARCH –BASED PRACTICES

Guidelines for Choosing Literature to Enhance Content Area Reading Instruction

- Consider the authenticity of the text and the background knowledge of the author. Are you sure the factual content is accurate? What are the credentials of the author?
- Examine the usefulness of the structural features such as table of contents, headings, subheadings, font size, use of bold text, use of italics, and glossary. Is the organization logical?
- Examine the graphics, including the illustrations, photographs, graphs, charts, and diagrams. Are they clear? Do they provide engaging information?
- Examine the interest level of the author's style. Is it engaging? Does the author provide meaningful examples? Will the students be motivated to learn from the text?
- Consider the readability of the text. Will the students be able to read it independently, or will it best be used as a read-aloud?

Figure 10.5 Lesson Guidelines for Engaging Readers in Content Area Lessons Using Literature

1. *Select the standards(s)* that you plan to teach based on your content area. It can be helpful to select a theme that addresses several standards. Examples of a social studies theme for first graders might include community helpers, neighborhoods, families, or community jobs.

2. *Decide on your purpose* for using literature and how you will use the literature to enhance the content of your lessons. Consider the specific goals that you want to address by using the literature you have selected. Are your goals to activate prior knowledge? Build background knowledge? Teach vocabulary associated with the content area? Share concepts in more vivid ways?

3. *Gather your books.* For beginning teachers, an efficient way to gather books is to enlist the help of a local children's librarian. By calling ahead, you can request that a collection of books be gathered by giving the librarian your needs and criteria; for example, "I need 20 books about communities that would be appropriate for first graders. Some of the books should be on a first- or second-grade reading level for independent reading; others can be for read-alouds. Please balance the collection with approximately a third of the books being fictional; the others should expose the students to real-life community issues." As teachers

continue to teach specific grade levels, writing grants that support literature-based content area instruction is another option. Browse the Martha Holden Jennings website for educators (www.mhjf.org/grants-to-educators) for classroom grants you may tap to help you gather content area literature resources.

4. *Develop a plan.* For example, will you use a read-aloud for each aspect of your theme? Will you select books in which the students can do independent reading? How will you introduce the children to the literature? Will you conduct book-talks in which you briefly share the nature of each book?

5. *Consider your assessment strategies* based on using literature in your content area classroom. Will your students conduct poster sessions about what they learned? Will they conduct their own book-talks that address the content? Will they develop artistic representations of what they learned? Will they gather journal entries for which you have developed specific criteria? Although there are myriad ways to assess student learning outcomes when teachers engage their students with literature-based content learning, you need to establish guidelines at the outset to ensure that your students are demonstrating the standards that you expected them to learn when you planned your lessons.

Instructional Strategies for Engaging Students in Reading Informational Text Prior to Reading

■ **Model strategies that prepare students to read informational text.**

Many strategies—such as QARs, reciprocal teaching, and think-alouds—can be implemented with narrative as well as informational text. Here we expound on strategies that assist students in understanding, examining, and interpreting nonfiction text prior to reading.

Determining the Structure of Informational Text

Informational text often includes identifiable features, such as headings and subheadings, a table of contents, a glossary, an index, illustrations, graphs, charts, labels, and definitions. Previewing the format of a textbook is an excellent way to help students get a "picture" of the content of a course. Garber-Miller (2007) offers a number of motivating ways to do just that, including gamelike activities such as "Name That Feature" and "Textbook Scavenger Hunt." In Figure 10.6, we share modifications of some of Garber-Miller's strategies.

Text structure also refers to how the topics are written. When students understand the organization of expository text, they are able to read with more efficiency and see how ideas are connected. Text structure is typically characterized as descriptive, sequential, or written to explain causes and effects or problems and solutions, or to compare and contrast information.

Figure 10.6 Strategies for Text Previewing

- *Textbook Scavenger Hunt.* Provide prompts such as the following and have students work individually or in small groups to locate the information:

  Who are the authors of the book, and where are they from?

  On what page will you find out about _____?

  What is the definition of _____?

  In the summary of Chapter _____, what do the authors say about _____?

  How many subtopics are there in Chapter _____?

  Prompts should be designed based on the features of the text.

- *Sticky Note Votes.* Have the students skim through the book and place sticky notes next to features they think will be helpful when they read the text. Next, divide the class into small groups to compare and contrast their findings. Have them rank order the findings according to importance by voting. Each group can share with the class as discussion occurs about each feature.

- *Textbook Sales Pitches.* Divide the class into groups of three. Have each group skim the book for at least three interesting features. They can use sticky notes to highlight the features. Next, have each group develop a scenario in which group members act as salespeople for the textbook. Allow time for each group to share its scenario while the rest of the class asks questions of the salespeople.

- *What's Old/What's New.* Divide the class into small groups, and assign a chapter to each. Have students preview the chapters listing special features. Next, have them mark each item as a feature they have seen before in other texts as "old," or as a feature they find unique as "new." List each feature in columns as the groups share and discuss any differences among them.

It is critical that teachers work with students so that they understand the various structures they will encounter when reading expository text. It can be effective for teachers to model how to diagram a text structure through graphic organizers. The visuals assist students in recognizing the organization of the expository text. Figure 10.7 shows four graphic organizers that reflect expository text structure. Dreher and Gray (2009) report that explicitly teaching the compare–contrast text structure works particularly well for ELLs. They provide an extensive list of books for this purpose, including *Country Kid* by J. Cummins (2002), *The Sun, the Wind, and the Rain* by L. W. Peters (1990), and *Are Trees Alive?* by D. S. Miller (2002).

Figure 10.7 Graphic Organizer Types

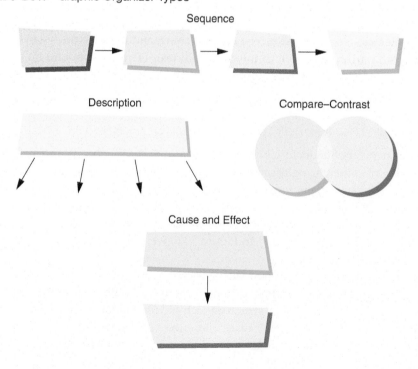

2017 ILA Standard

2.2

Common Core State Standards

CCRA.R.2, CCRA.R.5

In addition to teaching the structure of informational text, making students aware of **signal words** is important. Signal words indicate how the author is connecting ideas. For example, the following words denote a sequence: *first, second, next, then, first of all, last*; examples of cause and effect words are: *because, therefore, due to, resulting from, consequently*; examples of compare-contrast words are: *best, same, different, less, more than, but, yet.* A Google search of signal words provides multiple lists and phrases that can be sorted by purpose and used to develop matching activities with the graphic structures of text.

Frame of Reference

Teachers can help students learn new ideas by giving them a frame of reference as they get ready to read. A frame of reference is actually an anchor point; it reflects the cognitive structure students need to relate new information to existing knowledge. Helping students organize what they know and showing them where and how new ideas fit are essential for learning to take place.

Start previewing with a group of children or young adolescents by modeling some questions that all readers ask to prepare for reading. *Previewing*, after all, should help students become aware of the purposes of a reading assignment. What kind of reading are we going to do? What is our goal? Should we try to remember details or look for the main ideas? How much time will this assignment take? What things do we already know about _____ (the solar system, for example)? What do we still need to find out? Such questions prepare students for what's coming. Raising questions and setting purposes is the beginning of efficient processing of information. It calls for further explicit instruction in previewing.

First, select a subject area for which your textbook contains aids that are obviously visual. The textbook writer often incorporates a number of organizational and typographic aids as guideposts for readers. Point out how the table of contents, preface, chapter introductions or summaries, and chapter questions can give readers valuable clues about the overall structure of a textbook or the important ideas in a unit or chapter. Previewing a table of contents, for example, not only creates a general impression, but also helps readers of all ages distinguish the forest from the trees. The table of contents gives students a feel for the overall theme or structure of the course material so that they may get a sense of the scope and sequence of ideas at the very beginning of the unit. You can also use the table of contents to build background and discuss how the parts of the book are related. Model for students the kinds of questions that should be raised: Why do the authors begin with _____ in Part One? If you were the author, would you have arranged the major parts in the text differently? Why?

Here are some rules or steps to follow when previewing:

1. Read the title, converting it to a question.
2. Read the introduction, summary, and questions, stating the author's main points.
3. Read the heads and subheads; then convert them to questions.
4. Read the highlighted print.
5. Study the visual materials; what do pictures, maps, and other displayed elements tell about a chapter's content?

SKIMMING   Learning how to skim content material effectively is a natural part of previewing. *Skimming* involves intensive previewing of the reading assignment to see what it will be about. To help students get a good sense of what is coming, have them read the first sentence of every paragraph (often an important idea).

An effective motivator for raising students' expectations about their assigned text material is to direct them to skim the entire reading selection rapidly, taking no more than 2 minutes. You might even get a timer and encourage the students to zip through every page. When time is up, ask the class to recall everything they've read. Both you and the students will be surprised by the quantity and quality of the recalls.

Previewing and skimming are important strategies for helping students develop knowledge of textbook aids and for surveying texts to make predictions. They help get a general understanding as students learn how to size up material, judge its relevance to a topic, or gain a good idea of what a passage is about.

Organizers

To prepare students conceptually for ideas to be encountered in reading, help them link what they know to what they will learn. An **organizer** provides a frame of reference for comprehending text precisely for this reason—to help readers make connections between their prior knowledge and new material.

There's no one way to develop or use an organizer. They may be developed as *written previews* or as *verbal presentations*. Whatever format you decide to use, an organizer should highlight key concepts and ideas to be encountered in print. These should be prominent and easily identifiable in the lesson presentation. Another key feature of an organizer activity should be the explicit links made between the children's background knowledge and experience and the ideas in the reading selection.

An organizer may be developed for narrative or expository text. It can be used for difficult text selections when the material is unfamiliar to students, including those from diverse backgrounds, because of limited schemata. Organizers can also assist students as they learn to sort through complex information on the web. An organizer can be constructed by following these guidelines:

- Analyze the content of a reading selection, identifying its main ideas and key concepts.
- Link these ideas directly to students' experiences and storehouse of knowledge. Use real-life incidents, examples, illustrations, analogies, or anecdotes to which student readers can relate.
- Raise questions in the organizer that will pique interest and engage students in thinking about the text to be read.

Key concepts or main ideas in the material being studied can also be displayed as a **graphic organizer**, in which ideas are arranged to show their relationships to each other (see Figure 10.8 for an example).

Anticipation Guides

By creating anticipation about the meaning of what will be read, teachers facilitate student-centered purposes for reading. An **anticipation guide** is a series of oral or written statements for individual students to respond to before they read the text assignment. The statements serve as a springboard into discussion. Students must rely on what they already know to make educated guesses about the material to be read: They must make predictions. Anticipation guides work well for science, history, and social studies. Adams and Pegg (2012), for example, demonstrate how they worked in science classes. Here are the guidelines that one teacher followed in constructing and using anticipation guides:

1. Analyze the material to be read. Determine the major ideas, implicit and explicit, with which students will interact.

Figure 10.8 A Graphic Organizer

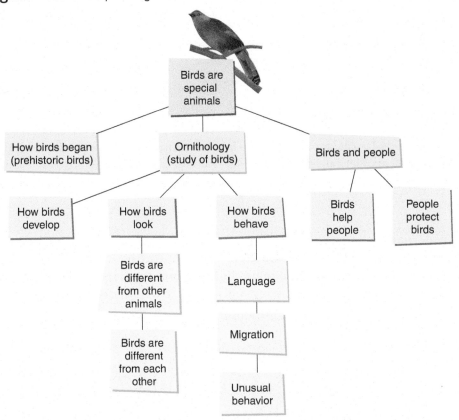

Figure 10.9 Anticipation Guide about Plant Life for Fourth Grade

Place a plus sign (+) next to the statements you think are true. Place a minus sign (–) next to the statements you think are not true.		
Before Reading		**After Reading**
1. _____	All plants have green leaves.	_____
2. _____	All plants bloom in the summer.	_____
3. _____	All plants need a lot of sun.	_____
4. _____	Plants need water.	_____
5. _____	Some plants come back to bloom every year.	_____
6. _____	All plants make food.	_____
7. _____	You can eat most plants.	_____
8. _____	Shrubs are a kind of plant.	_____

2. Write those ideas in short, clear declarative statements.
3. Put these statements into a format that will elicit anticipation and prediction making.
4. Discuss readers' predictions and anticipations prior to reading the text selection.
5. Assign the text selection. Have students evaluate the statements in light of the author's intent and purpose.
6. Contrast readers' predictions with the author's intended meaning.

See Figure 10.9 for an example of an anticipation guide based on plant life for a fourth-grade class.

Brainstorming

As a prereading activity, brainstorming is especially helpful in getting students to generate ideas they can use to think about the upcoming reading material. The brainstorming procedure involves two basic steps: (1) identifying a broad concept that reflects the main topic to be studied in the assigned reading; and (2) having students work in small groups to generate a list of words related to the broad concept within a specified length of time. After brainstorming, students can categorize the words into subtopics. See how one group of students initially brainstormed about transportation:

bus	canoe	helicopter	truck	trolley	bike	tugboat
plane	yacht	subway	van	semi	rocket	sailboat
train	jet	limousine	walking	stroller	running	motorcycle
boat	taxi	kayak	elevator	tricycle	skipping	carriage

They decided to categorize the words into ways to get around: air, land, and water. Can you think of other categories?

2017 ILA Standard

2.2

Brainstorming sessions are valuable not only from an instructional perspective but from a diagnostic one as well. Observant teachers discover what knowledge their students possess about the topic to be studied. Brainstorming also helps *students* become aware of how much they know, individually and collectively, about the topic.

Check Your Understanding 10.4: Gauge your understanding of the skills and concepts in this section.

Extending Content Learning Through Reading and Writing

■ **Demonstrate informational text strategies that include reading and writing connections.**

Next we examine several teaching strategies that increase concept learning as students read informational text. The strategies encourage students to read critically and analytically as they examine how to grasp the essential knowledge that informational texts impart.

Close Reading

Close reading involves reading complex text multiple times for different purposes. As students read informational text, they are given text-specific questions to which they provide evidence-based responses that reflect the author's intent. For example, one reading of the text might be to learn what the author means when a specific scientific term is used. The response must not only include "what the author meant," but also "how do you know that?" Was the text in italics? Was it in bold print? The purpose of re-reading the same text might be to explain the sequence of a scientific phenomenon; followed by a question such as, "How does the author tell you that the sequence is essential to understanding the concept?" "What signal words does the author use?" Teachers need to read the text closely ahead of time to determine the significance of what the author is saying prior to developing strategic questions; this is a critical step for effectively engaging students in a close reading of any text.

FOCUS ON CLOSE READING

Watch this **video** (http://www.youtube.com/watch?v=2anzoCrsgfw) to learn how teachers orchestrate close reading in their classrooms. What are the similarities and differences in what teachers use?

Figure 10.10 A Coding Example for Annotating Text

CODE	PURPOSE
Underline	To indicate key points
Circle	To indicate key academic vocabulary
Question Mark ?	To indicate confusion
Star	To indicate signal words
Arrow	To indicate a marginal note or query

Figure 10.11 Discussion Prompts

I believe the author means …
I see what the author is saying.
I understand why the author said this.
The author is proving a point here.
In the text the author mentions …
I found evidence here …

As students read the informational text, they need to annotate or write "all over" the page. Although there is no one particular way to annotate, teachers generally provide a code for marking. The purpose is to provide reference points that subsequently will be used as evidence for the text-specific questions. See Figure 10.10 for a coding example.

Discussion or collaborative conversations (Fisher, Frey, & Lapp, 2016) are another a key component of close reading. When students are guided in purposeful talk about informational text, they have the opportunity to verify their thinking, as well as understand the process of learning from their peers. Using their annotated text, for example, students can discuss the evidence they found in the text regarding main ideas, talk about the vocabulary, and indicate points of confusion. Discussion frames are useful when modeling how to carry on a conversation after reading (Fisher et al., 2016). See Figure 10.11 for examples of discussion prompts.

KWL

Ogle (1986) described **KWL** as a three-step teaching plan designed to guide and motivate children as they read to acquire information from expository texts. The strategy helps students think about what they know or believe they know about a topic, what they need to find out by reading the text, what they learned by reading, and what they still need and want to learn about the topic from other information sources. The KWL model is outlined on a chart, screen, or teacher-made handout that children use as they proceed through the steps of the strategy (see Figure 10.12).

The first two steps in the model are prereading activities. The beginning step (K—What do you *know*? or What do you think you know?) involves brainstorming with a group of students to help them focus on their current knowledge of a topic. The teacher's questions should lead children to think about and to respond *specifically* to the topic

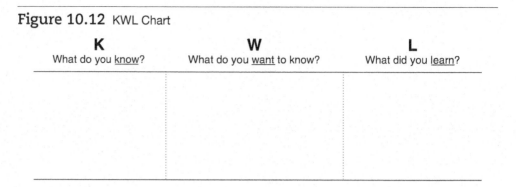

Figure 10.12 KWL Chart

K	**W**	**L**
What do you <u>know</u>?	What do you <u>want</u> to know?	What did you <u>learn</u>?

being discussed. Teachers of students with multicultural backgrounds need to be aware of their students' cultures and schemata in order to "tap" their prior knowledge about a topic. The purpose of this brainstorming process is to activate children's prior knowledge to help them understand what they will read in the text. The children's responses are recorded on the chart, screen, or worksheets.

2017 ILA Standard

2.2

The next step (W—What do you *want* to find out?) evolves naturally from assessing the results of the brainstorming and categorizing activities. As children identify areas of controversy or key categories that contain little or no information, a purpose for reading is developed. Although this step is done mainly as a group activity, each student writes the questions that he or she is most interested in learning about on the worksheet. Students' personal interests guide and motivate their reading.

During the final step of the KWL process (L—What did you *learn*?), the students record their findings on their worksheets. They have the option of writing down information either as they read or immediately after they finish reading. With teacher guidance and assistance, the students assess whether their questions and concerns were satisfactorily answered by reading the text. When students need or want additional information about a topic, they should be guided to other sources of information. In Figure 10.13, examine the KWL chart on chipmunks that was developed by a third-grade class.

Point-of-View Guides

Point-of-view guides provide students with the opportunity to express content knowledge by answering questions presented in an interview format. After reading an informational text selection, trade book, or online information, students role-play by writing in the *first person* to express points of view based on the content that has been read. First, the teacher presents a scenario; next the teacher poses the interview questions. When teachers scaffold this activity, different perspectives are encouraged. In answering the interview questions, students actively contribute their own thoughts about the role, which ultimately enhances their recall and comprehension. These questions allow students to elaborate and speculate. The purpose of the point-of-view guide is to develop mental elaboration (students add their own information as they read) and mental recitation (students put new information in their own words, merging text-based and reader-based information). In this way, students learn the content of the reading selection. Figure 10.14 depicts a point-of-view guide based on a fourth-grade science lesson about plants.

Figure 10.13 Completed KWL Chart

K	W	L
What do you <u>know</u>?	What do you <u>want</u> to find out?	What did you <u>learn</u>?
1. They run fast.	1. Do they come out in the daytime or at night?	1. I learned they live under rocks.
2. They eat nuts.	2. How old are they when they live on their own?	2. Their holes are 20 to 30 feet long.
3. They dig holes.	3. How long do they live?	3. Cats eat them.
4. They climb trees.	4. What colors are they?	4. Baby chipmunks grow up in one month.
5. They are afraid of people.	5. How fast can they dig?	5. Chipmunk is an American Indian word.
6. Some are brown.	6. How fast can they run?	6. They have two pouches for storing food.
	7. How deep can they dig?	7. They work, play, and rest at different times during the day and night.
		8. They have eyes on the sides of their heads.
		9. They have sharp claws and teeth.
		10. They are good at hiding.
		11. They nibble on leaves.

Figure 10.14 Point-of-View Guide for a Fourth-Grade Lesson About Plants

Text: Plants need sun and shade to survive. Some plants need a lot of sun. If they don't get enough sun, they will have trouble living. Other plants need mostly shade because that is what helps them live longer.

Plants also need water because they will wilt without it. Some plants need more water than others. Some plants need less water because they hold water in their stems to keep them alive.

Plants also need good soil. The soil gives them nutrients that they need to be healthy and strong.

Scenario: You are a plant that lives on a patio. You need lots of shade and water. It has been a hot summer with not much rain. You are having a difficult time living.

Interview questions:

1. How has the weather been this summer?
   Response: It has been so hot that I wish it would snow. I need something cool over me.
2. How do you feel about that?
   Response: It's sad. I really need to move to another place, and I need some water to drink.
3. Why?
   Response: Because it's too hot. It is very, very hot here, and I don't like it. There is too much sun, and I'm thirsty.
4. How could your life be better on the patio?
   Response: I think if I could move to the shade it would be better. Maybe somebody could water me with a hose. I think that would feel good.

Although this is a simple example, interview questions can be posed that help students argue, critique, and synthesize sophisticated content area concepts.

Teachers need to guide students in the organizational differences that Internet reading demands.

Annie Pickert Fuller/Pearson Education

Idea Circles

Idea circles are small peer-led group discussions of concepts fueled by multiple text sources. They are composed of three to six students. After introducing students to a concept, they each read different informational books, bringing unique information to the idea circle. In the circle, they discuss facts about this concept and relations among the facts and explanations. The teacher provides a chart to guide collaborative discussion, such as the one on lakes in Figure 10.15. The goal of the idea circle needs to be communicated explicitly. Teachers should tell students what they are expected to accomplish in an allotted time for discussion (Guthrie & McCann, 1996).

Idea circles can be easily adapted to reading content information on the web. Teachers can design questions for middle school students based on selected websites. Here is how a web-based idea circle works. Each small group is given a chart similar to the format in Figure 10.14. The group also receives an accompanying sheet with the same number of related websites as there are members of the group. Each group member selects a website from the list, making sure that everyone has selected a different site. The students are instructed to browse the web in search of answers to the questions on the chart. After an allotted amount of time or class periods, the students share their findings in small discussion groups. When teachers develop different questions about related topics for each group, the students in each group can pool their information and design a PowerPoint presentation for the rest of the class.

Curriculum-Based Reader's Theater

Another way to engage students in learning content from informational text is to adapt reader's theater by developing scripts that are based on curriculum content (Flynn, 2004, 2005). This strategy involves having the students read sections of text and, working in small groups, they rewrite the main ideas in the form of an entertaining script.

Figure 10.15 Chart to Guide Collaborative Discussion in an Idea Circle

Subject: Social Studies	**Topic:** Lakes	Grade 4

Ask your friends and family members if they have ever gone to a lake. What did they do there? Write your responses here. We will share these responses with the class as a whole.

Find the following information using your book about lakes. It is possible that the book you are using will not include all of the answers. You may have to get some of this information from others in the idea circle.

What is a lake?

What is a freshwater lake? Give an example of one. What is a saltwater lake? Give an example of one.

What are lakes used for?

What about lakes and pollution?

BOX 10.7 | STEP-BY-STEP LESSON

Implementing a Curriculum-Based Reader's Theater

1. Select a CCSS from your content area that specifies a particular knowledge base with details related to that topic. This concept will be used to scaffold students' writing of a curriculum-based script.
2. Next, introduce the concept of dialogue by modeling simple conversations with the students. For example, use probing questions such as, "What do you like to do in your free time?" "Why is that fun for you?" Provide the students time to share conversations with a partner, and explain that conversations express ideas. Have students share the main ideas and details of the conversations.
3. Next, introduce the idea of scripts and how scripts are like conversations in movies and videos written down. Introduce the idea of writing scripts.
4. Model how to write a script using the SMART Board or computer so that students can see the format. Select a simple concept at first. An example might be a conversation about going to a baseball game and watching the last inning of a game that has been tied; one team finally wins when a player makes a home run:

Joe: This game is driving me crazy!
Kim: Me, too! It's the last inning and still tied!

Joe: Oh, here comes Mason at bat. Let's see what happens!
Kim: Gee whiz! Strike one!
Joe: Gosh! Oh, no! Strike two!
Kim: Wow! Would you look at that! Mason's hit it out of the park!
Joe: Whew! What a game! Wish we could meet Mason!

5. Next, model a script about a concept in your content area in which the information comes alive through dialogue. See Figure 10.16 for an example of a curriculum-based reader's theater script on Mars.
6. Next, introduce the content area topic that you initially selected. Activate prior knowledge about the content, and divide the students into small groups. Either have them read assigned pages in a text or choose sections. Have the students brainstorm a conversation and create a script that demonstrates the main ideas. Circulate among the groups, and scaffold the writing.
7. Have the students share scripts and main ideas based on the content. They can read and dramatize the concepts and compare, contrast, and critique information. This provides the students with a way to demonstrate their understanding of content area topics. When the students read the scripts over and over, it also enhances fluency.

The benefits of a **curriculum-based reader's theater** are threefold: increased fluency, enhanced understanding of content, and motivation to read.

See the step-by-step lesson featured in Box 10.7 for one way to conduct a curriculum-based reader's theater. See Figure 10.16 for an excerpt of a script about Mars.

USING THINK-ALOUDS   In addition, using think-alouds can be an effective way to scaffold students' understanding of how we navigate online text. McKeon (2010a, 2010b) suggests a think-aloud framework to teach comprehension strategies that we

Figure 10.16 Partial Sample of Curriculum-Based Reader's Theater Script on Mars

Setting: Outer Space
Characters: Earth, Moon, Mars, Comet, Crater
Earth: Gee, you guys sure have more craters than I do! I'm *so* jealous! (exaggerated body language)
Moon: Not to worry, Earth. It's *really* not all that great.
Mars: Right on. Craters leave scars on us when objects from outer space crash!
ALL: Ouch! (Loud)
Earth: Yeah, I remember when a comet fell on me. Rather painful. Left a dent.
ALL: Ouch! (Loud)
Comet: Oh, brother, Earth. It wasn't *that bad*! It was sort of exciting to all those on Earth.
Crater: Yeah, Comet, I remember you made the headlines on that Earth thing they call a lewspaper.
Earth: I think you mean *newspaper*!
Crater: Whatever. Comet was *so* famous!
Earth: Well, anyway, I still am a bit jealous of all of your craters, Mars and Moon.
Moon: Well, I'm jealous of all the water you have! Almost three-fourths of you is water!
ALL: Yeah! Yeah! Water, water everywhere! Almost three-fourths of Earth is water! (Shout as a cheer, and repeat three times with cheering actions.)

use when we read online information. Teacher *preparation* for conducting the online think-aloud looks like this:

- Select a topic of inquiry that aligns with at least one content standard that you are expected to teach, for example in social studies, and fine-tune the purpose of your inquiry in terms of a question or questions.
- Locate two or three appropriate websites that address the content standard(s) and address your questions. Professional teaching organizations typically include content-specific information based on content standards and grade levels, but other web searches can be equally informative.
- After reviewing the website(s), note links that would be appropriate for conducting a think-aloud that relates to the information you want the students to navigate in order to answer the questions you have posed.
- Develop an open-ended graphic organizer so that you can record how you gather and record information as you surf the web, and complete it as you conduct the think-aloud.

See a sample think-aloud using web-based inquiry in Box 10.8.

BOX 10.8 | TRANSLITERACY

Using a Think-Aloud While Navigating the Web

Miss Kim is a fourth-grade teacher who believes that her students need to learn web-based navigation tools so they will know how to critically read and learn using the Internet. She has focused several lessons on rivers, which have included their utility for agriculture, housing, and wildlife. In the following lesson, she uses a think-aloud to explore a vacation topic about rivers using the web.

Miss K: We have been learning about rivers in our textbook and by reading trade books. I enjoyed learning about rivers and how useful they are for wildlife. What did you enjoy learning?

Adam: I liked that, too. I really liked learning how rivers are important for beavers!

Joe: My favorite was the river otters. Boy! They can dive really, really deep!

Miss K: Yes, all kinds of animals use rivers to survive. We also learned that rivers can be very big and long and that some rivers can be dangerous. I'm wondering about the dangers. I'm thinking it would be scary to live by a river that might overflow. What else do you think about rivers?

Adam: I know that sometimes they dry up. I think that's kind of weird.

Miss K: Yes, I wonder what the animals do if their river dries up? What do think?

Adam: Some of them might die.

Emily: They might find a puddle or another river for water.

Miss K: Yes, or maybe they would find a pond nearby. I like the way you are thinking about the information we learned about rivers. Since we've learned a lot about rivers, I was wondering whether visiting a river would be fun for a vacation. I think it would be fun to swim in a river. What do you think you could do if you were on a vacation by a river?

Emily: I would love to go rafting on a river. I saw a movie about that!

Joe: My uncle did white-water rafting in Tennessee!

Adam: I think fishing in a river would be lots of fun. You could cook the fish and eat them!

Miss K: Okay, here are two questions we can think about: Where are rivers in the United States that would make good vacation spots? What vacation activities are there to do by rivers? We are going to use the Internet to explore answers to these questions. I am going to tell you what I am thinking as we search for links. Let's begin our search for answers to these questions and see what we can find. *(Miss Kim posts the questions on the marker board.)*

Miss K: First, I think I will type a search "vacations by rivers in the United States." I think that's what I want. *(Miss Kim types the search words.)*

Miss K: Oh, my! Most of the links are about river cruises. I don't think I want a vacation that is a cruise down a river. I think that would be too expensive. I think I'll try another search. How about "land river vacations in the United States"? *(Miss Kim types the search words.)*

Miss K: Gee, this search gives me too many choices. Some of the choices, however, mention different states. Maybe I should type in a state. Let's try the state of Tennessee. That's where Joe said his uncle went white-water rafting. Let's try to focus on that state and see what we find. *(Miss Kim searches "river vacations in Tennessee.")*

Miss Kim: Oh, look! There are a lot of vacation places in Tennessee! They list all kinds of activities that you can do at these river vacation spots: horseback riding, rafting, hiking, fishing, boating. Let's pick an activity that we might want to do near a river in Tennessee and see what we can find. What kind of activity should we search for?

Joe: Let's do rafting, white-water rafting.

Emily: I choose rafting, too! I've always wanted to go rafting on a river.

Adam: What about fishing? That's my choice.

Miss K: Okay, let's try to search both ideas for vacations in Tennessee on a river. How should we search?

Adam: We could type "fishing in Tennessee."

Emily: We could type "fishing and rafting in Tennessee."

Miss K: Okay, I think we could combine your ideas. Let's type "fishing and rafting vacations in Tennessee." *(Miss Kim types the search words.)*

Miss K: Oh, my! Most of the sites are about rafting! I think if we want to go rafting and fishing, we might have to search further.

Miss Kim continues to think aloud and model what she is thinking as she searches for information on a Tennessee vacation. Her modeling explicitly demonstrates that you need to ask questions as you search the web.

As content area teachers implement and scaffold before, during, and after reading and writing strategies, many of which can be modeled and taught with traditional, as well as electronic texts, they also need to bear in mind that the literacy needs of today's students go far beyond strategy instruction. Next we explore additional challenges and skills that teaching the content areas involves in terms of twenty-first-century digital literacy.

Check Your Understanding 10.5: Gauge your understanding of the skills and concepts in this section.

Digital Literacy

■ **Understand and explain the importance and complexity that digital literacy holds for content area teachers.**

Digital literacy, also known as transliteracy, refers to the technological and communication skills that are needed in order to be productive citizens in our ever-evolving, twenty-first-century technological world. The competencies include the knowledge and abilities to use such tools as social networking and Internet resources, as well as the ability to read, comprehend, analyze, critique, and use online text and multimedia applications. Indeed, the CCSS (2010a) make it clear that students need to be able to locate, evaluate, and integrate online information, as well as utilize digital technologies in order to be college and career ready. As Don Leu and others remind us, however, the nature of digital literacy rapidly changes as new technologies develop (Leu, 2000; Leu et al., 2011).

2017 ILA Standard

5.2

Common Core State Standards

CCRA.R.7, CCRA.W.8, CCRA.SL.5

Needless to say, new technologies will continue to change the landscape of what it means to be literate. Although the skills needed to recognize print will probably not change in our lifetime (i.e., the ability to decode words), comprehending new vocabulary, understanding and using sophisticated information, interpreting new symbols of communication, and being able to navigate more complex digital technologies will surely challenge educators and students.

Equally important is the wide range of ever-growing available information on the Internet that content area teachers need to consider, along with how the information aligns with the content standards. Not only are the concepts complex, but the high levels of learning and thinking needed to use the information require significant scaffolding.

So, what are content area teachers to do? They need to take charge, lead, and continue to forge ahead with continuous professional development that not only keeps them up-to-date on current subject area content, but also keeps them informed about new technologies. Hence, we suggest several areas that content area teachers need to think about.

Informational Text and the Internet

Whether you are a first-grade teacher developing basic concepts about communities with your students, or a middle school teacher crafting thoughtful projects about how to improve the recycling habits of community members, you have access to countless websites when you search for online information and instructional ideas on the Internet. In fact, when you Google for information or lessons, there are boundless resources and you can easily become overwhelmed.

One way to narrow the scope of your search for content material and lessons is to utilize the professional associations linked to your subject areas. The International Literacy Association (ILA) and the National Council of Teachers of English (NCTE), for example, are two organizations affiliated with the language arts. Today many educational professional associations have lessons that align with the content standards. See, for example, the **ReadWriteThink** website sponsored by the ILA and NCTE for lessons that focus on reading, writing, listening, speaking, and viewing. In addition, there are innumerable links to student resources (http://www.readwritethink.org/).

Internet Inquiry

At the very least, when students use the Internet for learning about content area subjects, they need to understand that the organizational patterns of websites differ significantly from those of textbooks. Information, for example, is made available through a menu that is displayed on a home page rather than a table of contents. Instead of locating information using an index, a home page often provides hyperlinks to related topics of inquiry. Students, however, can easily get lost on the web as they "surf" for information. Haphazard web surfing can be counterproductive, whereas carefully orchestrated activities can result in creative and high-level critical thinking skills.

When teachers engage their students in **Internet inquiry**, they also need to consider the difference between knowledge and information. In other words, as teachers guide students in Internet inquiry, they need to ensure that students are not simply consumers of information but are instead learning how to use information technology to actively learn.

WebQuests, first developed by Bernie Dodge and Tom March at San Diego State University in the 1990s, are one way to organize Internet inquiry. The **WebQuest** model features systematic searching and focuses on supporting students' learning through synthesis, evaluation, and analysis.

WebQuests typically involve an introduction that is intended to motivate students, a task that describes the final project, steps that students take to accomplish the final project, a list of web-based resources to use during the process, a rubric for student evaluation, and a conclusion that focuses on reflection and discussion. McKeon (2010a, 2010b) suggests how to introduce students to WebQuests using think-alouds. Sox and Rubinstein-Avila (2009) suggest how WebQuests can be adapted for ELLs by synthesizing information, providing supplemental checklists for completion, and pre-teaching vocabulary. You can go to the **WebQuests** website to view sample WebQuests.

As teachers include Internet inquiry in purposeful ways to enhance content area learning, they will undoubtedly realize that this form of electronic text lends itself to new ways of defining literacy and subject matter learning. New skills will need to be honed. Skills such as skimming, scanning, evaluating sources of information, and synthesizing content take on new meaning when web searching is included in content area learning.

BOX 10.9 | TRANSLITERACY

Digital Media Concept Maps to Strengthen Comprehension

Graphic organizers are great tools students can to use to monitor their reading and comprehension of informational texts. Traditionally, teachers have created paper-based templates for students to use to organize their thinking around text. In a transliterate society, there are a number of web-based concept mapping tools and apps that teachers can employ in their classrooms to help support comprehension of informational text.

Popplet (http://popplet.com) is a concept mapping tool that supports students as they organize facts, ideas, and evidence around a topic. Available as a browser-based tool and as an iOS app, students create a primary "popple" and can then attach additional "popples" that can include text, photos, and videos. Support for embedded digital media, such as YouTube videos or royalty-free photos, is a key feature of Popplet and other concept mapping tools, like Mindmeister (http://www.mindmeister.com) and SimpleMind (http://www.simpleapps.eu/simplemind).

In an elementary classroom, you may ask students to independently read a selection of informational text about Arctic animals, and as they read, they can periodically stop, think, and react to what they are reading by inserting text and embedding digital media into a Popplet. When students embed media in their concept maps, they are taking a small snippet of HTML code from the source and adding that code into the concept map. This HTML code is what powers the media player and allows the digital media to be viewed by others.

The skills associated with working with small amounts of HTML code to embed digital media are becoming increasingly important in our hyperlinked, connected world. When students link and embed digital media in concept maps, it makes their thinking and learning more transparent for others and allows teachers an opportunity to gain insight into how students are comprehending informational text. As students get older and begin to write in online spaces like blogs and websites, embedding media, especially to source documents and referenced materials, will bring more credibility to students' written work.

Online Reading Comprehension Skills

When students use the Internet to locate information based on a content area topic, they have the opportunity to experience new levels of reading comprehension. Gathering information on the web involves searching through multiple types of text, including hyperlinks, videos, audios, and visual presentations of material. In addition, students need to evaluate the sources of the information and synthesize what they have learned, often creating multimedia presentations that reflect interrelated concepts. This includes learning how to create graphics and images that capture the essence of concepts. In Box 10.9, Jeremy Brueck suggests using digital graphic organizers to enhance reading comprehension.

In addition, students have the opportunity to use social network to communicate ideas and collaborate with others to problem solve. Blogs, wikis, and Twitter are only a few of the tools that are available to students as they interact with others via the web. Much like texting, social networking involves summarizing ideas in ways that make sense to the recipient(s). In essence, students need teachers who can scaffold online reading comprehension. Hence, teachers need to experience and practice how to gather, organize, synthesize, communicate, and present web-based information in unique formats. We suggest that teachers work with one another as they plan technology-based lessons and discuss with each other the procedures they use to search for new information, make sense of it, and ultimately use it.

Check Your Understanding 10.6: Gauge your understanding of the skills and concepts in this section.

RTI for Struggling Readers

Informational Text and *Response to Intervention*

For many readers, young and old alike, reading content material is challenging. The massive amount of new information that is generated each day on the Internet alone, for example, is daunting. In addition to content area reading on the web, most school systems use textbooks as a source of content information. Students who struggle in reading, in particular, may be challenged with understanding the amount of information both in textbooks and on the Internet. How teachers at the elementary and middle school levels teach with these texts can ultimately affect how students learn the content.

Given the comprehensive and complex skills necessary to prepare students for college, careers, and citizenship in the twenty-first century (National Governors Association Center for Best Practices, Council of Chief State School Officials, 2010a), it becomes critical that teachers rethink how we address continued support for ensuring that all students will achieve these high standards.

RTI, in theory, focuses primarily on the early years of prevention and intervention for struggling readers; although there is much contemporary literature on the topic, there are no definitive ways to implement and organize RTI. In fact, Ehren (2013) points out that while there are schools that exhibit successful implementation of RTI, we need more than good teachers and schools; we need excellent leaders who can expand upon these "pockets of excellence" (p. 449). We need professional development, collaborations among educators, and, perhaps most important, exceptional front-runners who can spearhead leadership that focuses on the needs of all students K through 12.

2017 ILA Standard

6.1

In addition to thinking beyond the original intent of RTI, which focuses on prevention at the elementary levels, we need to remember that when students enter middle school, they are primarily in content area classes. We agree with Brozo (2009/2010) that it then becomes the role of content area teachers to ensure that all students will be able to learn, think about, analyze, and ultimately use informational text about the subjects. Hence, there is the need for professional development, collaborations among experts who can constructively guide practices, and programs that will help all children succeed, as well as excellent teachers who know their content, how to teach it, and how to assess knowledge growth (Wixson & Lipson, 2012). The stakes are high, and they are challenging on multiple levels; there is no one size that will fit all. However, if we are to address these complex challenges, we must all become leaders at some level. We owe it to our students, for one day they will be *our* leaders.

What About . . .

Standards, Assessment, and Content Area Texts?

The CCSS (2010a) delineate a wide range of literacy skills across the curriculum that teachers need to address at all grade levels. Beginning in the early years, these competencies include being able to read, analyze, and synthesize informational text. Although content area textbooks are still used to foster learning in the subject areas in schools, it is critical that students be competent in reading multiple information sources that include online resources and multimedia formats. As teachers develop students' competencies to critically read subject matter, they must use their professional knowledge and experience as they scaffold learning. How students are assessed on the skills delineated in the CCSS (2010a), however, is a much debated topic. The Learning First Alliance, a consortium of professional organizations and stakeholders invested in the implementation of the Common Core, and Partnership for Assessment of Readiness for College and Careers (PARCC), a large assessment consortium, are two groups at the time of this printing that have a vested interest in implementing the CCSS and how to assess student achievement. In addition, there is considerable discussion among professionals regarding the lack of online reading skills necessary to be productive members of society in the twenty-first century that are included in the CCSS (Drew, 2012/2013; Leu et al., 2011).

Our advice for preservice and classroom teachers is to keep abreast of resources, research, and professional development opportunities regarding how to implement the Common Core competencies in classrooms and how to assess the results of instruction. There is not a clear-cut set of answers. It will be up to teachers who are willing to be leaders as they address the complex issues that the CCSS pose in terms of implementation and assessment. In essence, teachers need to become involved on multiple levels in order to address the content literacy skills that students will require when they enter the real world after graduation.

In addition, we suggest that teachers consider how they will address differentiated instruction including modifications for ELLs, as well as how they will provide the students with choices during the instructional and assessment phases of the lessons.

Summary

- Initially this chapter addressed issues about a variety of concerns that make informational text difficult to read. Topics included the format and organization of textbooks, the readability levels on which they are written, the vocabulary, and the styles of writing.

- Next, we shared ways to organize textbook reading. These included cooperative learning activities with designated assignments to provide students with specific purposes for reading textbook selections, such as informational text circles and jigsaws. In addition, we discussed how to use graphic organizers and sticky notes to help organize textbook reading.

- We discussed a variety of considerations regarding using literature and informational trade books in the content areas. Not only did we share the benefits of

- using nonfiction literature, but we also suggested guidelines and strategies for implementing trade books in content area classrooms.

- Next, we explored reading strategies that can assist students prior to reading text selections. These include previewing, skimming, organizers, anticipation guides, and brainstorming.

- We shared techniques for including writing as a significant piece of content area learning. These include close reading, KWL, point-of-view guides, idea circles, and curriculum-based reader's theater.

- Finally, we focused on new skills and challenges that teachers must address regarding digital, online reading in the content areas. Issues include technological skills and professional development.

Teacher Action Research

1. Contact curriculum directors from two different school districts, and ask them to loan you the textbooks for a particular content area (e.g., world history). Examine the textbooks in terms of the issues discussed in this chapter regarding what makes a textbook difficult for students. Compare and contrast the textbooks, and share with your classmates or colleagues. Use your findings as a springboard for discussing the pros and cons of using textbooks in the classroom.

2. Select a content area, and interview two teachers in two diverse school settings (for example, teachers in classrooms with high and low incidences of ELLs, respectively, or high and low numbers of multicultural students, or high and low poverty rates). Develop a questionnaire in which you ask the teachers how they differentiate and organize instruction for their students in the content area that you have selected.

Synthesize your findings by comparing and contrasting the teachers' responses.

3. Select a topic from a content area book. Divide the topic into subtopics. Locate children's literature—fiction and nonfiction—that could be used to teach the subtopics. Plan a lesson based on one of the subtopics, and teach it to a group of children. Take anecdotal records in which you record the students' reactions to the lesson. Write a reflection about what you observed.

4. Select a human interest story from the newspaper, and develop an anticipation guide based on the featured story. Distribute the anticipation guide to your colleagues; have them complete the guide individually or in groups. Next, distribute copies of the feature article. After allowing time for reading the article, have your colleagues compare and contrast how they completed the anticipation guide. Use the activity to

discuss the logistics of this strategy and how it worked or did not work for them.

5. Select a short, complex piece of informational text and develop text-dependent questions. Conduct a "close reading" of the text with your colleagues, and discuss the nature of the text-dependent questions.

6. Research professional development opportunities and workshops at the university you attend, in the school district in which you teach, or in the community in which you live that focus on new technologies. Compare and contrast the opportunities that are available to you. Select one of the resources that fits your schedule, and commit yourself to learning a new technological skill. Keep a diary of what you learn to share with colleagues.

Through the Lens of the Common Core

Beginning in the early years, the CCSS (2010a) focus on the importance of engaging students in reading nonfiction and complex text. The skills involve high-order thinking abilities such as analyzing, interpreting, synthesizing, evaluating, and using information. Teachers need to craft lessons in which they model and scaffold these skills so that students will be successful in adapting them to real-life situations.

In the primary years, teachers can begin to develop students' abilities to understand the formats of informational text through read-alouds. When they highlight features such as the table of contents, index, glossary, headings, and subheadings, they help young children understand that informational text is read differently than narrative stories.

As children enter the middle grades, teachers need to provide students with more sophisticated strategies for reading informational texts and online information. Not only do teachers need to scaffold deep thinking about content, but they also need to provide opportunities for students to integrate multiple resources and demonstrate competencies that focus on problem solving and collaboration.

Needless to say, the demands that the CCSS (2010a) place on content area teachers require expertise and proficiency in teaching not only complex subject matter but also multifaceted literacy skills. We believe that ongoing professional development, along with collaborations among reading specialists and teachers, will be critical in light of the aspiration to prepare all students for college, careers, and citizenship in the twenty-first century.

Chapter 11
Reading–Writing Connections

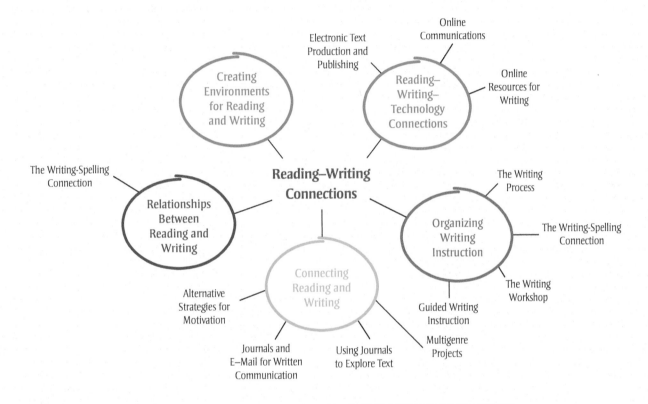

Learning Outcomes

In This Chapter, You Will Discover How to

- Explain the relationships between reading and writing.

- Demonstrate how to foster a classroom environment that supports reading–writing connections.

- Scaffold strategies for students that connect reading and writing, including journal writing, e-mail, and alternative approaches such as multigenre projects and writing nonfiction.

- Explain the writing process, and demonstrate how to organize writing instruction, including how to conduct writing workshops.

- Demonstrate an understanding of the importance of integrating technology into the language arts curriculum, including effective strategies for teaching twenty-first-century communication skills.

Activating Your Schema

Think of times in your life (past or present) when you wrote or when you now write. Categorize your recollections into two columns: academic writing and personal writing. Academic writing might include essays, theses, journals, reflections, or lesson plans. Personal writing might include e-mail, greeting card messages, and to-do lists, to name a few. After brainstorming, rate each writing entry with a plus sign (+) for a positive writing experience in your life, or a minus sign (−) for a negative experience in your life. Share your responses with a partner. What do you realize about yourself as a writer based on this activity?

2017 ILA Standards Found in This Chapter

1.2	2.2	3.2	5.3

Common Core State Standards: English Language Arts

CCRA.R.5	CCRA.W.3	CCRA.W.6	CCRA.W.9
CCRA.W.1	CCRA.W.4	CCRA.W.7	CCRA.W.10
CCRA.W.2	CCRA.W.5	CCRA.W.8	

Key Terms

brainstorming	minilesson
buddy journal	multigenre project
dialogue journal	plot scaffold
double-entry journal	reading journal
electronic texts	response journal
group share session	six traits-plus writing model
guided writing	writing notebooks
invented spelling	writing process
key pal correspondence	writing workshop

Livia is a fourth grader who loves to read stories. When given choices, she often selects books that she says are "magical" to her. Livia likes to read about princesses, fairytales, and make-believe stories that explore enchanted adventures.

When her teacher, Mrs. Peters, was conducting an introductory lesson for her fourth graders on *writing* stories, Livia raised her hand and said, "Mrs. Peters, I like to read stories, but I'm not an author. I can't write a book. I can't even write a story! I'm not an author!" Livia was actually quite vocal about her lack of ability to write a story. Mrs. Peter's initial response to Livia was, "Okay, we can talk about this later."

Mrs. Peters thought about Livia's comments and how she was an avid reader but declared her lack of confidence in actually writing her own story. She decided that one approach she would try to engage Livia in writing was to have the class compose a story together. Using the smartboard, Mrs. Peters worked with her students as they created a narrative about a lost puppy that was found by an old lady who decided to welcome him into her home. Livia contributed to the final draft of the story by adding that the woman was a *spinster* who was lonely and that the lost but now found puppy brought *delight* to the new owner. She also shared that the lady was *cranky* at first and at the end of the story she became a *warm* and *affectionate* character. Livia's colorful use of vocabulary added to the descriptive nature of the story. One of her classmates even commented, "Livia, you use good words!" Livia replied, "Words are fun; they make a picture in your mind!" Mrs. Peters couldn't help but smile. Maybe Livia will enjoy writing after all. When teachers provide support for students and scaffold their efforts to write by working together, they provide a path toward building confidence for reluctant writers.

Our emphasis throughout the chapter is on the strong bonds that exist between learning to write and learning to read. These connections are powerful enough to suggest that children probably learn as much about reading by writing as they learn about writing by reading.

Relationships Between Reading and Writing

■ **Explain the relationships between reading and writing.**

Common sense tells us that writing is intended to be read. When children are writing, they can't help but be involved in reading. Before writing, they may be collecting and connecting information from books, digital texts, or online communications. Depending on the nature of the writing, children might be revising, proofreading, and sharing their work with others, or they might simply be communicating thoughts about what they have read. No matter what the nature of the writing, children and young adolescents should be invited to write about what they are reading and to read about what they are writing. Therein lies a real value of *reading–writing connections* (Shanahan, 1990; Tierney & Shanahan 1991).

In the past, reading and writing were taught separately and sequentially. The premise underlying this instructional path was that reading ability develops first and writing ability follows. Supported by new knowledge about literacy development, today's teachers recognize that when young children are engaged in writing, they are using and manipulating written language. In doing so, children develop valuable concepts about print and how messages are created.

There is compelling historical evidence to suggest that writing and reading abilities develop concurrently and should be nurtured together. Marie Clay (1975, 1979, 1988, 1991, 2001) a seminal linguist, supported the powerful bonds between reading and writing. She saw them as complementary processes. Contemporary research confirms the intricate relationships between reading and writing, but also suggests that reading and writing in the twenty-first century demand new literacy connections and skills that are necessary for communication (Harris, Graham, Friedlander, & Laud, 2013; Hutchison, Beschorner, & Schmidt-Crawford, 2012; Larson, 2010; Peterson & Taylor, 2012). In addition, Eugene Garcia (2002) contends that teachers need to understand that the reading and writing connections for students from diverse backgrounds ought to be based on the roles reading and writing play in the social lives of people of various cultures. Judith Irvin (1998) underscores the importance of making the reading and writing connection explicit for the middle school student. She pointed out that the young adolescent is undergoing a transitional stage of language development and that language instruction needs to be integrated. Needless to say, literacy instruction ought to engage students in reading and writing concurrently for a variety of reasons.

2017 ILA Standard

1.2

The following are some of the conclusions that can be drawn about the relationships between reading and writing:

- Reading and writing processes are correlated; that is, good readers are generally good writers, and vice versa.
- Students who write well tend to read more than those who are less capable writers.
- Wide reading may be as effective in improving writing as actual practice in writing.
- Good readers and writers are likely to engage in reading and writing independently because they have healthy concepts of themselves as readers and writers.

These conclusions suggest that the two processes share many of the same characteristics: Both are language and experience based, both require active involvement from language learners, and both are viewed as acts of making meaning.

The Writing-Spelling Connection

How does spelling fit into the process of writing? Carol Chomsky (1970, 1979) was one of the first linguists to advocate that children write first and read later. She contended that writing is a beneficial introduction to reading because children acquire letter and word knowledge through *invented spellings*. Typically, very young children scribble and draw pictures when given writing tools such as crayons, markers, and pencils. Once they become aware of the alphabetic principle, they attempt to use symbols that resemble letters. Next we examine the early stages of writing beyond scribbling and pictures.

INVENTED SPELLING   When children attempt to write words based on their emerging knowledge of letter-sound associations, they are engaged in **invented spelling**. Most children don't begin school having mastered letter–sound correspondences; yet they come to school with varying degrees of knowledge about the structure of written language because of their early experiences with reading. Additionally, when they begin to write, children expect their writing to make sense and have meaning.

During the early stages of invented spelling, children typically attempt to write the first sound that is heard and enunciated by the mouth. For example, the word *bat* would be represented as **b** or **B**. Next, the final sound is characteristically heard and written; *bat* might be written as **bt** or **Bt** or **BT** or **bd**. The last sound typically attempted is a vowel sound; **bt** might emerge as **bet**, **bit**, **bot**, **but**, or **bat**. Hence, invented spellings signal that children are beginning to analyze speech sounds and represent them in writing. These early stages are characterized as *letter name-alphabetic spelling* (Bear, Invernizzi, Templeton, & Johnston, 2008).

When children have opportunities to explore letter–sound associations in their attempt to write "what they want to say" by using invented spelling, they begin to realize that writing is a way to communicate a message or a thought. A key concept for children is that their ideas can be written down. This is a critical perception when working with young children; they need to realize that what they think about can be expressed in writing; hence, when young writers are encouraged to write using invented spelling, they are free to get their thoughts down on paper.

The gradual sophistication in children's invented spellings should be celebrated by teachers and parents as a display of emerging competence with written language. Invented spellings help children place ideas before notions of correctness. When children are bound by a need to be correct, writing becomes a laborious undertaking rather than a meaning-making act. If teachers want their students to write, and they correct everything the children create, the task of writing becomes a "right" or "wrong" process. On the other hand, a supportive learning environment encourages beginners to try to spell words as best they can during writing and to experiment with written language without the restrictions imposed by demands for accuracy and correction. This helps young writers develop confidence in their ability to write and to recognize the value of taking risks.

It is, of course, important that teachers facilitate a transition from invented spelling to correct spelling. This transition typically occurs at the end of first grade and continues into second or even third grade. There are many ways that teachers can assist in this transition. A teacher, for example, might display a word wall of high frequency words for reference; a desktop personalized dictionary can be developed for each student that alphabetizes the frequently misspelled words a student uses; words that children like to use in their stories can be recorded in individualized word banks. For example, if Joey likes to write about *dinosaurs*, his word bank might include the correct spelling of "dinosaur"; whereas if Christina enjoys writing about *soccer*, then the correct spelling of "soccer" would be included her word bank. There is, however, no one particular strategy, program, or approach that is best to assist children as they make the transition from invented spelling to conventional spelling. Teachers need to observe the way each student spells words, examine the letter–sound correspondences that are used, and determine which grapheme–phoneme letter relationships should be taught next. Additionally, it is important that teachers consider the nature of the writing task. Is the task to write about ideas, or is the task to write a correctly spelled response to an academic question?

LATER DEVELOPMENTAL SPELLING PHASES   As young children advance in their writing skills, they typically proceed through levels of development in their spelling skills. After *letter name-alphabet spelling*, children transition to the *within word pattern stage*, in which they experiment with long and short vowel patterns, *r*-controlled vowels, diphthongs, and other vowel sounds.

The next level, the *syllables and affixes spelling stage*, typically occurs in the intermediate grades and is characterized by working with as prefixes and suffixes and inflected endings. The final stage is *derivational spelling* and is typified by work with bases and root words, as well as more work with affixes and their meanings. *Derivational spelling* occurs in the middle and high school years and beyond (Bear, et al., 2008).

Check Your Understanding 11.1: Gauge your understanding of the skills and concepts in this section.

Creating Environments for Reading and Writing

■ **Demonstrate how to foster a classroom environment that supports reading–writing connections.**

When children are immersed in an environment conducive to learning, not only do they write and read more, but they also take greater control over and responsibility for their writing and reading. Students need much less external motivation from their teachers to write and read when they have time to read and write and have the chance to select their own writing topics or reading material. See Box 11.1 to read what seventh grader Bethany has to say about reading and writing.

Classroom environments that are motivating include physical spaces that allow personal writing, collaborative writing, and sharing. In addition, when children believe in themselves as writers, are presented with expectations that they can achieve, are provided with opportunities in which they have choices, and receive positive feedback regarding their efforts, they are likely to blossom as writers. Moreover, children are likely to develop competence when they are provided with direct instruction, clearly defined goals, and strategies for planning, drafting, and revising (Graham & Harris, 2016). It is equally important that teachers model their enthusiasm for writing by sharing the value and importance of the written word (Zumbrunn & Krause, 2012).

BOX 11.1 | STUDENT VOICES

Bethany is a 12-year-old seventh grader who "personally would like to be famous for writing!" She comes from a home in which she receives continuous support for literacy activities; her proactive literacy home environment began at a very young age. Her parents are teachers who have always understood the importance of providing Bethany with multiple experiences in recognizing the value of reading and writing, and their support began when she was a young toddler.

During her interview Bethany was very thoughtful about her development as a writer. Regarding early perceptions of herself, she said, "Back then I used to write mostly sentences, basic sentences, more than longer paragraphs or stories. I think my writing now is more based on bigger words than when I was younger." [Back then], "I tried to learn sentences like 'I like my dog. I like my cat.' I now use full detail after reading lots of books. That helped my perspective because I have learned more from reading books." Bethany added, "When I write [for school] I write about the books and stories I've read. I also like to get the ideas from them, and I like to go into detail and write more about the characters and how I think they'd go on or other things they would do."

Then Bethany clarifies some of her thoughts about writing assignments about books. "It's okay. I like that you know what you can write about because you just read about it and you can just write about it. But I don't like that a lot because it's not something I really want to write about. It's just something they want me to write. I prefer to write about topics that I like to write about. I don't really like it when I'm told what to write about." For example, Bethany adds, "I had to read some books and they were really boring; I felt like they were boring and seemed to go on forever. I couldn't wait to get through a chapter just to be done with it. A couple of weeks ago we had to write about Dr. Seuss, and I didn't like it. Sometimes I just don't like the topic, especially if I don't know anything about it. I didn't get that particular Dr. Seuss story."

When probed about what she likes to write about, Bethany shared, "I'm gonna have to say 'What you did over Christmas break . . . or over vacation . . . or over the weekend.' I like writing about my favorite things. I also like journaling. The other day we wrote about school uniforms, and we had to write for a specific amount of time. I didn't like it because it seemed like a long time to write about that topic. I didn't like to write about that." She would rather teachers allow students to write about "fun topics and sensible topics like parties . . . fun stuff, interesting things . . . Girls would probably like to write about shopping . . . guys would probably like writing about sports."

Bethany's interview ended with the following powerful comments: "I would like to be known for my writing. I'd like to publish a book. I haven't actually written a book yet but I'd like to write a book someday. I also want to keep journaling, and maybe one day my diaries will give me some ideas."

It is apparent from Bethany's interview that her teachers have tried to connect reading with writing. Her comments about writing, however, clearly indicate that she would rather write about topics that interest her. Although teachers often try to develop writing assignments that are homogeneous so they can perhaps be based on rubrics or other measures of assessment, Bethany's message clearly says that students need choices about what they write. She wants to write. Her teachers need to recognize that desire and offer her opportunities to develop that desire.

In addition, a teacher's positive attitude toward invented spellings contributes greatly to children's writing development. Concerns for the form and mechanics of writing matter but should be viewed from a developmental perspective (Richgels, 2013). It is likewise important that teachers provide middle school students with opportunities to write freely in any form they choose without initial intense concern about grammar and punctuation. In order to develop their writing skills, all students need the chance to develop a writing voice (Zumbrunn & Krause, 2012).

2017 ILA Standard

1.2

ENCOURAGING CLASSROOM WRITING   Examine the following eight suggestions for encouraging classroom writing, and note the italics, which underscore connections between writing and reading. These recommendations are equally important for elementary and middle school students.

1. Use students' experiences, and encourage them to write about things that are relevant to their interests and needs. Students must choose topics they care about. Yet a fear teachers often harbor is that students will have nothing to say or write about if left to select their own topics. Rarely is this the case. Students want to write. Before students begin, they should have good reason to believe that they have

something to say. How can you help? Guide students to choose topics they have strong feelings about; *provide opportunities for reading literature, surfing the Internet, and brainstorming ideas* before writing; show students how to plan and explore topics by using lists, jotting notes, and clustering ideas.

2. Develop sensitivity to good writing by reading poetry and literature to students. All writers need to listen to written language. *Although literature is a mirror that reflects good writing, the writings of other students also serve as a powerful model.* Sharing good literature and students' writing helps writers feel that they are capable of producing similar work. Ehmann and Gayer (2009) offer an excellent reference of children's literature that provides teachers with multiple examples of books for teaching writing elements such as alliteration, hyperbole, personification, simile, metaphor, and much more.

3. Invent ways to value what students have written. Students need praise and feedback, the two mainstays of a built-in support system for classroom writing. *Sharing writing in progress* is an important way to ensure response, or feedback, in the classroom. *Displaying and publishing writing electronically* is another.

4. Guide the writing personally. As students are writing, you should circulate around the room to help and encourage. Conferencing then becomes the primary means by which to respond and to give feedback in the writer's environment. Teacher–student and peer-led conferences help create a collaborative, noncompetitive environment to write and *share what has been written with others.* Consider multiple ways in which technological communications can serve as collaborative ways to share writing.

5. Write stories and poetry of your own, and share them with your students. *Sharing your writing with students* or discussing problems you are having as a writer signals that writing is as much a problem-solving activity for you as it is for them.

Common Core State Standards

CCRA.W.10, CCRA.R.5, CCRA.W.6

6. Tie in writing with the entire curriculum. Content area activities may provide the experiences and topics that can give direction and meaning to writing. *Writing to learn will help students discover and synthesize relationships among the concepts they are studying in social studies, science, mathematics, art, music, and health.*

7. Start a writing center in your classroom. A writing center is a place where young writers can go to find ideas, contemplate, or *read other students' writing.* The center can be equipped with lined paper of various sizes and colors; lined paper with a space for a picture; drawing paper of all sizes; stationery and envelopes; a tag board; index cards; a picture file; pencils, colored pencils, crayons, and markers. A writing center isn't a substitute for having a classroom program in which students work every day at developing the craft of writing. Instead, the center is a visible support that enhances the writing environment in your classroom.

8. Create a relaxed atmosphere in which students are given the opportunity to write for a variety of purposes as you demonstrate and scaffold text structures. This is especially beneficial for English language learners (ELLs) (Pavlak, 2013). Although students need challenging and motivating assignments, they must feel comfortable with making mistakes.

When a teacher encourages students to write, they engage in reading activities in varied and unexpected ways. An environment that connects writing and reading provides students with numerous occasions to write and read for personal and academic reasons, some of which are suggested in Figure 11.1.

Check Your Understanding 11.2: Gauge your understanding of the skills and concepts in this section.

Figure 11.1 Occasions for Writing and Reading

- Pen pal arrangements with other classes within the building
- Pen pal and "key pal" (Internet correspondence through e-mail) arrangements with a class from another school in the same district or in classrooms around the world
- Writing stories for publication on the Internet
- Writing for a school or class newspaper
- Writing for a class, school, or electronic magazine on the Internet
- "Author of the Week" bulletin board that features a different student writer each week
- Entering writing contests in the local community or on the Internet
- Opportunities for students to read pieces of writing over the school's public address system
- Opportunities for students to read selected pieces of writing to a younger class
- Outings where students can read selected pieces of writing to children in a day-care center
- Displays of student writing in the classroom, on a classroom homepage, and in the corridors of the school
- Videotapes of students reading their writing
- Multimedia authoring presentations of students' projects
- Play festivals featuring student-authored scripts
- Student-made publicity for school events
- Student-written speeches for school assemblies and programs
- A "Young Author Festival" to highlight student-authored books
- Student-prepared speeches in the voices of characters from stories or from social studies
- Daily journals and diaries
- Biographical sketches based on interviews or research
- Songwriting
- Reviews of movies or television programs
- Cartoon scripts

Connecting Reading and Writing

■ **Scaffold strategies for students that connect reading and writing, including journal writing, e-mail, and alternative approaches such as multigenre projects and writing nonfiction.**

Since teaching reading and writing are intricately related as complimentary processes, teachers need to deliberately craft meaningful experiences in which these connections support students as they are learning to read and write. Having students engage in writing their thoughts through journals can be a powerful venue for providing children with opportunities to express their thoughts on paper without a highly structured format.

Early childhood teachers can provide young children with notebooks in which they write thoughts using invented spelling. Spiral notebooks with the dates sequentially recorded at the top of each page can serve as a way to systematically examine children's progress over the year. Mrs. Burns, for example, noticed that first grader Quinn frequently chose to write about his pet dog, Tasha. Over a span of several weeks, she observed that Quinn's spelling of *dog* progressed from **bg** to **dg** to **dag**. He initially spelled Tasha as **TA** and **TOSA**. Mrs. Burns decided to help him write the conventional spellings for *dog* and *Tasha*. Quinn added those words to his word bank for easy reference. It is evident that Quinn's knowledge of sounds and symbols was developing as he attempted to spell words that were important to him.

As children develop more sophisticated ways to express themselves in writing, journals can serve as part of the writing environment in which they write about things that are important to them as they examine their personal lives and record their thoughts and feelings. All forms of written expression are welcomed in journals—doodles, comments, poems, and letters; journals are a gold mine for generating ideas.

Using Journals (and E-mail Correspondence) for Written Conversation

Journals can be handwritten or electronic in nature. Regardless of the medium, teachers should decide how they will be shared. Teachers can set aside time to read and respond to children's entries on a regular basis. It can be helpful to develop a system where you collect or retrieve, read, and respond to several journals a day rather than attempting to read the journal entries of an entire class at one time.

DIALOGUE JOURNALS   The **dialogue journal** provides a natural setting in which the child and teacher converse in writing. A teacher's response to children's entries may include comments, questions, and invitations to children to further express their ideas. The research-based practices featured in Box 11.2 offer guidelines for using dialogue journals in the classroom. In Figure 11.2, see how second-grade teacher Mrs. Simons responded to Brin's electronic journal entry.

2017 ILA Standard
2.2

BOX 11.2 | RESEARCH–BASED PRACTICES

Guidelines for Using Dialogue Journals

Dialogue journals provide opportunities for students to gather their thoughts and write in a natural, free-flowing manner. As the conversations continue, the students have occasions to define themselves, their interests, and their issues of concern.

1. Decide on the mode of communication (paper and pencil or electronic), and decide how often the journal entries will be recorded and read. Be sure to allow for ample time for response writing.
2. Explain that the purpose of the journal writing is to get to know each other and to share thoughts in a letter-type format.
3. Ensure that there is an understanding that the entries are just between the teacher and the students. They will not be graded on grammar, spelling, or content (although content must be appropriate).
4. Use prompts or questions that encourage students to write more, such as "What else can you tell me?"
5. Take the opportunity to make positive statements about what the students write, such as "Nice thoughts!" or "I like what you wrote!"

Figure 11.2 Brin and Mrs. Simons's Electronic Dialogue Entries

Dear Mrs. Simons, I realy like the stori we read about the beach. I alwys go to the bech in the summer and I luv to cllect shells. I have a hole cllction on a shlf in my room.

I hope we read mre storis about beches. My favorite bech is in south crlina.

My brother Joe is getting mried on the beach.

Love Brin

Dear Brin,

I am very happy that you enjoyed the story about the beach. It is very cool that you go to the beach every summer. Sometimes I go to the beach in the summer, too. I like to build sandcastles. It is exciting that your brother, Joe, is getting married on the beach! When is the wedding? Do you know the name of the beach?

Yes, we will be reading another story about a beach. It is in Maine. Do you know where Maine is?

I will talk with you later.

Your friend,
Mrs. Simons

Dialogue journals can be especially meaningful for middle school students because they provide an authentic avenue for expressing concerns that young adolescents typically have. Stowell (2000) describes how a diverse class of seventh-grade students effectively communicated through dialogue journals with preservice teachers. She found that the middle school students benefited from the individualized nature of the project in multiple ways. They were able to write about themselves reflectively, and they corresponded about issues that were important to them, such as friendships, fears, and difficulties at home.

BUDDY JOURNALS   A **buddy journal** is a variation of the dialogue journal. However, instead of a teacher engaging in written conversation with a student, a buddy journal encourages dialogue between children. Before beginning buddy journals, children should be familiar with the use of journals as a tool for writing and also be comfortable with the process of dialoguing with a teacher through the use of dialogue journals. To get buddy journals off and running, organize the students in pairs. Buddies may be selected randomly by drawing names from a hat. To maintain a high level of interest and novelty, children may change buddies periodically. Buddies may converse about anything that matters to them—from sharing books they have been reading to sharing insights and problems. Their journals can occur with paper and pencil or as electronic text.

Van Sluys and Laman (2006) found that when written conversations between classmates took place, much like online chats, the students wrote jokes and exaggerated stories, talked about books they were reading together, used language from comics and videos, and utilized unusual handwriting to convey messages.

ELECTRONIC MAIL (E-MAIL) CONVERSATIONS   E-mail communication engages students in written conversations with others in the same learning community, at a neighboring school, or anywhere in the world. When students use e-mail, reading–writing connections are both personal and social (through **key pal correspondence**—the electronic equivalent of pen pals) and educational (through Internet projects—a collaborative approach to learning on the Internet).

Key pal correspondence creates opportunities for students to communicate with other students from around the world, learn about different cultures, ask questions, and develop literacy skills. When students communicate with key pals from other countries or communities, they have the opportunity to broaden their knowledge of diverse cultures, dispel misconceptions about cultures that differ from their own, and develop understanding of and respect for differences.

Internet projects also promote global conversations and learning connections between students through online communication in the form of blogs, chats, texting, wikis, and social networking (Leu et al., 2011).

In one Internet project in northeastern Ohio, preservice teachers engage in semester-long e-mail conversations with third and fourth graders. The collaborative project revolves around conversations about trade books and social dialogue. Not only does the e-mail collaboration serve to make reading–writing connections during the literature discussions, but the partners learn about each other socially as they share information and ask questions about college life, hobbies, interests, and family life. The social nature of e-mail can also motivate reluctant readers, enhance self-confidence, provide students with opportunities to take ownership of their reading and writing, and help them make decisions about what they will read and write (McKeon, 2001). In Figure 11.3 see how one preservice teacher and third grader dialogue socially.

Using Journals to Explore Texts

Journals create a nonthreatening context for children to explore their reactions and responses to literary and informational texts. Readers who use journals regularly are

Figure 11.3 Introductory Social E-mail Dialogue between a Preservice Teacher and a Third Grader

Dear Jimmy,

Hello! I am studying to be a teacher, and I will be your e-mail buddy this semester! I am excited to get to know all about you! I will tell you a little about myself. I am 21 years old and I hope to teach little children one day. I only have one more year at college, so I hope to be a teacher after that!

I have one younger sister, and she is in third grade, just like you! I am going to tell her all about our project together. Do you have any siblings? I also have a dog. Her name is Nemo. She is a golden retriever and is very friendly. Do you have any pets?

I have some other things to tell you. I love to read and do crossword puzzles. My favorite color is blue, and my favorite food is ice cream. I especially like chocolate. Do you have any hobbies? What is your favorite food?

One other interesting thing about me is that I wear a hearing aid. It is very small, and you can hardly notice it. It helps me hear better and that helps me a lot, especially when I am trying to listen to my teachers in the classroom.

Well, I will sign off now. I can't wait to hear from you!

Your new buddy,

Morgan

Dear Morgan,

Thank you for your e-mail. I can't wait to be your partner. I think we be good friends because my favorite color is blue. I like ice cream to and my favrit is choclate but I like it mixed with marshmallow.

I think its fun becase you have a sister or brother in my grade. What school do they go to? I go to Greenberry. Maybe they go to my school. I have a baby brother and he's 1 yr old. Hes cute but somtimes he takes my things. Its ok becase he is just 1.

My hobby is baseball. I play first. we didnt start yet. Maybe you come to one of my games. I'm sorry that you cant here too well. I where glasses to help me see. I gess thats life.

Plese write back to me. I can't wait.

Bye from Jimmy your friend

involved actively in the process of comprehending as they record their feelings, thoughts, and reactions to various types of literature. Journals create a permanent record of what readers are feeling and learning as they interact with texts; as a result, they have also been called *logs* because they permit readers to keep a visible record of their responses to texts. Such responses often reflect thinking beyond a literal comprehension of the text; they engage students in inferential and evaluative thinking.

Providing time for literature response journal writing is also an effective way to engage students from diverse backgrounds in writing. When students respond to multicultural books that reflect the values of their cultures, for example, they have the opportunity to explore writing about what they know. When they read about the cultures of others, students gain an appreciation for values and beliefs that differ from their own. Writing about those beliefs in journals fosters reflective thinking, and entries can be used as a stimulus for discussions about diversity (Laier, Edwards, McMillon, & Turner, 2001).

Several types of journals may be used to explore texts: **double-entry journals**, **reading journals**, and **response journals**. What do these different types of journals have in common? Each integrates reading and writing through personal response, allowing readers to feel and think more deeply about the texts they are reading.

DOUBLE-ENTRY JOURNALS   A double-entry journal provides students with an opportunity to identify text passages that are interesting or meaningful to them and to explore—in writing—why. As the name of the journal implies, students fold sheets of paper in half lengthwise, creating two columns for journal entries. In the left-hand column, readers select quotes from the text—perhaps a word, a phrase, a sentence or two—that they find interesting or evocative. They then copy the text verbatim and identify the page from which each text quote is taken. In instances in which the quoted passage is several sentences or a paragraph long, the student may choose to summarize rather than copy the passage.

Across from each quote, in the right-hand column, readers enter their personal responses and reactions to the text quotes. As Yopp and Yopp (1993) explain, students' responses to a text will vary widely: "Some passages may be selected because they are funny or use interesting language. Others may be selected because they touch the student's heart or remind the student of experiences in his or her own life" (p. 54).

The payoffs from using such journals will be readily evident in class discussions. One of the benefits of a double-entry journal is that it encourages interactions between reader and text. Another benefit is that children become sensitized to the text and the effect the author's language has on them as readers. A third payoff is that students explore texts for personally relevant ideas.

Electronic double-entry journals can be used as students respond to online informational text. Students first set up a word file for responses to a particular topic or query. The entry pages are in a two-column format. As the students research a topic, they cut and paste the URL as well as the passage to which they want to respond. In the second column they type their reactions. Responses can feature facts they found interesting, information they wonder about, or data they find significant. In Box 11.3,

BOX 11.3 | STEP-BY-STEP LESSON

Fourth-Grade Teacher Miss Kim Models an Electronic Double-Entry Journal

Miss Kim: Boys and girls, since it is almost spring, I think we might like to plant a vegetable garden that we could enjoy all summer. Our garden could be in the area next to the playground. What do you think?

Rick: I would like that! I've never had a garden before!

Leslie: Me, too!

Sue: Let's do it! How could we start?

Miss Kim: Let's begin by researching on the web. We can keep a class double-entry journal as we find important information about growing a vegetable garden.

Miss Kim: First, let's set up a file to record all of the information we can use.

Miss Kim opens a new Word document, entitles it "Our gardening journal," and formats the document in two columns. This is displayed on a screen for all of the students to see.

Miss Kim: Next, let's Google for information on the web. What key words do you think we should type?

Rick: I think we should just type "how to grow a vegetable garden."

Miss Kim: Good idea, Rick. Let's try that.

Miss Kim types the key words, and the students help her decide which websites to search. As they locate important information

together, she models how to cut and paste the URL and important information for the left side of the journal, and the students dictate important information gleaned from each website for the right side of the journal. After 20 minutes the class reviews its findings.

Miss Kim: Let's see what we learned so far about growing a vegetable garden and what we need to do to get started.

Leslie: It needs to be in a pretty sunny spot!

Sue: And we need to get some good soil.

Rick: I think we've gotta have soil with vitamins.

Miss Kim: Yes, the soil needs to have nutrients.

Rick: I meant nutrients.

Miss Kim: Good job, Rick. What else have we learned?

Sue: It says here something about irrigation. What was that again?

Leslie: It's about water. We wrote down water next to that section.

Miss Kim: Good job, Leslie. You looked at our notes. We'll have to see whether there is a space outside that is sunny and also close to a spigot.

The lesson continues over the next several days as the fourth graders gather information about growing a vegetable garden and recording words and phrases that they will need to consider.

see how a fourth-grade teacher, Miss Kim, models how to use an electronic double-entry journal as she researches information on gardening in the step-by-step lesson.

READING JOURNALS   In contrast to double-entry journals, reading journals provide students with more structure and less choice in deciding what they will write about. The teacher often provides a prompt—a question, for example—to guide students' writing after a period of sustained reading. Reading journals are usually used with a common or *core* text that everyone in a class or small group is reading or listening to.

Prompts may include generic "process" questions such as the following: What did you like? What, if anything, didn't you like? What did you think or wonder about as you were reading? What will happen next? What did you think about the story's beginning? The ending? What did you think about the author's style? Did anything confuse you? At times, reading journals use prompts that are more content-specific, asking readers to focus on their understanding of an important concept or some relevant aspect of plot, setting, character, or theme.

RESPONSE JOURNALS   The main difference between a reading journal and a response journal is the amount of prompting that teachers use to elicit students' reactions to a text. Response journals invite readers to respond to literary texts freely, without being prompted.

Sixth-grade teacher Gloria Reichert introduces students to response journals with a letter at the beginning of the school year. In one section of the letter, she explains response journals this way:

> I'm sure you are wondering about what a response journal is. It is a place where you will be able to write about books and stories that you will be reading throughout the year in our class. The response journal will be a great way to help us explore what we are feeling and thinking about what we are reading.
>
> What will you be writing in your response journals? You can write anything you want about the book or story you are reading. You can express your thoughts, your feelings, or your reactions. How do you feel about the book? What does the book make you think about? What do you like or dislike about it? Who are the characters? Do you like them? Can you relate to their problems? What does the story mean to you?

Gloria then shows the class some different types of responses she has collected from past students who read Wilson Rawls's *Where the Red Fern Grows*. One entry she shows mixes literary commentary with personal involvement in the story:

> I thought Chap. 5 was very good. I'm glad Billy got the dogs. I thought it was really, really mean that all the people were laughing at him because he was carrying the pups in the gunny sack. I mean, come on. He had nothing to carry them in, and they needed air to breathe. I can't believe a fight would actually start because it got so bad. The part where the mountain lion came, and the two pups saved Billy by howling was amazing. I thought the chapter had good action.

Another entry critiques a chapter from the perspective of someone who has dogs as pets:

> I didn't like chapter two. How can a kid get so sick from just not having a dog. Dogs are not always perfect anyways. They wake so early in the morning by barking there head off and sometimes they run around the house making a ruckus.

Regardless of format, journal writing allows children to use language as if they are engaged in talk. Such writing does not place a premium on perfection or mechanics—spelling, punctuation, or grammar. Teachers encourage students to write freely in journals, placing their reactions and responses ahead of concerns for correctness.

Digital tools such as web 2.0, e-books, iPads, digital storytelling, message boards, and blogs between students and teachers and among classmates extend the objectives of response journals to include the technological and collaborative skills necessary for

BOX 11.4 | RESEARCH–BASED PRACTICES

Advantages and Implications of Using Technological Responses to Text

- They foster the social nature of literacy practices.
- They promote motivating engagement with text.
- They allow for a broader reading and writing audience.
- They encourage collaboration.
- They afford opportunities for reading and responding to multiple points of view.
- They provide multiple opportunities for altering text and adding graphics, video, and sound.

- They foster spontaneity with minimal attention to spelling and grammar, but can also offer online support for writing mechanics.
- They demonstrate an authentic use of technological skills.
- They provide opportunities for real-time discussions and questions.

the twenty-first century (Hancock, 2008; Handsfield, Dean, & Cielocha 2009; Hutchison et al., 2012; Larson, 2008, 2009, 2010; Sylvester & Greenidge, 2009). For example, Hutchison, Beschorner, and Schmidt-Crawford (2012) found that iPad apps provided fourth graders with opportunities to creatively respond to stories through graphics. Larson's research (2010) with second graders demonstrated the effective use of e-books and digital note responses to literature. Handsfield, Dean, and Cielocha (2009) described how blogs can successfully serve as social avenues for reader response. In Box 11.4 we highlight some of the advantages and implications of using technological responses to text.

2017 ILA Standards

5.3

Common Core State Standards

CCRA.W.1, CCRA.W.2, CCRA.W.3, CCRA.W.6, CCRA.W.7

Alternative Strategies That Motivate Students to Write

Just as journal writing is a vehicle for developing writing fluency, alternative genres can provide students with motivating and creative ways to express themselves in writing. The Common Core State Standards (CCSS) (2010) specifically state that students need to be able to write arguments, informational and narrative text, and conduct and write research. In the following sections, we discuss ways to encourage students to gather ideas for writing; we also discuss multigenre projects, writing nonfiction, and using plot scaffolds for creative writing.

GATHERING IDEAS   It is well recognized that students are motivated when they are given choices about what to read and write. In order to help students gather ideas that they might choose to craft as writing drafts, Olness (2005) recommends Ralph Fletcher's (1996) idea of providing students with **writing notebooks** in which they gather observations, thoughts, reactions, ideas, unusual words, pictures, and interesting facts that might later spur them to write. Unlike journals, the notebooks are meant to provide students with a place to collect thoughts for future writing. Similar to writing notebooks, Rog (2007) suggests providing children with large envelopes, "topics in your pocket," in which they jot down ideas and collect pictures or drawings about which they might like to write.

Regardless of the manner in which students gather writing ideas, teachers need to provide students with choices.

Multigenre Projects

A **multigenre project** or paper is a collection of genres that reflects multiple responses to a book, theme, or topic (Romano, 2000). Students are given choices about which genres to use, and they experiment with writing in a variety of ways.

Gillespie (2005) suggests over 50 genres, including advice columns, biographies, comic strips, death notices, greeting cards, posters, prayers, and talk show transcripts. After reading *A Single Shard* (Park, 2001), a story that takes place in a twelfth-century Korean village about a homeless man and an orphan boy, one of her seventh graders chose to develop a crossword puzzle to review new vocabulary words. Another student designed a map of the locale; another wrote a letter to one of the main characters. Gillespie requires that her students develop ten pieces and experiment with at least seven different genres, as well as write a reflection about each piece. A final activity is to organize the project into a booklet and provide time for students to share.

WRITING NONFICTION   Some children do not enjoy writing stories, but are motivated to write nonfiction. Although all children should experience crafting nonfiction pieces, struggling readers often enjoy writing more when they are encouraged to write expository text (Olness, 2005).

Sharing nonfiction books is a critical component when introducing children to this type of writing. Teachers can use read-alouds and point out the features of nonfiction writing and the variety of text-based characteristics such as a table of contents, index, glossary, bold print, and subheadings. Read (2005) suggests having emerging writers create informational texts in pairs because collaborative partnerships take advantage of the "social nature of learning" (p. 43). For young writers, an "all about" book can be a simple way to begin writing expository text (Olness, 2005). If the children have gathered interesting pictures, they might select a topic based on a picture of their choice. Kletzien and Dreher (2004) suggest a variety of informational or nonfiction texts that young children can write, including descriptions of objects, personal events, and how to construct something.

For young adolescents, Pullman (2000) suggests that students work in pairs to develop "wanted posters" based on influential historical figures. After reading information and taking notes, the partners design a character sketch, create a nickname for the figure, write a final draft, and orally present the information learned. Baines (2000) suggests a group activity in which students develop fact sheets about a controversial topic and present the facts to different audiences. For example, a school dress-code issue might be presented to parents, peers, and a clothing store.

Common Core State Standards

CCRA.W.1, CCRA.W.2

PLOT SCAFFOLDS   A **plot scaffold** is an open-ended script in which students use their imaginations and creative writing in a playful manner (O'Day, 2006). The open-ended scripts include characters, setting, problem, and resolution with spaces for the students to write additional descriptions and problem-solving dialogue. For example, if the script read, "The house was dark," the students might be instructed to "describe the house and why it was dark." If the script read, "Joe spoke to Teresa," the students might be instructed to "describe how Joe spoke and what he said."

Prior to working with plot scaffolds, the students are taught that story plots have more than a beginning, middle, and end; they include the answers to three questions: "What if (the problem is stated)? What is the catch (what makes the problem worse)? What then (how is the problem solved)?" (O'Day, 2006, p. 11).

Figure 11.4 provides an example of a plot scaffold.

Figure 11.4 Sample Plot Scaffold

A Monster in the Chimney

Characters: Monster, Child 1, Child 2, Child 3

Narrator/Writer: The scene takes place in a house. Three children are playing, and they hear a sound. *(What does the house look like and where is it? What are the children playing and where? What kind of sound do they hear?)*

_____

_____

Child 1: What was that? *(Give the child a name, describe how the child is talking, and describe the situation.)*

_____

_____

Child 2: I don't know. *(Give the child a name, and describe the situation.)*

_____

_____

Child 3: I think the sound is from over there. *(Give the child a name, and describe where the child thinks the sound is coming from.)*

_____

_____

Monster: Help me! Help me! I'm stuck in your chimney! *(Describe the scene and the children's reaction.)*

_____

_____

Child 1: Who are you? *(Describe the child's reaction to hearing the monster speak.)*

_____

_____

Monster: *(What does the monster say, and how does he or she say it?)*

_____

_____

Child 2: *(What does the child say, and how does he or she say it?)*

_____

_____

Child 3: I'm scared. *(Describe the situation.)*

_____

_____

Monster: Call someone! Call someone quickly! *(Describe the situation.)*

_____

_____

Child 1: I'm calling the police.
Child 3: I think we should call the fire department!
Child 2: I think we should call 911!
Monster: *(What does the monster say?)*

_____

_____

Narrator/Writer: *(What happens next? Add new characters.)*

_____

_____

Monster: *(What does the monster say, and how does he or she say it?)*

_____

_____

Child 1: *(What does the child say?)*

_____

_____

Figure 1.4 *(Continued)*

Child 2:	*(What does the child say?)*
Child 3:	*(What does the child say?)*
Narrator/Writer:	*(Describe how the problem is solved. Add your own dialogue.)*

Open-ended scripts work well for students of all writing abilities since the children can work in groups. In addition, the strategy is particularly useful for ELL students because they can share their ideas on a level at which they are comfortable (O'Day, 2006).

Although there are multitudes of ways to engage students in writing, children need to take ownership of what they compose. Providing students with choices and scaffolding creative options are two key elements that will foster effective instruction.

Check Your Understanding 11.3: Gauge your understanding of the skills and concepts in this section.

Organizing Writing Instruction

■ **Explain the writing process, and demonstrate how to organize writing instruction, including how to conduct writing workshops.**

No two teachers organize writing instruction the same way; nor should they. Routines vary depending on numerous considerations, including classroom size, time allotted for language arts instruction, the developmental levels of the students, the students' needs, resources available, and the goals of instruction, to name a few. Preschool teachers, for example, can effectively scaffold young children's writing development with individual instruction based on their knowledge of writing conventions and sound–symbol relationships (Cabell, Tortorelli, & Gerde, 2013); and kindergarten teachers can guide students' writing with exemplary stories and by encouraging personal responses to literature (VanNess, Murnen, & Bertelsen, 2013). Read (2010) organizes her writing instruction based on genre.

Some teachers have their students keep writing samples in folders; some teachers have students gather their *best* writing in portfolios; some teachers use electronic collections of students' work. However teachers manage to collect and evaluate students' writing, we believe that writing instruction needs to be thoughtfully planned and that teachers need to deliberately scaffold instruction so that students are not simply given writing assignments.

Next, we highlight several important factors that teachers need to take into account with respect to writing instruction, including the stages of the writing process, the qualities of exemplary writing, and effective ways to organize writing instruction.

The Writing Process

It makes sense that teachers begin to organize writing instruction with a plan. One overall plan has been characterized as stages of the **writing process**. Traditionally, and included in the CCSS (2010a), these stages include having students:

1. Brainstorm what they want to write about.
2. Draft their thoughts.

3. Revise their thoughts after input from the teacher or peers.
4. Edit their writing for errors and such.
5. Publish their writing.

Vacca, Vacca, and Mraz (2014) characterize the stages of the writing process in terms of *discovery*, finding a topic and writing preliminary ideas; *drafting*, getting ideas down on paper; and *revising*, making it right. We concur that these overall "categories" capture a synthesis of the traditional stages of the writing process. In addition, we suggest that teachers need to scaffold students during writing lessons by:

- Providing students with exemplary examples of how authors write
- Encouraging students to write in multiple genres
- Assisting students *as* they write

Next we elaborate on the stages of the writing process.

BRAINSTORMING   Brainstorming is everything that writers do before the physical act of putting ideas on paper or on the screen for a first draft. "Getting it out" is a useful mnemonic because it helps us remember that brainstorming means activating background knowledge and experiences, getting ideas out in the open, and making plans for approaching the task of writing.

Brainstorming is a time to generate ideas, stimulate thinking, make plans, and create a desire to write. In other words, brainstorming is what writers do to get energized, to explore what to say and how to say it: What will I include? What is a good way to start? Who is my audience? What form should my writing take?

DRAFTING   "Getting it down" is an apt way to describe drafting. Once writers have brainstormed, explored, discovered, planned, and talked (and done whatever else it takes to get ideas out in the open), they are ready to draft a text with a purpose and an audience in mind. A student is reading when drafting. As students draft, the teacher regulates and monitors the process.

Drafting is a good time to confer individually with students who may need help using what they know to tackle the writing task. The teacher can serve as a sounding board, ask probing questions if students appear to be stuck, and create opportunities for a student to read what he or she is writing. A teacher may want to ask the following questions:

- How is it going?
- What have you written so far?
- Tell me the part that is giving you a problem. How are you thinking about handling it?
- I am not clear on _____. How can you make that part clearer?
- Are you leaving anything out that may be important?
- What do you intend to do next?
- How does the draft sound when you read it out loud?
- What is the most important thing you're trying to get across?

Once completed, a first draft is just that—a writer's first crack at discovering what he or she wants to say and how he or she wants to say it.

REVISING   Each interaction that occurs when a writer seeks a *response*, either from the teacher or from another writer in the class, constitutes a *conference*. Students have many opportunities to read their work critically during conferences. Simply stated, a conference may be held when a writer needs feedback for work in progress. The conference may last 5 seconds or 5 minutes, depending on the writer's needs. However, once a student decides to rework a first draft, conferencing becomes a prominent aspect of *revising* and *editing*. To conduct a teacher–student conference, a teacher must learn to define his or her role as listener.

To elicit clarification of a piece of writing, a teacher might focus the conference with a specific question or two appropriate to the writer's needs. The following general steps will help in conducting a conference.

1. The writer *reads* the draft out loud.
2. The teacher *listens* carefully for the meaning of the draft.
3. The teacher then *mirrors the content* ("Your draft is about . . ."), *focuses praise* ("The part I liked the best about your draft is . . ."), *elicits clarification* ("Which parts are giving you the most trouble?"), *makes suggestions* ("I think you should work on . . ."), and *seeks the writer's commitment* ("Now that we have talked, what will you do with the draft?").

Dix (2006) acknowledges that students tend to revise in a variety of ways. For example, one early childhood student was asked "what happens in her head" when writing, and she replied:

> Probably, either there are two . . . I think there are two sort of, like, columns in my head, and if I don't like it then I put it in one column and I say, "I don't like it," and I just put it away—forget about it. . . . Then the ones I do like, I write them down. So I think in my head first before I write it down. (Dix, 2006, p. 570)

When asked to describe the process of writing a poem, another student shared:

> Well, just say if the thing I was writing about was trees, I just go, "What shall I write about? What color are the leaves? Or how many rings do they have to say how old they are? And what shape they are, what shape different types of trees are. (Dix, 2006, p. 571)

As students revise, it is useful for teachers to observe, ask questions, and note how students approach the task. This can provide teachers with useful information for minilessons to share with the rest of the class. Teachers can ask questions such as: "What goes on in your mind as you write? What pictures do you have in your head when you write?" See Box 11.5 to see how one literacy coach assists a teacher in organizing the writing process.

EDITING   During revision, students will be messy in their writing, and they should be encouraged to be messy. They should be shown how to use carets to make insertions and be allowed to make cross-outs or to cut and paste sections of text, if necessary. The use of arrows will help students show changes in the position of words, phrases, or sentences within the text.

Once the content and organization of a draft are set, students can work individually or together to edit and proofread their texts for spelling, punctuation, capitalization, word choice, and syntax. Accuracy counts. "Polishing" or "cleaning up" a revised draft shouldn't be neglected, but students must recognize that *concern for proofreading and editing comes toward the end of the writing process.* This is particularly true for struggling writers and ELL students who need to be encouraged to take risks with the writing process.

Students should edit for skills that are appropriate for their ability and stage of development as writers. An editing conference should provide a *focused evaluation* in which one or two skill areas are addressed. If students have edited their writing to the best of their ability, the teacher may then edit the remainder of the piece for spelling and other conventions.

PUBLISHING   If writing is indeed a public act, it is meant to be shared with others. Writing is for reading, and students learn quickly to write for many different audiences. Opportunities to publish writing for a specific audience engage early childhood, elementary, and middle school students in exciting purposes for writing.

The pride and sense of accomplishment that come with *authorship* contribute powerfully to a writer's development. Publishing provides a strong incentive for children

BOX 11.5 | VIEWPOINT *THE LITERACY COACH*

Organizing Writing Instruction

Jackie, a fourth-grade teacher, has been struggling with how to effectively provide writing instruction during her language arts class. During a 45-minute class, Jackie typically allows the students one-half hour to write as she walks around the room to monitor and assist individual students. She is frustrated, however, because this time does not seem focused. Although the students seem to be writing, Jackie does not feel that she is providing effective writing instruction. She asked Marla, her school's literacy coach, to assist her. Marla suggested that Jackie consider the following:

- First, examine the purposes for which you are having the students write. Have you discussed the audience for whom the pieces should be written?

- Do the writing assignments involve a prompt? If so, do the students know the expectations of the assignments?
- Do the assignments involve choices? Are the students permitted to write fiction or nonfiction or multigenre pieces? Poetry?
- Are the students writing in response to pieces of literature, or are the assignments to compose creative pieces?
- Have you modeled the types of writing you expect? How did you scaffold instruction?

Marla developed the following template to help Jackie organize her writing instruction constructively.

Grade-Level Standard and Indicator	Purpose of the Writing Assignment	How Will I Scaffold Instruction?	Choices for Completing the Assignment	Conference Options	Evaluation
			☐ Poetry ☐ Narrative ☐ Nonfiction ☐ Multigenre ☐ Self-selected	☐ Teacher–small group ☐ Teacher–individual ☐ Peer partners ☐ Small group ☐ Peer sharing	☐ Checklist ☐ Rubric ☐ Peer evaluation ☐ Self-reflection ☐ Other

to keep writing and rewriting. But more than anything else, publishing in the classroom is fun. Young people take great pride in writing and illustrating their own books. Producing a book often provides the impetus for writing and justifies all the hard work that goes into the final product. Writing a book creates a meaningful context and motivates youngsters to revise and edit stories, focusing on content, organization, sentence structure, interesting words, and correct spelling. Young writers are especially inspired to write books when they are exposed to children's literature on a regular basis. They are also eager to make books when they can choose the type of book they want to write. Some possibilities for bookmaking are illustrated in Figure 11.5.

Move the slider to view directions for making bound cloth books.

For older students, class-produced newspapers, magazines, anthologies, and books are excellent ways to publish student writing. The students should be involved in all phases of the publication's production. We suggest that students not only participate as writers but also work in groups to assume responsibility for editing, proofreading, design, and production. Production of a class publication need not be elaborate or expensive. Photocopied or computer-generated publications have the same effect on student writers as more elaborate presentations when they see their work in print. Finally, be sure to display student writing. Establish an authors' day or a reading fair in which students circulate around the room reading or listening to as many pieces as they can.

The Qualities of Exemplary Writing

In addition to understanding the process of guiding students through the stages of writing, teachers need to scaffold children and guide them with explicit criteria for evaluating their writing. The **Six-Traits-Plus Model** is one example of an exemplary representation of the qualities of writing that focuses on the following elements: ideas, organization, voice, word choice, fluency, mechanics, and presentation (Spandel, 2013).

Ideas represent the core themes central to the writing, whether it is narrative or expository; they should be supported by clearly written details. The organization of a piece of writing refers to the structure of the content; it should be arranged logically

Figure 11.5 Ideas for Making Books

Type of Book	Sample	Construction
Shape books Stories about animals, objects, machines, people, etc.; poems; nursery rhymes; innovations		Make pages in the shape of your book. Bind together with staples or masking tape or lace with yarn.
Ring books Group stories; word fun; poems; collection of poems		Punch holes in pages and use notebook rings or shower curtain rings to bind together.
Stapled books Individual stories; group contributions; alphabet books; word books; poems		Pages and cover are stapled together, then bound with masking tape for added durability.
Fold-out books Poems; patterns; sequences; stories		Pages are folded accordion-style and then stapled or glued to covers.
Bound cloth books Poems; collections of poems; stories that have been edited and prepared for printing		(See extended directions on the next page.)

(Continued)

Figure 11.5 Ideas for Making Books *(Continued)*

Extended Directions for Bound Cloth Books

Supplies: 1 piece of lightweight fabric (approximately ½ yard), several needles, white paper, dry-mount tissue, cardboard, masking tape, an iron, and an ironing area.

1. Each child should have 6 or 7 sheets of paper. This will make a finished book with 10 to 12 pages but will not be too difficult to sew. Fold each sheet of paper in half (one by one). (Fig. 1)

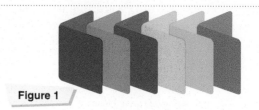

Figure 1

2. Bring the sheets together and sew along the fold. **Hint:** Start on the outside of the fold so that the knot will not be seen when binding is finished. (Fig. 2)

Figure 2   Stitches

3. Cut out the fabric to measure 12" x 15". Prepare some templates from cardboard for students to use as guides. (Fig. 3)

4. Spread out the materials as pictured. (Fig. 3)

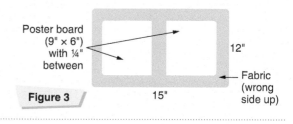

Poster board (9" × 6") with ¼" between

12"

Fabric (wrong side up)

Figure 3   15"

5. Fold the edges of the fabric over the two boards, and tape in place at the corners. (Fig. 4)

Figure 4

6. Now make a sandwich using the cover, then a piece of dry-mount tissue (8½" x 11"), then the sewn pages, and iron in place as pictured. Iron only on the endpapers since the pages can be scorched. (Fig. 5)

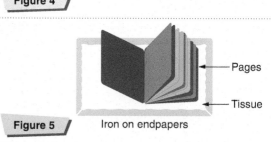

Pages

Tissue

Figure 5   Iron on endpapers

---

and follow a predictable pattern, for example: cause and effect, comparing and contrasting, or a sequential order. Voice denotes the author's tone or how the writer feels about the topic; the piece should reflect a passionate point of view. Word choice indicates the nature of the vocabulary and how it is used to express the core ideas. If the piece is descriptive, does the writer use effective imagery? If the piece is argumentative, does the author convince the reader? Or if the piece is informative, does the reader clearly understand the content? Fluency refers to the flow of the text—how it sounds. Does it read smoothly? Conventions denote correct grammar, spelling, punctuation, and capitalization. Presentation signifies the visual impact that the reader receives when viewing the product. Is it neatly written? If technology is used, is the font appropriate? Are graphics used effectively?

In this **video** (www.youtube.com/watch?v=oAp5w-ZKeXk), you will learn more about the six traits of writing and what they mean. Can you describe each one?

There are a variety of rubrics available for evaluating students' writing, many of which include the above qualities. Depending on the nature of the writing, rubrics may include features of writing such as text and digital citations, length of the assignment, revision considerations, or sufficient evidence to back a conclusion. It is useful for teachers to work with their students to help determine the criteria they should strive for as they write. Sharing examples of excellent, adequate, and poor writing is also beneficial. Additionally, it is wise if rubrics initially focus on several qualities, rather than a wide range of expectations. Less is more should be the rule of thumb. When the expectations of "excellent" writing include too many elements, students can be overwhelmed and thus unfocused. An example of a rubric that fourth graders developed for their narrative writing of a story can be found in Figure 11.6

Instructional Decision Making 11.1: Apply your understanding of the concepts in this section.

The Writing Workshop

Many teachers think about writing time each day as a workshop; the classroom is the student writer's studio. The **writing workshop** begins by providing students with the structure they need to understand, develop, or use specific writing strategies or by giving them direction in planning their writing or in revising their drafts. The **minilesson**, as the name implies, is a brief, direct instructional exchange (usually no longer than 10 minutes) between the teacher and the writing group (which may include the whole class). The exchange isn't a substitute for individual guidance; instead, it is meant to get students started on a writing project or to address their specific problems or needs. For example, a minilesson can stimulate topic selection, brainstorm ideas for writing, demonstrate interesting writing, model literary style by reading passages from literature, illustrate good sentence and paragraph structure, model strategies for revision, or teach a mechanical skill.

Following the minilesson is the actual time the students spend "in process," whether they are collecting information, drafting, revising, or editing their work. For part of this time, you may find yourself working on your own writing. Your role is

Figure 11.6 Fourth-Grade Rubric for Evaluating Story Writing

	3 Superior	2 Acceptable	1 Unacceptable	Rubric Score
Content	The topic of the story is very engaging and interesting to read.	The topic of the story is interesting and adequately engages the reader.	The topic of the story is not interesting and does not engage the reader.	
Organization	The paragraphs are clearly written. They follow a logical order with main ideas and details that are evident.	The paragraphs follow a somewhat logical order. The main ideas and details are primarily evident.	The paragraphs are not clearly written. The order is not logical or the main ideas and details are not evident.	
Conventions	Spelling, grammar, punctuation, and capitalization are primarily correct.	Spelling, grammar, punctuation, and capitalization errors are minimal.	Poor spelling, grammar, punctuation, or capitalization interfere with understanding the story.	

primarily to facilitate the workshop by responding to the needs of writers as specific situations demand. Hence, this would be the time to circulate among students and conduct individual or group conferences about initial drafts, questions, revisions, and final products.

One plan that teachers can follow in facilitating the writing workshop might go as follows:

A Writing Workshop Plan

1. Minilesson (3–10 minutes)
2. Writing process (45–120 minutes)
3. Group share session (10–15 minutes)

2017 ILA Standard

2.2

Ideally, the students need to have a significant amount of time to write. Teachers can certainly vary a writing workshop time frame to suit the needs of students and to accommodate different language arts schedules. For example, teachers might decide to have a group share session once a week, but for a longer period of time. Other teachers may find that they need a longer time to conduct minilessons for ELLs or struggling or advanced writers.

A main purpose of a **group share session** is to have writers reflect on the day's work. Process discussions focus on concerns implicit in the following questions:

- How did your writing go today? Did you get a lot done?
- Did you write better today than yesterday?
- Was it hard for you to keep your mind on what you were writing?
- What do you think you'll work on tomorrow?
- What problems did you have today?

Calkins (1983, 1994) provided these guidelines to facilitate reading and discussion of students' drafts:

- *Raising concerns*: A writer begins by explaining where he or she is in the writing process and what help he or she needs. For example, a student might say, "I'm on my third draft, and I want to know if it's clear and makes sense," or "I have two beginnings, and I can't decide which is best."
- *Reading aloud*: Usually, the writer then reads the writing (or the pertinent section) out loud.
- *Mirroring the content and focusing praise*: The writer then calls on listeners. A classmate begins by retelling what he or she has heard: "I learned that . . ." or "Your story began . . . ." Sometimes a listener may begin by responding with praise or showing appreciation for the writing.
- *Making suggestions*: Questions or suggestions are then offered about the concern raised by the writer. Sometimes other things will come up as well.

Besides reflecting on the day's writing, reserve the share session to celebrate finished work. Ask volunteers to share their writing with an audience. For elementary students, the author's chair is an integral part of the sharing experience. The celebration that students take part in reflects their payoff for the hard work that writers go through to craft a piece of work to their satisfaction. Instead of using the author's chair, at the end of writing time, Heffernan (2004) implements "Circle Check Out." The students sit in a circle and share "snapshots" of their writing that reflect examples of the concept taught during the minilesson. See how one teacher implements a practice writing workshop in the step-by-step lesson in Box 11.6.

BOX 11.6 | STEP-BY-STEP LESSON

How One Teacher Implements a "Practice Writing" Workshop

I introduce a skill to the entire class that will be the focus of what I call "writing practice." For example, when we are learning how to compose stories, I might base a lesson on writing about the setting, character development, or dialogue. Depending on the ability of my students, the time spent on the minilesson will vary from 5 to 15 or even 20 minutes.

Initially, the students typically work in pairs to practice the skill. I call this step "practice writing." They are given choices regarding the topic related to the skill.

For example, if the skill is to compose a dialogue, choices might be to write conversations in which two characters are expressing surprise, arguing, planning an event, discussing a problem, or explaining a procedure, to name a few. Typically I instruct the students to practice the skill multiple times. In the above instance, partners might decide to first compose an argument about who is responsible for a broken window, next write a conversation in which a movie has a surprise ending, and finally write a dialogue in which two characters are discussing how to build a kite.

This practice writing phase of my writing workshop ranges from 45 minutes to an hour. During this time I conference with partners, make suggestions, and scaffold their writing as needed.

At the conclusion of a typical practice writing workshop, I provide time for partners to share what they have written or share decision-making processes that they encountered during the writing process. Sharing is open-ended; partners decide whether they have something to share with the class and, if so, what they would like to share. Sometimes students will simply share comments such as, "We had a hard time getting started. We couldn't decide on a topic to write about that gets into that skill." These partners might explain how they resolved the issue. On the other hand, other partners may decide to dramatize what they have written. Time allotted for this step of practice writing varies. Sometimes we share for 5 minutes; other sessions may last longer. The time span for sharing is very much dependent on the students' choices and enthusiasm for sharing.

In essence, my practice writing workshop is very flexible. I have goals that match my English language arts curriculum, but I also craft my lessons to meet the needs and interests of my students.

Providing my students with choices as we practice writing skills is an essential part of my lesson plan development.

A DAY IN THE LIFE OF OUR WRITING WORKSHOP

In this **video** (www.youtube.com/watch?v=zPRM2ZXyrS0&list=PLb5RXypPqP5sNAY NUDEfwaq2QYPauhCcc), you will see how a first-grade teacher implements a writing workshop in her classroom. Observe the characteristics of a typical writing workshop.

Guided Writing Instruction

Guided writing is an instructional framework in which teachers scaffold students' writing *as* they write. The framework, developed by Sharan Gibson (2008/2009), assumes the social nature of writing and the need to explicitly assist students as they craft their work. Guided writing involves teaching skills that are needed by students based on actual observation, engaging the students in conversations as they write, and using prompts to guide instruction.

Critical components of guided writing include focused attention to writing tasks such as developing a main idea, providing immediate input *while* the students write, and allowing time to *complete* a piece of writing during the lesson. A premise of the framework is that:

> Teachers should lean in and assist with what each student is *currently* constructing in his or her writing, providing strong "feed forward" for the individual writer. Feedback evaluates what the writer has already written. In contrast, feed forward focuses the writer's attention on what strategies to use next. (Gibson, 2008/2009, p. 328)

Prompts are meant to foster conversations between the teacher and student *during* writing. They can range from general comments, such as, "What do you think you should write next?" to more specific guidance, such as, "Can you think of a word to describe what you mean?" Guiding writing is not meant to replace whole group instruction or ways to organize writing such as writing workshop. It is a framework that elaborates on the necessity for teachers to scaffold and coach students *as they write.*

How would you assess the effectiveness of guided writing? Gibson (2008/2009) recommends anecdotal notes that document students' writing behaviors *during* the writing process and students' responses to the teacher's attempts to scaffold instruction. Gibson also suggests periodically examining what the students have written based on the skills on which you are focusing your scaffolding. Is there evidence of student learning? Do students need more scaffolding? Where should your next steps in guided writing instruction take you with each student?

2017 ILA Standards

3.2

Check Your Understanding 11.4: Gauge your understanding of the skills and concepts in this section.

Reading–Writing–Technology Connections

■ **Demonstrate an understanding of the importance of integrating technology into the language arts curriculum, including effective strategies for teaching twenty-first-century communication skills.**

Advances in technology have changed how we communicate and disseminate information in the twenty-first century and will continue to transform how we think about teaching reading and writing. Technology, integrated into the curriculum for meaningful learning, is a necessary and powerful tool in students' literacy development, and it is critical that teachers guide students in how to retrieve and produce digital, online communications (National Governors Association Center for Best Practices, Council of Chief State School Officers, 2010a). Hence, the digital forces of the technology have paved the way for an information age that affects the literacy learning of today's generation of students like no other generation before it. **Electronic texts**, which are constructed and displayed on a computer screen, are an integral part of students' literacy lives in *and* out of classrooms. These texts are not fixed entities, set in print. They are fluid, interactive, and engaging.

Teachers must provide instruction in these new literacies by helping students recognize significant questions as they search for writing topics online and critically evaluate topic-related information. In addition, today's technology is redefining the sense of community as students communicate with others worldwide and participate in community-based projects that can be shared online (Leu et al., 2011).

Electronic Text Production and Publishing

Often students find when using computers to write—whether it is on desktop computers, laptops, or tablets—that their work may be less organized and need more revision than when using paper-and-pencil writing. This free, continuous writing followed by reflection and revision is one of the best ways to compose. In addition, students can store their work in electronic folders or electronic portfolios or on CDs or flash drives, which can make the revision process easier. Electronic portfolios can also store biographical information, PowerPoint presentations, research references, electronic communication, favorite websites—and the list goes on.

Used correctly, computers can help students write. Words are not carved in stone; they are painted in light, permitting effortless manipulation. The more students intelligently manipulate text—the more they read their work and revise—the better writers they will become.

Supporting students' writing of electronic texts is one of the important reading–writing–technology connections that can be made in the classroom. Using computers to construct electronic texts helps students examine ideas, organize and report information and inquiry findings, and communicate with others. Word processing, desktop publishing, and authoring software programs, for example, allow students to use and develop literacy skills to publish writing in creative ways and prepare multimedia reports and presentations relevant to curriculum objectives. The technology available today makes it possible for students to connect what they are reading and writing about to sound, graphics, illustrations, photographs, video, and other nonprint media in multimedia environments.

Online Communications

Today's information and communication technologies (ICTs) reinforce the critical importance of the social nature of reading and writing. In fact, today's students currently connect with others via a wide variety of online communications including e-mail, blogs, text messaging, wikis, online forums, and Twitter, to name a few (Sweeney, 2010). These avenues of interaction provide teachers with diverse opportunities to engage students in real-time reading, writing, and problem-solving skills that they will need to meet the communication competencies and expectations necessary for the twenty-first century.

Although teachers may have initial concerns regarding the nature and formats of online communications, creating guidelines beforehand can help monitor appropriate interactions (Sweeney, 2010). Once rules have been established, the range of writing connections is endless. Students can communicate with the teacher; they can dialogue with peers in the classroom, across the country, and throughout the world; they can reach out to professionals, ask questions, address concerns, and ask for advice. Online communications can provide workspaces to discuss books, share original writings, collaborate on research projects, address queries about interesting topics, exchange creative ideas, work with others to design presentations, and much more. A significant factor regarding ICTs is that they afford readers and writers an authentic audience for sharing knowledge, skills, and creative endeavors on a wide range of levels, and they foster collaboration beyond the walls of the classroom.

Online Resources for Writing

As students learn to develop the myriad writing skills that are necessary to be productive members of society today and in the future, access to online resources provides them with a multitude of ways to retrieve assistance. Teachers can incorporate these resources into whole class lessons, small group minilessons, or individualized tutorial sessions.

Online graphic organizers can help students craft their writing, spreadsheets can assist students in collecting data, and statistical software can support research and data analysis. Resources are also available that aid students in the logistics of writing, including grammar, spelling, and word choices (online thesauruses); editing assistance; and how to cite resources. Indeed, the online assistance available for all writers provides support they can use to efficiently organize, revise, edit, and communicate information in multiple genres (research reports, argumentative essays, narrative compositions, and more).

In addition, there is an ever-growing body of resources and lessons available through educationally sponsored as well as commercial websites that foster reading

BOX 11.7

Twitter Brainstorming

Educators should exemplify how an individual uses digital tools and resources to become a skilled communicator, collaborator, and devoted lifelong learner. Modelling the use of a range of transliteracy tools is something teachers need to engage in on a daily basis. Most educators are familiar with Twitter, but many wonder how to actually put it into classroom practice. Twitter brainstorming is one way to begin, even in the early grades, because it does not require students to have individual Twitter accounts.

To get started, teachers will need to create their own free Twitter account. When setting it up, identify your Twitter account as an education-related account and make sure your profile includes the grade you teach and where you are located, as this helps other educators with similar teaching positions connect and share with you. From there, you'll want to create a classroom hashtag. Hashtags are critical, as they allow Twitter users to sort and filter out irrelevant and potentially inappropriate Twitter content (tweets). A hashtag is a word or phrase that begins with the # symbol that is used to denote keywords or topics. In this case, you'll want to create a hashtag that identifies your classroom, school, or specific course. If I was a third-grade teacher, my hashtag might be something like #MrBrueckG3 or #3brueck3. You can be creative here, but ideally, the shorter the better.

Now that you've got your Twitter account and hashtag set up, you are ready to tweet! In this scenario, we'll be using Twitter to model for students how to leverage the social media platform to help generate ideas for writing narrative and expository texts. Let's say, as a class, students have generated and stated an opinion that it is important to conserve the world's water supply, and you are working to brainstorm ideas that support this opinion (CCSS.ELA-LITERACY.W.3.1.B). On your classroom Twitter account, you could post a tweet such as,

Grade 3 class discussing water conservation. Help us brainstorm! Why is conserving water so important? Include #3brueck3 in your reply!

Once your tweet goes out to all the Twitter followers (parents, community members, other classrooms, and teachers), you can track replies to your question with a hashtag using a free service like Tweetwall (https://tweetwall.com). Display the results for students in real time on your computer screen or project on your whiteboard so students can record and discuss the responses.

Vetted responses that can back up the students' opinions can then be transferred to a graphic organizer or online mind map like Popplet (http://popplet.com) to help students organize their thoughts before writing. Using Twitter as a mechanism for asking questions, gathering data and sharing ideas is a great way to bring many transliteracy skills into your classroom and help students generate ideas for writing!

and writing activities to enhance and support writing instruction. Authors also have resources that include writing tips and suggestions for young writers.

In essence, the range of resources available for students to publish their work, communicate in real time about their ideas, and receive technical assistance as they write provides teachers with an insurmountable number of ways to integrate writing instruction with twenty-first-century technology supports for writing. See Box 11.7 for Jeremy Brueck's commentary on how transliteracies enhance students' abilities to generate ideas for writing narrative and expository text.

Common Core State Standards

CCRA.W.6, CCRA.W.8

Check Your Understanding 11.5: Gauge your understanding of the skills and concepts in this section.

RTI for Struggling Readers

Generous Reading and *Response to Intervention*

ELLs experience multiple challenges that include understanding, speaking, reading, and writing the second language. They also bring unique schemata and cultural understandings to the classroom. With respect to writing, these experiences ought to be considered when evaluating ELLs' attempts to write. Benchmarks for writing include specific standards, and teachers very often assess students' progress using rubrics based on the number of errors that occur in sample writings. *Generous reading* of students' writing, on the other hand, implies a different approach to looking closely at how ELLs write and about what they write (Spence, 2010). We concur with Spence and think that this notion of generous reading fits well within the concept of RTI.

What is generous reading? According to Spence (2010), it involves teachers reading students' writing with a closer understanding of the students' backgrounds, the students' grasp of concepts and ideas, and the context in which the students write. This means looking beyond errors and examining the writers themselves and giving them choices about what to write. What are they saying about themselves as they write? What cultural understandings are reflected in their words? What sorts of first-language connections are evident in the writings?

Since reading and writing are integrally connected and because a focus of RTI is assessing students, we suggest that generous reading be considered as a component of the evaluation process. It doesn't make sense to count student errors and use that information as the sole criterion to measure students' progress, particularly with ELLs.

What About . . .

Standards, Assessment, and Reading–Writing Connections?

The CCSS (2010a) for K through 12 students indicate that students need to be able to read and write clearly and effectively in a variety of situations, must be able to adjust their written communication skills to a wide variety of audiences, and must know how to write for a range of purposes. In addition, students must know the conventions of written communication, including spelling and punctuation, and they must be able to generate and synthesize ideas via the written word.

Olness (2005) recommends rubrics that rate writers on a scale of 5 (strong) to 3 (developing) to 1 (weak). For example, when evaluating *voice*, a student whose writing is convincing, includes an appropriate tone, and demonstrates feeling would rate a 5. A student whose writing is not individualized and includes more "telling" than "feeling" would rate a 3. A rating of 1 means the reader could not tell what the writer means or cares about.

Regardless of the rubric used to evaluate student writing, teachers must ask themselves whether the students are meeting the standards. Proficiency assessments, especially test situations in which students must respond to open-ended questions or write extended essays, evaluate both the content and the process by which students produce a piece of writing. Often, this type of writing assessment is evaluated using holistic scoring. In holistic scoring, a rubric is typically used to assess the quality of writing. The rubric might ask test evaluators to judge the piece of writing based on a general impression of its overall effectiveness or to assess more specific skills. We certainly do not advocate practices that "teach to the test," but we do suggest that teachers inform themselves about the statewide assessment practices that are used to evaluate their students' proficiency in writing. How specifically are your students evaluated on their writing skills via your statewide tests? What are the standards? These are some questions teachers need to consider.

Summary

- In this chapter, we initially discussed the relationships that capture how reading and writing are integrally related, including the social nature of language. In addition, good readers tend to be good writers, and good writers tend to be good readers. Wide reading can also lead to improved writing. Hence, reading and writing instruction should be integrated throughout the curriculum. We also discussed the connections between spelling and writing.

- We explored the characteristics that foster an engaging reading and writing classroom environment, including the importance of offering students choices, tying writing to the curriculum, and guiding writing.

- We presented strategies that demonstrate strong reading–writing connections, including journal writing, e-mail, multigenre projects, writing nonfiction, and plot scaffolds, and highlighted ways to integrate technology.

- We discussed the writing process, including the six traits-plus model, and ways to organize writing instruction, including writing workshop and guided writing so that you will have frameworks for organizing writing instruction you can adapt to your own students' needs.

- We highlighted the importance of incorporating technology into the language arts curriculum in order to prepare students for the communication skills they will need for success in the twenty-first century. Electronic text production and publishing experiences help students examine, organize, and report information on a variety of levels. In addition, we also discussed how online communications such as blogs, e-mail, wikis, and Twitter can assist students in collaborative and problem-solving skills. Finally, we shared the significance of online resources that students can access, such as graphic organizers and editing websites. These resources provide tools that can enhance teaching the writing process in multiple ways.

Teacher Action Research

1. Interview a small group of middle-grade students to assess their understanding of reading–writing connections. Ask them questions such as: How do you read? How do you write? What strategies do you use when you read? What strategies do you use when you write? Can you tell me how you connect your writing to your reading? What kinds of assignments help you connect reading and writing? Adapt your interview to encourage open-ended responses. Next, analyze the students' responses and synthesize an understanding of your findings to share with your colleagues.

2. Ask a teacher whether you may talk with several of her or his students individually about writing, or use your own students. Develop interview questions such as the following and record the students' responses:

   - Do you like to write? Why or why not?
   - What things does your teacher do in the classroom that you like when you write?
   - What are your favorite writing assignments in class?
   - Are there any things you do not like about writing in class? Tell me more.

   After conducting several interviews, analyze the responses in terms of positive statements and negative statements. What are your conclusions about the students' perceptions of the classroom writing environment?

3. Select a grade level. Using the English language arts standards for your state, design a 15-minute writing minilesson that addresses a specific expectation for the standard that you selected. Peer-teach the lesson to your classmates, and gather reflections about the nature of your lesson. Ask your colleagues:

   - What was the goal of my minilesson?
   - Were my goals evident?
   - Were you engaged during my lesson?
   - How might you adapt my lesson?

   After reading your classmates' reflections, write a reflective piece that captures how your lesson might improve or change.

4. Locate a classroom in which process writing, including conferences, is used. Observe the interactions that occur when writers seek a response to their writing, from the teacher or other writers in the class. Do the

students seem to have sufficient opportunities to read their work critically during conferences? How long do the conferences tend to last? In a week or two, collect the same type of data based on observations in another classroom either at the same or another grade level. Or revisit the same classroom each week for the same amount of time during the course of a month. Do you notice any changes in the conduct of the conferences or the interactions among the students?

5. Interview a teacher who has a limited number of computers in his or her classroom and a teacher who uses a computer lab as the primary vehicle for using technology. Ask the teachers the following questions:

- Do you organize time for children to explore writing assignments on the computer? If so, how?
- If you use the computer for writing assignments, what is the nature of the assignments? Do the students have choices, or do you assign topics?
- If your students use the computer to develop their writing skills, how do you evaluate their work?

Through the Lens of the Common Core

In this chapter we discussed the wide variety of writing skills that are expected of students as delineated in the CCSS (2010a). Students need to be able to compose argumentative pieces, write narrative and expository selections, and conduct and develop research. It is also essential that students be adept at documenting, organizing, synthesizing, and revising text. In addition, the CCSS (2010a) affirm that students need to be able to effectively use and integrate technology throughout the writing processes. In this chapter, we emphasized the important role that technology plays in communicating ideas, opinions, responses, and solving problems.

Chapter 12
Bringing Children and Text Together

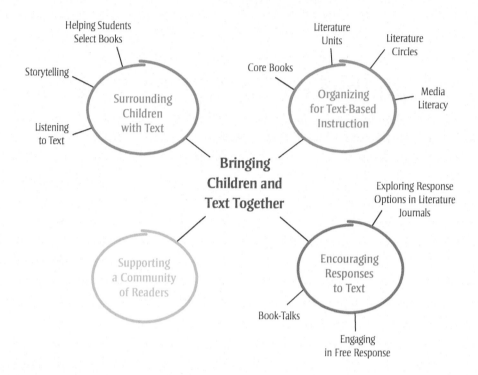

Helping Students Select Books

Storytelling

Surrounding Children with Text

Listening to Text

Literature Units

Literature Circles

Core Books

Organizing for Text-Based Instruction

Media Literacy

Bringing Children and Text Together

Exploring Response Options in Literature Journals

Supporting a Community of Readers

Encouraging Responses to Text

Book-Talks

Engaging in Free Response

Learning Outcomes

In this chapter, you will discover how to:

- Explain that literacy development is personal and that readers benefit from a supportive environment in order to create a community of readers.

- Choose books and classroom activities to surround children with print and nonprint material.

- Organize classroom instruction around narrative and informational text.

- Design strategies for encouraging readers to respond to text.

Activating Your Schema

Think about the different types of books you have read. Which genre did you like the most? The least? How did you access the books? How have your reading habits changed over time? Explain why the changes happened.

Think about the various classroom environments that you engaged in during your experiences in school. Describe the physical and psychological elements of the classroom that encouraged you to develop your reading skills.

Think about the changes in technology that have affected the use of literature. How has technology changed how teachers use or provide literature in the classroom?

2017 ILA Standards Found in This Chapter

1.3	4.2	5.1	5.4
1.4	4.3	5.2	6.1
4.1	4.4	5.3	

Common Core State Standards: English Language Arts

CCRA.R.5	CCRA.R.7	CCRA.R.10	CCRA.SL.2	CCRA.SL.4
CCRA.R.6	CCRA.R.9	CCRA.SL.1	CCRA.SL.3	CCRA.SL.5

Key Terms

aesthetic stance	literature circles
book-talks	literature journals
community of readers	literature units
core books	media literacy
critical literacy	read-aloud
efferent stance	reader-response theory
free response	storytelling
integrated instruction	thematic instruction

Tim, an on-level reader in Michelle Balderson's second-grade classroom, loved to read fictional stories. When they explored nonfiction, Michelle would catch Tim reverting back to fictional stories. This was a struggle. His mom also shared her frustrations, as she was also trying to get him to read some nonfiction material to support the second-grade reading curriculum. Things changed in early January when the class had a student book exchange. Tim was given a fictional story about a boy who would drift off at night and visit the planet Mars. He had all kinds of adventures there. Tim's mother informed his teacher that almost everyone in their family had the book memorized because Tim read it to them nightly. He *loved* this fictional book. When Tim was "student of the week" in his classroom, he asked to read the story to the class. After reading the story, Michelle pulled him aside and told him how well he read and that Mars sounded like a cool place. She asked him whether he would like to learn more about the planet Mars. He quickly exclaimed, "Yes!" That afternoon during recess time, Tim stayed in the classroom with his teacher and they pulled up pictures of Mars on the smartboard. The pictures led to a great discussion about outer space. He asked whether she had books about Mars. They walked hand in hand to the school library and checked out two books about Mars. The following week Tim returned the books and asked for more! His mother sent the teacher a letter stating, "I don't know what you did, but Tim will not put down the nonfiction reading books about Mars. Way to go!" Michelle believed that it was Tim who was inquisitive about Mars and had a desire to learn more. Over the next few weeks, Tim continued to check out books about outer space and asked whether he could tell the other children about his findings. He wrote a book report and made a poster. He then decided he wanted to make a 3-D model, so one day after school, Tim and his teacher made a model of outer space constructed with Styrofoam balls and tempera paint. Tim was proud of himself, and Michelle was proud of

Tim. He not only shared his model with the second-grade students, but with the third-and fourth-grade classes as well. He felt empowered, and by embracing his interest, he eventually raised his reading two levels.

Tim's story is not unlike that of students in other schools and in other classrooms whose path to literacy, for one reason or another, is rough and uncertain. Yet within the literacy community of Michelle's classroom, there is an air of confidence that all of the children will find their way to literate activity. How to reach them is the challenge she faces. Her 18 years of teaching experience with literacy beginners helped Michelle realize that she must first establish a level of trust in the classroom and then find a "hook" that will connect literacy to the lives of the children. For many teachers, like Michelle, literature is the hook.

Stephanie Sage also was able to hook her students with literature. Matt, a fifth-grade student with suspected learning disabilities, was a loner at the beginning of the school year. He was overlooked by other students because of some annoying behaviors and didn't contribute much to class discussions. About three months into the school year, Stephanie's class was reading a poem entitled "Reggie." This poem was about a boy who idolized Kareem Abdul-Jabbar. After reading the poem aloud to the students, Stephanie asked them who knew who Kareem was. Matt's hand was the only one in class to soar high in the air. She couldn't believe it! Matt offered correct information about the basketball hero and engaged the other students in the information he was offering. He was excited and wore a big smile as he educated the other students. At this moment Stephanie realized the vast knowledge Matt possessed about sports. This was the first time all year that he had responded to a poem and showed interest in class work. She then showed him literature of various genres that she had available in the classroom relating to sports and sports figures. Matt began to read, the best that he could, and discovered more facts about sports figures that he shared with the class. This was a huge success for Matt as the students now viewed him as a contributor to literacy in their classroom.

The stories of Tim and Matt illustrate convincingly that at its best, literacy is a personal and self-engaging activity. Students who view themselves as contributing members of a classroom of readers and writers develop a sense of self-worth and commitment. Bringing children and books together in a literate community fosters the ability not only to think better but also to feel and to imagine.

Reading text requires students to respond to books affectively as well as cognitively. Students respond emotionally to the literary text as a whole. These feelings are unique and tied to each reader's life experiences. Emphasizing personal involvement in literature develops in students an imagination, a sense of wonder, and an active participation in the literary experience. To our mind, bringing students and text together is one of the highest acts of humanity in the classroom.

How teachers capture students' interest in books and bring them into a supportive community of readers is the subject of this chapter. Examine the concept map, which depicts connections among several key concepts related to bringing books and children together. It is important to surround students with books, including those with a multicultural perspective, in order to immerse young children, as well as middle school students, in hearing various types of text and to help them find books they want to read.

We also emphasize in this chapter the importance of children's responding personally to text as a way to extend critical thinking and make connections to other readers. We look at how to organize the classroom so that students can authentically respond to print and nonprint materials. Finally, students' freedom to choose what they read is considered in relation to different ways of organizing for instruction.

Supporting a Community of Readers

■ **Explain that literacy development is personal and that readers benefit from a supportive environment in order to create a community of readers.**

Society has an impact on what is considered a proper text to be read by students and used by teachers for instruction. What is considered the appropriate text has changed due to external mandates, standards, and advanced technology. With the curricular changes, there is no longer a primary spotlight on literature alone. It has been broadened to include more reliance on including informational text especially integrated across disciplines. The criteria established by the Common Core State Standards (CCSS) emphasize the need for the use of 50 percent literature and 50 percent informational text across disciplines (Coleman & Pimentel, 2012). Within these categories a variety of genres is recommended to be incorporated across disciplines.

Additionally, the CCSS focus on utilizing more complex challenging text at each grade level for developing reading and writing skills and strategies. The International Reading Association (2012) reports that merely adding challenging text to the curriculum is not the intention of the CCSS. Rather, using a variety of text to help students reach more advanced levels of reading development is the purpose. This includes children reading text at their level as well as above in order to stretch their literacy achievement. Wixson and Valencia (2014) stress the need for elementary students to go beyond reading leveled texts. They need more interaction with texts that are on multiple levels of difficulty. Using text at various levels requires the teacher to provide more support, as well as developing critical reading and higher levels of thinking.

Technology has also changed the use of books in the classroom. Online reading, multimedia text productions, and electronic messaging have influenced classroom reading and reading instruction. Reading also takes place on computers, Kindles, Nooks, iPads, phones, and many other screens. No matter the mode of text, Serafini (2012) stresses that the reader needs to decode text, use text structures, and interpret images and figures. In order to create meaning, the students need to be active, critical readers.

There are long-term benefits implicit in bringing students and print and nonprint materials together on a regular basis. First, reading expands children's experiential backgrounds. Children who have never milked a cow and been awakened by a rooster or never lived in a tenement apartment and played in the alley of a big city can expand their world through reading. Second, text provides readers with good models of writing. These models are valuable in children's own writing development and teach the unique characteristics of written language. Third, students learn to read by reading, a theme we have repeated throughout this text. When they are encouraged to read books regularly, children are more likely to develop patience with print, and thus they gain valuable practice in reading. Fourth, when the prime purpose for reading is pleasure, children want to understand what they are reading and are likely to select books with familiar topics, themes, or characters. These natural reading situations will promote students' use of reading strategies. And fifth, wide reading provides opportunities for children to develop vocabulary knowledge. Readers learn the meaning of words by meeting them again and again in a variety of contexts.

Integrating various texts in the classroom has the potential for success with all types of students, but particularly with struggling readers like Tim and Matt, who can easily slip through the cracks without a supportive environment for literacy development. Supporting a community of readers enhances the development of reading and writing skills for all ages. Ivey and Fisher (2006) stress that for struggling adolescents, exposure to appropriate literature can help them to "stimulate their minds—make them laugh, puzzle, empathize, question, or reconsider previously held notions" (p. 17). Children who speak limited English have also made great gains in reading when immersed in their new language (Vardell, Hadaway, & Young, 2006). Free reading of second-language texts, as reported by Krashen (2003), contributes to advanced second-language development. In addition, reading is a way for ELLs to make connections with peers because they have conversations about books and share cultural experiences (Protacio, 2012).

Common Core State Standard

CCRA.SL.1

Providing all students with many and varied opportunities to read high-quality text is essential. As the International Reading Association has aptly stated, "Children who read more, read better" (2002b, p. 6). Moreover, encouraging students to read and write and integrating various texts create a **community of readers**. Hepler and Hickman (1982) proposed the idea of a community of readers to characterize how students, in alliance with their friends and teacher, work together in classrooms in which school reading becomes like adult reading, where adults are motivated to read. In these classrooms, students informally and spontaneously talk over their experiences with books and recommend books to each other. The interactions that students experience help them to learn from each other and share their confidence as readers.

2017 ILA Standards

5.2, 5.4

Classrooms where students support each other as readers and writers do not arise spontaneously. Rather, they are structured where students are given the opportunity to choose texts and share what they have learned in a low-risk environment. Galda and Beach (2004) believe that encouraging students to read and talk with others supports them as they make sense of text and the world they live in. Additionally, teachers are providing various instructional strategies, along with read-alouds, modeling, and strategy development, to help shape and develop a community of readers (Regan & Berkeley 2012). In a classroom with a community of readers, the students' responses to print and nonprint material are livelier and more positive, and their choices of books seem to be made with more care.

Common Core State Standard

CCRA.SL.1

Hooking students on books helps them realize their literacy potential. As Johnny emphasizes (see Box 12.1), the teacher plays a critical role in creating a literate environment that motivates students to read. In addition to Johnny's recommendations, we explore in this chapter some additional hooks (see Figure 12.1) that support a community of readers in primary and middle school classrooms.

BOX 12.1 | STUDENT VOICES

Johnny is a high-achieving middle school student. He likes school and especially enjoys science, but dislikes social studies. His explanation for his likes and dislikes is related to the instructional strategies that the teachers utilize. Johnny believes that more student interaction, clearer explanations, and realistic expectations help to motivate students to want to learn a specific topic area or subject.

Johnny considers himself a reader, and he reads more now than ever. His favorite books are related to sports, and he believes Mike Lupica is a great author because "he writes a lot of sport books and his books have a lot of people with problems." Mike Lupica's books include *The Batboy, Travel Team, Heat, Miracle on 49th Street*, and *Summer Ball*.

Reading in the middle school is not considered "cool." Johnny explains that "people think it is not cool to read, and people want to be cool so they don't read." He further explains

that in order to encourage students to read more, teachers should "help students find books they can enjoy." He emphasizes that "Teachers should have every kind of book from different authors because kids like different books and authors." Johnny believes that middle school classrooms should have shelves of books with easy access for the students to choose from during sustained silent reading and when they are finished reading their own book.

Johnny's insights are important for teachers to consider as they plan their own classrooms. At the middle school level, reading and the motivation to read, as Johnny has explained, need to be supported by the teacher. The teacher plays a critical role by choosing and recommending various books and authors, providing easy access to books, and encouraging students to read by setting expectations and creating opportunities for the students to read.

Figure 12.1 Hooking Students on Books

Immerse Students in Literature

- Create a classroom climate in which literature is an integral component.
- Use many genres of children's books with multicultural perspectives, including folktales, poetry, realistic fiction, historical fiction, and informational books.
- Select and organize a classroom collection of books.
- Read and tell stories. Show films and videoclips of literature selections.
- Integrate talking books.

Use Instructional Time to Show the Value of Reading

- Find classroom time for students to read books of their choice.
- Model reading behavior and become a reader of children's books.
- Encourage students to respond to the aesthetic dimensions of literature.

Help Students Find and Share Books They Want to Read

- Help students find books of interest at the appropriate level.
- Tell or read the beginning of interesting stories.
- Develop annotated lists of books worth reading.

Check Your Understanding 12.1: Gauge your understanding of the skills and concepts in this section.

Surrounding Children with Text

■ **Choose books and classroom activities to surround children with print and nonprint material.**

Teachers who make a point of talking about their own favorite books or stories or are themselves engrossed in a new book often find their students wanting to read those same books for themselves. These teachers also show personal interest in books in other ways. Some teachers share autographed copies of books from their own collections or display book-related items such as ceramic or stuffed toy characters or posters designed by a picture-book artist. No matter how the teacher's enthusiasm is expressed, it creates a setting in which students know that attention to the world of books is authentic and desirable. This is especially important for students in high-poverty areas and for English language learners (ELLs), for whom there are limited print and nonprint resources outside the school. Classroom environments where reading is valued and encouraged are motivating for all students.

2017 ILA Standards

1.4, 4.3, 5.1

Selecting a Classroom Collection of Books

With the implementation of the CCSS, teachers need to include both literature and information text in their classroom collections. Literature books typically include the utilization of a variety of genres such as stories, dramas, and poetry. Recommended informational text includes nonfiction, historical, scientific, and technical readings. Books need to inform, have the appropriate complexity, and be of high interest. Other material—both nonprint and print—may include but is not limited to books, articles, websites, videos, and newspapers. A major classroom characteristic that brings children and books together is many carefully selected readings. These books come from different sources—the teacher's personal collection, the school library, the public library, and paperback book clubs. Although the core collection is permanent, many of the borrowed titles change frequently, so there is always something new to encourage browsing.

Common Core State Standards

CCRA.R.5, CCRA.R.6, CCRA.R.7

Another way to encourage browsing is to include a selection of e-books (e.g., talking books, CD-ROM stories, interactive books). Simple e-books consist of computer files that include text, title, pages, chapters, illustrations, and internal hyperlinks that allow maneuvering through the text (Roskos & Brueck, 2009). More complex e-books contain multimedia additions such as sound, animation, video, a read-aloud capacity, highlighted text, hyperlinks, hotspots, and interactive tools. This complexity helps to increase comprehension and critical thinking skills. Teachers are encouraged to familiarize themselves with the various e-books and elements of e-books by reading versions of notable children's and young adult books. Books chosen for a classroom collection, no matter what type, should not be chosen for the sake of quantity. Rather, books should be carefully chosen for a variety of reasons. Marcy Zipke (2014) warns that when choosing e-books, focus on literacy experiences rather than distractions such as movies and games. The stories, illustrations, content appeal, and motivation to develop imagination and abilities are just a few reasons for choosing books.

2017 ILA Standards

5.2, 5.3

An additional feature of text selection is to choose books so that each title bears some relationship to others in the collection. Students will pick familiar books. There may be multiple books by an author or an illustrator or several books that represent a genre such as modern fantasy. For example, a classroom that contains Rowling's *Harry Potter* books would also have *A Series of Unfortunate Events* by Lemony Snicket. Other connections may be based on a content theme, such as spooky books, nature books, or survival books. *The Hunger Games* by Collins (2010) is another popular series.

CHOOSING CLASSROOM TEXTS   To be able to choose books for classroom collections and to give guidance to students as they choose books to read, a teacher needs to be familiar with children's and adolescents' books. Because the use of text has expanded extensively in the past 20 years, this is a formidable task.

Several strategies can be used to help choose classroom literature. Here are some tips on how to avoid being overwhelmed as you become familiar with various texts:

- *Read and enjoy children's and adolescents' books yourself.* The best way to become familiar with students' books is not to read anthologies or reviews but to read the books themselves. It is a good idea to keep a card file on the books you have read to jog your memory later. This card file can be used with students to help them in choosing books to read. It can also be used as you share your feelings about particular books with other teachers.

- *Read children's and adolescents' books with a sense of involvement.* Only by reading books thoroughly can you prepare yourself to share them honestly with students.

- *Read a variety of book types.* There are various classifications of genres or types of books. By being familiar with specific books in each of the different genres, you can be more helpful when students ask for such things as "a scary mystery" or "something true to life."

- *Read books for a wide variety of ability levels.* Students at any grade level vary tremendously in their reading abilities and interests. For example, Haywood's *B Is for Betsy* is read avidly by some second and third graders. Other students at the same grade level will read somewhat more difficult books, such as Sobol's *Encyclopedia Brown Lends a Hand* and Blume's *Tales of a Fourth Grade Nothing*. Still others may benefit from spending time with picture books such as *Where the Wild Things Are* by Sendak or *The Great Thumbprint Drawing Book* by Emberley.

- *Share how your students respond to particular books with other teachers or other university students.* A book-reporting system can be developed in any school. Seek the assistance of the librarian or media specialist. Anyone who reads a book and uses it with students can fill out a review card, which includes a brief summary, a rating, comments on the book's unique value, and recommendations for suggested ability levels. Teachers can use these cards to help select texts for their classrooms. Not unexpectedly, with this teacher-sharing system in place, the students will read more, as will the teachers.

- *Start by reading several books of good quality.* Look for Newbery Medal and Caldecott Medal award winners. As you read these and begin using them with students, you will begin to know books to which children in your class will respond favorably. For a list of recommended books for multicultural reading experiences, refer to Appendix D.
- *Search the Internet.* Review various sites on the Internet for book lists, e-books, videos, and other nonprint materials that facilitate conceptual development.

DETERMINING GOOD TEXT   A teacher's first priority is to choose books that students will like and will read. It is important to take into consideration students' diverse backgrounds, academic abilities, and interests. To choose such a collection of books, teachers must be knowledgeable of and enthusiastic about children's and adolescents' literature and informational text. Through reading books and talking about books with students, teachers learn which books to use in their classrooms. Five criteria to use in building a balanced collection of books are described in the following list:

2017 ILA Standard

6.1

1. *The collection needs to contain modern, realistic literature as well as more traditional literature.* In recent years, some critics have voiced concern about the appropriateness of realism in some children's literature. Other observers feel that realism is justified because it depicts problems children must face while growing up. Each teacher and school must decide whether to include books that deal with divorce, death, and drug use—issues that touch the lives of many of today's children. Traditional literature, which children have delighted in for many years, should also be a part of the classroom collection of books. "These books not only have artistic and literacy merit but also generate strong personal response and have universal appeal" as Livingston and Kurkjiam point out (2003, p. 96).
2. *The collection needs to contain books that realistically present different ethnic and minority groups and nontraditional families as well as mainstream Americans.* Refer to Appendix D for book suggestions.
3. *The collection needs to contain books with different types of themes and books of varying difficulty.* Students generally choose books based on reading level, content, and style (Ivey & Fisher, 2006). For ELLs book selection is more complex. Teachers need to consider language and writing complexity and use of visualization. The classroom library needs traditional literature, fantasy, poetry, historical fiction, nonfiction, and picture books. Even middle school classroom collections should have some picture books. Picture books often have a good story plot and provide a way to get less enthusiastic students into reading. A few picture books appropriate for middle school students are *Amazing Grace* by Mary Hoffman, *Baseball Saved Us* by Ken Mochizuki, and *Grandfather's Journey* by Allen Say.
4. *The collection needs to include nonfiction.* Students from all grades should have access to a wide selection of high-quality information books (Saul & Dieckman, 2005). The use of nonfiction trade books is common in middle school classrooms (Moss & Hendershot, 2002). However, this does not seem to be especially true in primary grades, where fiction is dominant. With the emphasis from the CCSS on using a variety of text—especially informational text—teachers in primary grades as well

as in middle school need to increase informational text utilization that includes simple and complex concepts, various topics, and a wide range of reading levels.

2017 ILA Standards

5.2, 5.4

5. *The collection of books needs to include e-books.* A collection of e-books needs exciting features along with quality stories, interesting subject matter, developmentally appropriate themes, and encourage language usage. When online, the students should want to read rather than watch a movie or play a game (Zipke, 2014).

TEXT WITH MULTICULTURAL PERSPECTIVES   In a multicultural society made up of diverse groups who maintain their own cultural traditions and experiences, books help us celebrate our distinctive differences and understand our common humanity. Culturally diverse books in the United States typically tell the stories of people of color—African Americans, Native Americans, Asian Americans, and Hispanic Americans. These stories are told through poems, folklore, picture books, realistic and historical fiction, biography, and nonfiction. Culturally diverse books also may represent the literature of regional white and religious groups—for example, Appalachian, Ozark, Jewish, Muslim, or Amish cultures—or the cross-cultural stories of people from other nations. What all culturally diverse books have in common is that they portray what is unique to an individual culture and universal to all cultures.

2017 ILA Standards

4.2, 4.3, 4.4

Common Core State Standard

CCRA.R.6

The power of multicultural literature lies in the human connections that we make. Not only do books about people of color or distinct cultural groups help us understand and appreciate differences among people, but they also show how people are connected to one another through human needs, desires, and emotions (Cullinan & Galda, 1994). A few text examples that exemplify the personal connection are *Pullman Porter: An American Journey* by Vanita Oeschlager (2014); *Terezin: Voices from the Holocaust* by Ruth Thomson (2011); and *Pablo Neruda: Poet of the People* by Monica Brown (2011). These texts, like other multicultural books, both narrative and informative, have an important role in developing critical literacy skills.

There are fundamental social and educational reasons why multicultural literature should be woven into the fabric of children's home and school experiences. In Box 12.2, Peter Schneller passionately expresses the need for teachers to integrate multiple perspectives in the curriculum using multicultural literature. He emphasizes that utilizing multicultural literature broadens the students' perspectives of themselves and their culture. Understanding of oneself helps to create an awareness of diversity and acceptance of others. This leads to an appreciation of the complex world and provides a foundation for learning about others and their cultural experiences.

Multicultural literature helps readers understand, appreciate, and celebrate the traditions and experiences that make each culture special in its own way. It is especially important to provide access for middle school students because they often have little or no exposure to multicultural literature. Teachers need to make specific efforts to include books that involve multicultural characters and discuss issues related to race and diversity (Koss & Teale, 2009). Multicultural literature opens doors to other cultures and introduces readers to ideas and insights they would otherwise not have encountered (Landt, 2006). When students read books that depict cultural differences,

BOX 12.2 | VIEWPOINT

Peter L. Schneller
Literature and Multiple Perspectives

Peter Schneller is a professor of education at the University of Mount Union.

I'm afraid that most Americans are becoming comfortable in horseradish. In a world that's becoming increasingly global, we tend to immerse ourselves in the routine and familiar; whether it's horseradish or ketchup, if it's familiar, we relish it. Admit it; the American perspective is often limited—myopic and xenophobic. So here's my command to teachers: Use literature to broaden your students' perspectives.

And it's easy. There is a plethora of literature that can provide multiple perspectives for students of all ages. An excellent example is *The True Story of the 3 Little Pigs!* by Jon Scieszka and Lane Smith. It enables students to think about the standard nursery rhyme through the eyes of the wolf, who is perhaps the most maligned archetype utilized by the seemingly unbiased and always good Mother Goose. Another picture book that offers a point of view rarely imagined is *Baseball Saved Us* by Ken Mochizuki and Dom Lee. It takes readers to the Japanese internment camps in Idaho during World War II and stimulates us to envision life through the eyes of a young Japanese American who's been imprisoned unjustly, yet intermittently is freed through playing the great American pastime. For older readers there's *Flip-Flop Girl* by Katherine Paterson. Paterson delicately permits us to walk in the shoes of Vinnie, a social outcast with complex life problems. The book dishes out generous doses of bibliotherapy; it's ideal for building a classroom community that honors students of all backgrounds. All teachers should read

and share with their students Mark Haddon's *The Curious Incident of the Dog in the Night-Time.* Haddon's point of view enlightens the reader through the inner life of an autistic child. It's also a nifty narrative filled with delightful literary intricacies.

Unless teachers integrate multiple perspectives into the curriculum, what's familiar may smother us. Gary Howard, author of *We Can't Teach What We Don't Know*, and the **Respecting Ethnic and Cultural Heritage Center (REACH)** have developed curricula for all grade levels that convey multiple perspectives as a foundation for increasing an awareness of diversity. Teachers should be obligated to examine REACH's ethnic perspectives series, which presents views of American history via American Indians, African Americans, European Americans, and Japanese Americans. It's a profound first step in developing cultural competency.

Mark Twain claims that "Travel is fatal to prejudice, bigotry, and narrow-mindedness, and many of our people need it sorely on these accounts" (1897, p. 444). Although there is no education quite like travel, books can be luxurious vehicles for vicarious sightseeing. Emily Dickinson was correct when she wrote, "There is no frigate like a book, To take us lands away . . . " We must help our students understand the dimensions of a multicultural United States that is globally interdependent. Exposing students to multiple perspectives through good books may be the way to a better, albeit increasingly smaller, world.

---

they not only view the world from another's perspective but also learn more about themselves.

When selecting multicultural books for the classroom, teachers should be aware of the country of origin, language, and traditions. Include readings that are current, accurate, and sensitive to the cultural group and the social conditions in which they live that influence their lives. Also, it is important to choose books to represent a variety of cultures. These books and many others may easily be incorporated into a classroom rich in books.

DESIGNING THE CLASSROOM LIBRARY   Access to books in classroom libraries affects students' reading. Morrow (2003) reports that students will read 50 percent more books in classrooms with libraries than those who don't have such access. A wide range of books on various reading levels is essential. As a classroom collection is compiled, the science, math, art, social studies, and music curricula need to be considered. Include books on topics that will be studied in these subject areas. Again, make materials on specific topics available in a wide range of reading levels because of the different reading abilities of students in the same grade level.

As the classroom collection develops, pay attention to the area of the classroom that houses the library. The classroom library should be highly visible; this communicates that it is an important part of the classroom. Clear boundaries should set the library area apart from the rest of the classroom. The library is a quiet place for five or six children to read away from the rest of the classroom. It should afford comfortable seating—perhaps carpet pieces, beanbags, or special chairs. It should hold five or six books per child. Multiple copies of favorites are included. A variety of genres and reading levels should be available, arranged on both open shelves to display attractive covers and shelves to house many books with the spine out. Books in the library are organized and labeled by genre, theme, topic, author, reading level, content area, or some combination of these features. Book-oriented displays, such as flannel boards, puppets, book jackets, posters, and talking books, boost interest and enthusiasm. Once the classroom library is in place, the use of the books needs to be considered. A major part of establishing a literate environment includes reading aloud and telling stories to children.

2017 ILA Standards

5.2, 5.4

Listening to Text

Teachers naturally seem to know that there is no better way for students to become interested in the world of books than through listening to stories and poems. In this way, students learn that books are a source of pleasure. When they listen to literature and informational text, students—especially those from culturally and linguistically diverse backgrounds—are exposed to stories, information, and poems they cannot, or will not, read on their own. Often, once students are excited by hearing a selection, they want to read it for themselves.

Through hearing stories and poems, students develop a positive disposition toward books. Cumulative experiences with hearing stories and poems are likely to improve reading comprehension and vocabulary development. Listening to stories and poems can also provide a basis for group discussion, which often leads to shared meanings and points of reference. Vasquez (2010) believes reading aloud goes beyond developing an interest in reading; with teacher support and critical literacy development, students can expand their literacy abilities. Galda, Ash, and Cullinan (2000) also conclude that being read aloud to helps students develop literacy and language skills and interest in reading, as well as provides opportunities for social interactions. For these reasons, listening time can be one of the most productive times in the school day. Sharing books with students is not a "frill."

It is important to note that although teachers may read aloud to students to fill odd moments between a completed activity and the bell or schedule reading aloud as a calming-down activity, sharing literature is not a time filler. It is too serious and central to the reading program as a whole to be treated in an offhand way. Reading aloud needs to be incorporated into all aspects of the curriculum and followed with interactive activities to develop better literacy skills.

2017 ILA Standards

1.3, 5.1, 5.4

CHOOSING TEXTS TO READ ALOUD   What kind of thought and planning go into deciding which books to share? Why not go to the library, pull some books from the shelf, and, when **read-aloud** time arrives, pick up a book and read? In classrooms where students become enthusiastic about listening to books, the teachers have carefully selected which books to read. They have considered the age, background, and interests of the students. They also present different types of genre. Often books read aloud are related to each other in some way. For example, a middle school teacher read several books by Russell Freedman: *The Adventures of Marco Polo* and *Freedom Walkers:*

The Story of the Montgomery Bus Boycott. Soon the students could recognize a Freedman book by his writing style.

Teachers can also share with students books in which authors show what the characters are like by describing what they do and how they interact with others. Even books for the very young do this. For example, in *Sam* by Ann Herbert Scott, Sam tries to interact with his mother; his brother, George; his sister, Marcia; and his father, all of whom are too preoccupied with their own concerns. Finally, the family responds. All the characters are developed skillfully by the author and portrayed in subtle monochromatic illustrations by Symeon Shimin. In hearing and discussing such books, children gain an awareness of how authors portray characters.

2017 ILA Standards

4.1, 4.2, 4.3, 4.4

Folktales in which the plot is generally very important can be read to illustrate simple characterization. Other authors give vivid physical descriptions. Consider this description from Judy Blume's *Are You There, God? It's Me, Margaret* (1970):

> When she smiles like that she shows all her top teeth. They aren't her real teeth. It's what Grandmother calls a bridge. She can take out a whole section of four top teeth when she wants to. She used to entertain me by doing that when I was little . . . When she smiles without her teeth in place she looks like a witch. But with them in her mouth she's very pretty. (pp. 15, 18)

No matter what type of text to be read aloud, teachers should consider the complexity of the ideas, development of characters, language, and visuals integrated throughout the book (Hoffman, 2011). When choosing text to read aloud for ELLs, it is important to choose books with topics of familiarity, simple sentence structure, and illustrations. For older readers, go beyond chapter books to include nonfiction, picture books, Internet articles, newspapers, and magazines to accommodate interest and reading abilities. Some teachers also include audiobooks during read-alouds as a way to introduce technology-based formats to students.

 This **video** (www.youtube.com/watch?v=xw4ebg0jV4o) presents tips on how to read aloud and how to choose a book. What tips were most beneficial for you?

PREPARING TO READ ALOUD   Teachers need to prepare for story time. First, before reading a book aloud to the class, they should be familiar with the story's sequence of events, mood, subject, vocabulary, and concepts. Second, teachers must decide how to introduce the story. Should the book be discussed intermittently as it is read, or should there be discussion at the conclusion of the reading? Furthermore, what type of discussion or other type of activity will follow the reading?

SETTING THE MOOD   Many teachers and librarians set the mood for book-sharing time with a story hour symbol. One librarian used a small lamp—when the lamp was lit, it was time to listen. Deliberate movement toward the story-sharing corner in the classroom may set the mood for story time. Some teachers create the mood with an iPod, CD, or by playing a keyboard. As soon as the class hears a specific tune, they know that it is time to come to the story-sharing corner. Other ideas to help set the mood include dressing up as a character, creating bulletin board displays, or spotlighting websites that connect the story to similar books, themes, and authors, as well as changing the physical environment. These and many other options help to connect the story to their prior knowledge and experiences as well as to ignite interest in the story.

INTRODUCING THE STORY   The purpose of introducing the story is to set the purpose and provide support as the students listen to the book (Labadie, Wetzel, & Rogers, 2012). Labadie, Wetzel, and Rogers (2012) continue to stress that when planning the introduction, consider the students' background experiences, as well as the challenges and complexity of the story. There are numerous ways to introduce stories. The story-sharing corner could have a whiteboard or an easel bearing a question relating to the story to be shared or a picture of the book to focus the students' attention. Many teachers effectively introduce a story with objects. For example, a full-length coat may be used to introduce *The Chronicles of Narnia* by C. S. Lewis. A good way to introduce folktales is with artifacts from the appropriate country.

Other ways to introduce a story would be to ask a question, to tell the students why you like a particular story, or to have the students predict what will happen in the story using the title or the pictures. You might tell them something interesting about the background of the story or its author. It is advantageous to display the book, along with other books by the same author or with books on the same subject or theme. Introductions, however, should be brief and should vary from session to session.

ACTIVITIES AFTER READING ALOUD   There are many different ways to encourage students to respond after hearing the text; the more direct ways such as literature circles, book-talks, free response, and literature journals are discussed later in this chapter. A more informal approach to reader response is simply to encourage children to react privately to what they have heard. Davis (1973) calls this the *impressional approach.* The basic idea is that students will take from an experience whatever is relevant to them; therefore, each child will benefit from the listening experience. Encourage the students to freely discuss their thoughts and feelings as a whole class, small group, or with a peer. Sipe (2008) emphasizes the importance of encouraging students to freely respond because students will make connections from their own insights during interactive discussions. The format of only responding to teacher questions is conforming. There is no particular reason for the teacher to know precisely what each child gets from each listening experience. Too many discussions and other follow-up activities may diminish interest; too little will diminish the impact of the reading. Therefore, teachers should strike a balance between formal and informal approaches.

Common Core State Standard

CCRA.SL.3

Storytelling

Storytelling is the act of telling a story orally without the use of a text. It is a natural way to present literature and oral traditions to both young and older students. It provides the opportunity for students to learn about oral tradition of literature, enhance speaking and listening skills, and develop an interest in personal expression. Each of these reasons is important. Students are sure to be spellbound by a well-told story. Close eye contact, the storyteller's expressions, ingenious props, and the eliciting of the children's participation contribute to the magic. Although we cannot expect everyone to acquire a high level of expertise for a large number of stories, storytelling is a skill one can master with practice, a story at a time.

2017 ILA Standards

1.3, 4.1, 4.2, 4.3, 4.4

SELECTING THE STORY TO TELL   Beginning storytellers should choose selections they like and with which they feel comfortable. Simple stories are often the most effective for storytelling. Stories with which many children are familiar and can help with the dialogue are excellent choices for younger children. "The Three Bears," "The Three

Little Pigs," and "The Three Billy Goats Gruff" fit in this category. Because ancient and modern fairy tales usually appeal to primary students, consider stories such as "The Elves and the Shoemaker," "Rumpelstiltskin," and "The Bremen Town Musicians." Middle school students frequently prefer adventure, so myths, legends, and epics such as "How Thor Found His Hammer," "Robin Hood," "Pecos Bill," and "Paul Bunyan" tend to be popular choices.

One of the purposes of storytelling is to give students an understanding of the oral tradition. Even very young children can understand that today stories are usually passed down in books, whereas many years ago they were handed down orally.

An effective way to help students gain this understanding is to tell stories that are similar in plot, such as "The Pancake" from Norse tales included in Sutherland's *Anthology of Children's Literature* (1984) and *The Bun* by Brown. Both of these stories have some kind of personified edible goodie chased by a series of animals and eaten by the cleverest animal. Jane, a kindergarten teacher, read these stories to her class and then guided her students in making a chart showing how the stories were alike and different. The class then dictated a story titled "The Pizza." In the class's story, the pizza rolled and was chased by the school nurse, some first graders, and the principal. Its fate, of course, was to be gobbled by the kindergartners. Through their experiences, the kindergarten class developed a story using elements from school life, just as story-tellers in the oral tradition did from their personal experiences.

PREPARING A STORY FOR TELLING   The task of memorizing a story may seem formidable. How can teachers or children prepare for telling a story in front of others? Actually, stories do not need to be memorized. In fact, the telling is often more interesting if the story unfolds in a slightly different way each time. Refer to Box 12.3 for helpful steps in preparing to tell a story.

Once you have prepared the story, decide how to set the mood and introduce it, just as you would before reading any text. Effective storytelling does not require props, but you may want to add variety and use flannel boards and flannel board figures or puppets. These kinds of props work well with cumulative stories containing a few

BOX 12.3 | STEP-BY-STEP LESSON

Preparing a Story for Telling

The following steps are helpful in preparing to tell a story.

1. Read the story two or three times so that it is clear in your mind.
2. List the sequence of events in your mind or on paper, giving yourself an outline of the important happenings. Peck (1989) suggested mapping the story to show the setting, the characters, the beginning event, the problem and attempts at solving it, and the solution. This structure enables students to tell stories without stilted memorization of lines.
3. Reread the story, taking note of the events you didn't remember. Look for lines of text you do need to memorize, such as "Mirror, mirror, on the wall, who's the fairest of them all?" from "Snow White." Many folk- and fairy tales include elements like this, but such passages are not difficult to memorize.
4. Go over the events again, and consider the details you want to include. Think of the meaning of the events and how to

express the meaning, rather than trying to memorize the words in the story. Stewig (1980) recommends jotting down the sequence of events on note cards and reviewing the cards whenever possible. With this technique, he reports, it seldom takes longer than a few days to secure the story elements.

5. When you feel you know the story, tell the story in front of a mirror. After you have practiced it two or three times, the wording will improve, and you can try changing vocal pitch to differentiate among characters. Also, try changing your posture or hand gestures to represent different characters.

Be sure to be aware of the students' abilities and language competency, especially that of the ELL. It may be necessary when telling the story to be sure to use simple language, use familiar words, and slow the pacing of the telling. Also, visuals and a print version of the story to follow along with may be used. Teachers need to be flexible regarding the steps they take to assure that a connection is made with all students.

characters. Jessica, a first grader, told how her teacher had a puppet of "The Old Lady Who Swallowed a Fly" with a plastic see-through window in her stomach. As the story was told, the children delighted in seeing the different animals in the old lady's stomach and helping the teacher tell the repetitive story. Telling stories through digital movie format is another option.

> ▶ In this **video** (www.youtube.com/watch?v=mOA8mUflH-Q), Sean Buvala, national storyteller and coach of storytelling, shares storytelling tips and techniques. What tips were most beneficial for you?

Common Core State Standard

CCRA.R.7

Helping Students Select Books

One trait of independent readers is the ability to select books they can enjoy and from which they can get personally important information. In fact, Anderson, Higgins, and Wurster (1985) find that good readers know how to select literature relevant to their interest and reading level, whereas struggling readers do not. More often than not, a teacher will hear a child moan, "I can't find a book I want to read." Comments like this usually reveal that students do not feel confident about finding good books by themselves. We have alluded to ways for students to become acquainted with specific books: Teachers can tell exciting anecdotes about authors, provide previews of interesting stories, show videos about stories, suggest titles of stories that match students' interests, encourage author searches on the Internet, share leveled book listings, or compile teacher-or student-annotated book lists. To be able to do these things well, teachers need to be well versed in children's and adolescents' literature and informational text, as well as know their students.

2017 ILA Standards

5.1, 5.4

Beyond this, students need to be shown how to choose books. Hansen (1987) proposes that children be asked to choose and read books of three different difficulty levels. Students should have an "easy book" on hand to encourage fluent reading and the "I can read" feeling. Second, children need a "book I'm working on," in which they can make daily accomplishments by working on the hard spots. Finally, they need a "challenge book," which they can go back to repeatedly over a period of time. This helps them gain a sense of growth over a long period. By letting children know we expect them to read at all levels, they learn to judge varying levels themselves and to give honest appraisals of how well books match their reading ability.

The picture-book format, with its dependency on interpreting text and pictures, is appropriate for readers of all age levels. Picture books can engage students in the text and meaningful discussion, especially struggling readers and ELLs. According to Martinez, Roser, and Harmon (2009), "Picture books may be just what the struggling reader in upper elementary or middle school needs for independent reading" (p. 297). However, they caution that there may be a stigma attached to using picture books with older readers. In order to reduce the stigma, it is important that picture books are utilized in other curricular areas so students value their importance.

For independent readers, book choice is related to reading purposes and intentions as they read the book. Rick may decide to read *A Wind in the Door* because he liked *A Wrinkle in Time* by the same author, Madeleine L'Engle. When he begins to read, he compares the two books. As he becomes engrossed in the book, he reads to see how the story unfolds. Students need to discuss with each other and their teacher why they chose a specific book and what they are thinking about as they read it. Roskos and Neuman (2014) emphasize the need for providing various texts, including texts from multiple genres. They explain that having exposure to various genres provides students opportunity to learn information, develop imagination, and spark their thought processes and motivate them to learn.

The use of dialogue journals is an effective tool used by teachers to get to know how students feel about their reading and to guide students to "the right book." Jan, a fifth-grade teacher, has her students write daily in a journal. One of her students wrote, "I like it when the whole class reads together. I think it makes me want to read more." Jan responded with, "I'm glad." Another student made the following journal entry: "My favorite book was *Florence Nightingale*. I liked it because of the way she improved the hospitals and made them stay clean. Also she acted differently than any other person I've read about" (Smith, 1982, p. 360). In response to this journal entry, Jan suggested that the student read other biographies of courageous women.

Dialogue journals seem to work well at the beginning of the school year in providing a response to children concerning their thoughts and feelings about the books they are choosing and reading. Later in the year, buddy journals can be instituted. Sometimes students will begin recommending books to each other in their buddy journals. Peer recommendations make the act of choosing a book more efficient and less risky. Recommendations from friends are a good way to connect books and readers.

Smith (1982) encouraged children to ask for suggestions about which books are interesting. But each reader needs to decide whether a book is too hard, too easy, or interesting enough to be read cover to cover. Of course, there are times when students need to be nudged to finish a book or to make the next "book I'm working on" a bit more challenging. The teacher is critical in motivating the students to read. Therefore, surrounding the students, especially the struggling reader, with books on topics of interest is essential.

Check Your Understanding 12.2: Gauge your understanding of the skills and concepts in this section.

Organizing for Text-Based Instruction

■ **Organize classroom instruction around narrative and informational text.**

Organizing patterns for text-based instruction vary from structured whole class studies of **core books** to independent reading of self-selected books in **literature units** and **literature circles**. Media literacy and the integration of the technology are also an organizational consideration. Just as time, response, and choice are important in writing, these factors are also critical to the success of text-based instruction.

Core Books

Sometimes teachers will organize instruction around the study of core books. In some schools, a set of core books forms the nucleus of the reading program at each grade level (Routman, 1991). A curriculum committee of teachers throughout the district is often assigned to develop a collection of books at each grade that is judged to be age-appropriate and of high quality. Core books are taught within the framework of whole class study across disciplines. Students have little or no choice in the selection of core books. As part of a whole class study, teachers assign various activities and use a variety of instructional strategies to support students' interactions with the texts.

Often teachers use core books as springboards for independent reading in which students choose books with related themes and situations or decide to read other works by an author they have studied. For example, when Brenda Church taught in inner-city fifth grade in Akron, she introduced a unit on survival by having her students do a whole class study of Jean George's *Julie of the Wolves*. As the unit evolved, the students also read novels in groups. They would select a novel from the choices that Brenda gave them from a book list.

Common Core State Standard

CCRA.R.10

A major problem with utilizing core books is the risk of "basalizing" reading. Core books and novels should not be treated like basal textbooks, whose major purpose is to organize instruction around the teaching of reading skills. Basalization could lead to students' completing worksheets, responding to literal comprehension questions, and engaging in round-robin reading (Zarrillo, 1989). Also, it limits the selection of books for struggling readers.

Literature Units

Teachers also organize instruction around literature units. Literature units, also known as **thematic instruction** and **integrated instruction**, usually have a unifying element such as the study of a genre, an author, or a conceptual theme. With literature units, a teacher usually chooses the theme (or negotiates one with the students) and pulls together a collection of books relating to the theme; the students, however, have options as to what books to choose from the collection and what activities they might pursue. It is important to note with the implementation of the Common Core State Standards (CCSS) text selection for literature units needs to include a variety of both narrative and informational texts. Also, successful literature units strike a balance between whole class, small group, and individually selected activities.

Literature Circles

Historically, teachers grouped students on the basis of measured reading ability. However, educators have questioned that practice because such grouping limits student choice, interest, and motivation. The criticism of grouping students by ability has led teachers to experiment with heterogeneous groups reading a common text and whole class models such as the previously described use of core books. Further, teachers and researchers have been collaborating on how to work with groups of children leading their own discussions. By studying transcripts of students participating in student-led literature groups (McMahon, 1997), two such teacher-researchers, Deb and Laura, became aware that students they perceived as "average" and "weak" readers were quite articulate when orally expressing their ideas in student-led groups. At the same time, some of the "good" readers responded to their classmates in these groups in ways that were extremely text based and thus did not connect what they read to other reading or to their own or others' experiences.

With the implementation of the CCSS, many teachers now seek to move beyond just developing reading fluency and comprehension to include language skills. They want to provide students with time and opportunity to use language to express their ideas, practice their speaking and listening skills, and explain their thinking to each other, which in turn extends the students' thinking. Teachers see literature circles as a way to do this for all students, including linguistically and culturally diverse learners (Protacio, 2012; Samway & Whang, 1996) and learners with special needs (Gilles, 1990). Teachers who implement literature circles (also known as *literature study groups* and *book clubs*) rely on cooperative learning strategies that show students how to work together and discuss books on the basis of their personal responses to what they have read.

In this **video** (www.youtube.com/watch?v=ltkprzZhyel), a fifth-grade teacher demonstrates a literature circle using the book *Boy in Striped Pajamas*. Various roles are utilized. What roles were demonstrated?

Gay, a third-grade teacher, organizes literature circles in her classroom. Gay introduces to the class potentially worthwhile books for discussion. If a book is fictional, she builds interest in the story by overviewing its plot, acquainting the students with characters, and reading parts of the story aloud. If the book is informational, she builds anticipation by overviewing the content, reading aloud, and showing the students illustrations from the text. The students then select the books they want to read. Teams are formed not by ability level but by choice of reading material (Vacca & Rasinski, 1992).

Thus in the ideal classroom, the size of the literature circle is determined by the number of students who freely choose a particular book. In real classrooms, some decision making and negotiation may be necessary to achieve groups of productive size. Arranging for about four students per circle allows for a productive mix of perspectives and roles without distractions and inefficiencies.

Marcus is a fourth-grade teacher who is enthusiastic about literature circles. When it is time for literature circles, students bring three items to the group: the book their circle is reading, response journals and drawings reflecting their ideas about their reading, and completed role sheets for the roles Marcus chose for the circles. On this day, the roles were *discussion leader, passage monitor, connector*, and *illustrator*. The roles utilized in literature circles vary depending on the purpose of the circle, the reading, and the students. Generally there will be a leader who has the responsibility to lead the discussion, a student who monitors the text to assure that the discussion relates to specific sections of the text, and a student who tries to connect the discussion to real-life experiences and other literature. Finally the illustrator creates a visual representing the group's responses. After a few minutes of settling and joking, the groups in Marcus's class began working. For the next 30 minutes, these 10-year-olds conversed with each other using open-ended questions and read passages to prove points or settle disagreements. They kept one eye on the clock to make sure everyone got a fair share of talking. Some of the books discussed in these literature circles were Katherine Paterson's *Bridge to Terabithia*, Daniel Keyes's *Flowers for Algernon*, H. G. Wells's *War of the Worlds*, and Beverly Cleary's *Dear Mr. Henshaw*.

Let's explore further how a teacher can give students of all abilities the opportunity to read and discuss literature in student-led groups by looking at how to share and what to share in literature circles.

STUDENT-LED LITERATURE CIRCLES: HOW AND WHAT TO SHARE   Teachers whose students lead their own literature circles need to explain clearly that these groups help participants explore different perspectives that each person brings to the discussion. Students are to evaluate, critique, and revise their own individual responses in light of the perspectives their peers express. To clarify how to participate in literature circles, emphasize the differences between "school talk" and "outside-school talk." Through discussion, students will conclude that in most classroom interactions, the teacher asks questions and students answer. Outside-school talk is characterized by talking when someone has an idea to share; thus sometimes there is overlapping talk. Further, it is important to note that different members of the group informally assume responsibility for maintaining the conversation. In the literature circles, the students share what they learned from the reading, clarify any questions, and make connections with personal experiences.

How to share and what is to be shared can be modeled and explored in whole class discussions while watching a tape of a literature circle in action. Also, as students talk to each other in student-led literature circles, the teacher can walk from group to group,

Figure 12.2 Self-Assessment in Literature Circles

Name: _____   Book: _____

Looking Back and Forward

	Date	Date	Date	Date
Did I share during literature circles?				
Were my comments relevant to the discussion?				
Did I let others have a turn?				
Did I listen to others?				
Did I offer to help when it was needed?				

Important comments: (What would I do the same and different the next time?)

facilitating the use of these conversational skills. Sometimes the students' conversations will wander to topics other than the book, and at other times members will be silent and need to be encouraged to participate. The teacher joins a group just long enough to help members identify the problem and solve it. Laura and Deb found that this modeling and analysis of the literature groups took up significant instructional time at the beginning of the school year; however, as students learned to assume responsibility for their own discussions, the need for modeling, discussion, and intervention diminished.

Common Core State Standard

CCRA.SL.3

Another way to guide students to take responsibility for their own literature discussion is through the use of self-assessment (see Figure 12.2). Students complete the form, and then the teacher helps them see how to solve their own dilemmas and what they could do the next time the group meets (McMahon, 1997).

ADAPTING LITERATURE CIRCLES FOR THE PRIMARY GRADES With primary grades the traditional roles in literature circles vary based on students and familiarity with the process. It is recommended that the group of children sit in a circle and take turns reading the book aloud to each other. Use picture books, simple stories, and child-made books. Then they take a few moments to make some notes on their role sheet using invented spellings or drawings. All children are encouraged to share and participate in the discussions. For young children it is recommended that each group has a leader to begin and guide the discussion. As is true of literature circles with middle school students, the discussion is natural and spontaneous. The entire process of selecting books, forming groups, reading, and discussing the books takes about 45 minutes. Time duration will depend largely on the age of the students and the books being discussed. When working with the young children, flexibility of the process must be considered.

Media Literacy

All types of media are an important aspect of a literate classroom. Online reading, multimedia presentations, and electronic messaging have changed the way students read. With the ever-changing types of media that students have access to, the understanding of what is literacy is also changing. The National Council of Teachers of English (NCTE) (2008) has defined **media literacy** in a position statement emphasizing that "media literacy is the capacity to access, analyze, evaluate and communicate messages in a variety of forms" (para.1 in **NCTE's position statement**).

2017 ILA Standards

5.2, 5.3

Common Core State Standard

CCRA.R.9

Children can use various modes of technology to develop their literacy skills.

Annie Pickert Fuller/Pearson Education

When thinking of media literacy, focusing on both breadth and depth is necessary. The breadth of media literacy is demonstrated by technology being embedded in all discipline areas. Because critical reading is required for the different forms of print, deep reading is necessary. Tate (2011) believes that "the twenty-first century classroom demands that students possess a wide range of abilities from reading on-line articles to participating in virtual classrooms" (p. 184). When reading the broad body of text, readers need to construct, analyze, evaluate, and interpret text. Freebody and Freiberg (2011) believe this body of curricular knowledge, termed **critical literacy**, is "the most significant and portable knowledge a learner can take from educational experiences" (p. 447). They continue to emphasize the importance of this complex thinking, stressing that students need to learn to evaluate their interpretations and think about their own experiences when using various texts.

Common Core State Standards

CCRA.R.10, CCRA.R.7

In spite of the push for incorporating new technologies, teachers need to make decisions regarding what to use and how. They need to think through and carefully plan technology usage. Blanchard and Farstrup (2011) suggest when planning reading instruction to think about the use of the new technologies, and they recommend that technology should not be used to supplement; rather it should be used in concert with instructional strategies and integrated in order to provide a student-centered classroom.

INTEGRATION OF THE INTERNET Teachers should make some critical decisions regarding their understanding of technology, the students' understanding of technology, and the integration of technology in order to develop literacy skills. Teachers also need to think through how technology can be used as text as well as the critical thinking skills required in order to create meaning from technology. Planning instruction utilizing the Internet to develop standards may be an option. The Internet is educationally important in relation to teacher and student use (Maloy, Verock-O'Loughlin, Edwards, & Woolf, 2014). More specifically Leu (2008) believes that the Internet is a useful tool for literacy and learning. Students can travel to new places and experience richer and more powerful responses to children's literature when the Internet is integrated within the classroom (Leu, Castek, Henry, Coiro, & McMullan, 2004). Lessons that rely on the students searching specific Internet sites facilitate conceptual development, critical thinking skills, and response opportunities, and provide opportunities to help students better understand cultural diversity. Utilizing digital tools from the Internet can help the teacher be more effective. Jeremy Brueck explains a few selected tools in Box 12.4.

BOX 12.4 | TRANSLITERACY

Responding to Literature Using Google Hangouts

The CCSS emphasize the need to "prepare all students for success in college, career, and life." In today's workplace, that means communicating across a variety of platforms. Jobs are no longer location-based, with all members of the workforce in the same building at the same time. Instead, a number of digital tools, such as email, voice-over-Internet calling and web-conferencing software, help colleagues connect across space and time. These tools can be put to effective use in the classroom, too!

One way to share the love of reading with others is through video conferencing. Teachers can begin to build the transliteracy skills students need to connect and collaborate with digital tools using a free resource like Google Hangouts (https://hangouts. google.com). Hangouts is a powerful tool that offers an opportunity to introduce a wider world to your students by connecting with classes in another state or country.

Teachers and students can use Hangouts to send messages, make voice and video calls, and share photos. Whether you are connecting to another classroom in your school or have found another classroom across the globe, using Google Hangouts to discuss literature can enhance the book experience by encouraging a broader audience. When teachers and students connect with another classroom via Hangouts, they are creating an interactive environment that promotes literary response. Classes that are reading the same book or genre can discuss the literature together and also suggest books to one another.

Before The Hangout Teachers should work with their respective classes to brainstorm a set of questions they want to ask their Hangout partners. Once the question sets are completed, send them to the partner class through e-mail to allow adequate time to organize answers.

During The Hangout Students should take turns asking and responding to the questions. If students have not "met" the partner class, make sure students take time to identify themselves prior to speaking. Consider recording the Hangout and exporting it to YouTube for review at a later time.

After The Hangout Each class can provide constructive feedback on the response to literature based on the Hangout dialogue. Each class can send their feedback through e-mail, they could post it on a class blog, or they could leave the feedback in the Comments section of the YouTube video.

The possibilities for using Hangouts are limited only by teacher and student creativity. Get started by connecting locally, and as you and your students gain experience with the tool, look to build connections with classrooms from other geographic areas. Hangouts is available as a browser-based tool for desktops and laptops and as a mobile app for Android and iOS devices. This transliteracy tool is a capable resource for strengthening the appreciation of and response to both narrative and informational text.

Check Your Understanding 12.3: Gauge your understanding of the skills and concepts in this section.

Encouraging Responses to Text

■ **Design strategies for encouraging readers to respond to text.**

After reading a book or seeing a movie, we may share the experience by briefly describing the plot. Most often, though, we tell how we felt and why. We point out something in the film or text or our personal histories that made us feel the way we did. We give examples from our lives and retell parts of the story. Yet when discussion shifts to the classroom, what usually happens? Often teachers ask questions to elicit a "right answer." Because we have often tried to evaluate what and how much students have understood about the text, teachers spend little time helping students explore, defend, or elaborate on ideas. In this section, we explore the need to lead students in classroom experiences in which they analyze their *personal* reactions to what they have read. Such action supports a **reader-response theory**, a theory that proclaims that *the reader is crucial to the construction of the literary experience.*

Louise Rosenblatt (1982) was one of the earliest proponents of a reader-response theory. She believes that the reader actively creates meaning by relating to his or her knowledge as well as past experiences. The reader is thinking about, predicting, and verifying those predictions while actively creating meaning.

Every reading event or transaction involves a reader and a text (a set of signs capable of being interpreted as verbal symbols); meaning that results from the transaction are dependent on both entities (Rosenblatt, 2004). They are not mutually exclusive. Rosenblatt took her analysis of reading one step further into implications for classroom literature discussions. In any reading event, the reader adopts one of two stances: the **efferent stance** or the **aesthetic stance**. Supporting Rosenblatt, Hancock (2007) refers to the response reading as the interaction between text and the reader's mind and heart. The reader's response deepens students' literacy experience.

When a reader approaches a reading event with an efferent stance, attention is focused on accumulating what is to be carried away from the reading. Readers using this stance may be seeking information, as in a textbook; they may want directions for action, as in a driver's manual; or they may be seeking a logical conclusion, as in a political article. In an aesthetic stance, however, readers shift their attention inward to center on *what is being created during the reading*. Reading is driven by personal feelings, ideas, and attitudes that are stirred up by the text.

In most reading situations, there is both an efferent and an aesthetic response to the text. In reading a newspaper article, for example, a reader may take a predominantly efferent stance, but there may be an accompanying feeling of acceptance or doubt about the evidence cited. Readers' response to literature is typically thought of with literary texts (narrative, poetry, drama, etc.); however, Fisher, Lapp, and Frey (2011) stress that it can be also used with certain forms of informational text. Although one stance usually predominates in most reading events, the text itself does not dictate a reader's stance. A text is chosen because it satisfies a reader's intended purpose.

2017 ILA Standard

5.2

Teachers create responsive environments in their classrooms by inviting students of all abilities and from diverse backgrounds to react to text through various symbol systems and modes of expression: art, movement, music, creative drama, talk, and writing. Alternative forms of communication such as art or movement are especially appealing for students who may have difficulty expressing their feelings and thoughts in words. When students connect drawing with reading, for example, their artwork often helps them discover and shape their response to a story. Various visual arts media—pencil drawings, chalk, markers, crayons, paint, cardboard, paper construction, computer-based art, and paint programs—can be used to encourage responses to literature. In addition, students can design book jackets, mobiles, posters, or comic strips, or utilize the Internet to set up discussions to capture the personal appeal or meaning that texts evoke. Creating multimodal productions such as PowerPoint, Prezi, or YouTube presentations encourages students to represent their thoughts in a creative format that can be assessed by others (Serafini & Youngs, 2013).

2017 ILA Standards

5.2, 5.4

Common Core State Standards

CCRA.SL.4, CCRA.SL.5

Setting up blogs is another interesting way to provide opportunities to communicate responses to books. Blogs are websites that provide a space for online conversations and comments. Text, pictures, and online audio recordings also can be included on blogs. Individuals, pairs of students, and groups of students can be encouraged to discuss their readings and to post comments.

Drawing, creative drama, role playing, and computer-generated projects often serve as springboards for oral and written responses. Students, especially at the primary level, gravitate naturally to drawing or dramatically performing a story before they talk or write about it.

Sparking Discussion with Book-Talks

Whole class study of core books and literature circles provide numerous opportunities for children to talk about books. Having **book-talks** is a great way to evoke children's responses to literature. The different types of discussions that evolve from student- or teacher-led small group or whole class formats lead students of all grades to acquire language skills and response strategies for the appropriate discussion genres (Galda & Beach, 2004). Utilizing the various discussion types also provides ELLs the opportunity to develop language, literacy, and critical thinking skills. Here are seven suggestions to spark book discussions:

1. Depending on the text, ask questions such as, "Did anything especially interest you? Frighten you? Puzzle you? Seem familiar? Seem weird?" Have students tell which parts of the text caused these reactions, and have them compare these experiences to their real-life experiences (Rosenblatt, 1982).
2. Have the students tell about the most memorable incident, character, or setting of the book. Then have them share with each other the specific parts of the text they recalled most clearly after hearing or reading the story (Benton, 1984).
3. Ask students to tell about the part of the story or character they remember most vividly. For example, "How did that character feel in this part of the story?" "Have you ever felt like this?" "Describe the situation you were in."
4. Read the opening of a story. Immediately afterward, tell students to jot down what was going on in their heads—pictures, memories, thoughts—during the reading. The jottings should be in a stream-of-consciousness style. Then share the responses and distinguish the common responses from the idiosyncratic ones. This shows students that reading has shared elements as well as highly individual ones and that sharing reactions is a valid way of talking about literature (Benton, 1984).
5. Ask students, "What pictures do you get in your mind of this character, setting, or event?" "If character X were to come through the door now, what would he or she look like?" "If you went to the place where the story occurred (i.e., setting), what would you see?" "Why do you say so?"
6. Ask, "What do you feel about this character? This setting? This event? Why?"
7. Ask, "What opinions do you have of this character? This setting? This incident? The way the story was told? Why?"

Book-talks encourage children to go beyond a literal retelling of a story. The collaborative nature of book-talks helps students relate reading to prior knowledge, construct meaning, critique related texts, and share personal responses (Raphael et al., 1992). Book-talks can be used in concert with a free-response heuristic to help students discover and shape their responses to literature. A heuristic, by its nature, is any kind of a prompt that stimulates inquiry and speculation.

Common Core State Standards

CCRA.SL.1, CCRA.SL.3

Engaging in Free Response

Free response encourages active involvement in reading and an integration of students' background knowledge with the selection's meaning. This technique generates a spirited discussion going far beyond the recall of information. Inferential, evaluative, and analytic thinking are the rule when students' free responses are discussed (Santa, Dailey, & Nelson, 1985).

Free response works well with text selections that generate diversity of opinion or emotional reactions from readers. The first time a group of students is guided through free response, they hear a portion of a narrative and then stop to respond in writing. Primary students, for example, might be given 3 minutes to respond in writing, and middle school students 5 minutes. Analyzing the structure of a particular story is useful in determining where to make the breaks for students to respond.

2017 ILA Standard

5.2

Mrs. Nowak used a free-response heuristic with her second-grade class for *Thomas' Snowsuit* by Robert Munsch (1985) and illustrated by Michael Martchenko. This story is a humorous treatment of power struggles between Thomas, who does not want to wear his new snowsuit, and his mother. The power struggle concerning whether he should wear his snowsuit continues with his teacher and the principal at school.

Mrs. Nowak introduced the story to her class by asking whether the children could recall not wanting to wear some clothing they were supposed to wear. A lively discussion ensued. Then Mrs. Nowak asked what they thought *Thomas' Snowsuit* would be about, and the children had no difficulty predicting that Thomas didn't want to wear his snowsuit. Mrs. Nowak stopped reading and asked her students to write down their reactions to what they had just heard. She emphasized that "any thought related to the story is correct; there are no wrong responses." After several segments of reading and responding, Mrs. Nowak led a discussion in which the children shared their free responses. When she asked their reactions to Thomas's telling his mother, "NNNNNO," Jeremy said, "He's going to get into trouble!" Sue said, "I wouldn't want to wear an old brown snowsuit, either." After each response, Mrs. Nowak probed, "Why do you think so?" Mrs. Nowak remained impartial, and the children's responses became a catalyst for discussion. Mrs. Nowak then read *No, David!* by David Shannon (1998). They had a discussion on why David's mother told David "no" throughout the story. Then the children talked about when their mother has told them "no." Finally, they talked about both stories and the use of the word *no*.

Prompts such as "I agree with," "I am confused with," "I think," and "I feel" help to develop free responses. These heuristic situations prompt students to view reading as a problem-solving activity. As such, free response is easily incorporated into the use of reading journals that help students explore and clarify their responses to text. Various kinds of reading journals encourage students to solve problems as they respond to meaning during reading. Response journals, in particular, invite students of all abilities and from diverse backgrounds to respond to text freely and personally. Their responses vary from monitoring understanding to plot and character involvement to literary evaluation.

Common Core State Standards

CCRA.SL.1, CCRA.SL.3

Exploring Response Options in Literature Journals

Literature journals provide readers with the freedom to express their feelings and perceptions about literary texts. They help students to communicate their thoughts during and after reading as well as before discussion (Galda & Beach, 2004). The potential for students to do more than summarize the text is omnipresent when they are invited to write freely as they engage in reading. Research on the content of literature journals shows that readers often expand their ways of thinking about a text beyond retelling when they write journal entries or literary letters on a regular basis (Hancock, 1993a, 1993b; Wells, 1993).

The use of technology can also be utilized to enhance responses. Blogs, short for weblogs, are online journals that typically include personal accounts. The teachers can have the students read preselected blogs, make comments, create class blogs, and post information related to education and learning. Using electronic communication such as e-mail also allows the writer to compose, revise, and craft messages based on the class assignment (Maloy et al., 2014).

2017 ILA Standard

5.3

Common Core State Standards

CCRA.SL.2, CCRA.R.9, CCRA.R.10

Teachers can increase the variety of reader responses by making children aware of the various options for responding in a literature journal. Students are encouraged to make predictions, make inferences, and express personal opinions. Writing about the elements of story with a specific focus on character and plot is another option. Students are also encouraged to critically review the text by judging or evaluating the author or content. For young children the use of drawings, charts, or graphic organizers is encouraged.

In addition, one of the most effective ways to extend response options is to start a dialogue with students in their journals. A teacher's comments in response to a journal entry will help students reexamine their responses to the text. When responding to journal entries, it is best to be nonjudgmental, encouraging, and thought-provoking. Once a supportive comment is written, the teacher may decide to direct a student toward an unexplored area of response. Interactive comments help students refocus and redirect their responses to literary text; they pave the way to personal meaning making.

Check Your Understanding 12.4: Gauge your understanding of the skills and concepts in this section.

RTI for Struggling Readers

Learners, Text, and *Response to Intervention*

Providing access to text that relates to each individual student's interests, needs, and abilities is essential in an environment that supports a community of readers. It is also important to provide opportunities for readers to share and learn from books.

When working with readers, especially struggling learners, it is necessary to match student and text. Teachers should encourage readers to read books from a variety of genres at their independent reading level. Teachers can help students choose these books, but, more important, it is essential to help readers self-select the most appropriate piece of literature.

Once the books have been chosen and students have access to them, it is important that teachers support all readers, especially the struggling learners, by creating occasions to share and respond to text. In a literacy-rich environment, whole class, small group, and individual time are reserved for sustained silent reading and various reading modeling opportunities: teacher read-aloud, peer read-aloud, buddy reading, books on tape, and book-talks. Literature circles, fishbowl discussions, and book buddies provide opportunities for the students to share insights. Time set aside for individual conferences also helps encourage teachers and students to share and exchange reflections about books, authors, illustrators, and writing styles. Finally, in a literate environment, students are encouraged to respond to texts in their own way and enhance their critical reading skills. The use of free-response journals in formats made appropriate for the individual struggling learner's abilities, such as the use of invented spelling and artwork, needs to be accepted and encouraged.

2017 ILA Standards

5.1, 5.2, 5.3, 5.4

Supporting a community of readers, especially struggling learners, is essential. Surrounding students with various texts and providing opportunities for sharing and learning from all forms of print and media in the various RTI tier formats are important in all classrooms for literacy development.

What About . . .

Standards, Assessment, and Text?

Creating a literate environment is important for the enhancement of reading and writing skills as well as to develop the CCSS. Key components of the literate environment include:

- The physical environment is designed to optimize students' use of traditional print and online resources.
- The social environment is low-risk, motivational, and supportive so students feel comfortable to collaborate and respond to literature in both efferent and aesthetic stances.
- Roles and routines are understood for the various text-based activities.
- Various classroom configurations (whole class, small group, pairs, and individual) are utilized in order to bring students and books together.
- Authentic assessments are utilized to assess understanding of text while students are responding in various literacy activities, such as book-talks, literature circles, discussions, and journals.
- Time is provided daily for reading and writing.

2017 ILA Standards

5.1, 5.2, 5.3, 5.4

Teachers create a literate environment that fosters reading and writing by integrating various practices, materials, books, and appropriate use of assessment.

Summary

- Literacy development is personal. Supporting readers and making reading personal in an environment that brings students and text together were discussed. It is important to choose text that students can connect with and to create a classroom that encourages and provides access to carefully selected readings.

- Teachers facilitate an environment supportive of a variety of print and nonprint materials by carefully structuring the classroom, selecting a collection of materials, and creating settings and predictable routines. Hooking students on books, storytelling, and classroom libraries all assist children in reading more both in and out of the classroom.

- Organizing for text-based instruction revolves around (1) studies of core books (a collection at each grade level judged to be age-appropriate and of high quality), (2) literature units (around a theme), (3) literature circles (which may be student-led), and (4) media literacy and the use of technology such as the Internet.

- We explored strategies for responding to text, such as book-talks, conferences, and response journals, which encourage students to extend their individual thoughts and feelings about books they read through a variety of response options.

Teacher Action Research

1. Reread the viewpoint in Box 12.2, Literature and Multiple Perspectives, and reflect on the author's thoughts. Discuss your reactions. How do the author's thoughts reflect your philosophy of teaching reading? How do the author's thoughts influence how you will set up your classroom for a community for readers?

2. Work with a group of students, and guide them in dramatizing a story after they have read it or heard it read aloud. Take video of the dramatization, and encourage students to reflect after viewing it. Have students discuss their reactions in pairs to the characterization, story elements, and overall feelings regarding the dramatization.

3. Collaborate with a fellow student or a classroom teacher to set up a book display to interest students, including those with limited English proficiency, in reading. Decide on a theme and ways to introduce the students to books related to that theme. If possible, observe what happens in the classroom and talk with the teacher about the students' use of the display. Or compile a list of things you would expect to see and questions you would like to have the classroom teacher answer.

4. Prepare a bibliography of children's and adolescents' literature that would be appropriate for a particular grade level's classroom library. Use the school librarian, classroom teachers' recommendations, and bibliographies from journals such as *Language Arts, Journal of Adolescent & Adult Literacy*, and *The Reading Teacher* as resources. What books would be the core of the library? What books could be added over time? Include annotations that would explain why each book was chosen. For example, which books would be useful in content area instruction? Which books would help teach letter–sound correspondence?

Through the Lens of the Common Core

With the integration of the Common Core State Standards for English Language Arts, the materials needed for instruction have been modified for all classrooms across all disciplines. There is now more than ever a need to include a variety of text, different media, text that requires critical thinking, and text that meets the abilities of all ages. Narrative and informational text has become the staple of all classrooms. Teachers need to select the appropriate text, organize various instructional activities that utilize the text including technology, and encourage the students to think about and learn from the readings. Encouraging the students to construct, analyze, evaluate, and interpret text in a community of readers is the essence of a literate classroom.

Chapter 13
Instructional Materials

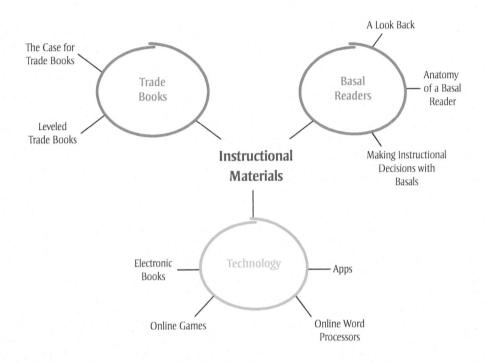

Trade Books
- The Case for Trade Books
- Leveled Trade Books

Basal Readers
- A Look Back
- Anatomy of a Basal Reader
- Making Instructional Decisions with Basals

Instructional Materials

Technology
- Electronic Books
- Online Games
- Apps
- Online Word Processors

 ## Learning Outcomes

In This Chapter, You Will Discover How to

- Identify the role and features of a basal reading program.

- Learn how leveled trade books are used for instruction.

- Explore technology-based materials.

- Evaluate components of instructional materials in relation to curriculum goals.

Activating Your Schema

Think back to your school days. What instructional materials did your teachers use? Maybe your teacher used big books, and you gathered around as she read them and pointed to the text. Or perhaps you worked independently at computers, reading books online and taking assessments following each story. Did the whole class have the same book, or did each group read from different books? Recalling such experiences will help you as you read this chapter and think about the variety of instructional materials available to teachers today.

2017 ILA Standards Found in This Chapter

1.1	2.2	5.2	6.4
2.1	2.3	5.3	

Common Core State Standards: English Language Arts

CCRA.R.1	CCRA.R.10	CCRA.L.4
CCRA.R.5	CCRA.R.9	CCRA.L.5

Key Terms

basal readers

core reading program

e-books

scope and sequence

supplemental materials

trade books

Han has been asked to be on the textbook selection committee along with teachers, literacy coaches, administrators, and one parent from across the district. The first meeting with the adoption committee was positive. "We spent the first meeting setting goals by listing the concerns and needs of the district. We came to the conclusion that the greatest need across the district was to find a set of literacy instruction materials that would help us teach to the Common Core State Standards (CCSS) and would have a lot of informational text and supplemental text we could use for interventions.

"At the second meeting, we spent time reviewing what the latest research had to say about reading instruction. We were given a set of articles to read prior to the meeting so the conversation was rich and informed. Our next step is to select or create our own tool to use to evaluate the different programs. That has been a real challenge because we need a tool that doesn't take a ridiculous amount of time, yet one that gets at depth. We don't just want a checklist that identifies whether things are included or not; we want to really examine the materials. We don't want to spend money on a program that simply has new stickers on old materials claiming it meets the CCSS. We really need to choose carefully."

Han's district is going about the adoption process the right way. The committee is putting a great deal of thought into establishing district needs and goals and taking the time to learn about the latest research on reading instruction. By doing this, everyone on the committee is informed about what the research says—not by personal philosophies that may differ. Following these preliminary tasks, Han's committee will either select an evaluation tool the members think measures the components of the program that are most important to them, or they will have to create one themselves. Either way, Han's district is going about the adoption process thoughtfully and with purpose.

The goal of reading instruction in elementary school is to help students acquire the skills and knowledge they need to read text fluently and with good comprehension. Research continues to reaffirm it is the teacher's knowledge and experiences that are vital in the production of positive student outcomes, rather than a simple focus on teaching materials. However, good instructional materials do matter; we need well prepared teachers, and we need high quality tools to support their teaching. In some schools, choices available to teachers for reading instruction include a basal reading series, an extensive library of leveled books, online programs, and other resources the teacher wishes to use, or a combination of any of the above. In other schools, teachers are required to use specific commercial materials to teach reading and are expected to follow them closely. The primary instructional tool that teachers use to teach children to learn to read is referred to as the **core reading program**. In some schools, the core program consists of many leveled books of varying genres.

In others, a core program is a basal reading program. Still others are adopting online, leveled e-books as their primary program. Whatever is used, the core program should address the instructional needs of most students in a respective school or district. Core material will be used by the majority of elementary children, but teachers also use many **supplemental materials** as enrichment for some children and as reinforcement of basic skills for students who struggle. Most are selected to provide small group, targeted support to help students catch up to their peers, providing direct instruction and more practice. There is no shortage of supplemental materials available on the market today. A recent walk through the exhibit hall at the Annual Conference of the International Reading Association demonstrated the many forms of supplemental materials: games students can play, reader's theater scripts, materials for listening centers, software for smartboards, online activities, mobile devices, comprehension packets, phonics and word study kits, interactive programs, and on and on. The choices were overwhelming.

This chapter is divided into three main categories of instructional materials. First, **basal readers** are explored in depth since they are the most popular materials used for reading instruction. Next we consider trade books and leveled readers as instructional materials, and then online resources, which are prominent in classrooms today. The chapter closes with a look into several ways of evaluating and selecting instructional materials for classroom use, whether print based or online. In Box 13.1, teachers from across the nation share what materials they use to teach reading today.

BOX 13.1 | VIEWPOINT

Survey of Classroom Materials

At the most recent Annual Conference of the International Reading Association (L. Lenhart, personal communication, July, 2015), we asked teachers from all over the country about the instructional materials used in their schools and districts. Here are some of the responses we had:

Texas: I am an English as a second language teacher for fifth and sixth graders. We have pacing guides and suggested resources, but at my school we can use what we want. Some of our available resources are Texas Treasures Literature books, novel sets (all genres and various levels), and I-Station, an e-learning program.

Illinois: I have a lot of latitude in what I can use. Some of the materials I use most are trade books, a basal reader, my leveled literacy intervention (LLI) kit. I use Reading A-Z, too.

Missouri: Our district has created units with a lot of resources as options. The units are created around trade books and include whole class and small group and strategy group activities.

Washington: Since Washington is a local control state, school districts have a lot of autonomy in making decisions about instructional programs to use. My district adopted a reading program grades K–5. It comes with teacher books, student books, big books, workbooks, leveled readers, and lots of other materials, and we are expected to use them.

Oregon: Our core reading program is a basal, but we have freedom to supplement. Our new superintendent has given us that freedom to make choices. Her focus is on quality, and believes it's okay to not get to everything in the basal. We also have a weekly magazine we use as text.

Tennessee: We use a basal reading series from a major publishing company. We are encouraged to use the materials given. Our school does but we have heard others in our county don't. It is a ton of stuff to get in and can be overwhelming. Our county scope and sequence follows the order of the curriculum as well as a letter a week and sight word a week.

Georgia: I am very lucky. My school has a pretty large book room with lots of leveled books that I use for guided reading. We also use a basal series, and it comes with two boxes of sets of books for small group instruction. I also use materials from the Internet; there are some free, printable books available online.

Maine: I teach for an online academy. A lot of the material is posted online, but students also have print materials sent to their homes. I have traditional teacher's editions of those materials and can assign lessons from them. For the online materials all of the lessons, activities, videos, and worksheets are online and available for me to access as needed for each student. I do this from my dashboard.

Basal Readers

■ **Identify the role and features of a basal reading program.**

Basal reading programs are the most popular materials used for reading instruction in this country, and some think this is with good reason. Commercially published materials that are well-designed tend to offer more thorough and explicit instruction than many teachers can provide on their own, and this is especially true for newer teachers. A basal program also offers greater continuity from class to class and grade level to grade level, providing both vertical and horizontal articulation. Additionally, these programs can save teachers valuable time planning and searching for materials, which gives them more time and attention to their students. Critics of basal reading materials say they aren't flexible enough, powerful enough, or motivating enough to enable all students to read important reading goals. The fact remains the largest percentage of educators ever—84 percent—have a commercially published core/basal reading series (Education Market Research, 2011). This compares to a previous high of around 80 percent in 2000 and low- to mid-70 percent range in 2004. Only 16 percent say they do not use a basal reading series.

Knowing and understanding how these sets of materials can support students' literacy development is essential given the "staying power" of basal reading programs in our schools. Teachers need to assess which educational opportunities are best offered by the reading series and then look for other reading and skill activities to support instruction. Most teachers view the basal reading program as just one instructional tool to be used in a variety of ways, and adoption of a basal program does not imply that other materials and strategies are not used to provide a rich, comprehensive program of instruction to meet the needs of all children.

A Look Back

Basal reading programs have a long history in the United States. Historically, they have been referred to as basal reading programs because they serve as the "base" for reading instruction. *The New England Primer*, first published for American colonists in the late 1600s, followed a strong bottom-up model of instruction. The alphabet was taught first; then vowels, consonants, double letters, italics, capitals, syllables, and so on were presented for instruction, in that order. Words were not introduced systematically in basal readers until the mid-1800s. This means colonial children might be introduced to 20 to 100 new words on every page! The 1860s saw the first mainstream use of basal readers with words systematically introduced in a series written by William McGuffey called the *McGuffey Readers*. These readers pioneered the first "levels" of reading material, contained many colored pictures, and followed a phonics-based approach to teach reading. A teacher's manual and student "work pad" was introduced for seatwork and skills practice. Over time, readers were then created for older students, which focused more on skills in oral reading and presentation. The readers for older students contained poems, stories, and Bible passages.

The most famous basal series was the "Dick and Jane" series by Scott Foresman, which began in the 1930s. This series featured the method of teaching reading by memorizing whole words and using repetition without teaching phonics like the McGuffey readers did before.

Today's commercially published reading programs attempt to satisfy every consumer's appetite when it comes to reading instruction. Our nation's school districts invest billions of dollars in textbooks *every year*. The latest trends have now been incorporated into most reading programs sold by various publishers. For example, the implementation of the CCSS has generated a tremendous amount of interest for publishing companies and vendors. Basal readers have been revised with new editions that focus on critical skills required by the Common Core, such as close reading or text complexity. There is also more nonfiction now because CCSS call for an equal emphasis on literature and informational text in elementary school (Coleman &

Pimental, 2012). This shift is due to the belief that students who are able to answer questions related to complex text will do better in introductory college courses (Goodwin & Miller, 2013). Progress monitoring, differentiated instruction, technology integration, and suggestions for working with English language learners (ELLs) are also hot topics in current basal reading programs.

Common Core State Standard

CCRA.R.10

Terminology of Basal Reading Programs   There are certain concepts and terms germane to basal reading programs. Figure 13.1 presents key terms and definitions that should prove helpful in understanding some key concepts. The terms may vary from series to series, but it is safe to assume that certain major components will be found in most programs. As programs have evolved, they have tried to provide every tool necessary to teach all students to read.

Anatomy of Basal Readers

More significant than similarities and differences among reading series are improvements in components over the past decades. Overall physical appearance, literary

Figure 13.1 The Language of Basal Instruction

Anthologies Anthologies are collections of stories, poems, and nonfiction selections bound together in a book and usually organized by themes that tie the content and materials together. Today's **anthologies** contain authentic text from all genres and include more nonfiction than ever before, signaling a shift in focus and philosophy. Traditional components such as a teacher's guide, student texts, and practice books are still offered.

Decodable Text This is text that is written for beginning readers. It contains a high number of regularly spelled, decodable words and high-frequency words.

Differentiating Instruction To adapt teaching for all learners (gifted students, visual learners, ELLs, struggling readers, etc.), suggestions are given for tailoring instruction to individual needs. Many programs have additional resources for differentiating instruction for particular groups of students.

Extension (Integrating Across the Curriculum) After the text is read and the main parts of the suggested lesson framework are completed, teachers continue or extend themes and make cross-curricular connections with projects and activities. Art, music, and writing are catalysts for the **extension** of ideas and concepts initiated during the lesson.

Guided Reading A teacher guides small groups of students in reading short, carefully chosen texts in order to build independence, fluency, comprehension skills, and problem-solving strategies. The teacher often begins by introducing the text and modeling a particular strategy. Then students read to themselves in quiet voices as the teacher listens in, noting strategies and obstacles, and cuing individual students as needed. Students then discuss content and share problem-solving strategies. Guided-reading materials usually become increasingly challenging and are often read more than once. The teacher regularly observes and assesses students' changing needs, and

adjusts groupings accordingly. Guided reading allows a teacher to provide different levels of support, depending on the needs of the students.

Levels Each level provides a sequential arrangement of student books (readers), teacher's editions, and ancillary materials and builds on those that come before it; corresponding to a grade level. There may be more than one book for some grade levels, making continuous progress possible.

Pacing Guide A guide is designed to help teachers in pacing instruction of what students are expected to know and be able to use in language arts/reading for the entire year. A pacing guide explains not just how long you will be teaching a topic, but also the scope (all the topics) and sequence (the order of the topics) of the topics you will be teaching. Pacing guides help teachers teach consistently across a school or district and provide teachers with a framework from which to plan their daily lessons. Pacing guides are like timelines showing what each teaching team plans to cover over the course of a year. Each subject area follows a logical sequence within a grade level and between grade levels.

Reinforcement To ensure that skills have been learned, exercises involving similar and contrasting examples are used for **reinforcement** of the learning. This re-teaching cycle includes the use of extension activities.

Scope and Sequence This general plan is for the introduction of skills in a sequential way. *Scope* refers to the depth of coverage given to a certain skill that will increase over time. *Sequence* is the order in which the skills are taught. Students move up through the levels and across within each level.

Skills Skills, such as sequencing, cause and effect, homonyms and vowel patterns, are not presented only once. They are introduced at one level and then repeated and reinforced at subsequent levels with increasing depth throughout the program. Skill building follows this design: introduction of a skill, reinforcement of the skill, and review of the skill.

variety, and efforts to be inclusive and respect diversity deserve special recognition. In general, components have become more comprehensive, thorough, or complex, depending on one's viewpoint.

STUDENT BOOKS   Anthologies, trade books, e-books, and leveled books are just some of the physical components now available for students. Emergent literacy programs are often organized thematically, include a variety of support materials, and capitalize on children's curiosity about print to get them excited about reading and making predictions.

For older students, there is typically a hardcover anthology—a bound collection of reading selections such as stories, poems, and informational text—in each program and then small, leveled readers for each student. Stories are chosen to illustrate and develop specific skills, which are taught in a predetermined sequence. Over the years the quality of literature has improved to include whole chapters from novels and original illustrations. Teachers remain the most important decision makers in terms of critically evaluating and deciding what is appropriate and valuable for their students to read. When the experience of culture isn't addressed in the illustrations or text of a basal series, children many not become motivated for meaningful learning. Culturally relevant teaching (Ladson-Billings, 1992) celebrates and builds on the cultural background of students. Such teaching helps students examine their reading critically, helping them ask, "How does this compare to my experiences? My knowledge? My feelings?" The validity and logic of what we read in school can be assessed in terms of our own beliefs and assumptions and also of people with world views different from our own.

LEVELED READERS   Leveled books are student books that are included in the program and used during guided reading. Children are matched with text at, below, or above grade level to help meet the needs of each student.

TEACHER'S EDITIONS   Teacher's editions provide an instructional guide and in-service support. Three important features of the teacher's edition are the scope and sequence chart, a reduced version of the student text, and suggested lesson plans. Lessons and activities designed to promote strategic reading and to teach strategies for making informed decisions are featured. With so many marginal notes, highlights, features, and extensions, lesson plans in a teacher's manual can be perplexing. What was once one large spiral-bound resource is now divided into multiple volumes organized by units. With an abundance of teaching options and directions, the size of a typical teacher's edition for one unit today is the size of former editions for the entire year! The confusing nature of so many options could be overwhelming to novice teachers, but many others have become discriminating consumers who realize they need not slavishly follow the teacher's manual.

Lesson Framework   Most teacher's editions of basal readers have lessons for whole group, small group, and independent activities. A typical lesson follows a before, during, and after reading framework for teaching a selection over a number of days.

Common Core State Standards

CCRA.L.4, CCRA.L.5

- **Before Reading** Before reading is a time to motivate students and build background knowledge. This aspect of the lesson involves getting ready to read. It is sometimes referred to as the prereading phase of instruction. The teacher attempts to build interest in reading, set purposes, and introduce new concepts and vocabulary.

- **During Reading** During reading the teacher guides the students through the text, usually in small groups. Depending on the grade level, a selection may be read on a section-by-section basis (in the primary grades) or in its entirety.

Following silent reading, children may be asked to read the story aloud or orally read specific parts to answer questions. The guided reading phase of the lesson focuses on comprehension development through questioning. Strategic reading, including explicit comprehension and vocabulary skill instruction, is explained in the teacher's guide, along with prompts interspersed throughout the teacher's copy of the story.

- **After Reading** After reading is a time for the teacher to determine whether students understand main concepts and can incorporate what they just read into their core knowledge. It is a time to clarify, reinforce, and extend concepts. Teachers might ask students to confirm predictions or discuss comprehension questions, or provide skill development and practice activities centered on direct instruction of reading skills, arranged according to **scope and sequence**. Activities and exercises from the various practice books that accompany the basal might be used to reinforce skills in the broad areas of word analysis and recognition, vocabulary, comprehension, and study skills.

WORKBOOKS Workbook content has changed a great deal since the work pads that accompanied early basals. While still providing practice in spelling, phonics, or decoding skills in the primary grades and comprehension or study skills in the intermediate grades, there are opportunities for open-ended, personal, and creative responses, too. A wide range of practice books in every area such as phonics, vocabulary, writing, CCSS, and handbooks for ELLs are included. Some workbooks are in the form of online activities that are completed and uploaded into a teacher's dropbox. No longer must teachers simply decide how many workbook pages to assign; today's question is: *What do I choose from the many available resources to differentiate for each child?*

ASSESSMENTS Basal reading programs include a comprehensive set of assessments to help teachers assess students' strengths and needs, determine ability levels, pinpoint foundational skill gaps, and challenge advanced learners. Assessments include screening, progress monitoring, and benchmark and unit tests. They are usually offered in print form but are also typically available online and include scoring and data reporting that provides immediate feedback. The automaticity with which data can be managed and organized online makes instructional planning more efficient and effective for teachers if used and interpreted correctly. As with all materials, teachers must have the knowledge to carefully select what assessments they need and for what purpose in order to gain information that will assist with student achievement.

TECHNOLOGY AND ONLINE LEARNING Basal readers have gone digital and, if used correctly, can offer opportunities to personalize and differentiate learning to meet the needs of individual students. Online versions now accompany print programs where students can simply navigate through different pages and titles, and are often available as part of a contemporary commercial program. Vocabulary cards, practice activities, writing assignments, and other support materials are included in digital format. Some offer online quizzes that accompany the print-based text. Most programs offer online management tools for teachers, such as search features to customize skill instruction, online lesson planning, and even online coaching.

The largest contribution technology has made to basal reading is the immediate, real-time assessments and data reporting system now part of most programs. Vendors offer online formative and summative tools that provide screening, progress monitoring, and summative feedback.

Watch this **video** (www.youtube.com/watch?v=In-g6elvUG4) to see a tutorial on the online portion of a basal reader. Follow along as she navigates through the website. What resources are available online to support the print version of the program?

INTERVENTION Basal programs provide options such as practice books, diagnostic assessments, games, and online interactive resources to reteach skills to students who do not demonstrate mastery on assessments. Leveled books in a series allow students to read on, above, or below grade level. There are small group lesson suggestions that provide more intense instruction focused on priority skills for strategic intervention. Many programs also come with ELL kits and materials such as practice books or language support activities for struggling readers.

Making Instructional Decisions with Basals

2017 ILA Standard
2.1

The basal lesson can be a tool at our command, or it can dominate our classroom actions. Can you imagine the enormity of the task of creating and organizing a reading curriculum on your own? You'd need to put together a whole year of texts at multiple levels, vocabulary words and instruction for them, lessons on decoding strategies, tiers of instruction, and on and on. The tasks would be endless! A commercial reading program provides a starting point for making sound instructional decisions.

Teachers must make informed decisions about using, not using, or supplementing basal reading programs. Basal programs, no matter how comprehensive they are, cannot differentiate instruction on their own. Teachers must be judicious about selecting materials to use for the core reading program and the plethora of supplemental materials that accompany it. See Box 13.2 to read how one literacy coach, Jane Hallisy, supports teachers who use a basal.

2017 ILA Standards
2.1, 5.2

BOX 13.2 | VIEWPOINT

Jane Hallisy
Supporting Teachers Who Use a Basal

Jane Hallisy is an educational consultant.

At times I have worked with teachers to help them plan the use of their core reading programs. I mainly focus on helping them understand the layout of the manual and how to differentiate for various needs. Often teachers think they need to teach everything on the page and use all of the materials, so my job is to help them sort through all of the resources available. We spend quite a bit of time discussing the many components of their district's selected reading program and what materials might work best for the different abilities in small, flexible groups. For example, I help teachers understand how to use the various leveled books to assist students with reading at their ability level. The focus skill remains the same for all groups. However, the activity or materials used are differentiated to meet the students' needs. Extra support materials assist struggling readers' instruction while advanced readers utilize materials and activities that are more challenging.

Within the core or basal teacher's manual, strategies such as questioning the author are presented. Sometimes we provide a more in-depth study of a strategy. For example, we might use the same strategy with a professional journal article. We have teachers walk through the steps and then discuss how they could use the strategy with their students.

When presenting professional development on a particular topic such as the five essentials, we have the teachers go through their core program teacher's edition and materials, search for these components, and determine how that specific component was stressed. Then we have them plan for the week. Using the suggestions from the manual, teachers plan how they will explicitly teach the essentials or how they might extend the practice in it through center activities.

Watch this **video** (www.youtube.com/watch?v=d6DvFPc9FM8) to see how one school is using a basal reading program. Notice what the teachers say they like about having a basal program. What did they do at this school to learn how to use the program effectively?

Common Core State Standard

CCRA.R.1

Let's consider how two primary teachers handle their teacher's manuals. LeAnn has been teaching for 10 years. She follows the lessons in her basal reading program assiduously, lesson by lesson and page by page from the teacher's manual. Her compliance, she suggests, is based on a couple of factors. The basal program, she says, was put together by experts "who know far more than I ever will about reading." But do these experts know her students as well as she does? Do they know her children's reading strategies? Their diagnostic results? LeAnn replied, "Perhaps not. But the lessons must be good or they wouldn't be in the book, and the publisher has aligned the materials with the CCSS, and it says it's research-based. I like that I don't have to think about that. It saves me hours of planning time. If I follow the book, I know I'm getting it all in there."

By contrast, Lori is a 12-year veteran. She has a basal program adopted by her district and uses it but "reorganizes parts to fit what I think my students need based on assessment data." When asked whether it takes time to do this, Lori replied, "It does. But I think it's time well spent. Sometimes I use supplemental materials if I think that will better target a skill or concept my students need, but I think it's worth the extra time."

As teachers reflect on why and how they use basals, they will find additional opportunities to use their knowledge and skills more fully and effectively. Modifications of basal reading lessons allow teachers to rely on their own strengths as well as those of the students. After all, teachers should not have to face an "either–or" dilemma in using basals to teach reading. Rather, they need to decide where to place instructional emphasis.

2017 ILA Standards

1.1, 2.1, 2.2, 2.3

It is not unusual to discover very different kinds of reading instruction going on in the same elementary school. Even when a school uses just one reading program, instructional emphasis often varies from teacher to teacher. It is clearly impossible to teach every activity suggested in a basal reading lesson. There isn't enough time in the day; moreover, we wonder whether a teacher would need to do so to produce proficient readers. From an instructional point of view, the question is not, "Am I going to do everything as suggested in the teacher's manual?" The more appropriate question is, "What am I going to use in order to meet the instructional needs of my students?"

As teachers of reading become more familiar with instructional strategies in this text and others, they try them out in their classrooms. Many will use alternative strategies in conjunction with their basal programs. They may prefer to follow the basic lesson framework, incorporating some alternatives into this structure.

Modifying lessons personalizes reading instruction for teachers and students. The reasons behind this lesson planning are varied, but the most important one is the need to adapt in order to meet the special needs of students. The nature of students as readers, and as individuals within a social situation in which language plays a large role, causes teachers to modify instruction.

Children who are reluctant to read, who are just learning English, who are in some way gifted, or who face developmental or other challenges benefit when teachers plan lessons with them in mind. Sometimes lessons may simply be rearranged; at other times, parts might be omitted or expanded.

Check Your Understanding 13.1: Gauge your understanding of the skills and concepts in this section.

Trade Books

■ **Learn how leveled trade books are used for instruction**

2017 ILA Standard

1.1

Common Core State Standard

CCRA.R.9

At the beginning of this chapter, we stated that the majority of schools in the United States adopt a commercial reading program as their primary means of literacy instruction. However, many teachers and districts embrace a teacher-constructed or student-centered program such as readers' workshop or guided reading and engage students with **trade books**, which are books designed for the general public and available through an ordinary bookstore. Some teachers use trade books as their core instructional materials and do not have a basal at all. Others may supplement their basal program with the use of trade books for small group time, to read aloud, to engage students in literature discussion groups, for independent reading, as models for writing, or for various other activities that make up the language arts portion of the day.

The Case for Trade Books

While most teachers use trade books in some way in their classrooms, proponents of trade books as the core curriculum have various reasons for selecting them over a commercially published basal. Some believe that without real engagement with quality, meaningful books, students will not want to read. This matters because the availability of reading material is related to how much students read, and that how *much* they read is related to how *well* they read. For this reason many teachers want the freedom to use a variety of texts—not a prepackaged set of materials—to provide a rich experience for each student.

Another reason for the preference of trade books is the belief that they can better respect the linguistic, social, and cultural heritages of their students by surrounding them with culturally appropriate and relevant trade books that capitalize on background knowledge and experiences. By connecting their students with meaningful multicultural books they can relate to, teachers validate and build on their students' cultural and world knowledge. A rich classroom collection of multicultural trade books acknowledges the background experience of all students and enhances their engagement in reading.

Still others believe there is simply no substitute for a real, hardbound book to encourage interest in reading or a lifelong love of reading. In fact, according to the latest Scholastic Kids and Reading Report (2015), most students still prefer to read in print form. Additionally, students across all grade levels said their favorite books—and the ones they are most likely to finish—are the ones they pick out themselves.

Many teachers believe the key to teaching all students to read is engagement in a literate atmosphere that stimulates and supports reading. They facilitate engagement in reading by modeling their own love of reading, reading aloud, book talking, providing access to a wealth of trade books, engaging students in a variety of activities with diverse texts, including daily independent reading of self-selected trade books, and providing book-related incentives that recognize students for their reading and emphasize the value of reading.

Leveling Trade Books

In many classrooms where trade books are used, each book is assigned a level to help the teacher identify which book offers just the right level of support and challenge for the reader. A leveled book collection is a set of trade books organized in levels of difficulty from the easy books that an emergent reader might begin to the longer, complex books that advanced readers will select. In some schools, the collection is housed in a central area such as the library or a book room where there are multiple copies of many books. To obtain levels, books are analyzed for text difficulty by evaluating features such as language use, sentence structure, story elements, and more. Leveled books are intended to guide young readers as they reach certain skill levels since they begin with simple sentences and concepts and progress into more complex content as children are ready to move on to the next stage of reading. Teachers use leveled books for small group instruction known as guided reading groups, and the books are also used for independent reading. There are numerous online resources that have already leveled thousands of books according to different leveled reading systems such as Guided Reading Level (GRL), Developmental Reading Assessment (DRA), and Lexile levels.

Recently there has been a growing concern over the heavy use of leveled books in the classroom. Morgan, Wilcox, and Eldridge (2000) did a study with three groups of struggling readers, each with texts of a set difficulty level. All three groups improved, but the greatest gains were made by the group using text that was two years above the instructional level. Moreover, Fisher and Frey (2014), longtime advocates of leveled text, reexamined the research around it. They found that the use of leveled text beyond the very first years of school produced no achievement gains in students. The belief that young readers should only be taught from texts that they understood to a level of 95 percent or higher oral reading accuracy has been found to be mistaken; there was no compelling evidence. What they did discover was plenty of research to support the use of more difficult reading material. They found numerous studies suggesting students learn more when taught with texts that are above their instructional level.

To be clear, this does not mean teachers should abandon the practice of having students read leveled text at their instructional level. It does, however, mean that students should read texts not only at their instructional level and their independent level, but at times read text that is at their frustration level in order to grow. For this to happen, teachers will need to scaffold the more difficult text for students.

> During this **video** (https://www.youtube.com/watch?v=vXvefHR9qWI), you will observe a teacher in small, guided reading lessons. What strategies does the teacher use to ensure that students who read on different levels are working at the appropriate level? What type of instructional materials does she choose?

Check Your Understanding 13.2: Gauge your understanding of the skills and concepts in this section.

2017 ILA Standards

5.2, 5.3

Technology

■ **Explore technology-based materials**

As we already know, most elementary teachers use supplemental instructional materials in addition to or in place of the basal reading program or trade books to teach reading.

BOX 13.3 | STUDENT VOICES

Jack is nine years old. He loves school and loves books. His mom has read to him all of his life, and the library is a big part of his life. Right now, he is a fan of the *Percy Jackson* books by Rick Riorden. He follows him on Twitter and likes to check out his Facebook page when he can. "It has lots of cool stuff on it, and you get to hear from the author and find out what he's doing and stuff. On his website, you can ask him questions and he will answer them," Jack says. For Jack, technology is a natural part of his young life, and he uses social media to connect with his favorite books and authors.

Jack and other twenty-first-century kids like him are savvy when it comes to electronic devices, the Internet, and social media. Twenty-first-century teachers need to use instructional materials that continue to interest and motivate young readers.

This willingness to broaden the materials used for instruction is a double-edged sword: There is a lot to choose from and not a lot of guidance on how to go about it. This is especially the case when it comes to electronic materials. Undoubtedly the fastest area of growth in instructional materials, new technologies for literacy learning are at an all-time high and show no sign of slowing down. The International Literacy Association (ILA) asserts that to be fully literate, students must become proficient with technology, and teachers must integrate it into the curriculum. As the endless options for integrating digital technologies into literacy instruction continue, it will be more important than ever for teachers to make careful choices around classroom instruction. Both teachers and students (such as Jack in Box 13.3) are increasingly aware of the possibilities for reading and learning with technology. As teachers begin to select technologies that are viable learning tools for their classrooms, they must consider that digital technology should enhance curricular goals and support student learning in new and transformative ways (Hutchison & Reinking, 2011). Further, ELLs and students with disabilities can benefit greatly from the use of technology in the classroom because lessons can be personalized to a student's individual needs.

A theoretical framework that supports the integration into literacy and other content areas is the Technological Pedagogical Content Knowledge (TPACK) framework (Mishra & Koehler, 2006; Thompson & Mishra, 2007/2008). Using technology for teaching requires knowledge and skills about technology, in addition to all the other skills and knowledge that teachers already possess. To be effective, Mishra and Koehler believe teachers must be skilled in three domains—technology, pedagogy, and content—and be able to integrate all three. If teachers design instruction with the components of the TPACK framework in mind, technology has the potential to help teachers meet objectives and at the same time provide students with the opportunity to learn new technologies by interacting with and responding to text in new ways. Brueck and Lenhart (2015) caution that ongoing, professional learning is key to staying apprised of digital advances and emerging technologies.

The Internet has transformed our literacy lives, providing instant access to online information, resources, digital tools, and one another. Students can gather information on every imaginable topic, publish their research reports, ask questions of experts, and have a spoken conversation with students around the world using software applications. Students can record their reading fluency and send it off to their teacher or create a movie trailer in place of a traditional book report. Teachers can access the Internet on their interactive whiteboards and take students on guided tours of lands far away to explore different places, such as the Swiss Alps or the Australian outback. They can watch live footage of puffins in Maine or create voice-over tutorials for their students. The possibilities are endless, but instructional time is not. This means teachers have to make wise choices that maximize student learning. Today's teachers use Internet and technology as viable learning tools in their classroom, enhancing curricular goals and supporting student learning in new ways (Hutchison & Reinking, 2011). In Box 13.4, Jeremy Brueck provides criteria teachers can use to select appropriate technology tools for the literacy classroom.

BOX 13.4

Selecting and Teaching with High-Quality Digital Texts

What makes a good, workable, instructive, enjoyable e-book for young children? Certainly the established criteria of quality children's literature apply to e-book texts. Strong features of good storybooks over the ages are similarly the features of enduring e-books into the future: Age-appropriate material that interests children, strong plots, and rich characterizations of the human condition are most likely the types of features we'd hope to find in a high-quality e-book. In this way, e-books are very much like traditional books, and their literary or informational content can be judged by the same general criteria.

However, the addition of electronics impacts reading in new ways. An e-book, for example, can have background music, whereas a traditional book cannot. E-books can provide mini-tutorials in hotspots, hyperlinks, and virtual assistants who instruct and explain on-the-spot—in essence, "teaching" children early literacy skills such as phonological awareness and vocabulary.

When selecting e-books for use in the classroom, teachers need to pay close attention to the scaffolds and tutors provided for learning to read, such as decoding helpers, animations, and audio. During their evaluation, teachers should make sure that common e-book design mistakes are avoided, such as confusing taps, swipes, and page turns or lack of easy access to the menu and controls. Additionally, when selecting an e-book, teachers need to consider what types of devices (desktop computers, laptops or tablets) to use to maximize children's participation throughout the e-book reading experience.

Using e-books to support learning in the early elementary classroom is much like teaching with traditional books, a practice that is familiar to all early elementary teachers.

1. Select a quality e-book.
2. Gather a small group of children around a touchscreen computer or a tablet.
3. Explore the e-book together.

Teachers can use a number of familiar shared reading activities with e-books—the application of the before-during-after framework, for example—and the introduction to the title, author, and illustrator on the initial screen page of the e-book. Evidence-based instructional techniques are retained, such as making predictions, asking/answering questions, learning new words, linking to prior experience, and discussing print and picture. After reading, make sure you take the additional step of modeling the proper use of devices for independent book browsing and re-reading, and helping children to engage in responsible e-book reading on their own or with a friend.

As you are getting started with e-books in your classroom, remain open to new procedures that expand the e-book reading experience, such as modeling the digital features of the e-book first! Be thoughtful and patient as you begin to incorporate e-books into your early literacy curriculum. Choose e-books wisely, and start to build up a library. Use the electronic capabilities of e-books, like hotspots and virtual assistants, to help you teach early literacy skills. Show your students how to navigate apps and e-books effectively and encourage lots of e-book browsing and sharing. As you follow these tips to select and incorporate high-quality digital texts in your classroom, you will begin to see the potential of e-books for increasing the resources and opportunities for early reading experience.

Electronic Books

Initially used only on devices called e-readers, **e-books** contain text that can be downloaded or viewed online from most any device. The text is presented to readers visually in a variety of ways. Many provide opportunities for students to interact with and manipulate texts and to transform texts to meet their needs and interests. This can make the reading experience more engaging for students. E-books that embed prompts, hints, model answers, and instant feedback into the text to provide individualized instruction are available. Some come equipped with adjustable font sizes and text captioning. Others include translations for ELL students.

The growing use of online technologies that contain leveled e-books are becoming popular among teachers and students in districts and schools across the country because, like print based commercial program, they are becoming increasingly comprehensive. Some school districts are adopting these subscription-based texts and accompanying materials as their core reading program; others are using them as a supplement. Once a subscription is purchased, students have access to hundreds if not thousands of texts that span reading levels. Teachers can view or download lesson plans and other instructional materials from a "dashboard" as well as select text to be placed into each student's account. Students can then access and read teacher selected books, take quizzes, and complete activities. Teachers can monitor student progress on quizzes, track books read, and listen to student oral reading all from the dashboard.

Instructional Decision Making 13.1: Apply your understanding of the concepts in this section.

Online Games

Online games and virtual learning experiences can be used as text for students, providing a new and different context for disciplinary knowledge that is highly motivating for students. Kozdras, Joseph, and Schneider (2015) have described how online games were used for teaching literacy skills and strategies, all scaffolded by the teacher. Using the games, teachers taught close reading, modeled think-alouds, asked text-dependent questions, previewed text, introduced vocabulary, and led discussions. To further engage students, they implemented literature circles—or, in this case, game circles—as a way for students to teach strategies to their peers and ask text-dependent questions.

Online Word Processors

Online word processors, such as Google Docs, allow for collaborative writing in real time. Students are able to use a Student Response System (SRS) on their cell phones to deliver lesson reflections or to submit predictions onto a class document that is projected for whole class discussion. Other teachers have students work collaboratively on projects and use document features to respond to student work, or put text into a document for close reading and have students highlight or underline text. Online documents allow teachers to easily track work and collaborate with students in real time.

Apps

An application—or an app, as it's generally called—is a type of software that allows you to perform specific tasks. There are desktop or laptop apps but there are also mobile apps that can be used on handheld devices like phones. When you open an app, it runs inside the operating system of the computer or device until you close it. There are thousands of apps available just for teachers of reading, from those that provide practice on individual skills such as ABCs and prefixes to others that allow students to create graphic novels to tell their stories. There are apps that read books to students, record their stories, help students create QR-coded book reviews (smartphone-readable code consisting of an array of black-and-white squares), and learn grammar. Teachers are using apps in all kinds of ways to explicitly teach literacy content, for guided and independent practice and to check understanding. They are especially popular during center or work station time, when students need to work independently in order for the teacher to meet with small groups of students. Neuman (2015) found that mobile apps in preschool classrooms guided by the teacher may help improve early literacy skills and boost school readiness for low-income children.

> ▶ In this **video** (www.youtube.com/watch?v=dE7Ojjs4dWg), an online reading series is introduced. What are some of the features of this program that stood out to you? How would you compare this to a traditional commercial reading program?

Many variables could account for a teacher's decision to favor one type of reading material over another for instruction. Grade level, school district policy, influence of colleagues, curriculum objectives, and available resources are some that come to mind. Figure 13.2 displays the pros and cons of basals, trade books, and online resources.

Figure 13.2 Pros and Cons of Core Instructional Materials

Type	Pros	Cons
Basal Reader	• Scope and sequence • Explicit, detailed lesson plans • Ease of teacher planning	• Predetermined, one-size-fits-all • Too comprehensive to sort through and determine what to use • Loss of teacher choice in selection of text
Trade Books	• Authentic text in unadapted form • Student choice in text • Teacher decision-making • Culturally relevant	• Teacher must plan lessons; time consuming • No scope and sequence; issues of continuity between classes and grade levels • Unstructured assessments
Technology	• Highly motivating • Detailed report of student progress • Large library of e-books • Real-time opportunities	• No scope and sequence • Teacher must plan lessons; time consuming • Unlimited resources with little guidance

Complete the drag-and-drop activity to test your understanding of the material.

Common Core State Standard

CCRA.R.5

Check Your Understanding 13.3: Gauge your understanding of the skills and concepts in this section.

Evaluating Reading Materials

■ **Evaluate components of instructional materials in relation to curriculum goals**

Like Han in the chapter's opening vignette, many teachers have served on textbook selection committees. Some probing would reveal the sophistication of the process: Did the committee seek and obtain information from the various stakeholder groups such as parents, administrators, students, and other teachers? Were there presentations and question-and-answer sessions with company representatives? Was there ample time to pilot one or two of the finalists in classrooms?

At the beginning of this chapter, we told you that basal reading programs are the most widely used reading materials in schools nationwide. This means that the decisions that go into selecting core materials should be of supreme importance to a district: These are the texts and instructional materials that will be used to teach so many important skills and strategies like reading comprehension and fluency and supply intervention strategies. Districts cannot rely on publishing companies, which have become so attuned to this process that they mount high-power, professional presentations to convince school districts to adopt a particular program. One selling strategy used by publishing companies is offering districts assistance in getting federal funding, as described in Figure 13.3. Because of how important core programs are to any school, it is critical to put a great deal of time and thought into selecting a set of materials.

2017 ILA Standard

6.4

Social trends such as treatment of women and minorities, return to basics, and increasing involvement of parents have varying degrees of impact on curriculum development and materials selection. Depending on the community, other issues need to be considered. Censorship is probably the most pervasive issue because it deals with people's values. Examining publications for objectionable matter is not the intended mission of most educational materials selection committees. Yet there is a

Figure 13.3 Federal Funding

Publishers of instructional reading materials are now partnering with districts that seek federal funding. Most of the publishing companies of core reading materials offer assistance to districts in the form of grant writing, free webinars to assist grant writing, sample grants, professional development, and many products and services that align to the federal requirements.

Federal funding is distributed two ways to schools: formula funds and competitive grants. Formula funds are allocated based on a per-student amount multiplied by the number of students who are eligible. Some examples of federal formula funds are

- *Title I.* Based on the number of students living in poverty
- *Title III.* Based on the number of English language learners
- *Individuals with Disabilities Education Act (IDEA).* Based on the number of students with disabilities

School districts that serve high-poverty populations are eligible for additional funding. To receive a competitive grant, districts must respond to a Request for Proposal and describe in detail how they would use the grant funding. Some examples of federal grants are

- *Enhancing Education Through Technology (EETT).* Focused on technology integration and professional development
- *21st Century Community Learning Centers.* Focused on K.–12 before- or after-school programs for children in low-performing schools

fine line between examining materials for their contribution to instructional goals and banning materials for their conveyance of implicit or explicit messages to students.

Another issue is the increased accountability as both the federal and state governments demand that schools boost test scores, which has garnered media attention. Newspapers run feature articles comparing local school districts to one another based on percentages of students passing these tests. Pressure is then put on the school board and administrators of a district to improve their scores. As this filters down to the individual classroom level, teachers devote more instructional time to practicing for the test, because in many states teacher evaluations now partially depend on student scores from state assessments. How does this affect the use of the various types of instructional strategies and reading materials? Will teachers, for example, feel free to have sustained silent reading time or use that block of time to drill and practice skills that will appear on state assessments?

Publishing companies mount organized campaigns to convince school districts to adopt their particular program. School districts and even states have in turn developed extensive evaluation forms to keep track of and compare the programs' elements. Publishing companies and vendors are responsible for developing quality products, but the ultimate burden falls on educators to thoroughly evaluate the deluge of instructional materials flooding the market.

A thorough evaluation of a program currently in use is beneficial for assessing the instructional program in relation to the curriculum goals of the school district. Teachers who participate in answering these questions gain the professional development so often neglected when it comes to reading materials. The steps in this process should be done before deciding whether to consider new programs; it's important to have this information as baseline data.

1. What is the overall philosophy of the program? How is reading discussed in the teacher's guide?
2. What kind of learning environment does the program recommend? Is it child-centered? Teacher-centered? Literature-centered? Skills-based? Scientific?
3. Describe the emergent literacy program in detail. How does it provide for communication between school and home?
4. Describe the instructional program in detail. How are lessons structured to teach phonemic awareness, word identification, vocabulary, reading fluency, comprehension, and writing?
5. Describe the literature of the program. Are the selections in unabridged form? Are different genres included? Is there a strong presence of nonfiction text? How culturally diverse is the literature?

6. How well does the program integrate across the curriculum? In what ways is assessment connected to daily instruction? What opportunities are there for connections between the various language arts?

Checklists designed to evaluate reading materials are popular, because they are relatively easy to construct; teachers are more willing to spend the short amount of time it takes to develop a list to help them examine materials. Figure 13.4 provides a sample checklist that could be used for a preliminary review of materials in order to

Figure 13.4 Checklist for Examining the Potential Effectiveness of Materials

Statement	Yes	No	Unsure	Does Not Apply
1. Reading materials are consistent with:				
a. philosophy and goals of the program	___	___	___	___
b. standards	___	___	___	___
2. Materials are adequate for various phases of the program:				
a. oral language development	___	___	___	___
b. listening comprehension	___	___	___	___
c. word recognition	___	___	___	___
d. reading comprehension	___	___	___	___
e. fluency	___	___	___	___
f. study skills	___	___	___	___
g. phonics	___	___	___	___
h. vocabulary	___	___	___	___
3. The materials are				
a. interesting and stimulating	___	___	___	___
b. easy for children to use	___	___	___	___
c. durable	___	___	___	___
d. well organized	___	___	___	___
e. cost-effective	___	___	___	___
4. The materials accommodate the range of reading abilities.	___	___	___	___
5. A variety of cultures is depicted in illustrations and text content.	___	___	___	___
6. The technology integrates with the content and objectives.	___	___	___	___
7. The technology is motivating and thought-provoking.	___	___	___	___
8. The program is easy to operate.	___	___	___	___
9. I feel adequately prepared to use all materials available.	___	___	___	___

Teacher's Name:_____   Grade Level:_____

determine which programs the district would like to examine more closely. However, we believe that something as critical as the selection of the materials that will be used to teach your students to read and then teach them to read to learn is important enough to expect committee members to commit to an in-depth analysis. With the ongoing proliferation of electronic materials and continuing efforts to develop multi-cultural, diverse, and authentic materials that meet every possible student need, teachers need to be more aware than ever about what they are using in instruction.

Check Your Understanding 13.4: Gauge your understanding of the skills and concepts in this section.

Dewitz, Leahy, Jones, and Sullivan (2010) provide a procedure for selecting a core reading program that goes beyond the basic checklists that often result in only a cursory view of materials. Their detailed set of guidelines allows districts to make informed decisions about textbook adoption.

1. *Form a textbook adoption committee.* The committee should be diverse and reflect the demographics of that particular district. Decide who on the committee will be responsible for the ultimate decision and who will just have input during the process.
2. *Set objectives.* Before even looking at texts, the committee should review board policies, state laws, and district guidelines. They should then compile a set of expectations, paying particular attention to those recommendations that are common to all sources reviewed.
3. *Study effective reading instruction.* By reading and discussing the same research on reading instruction, the committee will have a like-minded focus.
4. *Order core reading programs to review.* Select a few programs to review. Publishers will be quite willing to make presentations on their programs.
5. *Evaluate the core reading programs.* Spend time reading each grade level of each program. Compare the pros and cons of each program, and narrow the list to just two. Then pilot those two programs for a month or two.
6. *Present recommendations to the board of education.* If appropriate, select members of the committee to make a presentation to the school board.

Although the selection process is completed at this point, the work has just begun. Teachers are the ones who will actually use the materials to make critical decisions that will benefit their students. Dewitz, Leahy, Jones, and Sullivan (2010) remind us that teachers will need professional development and training on how to make informed instructional judgments when using the program.

RTI for Struggling Readers

Technology and Response to Intervention

Students are highly motivated when learning is technologically based, and many educators believe technology offers great potential for supplemental instruction for RTI. Students who need additional support beyond core instruction receive small-group (Tier 2) or individualized (Tier 3) interventions in addition to the daily classroom instruction. Lessons and intervention suggestions can be used to personalize learning for small groups and individual children as needed. For example, a teacher can assign additional, specific instruction for a student to practice blending and segmenting words or to build vocabulary. This can be done on a computer, tablet, or desktop with an app from the Internet or, as noted earlier in this chapter, from the online portion of the basal program. Many have intervention and practice materials included. When technology is used, students receive immediate feedback, and teachers, who need to continually progress monitor students to determine if they need additional reading instructional support, receive a detailed report of student progress. Teachers can target instruction and increase students' reading and writing abilities by combining intervention and technology.

What About . . .

Standards, Assessment, and Instructional Materials?

The Common Core State Standards Initiative (CCSSI) is a state-led effort coordinated by the National Governors Association Center for Best Practices (NGA Center) and the Council of Chief State School Officers (CCSSO). The CCSS, developed in collaboration with educators, establish goals for learning within K through 12 education. Most states have adopted the CCSS in their entirety and include the core in at least 85 percent of the state's standards in English language arts and mathematics.

As a result, publishers of basal readers are working to provide materials that offer full coverage of the standards. For example, reader-response questions are now being replaced by those that require students to use examples from the text to justify answers (Sawchuk, 2012).

In addition to aligning materials, many large publishing companies also provide professional development to districts in order to assist in the transition to the CCSS. By doing this, publishers hope districts will be more likely to adopt their programs.

Summary

- In this chapter, we began by examining basal reading programs past and present, concluding that a teacher must be judicious and make decisions daily about instruction that is best suited to the students in his or her classroom. Today's commercial programs have more workbooks, assessments, questions, and activities than a teacher could possibly use.

- Trade books as instructional materials were presented along with a discussion on leveled trade books. Students need to read at various levels for different purposes, and teachers need to know how to match students to texts.

- We discussed the huge impact technology has had in the classroom, and there are unlimited resources from which to choose with very little guidance. As with all instructional materials, teachers must select from these new technologies for literacy learning intentionally.

- Teachers are often selected to be on adoption committees to select reading materials for their school or district. Knowing how to evaluate instructional materials in relation to curriculum goals is important. We provided some helpful guidelines to assist with this process.

Teacher Action Research

Teachers have thousands of choices available to them when it comes to instructional materials. Action research is one way for teachers who want to learn more about making smart choices about materials to use with their students. Several ideas are presented here.

1. Select a teacher who has a basal reading program. Interview the teacher about his or her attitude toward basal instruction. How closely is the teacher's manual followed? How does the teacher use the basal workbooks? In what ways, if any, does the teacher deviate from the suggested steps in the man-

ual? What reasons does the teacher give for making modifications?

2. Every teacher wants a library of trade books for a classroom library. But where can you to find free or low-cost trade books for your classroom? There are a number of national nonprofit organizations you can turn to for help. Go online and search programs such as *First Book*, *International Book Project*, or *Kids Need to Read*. Who do they distribute books to? What other organizations can you find that might supply trade books to your classroom?

3. Suppose you work in a school where you are allowed to use whatever instructional materials you want to teach your students. What would you use as your core instructional materials, and why? Would technology be the core instructional material, or would you use it as supplemental? What technologies would you use in your classroom?

4. Look at the checklist included in this chapter for examining the effectiveness of materials. What other items would you include? Are there some you would delete? Compare your findings with a classmate, and compose another checklist.

Through the Lens of the Common Core

The CCSS have generated a large amount of interest for publishers of basal readers and other textbooks. In this chapter we addressed the impact the CCSS have had on the shaping of basal readers and other instructional materials. We discussed the shifts basals have incorporated to update their product, such as text-based responses after reading. While strong instructional materials matter, nothing takes the place of a knowledgeable teacher in the classroom. For this reason we encourage teachers to be judicious users of all materials promising to meet every need for every student.

Appendix A
Beliefs About Reading Interview

Determining Your Beliefs About Reading

To determine your beliefs about reading, study the sample responses in this appendix. Then compare each answer you gave to the interview questions in Box 2.2 in Chapter 2 to the samples given here. Using the form in Figure A.1, categorize each response as *bottom-up* (BU) or *top-down* (TD). If you cannot make that determination, check NI, for *not enough information.*

Ask yourself as you judge your responses, "What unit of language did I stress?" For example, if you said that your major instructional goal is "to increase students' ability to associate sounds with letters," then the unit of language emphasized suggests a bottom-up response. Bottom-up responses are those that emphasize *letters* and *words* as the predominant units of language.

By contrast, a top-down response would be appropriate if you had said that your major instructional goal is "to increase students' ability to read library books or other materials on their own." In this response, the unit of language involves the entire selection. Top-down responses emphasize *sentences, paragraphs*, and the *selection itself* as the predominant units of language.

An example of a response that does not give enough information is one in which you might have said, "I tell the student to figure out the word." Such a response needs to be probed further during the interview by asking, "How should the student figure out the word?"

The following rating sheet will help you determine roughly where you lie on the continuum between bottom-up and top-down belief systems. After you have judged each response to the interview questions, check the appropriate column on the rating sheet for each interview probe.

Figure A.1 Rating Sheet for Beliefs About Reading Interview

	Rating Scale		
	BU	TD	NI
1. Instructional goals			
2. Response to oral reading when reader makes an error			
3. Response to oral reading when a student does not know a word			
4. Most important instructional activity			
5. Instructional activities reader should be engaged in most of the time			
6. Ordering of steps in a reading lesson			
7. Importance of introducing vocabulary words before students read			
8. Information from testing			
9. How a reader should respond to unfamiliar words during silent reading			
10. Rationale for best reader			

Table A.1 Rating Chart

Bottom-up:	Gave 0 or 1 top-down response (the rest are bottom-up or not enough information)
Interactive:	Gave 3 to 5 bottom-up responses
Top-down:	Gave 0 or 1 bottom-up responses

An overall rating of your conceptual framework of reading is obtained from Table A.1, showing where you fall on the reading beliefs continuum in Figure 2.1 in Chapter 2.

Guidelines for Analyzing Beliefs About Reading Interviews

Directions: Use the following summary statements as guidelines to help analyze your responses to the questions in the interview.

Question 1: Main Instructional Goals

Bottom-Up Responses

Increase students' ability to blend sounds into words or ability to sound out words.

Increase knowledge of phonetic sounds (letter–sound associations).

Build sight vocabulary.

Increase ability to use word attack skills.

Top-Down Responses

Increase students' ability to read independently by encouraging them to read library or other books that are easy enough for them on their own.

Increase enjoyment of reading by having a lot of books around, reading aloud to children, and sharing books I thought were special.

Improve comprehension.

Increase ability to find specific information, identify key ideas, determine cause-and-effect relationships, and make inferences. (Although these are discrete skills, they are categorized as top-down because students use higher-order linguistic units—phrases, sentences, and paragraphs—in accomplishing them.)

Question 2: Teacher Responses When Students Make Oral Reading Errors

Bottom-Up Responses

Help students sound out the word.

Tell students what the word is and have them spell and then repeat the word.

Top-Down Responses

Ask, "Does that make sense?"

Don't interrupt; one word doesn't "goof up" the meaning of an entire passage.

Don't interrupt; if students are worried about each word, they won't be able to remember what they read.

Don't correct if the error doesn't affect the meaning of the passage.

If the error affects the meaning of the passage, ask students to reread the passage, tell students the word, or ask, "Does that make sense?"

Question 3: Teacher Responses When Students Do Not Know a Word

Bottom-Up Responses

Help students sound out the word.

Help them distinguish smaller words within the word.

Help them break down the word phonetically.

Help them sound out the word syllable by syllable.

Tell them to use word attack skills.

Give them word attack clues; for example, "The sound of the beginning consonant rhymes with _____."

Top-Down Responses

Tell students to skip the word, go on, and come back to see what makes sense.

Ask, "What makes sense and starts with _____?"

Questions 4 and 5: Most Important Instructional Activities

Bottom-Up Responses

Working on skills

Working on phonics

Working on sight vocabulary

Vocabulary drill

Discussing experience charts, focusing on the words included and any punctuation needed

Recording students reading and playing it back, emphasizing accuracy in word recognition

Top-Down Responses

Actual reading, silent reading, and independent reading

Comprehension

Discussion of what students have read

Book reports

Recording students reading and playing it back, emphasizing enjoyment of reading or comprehension

Question 6: Ranking Parts of the Directed Reading Procedure

Bottom-Up Responses

The following are most important:

- Introduction of vocabulary
- Activities to develop reading skills

The following are least important:

- Setting purposes for reading
- Reading
- Reaction to silent reading
- Introduction of vocabulary when the teacher stresses using word attack skills to sound out new words

Top-Down Responses

The following are most important:

- Setting purposes for reading
- Reading
- Reaction to silent reading

The following are least important:
- Introduction of vocabulary
- Activities to develop reading skills

Question 7: Introducing New Vocabulary Words

Bottom-Up Responses

Introducing new vocabulary is important because students need to know which words they will encounter in order to be able to read a story.

Previewing new vocabulary isn't necessary; if students have learned word attack skills, they can sound out unknown words.

Introducing new words is useful in helping students learn which words are important in a reading lesson.

Vocabulary words should be introduced if students don't know the meanings of the words; otherwise it isn't necessary.

Top-Down Response

Vocabulary words need not be introduced before reading because students can often figure out words from context.

Question 8: What a Reading Test Should Do

Bottom-Up Responses

Test word attack skills.

Test ability to name the letters of the alphabet.

Test sight words.

Test knowledge of meanings of words.

Test ability to analyze letter patterns of words missed during oral reading.

Test visual skills such as reversal.

Top-Down Responses

Test comprehension: Students should be able to read a passage orally, look at the errors they make, and use context in figuring out words.

Test whether students are able to glean the meanings of words from context.

Answer questions such as the following: Do students enjoy reading? Do their parents read to them? Do their parents take them to the library?

Have students read passages and answer questions.

Have students read directions and follow them.

Question 9: What Students Should Do When They Come to an Unknown Word During Silent Reading

Bottom-Up Responses

Sound it out.

Use their word attack skills.

Top-Down Responses

Look at the beginning and the end of the sentence and try to think of a word that makes sense.

Try to think of a word that both makes sense and has those letter sounds.

Skip the word; often students can understand the meaning of the sentence without knowing every word.

Use context.

Question 10: Who Is the Best Reader?

Reader A

Miscue is similar both graphically and in meaning to the text word.

Reader B

Miscue is a real word that is graphically similar but not meaningful in the text.

Reader C

Miscue is a nonword that is graphically similar.

Bottom-Up Responses

Reader C, because *ineff* is graphically similar to *ineffective.*

Reader B, because *inner* is a real word that is graphically similar to *ineffective.*

Top-Down Response

Reader A, because *defective* is similar in meaning to *ineffective.*

Appendix B
Texts and Phonics

Trade Books That Repeat Phonic Elements

Adams, P. (2007). *This Old Man.* Grosset & Dunlap.

Barrett, J. (2001). *Which Witch Is Which?* Atheneum.

Bridwell, N. (2000). *Clifford's Birthday Party.* Scholastic.

Campbell, R. (2007). *Dear Zoo.* Four Winds.

Cleary, B. (2008). *The Bug in the Jug Wants a Hug.* Lerner.

Cole, B. (2001). *The Giant's Toe.* Farrar, Straus and Giroux.

Cowley, J. (2006). *Mrs. Wishy-Washy.* Wright Group.

Dillon, L. (2002). *Rap a Tap Tap: Here's Bojangles.* Wright Group.

Eagle, K. (2002). *Rub a Dub Dub.* Charlesbridge.

Galdone, P. (2006). *The Little Red Hen.* Scholastic.

Hoberman, M. (2007). *A House Is a House for Me.* Puffin.

Janovitz, M. (2007). *Look Out, Bird!* North-South.

Kraus, R. (2000). *Whose Mouse Are You?* Macmillan.

Lies, B. (2006). *Bats at the Beach.* Houghton Mifflin.

Marshall, J. (2001). *The Cut-Ups at Camp Custer.* Puffin.

McPhail, D. (2001). *Big Pig and Little Pig.* Harcourt.

Moss, L. (2000). *Zin! Zin! Zin! A Violin.* Simon & Schuster.

Peek, M. (2006). *Mary Wore Her Red Dress.* Clarion.

Perez-Mercado, M. (2000). *Splat!* Children's Press.

Sadler, M. (2006). *Money, Money, Honey, Bunny.* Random House.

Seuss, Dr. (2005). *Wet Pet, Dry Pet, Your Pet, My Pet.* Random House.

Shaw, N. (2006). *Sheep in a Jeep.* Houghton Mifflin.

Strickland, P. (2000). *One Bear, One Dog.* Chronicle Books.

Udry, J. (2001). *Thump and Plunk.* HarperCollins.

Wood, A. (2007). *Silly Sally.* Harcourt.

Read-Aloud Books for Developing Phonemic Awareness

Ahlberg, A. (2001). *The Adventures of Bert.* Farrar, Straus and Giroux.

Bateman, T. (2001). *Farm Flu.* Albert Whitman.

Brown, M. (2001). *The Dirty Little Boy.* Random House.

Burg, S. (2006). *One More Egg.* North-South.

Carle, E. (2005). *10 Little Rubber Ducks.* HarperCollins.

Dunbar, J. (2006). *Where's My Socks?* Scholastic.

Grindley, S. (2003). *Mucky Ducky.* Bloomsbury.

Hilb, N., & Jennings, S. (2009). *Wiggle Giggle Tickle Train.* Annick.

Hoberman, M. (2000). *The Seven Silly Eaters.* Voyager.

Janovitz, M. (2007). *Look Out, Bird!* North-South.

Johnson, S. (2001). *Fribbity Ribbit!* Knopf.

Long, M. (2001). *Hiccup Snickup.* Simon & Schuster.

Martin, B. (2009). *Chicka Chicka Boom Boom.* Aladdin.

Martin, B. (2010). *Brown Bear, Brown Bear, What Do You See?* Holt.

Munsch, R. (2002). *More Pies.* Scholastic.

Richardson, J. (2002). *Grunt.* Clarion.

Root, P. (2005). *Quack.* Candlewick.

Rylant, C. (2001). *Mr. Putter and Tabby Feed the Fish.* Harcourt.

Schubert, L. (2010). *Feeding the Sheep.* Farrar, Straus and Giroux.

Van Leeuwen, J. (2001). *"Wait for Me!" Said Maggie McGee.* Penguin Putnam.

Appendix C
Recommended Books for Multicultural Reading Experiences

African and African American Books

Folklore

Aardema, Verna. *Bimwili and the Zimwi.* (P)

———. *Bringing the Rain to Kapiti Plain.* (P)

———. *Oh, Kojo! How Could You!* (I)

———. *Why Mosquitoes Buzz in People's Ears.* (P–I)

Bryan, Ashley. *All Night, All Day: A Child's First Book of African American Spirituals.* (P–I–A)

———. *What a Morning! The Christmas Story in Black Spirituals.* (P–I)

———. *Let It Shine: Three Favorite Spirituals.* (I–A)

Climo, Shirley. *The Egyptian Cinderella.* (P–I)

Grifalconi, Ann. *The Village of Round and Square Houses.* (P–I)

Hamilton, Virginia. *The All Jahdu Storybook.* Ill. Barry Moser. (P–I)

———. *The People Could Fly.* Ill. Leo Dillon and Diane Dillon. (I)

Keats, Ezra Jack. *John Henry.* (I)

Lester, Julius. *How Many Spots Does a Leopard Have?* (I)

———. *John Henry.* Ill. Brian Pinkney. (I)

———. *The Tales of Uncle Remus: The Adventures of Brer Rabbit.* (P–I)

McKissack, Patricia. *The Dark.* (I)

Mollel, Tololwa. *The Princess Who Lost Her Hair: An Akamba Legend.* (P–I)

San Souci, Robert. *Sukey and the Mermaid.* Ill. Brian Pinkney. (P–I)

Smith, Ronald. *Hoodoo* (I)

Steptoe, John. *Mufaro's Beautiful Daughters.* (P)

P = primary; I = intermediate; A = adolescent

Poetry

Adoff, Arnold. *All the Colors of the Race.* (I)

———. *Black Is Brown Is Tan.* (P)

———. *In for Winter, Out for Spring.* (P–I)

———. *My Black Me: A Beginning Book of Black Poetry.* (P)

Brooks, Gwendolyn. *Bronzeville Boys and Girls.* (P–I)

Bryan, Ashley. *Ashley Bryan's ABC of African American Poetry.* (P–I)

———. *Sing to the Sun.* (P–I)

Chocolate, Debbi. *Kente Colors.* (P–I)

Clifton, Lucille. *Everett Anderson's Goodbye.* (P)

———. *Everett Anderson's Nine Month Long.* (P)

———. *Some of the Days of Everett Anderson.* (P)

Feelings, Tom. *Soul Looks Back in Wonder.* (I–A)

Giovanni, Nikki. *Spin a Soft Black Song.* (P–I)

Greenfield, Eloise. *"Honey, I Love" and Other Love Poems.* (P–I–A)

Grimes, Nikki. *Come Sunday.* (P–I)

———. *Meet Danitra Brown.* (P–I)

Johnson, Angela. *The Other Side: Shorter Poems.* (P–I)

Johnson, James. *Lift Ev'ry Voice and Sing.* (P–I–A)

Myers, Walter. *Dean Harlem.* (I–A)

Price, Leontyne. *Aïda.* Ill. Leo Dillon and Diane Dillon. (A)

Steptoe, Javaka. *In Daddy's Arms I Am Tall.* (P)

Winter, Jeanette. *Follow the Drinking Gourd.* (P–I)

Picture Books

Barber, Barbara. *Saturday and the New You.* Ill. Anna Rich. (P–I)

Clifton, Lucille. *The Boy Who Didn't Believe in Spring.* (P)

———. *Everett Anderson's Christmas Coming.* (P)

———. *Three Wishes.* Ill. Michael Hays. (P)

Collier, Bryan. *Uptown.* (P–I)

Cosby, Bill. *Little Bill Books for Beginning Readers.* Ill. Varnette P. Honeywood. (P–I)

Crews, Donald. *Bigmama's.* (P)

Evans, Shane. *Underground: Finding the Light to Freedom.* (P–I)

Flowers, Art. *Cleveland Lee's Beale Street Band.* Ill. Anna Rich. (P–I)

Greenfield, Eloise. *Grandpa's Face.* (P)

———. *She Come Bringing Me That Little Baby Girl.* (P)

Grifalconi, Ann. *Darkness and the Butterfly.* (P)

———. *Osa's Pride.* (P)

Hamilton, Virginia. *Drylongso.* Ill. Jerry Pinkney. (I)

Hoffman, Mary. *Amazing Grace.* Ill. Caroline Binch. (P)

Hopkinson, Deborah. *Sweet Clara and the Dream Quilt.* Ill. James Ransome. (P–I)

———. *First Family.* Ill. A. G. Ford. (P–I)

Howard, Elizabeth Fitzgerald. *Aunt Flossie's Hats (and Crab Cakes Later).* Ill. James Ransome. (P)

Igus, Toyomi. *I See the Rhythm.* Ill. Michele Wood. (P–I)

Johnson, Angela. *One of Three.* Ill. David Soman. (P)

———. *Tell Me a Story, Mama.* Ill. David Soman. (P)

Keats, Ezra Jack. *A Snowy Day.* (P)

———. *Whistle for Willie.* (P)

King, Coretta Scott. *I Have a Dream.* (I–A)

Kurtz, Jane. *Trouble.* Ill. Durga Bernhard. (P–I)

———, and Christopher Kurtz. *Only a Pigeon.* Ill. E. B. Lewis. (P–I)

Lester, Julius. *What a Truly Cool World.* Ill. Joe Cepeda. (P–I–A)

McKissack, Patricia. *Flossie and the Fox.* (P)

———. *Mirandy and Brother Wind.* Ill. Jerry Pinkney. (P–I)

Mitchell, Margaree. *Uncle Jed's Barbershop.* Ill. James Ransome. (P–I)

Nelson, Vaunda. *Almost to Freedom.* (P)

Nolen, Jerdine. *Thunder Rose.* (P)

Pinkney, Brian. *Max Found Two Sticks.* (P)

Pinkney, Gloria Jean. *Back Home.* Ill. Jerry Pinkney. (P)

Polacco, Patricia. *Chicken Sunday.* (P)

———. *Mrs. Katz and Tush.* (P–I)

Ringgold, Faith. *Tar Beach.* (P–I)

Siegelson, Kim. *In the Time of the Drums.* Ill. Brian Pinkney. (P)

Steptoe, John. *Stevie.* (P)

Walker, Alice. *To Hell with Dying.* Ill. Catherine Deeter. (I–A)

Weatherford, Carole Boston. *Moses: When Harriet Tubman Led Her People to Freedom.* Ill. Kadir Nelson. (P–I)

Williams, Sherley Anne. *Working Cotton.* Ill. Carole Byard. (P)

Fiction

Booth, Coe. *Kendra.* (A)

Curtis, Christopher Paul. *Bud, Not Buddy.* (I)

———. *Elijah of Buxton.* (I)

Davis, Ossie. *Just Like Martin.* (I)

Draper, Sharon. *The Battle of Jericho.* (I)

———. *Copper Sun.* (I–A)

Greenfield, Eloise. *Koya De Laney and the Good Girl Blues.* (I)

Hamilton, Virginia. *Cousins.* (I)

———. *Drylongso.* Ill. Jerry Pinkney. (I)

———. *M. C. Higgins, the Great.* (I–A)

———. *Planet of Junior Brown.* (I–A)

———. *Zeely.* (I)

Johnson, Angela. *Heaven.* (I)

Kurtz, Jane. *The Storyteller's Beads.* (I–A)

Myers, Walter Dean. *Fast Sam, Cool Clyde, and Stuff.* (I–A)

———. *Hoops.* (A)

———. *Motown and Didi.* (A)

———. *Somewhere in the Darkness.* (A)

———. *Won't Know till I Get There.* (A)

———. *The Young Landlords.* (A)

Smothers, Ethel Footman. *Down in the Piney Woods.* (I–A)

Taylor, Mildred. *The Road to Memphis.* (A)

———. *Roll of Thunder, Hear My Cry.* (A)

Woodson, Jacqueline. *Locomotion.* (I)

Williams-Garcia, Rita. *Gone Crazy in Alabama* (I)

Yarbrough, Camille. *Cornrows.* (P)

Nonfiction

Anderson, Laurie. *Ndito Runs.* (P–I)

Andrews, Troy. *Trombone Shorty.* Ill. Bryan Collier (P–I)

Bunting, Eve. *Smoky Nights.* (I–A)

Feelings, Muriel. *Jambo Means Hello.* (P–I)

Haskins, James. *John Lewis in the Lead: A Story of the Civil Rights Movement.* (I–A)

Lester, Julius. *From Slave Ship to Freedom Road.* (I–A)

McKissack, Patricia, and Frederick McKissack. *Black Hands, White Sails.* (P–I)

———. *A Long Hard Journey: The Story of the Pullman Porter.* (I)

Musgrove, Margaret. *Ashanti to Zulu.* (P–I)

Myers, Walter Dean. *Now Is Your Time! The African-American Struggle for Freedom.* (I–A)

Nelson, Kadir. *Heart and Soul.* (I)

Pinkney, Andrea Davis. *Let It Shine! Stories of Black Women Freedom Fighters.* Ill. Stephen Alcorn. (P–I)

Sabuda, Robert. *Tutankhamen's Gift.* (P–I)

Biography

Angelou, Maya. *Kofi and His Magic.* (P–I)

Collier, Bryan. *Freedom River.* (I)

Cooper, Floyd. *Coming Home: From the Life of Langston Hughes.* (I)

Freedman, Florence B. *Two Tickets to Freedom: The True Story of Ellen and William Craft, Fugitive Slaves.* (I–A)

Hamilton, Virginia. *Anthony Burns: The Defeat and Triumph of a Fugitive Slave.* (I–A)

Haskins, James. *Bill Cosby: America's Most Famous Father.* (I)

———. *Diana Ross, Star Supreme.* (I)

Krull, Kathleen. *Wilma Unlimited.* (P–I)

Lester, Julius. *To Be a Slave.* (I–A)

Lorbiecki, Marybeth. *Jackie's Bat.* (I)

Nivola, Claire. *Planting the Trees of Kenya: The Story of Wangari Maathai.* (P–I)

Ringgold, Faith. *My Dream of Martin Luther King.* (P–I)

Asian and Asian American Books

Folklore

Birdseye, Tom. *A Song of Stars*. Ill. Ju-Hong Chen. (P)

Climo, Shirley. *The Korean Cinderella*. (P–I)

Coerr, Eleanor. *Sadako*. (I–A)

Demi. *The Empty Pot*. (P)

Ho, Minfong. *The Stone Goddess*. (I)

Louie, Ai-Ling. *Yeh-Shen: A Cinderella Story from China*. Ill. Ed Young. (P–I)

Mahy, Margaret. *The Seven Chinese Brothers*. (P)

San Souci, Robert. *The Samurai's Daughter*. (I)

Tan, Amy. *The Moon Lady*. (I)

Yacowitz, Caryn. *The Jade Stone: A Chinese Folktale*. Ill. Ju-Hong Chen. (I)

Yep, Laurence. *The Butterfly Man*. (I)

———. *The Rainbow People*. (I)

———. *Tongues of Jade*. Ill. David Wiesner. (I)

Poetry

Baron, Virginia Olsen. *Sunset in a Spider Web: Sijo Poetry of Ancient Korea*. (I–A)

Behn, Harry. *Cricket Songs*. (I–A)

Demi. *In the Eyes of the Cat: Japanese Poetry for All Seasons*. Ill. Tze-Si Huang. (P–I–A)

Lee, Jeanne. *The Song of Mu Lan*. (P–I)

Liu, Siyu, and Orel Protopopescu. *A Thousand Peaks*. (P–I)

Whelan, Gloria. *Yuki and the One Thousand Carriers*. Ill. Yan Nascimbene. (P–I)

Picture Books

Ashley, Bernard. *Cleversticks*. Ill. Derek Brazell. (P)

Bang, Molly. *The Paper Crane*. (P)

Breckler, Rosemary. *Hoang Breaks the Lucky Teapot*. Ill. Adrian Frankel. (P)

Coutant, Helen. *First Snow*. Ill. Vo-Dinh. (P)

Friedman, Ina. *How My Parents Learned to Eat*. (P)

Garland, Sherry. *The Lotus Seed*. Ill. Tatsuo Kiuchi. (P–I)

Ho, Minfong. *Peek!* Ill. Holly Meade. (P)

Levinson, Riki. *Our Home Is the Sea*. Ill. Dennis Luzak. (P–I)

Say, Allen. *Bicycle Man*. (P)

———. *El Chino*. (P–I)

———. *Emma's Rug*. (P–I)

———. *Grandfather's Journey*. (I)

———. *The Boy in the Garden* (I)

———. *The Lost Lake*. (I)

———. *Tree of Cranes*. (P–I)

Tejima. *Ho-limlim: A Rabbit Tale from Japan*. (P–I)

Turner, Ann. *Through Moon and Stars and Night Skies*. Ill. James Graham Hale. (P–I)

Wells, Rosemary. *Yoko*. (P)

Yashima, Taro. *Crow Boy*. (P–I)

———. *Momo's Kitten*. (P)

———. *Umbrella*. (P)

———. *Youngest One*. (P)

Fiction

Kadohata, Cynthia. *Kira-Kira: Weedflower*. (I–A)

Merrill, Jean. *The Girl Who Loved Caterpillars*. Ill. Floyd Cooper. (I)

Mochizuki, Ken. *Baseball Saved Us*. (I)

Moss, Marissa. *Barbed Wire Baseball*. Ill. Yuko Shimizu. (I)

Namioka, Lensey. *Yang the Youngest and His Terrible Ear*. (I)

Napoli, Donna Jo. *Bound*. (I–A)

Uchida, Yoshiko. *The Best Bad Thing*. (I)

———. *The Happiest Ending*. (I)

———. *The Invisible Thread*. (I)

———. *A Jar of Dreams*. (I)

Wong, Janet. *The Trip Back Home*. (P–I)

Yep, Laurence. *Child of the Owl*. (I–A)

———. *Dragonwings*. (I–A)

———. *Learning to Fly*. (I)

———. *Mountain Light*. (I–A)

———. *Sea Glass*. (I–A)

Nonfiction

Banish, Roslyn. *A Forever Family*. (I)

Brown, Tricia. *Lee Ann*. Photos by Ted Thai. (I)

Fugita, Stephen, and Marilyn Fernandez. *Altered Lives, Enduring Community*. (I)

Hoyt-Goldsmith, Diane. *Hoang Anh: A Vietnamese-American Boy*. Photos by Lawrence Migdale. (I)

Kajikawa, Kimiko. *Tsunami!* (P)

Maruki, Toshi. *Hiroshima no Pika*. (I–A)

McMahon, Patricia. *Chi-Hoon: A Korean Girl*. (P–I)

Meltzer, Milton. *The Chinese Americans*. (A)

Schlein, Miriam. *The Year of the Panda*. Ill. Kam Mak. (P–I)

Waters, Kate, and Madeline Slovenz-Low. *Lion Dancer: Ernie Wan's Chinese New Year*. (P–I)

Wolf, Bernard. *In the Year of the Tiger*. (I)

Biography

Huynh, Quang Nhuong. *The Land I Lost: Adventures of a Boy in Vietnam*. (I)

Kashiwagi, Hiroshi. *Swimming in the American*. (I)

Lord, Bette Bao. *In the Year of the Boar and Jackie Robinson*. (I)

Young, Ed. *My Mei ei*. (I)

Hispanic American Books

Folklore

Aardema, Verna. *Borreguita and the Coyote.* Ill. Petra Mathers. (Mexico) (P–I)

———. *The Riddle of the Drum: A Tale from Tizapan, Mexico.* (P–I)

Alexander, Ellen. *Llama and the Great Flood.* (Quechua story from Peru) (I)

Anaya, Rudolfo. *Roadrunner's Dance.* Ill. David Diaz. (P)

Belpre, Pura. *Once in Puerto Rico.* (I)

———. *The Rainbow-Colored Horse.* (Puerto Rico) (P–I)

de Paola, Tomie. *The Lady of Guadalupe.* (Mexico) (P–I)

de Sauza, James. *Brother Anansi and the Cattle Ranch.* (Nicaragua) (P)

Hall, Melisande. *Soon Come: A Ptolemy Turtle Adventure.* (P–I)

Hayes, Joe. *A Spoon for Every Bite.* (P–I)

Jaffe, Nina. *The Golden Flower.* (P–I)

Joseph, Lynn. *A Wave in Her Pocket: Stories from Trinidad.* Ill. Brian Pinkney. (I)

Kurtycz, Marcos. *Tigers and Opossums: Animal Legends.* (Mexico) (I)

Martinez, Reuben. *Once Upon a Time: Traditional Latin American Tales.* (I–A)

Schon, Isabel. *Doña Blanca and Other Hispanic Nursery Rhymes and Games.* (P–I)

Vidal, Beatriz. *The Legend of El Dorado.* (I)

Wolkstein, Diane. *Banza: A Haitian Story.* Ill. Marc Tolon Brown. (P)

Poetry

Carlson, Lori. *Red Hot Salsa: Bilingual Poems on Being Young and Latino in the United States.* (I)

de Gerez, Toni. *My Song Is a Piece of Jade: Poems of Ancient Mexico in English and Spanish.* (I–A)

Delacre, Lulu. *Arrorró, Mi Niño: Latino Lullabies and Gentle Games.* (P)

———. *Arroz con Leche: Popular Songs and Rhymes from Latin America.* (P–I)

Joseph, Lynn. *Coconut Kind of Day.* (P–I)

Soto, Gary. *A Fire in My Hands.* Ill. James Cardillo. (I)

———. *Neighborhood Odes.* Ill. David Diaz. (I)

Picture Books

Belpre, Pura. *Santiago.* Ill. Symeon Shimin. (P)

Bunting, Eve. *How Many Days to America?* Ill. Beth Peck. (I–A)

Cannon, Janell. *Verdi.* (P–I)

Cruz, Martel. *Yagua Days.* (P)

Czernicki, Stefan, and Timothy Rhodes. *The Sleeping Bread.* (P)

Dorros, Arthur. *Abuela.* Ill. Elisa Kleven. (P)

———. *Isla.* (P–I)

Ets, Marie Hall, and Aurora Latastida. *Nine Days to Christmas: A Story of Mexico.* (P)

Galindo, Mary Sue. *Icy Watermelon/Sandria Fria.* Ill. Pauline Rodriguez Howard. (P)

Garza, Carmen Lomas. *Family Pictures: Cuadros de Familia.* (P–I)

Gershator, David, and Phillis Gershator. *Bread Is for Eating.* Ill. Emma Shaw Smith. (P–I)

Havill, Juanita. *Treasure Nap.* Ill. Elivia Savadier. (Mexico) (P)

Isadora, Rachel. *Caribbean Dream.* (P)

Jordon, Martin, and Tanis Jordan. *Amazon Alphabet.* (P–I)

Marvin, Isabel. *Saving Joe Louis.* (P)

Mora, Pat. *Fiesta! Celebrate Children's Day/Book Day.* Ill. Rafael Lopez. (P–I)

Politi, Leo. *Pedro, the Angel of Olvera Street.* (P)

Reich, Susanna. *Jose! Born to Dance.* (P–I)

Roe, Eileen. *Con Mi Hermano: With My Brother.* (P)

San Souci, Robert. *Cendrillon: A Caribbean Cinderella.* Ill. Brian Pinkney. (P–I)

Fiction

Alvarez, Julia. *Before We Were Free: How the Garcia Girls Lost Their Accents.* (I–A)

Cameron, Ann. *The Most Beautiful Place in the World.* Ill. Thomas B. Allen. (P–I)

Carlson, Lori M., and Cynthia L. Ventura (eds.). *Where Angels Glide at Dawn: New Stories from Latin America.* Ill. José Ortega. (I)

Joseph, Lynn. *The Color of My Words.* (I)

Mohr, Nicholasa. *El Bronx Remembered.* (A)

———. *Felita.* (I)

———. *Going Home.* (I–A)

———. *In Nueva York.* (A)

———. *Nilda.* (A)

Paloma, Juanito. *Downtown Boy.* (I)

Ryan, Pam. *Becoming Naomi Leon.* (I–A)

———. *Neruda: A Novel.* (I–A)

Soto, Gary. *Baseball in April and Other Stories.* (I)

———. *Taking Sides.* (I–A)

Nonfiction

Ancona, George. *Bananas: From Manolo to Margie.* (P–I)

———. *Carnaval.* (P–I)

Anderson, Joan. *Spanish Pioneers of the Southwest.* (P–I)

Brown, Tricia. *Hello, Amigos!* Photos by Fran Ortiz. (P–I)

Brusca, Maria Christina. *On the Pampas.* (I)

Cherry, Lynn. *The Shaman's Apprentice.* (P–I)

Cofer, Judith. *An Island Like You: Stories of the Barrio.* (I–A)

Emberley, Rebecca. *My House: A Book in Two Languages/Mi Casa: Un Libro en Dos Lenguas.* (I)

Grossman, Patricia, and Enrique Sanchez. *Saturday's Market.* (P–I)

McDonald's Hispanic Heritage Art Contest. *Our Hispanic Heritage.* (P)

Meltzer, Milton. *The Hispanic Americans.* (A)

Perl, Lila. *Piñatas and Paper Flowers: Holidays of the Americas in English and Spanish.* (I–A)

Shalant, Phyllis. *Look What We've Brought You from Mexico.* (I)

Thomas, Jane. *Lights on the River.* (I)

Tonatiuh, Duncan. *Separate Is Never Equal: Sylvia Mendez & Her Family's Fight for Desegregation.* (I)

Zak, Monica. *Save My Rainforest.* Ill. Bengt-Arne Runnerstrom. Trans. Nancy Schimmel. (I)

Biography

Codye, C. *Luis W. Alvarez.* (I–A)

de Treviño, Elizabeth Borten. *El Guero.* (I–A)

————. *I, Juan de Pareja.* (A)

————. *Juarez, Man of Law.* (A)

Garza, Xavier. *Lucha Libre: The Man in the Silver Mask: A Bilingual Cuento.* (I–A)

Gleiter, Jan. *David Farragut.* (A)

————. *Diego Rivera.* (A)

Shorto, R. *David Farragut and the Great Naval Blockade.* (A)

American Indian Books

Folklore

Bierhorst, John. *Doctor Coyote.* (I)

————. *The Ring in the Prairie: A Shawnee Legend.* (I)

de Paola, Tomie. *The Legend of the Bluebonnet.* (P)

————. *The Legend of the Indian Paintbrush.* (P–I)

Dixon, Ann. *How Raven Brought Light to People.* Ill. James Watts. (P–I)

Goble, Paul. *Beyond the Ridge.* (P–I)

————. *Buffalo Woman.* (P–I)

————. *Crow Chief: A Plains Indian Story.* (I)

————. *Death of the Iron Horse.* (P–I)

————. *Her Seven Brothers.* (P–I)

————. *Iktomi and the Berries: A Plains Indian Story.* (P–I)

————. *Iktomi and the Buffalo Skull: A Plains Indian Story.* (P–I)

————. *Star Boy.* (P–I)

Goldin, Barbara. *The Girl Who Lived with the Bears.* (P–I)

Highwater, Jamake. *Anpao: An American Indian Odyssey.* (I–A)

Kusugak, Michael. *Hide and Sneak.* (P–I)

MacGill-Callahan, Sheila. *And Still the Turtle Watched.* Ill. Barry Moser. (P)

Monroe, Jean Guard, and Ray Williamson. *They Dance in the Sky.* Ill. Edgar Stewart. (I–A)

Osofsky, Audrey. *Dreamcatcher.* (P)

Oughton, Jerrie. *How the Stars Fell into the Sky.* Ill. Lisa Desimini. (P–I)

Renner, Michelle. *The Girl Who Swam with the Fish: An Athabascan Legend.* (P–I)

Rodanas, Kristina. *Dragonfly's Tale.* (P–I)

Siberell, Anne. *The Whale in the Sky.* (P–I)

Taylor, C. J. *How Two-Feather Was Saved from Loneliness.* (P–I)

Wisniewski, David. *Rain Player.* (P–I)

Poetry

Baylor, Byrd. *The Other Way to Listen.* (P–I)

Begay, Shonto. *Navajos: Visions and Voices Across the Mesa.* (I)

Bierhorst, John. *A Cry from the Earth: Music of the North American Indians.* (P–I)

Bruchac, Joseph, and Jonathan London. *Thirteen Moons on Turtle's Back: A Native American Year of Moons.* Ill. Thomas Locker. (P–I)

Clark, Ann Nolan. *In My Mother's House.* Ill. Velino Herrera. (P–I)

Jones, Hettie. *The Trees Stand Shining: Poetry of the North American Indians.* Ill. Robert Andrew Parker. (P–I)

Wood, Nancy. *Dancing Moon.* (I–A)

————. *Many Winters.* (I–A)

———— (ed.). *The Serpent's Tongue: Prose, Poetry, and the Art of the New Mexico Pueblos.* (I)

Picture Books

Baker, Olaf. *Where the Buffaloes Begin.* Ill. Stephen Gammell. (P)

Baylor, Byrd. *Hawk, I'm Your Brother.* (P–I)

Bruchac, Joseph. *Between Earth and Sky: Legends of Native American Sacred Places.* Ill. Thomas Locker. (I)

————. *Night Wings.* (P–I)

Buchanan, Ken. *This House Is Made of Mud.* Ill. Libba Tracy. (P–I)

Bunting, Eve. *Cheyenne Again.* Ill. Irving Toddy. (P–I)

Joosse, Barbara. *Mama, Do You Love Me?* Ill. Barbara Lavallee. (P–I)

Parsons-Yazzie, Evangeline. *Dzání Yázhí Naazbaa': Little Woman Warrior Who Came Home: A Story of the Navajo Long Walk.* Ill. Irving Toddy. (P)

Steptoe, John. *The Story of Jumping Mouse: A Native American Legend.* (P)

Yolen, Jane. *Encounter.* Ill. David Shannon. (I–A)

———. *Sky Dogs.* Ill. Barry Moser. (P)

Fiction

Dorris, Michael. *Morning Girl.* (I)

Erdrich, Louise. *The Birchbark House.* (I)

Goble, Paul. *Mystic Horse.* (I)

Hobbs, Will. *Bearstone.* (I–A)

O'Dell, Scott, and Elizabeth Hall. *Thunder Rolling in the Mountains.* (A)

Rohmer, Harriet, Octavia Chow, and Morris Vidaure. *The Invisible Hunters.* Ill. Joe Sam. (I–A)

Spinka, Penina Keen. *Mother's Blessing.* (I)

Strete, C. K. *Big Thunder Magic.* (P–I)

———. *When Grandfather Journeys into Winter.* (I)

Wosmek, Frances. *A Brown Bird Singing.* (I)

Nonfiction

Bruchac, Joseph. *Code Talker: A Novel about the Navajo Marines of World War Two.* (I–A)

———. *Pocahontas.* (I–A)

———. *Sacajawea.* (I–A)

Cherry, Lynn. *A River Ran Wild.* (P–I)

Freedman, Russell. *Children of the Wild West.* (I–A)

———. *Indian Chiefs.* (I–A)

Hoyt-Goldsmith, Diane. *Pueblo Storyteller.* Photos by Lawrence Migdale. (I)

Kendall, Russ. *Eskimo Boy: Life in an Inupiaq Eskimo Village.* (I)

Regguinti, Gordon. *The Sacred Harvest: Ojibway Wild Rice Gathering.* Photos by Dale Kakkak. (I–A)

Sneve, Virginia Driving Hawk. *Bad River Boys: A Meeting of the Lakota Sioux with Lewis and Clark.* (I–A)

Yolen, Jane. *Encounter.* Ill. David Shannon. (P–I–A)

Biography

Ekoomiak, Normee. *Arctic Memories.* (Inuit in Arctic Quebec) (I)

Freedman, Russell. *Indian Chiefs.* (I–A)

———. *The Life and Death of Crazy Horse.* (I–A)

Matthaei, Gay, and Jewel Grutman. *The Ledgerbook of Thomas Blue Eagle.* (I–A)

Books on Other Cultures

Appelt, Kathi. *Bayou Lullaby.* Ill. Neil Waldman. (P)

Archambault, John, and David Plummer. *Grandmother's Garden.* (P)

Beller, K. and Heather Chase. *Great Peacemakers: True Stories from Around the World.* (P–I)

Bunting, Eve. *Terrible Things.* (P–I–A)

Chin-Lee, Cynthia, and Terri de la Pena. *A Is for Americas.* (P)

Conrad, Pam. *Animal Lingo.* (P)

Durrell, Ann, and Marilyn Sachs (eds.). *The Big Book for Peace.* (P–I–A)

Fleishman, Paul. *The Matchbox Diary.* Ill. Bagram Ibatoulline. (I)

Goldin, Barbara. *The World's First Birthday: A Rosh Hashanah Story.* (P–I)

Gratz, Alan, Gruener, Ruth, and Gruener, Jack. *Prisoner B-3087.* (I–A)

Hooks, William. *The Three Little Pigs and the Fox.* Ill. S. D. Schindler. (P–I)

Igus, Toyomi. *Two Mrs. Gibsons.* Ill. Daryl Wells. (P)

Kimmel, Eric. *Baba Yaga: A Russian Folktale.* Ill. Megan Lloyd. (P)

Krensky, Stephen. *Hanukkah at Valley Forge.* Ill. Greg Harlin. (I)

Lacapa, Kathleen, and Michael Lacapa. *Less than Half, More than Whole.* (P–I)

Mayer, Marianna. *Baby Yaga and Vasilisa the Brave.* Ill. K. Y. Craft. (P–I)

Nanji, Shenaaz. *Child of Dandelions.* (I–A)

Parkinson, Siobhan. *Blue Like Friday.* (I–A)

Polacco, Patricia. *The Keeping Quilt.* (P–I)

———. *The Blessing Cup.* Ill. Patricia Polaco. (I)

———. *Fiona's Lace.* Patricia Polaco. (P)

Rosen, Michael. *Elijah's Angel: A Story for Chanukah and Christmas.* Ill. Aminah Robinson. (P–I)

Rosenblum, Richard. *Journey to the Golden Land.* (I–A)

Rosenstock, Barb, *The Noisy Paint Box: The Colors and Sounds of Kandinsky's Abstract Art.* Ill. Mary GrandPre (I)

Vagin, Vladimir. *Here Comes the Cat.* (P–I)

Wisniewski, David. *Golem.* (I)

Zusak, Markus. *The Book Thief.* (I)

Glossary

academic and cognitive diversity   The situation that results when children learn faster than, slower than, or differently from what is expected in school.

academic language   Refers to the words that are not typically used in everyday conversations, but rather vocabulary that relates to academic content.

accent   A linguistic variation in the pronunciations of sounds; the grammar remains standard.

active comprehension   Using prior knowledge, schemata, and metacognition to construct textual meaning; fostered by the use of questioning during reading.

additive approach   A thematic approach that addresses multicultural issues.

aesthetic stance   Focusing attention on personal responses to what is read.

alphabet knowledge   Knowing the names of letters, which is a strong predictor of success in early reading achievement.

alphabetic principle   Principle suggesting that letters in the alphabet map to phonemes, the minimal sound units represented in written language.

American Standard English   The grammar, vocabulary, and pronunciation that are appropriate for public speaking and writing.

analogic-based instruction   Sometimes referred to as *analogic phonics*, analogy-based instruction teaches children to use onsets and rimes they already know to help decode unknown words.

analogy   A comparison of two similar relationships.

analytic phonics   An approach to phonics teaching that emphasizes the discovery of letter–sound relationships through the analysis of known words.

anecdotal notes   Brief, written observations of revealing behavior that a teacher considers significant to understanding a child's literacy learning.

annotating text   A notetaking strategy in which students jot down thoughts within the actual text and margins that indicate their thoughts as they are reading.

anthologies   Bound collections of stories and poems in reading programs.

anticipation guide   A series of written or oral statements for individual students to respond to before reading text assignments.

antonyms   Words opposite in meaning to other words.

aptitude hypothesis   The belief that vocabulary and comprehension reflect general intellectual ability.

authentic assessment   Asking students to perform tasks that demonstrate sufficient knowledge and understanding of a subject.

autobiographical narrative   An instructional strategy to help students and teachers reflect on personal knowledge.

automated reading   A reading approach in which students listen individually to an audio recording while reading along with the written story.

automaticity   The automatic, almost subconscious recognition and understanding of written text.

basal readers   *Basal* comes from the word *base*, as the program acts as the basis for the lessons. Basal readers are highly organized reading textbooks used to teach reading and associated skills. Stories are chosen to illustrate and develop specific reading skills, which are taught in a predetermined sequence.

basal reading approach   A major approach to reading that occupies the central and broadest position on the instructional continuum. Built on scope and sequence foundations and traditionally associated with bottom-up theory, basal programs have been modified in recent years with the inclusion of language experience and literature activities.

belief system   A theoretical orientation and philosophical approach to the teaching of reading.

best practice   Thoughtful, informed, state-of-the-art teaching in which literacy-related practices are theoretically sound and supported by research.

big books   Enlarged versions of children's storybooks, distinguished by large print and illustrations, designed to offer numerous opportunities for interaction.

book-talks   Discussion opportunities for children to engage in conversations about their responses to reading books from class core study, reading workshops, or literature circles.

bottom-up model   A type of reading model that assumes that the process of translating print to meaning begins with the printed word and is initiated by decoding graphic symbols into sound.

brainstorming   A prereading activity that identifies a broad concept reflecting the main topic to be studied in an assigned reading and organizes students in small groups to generate a list of words related to the topic.

buddy journal   Written conversations between children in a journal format; promotes student interaction, cooperation, and collaboration.

categorization   Critical manipulation of words in relation to other words through the labeling of ideas, events, or objects.

checklist   A list of categories presented for specific diagnostic purposes.

choral reading   Oral reading, often of poetry, that makes use of various voice combinations and contrasts to create meaning or highlight the tonal qualities of a passage.

circular story maps   A visual representation using pictures to depict the sequence of events leading to the problem in a story.

class relationships   Conceptual hierarchies organized according to the superordinate and subordinate nature of the concepts.

close reading   Reading complex texts multiple times in order to gain multiple levels of meaning for different purposes through analysis.

cloze procedure   A strategy in which words or letters are omitted from the text and students are required to fill in the blanks using information from the passage.

code-switching   The process of moving from one variation of a language to another or between dialects and Standard English.

community of readers   The conceptualization of children, in alliance with their friends and teacher, working together in classrooms where school reading imitates adult reading; an effect created by literature-based reading programs.

comprehensive approach   An approach to instruction that adheres to the belief that teachers need to possess a strong knowledge of multiple methods for teaching reading so they can create the appropriate balance of methods needed for the children they teach.

concept circles   A vocabulary activity in which students identify conceptual relationships among words and phrases that are partitioned within a circle.

concept   A mental image of anything; can be used as the basis for grouping by common features or similar criteria.

considerate text   A textbook distinguished by its user friendliness, particularly in regard to organizational features and presentation of material.

constructivism   Learning theory associated with Jean Piaget that describes meaning-making as cognitively constructing knowledge by using prior knowledge and experience in interaction with the environment.

context clues   Words that surround an unknown word that assist the reader in word identification.

contextual search   A dictionary-related activity in which prediction of word meaning comes from reading the word in different contexts. The dictionary is used for verification of predictions.

contributions approach   A multicultural approach that typically includes culturally specific celebrations and holidays.

core books   Collection of books that forms the nucleus of a school reading program at each grade level; usually selected by a curriculum committee.

core reading programs   The primary instructional tool teachers use to teach children to learn to read. In some schools it is used interchangeably with the basal reader; in other schools it refers to the main piece of literature being used in the classroom.

criterion-referenced tests   Formal assessment designed to measure individual student achievement according to a specific criterion for performance (e.g., eight words out of ten spelled correctly).

critical literacy   Complex thinking to construct, analyze, evaluate, and interpret the various forms of text.

cross-checking   Using letter–sound information and meaning to identify words.

cross-age reading   A routine for fluency development that pairs upper-grade readers with younger children.

cultural diversity   Situation that results when a student's home, family, socioeconomic group, culture, and society differ from the predominant culture of the school.

curriculum compacting   An alternative way to accommodate gifted students in which the curriculum is compressed.

curriculum-based reader's theater   A strategy in which students work in small groups to create sections of content text in the form of an entertaining play.

decoding   The conscious or automatic processing and translating of the printed word into speech.

definitional knowledge   The ability to relate new words to known words; can be built through synonyms, antonyms, and multiple-meaning words.

Developmental Reading Assessment (DRA)   Reading assessment that includes a series of leveled texts that assess fluency and comprehension.

diagnostic test   Formal assessment intended to provide detailed information about individual students' strengths and weaknesses.

dialect   A variation of the same language spoken by members of a specific area, region, or community. The differences are typically characterized by distinctive sounds, pronunciations of words, grammar usage, and vocabulary.

dialogue journal   A journal written as a conversation between child and teacher that emphasizes meaning while providing natural, functional experiences in both writing and reading.

differentiated instruction   Teaching adapted for all learners to meet individual needs.

digital literacy   The technological and communication skills that are needed in order to be productive members of society in the twenty-first century, including the ability to locate and use Internet resources and social networking tools.

digital portfolio   A multimedia collection of student work stored and reviewed in digital format.

directed reading–thinking activity (DR–TA)   An activity that builds critical awareness of the reader's role and responsibility in interacting with the text through the process of predicting, verifying, judging, and extending thinking about text material.

disciplinary literacy   Fosters the notion that students need to be able to read math as mathematicians, history as historians, science as scientists, and so forth.

discussion webs   A strategy used in cooperative learning that requires students to explore both sides of issues during postreading discussions before drawing conclusions.

double-entry journal   A two-column journal format that gives students an opportunity to identify passages from texts and explore in writing why those passages are interesting or meaningful.

Dynamic Indicators of Basic Early Literacy Skills (DIBELS)   An assessment that includes a series of oral reading skill assessments. Short measures are used to monitor early literacy skills and provide feedback to inform instruction.

dyslexia A specific reading disability in which individuals have difficulty in processing the phonological components of language.

efferent stance Attention is focused on accumulating information from the text.

electronic texts Texts that are created and read on a computer screen.

embedded phonics instruction Often called *holistic, meaning-centered instruction,* embedded phonics teaches phonics within the context of stories that make sense to the children.

emergent literacy Children's literacy learning conceptualized as developmental, with no clear beginning or end, rather than as proceeding in distinct sequence. Thus children begin to develop literacy through everyday experiences with print long before they enter school.

environmental print Print that surrounds children in their everyday lives, such as traffic signs, restaurant signs, charts, and labels.

evaluative (or critical reading) questions Questions that focus on making a judgment about what is read.

explicit Based on stated information.

expository informational books Books that contain information that typically follows specific text structures such as description, sequence, cause and effect, comparison and contrast, and problem solving.

extension (integrating across the curriculum) Using activities such as art, music, and writing as catalysts to extend ideas and concepts initiated during a formal lesson.

fluency development lesson (FDL) An instructional framework designed to develop oral reading fluency. It incorporates the use of various repeated reading techniques such as choral reading and paired reading routines.

fluency The ability to read easily and well.

formative assessment An assessment that is used to gather information for teachers to adapt instruction to meet students' needs.

free response Active involvement or participation in reading through discussion or writing that includes inferential, evaluative, and analytic thinking about a book based on the reader's response.

graphic organizer Any diagram of key concepts or main ideas that shows their relationships to each other.

graphophonemic cues Letter–sound information that readers process during reading.

group share session Discussion period intended to help students reflect on the day's work. As part of a writing workshop plan, the session focuses on specific writing concerns.

guided reading A teaching approach designed to help individual readers build a system for processing increasingly challenging texts over time.

guided writing An instructional framework in which teachers guide students *as* they write.

high-frequency words Words that appear often in printed material.

high-stakes testing The practice of using a single test score for making education-related or personnel decisions.

idea circle A *literature circle* in which readers engage in discussions of concepts they have been exploring in trade books and other types of texts.

idea sketches Graphic organizers that students complete in small groups as they read textbook material.

implicit Based on unstated assumptions in conjunction with given information.

inclusion Incorporating the diverse needs and abilities of all students into classroom instruction.

incremental rehearsal A technique that uses flash cards to teach unknown words with a ratio of known words.

inferential questions Questions in which the reader uses background knowledge and information from the text.

inflected endings Suffixes that change the tense or degree of a word. Examples include /s/, /es/, /ies/, /d/, /ed/, /er/, /ier/, and /est/.

informal assessment Informal measures of reading that yield useful information about student performance without comparisons to the performance of a normative population.

informal reading inventory (IRI) An individually administered informal test, usually consisting of graded word lists, graded reading passages, and comprehension questions that assess how students orally and silently interact with print.

informational text Text that is explanatory in nature and conveys factual information to increase an individual's knowledge of subject matter.

informational text circles A cooperative learning strategy in which students assume different roles as they read in small groups.

inquiry learning A process in which students engage in experimentation and problem solving as they research issues and interests, gathering information from a variety of sources.

instructional conversations A teaching strategy in which the teacher scaffolds learning through divergent questions and students are encouraged to express their reactions to content on a personal level.

instructional scaffolding Providing enough instructional guidance and support for students so that they will be successful in their use of reading strategies.

instrumental hypothesis Belief in a causal chain between vocabulary knowledge and comprehension; that is, if comprehension depends in part on the knowledge of word meanings, vocabulary instruction should influence comprehension.

integrated approach A methodology that suggests the best way to teach reading is to use a combination of the greatest features of all of the approaches.

integrated instruction Another name for *literature units.*

integrated language arts approach An instructional approach in which reading, writing, listening, speaking, and viewing activities are connected through the use of literature.

interactive model   A type of reading model that assumes that translating print to meaning involves using both prior knowledge and print and that the process is initiated by the reader making predictions about meaning and/or decoding graphic symbols.

Internet inquiry   An instructional strategy designed to help students engage in research on the Internet based on the questions they raise or their interests in various topics of study.

interviewing   Periodic communication with individual students to assess reading interests and attitudes, self-perceptions, and understanding of the language-learning process.

invented spelling   When children attempt to write words based on their emerging knowledge of letter-sound associations, they are engaged in invented spelling.

invented spelling   Spellings children use early in their reading and writing development as they begin to associate letters to sounds.

jigsaw   A cooperative learning strategy in which students read selections of informational text and become experts in the topic. The experts share with members of small groups.

key pal correspondence   The electronic equivalent of pen pals.

key words   Words charged with personal meaning and feeling selected for use in helping beginning readers identify words quickly and easily.

kidwatching   See *observation.*

knowledge hypothesis   The suggestion that vocabulary and comprehension reflect general knowledge rather than intellectual ability.

KWL   (What do you *know*? What do you *want* to find out? What did you *learn*?) A three-step teaching model designed to guide and motivate children as they read to acquire information from expository texts.

language-experience activities   Activities using the natural language of children and their background experiences to share and discuss events; listen to and tell stories; dictate words, sentences, and stories; and write independently.

language-experience approach (LEA)   A major approach to reading, located on the holistic side of the instructional continuum, tied closely to interactive or top-down theory. Often considered a beginning reading approach, connections between reading and writing are becoming more prevalent in classrooms.

leveled books   Books that are categorized into stages of difficulty in order to select text based on ability.

linguistic awareness   Understanding the technical terms and labels needed to talk and think about reading.

linguistic diversity   The diversity that results when a student's first language, or language of communication at home, is not the language of instruction in the school.

literacy coach   An individual who provides professional development opportunities and resources. In-class coaching and support provide a variety of professional development activities while in a nonevaluative role.

literacy development   The stages of language experience.

literacy event   Any powerful, authentic instance of the use of language to convey meaning and understanding between a writer and reader.

literacy play center   A designated classroom area designed around familiar contexts or places and furnished with props to provide an environment in which children may play with print on their own terms.

literal questions   Questions that are based on explicitly stated information in the text.

literate environment   An environment that fosters and nurtures interest in and curiosity about written language and supports children's efforts to become readers and writers.

literature across the curriculum   Weaving an array of literature into meaningful and relevant instructional activities within the context of content area study.

literature circles   Discussions or study groups based on a collaborative strategy involving self-selection of books for reading; each group consists of students who independently selected the same book.

literature journals   Journals that invite readers to respond to literary texts; less structured than reading logs and other journals.

literature units   Lessons organized around book collections featuring unifying elements such as genre, author, or conceptual theme.

literature web   Any graphic device that illustrates the relationships between the major components in a unit of study.

literature-based instruction   A major approach to reading that encourages students to select their own trade books, with the sessions followed by teacher–student conferences at which students may be asked to read aloud from their selections; used by teachers who want to provide for individual student differences in reading abilities while focusing on meaning, interest, and enjoyment.

LOTEs   Acronym that stands for individuals who speak "Languages Other Than English."

macrocloze stories   Stories given to students with passages deleted from the text; students read the stories and discuss the missing text either orally or in writing.

media literacy   The capacity to access, analyze, evaluate, and communicate messages in a variety of forms.

metacognition   Awareness of one's own cognitive processes, including task knowledge and self-monitoring of activity.

minilesson   A brief, direct instructional exchange between teacher and students to address specific, observed learning needs of students.

miscue analysis   An informal assessment of oral reading errors to determine the extent to which readers use and coordinate graphic–sound, syntactic, and semantic information.

mixed-text informational books   Sometimes referred to as *combined-text trade books;* stories are narrated and factual information surrounds the story.

morpheme   The smallest meaningful unit of a word. For example, /un/ is a morpheme that means *not.*

multigenre project   A paper that is a collection of genres that reflect multiple responses to a book, theme, or topic. Examples of genres are postcards, letters, posters, and comic strips.

multiliteracies   Fluid representations of knowing beyond traditional text. Examples are drama, painting, photography, and technological representations.

multiple-meaning words   Words for which readers must rely on context in order to determine meaning.

multisensory activities   Activities that involve the senses, namely visual, auditory, kinesthetic, and tactile.

narrative informational texts   Books in which the author typically tells a story that conveys factual information.

narrative text   Literature that tells a story and is characterized as fiction.

new literacies   The knowledge, skills, strategies, and dispositions needed to use and adapt to the constantly changing information and communication technologies.

norms   Average scores of a sampling of students selected for testing according to factors such as age, sex, race, grade, or socioeconomic status; basis for comparing the performance of individuals or groups.

observation   An informal assessment by classroom teachers to document growth in learning by watching and recording students' literate behaviors.

onset   The initial part of a word (a consonant, consonant blend, or digraph) that precedes the vowel.

oral language comprehension   The ability to listen and accurately reconstruct what is said on the basis of understanding.

oral recitation lesson (ORL)   A lesson that makes use of direct instruction and student practice, including reading in chorus, as a means of incorporating fluency into daily reading instruction.

organizer   A frame of reference established to prepare children conceptually for ideas to be encountered in reading.

orthographic knowledge   Knowledge of common letter patterns that skilled readers use rapidly and accurately to associate with sounds.

paired reading   Structured collaborative work involving pairs of children of the same or different reading ability to foster reading fluency.

paired-word sentence generation   A teaching strategy that asks students to take two related words and create one sentence that correctly demonstrates an understanding of the words and their relationship to one another.

phonemic awareness   An understanding that speech is composed of a series of written sounds; a powerful predictor of children's later reading achievement.

phonemic segmentation   The ability to isolate and identify sounds in words.

phonics   Provides readers with a tool to pronounce words by associating sounds (phonemes) with letters (graphemes).

phonograms   Letter clusters that help form word families or rhyming words; see also *rime*.

phonological awareness   The ability to hear, recognize, and play with sounds in language. It involves hearing the sounds of language apart from meaning.

plot scaffold   An open-ended script in which students use their imaginations to create characters, a setting, a problem, and a solution.

point-of-view guide   An instructional activity for supporting comprehension in which readers approach a text selection from various perspectives or points of view.

portfolio   A compilation of an individual student's work in reading and writing, devised to reveal literacy progress as well as strengths and weaknesses.

predictable text   Literature that is distinguished by familiar or predictable characteristics of setting, story line, language patterns, or rhyme and consequently can promote fluency.

predictogram   A strategy that develops students' meaning vocabulary through the use of story elements.

prereading activities   Activities designed to help students activate prior knowledge, set purpose, and/or engage their curiosity before reading.

print knowledge   The understanding that words are represented by print, that letters of the alphabet are represented in different ways, and that letters can represent multiple sounds or the same sound represented by different letters.

professional knowledge   Knowledge acquired from an ongoing study of the practice of teaching.

progress monitoring   The process of monitoring students in order to determine growth and development of reading and writing skills and strategies. Student's performance as well as improvement or responsiveness to instruction are measured.

psycholinguistics   The study of the mental faculties involved in acting on and interacting with written language in an effort to make sense of a text.

question–answer relationships (QARs)   A comprehension strategy that enhances children's ability to answer comprehension questions by teaching them how to find the information they need to respond.

questioning the author (QtA)   A comprehension-centered instructional strategy designed to show readers how to question the author's intent while reading.

readability   The relative accessibility or difficulty of a text. Sentence length and word difficulty are among the elements used in formulas that assign grade-level readability scores for text materials.

read-aloud   Generally a group event in which literature is read orally.

reader's theater   The oral presentation of drama, prose, or poetry by two or more readers.

reader-response theory   The belief that responsibility for constructing textual meaning resides primarily with the reader and depends to a great extent on the reader's prior knowledge and experience.

reading journal A journal used in conjunction with literary texts. After a period of sustained reading, teachers use prompts to guide students' written responses to the text.

reading readiness The level of physical, mental, and emotional maturity that children need to reach to benefit from reading instruction.

reciprocal teaching An instructional strategy that builds readers' awareness of and expertise in the use of various comprehension skills and strategies.

reinforcement Exercises involving similar and contrasting examples that are used to reinforce learning in basal programs.

reliability Consistency of test results over time and administrations.

repeated readings Reading short passages of text more than once, with different levels of support, to develop rapid, fluent oral reading.

ReQuest Reciprocal questioning that encourages students to ask their own questions about material they have read.

response journal A journal entry without a teacher prompt.

response protocol A framework for teacher responses to English language learners when they respond to teacher questions.

retelling An assessment in which students identify and discuss integral parts of a story.

rime The part of the letter pattern in a word that includes the vowel and any consonants that follow; also called a *phonogram* or *word family.*

running record A method for marking miscues of beginning readers while they read.

scaffolded instruction Instruction in which teachers model strategies step by step and provide guided practice, followed by independent practice and application.

schemata Mental frameworks that humans use to organize and construct meaning.

scope and sequence General plan in basal reading programs for the introduction of skills in sequential or vertical arrangement.

scrambled stories Stories separated into parts and jumbled; students read the stories and put them back in order.

scribbling One of the primary forms of written expression; the fountainhead for writing that occurs from the moment a child grasps and uses a writing tool.

self-assessment An assessment in which students identify their strengths and weaknesses to help provide a plan for intervention.

self-monitoring Being aware of miscues, the pronunciation of unknown words, and comprehension processes during reading to develop the ability to correct oneself.

self-selection strategy A strategy that helps students monitor their own vocabulary growth by selecting unknown vocabulary words.

semantic cues The prior knowledge and experience that readers bring to a reading situation.

semantic gradients A collection of related words that go from one extreme to another, such as *hot, warm, cool, cold, freezing,* and *frigid.*

semantic mapping A strategy that shows readers and writers how to organize important information.

shared reading A strategy allowing all children in a classroom or small group to participate in the reading of a story, usually through the use of a big book with large print and illustrations.

shared writing A writing practice in which the teacher and child collaborate to compose text together, with both contributing their thoughts and ideas to the process. The teacher usually acts as a scribe and engages students in a rich discussion about the text.

Sheltered Instruction Observation Protocol (SIOP) A model for sheltered English that provides teachers with an instructional framework for teaching ELLs.

signal words Words that indicate how the author is connecting ideas.

Six Traits-Plus Model A model of writing that is characterized by the author's ability to generate ideas, effectively organize, express voice, select appropriate words, write with fluency, use correct conventions, and clearly present a piece of writing.

skill building The introduction, repetition, and reinforcement of skills at all levels of basal reading programs.

social-action approach A multicultural approach that provides students with opportunities to undertake activities and projects related to cultural issues.

sociolinguistics The study of the everyday functions of language and how interactions with others and with the environment aid language comprehension and learning.

spelling-based instruction Instruction that focuses on teaching students strategies for studying words they read and write; it is based on the idea that students need to be working on words that represent their levels of development.

standardized reading test A formal test of reading ability administered according to specific, unvarying directions; usually norm-referenced and machine-scored.

sticky-note folders A cooperative learning strategy that assists students in organizing and thinking about content area reading by providing them with a way to manipulate and group concepts, and add additional information from other resources, such as online texts and trade books.

story frames Skeletal paragraphs represented by a sequence of spaces tied together with transition words and connectors signaling lines of thought; frames can emphasize plot summary, setting, character analysis, character comparison, and problem.

story grammar The basic elements that make up a well-developed story, such as plot and setting.

story map An analysis of a story's organizational elements; used to strengthen instructional decisions.

story schema The underlying structure and relationships in a story that act as catalysts for constructing meaning and distinguishing important ideas and events.

storybook experiences Read-alouds, read-alongs, interactive reading, interactive writing, rereadings of favorite texts, and independent reading and writing.

storytelling   The act of telling a story orally without the use of text.

strands   Areas of skills developed at increasingly higher levels throughout basal reading programs.

structural analysis   A word recognition skill that involves identifying words in meaningful units such as prefixes, suffixes, and root words. Structural analysis also includes being able to identify inflected endings, compound words, and contractions.

subordinate   Inferior in rank, class, or status.

superordinate   Superior in rank, class, or status.

support reading strategy   A strategy designed to develop the ability to read fluently by combining several instructional elements.

survey test   A broad type of test that measures general performance only.

sustained silent reading   A structured activity in which children are given fixed time periods for reading silently.

synonyms   Words similar in meaning to other words.

syntactic cues   Grammatical information in a text that readers process, along with graphophonemic and semantic information, to construct meaning.

synthetic phonics   A building-block approach to phonics intended to foster the understanding of letter–sound relationships and develop phonic knowledge and skill.

technology-based instruction   An instructional approach that utilizes computers and their many capabilities.

text complexity   The difficulty of a text as measured by a quantitative measure of the text's readability, qualitative considerations of the language and clarity of the text, and the reader's ability to complete a reading task.

text connections   A comprehension strategy in which students are encouraged to share how texts relate to themselves, to other texts, or to the world.

text set   A group of trade books that have a common theme.

thematic instruction   Another name for literature units.

think sheet   A list of questions used to elicit responses about texts for discussion purposes.

think-alouds   A comprehension strategy in which students talk about their thoughts as they read aloud.

top-down model   A type of reading model that assumes that the construction of textual meaning depends on the reader's prior knowledge and experience.

trade books   Literature and informational books widely available in bookstores; used by teachers to supplement or replace sole dependence on textbooks in reading or content area instruction.

transformative approach   A multicultural approach that provides students with opportunities to read about cultural concepts and events that are different from their own, make judgments about them, think critically, and generate conclusions.

translanguaging   A view of English language learning that is characterized by speakers moving from one language (for example, English) to other languages when they communicate.

units of language   Categories of written language, ranging from the smallest unit (letters) to the largest unit (the whole text selection) that are emphasized for instructional purposes.

validity   The accuracy with which a test measures what it is designed to measure—the most important characteristic of a test.

vocabulary development   The introduction and repetition of words for reinforcement in basal reading programs.

vocabulary   The panoply of words we use, recognize, and respond to in meaningful acts of communication.

vocabulary-building skills   Linguistic skills that allow children to construct word meanings independently on the basis of context clues.

WebQuest   An electronic model in which Internet inquiry is organized to support student learning.

whole language   A theoretical perspective that focuses on the integration of all the language arts—reading, writing, speaking, listening—to create child-responsive environments for learning that are supported by literature-based instruction.

word banks   Boxes of word cards that individual students are studying as they relate to phonics, spelling, or vocabulary learning.

word knowledge rating   A strategy that helps students develop an awareness of how well they know vocabulary words by rating themselves on their knowledge of words based on a continuum.

word ladders   A game in which students add, delete, or replace letters using clues to make new words.

word part connections   A dictionary-related activity in which the unknown word is broken into word parts. The dictionary is used to verify the meaning of the word and/or word part.

word sorts   Vocabulary development through categorization activities with groups of words.

word walls   Words compiled on sheets of shelf paper hung on the wall of a classroom. Word walls are used by teachers to engage students in word study for a variety of instructional purposes.

words correct per minute (WCPM)   An assessment in which readers read aloud for 1 minute from materials used in their reading lessons. The teacher notes words read incorrectly. The assessment tracks changes in reading rates and accuracy over time and assesses the appropriateness of the text's difficulty.

words   Labels for concepts.

writing notebooks   Places where students can gather observations, thoughts, reactions, ideas, unusual words, pictures, and interesting facts for future writing.

writing process   The stages of writing, including rehearsing, drafting, revising and editing, and publishing.

writing workshop   Classroom writing time during which students are given the structure and direction they need to understand, develop, or use specific writing strategies in planning and revising drafts.

References

Aaron, R. L., & Anderson, M. K. (1981). A comparison of values expressed in juvenile magazines and basal reader series. *The Reading Teacher, 35*(3), 305–313.

Adams, A. E., & Pegg, J. (2012). Teachers' enactment of content literacy strategies in secondary science and mathematics classes. *Journal of Adolescent & Adult Literacy, 56*(2), 151–161.

Adams, M. J. (1990). *Beginning to read: Thinking and learning about print: A summary.* Urbana: University of Illinois, Center for the Study of Reading.

Adams, M. J. (2013). Common Core State Standards: Productivity is key. In S. B. Neuman and L. B. Gambrell (Eds.), *Quality reading instruction in the age of Common Core Standards* (pp. 204–218). Newark, DE: International Reading Association.

Afflerbach, P. (2004). *National Reading Conference policy brief: High-stakes testing and reading assessment.* Oak Creek, WI: National Reading Conference.

Afflerbach, P. (2007). *Understanding and using reading assessment, K–12.* Newark, DE: International Reading Association.

Afflerbach, P., & Cho, B. (2011). The classroom assessment of reading. In M. Kamil, P. Pearson, E. Moje, & P. Afflerbach (Eds.), *Handbook of reading research* (pp. 487–514). New York, NY: Routledge.

Afflerbach, P., Cho, B., Kim, J., & Clark, S. (2010). Classroom assessment of literacy. In D. Wise, R. Andrews, & J. Hoffman (Eds.), *The international handbook of English, language, and literacy teaching* (pp. 401–412). London, England: Routledge.

Agnew, A. T. (1982). Using children's dictated stories to assess code consciousness. *The Reading Teacher, 35*(4), 448–452.

Ahlness, M. (2005). Giving it away: The Earth Day groceries project. In R. A. Karchmer, M. H. Mallette, J. Kara-Soteriou, & D. J. Leu, Jr. (Eds.), *Innovative approaches to literacy education: Using the Internet to support new literacies* (pp. 28–43). Newark, DE: International Reading Association.

Allen, R. V. (1976). *Language experiences in communication.* Boston, MA: Houghton Mifflin.

Allington, R. L. (2009). If they don't read much . . . 30 years later. In E. H. Hiebert (Ed.), *Reading more, reading better* (pp. 30–54). New York, NY: Guilford.

Allington, R. L., & McGill-Franzen, A. (2003). The impact of summer reading setback on the reading achievement gap. *Phi Delta Kappan, 85*(1), 68–75.

Allington, R. (2004). Setting the record straight. *Educational Leadership, 61*, 22–25.

Allington, R. (2013a). What really matters when working with struggling readers. *The Reading Teacher, 66*(7), 520–530.

Allington, R. (2013b, April). The Reading Teacher: Literacy Research That Informs Practice. Speech presented at the International Reading Association Annual Conference, San Antonio, TX.

Allington, R. L. (1983). Fluency: The neglected reading goal. *The Reading Teacher, 36*, 556–561.

Allington, R. L. (2009). *What really matters in fluency.* Boston, MA: Pearson.

Altieri, J. L. (2011). Meeting the reading comprehension demands of each content area. In *Content counts!* (pp. 67–104). Newark, DE: International Reading Association.

Alvermann, D. E. (1991). The discussion web: A graphic aid for learning across the curriculum. *The Reading Teacher, 45*, 92–99.

Ammon, P., Simons, H., & Elster, C. (1990). *Effects of controlled, primerese language on the reading process* (Technical Report No. 45). Berkeley, CA, and Pittsburgh, PA: Center for the Study of Writing. ERIC Doc. No. ED 334542.

Anderson, R. C., & Freebody, P. (1981). Vocabulary knowledge. In J. T. Guthrie (Ed.), *Comprehension and teaching: Research perspectives.* Newark, DE: International Reading Association.

Anderson, R. C., Hiebert, E. H., Scott, J., & Wilkinson, I. A. G. (1985). *Becoming a nation of readers.* Washington, DC: National Institute of Education.

Anderson, R. C., Higgins, G. D., & Wurster, S. R. (1985). Differences in the free reading books selected by high, average, and low achievers. *The Reading Teacher, 39*, 326–330.

Angelos, S., & McGriff, N. (2002). Tracking students' reading progress. *Knowledge Quest, 30*(5), 44–46.

Anstey, M., & Bull, G. (2006). *Teaching and learning multiliteracies: Changing times, changing literacies.* Newark, DE: International Reading Association.

Armbruster, B. B., Echols, C., & Brown, A. L. (1982). The role of metacognition in reading to learn: A developmental perspective. *Volta Review, 84*, 45–56.

Armbruster, B. B., & Nagy, W. E. (1992). Vocabulary in content area lessons. *The Reading Teacher, 45*, 550–551.

Aronson, E. (1978). *The jigsaw classroom.* Beverly Hills, CA: Sage.

Ashton-Warner, S. (1959). *Spinster.* New York, NY: Simon & Schuster.

Ashton-Warner, S. (1963). *Teacher.* New York, NY: Simon & Schuster.

Ashton-Warner, S. (1972). *Spearpoint: Teachers in America.* New York, NY: Knopf.

Athans, S. K., & Devine, D. A. (2008). *Quality comprehension: A strategic model of reading instruction using read-along guides, grades 3–6.* Newark, DE: International Reading Association.

Atkinson, T. S., Matusevich, M. N., & Huber, L. (2009). Making science trade book choices for elementary classrooms. *The Reading Teacher, 62*(6), 484–497.

Atwell, N. (1998). *In the middle: New understandings about writing, reading, and learning* (2nd ed.). Portsmouth, NH: Heinemann.

Baildon, R., & Baildon, M. (2008). Guiding independence: Developing a research tool to support student decision making in selecting online information sources. *The Reading Teacher, 61*(8), 636–647.

Baines, L. (2000). Same facts, different audience. In L. Baines & A. J. Kunkel (Eds.), *Going Bohemian: Activities that engage adolescents in the art of writing well* (pp. 78–80). Newark, DE: International Reading Association.

Banks, J. A. (2014). *An introduction to multicultural education* (5th ed.). Boston, MA: Pearson.

Barone, D. (1996). Whose language? Learning from bilingual learners in a developmental first-grade classroom. In D. J. Leu, C. K. Kinzer, & K. Hinchman (Eds.), *Literacies for the 21st century: Research and practice* (pp. 170–182). Chicago, IL: National Reading Conference.

Barron, R. (1969). The use of vocabulary as an advance organizer. In H. L. Herber & P. Sanders (Eds.), *Research in reading in the content areas: First report* (pp. 29–39). Syracuse, NY: Syracuse University Reading and Language Arts Center.

Bauer, E. B. (2009). Informed additive literacy instruction for ELLs. *The Reading Teacher, 62*(5), 446–448.

Baumann, J. F., & Heubach, K. M. (1996). Do basal readers deskill teachers? A national survey of educators' use and opinions of basals. *Elementary School Journal, 96*(5), 511–526.

Bean, T. W., & Harper, H. (2011). The context of English language arts learning: The high school years. In D. Lapp & D. Fisher (Eds.), *Handbook of research on teaching the English language arts* (3rd ed., pp. 60–75). New York, NY: Routledge.

Bear, D. R., Helman, L., Templeton, S., Invernizzi, M., & Johnston, F. (2007). *Words their way with English language learners: Word study for phonics, vocabulary and spelling instruction.* Upper Saddle River, NJ: Pearson.

Bear, D. R., Invernizzi, M., Templeton, S., & Johnston, F. (1996). *Words their way: Word study for phonics, vocabulary, and spelling instruction.* Upper Saddle River, NJ: Prentice Hall.

Bear, D. R., Invernizzi, M., Templeton, S., & Johnston, F. (2000). *Words their way: Word study for phonics, vocabulary, and spelling instruction* (2nd ed.). Upper Saddle River, NJ: Prentice Hall.

Bear, D. R., Invernizzi, M., Templeton, S., & Johnston, F. (2008). *Words their way: Word study for phonics, vocabulary, and spelling instruction* (4th ed.). Upper Saddle River, NJ: Pearson.

Bear, D. R., & Templeton, S. (1998). Explorations in developmental spelling: Foundations for learning and teaching phonics, spelling, and vocabulary. *The Reading Teacher, 52,* 222–242.

Beaver, J., & Carter, M. (2005). *Developmental reading assessment* (2nd ed.). Upper Saddle River, NJ: Celebration Press/Pearson.

Beck, I. L., & Juel, C. (1995). The role of decoding in learning to read. *American Educator, 19*(2), 8, 21–25, 39–42.

Beck, I. L., McKeown, M. G., & Kucan, L. (2002). *Bringing words to life.* New York, NY: Guilford.

Beck, I. L., & McKeown, M. G. (1991). Social studies texts are hard to understand: Mediating some of the difficulties. *Language Arts, 68,* 482–490.

Beck, I. L., & McKeown, M. G. (2001). Text talk: Capturing the benefits of read-aloud experiences for young children. *The Reading Teacher, 55*(1), 10–20.

Beck, I. L., McKeown, M. G., Hamilton, R. L., & Kucan, L. (1997). *Questioning the author: An approach for enhancing student engagement with text.* Newark, DE: International Reading Association.

Beck, I. L., McKeown, M. G., & Kucan, L. (2008). *Creating robust vocabulary: Frequently asked questions and extended examples.* New York, NY: Guilford Press.

Beck, I. L., McKeown, M. G., & McCaslin, E. (1983). All contexts are not created equal. *Elementary School Journal, 83,* 177–181.

Beck, I. L., McKeown, M. G., McCaslin, E., & Burket, A. (1979). *Instructional dimensions that may affect reading comprehension: Examples of two commercial reading programs.* Pittsburgh, PA: University of Pittsburgh Language Research and Development Center.

Beck, I. L., McKeown, M. G., & Omanson, R. (1987). The effects and uses of diverse vocabulary instructional techniques. In M. McKeown & M. Cartis (Eds.), *The nature of vocabulary acquisition.* Mahwah, NJ: Erlbaum.

Beers, K., & Probst, R. E. (2013). *Notice & note: Strategies for close reading.* Portsmouth, NH: Heinemann.

Benjamin, R., Schwanenflugel, P., Meisinger, E., Groff, C., Kuhn, M., & Steiner, L. (2013). A spectrographically grounded scale for evaluating reading expressiveness. *Reading Research Quarterly, 48*(2), 105–133.

Bennett-Armistead, V., & Duke, N. K. (2003). *Reading and writing informational text in the primary grades: Research-based practices.* New York, NY: Teaching Resources.

Bennett-Armistead, V., Duke, N., & Moses, A. (2005). *Literacy and the youngest learner.* New York, NY: Scholastic.

Benton, M. (1984). The methodology vacuum in teaching literature. *Language Arts, 61,* 265–275.

Betts, E. A. (1946). *Foundations of reading instruction.* New York, NY: American Book Company.

Beyersdorfer, J. M., & Schauer, D. K. (1989). Semantic analysis to writing: Connecting words, books, and writing. *Journal of Reading, 32,* 500–508.

Biemiller, A. (2006). Vocabulary development and instruction. In D. Dickinson & S. B. Neuman (Eds.), *Handbook of early literacy research* (Vol. 6, pp. 41–51). New York, NY: Guilford Press.

Bissex, G. (1980). *GNYS AT WRK: A child learns to write and read.* Cambridge, MA: Harvard University Press.

Blachowicz, C., & Fisher, P. (1996). *Teaching vocabulary in all classrooms.* Columbus, OH: Merrill.

Blachowicz, C. L. (1986). Making connections: Alternatives to the vocabulary notebook. *Journal of Reading, 29,* 643–649.

Blachowicz, C. L. Z., & Fisher, P. (2000). Vocabulary instruction. In M. Kamil, P. Mosenthal, P. Pearson, & R. Barr (Eds.), *Handbook of reading research* (Vol. 3, pp. 503–523). Mahwah, NJ: Erlbaum.

Blachowicz, C. L. Z., & Fisher, P. (2010). *Teaching vocabulary in all classrooms* (4th ed.). Boston, MA: Pearson.

Blachowicz, C. Z., & Fisher, P. J. (2006). *Teaching vocabulary in all classrooms.* Upper Saddle River, NJ: Pearson Education.

Black, P., Harrison, C., Lee, C., Marshall, B., & Wiliam, D. (2004). Working inside the black box: Assessment for learning in the classroom. *Phi Delta Kappan, 86*(1), 8–21.

Black, R. W. (2009). English-language learners, fan communities, and 21st century skills. *Journal of Adolescent & Adult Literacy, 52*(8), 688–697.

Blair, T. R., Rupley, W. H., & Nichols, D. W. (2007). The effective teacher of reading: Considering the "what" and "how" of instruction. *The Reading Teacher, 60,* 432–438.

Blanchard, J. S., & Farstrup, A. E. (2011). Technologies, digital media, and reading instruction. In S. Jay Samuels & A. E. Farstrup (Eds.), *What research has to say about reading instruction* (4th ed.). Newark, DE: International Reading Association.

Blume, J. (1970). *Are you there, God? It's me, Margaret.* New York, NY: Dell.

Bomer, K. (2005). Missing the children: When politics and programs impede our teaching. *Language Arts, 82,* 168–176.

Bond, G., & Dykstra, R. (1967). The cooperative research programs in first-grade reading. *Reading Research Quarterly, 2,* 135–142.

Booth, D. (2001). *Reading and writing in the middle years.* Portland, ME: Stenhouse.

Bowman, B., Donovan, M., & Burns, M. (Eds.). (2001). *Eager to learn: Educating our preschoolers.* Washington, DC: National Academy Press.

Boyd, F. B., Causey, L. L., & Galda, L. (2015). Culturally diverse literature: Enriching variety in an era of Common Core State Standards. *The Reading Teacher, 68*(5), 378–387.

Boyd, F. B., & Ikpeze, C. H. (2007). Navigating a literacy landscape: Teaching conceptual understanding with multiple text types. *Journal of Literacy Research, 39,* 217–248.

Boyles, N. (2012, 2013). Closing in on close reading. *Educational Leadership, 70*(4), 36–41. Retrieved March 2016 from http://www.ascd.org/publications/educational-leadership/dec12/vol70/num04/Closing-in-on-Close-Reading.aspx

Bradley, J. M., & Talgott, M. R. (1987). Reducing reading anxiety. *Academic Therapy, 22,* 349–358.

Brassell, D., & Rasinski, T. (2008). *Comprehension that works: Taking students beyond ordinary understanding to deep comprehension.* Huntington Beach, CA: Shell Education.

Bromley, K. (1989). Buddy journals make the reading-writing connection. *The Reading Teacher, 43,* 122–129.

Bromley, K. (2007). Nine things every teacher should know about words and vocabulary instruction. *Journal of Adolescent & Adult Literacy, 50,* 528–537.

Brown, A. L. (1985). Metacognition: The development of selective attention strategies for learning from texts. In H. S. Singer & R. B. Ruddell (Eds.), *Theoretical models and processes of reading* (3rd ed., pp. 501–526). Newark, DE: International Reading Association.

Brown, M. (2011). *Pablo Neruda: Poet of the people.* New York, NY: Henry Holt.

Brown, R. (2008). The road not yet taken: A transactional approach to comprehension Instruction. *The Reading Teacher 61*(7), 538–547.

Brown, S. C., & Kysilka, M. L. (2002). *Applying multicultural and global concepts in the classroom and beyond.* Boston, MA: Allyn & Bacon.

Brozo, W. G. (2009/2010). Response to intervention or responsive instruction? Challenges and possibilities of response to intervention for adolescent literacy. *Journal of Adolescent & Adult Literacy, 53*(4), 277–281.

Brozo, W. G., & Tomlinson, C. M. (1986). Literature: The key to lively content courses. *The Reading Teacher, 40,* 288–293.

Brueck, J., & Lenhart, L. (2015). EBooks and TPack: What teachers need to know. *The Reading Teacher, 68*(5), 373–376.

Buehl, D. (2011). Mentoring students in disciplinary literacy. In *Developing readers in the academic disciplines* (pp. 1–30). Newark, DE: International Reading Association.

Buehl, D., & Moore, D. W. (2009). Linking research to practice in disciplinary instruction. *Journal of Adolescent & Adult Literacy, 52*(6), 535–537.

Bulion, L. (2006). *Hey there, stink bug!* Watertown, MA: Charlesbridge.

Burkins, J. M., & Croft, M. M. (2010). *Preventing misguided reading: New strategies for guided reading teachers.* Newark, DE: International Reading Association.

Bus, A., Van Ijzendoorn, M., & Pellegrini, A. (1995). Joint book reading makes for success in learning to read: A meta-analysis on intergeneration transmission of literacy. *Review of Educational Research, 65,* 1–21.

Butler, A. (1988). *Shared book experience.* Crystal Lake, IL: Rigby.

Butler-Pascoe, M. E., & Wiburg, K. M. (2003). *Technology and teaching English language learners.* Boston, MA: Allyn & Bacon.

Byers-Heinlein, K., Burns, T. C., & Werker, J. F. (2010). The roots of bilingualism in newborns. *Psychological Science, 21*(3), 343–348.

Cabell, S., Tortorelli, L., & Gerde, H. (May 2013). How do I write . . . ? Scaffolding preschoolers' early writing skills. *The Reading Teacher, 66*(8), 650–659.

Cabell, S. Q., Tortorelli, L. S., & Gerde, H. K. (2013). How do I write. . . . ? Scaffolding preschoolers' early writing skills. *The Reading Teacher, 66*(8), 650–659.

Calkins, L. M. (1983). *Lessons from a child.* Portsmouth, NH: Heinemann.

Calkins, L. M. (1994). *The art of teaching writing.* Portsmouth, NH: Heinemann.

Calkins, L., Montgomery, K., & Santman, D. (1998). *A teacher's guide to standardized reading tests: Knowledge is power.* Portsmouth, NH: Heinemann.

Calo, K. M., Woolard-Ferguson, T., & Koitz, E. (2013). Fluency Idol: Using pop culture to engage students and boost fluency skills. *The Reading Teacher, 66*(6), 454–458.

Cambourne, B. (2016, January 15). The "ideal" learning culture: Can the conditions of learning inform teaching practice? [Web log post] Retrieved from http://www.cambourneconditionsoflearning.com.au/conditions-of-learning-blog-spot/the-ideal-learning-culture-can-the-conditions-of-learning-inform-teaching-practice

Cambourne, B. (1988). *The whole story: Natural learning and the acquisition of literacy in the classroom.* Auckland, New Zealand: Ashton Scholastic.

Cambourne, B. (1993). *The whole story: Natural learning & the acquisition of literacy in the classroom.* New York, NY: Scholastic.

Cambourne, B. (2001). Conditions for learning. *The Reading Teacher, 54,* 784–786.

Carlisle, J. F., & Stone, C. A. (2005). Exploring the role of morphemes in word reading. *Reading Research Quarterly, 40,* 428–447.

Carrick, L. U. (2006). Readers theatre across the curriculum. In T. Rasinski, C. Blachowicz, & K. Lems (Eds.), *Fluency instruction: Research-based best practices* (pp. 209–230). New York, NY: Guilford Press.

Carrick, L. U. (2009). *The effects of readers theatre on fluency and comprehension: A study on fifth-grade students in a regular classroom.* Saarbrucken, Germany: VDM.

Cazden, C. (1983). Adult assistance to language development: Scaffolds, models, and direct instruction. In C. Cazden (Ed.), *Developing literacy: Young children's use of language.* Newark, DE: International Reading Association.

Chall, J. (1967). *Learning to read: The great debate.* New York, NY: McGraw-Hill.

Chall, J. S. (1983). *Stages of reading development.* New York, NY: McGraw-Hill.

Chapman, V. G., & Sopko, D. (2003). Developing strategic use of combined-text trade books. *The Reading Teacher, 57*(3), 236–239.

Chappuis, J. (2005). Helping students understand assessment. *Educational Leadership, 63*(3), 39–43.

Charron, N. N. (2007). "I learned that there's a state called Victoria and he has six blue-tongued lizards!" *The Reading Teacher, 60,* 762–769.

Chomsky, C. (1970). Reading, writing, and phonology. *Harvard Educational Review, 40,* 287–309.

Chomsky, C. (1972). Stages in language development and reading exposure. *Harvard Educational Review, 42,* 1–33.

Chomsky, C. (1976). After decoding, what? *Language Arts, 53,* 288–296, 314.

Chomsky, C. (1979). Approaching reading through invented spelling. In L. B. Resnick & P. A. Weaver (Eds.), *Theory and practice of early reading* (Vol. 2, p. 43). Mahwah, NJ: Erlbaum.

Christie, J., & Burstein, K. (February, 2010). The Literacy Coaching Institute, Oklahoma State University, Norman, OK.

Ciechanowski, K. M. (2009). "A squirrel came and pushed earth": Popular culture and scientific ways of thinking for ELLs. *The Reading Teacher, 62*(7), 558–568.

Clay, M. M. (1975). *What did I write? Beginning writing behaviour.* Portsmouth, NH. Heinemann.

Clay, M. (1992). *Early detection of reading difficulties* (3rd ed.). Portsmouth, NH: Heinemann.

Clay, M. (2005). *An observation survey of early literacy achievement.* Portsmouth, NH: Heinemann.

Clay, M. M. (1979). *Concepts about print test.* Portsmouth, NH: Heinemann.

Clay, M. M. (1985). *The early detection of reading difficulties: A diagnostic survey with recovery procedures.* Portsmouth, NH: Heinemann.

Clay, M. M. (1988). Exploring with a pencil. *Reading Today, 6*(20), 179–185.

Clay, M. M. (1991). *Becoming literate: The construction of inner control.* Portsmouth, NH: Heinemann.

Clay, M. M. (2001). *Change over time in children's literacy development.* Portsmouth, NH: Heinemann.

Clymer, T. (1963). The utility of phonic generalizations in the primary grades. *The Reading Teacher, 16,* 252–258.

Coaches, controversy, consensus. (2004 April/May). *Reading Today, 21*(5), 1.

Coiro, J. (2003). Exploring literacy on the Internet: Reading comprehension on the Internet: Expanding our understanding of reading comprehension to encompass new literacies. *The Reading Teacher, 56,* 458–464.

Coiro, J., & Castek, J. (2011). Assessment frameworks for teaching and learning English language arts in the digital age. In D. Lapp & D. Fisher (Eds.), *Handbook of research on teaching the English language arts* (3rd ed., pp. 314–321). New York, NY: Routledge.

Coiro, J., Knobel, M., Lankshear, C., & Leu, D. J. (2008). Central issues in new literacies and new literacies research. In J. Coiro, M. Knobel, C., Lankshear, & D. J. Leu (Eds.), *Handbook of research in new literacies* (pp. 1–21). Mahwah, NJ: Erlbaum.

Coiro, J., & Moore, D. W. (2012). New literacies and adolescent learners: An interview with Julie Coiro. *Journal of Adolescent & Adult Literacy, 55*(6), 551–553.

Cole, J. (1990). *The magic school bus: Inside the human body.* New York, NY: Scholastic.

Coleman, M., & West, T. (2009). *Roadmap to Pre-K RTI: Applying Response to Intervention in Preschool Settings.* A publication of the National Center for Learning Disabilities, Inc. New York, NY.

Coleman, D., & Pimentel, S. (2012). *Revised publishers' criteria for the Common Core State Standards in English language arts and literacy, grades 3–12.* Retrieved from the Common Core Standards Initiative at www.corestandards.org/assets/Publishers_Criteria_for_3-12.pdf

Coleman, D., & Pimentel, S. (2012). *Revised publishers' criteria for the Common Core State Standards in English language arts and literacy, grades K–2.* National Governors Association Center for Best Practices (NGA Center) and the Council of Chief State School Officers (CCSSO). Retrieved from www.corestandards.org/resources

Coleman, J. M., Bradley, L. G., & Donovan, C. A. (2012). Visual representations in second graders' information book compositions. *The Reading Teacher, 66*(1), 31–45.

Collins, S. (2008). *The hunger games.* New York, NY: Scholastic.

Confrey, J. (1990). What constructivism implies for teaching. In R. B. Davis, C. A. Maher, & N. Noddings (Eds.), *Constructivist views on the teaching and learning of mathematics* (pp. 107–124). Reston, VA: National Council of Teachers of Mathematics.

Connelly, F. M., & Clandinin, D. J. (1988). *Teachers as curriculum planners: Narrative of experience.* New York, NY: Teachers College Press.

Cooper, P., & Gray, P. (1984). *Teaching listening as an interactive process.* Paper presented at the International Reading Association Annual Convention, Atlanta.

Cornett, C. E. (2006). Center stage: Arts-based read-aloud. *The Reading Teacher, 60,* 234–240.

Cowley, J. (1991, October). Joy of big books. *Instructor, 101,* 19.

Cox, K. E., & Guthrie, J. T. (2001). Motivational and cognitive contributions to students' amount of reading. *Contemporary Educational Psychology, 26*(1), 116–131.

Cramer, R. L. (1975). Reading to children: Why and how. *The Reading Teacher, 28,* 460–463.

Cramer, R. L. (1978). *Children's writing and language growth.* Columbus, OH: Merrill.

Crotteau, M. (2007). Honoring dialect and culture: Pathways to student success on high-stakes writing assessments. *English Journal, 96*(4), 27–32.

Cullinan, B., & Galda, L. (1994). *Literature and the child* (3rd ed.). New York, NY: Harcourt Brace.

Cummins, J. (1986). Empowering minority students: A framework for intervention. *Harvard Educational Review, 56,* 18–36.

Cummins, J. (1989). *Empowering minority students.* Sacramento, CA: Association of Bilingual Education.

Cummins, J. (2011). Literacy engagement: Fueling academic growth for English learners. *The Reading Teacher, 65*(2), 142–146.

Cummins, J., Brown, K., & Sayers, D. (2007). *Literacy, technology, and diversity.* Boston, MA: Allyn & Bacon.

Cunningham, A. J., & Carroll, J. M. (2015). Early predictors of phonological and morphological awareness and the link with reading: evidence from children with different patterns of early deficit. *Applied Psycholinguistics, 36*(3), 509–531.

Cunningham, A. E., & Stanovich, K. E. (1998). What reading does for the mind. *American Educator, 22*(1/2), 8–15.

Cunningham, J. W., Cunningham, P. M., Hoffman, J. V., & Yopp, H. K. (1998). *Phonemic awareness and the teaching of reading: A position statement from the board of directors of the International Reading Association.* Newark, DE: International Reading Association.

Cunningham, P. (1987). Action phonics. *The Reading Teacher, 41,* 247–249.

Cunningham, P. M. (1995). *Phonics they use: Words for reading and writing* (2nd ed.). New York, NY: HarperCollins.

Cunningham, P. M. (2000). *Phonics they use: Words for reading and writing* (3rd ed.). New York, NY: Longman.

Cunningham, P. M. (2005). *Phonics they use: Words for reading and writing* (4th ed.). New York, NY: Pearson.

Cunningham, P. M. (2009). *Phonics they use: Words for reading and writing* (5th ed.). Boston, MA: Pearson.

Cunningham, P. M., & Cunningham, J. W. (2002). What we know about how to teach phonics. In A. E. Farstrup & S. J. Samuels (Eds.), *What research has to say about reading instruction* (pp. 87–109). Newark, DE: International Reading Association.

D'Alessandro, M. (1990). Accommodating emotionally handicapped children through a literature-based reading program. *The Reading Teacher, 44,* 288–293.

Daane, M. C., Campbell, J. R., Grigg, W. S., Goodman, M. J., & Oranje, A. (2005). *Fourth-grade students reading aloud: NAEP 2002 special study of oral reading* (NCES 2006-469). U.S. Department of Education. Institute of Education Sciences, National Center for Education Statistics. Washington, DC: Government Printing Office.

Dale, E. (1965). Vocabulary measurement: Techniques and major findings. *Elementary English, 42,* 895–901.

Dale, E., & Chall, J. (1948). A formula for predicting readability. *Educational Research Bulletin, 27,* 11–20, 28.

Dalton, B. (2013). Engaging children in close reading. *The Reading Teacher, 66*(8), 642–649.

Daniel, S. M., & Pacheco, M. B. (2015). Translanguaging practices and perspectives of four multilingual teens. *Journal of Adolescent and Adult Literacy,* 1–11. doi:10.1002/jaal.500

Daniels, H. (1994). *Literature circles: Voice and choice in one student-centered classroom.* York, ME: Stenhouse.

Danzak, R. L. (2011). Defining identities through multiliteracies: EL teens narrate their immigration experiences as graphic stories. *Journal of Adolescent & Adult Literacy, 55*(3), 187–196.

DaSilva Iddings, A. C., Risko, V. J., & Rampulla, M. P. (2009). When you don't speak their language: Guiding English-language learners through conversations about text. *The Reading Teacher, 63*(1), 52–61.

Davis, D. C. (1973). *Playway: Education for reality.* Minneapolis, MN: Winston.

Davis, F. B. (1944). Fundamental factors of comprehension in reading. *Psychometrika, 9,* 185–197.

Deighton, L. (1970). *Vocabulary development in the classroom.* New York, NY: Teachers College Press.

dePaola, T. (1973). *Charlie needs a cloak.* New York, NY: Simon & Schuster.

Dewitz, P., & Jones, J. (2013). Using basal readers: From dutiful fidelity to intelligent decision making. *The Reading Teacher, 66*(5), 391–400.

Dewitz, P., Leahy, S., Jones, J., & Sullivan, P. (2010). *The essential guide to selecting and using core reading programs.* Newark, DE: International Reading Association.

Dickinson, D. K., & Tabors, P. O. (2001). *Beginning literacy with language: Young children learning at home and school.* Baltimore, MD: Paul H. Brookes.

Dickinson, D., & Neuman, B. (Eds.). (2006). *Handbook of early literacy research: Volume II.* New York, NY: Guilford Press.

Dickinson, D., & Smith, M. (1994). Long-term effects of preschool teachers book readings on low-income children's vocabulary and story understanding. *Reading Research Quarterly, 29*(2), 105–122.

Dix, S. (2006). I'll do it my way: Three writers and their revision practices. *The Reading Teacher, 59,* 566–573.

Dobler, E. (2013). Authentic reasons for close reading: How to motivate students to take another look. *Reading Today, 30*(6), 13–15.

Dolch, E. W. (1948). *Problems in reading.* Champaign, IL: Garrard Press.

Donovan, C. A., Smolkin, L. B., & Lomax, R. G. (2000). Beyond the independent-level text: Readability of first graders' self-selections. *Reading Psychology, 21,* 309–333.

Dorn, L. J., & Soffos, C. (2001). *Shaping literate minds: Developing self-regulated learners.* Portland, ME: Stenhouse.

Dowhower, S. L. (1987). Effects of repeated reading in secondgrade transitional readers' fluency and comprehension. *Reading Research Quarterly, 22,* 389–406.

Dowhower, S. L. (1989). Repeated reading: Research into practice. *The Reading Teacher, 43,* 502–507.

Dowhower, S. L. (1991). Speaking of prosody: Fluency's unattended badfellow. *Theory into Practice, 30,* 165–176.

Dowhower, S. L. (1994). Repeated reading revisited: Research into practice. *Reading and Writing Quarterly, 10*(4) 343–358.

Downing, J. (1979). *Reading and reasoning.* New York, NY: Springer-Verlag.

Dray, M. (2005). *Dougal the garbage dump bear.* La Jolla, CA: Kane/Miller.

Dreher, M. J., & Gray, J. L. (2009). Compare, contrast, comprehend: Using compare–contrast text structures with ELLs in K–3 classrooms. *The Reading Teacher, 63*(2), 132–141.

Drew, S. V. (2012/2013). Open up the ceiling on the Common Core State Standards: Preparing students for 21st-century literacy—now. *Journal of Adolescent & Adult Literacy, 56*(4), 321–330.

Drucker, M. J. (2003). What reading teachers should know about ESL learners. *The Reading Teacher, 57*(1), 22–29.

Duin, A., & Graves, M. (1987). Intensive vocabulary instruction as a prewriting technique. *Reading Research Quarterly, 22,* 311–330.

Duke, N. K. (2004). What research has to say about reading: The case for informational text. *Educational Leadership, 61*(6), 40–44. Retrieved March 12, 2016, from http://www.ascd.org/publications/educational-leadership/mar04/vol61/num06/The-Case-for-Informational-Text.aspx

Duke, N. (2003). Reading to learn from the very beginning: Information books in early childhood. *Young Children, 58*(2), 14–20.

Duke, N. K., & Bennett-Armistead, V. S. (2003). *Reading and writing informational text in the primary grades: Research-based practices.* New York, NY: Scholastic.

Duke, N. K., Bennett-Armistead, V. S., & Roberts, E. M. (2002). Incorporating information text in the primary grades. In C. Roller (Ed.), *Comprehensive reading instruction across grade levels* (pp. 40–54). Newark, DE: International Reading Association.

Dupuis, M. M., & Snyder, S. L. (1983). Develop concepts through vocabulary: A strategy for reading specialists to use with content teachers. *Journal of Reading, 26,* 297–305.

Durkin, D. (1966). *Children who read early.* New York, NY: Teachers College Press.

Durkin, D. (1972). *Teaching young children to read.* Boston, MA: Allyn & Bacon.

Durkin, D. (1980). *Teaching young children to read* (3rd ed.). Boston, MA: Allyn & Bacon.

Durkin, D. (1988). *A classroom observation study of reading instruction in kindergarten* (Technical Report No. 422). Champaign, IL: University of Illinois, Center for the Study of Reading.

Durrell, D. D. (1963). *Phonograms in primary grade words.* Boston, MA: Boston University Press.

Duthie, C., & Zimet, E. K. (1992). "Poetry is like directions for your imagination!" *The Reading Teacher, 46,* 14–24.

Dymock, S. (2005). Teaching expository text structure awareness. *The Reading Teacher, 59,* 177–182.

Ebner, R. J., & Ehri, L. C. (2013). Vocabulary learning on the Internet: Using a structured think-aloud procedure. *The Reading Teacher, 56*(6), 480–489.

Echevarria, J., Vogt, M., & Short, D. J. (2008). *Making content comprehensible for English-language learners: The SIOP model* (3rd ed.). Boston, MA: Allyn & Bacon.

Echevarria, J., Vogt, M., & Short, D. J. (2012). *Making content comprehensible for English language learners: The SIOP model* (4th ed.). Boston, MA: Pearson.

Education Market Research. (2010). *Elementary reading market: Teaching methods, textbooks/materials used and needed, and market size.* Rockaway Park, NY: Author.

Edwards, P. A. (2010). Reconceptualizing literacy. *Reading Today 6* (27), 22.

Ehmann, S., & Gayer, K. (2009). *I can write like that! A guide to mentor texts and craft studies for writers' workshop, K–6.* Newark, DE: International Reading Association.

Ehren, B. J. (2013). Expanding pockets of excellence in RTI. *The Reading Teacher, 66*(6), 449–453.

Ehri, L. C. (1991). Development of the ability to read words. In R. Barr, M. L. Kamil, P. Mosenthal, & P. D. Pearson (Eds.), *Handbook of reading research* (2nd ed., pp. 383–417). New York, NY: Longman.

Ehri, L. C. (1994). Development of the ability to read words: Update. In R. Ruddell & H. Singer (Eds.), *Theoretical models and processes of reading* (4th ed., pp. 323–358). Newark, DE: International Reading Association.

Ehri, L. C. (1995). Teachers need to know how word reading processes develop to teach reading effectively to beginners. In C. N. Hedley, P. Antonacci, & M. Rabinowitz (Eds.), *Thinking and literacy: The mind at work.* Mahwah, NJ: Erlbaum.

Ehri, L. C. (2005). Learning to read words: Theory, findings, and issues. *Scientific Studies of Reading, 9*(2), 167–188.

Ehri, L. C. (2011). Teaching phonemic awareness and phonics in the language arts classroom. In D. Lapp & D. Fisher (Eds.), *Handbook of research on teaching the English language arts* (3rd ed., pp. 231–237). New York, NY: Routledge.

Ehri, L., Nunes, S., Willows, D., Schuster, B., Yaghoub-Zadeh, Z., & Shanahan, T. (2001). Phonemic awareness instruction helps children learn to read: Evidence from the national reading panel's meta-analysis. *Reading Research Quarterly, 36,* 250–287.

Eisner, E. (1997). Cognition and representation: A way to pursue the American dream? *Phi Delta Kappan, 78,* 349–353.

Enz, B. J., & Morrow, L. M. (2009). *Assessing preschool literacy development.* Newark, DE: International Reading Association.

Eurydice Network. (2011). *Teaching reading in Europe: Contexts, policies and practices.* Brussels, Belgium: Education, Audiovisual and Culture Executive Agency. Retrieved from eacea.ec.europa.eu/education

Evanchan, G. (2015). The development of fluency and comprehension literacy skills of second grade students by providing regular use of the fluency development lesson. Unpublished doctoral dissertation. The University of Akron: Akron, Ohio.

Fang, Z. (2008). Going beyond the Fab Five: Helping students cope with the unique linguistic challenges of expository reading in intermediate grades. *The Reading Teacher, 51*(6), 476–487.

Farr, R., & Tone, B. (1998). *Assessment portfolio and performance* (2nd ed.). Orlando, FL: Harcourt Brace.

Faver, S. (2009). Repeated reading of poetry can enhance reading fluency. *The Reading Teacher, 62*(4), 350–352.

Fielding, L. G., Wilson, P. T., & Anderson, R. C. (1986). A new focus on free reading: The role of trade books in reading instruction. In T. Raphael (Ed.), *The contexts of school-based literacy* (pp. 149–160). New York, NY: Random House.

Fillmore, L. W., & Fillmore, C. J. (n.d.). *Understanding Language: What does text complexity mean for English language learners and language minority students?* Retrieved January 2016 from http://ell.stanford. edu/sites/default/files/pdf/academic-papers/06-LWF%20CJF%20 Text%20Complexity%20FINAL_0.pdf

Fisette, D. (1993). Practical authentic assessment: Good kid watchers know what to teach next! *The California Reader, 26*(4), 4–9.

Fisher, D., Frey, N., & Lapp, D. (2016). *Text complexity: Stretching readers with texts and tasks* (2nd ed.). Thousand Oaks, CA: Corwin.

Fisher, D., & Frey, N. (2015). Scaffolded reading instruction of content-area texts. *The Reading Teacher, 67*(5), 347–351.

Fisher, D., Frey, N., & Lapp, D. (2012). *Raising rigor in reading.* Newark, DE: International Reading Association.

Fisher, D., Lapp, D., & Frey, N. (2011). Comprehension: The cooperation of many faces. In D. Lapp & D. Fisher (Eds.), *Handbook of research on teaching the English language arts* (3rd ed., pp. 258–263). New York, NY: Routledge.

Fisher, P., Blachowicz, C. L. Z., & Watts-Taffe, S. (2011). Vocabulary instruction. In D. Lapp & D. Fisher (Eds.), *Handbook of research on teaching the English language arts* (pp. 252–257). New York, NY: Routledge.

Fitzgerald, J., & Graves, M. F. (2004). *Scaffolding reading experiences for English-language learners.* Norwood, MA: Christopher-Gordon.

Fleming, N. D., & Mills, C. (1992). Not another inventory, rather a catalyst for reflection. *To Improve the Academy, 11,* 137.

Flesch, R. (1948). A new readability yardstick. *Journal of Applied Psychology, 32,* 221–233.

Flesch, R. (1955). *Why Johnny can't read—And what you can do about it.* New York, NY: Harper & Brothers.

Fletcher, R. (1996). *A writer's notebook: Unlocking the writer within you.* New York, NY: Avon.

Flippo, R. F. (2014). *Assessing readers: Qualitative diagnosis and instruction* (2nd ed.). Newark, DE: International Reading Association.

Flynn, R. M. (2004, 2005). Curriculum-based readers theatre: Setting the stage for reading and retention. *The Reading Teacher, 58,* 360–365.

Flynt, E. S., & Brozo, W. G. (2009). It's all about the teacher. *The Reading Teacher, 62*(6), 536–538.

Fosnot, C. (1996). *Constructivism: Theory, perspectives, and practice.* New York, NY: Teachers College Press.

Fountas, I. C., & Pinnell, G. S. (1996). *Guided reading: Good first teaching for all children.* Portsmouth, NH: Heinemann.

Fountas, I. C., & Pinnell, G. S. (2012). Guided reading: The romance and the reality. *The Reading Teacher, 66*(4), 268–284.

Fowler, G. L. (1982). Developing comprehension skills in primary students through the use of story frames. *The Reading Teacher, 36,* 176–179.

Fox, B. J. (2003). Teachers' evaluation of word identification software: Implications for literacy methods courses. In M. B. Sampson, P. E. Linder, J. R. Dugan, & B. Brancato (Eds.), *Celebrating the freedom of literacy: The twenty-fifth yearbook of the College Reading Association* (pp. 266–279). Commerce, TX: Texas A&M University.

Fox, B. J. (2004). *Word identification strategies: Phonics from a new perspective* (3rd ed.). Upper Saddle River, NJ: Pearson.

Fox, B. J., & Wright, M. (1997). Connecting school and home literacy experiences through cross-age reading. *The Reading Teacher, 50,* 396–403.

Fractor, J. S., Woodruff, M. C., Martinez, M. G., & Teale, W. H. (1993). Let's not miss opportunities to promote voluntary reading: Classroom libraries in the elementary school. *The Reading Teacher, 46,* 476–484.

Freebody, P., & Freiberg, J. (2011). The teaching and learning of critical literacy: Beyond the "show of wisdom." In M. Kamil, P. Pearson, E. Moje, & P. Afflerbach (Eds.), *Handbook of reading research* (pp. 684–710). New York, NY: Routledge.

Freeman, D., & Freeman, Y. (1993). Strategies for promoting the primary languages. *The Reading Teacher, 46,* 551–558.

Freeman, D., & Freeman, Y. (2003). Teaching English learners to read: Learning or acquisition? In G. Garcia (Ed.), *English learners: Reaching the highest levels of English literacy* (pp. 34–54). Newark, DE: International Reading Association.

Freeman, Y., & Freeman, D. (2004). Preview, view, review: Giving multilingual learners access to the curriculum. In L. Hoyt (Ed.), *Spotlight on comprehension: Building a literacy of thoughtfulness* (pp. 453–459). Portsmouth, NH: Heinemann.

Freeman, D. E., & Freeman, Y. S. (2006). Teaching language through content themes: Viewing our world as a global village. In T. A. Young & N. L. Hadaway (Eds.), *Supporting the literacy development of English learners: Increasing success in all classrooms* (pp. 61–78). Newark, DE: International Reading Association.

Friedman, T. L. (2005). *The world is flat: A brief history of the twenty-first century.* New York, NY: Picador.

Friend, M., & Bursuck, W. D. (2002). *Including students with special needs: A practical guide for classroom teachers* (3rd ed.). Boston, MA: Allyn & Bacon.

Friend, M., & Bursuck, W. D. (2011). *Including students with special needs: A practical guide for classroom teachers* (6th ed.). Boston, MA: Pearson.

Fry, E. (2002). Readability versus leveling. *The Reading Teacher, 56*(3), 286–291.

Fry, E. (2004). Phonics: A large phoneme-grapheme frequency count revised. *Journal of Literacy Research, 36*(1), 85–98.

Fry, E. B. (1968). A readability formula that saves time. *Journal of Reading, 11,* 513–516, 575–578.

Fry, E. B. (1977). Fry's readability graph: Clarifications, validity, and extension to level 17. *Journal of Reading, 21,* 242–252.

Fry, E. B. (1980). The new instant word list. *The Reading Teacher, 34,* 284–290.

Fry, E. B. (1998). The most common phonograms. *The Reading Teacher, 51,* 620–622.

Fuchs, D., Fuchs, L., & Burish, P. (2000). Peer-assisted learning strategies: An evidence-based practice to promote reading achievement. *Learning Disabilities Research and Practice, 15*(2), 85–91.

Fuchs, L. S., Fuchs, D., Hosp, M. K., & Jenkins, J. R. (2001). Oral reading fluency as an indicator of reading competence: A theoretical, empirical, and historical analysis. *Scientific Studies of Reading, 5,* 239–256.

Fuhrken, C., & Roser, N. (2010). Exploring high-stakes tests as a genre. In B. Moss & D. Lapp (Eds.), *Teaching new literacies in grades 4–6: Resources for 21st century classrooms* (pp. 186–198). New York, NY: Guilford Press.

Galda, L. (1993). *Language literacy and the child.* New York, NY: Harcourt Brace Jovanovich.

Galda, L., Ash, G. E., & Cullinan, B. E. (2000). Children's literature. In M. L. Kamil, P. B. Mosenthal, P. D. Pearson, & R. Barr (Eds.), *Handbook of reading research* (pp. 361–379). Mahwah, NJ: Erlbaum.

Galda, L., & Beach, R. (2004). Response to literature as a cultural activity. In R. B. Ruddell & N. J. Unrau (Eds.), *Theoretical models and processes of reading* (pp. 852–869). Newark, DE: International Reading Association.

Gambrell, L. B. (1985). Dialogue journals: Reading-writing interactions. *The Reading Teacher, 38,* 512–515.

Ganske, K., Monroe, J. K., & Strickland, D. S. (2003). Questions teachers ask about struggling readers and writers. *The Reading Teacher, 4*(2), 118–127.

Garan, E., & DeVoogd, G. (2008). The benefits of sustained silent reading: Scientific research and common sense converge. *The Reading Teacher, 62,* 336–344.

Garber-Miller, K. (2007). Playful textbook previews: Letting go of familiar mustache monologues. *Journal of Adolescent & Adult Literacy, 50,* 284–288.

Garcia, O. (2009). *Bilingual education in the 21st century: A global perspective.* Malden, MA: Wiley-Blackwell.

Garcia, E. (1999). *Student cultural diversity: Understanding and meeting the challenge* (2nd ed.). Boston, MA: Houghton Mifflin.

Garcia, G. E. (2000). Bilingual children's reading. In M. L. Kamil, P. B. Mosenthal, P. D. Pearson, & R. Barr (Eds.), *Handbook of reading research* (Vol. 3, pp. 813–834). Mahwah, NJ: Erlbaum.

Garcia, G. E., & Bauer, E. B. (2009). Assessing student progress in the time of no child left behind. In L. M. Morrow, R. Rueda, & D. Lapp (Eds.), *Handbook of research on literacy and diversity* (pp. 233–253). New York, NY: Guilford Press.

Garcia, G. G., & Beltran, D. (2003). Revisioning the blueprint: Building for the academic success of English learners. In G. G. Garcia (Ed.), *English learners: Reaching the highest levels of English literacy* (pp. 197–226). Newark, DE: International Reading Association.

Gardner, H. (1993). *Multiple intelligences: The theory in practice.* New York, NY: Basic Books.

Gardner, H. E. (2006). *Multiple intelligences: New horizons in theory and practice.* New York, NY: Basic Books.

Gaskins, I. W., Ehri, L. C., Cress, C., O'Hara, C., & Donnelly, K. (1997). Procedures for word learning: Making discoveries about words. *The Reading Teacher, 50,* 312–327.

Gee, J. (2004). Reading as situated language: A sociocognitive perspective. In R. B. Ruddell & N. J. Unrau (Eds.), *Theoretical models and processes of reading* (pp. 116–132). Newark, DE: International Reading Association.

Gelzheiser, L., Hallgren-Flynn, L., Connors, M., & Scanlon, D. (2014). Reading thematically related texts to develop knowledge and comprehension. *The Reading Teacher, 68*(1), 53–63 doi: 10.1002/trtr.1271

Gentry, J. R., & Henderson, E. H. (1980). Three steps to teaching beginning readers to spell. In E. H. Henderson & J. W. Beers (Eds.), *Developmental and cognitive aspects of learning to spell: A reflection of word knowledge* (pp. 112–119). Newark, DE: International Reading Association.

Gibson, S. A. (2008/2009). An effective framework for primary grade level guided reading instruction. *The Reading Teacher, 62*(4), 324–334.

Giff, P. R. (1980). *Today was a terrible day.* New York, NY: Viking.

Gilles, C. (1990). Collaborative literacy strategies: "We don't need a circle to have a group." In K. G. Short & K. M. Pierce (Eds.), *Talking about books: Creating literate communities* (pp. 58–68). Portsmouth, NH: Heinemann.

Gillespie, J. (2005). "It would be fun to do again": Multigenre responses to literature. *The Reading Teacher, 48,* 678–684.

Giroir, S., Grimaldo, L. R., Vaughn, S., & Roberts, G. (2015). Interactive read-alouds for English learners in the elementary grades. *The Reading Teacher, 68*(8), 639–648.

Glazer, S. M., & Brown, C. S. (1993). *Portfolios and beyond.* Norwood, MA: Christopher-Gordon.

Glenn, D., & Modla, V. (2010). Language experience stories gone digital: Using digital stories with the LEA approach. *The Thirty-First Yearbook of The College Reading Association, 31.* www.aleronline.org/resource/resmgr/yearbooks/yearbook_volume_31.pdf#page=267

Goatley, V. (1997). Talk about text among special education students. In S. I. McMahon & E. Raphael (Eds.), *The book club connection* (pp. 119–137). New York, NY: Teachers College Press.

Goldenberg, C. (2011). Reading instruction for English language learners. In M. Kamil, P. Pearson, E. Moje, & P. Afflerbach (Eds.), *Handbook of reading research* (pp. 684–710). Abingdon, Oxon, England: Routledge.

Goldman, S. R., Braasch, J. L. G., Wiley, J., Graesser, A. C., & Brodowinska, K. (2012). Comprehending and learning from Internet sources: Processing patterns of better and poorer learners. *Reading Research Quarterly, 47*(4), 356–381.

Gollnick, D. M., & Chinn, P. C. (2013). *Multicultural education in a pluralistic society.* (9th ed.). Boston, MA: Pearson.

Good, R. H., & Kaminski, R. A. (2002). *Dynamic indicators of basic early literacy skills* (6th ed.). Eugene, OR: Institute for the Development of Educational Achievement.

Goodman, K. S. (1973). Psycholinguistic universals in the reading process. In F. Smith (Ed.), *Psycholinguistics and reading* (pp. 21–27). Austin, TX: Holt, Rinehart and Winston.

Goodman, K. S. (1975). Do you have to be smart to read? Do you have to read to be smart? *The Reading Teacher, 28,* 625–632.

Goodman, K. S. (1986). *What's whole in whole language?* Portsmouth, NH: Heinemann.

Goodman, K. S. (1988). Look what they've done to Judy Blume! The basalization of children's literature. *New Advocate, 1,* 18–28.

Goodman, K. S. (2006). *The truth about DIBELS.* Portsmouth. NH: Heinemann.

Goodman, Y. M. (1978). Kid-watching: An alternative to testing. *National Elementary Principal, 10,* 41–45.

Goodman, Y. M., & Burke, C. L. (1972). *Reading miscue inventory manual: Procedure for diagnosis and evaluation.* Old Tappan, NJ: Macmillan.

Goodwin, B., & Miller, K. (2013). Research says: Nonfiction reading promotes student success. *Educational Leadership, 70*(4), 80–82.

Gordon, C. J., & Braun, C. (1983). Using story schemata as an aid to reading and writing. *The Reading Teacher, 37,* 116–121.

Goswami, U. (1986). Children's use of analogy in learning to read: A developmental study. *Journal of Experimental Child Psychology, 42,* 73–83.

Goswami, U., & Bryant, P. (1990). *Phonological skills and learning to read.* Mahwah, NJ: Erlbaum.

Gough, P. (1985). One second of reading. In H. Singer & R. Ruddell (Eds.), *Theoretical models and processes of reading* (3rd ed., pp. 26–27). Newark, DE: International Reading Association.

Gove, M. K. (1983). Clarifying teachers' beliefs about reading. *The Reading Teacher, 37,* 261–268.

Graham, S., & Harris, K. R. (2016). A path to better writing: Evidence-based practices in the classroom. *The Reading Teacher, 69*(7), 359–365.

Graves, D. H. (1983). *Writing: Teachers and children at work.* Portsmouth, NH: Heinemann.

Graves, D. H. (1994). *A fresh look at writing.* Portsmouth, NH: Heinemann.

Graves, M. F. (2006). *The vocabulary book: Learning & instruction.* New York, NY: Teachers College Press; Newark, DE: International Reading Association.

Graves, M. F., & Watts-Taffe, S. M. (2002). The place of word consciousness in a research-based vocabulary program. In A. Farstrup & S. Samuels (Eds.), *What research has to say about reading instruction* (pp. 140–165). Newark, DE: International Reading Association.

Greenlaw, M. J. (1988). Using informational books to extend the curriculum. *The Reading Teacher, 42,* 18.

Greenwood, S. C., & Flanigan, K. (2007). Overlapping vocabulary and comprehension: Context clues complement semantic gradients. *The Reading Teacher, 61*(3), 249–254.

Gregg, M., & Sekeres, D. C. (2006). Supporting children's reading of expository text in the geography classroom. *The Reading Teacher, 60,* 102–110.

Griffith, L. W., & Rasinski, T. V. (2004). A focus on fluency: How one teacher incorporated fluency with her reading curriculum. *The Reading Teacher, 58*(2), 126–137.

Griffith, P. L., & Olson, M. (1992). Phonemic awareness helps beginning readers break the code. *The Reading Teacher, 45,* 516–523.

Gruenberg, R. (1948). *Poor Mr. Fingle. More favorite stories.* New York, NY: Doubleday.

Gunning, T. G. (2000). *Best books for building literacy for elementary school children.* Boston, MA: Allyn & Bacon.

Guthrie, J. T., Hoa, L. W., Wigfield, A., Tonks, S. M., & Perence-vich, K. C. (2006). From spark to fire: Can situational reading interest lead to long-term reading motivation? *Reading Research and Instruction, 45,* 91–117.

Guthrie, J. T., & McCann, A. D. (1996). Idea circles: Peer collaborations for conceptual learning. In L. B. Gambrell & J. F. Almasi (Eds.), *Lively discussions! Fostering engaged reading* (pp. 87–105). Newark, DE: International Reading Association.

Hadaway, N. L., & Young, T. A. (2006). Changing classrooms: Transforming instruction. In T. A. Young & N. L. Hadaway (Eds.), *Supporting the literacy development of English learners: Increasing success in all classrooms* (pp. 6–21). Newark, DE: International Reading Association.

Haggard, M. R. (1986). The vocabulary self-collection strategy: Using student interest and world knowledge to enhance vocabulary growth. *Journal of Reading, 29,* 634–642.

Hakuta, K., Santos, M., & Fang, Z. (2013). Challenges and opportunities for language learning in the context of the CCSS and the NGSS. *Journal of Adolescent & Adult Literacy, 56*(6), 451–454.

Hall, A. K. (1995). Sentencing: The psycholinguistic guessing game. *The Reading Teacher, 49,* 76–77.

Halliday, M. A. K. (1975). *Learning how to mean: Exploration in the development of language.* London: Arnold.

Hancock, M. R. (1993a). Exploring and extending personal response through literature journals. *The Reading Teacher, 46,* 466–474.

Hancock, M. R. (1993b). Exploring the meaning-making process through the content of literature response journals: A case study investigation. *Research in the Teaching of English, 27,* 335–369.

Hancock, M. (2007). *A celebration of literature and response: Children, books, and teachers in K–8 classrooms* (3rd ed.). New York, NY: Prentice Hall.

Hancock, M. R. (2008). The status of reader-response research: Sustaining the reader's voice in challenging times. In S. Lehr (Ed.), *Shattering the looking glass: Challenge, risk, and controversy in children's literature* (pp. 97–116). Norwood, MA: Christopher-Gordon.

Handsfield, L. J., Dean, T. R., & Cielocha, K. M. (2009). Becoming critical consumers and producers of text: Teaching literacy with Web 101 and Web 102. *The Reading Teacher, 63*(1), 40–50.

Hanna, P. R., Hanna, J. S., Hodges, R. E., & Rudorf, E. H. (1966). *Phoneme-grapheme correspondences as cues to spelling improvement.* Washington, DC: U.S. Department of Health, Education, and Welfare.

Hansen, J. (1987). *When writers read.* Portsmouth, NH: Heinemann.

Harris, K. R., Graham, S., Friedlander, B., & Laud, L. (2013). Bring powerful writing strategies into your classroom. *The Reading Teacher, 66*(7), 538–542.

Harris, T. H., & Hodges, R. E. (1995). *The literacy dictionary: The vocabulary of reading and writing.* Newark, DE: International Reading Association.

Harris, V. (1993). Bookalogues: Multicultural literature. *Language Arts, 70,* 215–217.

Harste, J. C., & Burke, C. L. (1977). A new hypothesis for reading teacher research. In P. D. Pearson & J. Hansen (Eds.), *Reading: Theory, research, and practice* (pp. 32–40). Clemson, SC: National Reading Conference.

Harste, J. C., Woodward, V. A., & Burke, C. L. (1984). *Language stories and literacy lessons.* Portsmouth, NH: Heinemann.

Hart, B., & Risley, T. R. (1995). *Meaningful differences in the everyday experience of young American children.* Baltimore, MD: Paul H. Brookes.

Harvey, S., & Goudvis, A. (2000). *Strategies that work: Teaching comprehension to enhance understanding.* York, ME: Stenhouse.

Harvey, S., & Goudvis, A. (2007). *Strategies that work: Teaching comprehension to enhance understanding.* York, ME: Stenhouse.

Harvey, S., & Goudvis, A. (2013). Comprehension at the core. *The Reading Teacher, 66*(6), 432–439.

Hasbrouck, J. (2016). Are oral reading norms accurate with complex text? [Web log]. Retrieved from http://www.shanahanonliteracy.com/search/label/Jan%20Hasbrouck

Hasbrouck, J. (2006). For students who are not yet fluent, silent reading is not the best use of classroom time. *American Educator, 30*(2).

Hayes, J. (2007a). *Activities for newcomers.* Retrieved June 5, 2007, from www.everythingesl.net/inservices/september.php

Heffernan, L. (2004). *Critical literacy and writer's workshop: Bringing purpose and passion to student writing.* Newark, DE: International Reading Association.

Heisey, N., & Kucan, L. (2010). Introducing science concepts to primary students through read-alouds: Interactions and multiple texts make the difference. *The Reading Teacher, 63*(8), 666–676.

Helman, L. A. (2004). Building on the sound system of Spanish: Insights from the alphabetic spellings of English-language learners. *The Reading Teacher, 57*(5), 452–460.

Helman, L. A., & Burns, M. K. (2008). What does oral language have to do with it? Helping young English-language learners acquire a sight word vocabulary. *The Reading Teacher, 62*(1), 14–19.

Henderson, E. (1990). *Teaching spelling* (2nd ed.). Boston, MA: Houghton Mifflin.

Henry, G. (1974). *Teaching reading as concept development.* Newark, DE: International Reading Association.

Hepler, S. I. (1982). *Patterns of response to literature: A one-year study of a fifth- and sixth-grade classroom.* Unpublished doctoral dissertation, Ohio State University, Columbus.

Hepler, S. I., & Hickman, J. (1982). "The book was okay. I love you": Social aspects of response to literature. *Theory into Practice, 21,* 278–283.

Herman, J., & Baker, E. (2005). Making benchmark testing work. *Educational Leadership, 63*(3), 48–54.

Herman, P. A. (1985). The effect of repeated readings on reading rate, speech, and word recognition. *Reading Research Quarterly, 20,* 553–565.

Hernandez, D. J. (2011). *How third-grade reading skills and poverty influence high school graduation.* Baltimore, MD: Annie E. Casey Foundation.

Herrington, A. J. (1997). Developing and responding to major writing projects. In M. D. Sorcinelli & P. Elbow (Eds.), *Writing to learn: Strategies for assigning and responding to writing across the disciplines.* San Francisco, CA: Jossey-Bass.

Herrmann, B. A. (1988). Two approaches for helping poor readers become more strategic. *The Reading Teacher, 42,* 24–28.

Heward, W. L. (2012). *Exceptional children: An introduction to special education* (10th ed.). Boston, MA: Pearson.

Hickman, J. (1983). Classrooms that help children like books. In N. Roser & M. Frith (Eds.), *Children's choices.* Newark, DE: International Reading Association.

Hiebert, E. H. (Ed.) (2015). *Teaching stamina & silent reading in the digital-global age.* Santa Cruz, CA: TextProject, Inc.

Hiebert, E. H. (2013). Supporting students' movement up the staircase of text complexity. *The Reading Teacher, 66*(6), 459–468.

Hilden, K., & Jones, J. (2013). Effective interactive read-alouds build stronger comprehension. *Reading Today, 30,* 17–19.

Hinchman, K. A., & Moore, D. W (2013). Close reading: A cautionary interpretation. *Journal of Adolescent & Adult Literacy, 56*(6), 441–450.

Hoffman, J. (2011). Constructing meaning: Interactive literary discussions in kindergarten read-alouds. *The Reading Teacher (65)*3, 183–194.

Hoffman, J. V. (1985). *The oral recitation lesson: A teacher's guide.* Austin, TX: Academic Resource Consultants.

Hoffman, J. V., Roser, N. L., & Battle, J. (1993). Reading aloud in classrooms: From the modal to a "model." *The Reading Teacher, 46,* 496–503.

Holdaway, D. (1979). *The foundations of literacy.* Portsmouth, NH: Heinemann.

Hollenbeck, A. F., & Saternus, K. (2013). Mind the comprehension iceberg: Avoiding titanic mistakes with CCSS. *The Reading Teacher, 66*(7), 558–568.

Hudson, R. F., Lane, H. B., & Pullen, P. C. (2005). Reading fluency assessment and instruction: What, why, and how? *The Reading Teacher, 58*(8), 702–714.

Hunt, L. (1970). The effect of self-selection, interest, and motivation upon independent, instructional, and frustrational levels. *The Reading Teacher, 24,* 146–151, 158.

Hunt, N., & Marshall, K. (1999). *Exceptional children and youth* (2nd ed.). Boston, MA: Houghton Mifflin.

Hutchison, A., Beschorner, B., & Schmidt-Crawford, D. (2012). Exploring the use of the iPad for literacy learning. *The Reading Teacher, 66*(1), 15–23.

Hutchison, A., & Reinking, D. (2011). Teachers' perceptions of integrating information and communication technologies into literacy instruction: A national survey in the United States. *Reading Research Quarterly, 46*(4), 308–329.

Hutton J. S., Horowitz-Kraus, T., Mendelsohn, A. L., DeWitt T., & Holland S. K. (2015). Home reading environment and brain activation in preschool children listening to stories. *Pediatrics, 136* (3), 466–478. http://dx.doi.org/10.1542/peds.2015-0359

Hymes, D. (1974). *Foundations in sociolinguistics: An ethnographic approach.* Philadelphia, PA: University of Pennsylvania Press.

Ignoffo, M. (1980). The thread of thought: Analogies as a vocabulary building method. *Journal of Reading, 23,* 519–521.

Ikpeze, C. H., & Boyd, F. B. (2007). Web-based inquiry learning: Facilitating thoughtful literacy with WebQuests. *The Reading Teacher, 60,* 644–654.

International Dyslexia Association. (2002). *Definition of Dyslexia.* Retrieved February 14, 2016, from: http://eida.org/definition-of-dyslexia/

International Reading Association. (1999a). *High-stakes assessments in reading.* Newark, DE: Author.

International Reading Association. (1999b). *Using multiple methods of beginning reading instruction: A position statement from the International Reading Association.* Newark, DE: International Reading Association.

International Reading Association. (2000b). *Providing books and other print materials for classroom and school libraries: A position statement of the International Reading Association.* Newark, DE: Author.

International Reading Association. (2000c). *A tour and an invitation.* Retrieved June 8, 2007, from www.readingonline.org/newliteracies/lit_index.asp?HREF=wattspailliotet1/tour.html

International Reading Association. (2001). *Second-language literacy instruction: A position statement of the International Reading Association.* Newark, DE: Author.

International Reading Association. (2002a). *Integrating literacy and technology in the curriculum: A position statement of the International Reading Association.* Newark, DE: Author.

International Reading Association. (2002b). *What is evidence-based reading instruction: A position statement of the International Reading Association.* Newark, DE: Author.

International Reading Association. (2004). *The role and qualifications of the reading coach in the United States: A position statement of the International Reading Association.* Newark, DE: Author.

International Reading Association. (2009). New literacies and 21st-century technologies: A position paper of the International Reading Association. Newark, DE: Author.

International Reading Association. (2010a). *Response to intervention: A position paper of the International Reading Association.* Newark, DE: Author.

International Reading Association. (2010b). *Standards for reading professionals—Revised 2010.* Newark, DE: Author.

International Reading Association. (2012). Literacy research panel. Retrieved from www.reading.org/general/CurrentResearch/literacy_research_panel.aspx

International Reading Association and National Association for the Education of Young Children. (1998). *Learning to read and write: Developmentally appropriate practices for young children: A joint position statement of the International Reading Association and the National Association for the Education of Young Children.* Newark, DE, and Urbana, IL: Authors.

International Reading Association and National Council of Teachers of English. (1996). *Standards for the English language arts.* Newark, DE: International Reading Association.

International Reading Association and National Council of Teachers of English. (2010). *Standards for the assessment of reading and writing.* Newark, DE: Authors.

International Reading Association Common Core State Standards (CCSS) Committee. (2012). *Literacy implementation guidance for the ELA Common Core State Standards* [White paper]. Retrieved from www.reading.org/Libraries/association-documents/ira_ccss_guidelines.pdf

International Reading Association. (2013). *Formative assessment: A position statement of the International Reading Association.* Newark, DE: Author.

International Literacy Association. (2015). Advocacy Position on ESEA Reauthorization, February 17, 2015. http://www.literacyworldwide.org/docs/default-source/where-we-stand/esea-advocacy-position.pdf

Irvin, J. L. (1998). *Reading and the middle school student: Strategies to enhance literacy.* Boston, MA: Allyn & Bacon.

Irwin, J. W., & Davis, C. A. (1980). Assessing readability: The checklist approach. *Journal of Reading, 24,* 124–130.

Ivey, G., & Fisher, D. (2006). When thinking skills trump reading skills. *Educational Leadership, 64*(2), 16–21.

Jacobi-Karna, K. (1995). Music and children's books. *The Reading Teacher, 49,* 265–269.

Jimenez, R. T. (2004). More equitable literacy assessments for Latino students. *The Reading Teacher, 57,* 576–578.

Johns, J. L. (1985). *Basic reading inventory* (3rd ed.). Dubuque, IA: Kendall-Hunt.

Johns, J. L., & Lenski, S. (2010). *Improving reading: Interventions, strategies, and resources* (5th ed.). Dubuque, IA: Kendall Hunt.

Johnson, J., Christie, J., & Wardle, F. (2005). *Play, development and early education.* Boston, MA: Allyn & Bacon.

Johnston, F. R. (1999). The timing and teaching of word families. *The Reading Teacher, 53*, 64–75.

Johnston, P., & Costello, P. (2005). Principles for literacy assessment. *Reading Research Quarterly, 40*(2), 256–267.

Jones, M., & Shelton, M. (2011). *Developing your portfolio—Enhancing your learning and showing your stuff.* New York, NY: Routledge.

Joseph, L. M. (2006). Incremental rehearsal: A flashcard drill technique for increasing retention of reading words. *The Reading Teacher, 59*(8), 803–806.

Juel, C. (1988). Learning to read and write: A longitudinal study of fifty-four children from first through fourth grade. *Journal of Educational Psychology, 80*, 437–447.

Juel, C., & Minden-Cupp, C. (2000). Learning to read words: Linguistic units and instructional strategies. *Reading Research Quarterly, 35*, 458–492.

Justice, L., Meier, J., & Walpole, S. (2005). Learning new words from storybooks: An efficacy study with at-risk kindergartners. *Language, Speech, and Hearing Services in Schools, 36*(1), 17–32.

Kame'enui, E. J. (1993). A special issue on innovations in literacy for a diverse society. *The Reading Teacher, 46*, 539.

Kamii, C. (1991). What is constructivism? In C. Kamii, M. Manning, & G. Manning (Eds.), *Early literacy: A constructivist foundation for whole language.* Washington, DC: National Education Association.

Kamil, M. L., & Pearson, P. D. (1979). Theory and practice in teaching reading. *New York University Education Quarterly, 10*, 10–16.

Kara-Soteriou, J., Zawilinski, L., & Henry, L. A. (2007). Children's books and technology in the classroom: A dynamic combo for supporting the writing workshop. *The Reading Teacher, 60*, 698–707.

Karchmer, R., Mallette, M., Kara-Soteriou, J., & Leu, D. (2005). *Innovative approaches to literacy education: Using the Internet to support new literacies.* Newark, DE: International Reading Association.

Karchmer-Klein, R., & Shinas, V. H. (2012). Guiding principles for supporting new literacies in your classroom. *The Reading Teacher, 65*(5), 288–293.

Keegan, B., & Shake, K. (1991). Literature study groups: An alternative to ability grouping. *The Reading Teacher, 44*, 542–547.

Keene, E. O., & Zimmerman, S. (1997). *Mosaic of thought: Teaching comprehension in a reader's workshop.* Portsmouth, NH: Heinemann.

Kelley, M. J., & Clausen-Grace, N. (2006). R5: The sustained silent reading makeover that transformed readers. *The Reading Teacher, 60*, 148–156.

Kieffer, M. J., & Lesaux, N. K. (2007). Breaking down words to build meaning: Morphology, vocabulary, and reading comprehension in the urban classroom. *The Reading Teacher, 61*(2), 134–144.

Kieffer, R. D., & Morrison, L. S. (1994). Changing portfolio process: One journey toward authentic assessment. *Language Arts, 71*, 411–418.

Kincaid, J. P., Fishburne, R. P., Rogers, R. L., & Chissom, B. S. (1975). *Derivation of new readability formulas (Automated Readability Index, Fog Count, and Flesch Reading Ease formula) for Navy enlisted personnel.* Research Branch Report 8-75. Millington, TN: Naval Air Station Memphis.

Kinch, A., & Azer, S. L. (2002). *Promoting early childhood literacy: Highlights of state efforts.* Washington, DC: National Association for the Education of Young Children.

Kinzer, C. K. (2005). The intersection of schools, communities, and technology: Recognizing children's use of new literacies. In R. A. Karchmer, M. H. Mallette, J. Kara-Soteriou, & D. J. Leu, Jr. (Eds.), *Innovative approaches to literacy education: Using the Internet to support new literacies* (pp. 65–82). Newark, DE: International Reading Association.

Kist, W. (2005). *New literacies in action: Teaching and learning in multiple media.* New York, NY: Teachers College Press.

Kist, W. (2010). *The socially networked classroom: Teaching in the new media age.* Thousand Oaks, CA: Corwin Press.

Klein, G. (2006, May 1). iPods, Podcasts latest teaching tool in classrooms. *PotomacNews.com.* Retrieved July 19, 2007, from www.potomacnews.com/servlet/Satellite?pagename=?WPN/MGArticle/WPN_BasicArticle&c=MGArticle&cid=?1137835724174.

Klein, M. L. (1985). *The development of writing in children: Pre-K through grade 8.* Upper Saddle River, NJ: Prentice Hall

Klesius, J. P., & Griffith, P. H. (1998). Interactive storybook reading for at-risk learners. *The Reading Teacher, 49*, 552–560.

Kletzien, S. B., & Dreher, M. J. (2004). *Informational text in K–3 classrooms: Helping children read and write.* Newark, DE: International Reading Association.

Klinger, J. K., & Edwards, P. A. (2006). Cultural considerations with response to intervention models. *Reading Research Quarterly, 41*, 108–117.

Kobrin, B. (1995). *Eye openers II: How to choose and use children's books about real people and things.* New York, NY: Penguin.

Koskinen, P., & Blum, I. (1986). Paired repeated reading: A classroom strategy for developing fluent reading. *The Reading Teacher, 40*, 70–75.

Koskinen, P. S., Blum, I. H., Bisson, S. A., Phillips, S. M., Creamer, T. S., & Baker, T. K. (1999). Shared reading, books, and audiotapes: Supporting diverse students in school and at home. *The Reading Teacher, 52*, 430–444.

Koss, M. D., & Teale, W. H. (2009). What's happening in YA literature? Trends in books for adolescents. *Journal of Adolescent & Adult Literacy 52*(7), 563–572.

Kostelnik, M. J., Soderman, A. K., & Whiren, A. P. (2003). *Developmentally appropriate curriculum: Best practices in early childhood education* (3rd ed.). Alexandria, VA: Prentice Hall.

Krashen, S. D. (2004). *The power of reading: Insights from the research* (2nd ed.). Westport, CT: Libraries Unlimited; Portsmouth, NH: Heinemann.

Krashen, S. (2003). Three roles for reading for minority-language children. In G. Garcia (Ed.), *English learners: Reaching the highest levels of English literacy* (pp. 55–70). Newark, DE: International Reading Association.

Krashen, S. (2004a). False claims about literacy development. *Educational Leadership, 61*, 18–21.

Krashen, S. (2004b). *The power of reading.* Portsmouth, NH: Heinemann.

Kraus, C. (1983). The influence of first-grade teachers' conceptual frameworks of reading on their students' perceptions of reading and reading behavior. Doctoral dissertation, Kent State University, Kent, Ohio.

Kress, G. (2003). *Literacy in the media age.* London: Routledge.

Kuhn, M. R., Schwanenflugel, P. J., & Meisinger, E. B. (2010). Aligning theory and assessment of reading fluency: Automaticity, prosody and definitions of fluency. *Reading Research Quarterly, 45*(2), 230–251.

Kuhn, M. R., & Stahl, S. A. (2000). *Fluency: A review of developmental and remedial practices* (CIERA Rep. No. 2-008). Ann Arbor, MI: Center for the Improvement of Early Reading Achievement.

Kymes, A. (2005). Teaching online comprehension strategies using think-alouds. *Journal of Adolescent & Adult Literacy, 48*, 492–500.

Labadie, M., Wetzel, M., & Rogers, R. (2012). Opening spaces for critical literacy: Introducing books to young readers. *The Reading Teacher 66*(2), 117–127.

Labbo, L. D. (2000). 12 things young children can do with a talking book in a classroom computer center. *The Reading Teacher, 53*(7), 542–546.

Labbo, L. D. (2004). Author's computer chair. *The Reading Teacher, 57*(7), 688–691.

Labbo, L. D., Eakle, A. J., & Montero, M. K. (2002). Digital language experience approach: Using digital photographs and software as a language experience approach innovation. *Reading Online, 5*(8). Retrieved July 31, 2007, from www.readingonline.org/electronic/elec_index.asp?HREF=labbo2/index.html

Labbo, L., Love, M., & Ryan, T. (2007). A vocabulary flood: Making words "sticky" with computer-response activities. *The Reading Teacher, 60*(6), 582–588.

Labbo, L., & Teale, W. (1990). Cross-age reading: A strategy for helping poor readers. *The Reading Teacher, 43*, 362–369.

Ladson-Billings, G. (1992). Reading between the lines and beyond the pages: A culturally relevant approach to literacy teaching. *Theory into Practice, 28*, 312–320.

Laier, B. B., Edwards, P. A., McMillon, G. T., & Turner, J. D. (2001). Connecting home and school values through multicultural literature and family stories. In P. Ruggiano Schmidt & A. W. Pailliotet (Eds.), *Exploring values through literature, multimedia, and literacy events* (pp. 64–75). Newark, DE: International Reading Association.

Lamme, L. L. (1984). *Growing up writing*. Washington, DC: Acropolis.

Landis, D., Umolu, J., & Mancha, S. (2010). The power of language experience for cross-cultural reading and writing. *The Reading Teacher, 63*(7), 580–587.

Landt, S. (2006). Multicultural literature and young adolescents: A kaleidoscope of opportunity. *Journal of Adolescent & Adult Literacy, 49*(8), 690–697.

Lapp, D., Moss, B., Johnson, K., & Grant, M. (2013). *Teaching students to closely read texts: How and when?* Newark, DE: International Reading Association.

Larson, L. C. (2008). Electronic reading workshop: Beyond books with new literacies and instructional technologies. *Journal of Adolescent & Adult Literacy, 52*(2), 121–131.

Larson, L. C. (2009). E-reading and e-responding: New tools for the next generation of readers. *Journal of Adolescent & Adult Literacy, 53*(3), 255–258.

Lauritzen, C. (1982). A modification of repeated readings for group instruction. *The Reading Teacher, 35*, 456–458.

Lazar, A. M. (2004). *Learning to be literacy teachers in urban schools: Stories of growth and change.* Newark, DE: International Reading Association.

Lehman, B., Freeman, D., & Allen, R. (1994). Children's literature and literacy instruction: "Literature-based" elementary teacher's belief and practices. *Reading Horizons, 35*(1), 3–29.

Leland, C., & Fitzpatrick, R. (1994). Cross-age interaction builds enthusiasm for reading and writing. *The Reading Teacher, 47*, 292–301.

Lenhart, L., & Roskos, K. (2003). What Hannah taught Emma and why it matters. In D. M. Barone & L. M. Morrow (Eds.), *Research based practice in early literacy* (pp. 83–100). New York, NY: Guilford Press.

Lenski, S. D., Ehlers-Zavala, F., Daniel, M. C., & Sun-Irminger, X. (2006). Assessing English-language learners in mainstream classrooms. *The Reading Teacher 1*(60), 24–34.

Lenters, K. (2004/2005). No half measures: Reading instruction for young second-language learners. *The Reading Teacher, 58*, 328–336.

Leong, D. J., & Bodrova, E. (2012). Assessing and scaffolding make-believe play. *Young Children, 67*(1), 28–34.

Lesaux, N. K. (2013). PreK-3rd: Getting literacy instruction right. PreK-3rd Policy to Action Brief, 9. Retrieved from http://fcd-us.org/sites/default/files/PreK-3rd_Getting_Literacy_Instruction_Right.pdf

Leslie, L., & Jett-Simpson, M. (1997). *Authentic literacy assessment.* New York, NY: Longman.

Leu, D. J. (2000). Literacy and technology: Deictic consequences for literacy education in an information age. In M. L. Kamil, P. B. Mosenthal, P. D. Pearson, & R. Barr (Eds.), *Handbook of reading research* (Vol. 3, pp. 743–770). Mahwah, NJ: Erlbaum.

Leu, D. J., Castek, J., Henry, L. A., Coiro, J., & McMullan, M. (2004). The lessons that children teach us: Integrating children's literature and the new literacies of the Internet. *The Reading Teacher, 57*, 496–503.

Leu, D. J., Jr., & Kinzer, C. K. (2000). The convergence of literacy instruction with networked technologies for information and communication. *Reading Research Quarterly, 35*(1), 108–127.

Leu, D., Kinzer, C., Coiro, J., & Cammack, D. (2004). Toward a theory of new literacies emerging from the Internet and other information and communication technologies. In R. B. Ruddell & N. J. Unrau (Eds.), *Theoretical models and processes of reading* (pp. 1570–1613). Newark, DE: International Reading Association.

Leu, D. J., Jr., & Leu, D. D. (1999). *Teaching with the Internet: Lessons from the classroom* (2nd ed.). Norwood, MA: Christopher-Gordon.

Leu, D. J., McVerry, J. G., O'Byrne, W. I., Kiili, C., Zawilinski, L., Everett-Cacopardo, H., Kennedy, C., & Forzani, E. (2011). The new literacies of online reading comprehension: Expanding the literacy and learning curriculum. *Journal of Adolescent & Adult Literacy, 55*(1), 5–14.

Leu, D. L. (2008). *"The C's of change": An extended interview with the members of the New Literacies Research Lab.* Retrieved from http://www.ncte.org/magazine/extended

Liberman, I. Y., Shankweiler, D., Fisher, F. W., & Carter, B. (1974). Explicit syllable and phoneme segmentation in the young child. *Journal of Experimental Child Psychology, 18*, 201–212.

Livingston, N., & Kurkjiam, C. (2003). Timeless and treasured books. *The Reading Teacher, 57*, 96–103.

Lobel, Arnold. (1979). *Days with frog and toad.* New York, NY: HarperCollins.

Long, C. (2007). Podcasting the 1600s: Old world meets new when student podcasts bring the Jamestown settlement to life. *NEA Today.* Retrieved July, 19, 2007, from www.nea.org/neatoday/0703/features6.html.

Louie, B. Y. (2006). Guiding principles for teaching multicultural literature. *The Reading Teacher, 59*(5), 438–448.

Lynch, E. W. (2004). Developing cross-cultural competence. In E. W. Lynch & M. J. Hanson (Eds.), *Developing cross-cultural competence: A guide for working with children and their families* (pp. 41–77). Baltimore, MD: Paul H. Brookes.

Lyon, G. R., & Chhabra, V. (2004). The science of reading research. *Educational Leadership, 61*, 12–17.

Lyons, C., & Pinnell, G. (2001). *Systems for change in literacy education: A guide to professional development.* Portsmouth, NH: Heinemann.

Lysaker, J., & Hopper, E. (2015). Kindergartner's emergent strategy use during wordless picture book reading. *The Reading Teacher, 68*(8), 649–657.

MacGinitie, W. H. (1993). Some limits of assessment. *Journal of Reading, 26*, 556–560.

MacQuarrie, L. L., Tucker, J. A., Burns, M. K., & Hartman, B. (2002). Comparison retention rates using traditional drill sandwich, and incremental rehearsal flash card methods. *School Psychology Review, 31*, 584–595.

Maloch, B., & Beutel, D. (2010) "Big loud voice—You have important things to say": The nature of student initiations during one teacher's interactive read-alouds. *Journal of Classroom Interaction, 45*(3), 20–29.

Maloch, B., & Horsey, M. (2013). Living inquiry: Learning from and about informational texts in a second-grade classroom. *The Reading Teacher, 66*(6), 475–485.

Maloy, R. W., Verock-O'Loughlin, R-E. W., Edwards, S. A., & Woolf, B. P. (2014). *Transforming learning with new technologies* (2nd ed.). Boston, MA: Pearson.

Mandler, J., & Johnson, N. (1977). Remembrance of things parsed: Story structure and recall. *Cognitive Psychology, 9,* 111–151.

Manuel, L. (2006). *The trouble with Tilly Trumble.* Waterbury, CT: Abrams.

Many, J. E., Ariail, M., & Fox, D. L. (2011). Language arts learning in the middle grades. In D. Lapp & D. Fisher (Eds.), *Handbook of research on teaching the English language arts* (3rd ed.) (pp. 53–59). New York, NY: Routledge.

Manyak, P. C., & Bauer, E. B. (2008). Explicit code and comprehension instruction for English learners. *The Reading Teacher, 61*(5), 432–434.

Manzo, A. V. (1969). The request procedure. *Journal of Reading, 11,* 123–126.

Marsalis, W. (2005). *Jazz ABZ.* Cambridge, MA: Candlewick.

Martin, B., & Carle, E. (1996) *Brown Bear, Brown Bear What do you see?* Henry Holt and Co. New York, NY.

Martinez, M., Roser, N., & Harmon, J. (2009). Using picture books with older learners. In K. D. Wood & W. E. Blanton (Eds.), *Literacy instruction for adolescents* (pp. 287–306). New York, NY: Guilford Press.

Martinez, M., Roser, N. L., & Strecker, S. (1998/1999). "I never thought I could be a star." A reader's ticket to fluency. *The Reading Teacher, 52*(4), 326–334.

Mathers, P. (1995). *Kisses from Rosa.* New York, NY: Knopf.

McCabe, A. & Tamis-LeMonda, C. S. (2013). *Social policy report: Multilingual children beyond myths and toward best practices. Society for Research in Child Development,27*(4). Retrieved January 2016 from http://www.srcd.org/sites/default/files/documents/E-News/spr_27_4.pdf

McCaslin, N. (1990). *Creative drama in the classroom* (5th ed.). New York, NY: Longman.

McDonnell, G. M., & Osburn, E. B. (1978). New thoughts about reading readiness. *Language Arts, 55,* 26–29.

McEneaney, J. E., Lose, M. K., & Schwartz, R. M. (2006). A transactional perspective on reading difficulties and Response to Intervention. *Reading Research Quarterly, 1*(41), 117–128.

McGee L. M., & Richgels, D. J. (2012). *Literacy's beginnings: Supporting young readers and writers.* Boston, MA: Pearson Education.

McGinley, W. J., & Denner, P. R. (1987). Story impressions: A pre-reading/writing activity. *Journal of Reading, 31,* 248–253.

McKenna, M., & Picard, M. (2006/2007). Revisiting the role of miscue analysis in effective teaching. *The Reading Teacher, 60*(4), 378–380.

McKeon, C. A. (1999). The nature of children's e-mail in one classroom. *The Reading Teacher, 52*(7), 698–706.

McKeon, C. A. (2001). E-mail as a motivating literacy event for one struggling reader: Donna's case. *Reading Research & Instruction, 40*(3), 185–202.

McKeon, C. A. (2010a). Reading web-based electronic texts: Using think-alouds to help students begin to understand the process. In B. Moss & D. Lapp (Eds.), *Teaching new literacies in grades 4–6: Resources for 21st century classrooms* (pp. 245–257). New York, NY: Guilford Press.

McKeon, C. A. (2010b). Reading web-based electronic texts: Using think-alouds to help students begin to understand the process. In B. Moss & D. Lapp (Eds.), *Teaching new literacies in grades K–3: Resources for 21st century classrooms* (pp. 221–233). New York, NY: Guilford Press

McKeon, C. A., & Burkey, L. C. (1998). A literature-based e-mail collaborative. In E. G. Sturtevant, J. A. Dugan, P. Linder, & W. M. Linek (Eds.), *Literacy and community: The twentieth yearbook of the College Reading Association* (pp. 84–93). Commerce, TX: Texas A&M University.

McKeon, C. A., & Vacca, R. T. (2008). Adolescent literacy: Birds' eye views. In S. B. Wepner & D. S. Strickland (Eds.), *The administration and supervision of reading programs* (4th ed., pp. 90– 102). New York, NY: Teachers College Press.

McKeown, M. G., Crosson, A. C., Artz, N. J., Sandora, C., & Beck, I. L. (2013). In the media: Expanding students' experience with academic vocabulary. *The Reading Teacher, 67*(1), 45–53.

McKeown, M. G., & Beck, I. L. (2004). Direct and rich vocabulary instruction. In J. F. Baumann & E. J. Kame'enui (Eds.), *Vocabulary instruction* (pp. 13–27). New York, NY: Guilford Press.

McLaughlin, M., & Overturf, B. J. (2013a). *The common core: Teaching K-5 students to meet reading standards.* Newark, DE: International Reading Association.

McLaughlin, M., & Overturf, B. J. (2013b). *The common core: Teaching 6-12 students to meet reading standards.* Newark, DE: International Reading Association.

McLaughlin, M. (2012). Reading comprehension: What every teacher needs to know. *The Reading Teacher, 65*(7), 432–440.

McMahon, S. I. (1997). Book clubs: Contexts for students to lead their own discussions. In S. I. McMahon & T. E. Raphael (Eds.), *The book club connection* (pp. 89–106). New York, NY: Teachers College Press.

McQuillan, J. (1998). *The literacy crisis: False claims, real solution.* Portsmouth, NH: Heinemann.

McTigue, E., Thornton, E., & Wiese, P. (2012). Authentication projects for historical fiction: Do you believe it? *The Reading Teacher, 66*(6), 495–505.

Mesmer, H. A. (2001). Examining the theoretical claims about decodable text: Does text decodability lead to greater application of letter/sound knowledge in first-grade readers? In J. V. Hoffman, D. L. Schallert, C. M. Fairbanks, J. Worthy, & B. Maloch (Eds.), *Fiftieth Yearbook of the National Reading Conference* (pp. 444–459). Chicago, IL: National Reading Conference.

Mesmer, H. A. (2006). Beginning reading materials: A national survey of primary teachers' reported uses and beliefs. *Journal of Literacy Research, 38*(4), 389–425.

MetaMetrics. (2000). *The Lexile framework for reading.* Durham, NC: Author. Retrieved from www.lexile.com

Mezynski, K. (1983). Issues concerning the acquisition of knowledge: Effects of vocabulary training on reading comprehension. *Review of Educational Research, 53,* 258–279.

Mishra, P., & Koehler, M. J. (2006). Technological Pedagogical Content Knowledge: A new framework for teacher knowledge. *Teachers College Record, 108*(6), 1017–1054.

Moats, L. (2006, Winter). How spelling supports reading. *American Educator,* 12–22.

Mohr, K. A. (2003). "I want that book!": First-graders' preferences for expository text. In M. B. Sampson, P. E. Linder, J. A. R. Dugan, & B. Brancato (Eds.), *Celebrating the freedom of literacy: The twenty-fifth yearbook of the College Reading Association* (pp. 71–85). Commerce, TX: Texas A&M University.

Mohr, K. A. J., & Mohr, E. S. (2007). Extending English-language learners' classroom interactions using the response protocol. *The Reading Teacher, 60,* 440–450.

Moje, E. B. (2007). Developing socially just subject-matter instruction: A review of the literature on disciplinary literacy. In N. L. Parker (Ed.), *Review of research in education* (pp. 1–44). Washington, DC: American Educational Research Association.

Moje, E. B. (2008). Responsive literacy teaching in secondary school content areas. In M. W. Conley, J. R. Freidhoff, M. B. Sherry, & S. F. Tuckey (Eds.), *Meeting the challenge of adolescent literacy* (pp. 58–87). New York, NY: Guilford Press.

Mokhtari, K., Kymes, A., & Edwards, P. (2009). Assessing the new literacies of online reading comprehension: An informative interview with W. Ian O'Byrne, Lisa Zawilinski, J. Greg McVerry, and Donald J. Leu at the University of Connecticut. *The Reading Teacher, 62*(4), 354–357.

Mol, S. E., & Bus, A. G. (2011). To read or not to read: A meta-analysis of print exposure from infancy to early adulthood. *Psychological Bulletin, 137*, 267–296.

Moore, D. W., Bean, T. W., Birdyshaw, D., & Rycik, J. A. (1999). Adolescent literacy: A position statement. *Journal of Adolescent & Adult Literacy, 43*(1), 97–112.

Mora, J. K. (2006). Differentiating instruction for English learners: The four-by-four model. In T. A. Young & N. L. Hadaway (Eds.), *Supporting the literacy development of English learners: Increasing success in all classrooms* (pp. 24–40). Newark, DE: International Reading Association.

Morgan, A., Wilcox, B. R., & Eldridge, J. L. (2000). Effect of difficulty levels on second-grade delayed readers using dyad reading. *The Journal of Educational Research 94*(2), 113–119.

Morphett, M. V., & Washburne, C. (1931). When should children begin to read? *Elementary School Journal, 31*, 496–503.

Morris, D., & Nelson, L. (1992). Supported oral reading with low-achieving second graders. *Reading Research and Instruction, 31*, 49–63.

Morrow, L. (2003). Motivating lifelong voluntary readers. In J. Flood, D. Lapp, J. Squire, & J. Jensen (Eds.), *Handbook of research on teaching the English language arts* (pp. 857–867). Mahwah, NJ: Erlbaum.

Morrow, L. M. (1985). *Promoting voluntary reading in school and home.* Bloomington, IN: Phi Delta Kappa Educational Foundation.

Morrow, L. M. (1990). Preparing the classroom environment to promote literacy during play. *Early Childhood Research Quarterly, 5*, 537–554.

Morrow, L. M., & Gambrell, L. B. (2000). Literature-based reading instruction. In M. L. Kamil, P. B. Mosenthal, P. D. Pearson, & R. Barr (Eds.), *Handbook of reading research* (Vol. 3, pp. 563–586). Mahwah, NJ: Erlbaum.

Morrow, L., Kuhn, M., & Schwanenflugel, P. (2007). The family literacy program. *The Reading Teacher, 60*(1), 322–333.

Morrow, L. M., & Weinstein, C. S. (1982). Increasing children's use of literature through program and physical design changes. *Elementary School Journal, 83*, 131–137.

Moss, B. (1991). Children's nonfiction trade books: A complement to content area texts. *The Reading Teacher, 45*, 26–31.

Moss, B. (2002). *Exploring the literature of fact.* New York, NY: Guilford Press.

Moss, B., & Hendershot, J. (2002). Exploring sixth graders' selection of nonfiction trade books. *The Reading Teacher, 56*, 6–17.

Moss, B., & Loh, V. S. (2010). *35 strategies for guiding readers through informational texts.* New York, NY: Guilford Press.

Moustafa, M. (1997). *Beyond traditional phonics.* Portsmouth, NH: Heinemann.

Moustafa, M., & Maldonado-Colon, E. (1999). Whole-to-parts phonics instruction: Building on what children know to help them know more. *The Reading Teacher, 52*, 448–458.

Munsch, R. N. (1980). *The paperbag princess.* Toronto: Annick Press.

Munsch, R. N. (1985). *Thomas' snowsuit.* Toronto: Annick Press.

Murdoch, M. K. (2016). I can and so can you: A sibling's role in emerging literacy. (Unpublished doctoral dissertation). The University of Akron, Akron, Ohio.

Nagy, W. (1988). *Teaching vocabulary to improve reading comprehension.* Urbana, IL: National Council of Teachers of English.

Nagy, W., & Scott, J. A. (2000). Vocabulary processes. In M. Kamil, P. Mosenthal, P. Pearson, & R. Barr (Eds.), *Handbook of reading research* (Vol. 3, pp. 269–284). Mahwah, NJ: Erlbaum.

Nagy, W., & Scott, J. (2004). Vocabulary processes. In R. B. Ruddell & N. J. Unrau (Eds.), *Theoretical models and processes of reading* (pp. 574–593). Newark, DE: International Reading Association.

Nanji, S. (2008). *Child of dandelions.* Honesdale, PA: Boyd Mills.

National Association for the Education of Young Children (NAEYC). (2009). Where we stand on learning to read and write. Retrieved September 20, 2010, from www.naeyc.org/files/naeyc/file/positions/WWSSLearningToReadAnd?WriteEnglish.pdf.

National Council of Teachers of English. (2008, November). Code of best practices in fair use for media literacy education. Retrieved from http://www.ncte.org/positions/statements/fairusemedialiteracy

National Early Literacy Panel. (2008a). *Developing Early Literacy: Report of the National Early Literacy Panel.* Jessup, MD: National Institute for Literacy.

National Early Literacy Panel. (2008b). A Scientific Synthesis of Early Literacy Development and Implications for Intervention. National Institute for Literacy.

National Governors Association Center for Best Practices & Council of Chief State School Officers. (2010). *Common Core State Standards for English language arts and literacy in history/social studies, science, and technical subjects. Appendix B: Text exemplars and sample performance tasks.* Washington, DC: Authors

National Governors Association Center for Best Practices, Council of Chief State School Officers. (2010a). *Common core state standards.* Retrieved from www.corestandards.org/the-standards

National Governors Association Center for Best Practices, Council of Chief State School Officers. (2010b). *Common core state standards for English language arts and literacy in history, social studies, science and technical studies.* Washington, DC: Authors.

National Institute of Child Health and Human Development (2000). *Report of the National Reading Panel. Teaching children to read: An evidence based assessment of the scientific research literature on reading and its implications for reading instruction* (NIH Publication No. 00-4769). Washington, DC: U.S. Government Printing Office.

National Reading Panel. (2000). *Teaching children to read: An evidence-based assessment of the scientific research literature on reading and its implications for reading instruction.* Washington, DC: National Institute of Child Health and Human Development.

Neisser, U. (1976). *Cognition and reality: Principles and implications of cognitive psychology.* New York, NY: Freeman.

Neuman, S. B., & Wright, T. S. (2013). *All about words. Increasing vocabulary in the Common Core classroom, preK-grade 2.* New York, NY: Teachers College Press.

Neuman, S. B., (2015). *Literacy app improves school readiness in at-risk preschoolers.* Retrieved January 18, 2016, from http://www.sciencedaily.com/releases/2015/04/150419193725.htm

Neuman, S. B., Newman, E., & Dwyer, J. (2011). Educational effects of a vocabulary intervention on preschoolers' word knowledge and conceptual development: A cluster randomized trial. *Reading research Quarterly, 46*(3), 249–272.

Neuman, S. (2006). How we neglect knowledge and why. *American Educator*, Spring, 24–27.

Neuman, S. B., Caperelli, B. J., & Kee, C. (1998). Literacy learning: A family matter. *The Reading Teacher, 52*, 244–252.

Neuman, S. B., & Roskos, K. A. (1990). Play, print, and purpose: Enriching play environments for literacy development. *The Reading Teacher, 44*, 214–221.

Neuman, S. B., & Roskos, K. A. (1993). Access to print for children of poverty: Differential effects of adult mediation and literacy-enriched play settings in environmental and functional print tasks. *American Educational Research Journal, 30*, 95–122.

Neuman, S. B., & Roskos, K. A. (1997). Literacy knowledge in practice: Contexts of participation for young writers and readers. *Reading Research Quarterly, 32*, 10–32.

Neuman, S. B., & Roskos, K. (2012a). Helping children become more knowledgeable through text. *The Reading Teacher, 66*(3), 207–210.

Neuman, S. B., & Roskos, K. (2012b). More than teachable moments: Enhancing oral vocabulary instruction in your classroom. *The Reading Teacher, 66*(1), 63–67.

Neuman, S., Roskos, K., Wright, T., & Lenhart, L. (2007). *Nurturing knowledge: Building a foundation for school success by linking early literacy to math, science, art, and social studies.* New York, NY: Scholastic.

Newman, T. (2007). Factors that motivate fifth-grade students to read during sustained silent reading (SSR). Unpublished doctoral dissertation, University of Maryland, College Park. Retrieved from http://drum.lib.umd.edu/bitstream/1903/6738/1/umi-umd-4215.pdf

Nichols, W. D., Walker, B. J., & McIntyre, B. K. (2009). Assessing adolescent literacy. In K. D. Wood, & W. E. Blanton (Eds.), *Literacy instruction for adolescents* (pp. 248–268). New York, NY: Guilford Press.

Niguidula, D. (2005). Documenting learning with digital portfolios. *Educational Leadership, 63*(3), 44–47.

Nivola, C. A. (2008). *Planting the trees of Kenya: The story of Wangari Maathai.* New York, NY: Farrar, Straus and Giroux.

No Child Left Behind Act of 2001, U.S. Public Law 107-110, 107th Cong., 1st session (2002).

Noden, H., & Vacca, R. T. (1994). *Whole language in middle and secondary classrooms.* New York, NY: HarperCollins.

Nolte, R. Y., & Singer, H. (1985). Active comprehension: Teaching a process of reading comprehension and its effects on reading achievement. *The Reading Teacher, 39,* 24–28.

North Carolina Department of Public Instruction. (2004). *English language arts curriculum guide.* Retrieved October 17, 2004, from www.ncpublicschools.org/curriculum/languagearts Norton, D. E. (1980). *The effective teaching of language arts.* Columbus, OH: Merrill.

Oberman, S. (1994). *The always prayer shawl.* Honesdale, PA: Boyds Mills Press.

Oczkus, L. D. (2003). *Reciprocal teaching at work: Strategies for improving reading comprehension.* Newark, DE: International Reading Association.

O'Day, S. (2006). *Setting the stage for creative writing: Plot scaffolds for beginning and intermediate writers.* Newark, DE: International Reading Association.

Ogle, D. M. (1986). K-W-L: A teaching model that develops active reading of expository text. *The Reading Teacher, 39,* 564–571.

Olness, R. (2005). *Using literature to enhance writing instruction: A guide for K–5 teachers.* Newark, DE: International Reading Association.

Olness, R. (2007). *Using literature to enhance content area reading instruction.* Newark, DE: International Reading Association.

Opitz, M. F. (1999). Cultural diversity + supportive text = perfect books for beginning readers. *The Reading Teacher, 52*(8), 888–890.

Pacheco, M. B., & Miller, M. E. (2015). Making meaning through translanguaging in the literacy classroom. *The Reading Teacher, 1–5.* doi:10.1002/trtr:1390

Padak, N., & Rasinski, T. (2008). *Evidence-based instruction in reading: A professional development guide to fluency.* Boston, MA: Allyn & Bacon.

Padak, N., & Rasinski, T. (2009). The games children play. *The Reading Teacher, 62*(4), 363–364.

Palincsar, A., & Brown, A. L. (1984). Reciprocal teaching of comprehension-fostering and comprehension-monitoring activities. *Cognition and Instruction, 1,* 117–175.

Palmer, R., & Stewart, R. (2003). Nonfiction trade book use in primary grades. *The Reading Teacher, 57,* 38–47.

Paratore, J. R., & Jordan, G. (2007). Starting out together: A home-school partnership for preschool and beyond. *The Reading Teacher, 60*(7), 694–696.

Park, L. S. (2001). *A single shard.* New York, NY: Dell Yearling.

Pavlak, C. M. (2013). "It is hard fun": Scaffolded biography writing with English learners. *The Reading Teacher, 66*(5), 405–414.

Pearman, C. J. (2008). Independent reading of CD-ROM storybooks: Measuring comprehension with oral retellings. *The Reading Teacher 61*(8), 594–602.

Pearson, D., Hiebert, E., & Kamil, M. (2007). Vocabulary assessment: What we know and what we need to learn. *Reading Research Quarterly, 42*(2), 282–296.

Pearson, P. D. (1982). *Asking questions about stories.* New York, NY: Ginn.

Pearson, P. D. (1984). Guided reading: A response to Isabel Beck. In R. C. Anderson, J. Osborn, & R. Tierney (Eds.), *Learning to read in American schools: Basal readers and content texts* (pp. 21– 26). Mahwah, NJ: Erlbaum.

Pearson, P. D. (1996). Reclaiming the center. In M. Graves, P. Vanden Broek, & B. Taylor (Eds.), *The first R: Every child's right to read* (pp. 259–274). New York, NY: Teachers College Press.

Pearson, P. D., & Gallagher, M. (1983). The instruction of reading comprehension. *Contemporary Educational Psychology, 8,* 317–344.

Pearson, P. D., & Johnson, D. W. (1978). *Teaching reading comprehension.* Austin, TX: Holt, Rinehart and Winston.

Peck, J. (1989). Using storytelling to promote language and literacy development. *The Reading Teacher, 43,* 138–141.

Perfect, K. (1999). Rhyme and reason: Poetry for the heart and head. *The Reading Teacher, 52*(7), 728–737.

Peterson, D. S., & Taylor, B. M. (2012). Using higher order questioning to accelerate students' growth in reading. *The Reading Teacher, 65*(5), 295–304.

Piaget, J. (1970). *The science of education and the psychology of the child.* New York, NY: Orion Press.

Piaget, J. (1973). *The language and thought of the child.* New York, NY: World.

Pikulski, J. J., & Chard, D. J. (2005). Fluency: Bridge between decoding and reading comprehension. *The Reading Teacher, 58*(6), 510–519.

Pilgreen, J. (2006). Supporting English learners: Developing academic language in the content classroom. In T. A. Young & N. L. Hadaway (Eds.), *Supporting the literacy development of English learners: Increasing success in all classrooms* (pp. 41–60). Newark, DE: International Reading Association.

Pilonieta, P., & Medina, A. L. (2009). Reciprocal teaching for the primary grades: "We can do it, too!" *The Reading Teacher, 63*(2), 120–129.

Pinto, A. I., Manuela, P., & Aguiar, C. (2013). Effects of home environment and center-based child care quality on children's language, communication, and literacy outcomes. *Early Childhood Research Quarterly, 28*(1), 94–101.

Pollard-Durodola, S. D., Gonzalez, J. E., Simmons, D. C., Davis, M. J., Simmons, L., & Nava-Walichowski, M. (2011/2012). Using knowledge networks to develop preschoolers' content vocabulary. *The Reading Teacher, 65*(4), 265–274.

Pressley, M. (2000). What should comprehension instruction be the instruction of ? In M. L. Kamil, P. B. Mosenthal, P. D. Pearson, & R. Barr (Eds.). *Handbook of reading research* (Vol. 3, pp. 545–561). Mahwah, NJ: Erlbaum.

Pressley, M. (2006). *Reading instruction that works: The case for balanced teaching.* New York, NY: Guilford Press.

Pressley, M., Allington, R., Wharton-McDonald, R., Block, C. C., & Morrow, L. M. (2001). *Learning to read: Lessons from exemplary first grades.* New York, NY: Guilford.

Pressley, M., Rankin, J., & Yokoi, L. (1996). A survey of instructional practices of primary grade teachers nominated as effective in promoting literacy. *Elementary School Journal, 96,* 363–384.

Pressley, M., Wharton-McDonald, R., Rankin, J., Yokoi, L., & Ettenberger, S. (1996). The nature of outstanding primary grade literacy instruction. In E. McIntyre & M. Pressley (Eds.), *Balanced instruction: Strategies and skills in whole language* (pp. 251–276). Norwood, MA: Christopher-Gordon.

Price, L. H., Bradley, B. A., & Smith, J. (2012). A comparison of preschool teachers' talk during storybooks and information book read alouds. *Early Childhood Research Quarterly, 27,* 426–440.

Protacio, M. S., & Edwards, P. A. (2015). Restructuring sharing time for English language learners and their parents. *The Reading Teacher, 68*(6), 413–421.

Protacio, M. S. (2012). Reading motivation: A focus on English learners. *The Reading Teacher, 66*(1), 69–77.

Puig, E. A., & Froelich, K. S. (2007). *The literacy coach: Guiding in the right direction.* Boston, MA: Pearson Education.

Pullman, T. (2000). Wanted posters. In L. Baines & A. J. Kunkel (Eds.), *Going Bohemian: Activities that engage adolescents in the art of writing well* (pp. 75–77). Newark, DE: International Reading Association.

Randall, S. N. (1996). Information charts: A strategy for organizing student research. *Journal of Adolescent and Adult Literacy, 39,* 536–542.

Raphael, T. E. (1982). Question-answering strategies for children. *The Reading Teacher, 36,* 186–191.

Raphael, T. E. (1986). Teaching question-answer relationships, revisited. *The Reading Teacher, 39,* 516–522.

Raphael, T., McMahon, S., Goatley, V., Boyd, C., Pardo, L., & Woodman, G. (1992). Literature and discussion in the reading program. *Language Arts, 69*(1), 54–61.

Rasinski, T. V. (2003). *The fluent reader: Oral reading strategies for building word recognition, fluency, and comprehension.* New York, NY: Scholastic.

Rasinski, T. (2004a). *Assessing reading fluency.* Honolulu, HI: Pacific Resources for Education and Learning.

Rasinksi, T. (2004b). Creating fluent readers, *Educational Leadership, 61,* 46–51.

Rasinski, T. (2005a). *Daily word ladders: Grades 2–3.* New York, NY: Scholastic.

Rasinski, T. (2005b). *Daily word ladders: Grades 4–6.* New York, NY: Scholastic.

Rasinski, T. (2009). *Essential readings on fluency.* Newark, DE: International Reading Association.

Rasinski, T. (2010). *The fluent reader.* New York, NY: Scholastic.

Rasinski, T. (2012a, February 15). *Authentic and effective fluency instruction* [Podcast]. Newark, DE: International Reading Association.

Rasinski, T. (2012b). Why fluency instruction should be hot! *The Reading Teacher, 65*(8), 516–522.

Rasinski, T. (2015). Striking the right balance: Why silent and extended reading of challenging materials matters. In E. H. Hiebert (Ed.), *Teaching stamina & silent reading in the digital-global age (p.v).* Santa Cruz, CA: TextProject, Inc.

Rasinski, T. (2015b). The case against timed readings. [Web log]. Retrieved from http://www.scilearn.com/blog/the-case-against-timed-readings

Rasinski, T., Blachowicz, C., & Lems, C. (2012). (Eds.) *Fluency instruction: Research-based best practices* (2nd ed.). New York, NY: Guildford Press.

Rasinski, T., & Padak, N. (2004). *Effective reading strategies: Teaching children who find reading difficult* (3rd ed.). Upper Saddle River, NJ: Pearson.

Rasinski, T. V., & Fredericks, A. D. (1991). The Akron paired reading project. *The Reading Teacher, 44,* 514–515.

Rasinski, T. V., & Padak, N. D. (1996). *Holistic reading strategies: Teaching children who find reading difficult.* Columbus, OH: Merrill.

Rasinski, T. V., & Padak, N. D. (2001). *From phonics to fluency: Effective teaching of decoding and reading fluency in elementary school.* New York, NY: Longman.

Rasinski, T. V., Padak, N. D., Linek, W. L., & Sturtevant, E. (1994). Effects of fluency development on urban second-grade readers. *Journal of Educational Research, 87,* 158–165.

Rasinski, T. V., Reutzel, C. R., Chard, D., & Linan-Thompson, S. (2011). Reading fluency. In M. L. Kamil, P. D. Pearson, E. B. Moje, & P. Afflerbach (Eds.), *Handbook of reading research* (Vol. 4, pp. 286–319). New York, NY: Routledge.

Read, S. (2005). First and second graders writing informational text. *The Reading Teacher, 59,* 36–44.

Read, S. (2010). A model for scaffolding writing instruction: IMSCI. *The Reading Teacher, 64*(1), 47–52.

Reid, J. F. (1966). Learning to think about reading. *Educational Research, 9,* 56–62.

Reinking, D. (1995). Reading and writing with computers: Literacy research in a post-typographical world. In K. A. Hinderman, D. J. Leu Jr., & C. K. Kinzer (Eds.), *Perspectives on literacy research and practice* (pp. 17–33). Chicago, IL: National Reading Conference.

Reinking, D. (1998). Synthesizing technological transformations of literacy in a post-typographic world. In D. Reinking, M. McKenna, L. D. Labbo, & R. Kieffer (Eds.), *Handbook of literacy and technology: Transformations in a post-typographic world* (pp. xi–xxx). Mahwah, NJ: Erlbaum.

Reinking, D., McKenna, M. C., Labbo, L. D., & Kieffer, R. D. (Eds.). (1998). *Handbook of literacy and technology: Transformations in a post-typographic world.* Mahwah, NJ: Erlbaum.

Renzulli, J. S., & Smith, L. H. (1979). *A guidebook for developing individualized educational programs for gifted and talented students.* Mansfield Center, CT: Creative Learning Press.

Reutzel, D. R., & Cooter, R. B. (1991). Organizing for effective instruction: The reading workshop. *The Reading Teacher, 44,* 548–554.

Reutzel, D. R., & Cooter, R. B. (2002). *Strategies for assessment and instruction: Helping every child succeed.* Upper Saddle River, NJ: Merrill Prentice Hall.

Reutzel, D. R., Jones, C. D., & Newman, T. (2010). Scaffolded silent reading. In E. H. Hiebert & D. R. Reutzel (Eds.), *Revisiting silent reading: New directions for teachers and researchers* (pp. 129–150). Newark, DE: International Reading Association.

Reutzel, R., Jones, C., Fawson, P., & Smith, J. (2008). Scaffolded silent reading: A complement to guided repeated oral reading that works! *The Reading Teacher, 62*(3), 196.

Reyes, I. (2012). Biliteracy among children and youths. *Reading Research Quarterly, 47*(3), 307–327.

Rhodes, L. K., & Shanklin, N. (1993). *Windows into literacy: Assessing learners K–8.* Portsmouth, NH: Heinemann.

Richgels, D. J. (2013). Talk, write, and read: A method for sampling emergent literacy skills. *The Reading Teacher, 66*(5), 380–389.

Roberts, J., Jurgens, J., & Burchinal, M. (2005). The role of home literacy practices in preschool children's language and emergent literacy skills. *Journal of Speech, Language, and Hearing Research, 48,* 345–359.

Robinson, H. A., Faraone, V., Hittleman, D. R., & Unruh, E. (1990). *Reading comprehension instruction, 1783–1987: A review of trends and research.* Newark, DE: International Reading Association.

Roe, B. D. (2000). Using technology for content area literacy. In S. B. Wepner, W. J. Valmont, & R. Thurlow (Eds.), *Linking literacy and technology: A guide for K–8 classrooms* (pp. 133–158). Newark, DE: International Reading Association.

Rog, L. J. (2007). *Marvelous minilessons for teaching beginning writing, K–3*. Newark, DE: International Reading Association.

Romano, T. (1987). *Clearing the way: Working with teenage writers.* Portsmouth, NH: Heinemann.

Romano, T. (2000). *Blending genre, altering style.* Portsmouth, NH: Boynton/Cook.

Rosenblatt, L. M. (1978). *The reader, the text, the poem: The transactional theory of literary Work.* Carbondale, IL: Southern Illinois University.

Rosenblatt, L. (1982). The literary transaction: Evocation and response. *Theory into Practice, 21,* 268–277.

Rosenblatt, L. (2004). The transactional theory of reading and writing. In R. B. Ruddell & N. J. Unrau (Eds.), *Theoretical models and processes of reading* (pp. 1363–1398). Newark, DE: International Reading Association.

Rosenshine, B., & Meister, C. (1994). Reciprocal teaching: A review of the research. *Review of Educational Research, 64*(4), 479–530.

Roskos, K. & Neuman, S. (2014). Best practices in reading: A 21st century skill update. *The Reading Teacher, 67*(7), 507–511.

Roskos, K. A. (1986). *The nature of literate behavior in the pretend play episodes of four- and five-year-old children.* Unpublished doctoral dissertation, Kent State University, Kent, Ohio.

Roskos, K. A. (2013). The e-book goes to school: Shared reading 3.0. In S. B. Neuman & L. B. Gambrell (Eds.), *Quality reading instruction in the age of common core standards.* Newark, DE: International Reading Association.

Roskos, K. (2015). Storytime on a Screen: Reading E-Books with Young Children. https://www.noodle.com/articles/ebooks-for-preschoolers-how-to-use-digital-readers-with-young-kids

Roskos, K., Burstein, K., Shang, Y., & Gray, E. (2104). Young children's engagement with e-books at school: Does device matter? DOI: 10.1177/2158244013517244

Roskos, K., & Brueck, J. (2009). The eBook as a learning object in an online world. In A. G. Bus & S. B. Neuman (Eds.), *Multimedia and literacy development: Improving achievement for young learners* (pp. 77–88). New York, NY: Routledge.

Roskos, K. A., Tabors, P., & Lenhart, L. (2009). *Oral language and early literacy in preschool* (2nd ed.). Newark, DE: International Reading Association.

Rosow, L. (1992). The story of Irma. *The Reading Teacher, 45,* 525.

Routman, R. (1991). *Invitations.* Portsmouth, NH: Heinemann.

Rubin, D. I. (2016). Growth in oral reading fluency of Spanish ELL students with learning disabilities. *Intervention in School and Clinic.* doi:10.1177/1053451216630280

Rueda, R. (2011). Cultural perspectives in reading: Theory and research. In M. Kamil, P. Pearson, E. Moje, & P. Afflerbach (Eds.), *Handbook of reading research* (pp. 84–103). New York, NY: Routledge.

Rumelhart, D. E. (1982). Schemata: The building blocks of cognition. In J. Guthrie (Ed.), *Comprehension and teaching: Research reviews* (pp. 3–26). Newark, DE: International Reading Association.

Rupley, W. H., Logan, J. W., & Nichols, W. D. (1999). Vocabulary instruction in balanced reading programs. *The Reading Teacher, 52,* 336–346.

Rylant, C. (1991). *Henry and Mudge take the big test.* New York, NY: Simon & Schuster.

Rylant, C. (1997). *Poppleton the Pig.* New York, NY: Blue Sky Press.

Samuels, S. J. (1979). Method of repeated readings. *The Reading Teacher, 32,* 403–408.

Samuels, S. J. (1988). Decoding and automaticity. *The Reading Teacher, 41,* 756–760.

Samuels, S. J. (1994). Toward a theory of automatic information processing in reading, revisited. In R. Ruddell, M. Ruddell, & H. Singer (Eds.), *Theoretical models and processes of reading* (4th ed., pp. 816–837). Newark, DE: International Reading Association.

Samuels, S. J. (2012). Reading fluency: Past, present, and future. In T. Rasinski, C. Blachowitz, & K. Lems (Eds.), *Fluency instruction: Research-based best practices* (pp. 3–16). New York, NY: Guilford Press.

Samway, K. D., & Whang, G. (1996). *Literature study circles in a multicultural classroom.* York, ME: Stenhouse.

Sanden, S. (2014). Out of the shadow of SSR: Real teachers' classroom independent reading practices. *Language Arts, 91*(3), 161–175.

Sanders, W. (1998). Value-added assessment. *School Administrator, 11*(3), 24–27.

Santa, C. M., Dailey, S. C., & Nelson, M. (1985). Free response and opinion proof: A reading and writing strategy for middle grade and secondary teachers. *Journal of Reading, 28,* 346–352.

Santoro, L. E., Chard, D. J., Howard, L., & Baker, S. K. (2008). Making the *very* most of classroom read-alouds to promote comprehension and vocabulary. *The Reading Teacher, 61*(5), 396–408.

Saul, E., & Dieckman, D. (2005). Choosing and using information trade books. *Reading Research Quarterly, 40*(4), 502–513.

Savage, J. F. (2004). *Sound it out! Phonics in a comprehensive reading program* (2nd ed.). New York, NY: McGraw Hill.

Sawchuk, S. (2012, November). Retooled textbooks aim to capture common core. *Education Week.*

Scala, M. C. (2001). *Working together: Reading and writing in inclusive classrooms.* Newark, DE: International Reading Association.

Scarborough, H. S. (1998). Early identification of children at risk for reading disabilities: Phonological awareness and some other promising predictors. In B. K. Shapiro, P. J. Accardo, & A. J. Capute (Eds.), *Specific reading disability: A view of the spectrum* (pp. 75–119). Timonium, MD: York Press.

Scarborough, H. S. (2001). Connecting early language and literacy to later reading (dis)abilities: Evidence, theory, and practice. In S. Neuman & D. Dickinson (Eds.), *Handbook for research in early literacy* (pp. 97–110). New York, NY: Guilford Press.

Scharlach, T. D. (2008). START comprehending: Students and teachers actively reading text. *The Reading Teacher 62*(1), 20–31.

Schickedanz, J. A. (1986). *More than the ABCs.* Washington, DC: National Association for the Education of Young Children.

Schickedanz, J. A. (1998). What is developmentally appropriate practice in early literacy? Considering the alphabet. In S. B. Neuman & K. A. Roskos (Eds.), *Children achieving: Best practices in early literacy* (pp. 20–37). Newark, DE: International Reading Association.

Schickedanz, J., & Casbergue, R. (2009). *Writing in preschool: Learning to orchestrate meaning and marks* (2nd ed.). Newark, DE: International Reading Association.

Schickedanz, J., & Collins, M. (2013). *So much more than the ABCs: The early phases of reading and writing.* Washington, DC: National Association for the Education of Young Children.

Schleper, D.(2002). *Leading from Behind: Language Experience in Action.* Washington, DC: Gallaudet University, Laurent Clerc National Deaf Education Center.

Schmidt, P. R. (1998a). The ABCs model: Teachers connect home and school. In T. Shanahan & F. Rodriguez-Brown (Eds.), *Forty-Seventh Yearbook of the National Reading Conference* (pp. 194–208). Chicago, IL: National Reading Conference.

Schmidt, P. R. (1998b). The ABCs of cultural understanding and communication. *Equity and Excellence in Education, 31*(2), 28–38.

Schmidt, P. R. (1998c). *Cultural conflict and struggle: Literacy learning in a kindergarten program.* New York, NY: Lang.

Schmidt, P. R. (1999). KWLQ: Inquiry and literacy learning in science. *The Reading Teacher, 52,* 789–792.

Scholastic. (2015). *Kids & Family Reading Report (5th ed.)*. Retrieved on January 18, 2016, from http://www.scholastic.com/readingreport/

Schreiber, P. (1980). On the acquisition of reading fluency. *Journal of Reading Behavior, 12*, 177–186.

Schuele, M. C., & Boudreau, D. (2008). Phonological awareness intervention: Beyond the basics. *Language, Speech and Hearing Services in Schools, 39*, 3–20.

Schwanenflugel, P. J., & Benjamin, R. G. (2012). Reading expressiveness: The neglected aspect of reading fluency. In T. Rasinski, C. Blachowicz, & K. Lems (Eds.), *Fluency instruction: Research-based best practices* (2nd ed., pp. 35–54). New York, NY: Guilford Press.

Schwanenflugel, P. J., Hamilton, A. M., Kuhn, M. R., Wisenbaker, J., & Stahl, S. A. (2004). Becoming a fluent reader: Reading skill and prosodic features in the oral reading of young readers. *Journal of Educational Psychology, 96*, 119–129.

Serafini, F. (2013). Close readings and children's literature. *The Reading Teacher, 67*(4), 299–301.

Serafini, F. (2012). Expanding the four resources model: Reading visual and multimodal texts. *Pedagogies: An International Journal, 7*(2), 150–164.

Serafini, F., & Youngs, S. (2013). Reading workshop 2.0: Children's literature in the digital age. *The Reading Teacher, (66)*5, 401–404.

Seuss, Dr. (1957). *The cat in the hat*. New York, NY: Random House.

Sewell, G. T. (1987). *American history textbooks: An assessment of quality*. New York, NY: Educational Excellence Network, Teachers College, Columbia University.

Shanahan, C., & Shanahan, T. (2014). Does disciplinary literacy have a place in elementary school? *The Reading Teacher, 67*(8), 636–639.

Shanahan, T. (2016). Are oral reading norms accurate with complex text? [Web log]. Retrieved from http://www.readingrockets.org/blogs/shanahan-literacy/are-oral-reading-norms-accurate-complex-text

Shanahan, T. (1988). The reading-writing relationship: Seven instructional principles. *The Reading Teacher, 41*, 636–647.

Shanahan, T. (1990). *Reading and writing together. New perspectives for the classroom*. Norwood, MA: Christopher-Gordon.

Shanahan, T., Fisher, D., & Frey, N. (2012). The challenge of challenging text. *Educational Leadership, 69*(6), 58–62.

Shanahan, T., & Neuman, S. B. (1997). Literacy research that makes a difference. *Reading Research Quarterly, 32*, 202–210.

Shanahan, T., & Shanahan, C. (2008). Teaching disciplinary literacy to adolescents: Rethinking content area literacy. *Harvard Educational Review, 78*(1), 40–59.

Shanklin, N. L., & Rhodes, L. K. (1989). Comprehension instruction as sharing and extending. *The Reading Teacher, 42*, 496–501.

Shannon, D. (1998). *No, David!* New York, NY: Scholastic.

Sharpley, A. M., & Sharpley, C. F. (1981). Peer tutoring: A review of the literature. *Collected Original Resources in Education 5*(3), 7–11.

Shatz, E. K., & Baldwin, R. S. (1986). Context clues are unreliable predictors of word meanings. *Reading Research Quarterly, 21*, 429–453.

Shen, F. (2005). iPods fast becoming new teacher's pet. *The Washington Post*, p. B01.

Shonkoff, J., & Phillips, D. A. (2000). *From neurons to neighborhoods: The science of early childhood development*. Washington, DC: National Academy Press.

Simmons, D. C., & Kame'enui, E. J. (2006). *Guide to evaluating a core reading program grades K–3*. National Center to Improve the Tools of Educators (NCITE) and Institute for the Development of Educational Achievement (IDEA). Eugene, OR: University of Oregon.

Simons, H., & Elster, C. (1990). Picture dependence in first-grade basal texts. *Journal of Educational Research, 84*, 86–92.

Simpson, M. (1987). Alternative formats for evaluating content area vocabulary understanding. *Journal of Reading, 31*, 20–27.

Singer, H., & Ruddell, R. (Eds.). (1985). *Theoretical models and processes of reading* (3rd ed.). Newark, DE: International Reading Association.

Sipe, L. R. (2008). *Storytime: Young children's literary understanding in the classroom*. New York, NY: Teachers College Press.

Slapin, B. (1992). *How to tell the difference: A checklist for evaluating children's books for anti-Indian bias*. Philadelphia, PA: New Society.

Smith, F. (1977). The uses of language. *Language Arts, 54*, 638–644.

Smith, F. (1985). *Reading without nonsense* (2nd ed.). New York, NY: Teachers College Press.

Smith, F. (1988). *Joining the literacy club: Further essays into education*. Portsmouth, NH: Heinemann.

Smith, F. (1989). Demonstrations, engagement, and sensitivity: The choice between people and programs. In G. Manning & M. Manning (Eds.), *Whole language: Beliefs and practices, K–8* (pp. 48–59). Washington, DC: National Education Association.

Smith, L. B. (1982). Sixth graders write about reading literature. *Language Arts, 59*, 357–366.

Smith, N. B. (1965). *American reading instruction*. Newark, DE: International Reading Association.

Smith, R. J., & Johnson, D. D. (1980). *Teaching children to read*. Reading, MA: Addison-Wesley.

Smolen, L. A., & Ortiz-Castro, V. (2000). Dissolving borders and broadening perspectives through Latino traditional literature. *The Reading Teacher, 53*(7), 566–578.

Smythe, S., & Neufeld, P. (2010). "Podcast time": Negotiating digital literacies and communities of learning in a middle years ELL classroom. *Journal of Adolescent & Adult Literacy, 53*(6), 488–496.

Snow, C. E. (2013). Cold versus warm close reading: Building students' stamina for struggling with text. *Reading Today, 30*(6), 18–19.

Snow, C. E., Burns, M. S., & Griffin, P. (1998). *Preventing reading difficulties in young children*. Washington, DC: National Academy Press.

Soalt, J. (2005). Bringing together fictional and informational texts to improve comprehension. *The Reading Teacher, 58*, 680–683.

Solomon, G. (2002). Digital equity: It's not just about access anymore. *Technology and Learning, 22*(9), 18–26.

Sox, A., & Rubinstein-Avila, E. (2009). WebQuests for English language learners: Essential elements for design. *Journal of Adolescent and Adult Literacy, 53*(1), 38–48.

Spache, G. (1953). A new readability formula for primary-grade reading materials. *The Elementary School Journal, 53*(7), 410–413.

Spandel, V. (2013). *Creating writers: 6 traits, process, workshop, and literature* (6th ed.). Boston, MA: Pearson.

Spangenberg-Urbschat, K., & Pritchard, R. (Eds.). (1994). *Kids come in all languages: Reading instruction for ESL students*. Newark, DE: International Reading Association.

Spearitt, D. (1972). Identification of subskills in reading comprehension by maximum likelihood factor analysis. *Reading Research Quarterly, 8*, 92–111.

Spence, L. K. (2010). Generous reading: Seeing students through their writing. *The Reading Teacher, 63*(8), 634–642.

Spotlight on Literacy. (2000). New York, NY: Macmillan/McGraw-Hill.

Squire, J. R. (1984). Composing and comprehending: Two sides of the same basic process. In J. M. Jensen (Ed.), *Composing and comprehending* (pp. 23–31). Urbana, IL: National Conference on Research in English.

Stahl, S. A. (1983). *Vocabulary instruction and the nature of word meanings*. Paper presented at a meeting of the College Reading Association, Atlanta.

Stahl, S. A. (1986). Three principles of effective vocabulary instruction. *Journal of Reading, 29*, 662–668.

Stahl, S. A. (1992). Saying the "p" word: Nine guidelines for exemplary phonic instruction. *The Reading Teacher, 45,* 618–625.

Stahl, S. A. (2004). What do we know about fluency? Findings of the National Reading Panel. In P. McCardle & V. Chhabra, *The voice of evidence in reading research* (pp. 187–211). Baltimore, MD: Paul H. Brookes.

Stahl, S. A., Duffy-Hester, A. M., & Stahl, K. A. (1998). Everything you wanted to know about phonics (but were afraid to ask). *Reading Research Quarterly, 33,* 338–355.

Stahl, S. A., & Fairbanks, M. (1986). The effects of vocabulary instruction: A model-based meta-analysis. *Review of Educational Research, 56,* 72–110.

Stahl, S. A., & Heubach, K. (2005). Fluency-oriented reading instruction. *Journal of Literacy Research, 37*(1), 25–60.

Stanovich, K. E. (1986). Matthew effects in reading: Some consequences of individual differences in the acquisition of literacy. *Reading Research Quarterly, 21,* 360–407.

Stead, T., & Duke, N. (2005). *Reality checks: Teaching reading comprehension with nonfiction, K–5.* York, ME: Stenhouse.

Stein, N., & Glenn, C. (1979). An analysis of story comprehension in elementary school children. In R. Freedle (Ed.), *New directions in discourse processing* (pp. 53–120). Norwood, NJ: Ablex.

Stephens, K. E. (2008). A quick guide to selecting informational books for young children. *The Reading Teacher, 61*(6), 488–490.

Stewart, O., & Tei, E. (1983). Some implications of metacognition for reading instruction. *Journal of Reading, 27,* 36–43.

Stewart, R. A., Paradis, E. E., Ross, B. D., & Lewis, M. J. (1996). Student voices: What works in literature-based developmental reading. *Journal of Adolescent & Adult Literacy, 39*(6), 468–477.

Stewig, J. W. (1980). *Read to write* (2nd ed.). Austin, TX: Holt, Rinehart and Winston.

Stowell, L. (2000). Building alliances, building community, building bridges through literacy. In K. D. Wood & T. S. Dickinson (Eds.), *Promoting literacy in grades 4–9: A handbook for teachers and administrators* (pp. 77–96). Boston, MA: Allyn & Bacon.

Strachan, S. L. (2015). Expanding the range of text types used in the primary grades. *The Reading Teacher, 68*(4), 303–311.

Strickland, D. S. (1998). *Teaching phonics today: A primer for educators.* Newark, DE: International Reading Association.

Strickland, D. S. (2013). Linking early literacy research and the Common Core State Standards. In S. B. Neuman & L. B. Gambrell (Eds.), *Quality reading instruction in the age of Common Core Standards* (pp. 13–25). Newark, DE: International Reading Association.

Strickland, D. S., & Morrow, L. M. (1990). Family literacy: Sharing good books. *The Reading Teacher, 43,* 518–519.

Strickland, D. S., & Riley-Ayers, S. (2006, April). *Early literacy: Policy and practice in the preschool years.* NIEER Preschool Policy Brief, 10. Retrieved from http://nieer.org/resources/policybriefs/10.pdf

Strickland, D., & Schickedanz, J. (2009). *Learning About Print in Preschool* (2nd ed.). Newark, DE: International Reading Association.

Strickland, R. (1962). *The language of elementary school children: Its relationship to the language of reading textbooks and the quality of reading of selected children.* Bloomington, IN: Indiana University School of Education.

Sturtevant, E. G. (2001). What middle and high school educators need to know about language minority students. In J. A. Rycik & J. L. Irvin (Eds.), *What adolescents deserve: A commitment to students' literacy learning* (pp. 40–44). Newark, DE: International Reading Association.

Sulzby, E., & Teale, W. H. (1987). *Emergent literacy: Writing and reading* (Writing Research Series, Vol. 6). Norwood, NJ: Ablex Publishing.

Sutherland, Z. (Ed.). (1984). *The Scott, Foresman anthology of children's literature.* Glenview, IL: Scott, Foresman.

Sweeney, S. M. (2010). Writing for the instant messaging and text messaging generation: Using new literacies to support writing instruction. *Journal of Adolescent & Adult Literacy, 54*(2), 121–130.

Sylvester, R., & Greenidge, W. (2009). Digital storytelling: Extending the potential for struggling writers. *The Reading Teacher, 63*(4), 284–295.

Taberski, S. (2000). *On solid ground: Strategies for teaching reading K–3.* Portsmouth, NH: Heinemann.

Taberski, S. (2010). *Comprehension from the ground up K–3.* Portsmouth, NH: Heinneman.

Takacs, Z. K., Swart, E. K. & Bus, A.G. (2015). Benefits and Pitfalls of Multimedia and Interactive Features in Technology-Enhanced Storybooks: A Meta-Analysis. Retrieved from *Review of Educational Research* 0034654314566989, first published on January 27, 2015 doi:10.3102/0034654314566989

Tate, S. L. (2011). Media literacy. In D. Lapp & D. Fisher (Eds.), *Handbook of research on teaching the English language arts* (3rd ed., pp. 182–187). New York, NY: Routledge.

Taylor, B. M., Pearson, P. D., Clark, K., & Walpole, S. (2000). Effective schools and accomplished teachers: Lessons about primary-grade reading instruction in low-income schools. *Elementary School Journal, 101*(2), 121–165.

Taylor, D. (1983). *Family literacy: Young children learning to read and write.* Portsmouth, NH: Heinemann.

Taylor, D., & Dorsey-Gaines, C. (1989). *Growing up literate: Learning from inner-city families.* Portsmouth, NH: Heinemann.

Taylor, N. E., & Vawter, J. (1978). Helping children discover the functions of written language. *Language Arts, 55,* 941–945.

Teachers of English to Speakers of Other Languages (TESOL). (2006). *TESOL revises PreK–12 English Language Proficiency Standards (March 2006).* Retrieved May 31, 2007, from www.tesol.org/s_tesol/sec_document.asp?CID=1186&DID=5349

Teale, W. H. (1978). Positive environments for learning to read: What studies of early readers tell us. *Language Arts, 55,* 922–932.

Teale, W. H. (1986). Home background and young children's literacy development. *Emergent literacy: Writing and reading* (pp. 173–206). Norwood, NJ: Ablex.

Teale, W. H. (2009). Students learning English and their literacy instruction in urban schools. *The Reading Teacher, 62*(8), pp. 699–703.

Teale, W. H., & Sulzby, E. (1986). *Emergent literacy: Writing and reading.* Norwood, NJ: Ablex.

Templeton, S. (2011). Teaching spelling in the English/language arts classroom. In D. Lapp & D. Fisher (Eds.), *Handbook of research on teaching the English language arts* (3rd ed.) (pp. 247–251). New York, NY: Routledge.

Thelen, J. (1986). Vocabulary instruction and meaningful learning. *Journal of Reading, 29,* 603–609.

Thompson, A. D., & Mishra, P. (2007/2008). Breaking news: TPCK becomes TPACK. *Journal of Computing in Teacher Education, 24*(2), 38, 64.

Thomson, R. (2011). *Terezin: Voices from the Holocaust.* Somerville, MA: Candlewick Press.

Thorndyke, P. (1977). Cognitive structures in comprehension and memory of narrative discourse. *Cognitive Psychology, 9,* 77–110.

Thurstone, L. L. (1946). A note on a reanalysis of Davis' reading tests. *Psychometrika, 11,* 185–188.

Tiedt, I. M. (2000). *Teaching with picture books in the middle school.* Newark, DE: International Reading Association.

Tierney, R. J. (1998). Literacy assessment reform: Shifting beliefs, principled possibilities, and emerging practices. *The Reading Teacher, 51,* 374–390.

Tierney, R. J., & Shanahan, T. (1991). Research on reading-writing relationships: Interactions, transactions, and outcomes. In R. Barr,

M. L. Kamil, P. Mosenthal, & P. D. Pearson (Eds.), *Handbook of reading research* (2nd ed., pp. 246–280). New York, NY: Longman.

Tomlinson, C. A. (2001). *How to differentiate instruction in mixedability classrooms* (2nd ed.). Alexandria, VA: Association for Supervision and Curriculum Development.

Topping, K. (1989). Peer tutoring and paired reading: Combining two powerful techniques. *The Reading Teacher, 42,* 488–494.

Torgesen, J. K., Wagner, R. K., Rashotte, C. A., Herron, J., & Lindamood, P. (2010). Computer-assisted instruction to prevent early reading difficulties in students at risk for dyslexia: Outcomes from two instructional approaches. *Annals of Dyslexia, 60,* 40–56.

Townsend, D., & Kiernan, D. (2015). Selecting academic vocabulary words worth teaching. *The Reading Teacher, 69*(1), 113–118.

Trachtenburg, P. (1990). Using children's literature to enhance phonic instruction. *The Reading Teacher, 43,* 648–654.

Trelease, J. (1989). *The new read-aloud handbook.* New York, NY: Penguin.

Trelease, J. (2006). *The read-aloud handbook* (6th ed.). New York, NY: Penguin.

Trelease, J. (2013). *The read-aloud handbook* (7th ed.). New York, NY: Penguin Books.

Trilling, B., & Fadel, C. (2009). *21st century skills: Learning for life in our times.* San Francisco, CA: Jossey-Bass.

Tunmer W. E., & Nicholson, T. (2011). The development and teaching of word recognition skill. In M. Kamil, P. Pearson, E. Moje, & P. Afflerbach (Eds.), *Handbook of reading research* (pp. 405–431). New York, NY: Routledge.

Tunnell, M., Calder, J., Justen, J., & Waldrop, P. (1988). An affective approach to reading: Effectively teaching reading to mainstreamed handicapped children. *The Pointer, 32,* 38–40.

Turner, J. D., & Hoeltzel, C. C. (2011). Assessing every child. In D. Lapp & D. Fisher (Eds.), *Handbook of research on teaching the English language arts* (3rd ed., pp. 329–335). New York, NY: Routledge.

Twain, M. (1897). *The innocents abroad or the new pilgrim's progress: Being some account of the steamship Quaker City's pleasure excursion to Europe and the Holy Land.* Vol. II. New York, NY: Harper & Brothers.

U.S. Census Bureau. (2002). United States Census 2000. Washington, DC. Retrieved May 29, 2010, from www.census.gov/main/www/cen2000.html

U.S. Census Bureau. (2004). *Population projections.* Retrieved May 24, 2007, from www.census.gov

U.S. Census Bureau. (2012). U.S. Census Bureau projections show a slower growing, older, more diverse nation a half century from now. Retrieved from http://www.census.gov/newsroom/releases/archives/population/cb12-243.html

United States Census Bureau. (2015). *Census Bureau Reports at least 350 languages spoken in us homes.* Retrieved January 2016 from http://www.census.gov/newsroom/press-releases/2015/cb15-185.html

Vacca, R. (2006). They can because they think they can. *Educational Leadership, 63,* 56–59.

Vacca, R. T., & Rasinski, T. V. (1992). *Case studies in whole language.* Orlando, FL: Harcourt Brace.

Vacca, R. T., & Vacca, J. L. (2002). *Content area reading: Literacy and learning across the curriculum* (7th ed.). Boston, MA: Allyn & Bacon.

Vacca, R. T., & Vacca, J. L. (2005). *Content area reading: Literacy and learning across the curriculum* (8th ed.). Boston, MA: Allyn & Bacon.

Vacca, R. T., & Vacca, J. L. (2008). *Content area reading: Literacy and learning across the curriculum* (9th ed.). Boston, MA: Allyn & Bacon.

Vacca, R. T., Vacca, J. L., & Mraz, M. (2011). *Content area reading: Literacy and learning across the curriculum* (10th ed.). Boston, MA: Allyn & Bacon.

Vacca, R. T., Vacca, J. L., & Mraz, M. (2014). *Content area reading: Literacy and learning across the curriculum* (11th ed.). Boston, MA: Allyn & Bacon.

Valmont, W. J. (2003). *Technology for literacy teaching and learning.* Boston, MA: Houghton Mifflin.

Van Sluys, K., & Laman, T. T. (2006). Learning about language: Written conversations and elementary language learners. *The Reading Teacher, 60,* 222–233.

VanNess, A. R., Murnen, T. J., & Bertelsen, C. D. (2013). Let me tell you a secret: Kindergarteners can write! *The Reading Teacher, 66*(7), 574–585.

Vardell, S., Hadaway, N., & Young, T. (2006). Matching books and readers: Selecting literature for English learners. *The Reading Teacher, 59*(8), 734–741.

Vasquez, V. (2010). *Getting beyond "I like the book": Creating space for critical literacy in K–6 classrooms* (2nd ed.). Newark, DE: International Reading Association.

Veatch, J., Sawicki, F., Elliot, G., Flake, E., & Blakey, J. (1979). *Key words to reading* (2nd ed.). Columbus, OH: Merrill.

Venezky, R. L., & Massaro, D. W. (1979). The role of orthographic regularity in word recognition. In L. Resnick & R. Weaver (Eds.), *Theory and practice of early reading* (pp. 85–107). Mahwah, NJ: Erlbaum.

Villaume, S. K., Worden, T., Williams, S., Hopkins, L., & Rosenblatt, C. (1994). Five teachers in search of a discussion. *Language Arts, 47,* 480–489.

Viorst, J. (1972). *Alexander and the terrible, horrible, no good, very bad day.* New York, NY: Atheneum.

Vukelich, C., & Christie, J. (2004). *Building a foundation for preschool literacy: Effective instruction for children's reading and writing development.* Newark, DE: International Reading Association.

Vukelich, C., & Christie, J. (2009). *Building a foundation for preschool literacy* (2nd ed.). Newark, DE: International Reading Association.

Vukelich, C., Christie, J., & Enz, B. (2008). *Helping young children learn language and literacy.* Boston, MA: Allyn & Bacon.

Vygotsky, L. S. (1962). *Thought and language.* Cambridge, MA: MIT Press.

Vygotsky, L. S. (1978). *Mind in society.* Cambridge, MA: Harvard University Press.

Walker, B. J. (2008). *Diagnostic teaching in reading: Techniques for instruction and assessment* (6th ed.). Upper Saddle River, NJ: Pearson Education.

Walsh, K. (2003). Basal readers: The lost opportunity to build the knowledge that propels comprehension. *American Educator, 27,* 24–27.

Wasik, B. A., & Iannone-Campbell, C. (2012/2013). Developing vocabulary through purposeful, strategic conversations. *The Reading Teacher, 66*(2), 321–332.

Waters, J. (2007). Making things easy. *THE Journal, 34*(4), 26–33.

Weaver, C. (2002). *Reading process and practice.* Portsmouth, NH: Heinemann.

Wells, G. (1986). *The meaning-makers: Children learning language and using language to learn.* Portsmouth, NH: Heinemann.

Wells, M. C. (1993). At the juncture of reading and writing: How dialogue journals contribute to students' reading development. *Journal of Reading, 36,* 294–303.

Whaley, J. F. (1981). Story grammar and reading instruction. *The Reading Teacher, 34,* 762–771.

Wheeler, R. S., & Swords, R. (2006). *Code-switching: Teaching Standard English in urban classrooms.* National Council of Teachers of English.

Whelan, G. (2008). *Yuki and the one thousand carriers.* Farmington Hills, MI: Sleeping Bear.

Widdowson, D., Dixon, R., & Moore, D. (1996). The effects of teacher modeling of silent reading on students' engagement during sustained silent reading. *Educational Psychology, 16*(2), 171–180.

Wilfong, L. G. (2009). Textmasters: Bringing literature circles to textbook reading across the curriculum. *Journal of Adolescent & Adult Literacy, 53*(2), 164–171.

Willems, M. (2007). *There is a bird on your head!* New York, NY: Hyperion Books.

Williams, C., Phillips-Birdsong, C., Hufnagel, K., Hungler, D., & Lundstrom, R. P. (2009). Word study instruction in the K–2 classroom. *The Reading Teacher, 62*(7), 570–578.

Williams, T. L. (2007). "Reading" the painting: Exploring visual literacy in the primary grades. *The Reading Teacher, 60,* 636–642.

Willis, P. (1997). *Danger along the Ohio.* New York, NY: Houghton Mifflin.

Wixson, K. K., & Lipson, M. Y. (2012). Relations between the CCSS and RTI in literacy and language. *The Reading Teacher, 65*(6), 387–391.

Wolf, M. (2007). *Proust and the Squid: The Story and Science of the Reading Brain.* New York, NY: HarperCollins.

Wooten, D. A. (2000). *Valued voices: An interdisciplinary approach to teaching and learning.* Newark, DE: International Reading Association.

Wylie, R. E., & Durrell, D. D. (1970). Teaching vowels through phonograms. *Elementary English, 47,* 787–791.

Yanok, J. (1988). Individualized instruction: A good approach. *Academic Therapy, 24,* 163–167.

Yarosz, D. J., & Barnett, W. S. (2001). Who reads to young children? Identifying predictors of family reading activities. *Reading Psychology, 22,* 67–81.

Yashima, T. (1976). *Crow Boy.* New York, NY: Puffin.

Yokota, J. (1993). Issues in selecting multicultural literature for children and adolescents. *Language Arts, 70,* 156–167.

Yopp, H. K. (1992). Developing phonemic awareness in young children. *The Reading Teacher, 45,* 696–703.

Yopp, H. K. (1995). A test for assessing phonemic awareness in young children. *The Reading Teacher, 49,* 20–29.

Yopp, H. K., & Yopp, R. H. (2012). Young children's limited and narrow exposure to informational text. *The Reading Teacher, 65*(7), 480–490.

Yopp, R. H., & Yopp, H. K. (1993). *Literature-based reading activities.* Boston, MA: Allyn & Bacon.

Young, C., & Rasinski, T. (2009). Implementing readers theatre as an approach to classroom fluency instruction. *The Reading Teacher, 63*(1), 4–13.

Young, T. A., & Hadaway, N. L. (Eds.). (2006). *Supporting the literacy development of English learners: Increasing success in all classrooms.* Newark, DE: International Reading Association.

Zarrillo, J. (1989). Teachers' interpretations of literature-based reading. *The Reading Teacher, 43,* 22–28.

Zuidema, L. A. (2005). Myth education: Rationale and strategies for teaching against linguistic prejudice. *Journal of Adolescent Literacy, 48*(8), 666–676.

Zumbrunn, S., & Krause, K. (2012). Conversations with leaders: Principles of effective writing instruction. *The Reading Teacher, 65*(5), 346–353.

Name Index

Duffy-Hester, A. M., 152, 156, 157
Duin, A., 237
Duke, N., 78, 93
Duke, N. K., 93, 277, 290
Durkin, D., 87, 157, 175
Durrell, D. D., 161
Dwyer, J., 218
Dykstra, R., 47

E

Eakle, A. J., 43
Ebner, R. J., 228
Echevarria, J., 58
Echols, C., 21
Edwards, P. A., 57, 73, 321
Edwards, S. A., 361
Ehmann, S., 317
Ehren, B. J., 308
Ehri, L., 103
Ehri, L. C., 18–19, 27, 152, 154, 155–156, 160, 228
Eldridge, J.L., 379
Evanchan, G., 200–201, 206
Everett- Cacopardo, H., 271, 308, 320

F

Fadel, C., 267
Fang, Z., 55, 57, 61, 281
Farr, R., 115, 118, 125
Farstrup, A. E., 361
Faver, S., 200
Fawson, P., 209
Fielding, L. G., 240
Fishburne, R. P., 283
Fisher, D., 214, 280, 299, 345, 349, 363, 379
Fisher, P., 170, 214, 215, 216, 221, 222, 224, 225–226, 244
Fitzgerald, J., 251, 281
Flanigan, K., 170–171
Flesch, R., 283
Fletcher, R., 324
Flippo, R.F., 116, 117
Flynn, R. M., 302
Forzani, E., 271, 308, 320
Fosnot, C., 71
Fountas, I. C., 267
Fowler, G. L., 252
Fox, B. J., 77
Fox, D. L., 24
Fredericks, A. D., 203
Freebody, P., 215, 361
Freedman, R., 352–353
Freeman, D., 225
Freeman, Y., 225
Freiberg, J., 361
Frey, N., 214, 280, 363, 379
Friedlander, B., 313
Friend, M., 67, 69
Froelich, K. S., 15
Fry, E., 161, 165, 175–177
Fuchs, D., 201, 205
Fuchs, L., 201
Fuchs, L. S., 205

G

Galda, L., 66, 95, 346, 350, 352, 364, 365
Garan, E., 210
Garber-Miller, K., 293–294

Garcia, E., 68, 313
Garcia, G. E., 55, 141
Garcia, G. G., 117
Garcia, O., 55
Gardner, H., 68
Gaskins, I. W., 155–156, 160
Gayer, K., 317
Gee, J., 72
George, J., 358
Gerde, H., 327
Gibson, S. A., 333–334
Gilles, C., 358
Gillespie, J., 325
Giroir, S., 65
Glenn, D., 43
Goldenberg, C., 225
Goldman, S. R., 271
Gollnick, D. M., 61
Gonzalez, J. E., 292
Goodman, K. S., 22–23, 141
Goodman, M. J., 207–208, 210
Goodman, Y. M., 23, 137
Goswami, U., 160
Gough, P., 26
Gove, M. K., 34
Graesser, A. C., 271
Graham, S., 313, 315
Grant, M., 263, 267
Graves, M., 237
Graves, M. F., 215, 216, 226, 240, 251, 281
Gray, E., 95–96
Gray, W., 277
Greenidge, W., 324
Greenwood, S. C., 170–171
Gregg, M., 292
Griffin, P., 7, 80, 85, 87, 168
Griffith, L. W., 196
Grigg, W. S., 207–208, 210
Grimaldo, L. R., 65
Groff, C., 205
Guthrie, J. T., 208, 209, 302

H

Hadaway, N., 345
Hadaway, N. L., 55, 60, 64
Haddon, M., 351
Haggard, M. R., 242
Hakuta, K., 55, 57, 61
Hall, A. K., 170
Halliday, M. A. K., 22, 24
Hallisy, J., 376
Hamilton, A. M., 190
Hamilton, R. L., 260–261
Hancock, M. R., 324, 363, 365
Handsfield, L. J., 324
Hansen, J., 356
Harmon, J., 356
Harris, K. R., 313, 315
Harrison, C., 119
Harste, J. C., 34, 83
Hart, B., 79, 86
Hartman, B., 178
Harvey, S., 248, 256, 270
Hasbrouck, J., 195, 206, 207
Heffernan, L., 333
Heisey, N., 92
Helman, L., 156, 158

Helman, L. A., 158–159, 175
Hendershot, J., 349
Henry, G., 223
Henry, L. A., 305, 361
Hepler, S. I., 346
Herber, H., 277–278
Herman, J., 146
Herron, J., 103
Heubach, K., 195
Heward, W. L., 68, 71
Hickman, J., 226, 346
Hiebert, E., 216
Hiebert, E. H., 280, 283–284
Higgins, G. D., 356
Hilden, K., 93
Hinchman, K. A., 263
Hoa, L. W., 209
Hoeltzel, C. C., 119, 142
Hoffman, J., 202
Hoffman, M., 349, 353
Holdaway, D., 203
Hollenbeck, A. F., 255, 267
Hopper, E., 59
Horsey, M., 291
Hosp, M. K., 205
Howard, G., 351
Howard, L., 265
Hudson, R. F., 190, 205
Hufnagel, K., 184
Hungler, D., 184
Hunt, L., 209
Hutchison, A., 313, 324, 380
Hymes, D., 24

I

Iannone-Campbell, C., 225
Ignoffo, M., 235–236
Ikpeze, C. H., 292
Invernizzi, M., 156, 158, 164, 314, 315
Irvin, J. L., 313
Ivey, G., 345, 349

J

Jenkins, J. R., 205
Jett-Simpson, M., 118
Jimenez, R. T., 117
Johns, J. L., 130, 175
Johnson, K., 263, 267
Johnston, F., 156, 158, 164, 314, 315
Johnston, F. R., 156
Johnston, P., 116–117, 119, 145
Jones, C., 209
Jones, C. D., 209
Jones, J., 93, 386
Jones, M., 142
Joseph, L. M., 178
Joseph, 382
Juel, C., 103, 168
Justice, L., 92

K

Kamil, M., 216
Kamil, M. L., 28
Karchmer-Klein, R., 71, 271
Kelley, M. J., 209
Kennedy, C., 271, 308, 320, 334–335
Kieffer, M. J., 173

Subject Index